Knowledge, Information, and Expectations
in Modern Macroeconomics:
In Honor of Edmund S. Phelps

Knowledge, Information, and Expectations in Modern Macroeconomics: In Honor of Edmund S. Phelps

EDITED BY

PHILIPPE AGHION, ROMAN FRYDMAN,
JOSEPH STIGLITZ, AND MICHAEL WOODFORD

PRINCETON UNIVERSITY PRESS

Princeton and Oxford

Copyright © 2003 by Princeton University Press

Published by Princeton University Press,
41 William Street, Princeton, New Jersey 08540

In the United Kingdom: Princeton University Press,
3 Market Place, Woodstock, Oxfordshire OX20 1SY

Library of Congress Cataloging-in-Publication Data

Knowledge, information, and expectations in modern macroeconomics :
in honor of Edmund S. Phelps / edited by Philippe Aghion . . . [et al.].
p.   cm.
Includes bibliographical references and index.
ISBN 0-691-09484-5 (cl : alk. paper)—ISBN 0-691-09485-3 (pb : alk. paper)
1. Phelps, Edmund S.   2. Economists—United States—Congresses.
3. Macroeconomics—Congresses.   I. Phelps, Edmund S.   II. Aghion, Philippe.
HB119.P39 K66   2002
339—dc21   2002024341

British Library Cataloging-in-Publication Data is available

This book has been composed in Times New Roman and Trump Mediaeval
by Princeton Editorial Associates, Inc., Scottsdale, Arizona

Printed on acid-free paper. ∞

www.pupress.princeton.edu

Printed in the United States of America

1 3 5 7 9 10 8 6 4 2

CONTENTS

PART IV   Education, Technical Change, and Growth

CONTRIBUTORS

DARON ACEMOGLU, Department of Economics, Massachusetts Institute of Technology, Cambridge, Massachusetts 02142

PHILIPPE AGHION, Department of Economics, Harvard University, Cambridge, Massachusetts 02138

JESS BENHABIB, Department of Economics, New York University, New York, New York 10003

OLIVIER J. BLANCHARD, Department of Economics, Massachusetts Institute of Technology, Cambridge, Massachusetts 02142

GUILLERMO A. CALVO, Department of Economics, University of Maryland, College Park, Maryland 20742

OYA CELASUN, International Monetary Fund, Washington, D.C. 20431

JEAN-PAUL FITOUSSI, Observatoire Française des Conjunctures Économiques, F-75007 Paris, France

ROMAN FRYDMAN, Department of Economics, New York University, New York, New York 10003

MARK GERTLER, Department of Economics, New York University, New York, New York 10003

MICHAEL D. GOLDBERG, Department of Economics, University of New Hampshire, Durham, New Hampshire 03824

BRUCE GREENWALD, Graduate School of Business, Columbia University, New York, New York 10027

ROBERT E. HALL, Hoover Institute, Stanford University, Stanford, California 94305

JAMES J. HECKMAN, Department of Economics, University of Chicago, Chicago, Illinois 60637

BART HOBIJN, Domestic Research Function, Federal Reserve Bank of New York, New York, New York 10045

PETER HOWITT, Department of Economics, Brown University, Providence, Rhode Island 02912

HEHUI JIN, Department of Economics, Stanford University, Stanford, California 94305

CHARLES I. JONES, Department of Economics, University of California, Berkeley, Berkeley, California 94720

MICHAEL KUMHOF, Department of Economics, Stanford University, Stanford, California 94305

MORDECAI KURZ, Department of Economics, Stanford University, Stanford, California 94305

DAVID LAIBSON, Department of Economics, Harvard University, Cambridge, Massachusetts 02138

LARS LJUNGQVIST, Stockholm School of Economics, SE-113 83 Stockholm, Sweden

ROBERT E. LUCAS, JR., Department of Economics, University of Chicago, Chicago, Illinois 60637

N. GREGORY MANKIW, Department of Economics, Harvard University, Cambridge, Massachusetts 02138

DALE T. MORTENSEN, Department of Economics, Northwestern University, Evanston, Illinois 60208

MAURIZIO MOTOLESE, Istituto di Politica Economica, Universita Cattolica di Milano, 20123 Milan, Italy

STEPHEN NICKELL, Department of Economics, London School of Economics and Political Science, London WC2A 2AE, United Kingdom

LUCA NUNZIATA, Nuffield College, Oxford University, Oxford OX1 1NF, United Kingdom, and Department of Economics, University of Bologna, 40126 Bologna, Italy

WOLFGANG OCHEL, Department of International Institutional Comparisons, Ifo Institute for Economic Research, 81679 Munich, Germany

DAVID H. PAPELL, Department of Economics, University of Houston, Houston, Texas 77204

EDMUND S. PHELPS, Department of Economics, Columbia University, New York, New York 10027

CHRISTOPHER A. PISSARIDES, Department of Economics, London School of Economics and Political Science, London WC2A 2AE, United Kingdom

ROBERT A. POLLAK, Department of Economics, Washington University, St. Louis, Missouri 63130-4899

GLENDA QUINTINI, Centre for Economic Performance, London School of Economics and Political Science, London WC2A 2AE, United Kingdom

RICARDO REIS, Department of Economics, Harvard University, Cambridge, Massachusetts 02138

ANDREA REPETTO, Department of Industrial Engineering, University of Chile, Santiago, Chile

PAUL A. SAMUELSON, Department of Economics, Massachusetts Institute of Technology, Cambridge, Massachusetts 02142

THOMAS J. SARGENT, Hoover Institute, Stanford University, Stanford, California 94305

ROBERT M. SOLOW, Department of Economics, Massachusetts Institute of Technology, Cambridge, Massachusetts 02142

JOSEPH STIGLITZ, Department of Economics, Columbia University, New York, New York 10027

NANCY L. STOKEY, Department of Economics, University of Chicago, Chicago, Illinois 60637

LARS E. O. SVENSSON, Department of Economics, Princeton University, Princeton, New Jersey 08544

JEREMY TOBACMAN, Department of Economics, Harvard University, Cambridge, Massachusetts 02138

GIANLUCA VIOLANTE, Department of Economics, University College London, London WC1E 6BT, United Kingdom

MICHAEL WOODFORD, Department of Economics, Princeton University, Princeton, New Jersey 08544

Knowledge, Information, and Expectations
in Modern Macroeconomics:
In Honor of Edmund S. Phelps

Edmund Phelps,
Insider-Economists' Insider

PAUL A. SAMUELSON

Of Arms and the Man we Virgilians gather here to sing. Lest the keynote speaker steal in his overture the best tunes of the seminars that will appraise and praise the Ned Phelps feats of arms, my function now is to talk of the scholar himself as a person in his times.

In politics you know you are getting old when you hear yourself saying repeatedly, "I gave him his first job." Let the record show that Ned Phelps's rise to scientific fame owed nothing to interventions by me. However, that was not because of lack of trying on my part. When Phelps was a bright senior at Amherst, I lectured there solely in order to recruit him for MIT. His case was a no-brainer lay-down hand. But Ned was one of the fish that got away. And it was Yale's good fortune that he went there. One cannot deny that his was a good choice, for out of the ashes of Old Eli's glory in the days of Fairchild, Furness, and Buck—an interlude between the Gibbs and Irving Fisher era—Jim Tobin gathered to New Haven the refugee Cowles clan and many more. Eclectically, Ned learned from them and from the Fellner-Wallich-Triffin crowd too, and what he borrowed from his elders, he paid back at golden compound interest.

In no time at all he became known for golden rule theorems, for the Phelps-Koopmans permanent inefficiencies, for optimal intertemporal stochastic programming, for models of *endogenous* technological change, and for the concept of a natural rate of unemployment defined at the point where the algebraic rate of inflation passes from being permanently minus to permanently plus.

You might say this was Picasso's classical period. I knew of his innovations well, and not only because Solow and I were pedaling in the same bicycle marathon. Often I was a free rider boosted ahead by Ned's windbreaking lead efforts. Truly Phelps has been external-economy. Thus, my much-cited 1969 paper on optimal intertemporal portfolio programming opportunistically used the Bellman-Beckman-Phelps recursive techniques to analyze what defines the best qualitative asset-portfolio mix of the Phelps 1962 aggregate saving. It was not plagiarism but it was horning in on a created public good there for the taking.

The biography of a Phelps illuminates the nature of scientific advance and of innovators' behavior. Physics or mathematics or botany or anthropology, all of them are group efforts—you might call them overlapping generations of clique efforts. On the Midway at the University of Chicago, there stands a statue depicting Time, the work of Sculptor Lorado Taft (Senator-Professor Paul Douglas's father-in-law). It portrays the stationary figure of Time, before whom draped figures of succeeding generations pass from left to right. Etched in the marble base is the legend that I paraphrase from imperfect memory. "Time passes, you say? Ah no. 'Tis we who go."

The inner history of economics is a bit like that. Into the main ring of the circus each of us enters from the left and departs from the right. But it is not a simply ordered sequence ABC . . . XYZ: The better image is that of each epoch's chorus of scholars: Smith, Malthus, Ricardo, and the two Mills in the prime classical age. Then, in Victorian times, Jevons, Menger, Walras, Marshall, Pareto, Slutsky, Wicksell, and Cassel. Contemporaries of my teachers were Pigou, the Clarks, von Bortkiewicz, Keynes, Knight, Young, Viner, Schumpeter, and Hotelling—followed by the 1900+ vintages of Hayek, Haberler, Leontief, Hicks, Lerner, Kaldor, Robinson(s), Robertson, Tinbergen, Frisch, Ohlin, and Meade. Never are the hall lights so dimmed that a previous chorus can be replaced in one fell swoop by a new set of singers. Rather, imperceptibly new voices come on stage while old ones quietly slip off, humming ever more softly as they first linger and then fade away.

This construct enables me to place today's birthday boy in his generation. For a surprisingly long time most of our productive economists had their roots in the pre–World War II epoch. This is true of Tobin, Modigliani, Alexander, McKenzie, Arrow, Kaysen, Baumol, and Solow—to say nothing of Methuselahs like Bergson and me—and all of us had a head start over graduate students of the post-1945 years—the hot breath of ingenious youth at first burned less scorchingly on our necks.

But of course that could not last. The 1950s began with the Beckers, Ecksteins, Jorgensons, Grilicheses, von Wiezackers, Diamonds, Fishers, and Phelpses, all of whom were still singing soprano when the Pearl Harbor attack took place, and soon to come were the invading hosts of the Halls, Gordons, Stiglitzes, Mertons, Dornbusches, Fischers, and . . . but now I must stop because a countable infinity is still an infinity and a lunchtime speech is of finite duration, however boring it may become.

Returning to our rags-to-riches Horatio Alger, Jr., hero, Phelps established his credentials in the easy micro and macro of Hicks-Dantzig-Debreu: Santa Claus domains of convex sets and the differentiable calculus of variations. Would he advance into the unpromising lands of increasing scale returns, asymmetric information, lumpinesses, and all those other imperfections undreamed of in the philosophies of the equilibrium mongers?

The answer is a resounding, Yes. To sum up my hagiographic panegryic, I shall steal a few lines from Philippe Aghion, who "sees Phelps's contribution [to economics] as basically *one* project: *to introduce imperfect information and knowledge, imperfect competition, and market frictions* into macroeconomics"—and, I would add, into microeconomics as well. To polish Max Planck's dictum: Science does progress funeral by funeral—as the chorus of Phelpses and Stiglitzes explicates those many ways that palsy can afflict the invisible hand of Smith, Say, and Lucas.

Edmund S. Phelps and
Modern Macroeconomics

PHILIPPE AGHION, ROMAN FRYDMAN,
JOSEPH STIGLITZ, AND MICHAEL WOODFORD

It is not easy to summarize Ned Phelps's monumental contribution to economics. A first impression is likely to be of a vast array of original concepts and models developed over the years: the "natural rate of unemployment" and the expectations-augmented Phillips curve (1967, 1968, 1971), the "island" parable of search unemployment (1968, 1969, 1970), "incentive/efficiency wages" (1968), optimal inflation targeting over time (1967, 1972, 1978), the consequences of staggered wage setting for unemployment dynamics (1977, 1979) and for disinflation (1978), the "customer market" model of pricing (1970, 1994), the roles of education and technological diffusion in long-run growth (1966), "golden rules" for investment in physical capital (1961) and in research (1966), dynamic inconsistency in savings behavior (1968), statistical discrimination (1972), and "structuralist" models of endogenous variation in the natural rate of unemployment (1994).

Nearly all of these innovations have had a substantial impact, and some have been developed further by others in ways that have won considerable recognition. Thus the golden rule was further advanced in the "overtaking principle" of Weizsäcker; the Phelps-Koopmans dynamic inefficiency theorem led to results by Cass (1972); the "island" parable was used in the celebrated rational expectations business cycle model of Lucas (1972) and in the analysis of equilibrium unemployment by Lucas and Prescott (1974); Phelps's conception of equilibrium unemployment was further developed by Stiglitz (1973); the model of staggered wage setting was developed econometrically by Taylor (1979, 1980, 1993); the efficiency wage model was later extended to shirking by Calvo (1979) and Shapiro and Stiglitz (1984); the "customer market" model played a central role in the analysis of Okun (1981); the labor market hysteresis hypothesis was tested by Blanchard and Summers (1985); the Nelson-Phelps view of the role of education in technical progress has been an important theme of the recent Schumpeterian growth literature; the Phelps-Pollak time-inconsistent preferences have been built on by Laibson (1997) and others; the "Phelps problem" of optimal inflation planning has been extensively analyzed by several authors, including Taylor (1979) and Sargent (1999); the relation between population and technical progress is stressed in the recent work of Jones (1995) and others; the structuralist theory of an endogenous natural rate has been tested in econometric work by Blanchard, Bean, and others; and so on and on.

Yet we believe it is also possible to see Phelps's primary contribution as the unfolding of a *single* central project: *introducing imperfect information, with its associated market frictions, and imperfect knowledge, with its consequent complications, into macroeconomics*. This contribution has been of fundamental importance, not only to the development of macroeconomics over the past 35 years but to much of the most exciting work at the current research frontier, some of which is on display in this volume. True, Phelps was not the first economist to have attempted a break with the neoclassical paradigm of perfect information and knowledge. Among prewar theorists, Schumpeter, Knight, Keynes, and Hayek each stressed themes of this sort, though their ideas were not accepted by all and were certainly not assimilated into the core of mainstream economic theory. But it has been only since the 1960s and 1970s that it has begun to be possible to see how to revise the postulates of the neoclassical paradigm with regard to information and knowledge, while retaining a theory of comparable scope and power. Phelps has arguably been the pivotal figure in this new informational-expectational line of economic research; in particular, he was the first to stress the importance of reorganizing macroeconomic theory around issues of this kind and to show how this could actually be done.

1. THE "PHELPS PROGRAM" IN MACROECONOMICS

Here we try to briefly summarize the main steps of what we perceive as Phelps's unified *demarche*. In a first major effort, from the late 1960s, he pioneered the first generation of models of unemployment and inflation based on microfoundations, in which firms and employees have to make their current decisions before learning or inferring the average price, wage, and employment decisions made by others. This was followed in the 1970s by work on models with staggered wage or price commitments, so that a firm's effective expectational error could eventually become large even if there had originally been no misunderstanding of the firm's environment. In a more radical effort made in the early 1980s, Phelps explored models in which each firm used a model to form its expectations but did not assume that the expectations of others were based on the same model. Finally, his nonmonetary micro-macro models in the 1990s show that, even if we exclude both errors in expectations and delays in price adjustment, changes in the structure of the economy for exogenous reasons can generate large and fairly persistent shifts in the equilibrium path of unemployment. While these structuralist models stress the variation over time in the natural rate of unemployment, in the sense of a rate of unemployment that involves no expectational error, Phelps's work continues to stress the *inefficiency* of the equilibrium unemployment rate, owing to pervasive information asymmetries. Let us now consider some of these steps in more detail.

1.1. Incomplete Information, Expectations, and the Phillips Curve

Phelps is perhaps best known for his contributions to the analysis of the effects of purely nominal disturbances, owing, for example, to changes in monetary policy, upon real activity and employment. A perennial question in economic theory asks why an increase in the volume of nominal expenditure should result in a temporary increase in real activity and not simply in a proportional increase in all money wages and prices, with no effect at all upon relative prices or any real quantities. In Phelps's work, this is argued to result from the nature of wage and price setting in a non-Walrasian world, where no "auctioneer" coordinates the adjustment of wages and prices so as to instantaneously clear markets. In Phelps et al. (1970), he offers the parable of an economy in which goods are produced on separate "islands," each with its own labor market. Wages and employment decisions must be made on each island without an opportunity to observe what is being done on other islands. An increase in nominal expenditure across all of the islands owing to loose monetary policy need not be immediately recognized as such on individual islands, and as a result wages and prices need not immediately adjust to the extent required to neutralize any effect upon the real quantities produced and consumed.

A crucial feature of Phelps's analysis of decision making in such a setting is the attention he gives to average *expectations* as a key state variable, in addition to such directly measurable variables (for an econometric modeler, after the fact) as the actual levels of wages and prices. In the models of Phelps (1967, 1968a), firms' expectations of the level (or rate of change) of average wages and prices are critical determinants of their individual wage and price setting and thus of employment and output. This is important, in that it allows Phelps to explain how real variables can be affected by changes in nominal quantities—as was asserted in Keynes's discussion of the "aggregate supply" schedule, and in the interpretation of econometric Phillips curves, which had become popular in the 1960s—without having to violate the crucial precept of rational decision theory, according to which the absolute level of prices (as opposed to relative prices) should not affect people's choices. His solution to the puzzle was to argue that the aggregate supply schedule or Phillips curve should actually be specified as a relation between employment (or output) and the difference between *actual and expected* levels (or rates of change) of wages and/or prices.

A key implication of Phelps's analysis was the argument that while real effects of monetary disturbances could be important in the short run, they would have to be purely transitory. Subjective estimates of market conditions should not forever remain out of line with what actually occurs, and as a result both real activity and employment should return before long to their natural levels—the equilibrium levels in the case of fulfilled expectations—which depend solely upon real factors (Phelps, 1967). This *natural rate hypothesis* (also associated with Friedman, 1968) is surely one of the most important ideas in macroeconomics of the past 50 years. It has had profound consequences both for theory and for the practical conduct of monetary policy. Of course, Phelps's conception of the natural rate implies neither that it is constant over time (and hence easily knowable with accuracy) nor that it should be regarded as in any way optimal; but its existence implies an important limit to what one can expect to achieve with monetary policy alone.

The recognition that inflation expectations are a crucial state variable has implied that banks must be more conscious of how their actions may shift expectations. Phelps (1972a) argues that as a result monetary policy must be conceived as an *intertemporal* planning problem, with policy at each time being judged partly on the basis of its effects upon the evolution of inflation expectations (modeled there in terms of a simple adaptive expectations rule) and hence the location of future short-run Phillips-curve trade-offs. This sort of intertemporal planning approach to monetary policy analysis is now at the heart of the approaches to policy making used by inflation-targeting central banks in particular. The problem of how optimizing monetary policy should take account of private-sector learning dynamics (including the problem of how best to model those dynamics) remains an important topic of current research.

1.2. Determinants of Equilibrium Unemployment

Phelps's concept of a natural rate of unemployment is important not only because of its emphasis upon the limits to the degree to which purely monetary disturbances can be expected to affect unemployment. It also directs attention to the *real* determinants of equilibrium unemployment, which have been an increasing focus of Phelps's attention in recent years.

The real determinants of the natural rate are first addressed in Phelps (1968a). This model of expectational disequilibrium focuses on the labor market. Owing to the problem of employee turnover, a wage-wage spiral of unexpected and accelerating wage inflation is predicted to arise if the unemployment rate is maintained below its equilibrium path. Letting w_t denote the log of the average nominal wage, Phelps derives a wage-setting equation of the form

$$w_t = \log \, \psi(U_t, dN_t/dt) + w_t^e,$$

where ψ is a decreasing function of both the current level of unemployment, U_t, and the speed with which hiring is increasing employment N_t. A consequence of this relation is that, taking the labor force to be fixed, there is only one *steady* level of unemployment at which no expectational error will result—the rate at which

$$\psi(U^*, 0) = 1.$$

Phelps shows that this steady equilibrium unemployment rate should generally be positive. A policy experiment of maintaining the unemployment rate at a sufficiently low level should cause workers to quit more readily, and that in turn would cause firms to attempt to outpay one another in order to protect their costly investment in their employees—a state of unexpected wage inflation. The argument given here for equilibrium unemployment was an early example of what came to be known as *efficiency wage* models.

While this steady-state natural rate is a constant, Phelps's work has from the beginning stressed dynamic elements in the determinants of the natural rate, and not just in the dynamics of temporary deviations from expectational equilibrium. The model just sketched actually implies that the natural rate should be time varying. Equating w_t to w_t^e in the above relation yields a differential equation for the equilibrium unemployment rate *path* originating from the current unemployment rate, which changes only gradually with costly hiring and employee attrition and which converges to the steady equilibrium rate. The paper also includes a relatively formal analysis of an individual firm's optimum rate of hiring under rising marginal hiring costs.

Phelps (1972a) further extends the analysis of dynamic aspects of natural rate theory and introduces the idea of *hysteresis* in unemployment rate, according to which a drop in employment (perhaps originally due to expectational disequilibrium) might prove partially irreversible as a result of a loss in skills or morale. As noted earlier, this idea has stimulated a great deal of subsequent work, especially following the observed persistence of the increase in European unemployment rates in the 1980s.

1.3. Customer Markets

A distinguishing feature of Phelps's research program was that it attempted to use simple, plausible *microeconomic* models of the firm, based on imperfections of competition and information, to explain widely observed macroeconomic phenomena that were hard to reconcile with standard neoclassical theory. In the previous section, we showed how, beginning with an attempt to explain why nominal shocks to the economy had real effects, he at the same time developed a far more sophisticated understanding of the relationship between inflation and unemployment. Another long-standing puzzle has been the movement of markups over the business cycle. Phelps and Winter (1970) developed an explicit model of imperfectly competitive pricing behavior, in order to explain why prices need not fully reflect short-term fluctuations in marginal costs of supply.

In the Phelps-Winter model of customer markets, firms have substantial power to vary their prices in the short run (owing to imperfect knowledge of the distribution of currently available prices), but no long-run market power, as a price that is at all higher than that of other firms will eventually result in a complete loss of customers. There was a clear parallel between his earlier work in the labor market, where firms that paid too low a wage lost their workers, and this work on the product market, where firms that charged too high a price lost their customers. In a world with perfect information, of course, the trade-offs—and the complicated dynamic optimization to which they give rise—would simply not occur. A firm that paid any less than its competitors or charged any more than its rivals would lose all of its workers or customers.

Imperfectly competitive models of price setting are now commonplace in modern macroeconomic models, and the idea that business fluctuations involve variations in the relation between price and marginal cost is widely accepted as well, although there is now a plethora of models, with quite differing patterns of movement in markups, perhaps reflecting differences in the markets in which the firms interact (see, e.g., Stiglitz, 1984, and Rotemberg and Woodford, 1999). Even the specific model of dynamic markup variation developed by Phelps and Winter continues to be used to explain a variety of phenomena, and it is used extensively in the later models of equilibrium fluctuations in Phelps (1994).

1.4. New Keynesian Models and Staggered Contracts

The consequences of imperfect information became a central theme of the "new classical macroeconomics" of the 1970s, as a consequence of the celebrated Lucas (1972) model of how business fluctuations result from monetary surprises. Lucas adopts the island setting suggested in Phelps et al. (1970), but introduces the assumption of rational expectations—the postulate that expectations of all agents are at each point in time given by Bayesian updating, starting from a prior that is consistent with the data-generating process implied by the model and conditioning upon all information that is observable on the individual agent's island. This elegant development of the consequences of informational decentralization verified Phelps's basic insight that monetary surprises could have temporary real effects in such a setting without any need for nominal rigidities and also demonstrated the logic of the Phelps-Friedman natural rate hypothesis.

Nonetheless, the new classical macroeconomics often stressed strong implications of this particular model that Phelps himself was reluctant to endorse. For example, it was argued that monetary policy could affect real activity *only* to the extent that it was purely random, and not a systematic response to aggregate conditions, and thus that monetary stabilization policy would be pointless. Phelps found this implausible and led the development of a new Keynesian macroeconomics (though he did not himself introduce this term) in which monetary stabilization policy could mitigate the effects of real disturbances even under the assumption of rational expectations.

The key idea was the recognition that in reality, wages and prices are not continually readjusted. While Phelps's early papers about the consequences of imperfect information stressed the fact that this could give rise to real effects of monetary policy even in the absence of any such delays—in the introduction to the Phelps volume (Phelps et al., 1970, p. 3) he states that the new theory "does not fundamentally require that price-setters economize on their decision time"—he also always made it clear that in reality such delays existed. (On the page just cited, he states that "quarterly or annual reviews" of wages or prices "are frequently the rule," rather than more frequent reviews.) In the third part of Phelps (1968a), he assumes "that wage negotiations are annual and are evenly staggered across firms over the year" (p. 698) and points out that, although the inflation rate may still jump in response to a monetary disturbance, the size of such a jump is reduced by the fact that existing wages are not immediately reconsidered.

In the mid-1970s, Phelps incorporated these insights into rational expectations models of wage setting, in collaboration with two younger colleagues at Columbia, John Taylor and Guillermo Calvo, showing that even if expectations were rational, a negative shock to aggregate demand could generate a prolonged shortfall of output from the natural rate. The first of these papers (Phelps and Taylor, 1977) studied a simple setup in which a firm, though possessing rational expectations, has to decide its fall price by the start of the previous spring and analogously its spring price—too soon to observe the events and outcomes of the spring season. Phelps (1978a,b, 1979) examined the consequences of staggering the timing of wage revisions across firms and showed that such staggering could greatly increase the degree of persistence of the real effects of a monetary disturbance, allowing real effects to last longer than the time by which all wages would have been revised following the shock. Taylor (1979, 1993) then showed how this insight could be incorporated into econometric models of wage/price and output dynamics that incorporated rational expectations. Finally Calvo (1983) showed the consequences of modeling overlapping prices in a similar way. This particular model of price adjustment has since become the most common specification in new Keynesian analyses.

1.5. Imperfect Knowledge and Learning Dynamics

While much of Phelps's work since the period just discussed has made use of the assumption of rational expectations, he has also expressed frequent skepticism about the realism of assuming the degree of conformity between individual beliefs and the predictions of the economist's model that this postulate presumes, especially when analyzing the short-run effects of disturbances. Phelps (1983) argued that fully rational expectations were especially unlikely in contexts where individuals' optimal actions depend not simply on their own beliefs about aggregate conditions but also on their beliefs about *others' beliefs,* and so on in an infinite hierarchy of "higher-order beliefs." He suggested that higher-order beliefs were especially unlikely to be revised quickly following a disturbance, given the difficulty of knowing how others might perceive what had just occurred, even if one's own awareness of the current state were believed to be fairly precise. This provided a further reason for slow adjustment of wages and prices to a nominal disturbance and, hence, for the real effects of monetary policy to be greater and longer-lasting than the new classical models of the 1970s implied.

A conference that Phelps organized with Roman Frydman in 1981 (Frydman and Phelps, 1983a) gave an important early impetus to work on explicit models of the way in which economic agents learn about the laws of motion of the variables that they need to forecast and the consequences of such learning for macroeconomic dynamics. Frydman and Phelps (1983b) argue forcefully in the introduction to the volume that individual rationality alone provides no guarantee of the coordination of beliefs that is assumed in a rational expectations equilibrium and stress the need for a model of learning as an element of a convincing model of aggregate dynamics. By the 1990s, this point of view had been adopted even by leading proponents of the new classical macroeconomics (e.g., Sargent, 1993), and work on the macroeconomic consequences of learning dynamics is now at the forefront of current developments in macroeconomics.

1.6. Intertemporal General Equilibrium Models of Unemployment

In recent years, the central focus of Phelps's research has been understanding the causes of unemployment, especially relatively persistent increases in unemployment such as those seen in much of the European Union since 1980. An interest in "long swings" in unemployment of this kind has led to a deemphasis in the later work on the problem of expectational disequilibrium (or monetary factors more generally) that occupied Phelps's earliest work on labor markets. Instead, he has directed increased attention to the real determinants of changes in the natural rate of unemployment, a topic that he considers, in his work from the 1990s, in the context of complete intertemporal general equilibrium models. The structuralist viewpoint to which this work has led is expounded in great detail in Phelps (1994) in particular.

While the emphasis on nonmonetary models, the effects of real disturbances (including technology shocks), general equilibrium effects, and the dynamics of capital accumulation are all features that Phelps's more recent work shares with the real business cycle theory developed by Kydland and Prescott, Plosser, and others in the 1980s, Phelps's structuralist approach differs from real business cycle theory in important respects. Notably, whereas these latter models tend to assume a highly efficient system of frictionless competitive markets—and often compute the implied equilibrium responses to shocks by solving a planning problem, confident that the equilibrium response should in fact be an optimal one—Phelps's work has continued to stress the market frictions resulting from information imperfections. In particular, his models of unemployment assume that unemployment is involuntary and inefficient; an inefficient level of unemployment generally exists owing to efficiency wage concerns of one type or another, such as the need to pay high wages to avoid an inefficient rate of turnover, as in Phelps (1968a). Many of his models also assume imperfectly competitive product markets, incorporating the dynamics of customer flow first assumed in Phelps and Winter (1970). Variation in the desired markup of prices over marginal cost then becomes a crucial element in the effects of various types of real disturbances on the equilibrium level of employment.

A central theme of much of Phelps's structuralist writing has been the importance of changes in the real rate of interest (and asset prices more generally, such as the level of stock prices) on the equilibrium unemployment rate. This is a key element in his analysis of how many kinds of real disturbances should ultimately affect unemployment, and it is an issue that comes into focus only in the kind of intertemporal general equilibrium analysis that he develops. High real interest rates are argued to reduce equilibrium unemployment by discouraging investment-like activities of many kinds: investment in the retention of a larger work force (e.g., by paying higher wages) on the part of firms that face costs of recruiting or investment in a larger customer base by lowering current price markups, in addition to investments that would increase the productivity of the firm's workforce. Phelps's interest in this theme goes back to his relatively early work (Phelps, 1972b) on the effects of the government's fiscal stance (and the central bank's balance sheet) on aggregate supply. Here Phelps argued that equilibrium employment is reduced by government actions that push up the real interest rate and so reduce firms' labor demand at a given real wage and also by actions that push up the wealth of the working-age population, hence raising the real wage that workers demand. An important further development of the theme came in the work of Fitoussi and Phelps (1986, 1988), which set out a series of models in which an increase in the world real interest rate reduces firms' willingness to hire, to increase or maintain their stock of customers, or to add to their stock of fixed capital.

The full theory presented in *Structural Slumps: The Modern Equilibrium Theory of Unemployment, Interest and Assets* (Phelps, 1994) develops this theme more rigorously and in greater detail. The models presented there also consider a number of other important types of general equilibrium effects. These include the consequences for unemployment of a secular accumulation of private wealth by nationals; of an increase in what Phelps calls the "social wealth" provided by public entitlement programs; of labor-intensive public expenditure and taxes, particularly payroll levies and the income tax, to the extent that they effectively fail to tax nonwage income. In subsequent work, Phelps and his collaborators have explored the effects of changes in demographic factors, such as the distribution of educational attainments and age, and the effects of changes in expectations of *future* productivity developments, as measured by the level of stock prices. All of these factors can produce persistent swings in equilibrium employment at a given real wage; when they are combined with a theory of real wage rigidity owing to efficiency wage considerations, Phelps shows how substantial variations over time in (inefficient) unemployment can be understood.

1.7. Education and Technological Change

Another important part of Phelps's contributions to economics has been his work on models of long-run economic growth. It would take us too far from the main themes of this volume to attempt to survey all of his work on aspects of growth theory. But we do wish to draw particular attention to certain aspects of that work in the 1960s that have proven to have been ahead of their time.

It is only recently, in particular with the Schumpeterian growth literature of the 1990s, that the profession has fully realized the importance of the Nelson and Phelps (1966) paper on education and technical change. Departing from the view that education affects growth primarily through its effects on the rate of human capital accumulation, Nelson and Phelps describe growth as being determined by the consequences of the stock of human capital (or the education level) for a country's ability to innovate or to adapt to more advanced technologies. Differences in growth rates across countries then result primarily from differences in human capital stocks (rather than in rates of human capital accumulation) and thereby in countries' ability to achieve productivity gains. This approach predicts that the return to education is an increasing function of the rate of technological progress and suggests that the average level of education in a country should be increased not only directly through education policy but also indirectly through research and development policy. The Nelson-Phelps approach relating educational skills to technical progress is particularly helpful in explaining the upsurge in wage inequality during the past 20 years. While it has been widely recognized that much of the increased inequality has come from increased returns to education, the increased returns to education have also increased the relative supply of skilled workers, which in turn has increased the pace of innovation, which in turn has increased the relative returns to the educated.

2. PHELPSIAN THEMES IN CONTEMPORARY MACROECONOMIC DEBATE

The work that we have just sketched is worth recalling not only because it is an important stepping-stone in the development of current macroeconomic theory; but also because it continues, to an impressive degree, to provide the agenda for current work on the frontiers of macroeconomic theory. The chapters in this volume, which represent the proceedings of a conference in Ned Phelps's honor held at Columbia University on October 5–6, 2001, amply illustrate this. Here we briefly review the topics treated in the following pages and the ways in which they recall themes in Phelps's own work.

2.1. Information, Wage-Price Dynamics, and Business Fluctuations

Part I illustrates the continuing relevance to current work of a central theme of the conference that Phelps organized in 1969, the proceedings of which were published in Phelps et al. (1970), the famous Phelps volume—the role of incomplete information in explaining the real effects of monetary disturbances. As noted previously, a major strand of the new Keynesian literature has instead focused primarily on delays in the adjustment of wages and/or prices as a source of real effects of monetary policy (and this development as well had its origins in Phelps's work). In recent years, sticky wages and prices in this sense have been incorporated into quite sophisticated intertemporal equilibrium models, and the consequences of this hypothesis for the optimal conduct of monetary policy have been explored in some detail.

But such optimizing models with sticky wages and prices, at least the simplest and most familiar versions, have difficulty explaining certain aspects of observed wage-price dynamics. In particular, while the models allow for stickiness of the absolute *levels* of wages and prices, they tend to imply that the *rates of inflation* of both wages and goods prices should be determined largely by current and expected future conditions rather than by the rate of inflation that may have prevailed in the recent past. This prediction is difficult to reconcile with evidence of apparent inertia in the rate of inflation—for example, with the fact that nominal disturbances appear to have their greatest effect upon the rate of inflation *after*, rather than before, they have their greatest effect upon real activity. (See the chapter by Woodford in this volume for further discussion.)

The chapters by Calvo, Celasun, and Kumhof; Mankiw and Reis; and Woodford presented here all seek, in different ways, to provide explanations consistent with optimizing behavior for this apparent "inflation inertia." While the models of wage and price dynamics offered in each case differ in their details, all three chapters share the theme of explaining inflation inertia as being due *not* to any mechanical effect of past inflation as such on the determination of current inflation but rather to the continuing effect of *past inflation expectations*. It is really expectations regarding the rate at which others' prices are being increased (and hence the rate at which it is desirable to increase one's own prices) that are inertial in these models; and the reason for this, essentially, is the imperfect information—in particular, the incomplete knowledge of *the minds of others*—that Phelps has always stressed.

In the Calvo-Celasun-Kumhof model, prices are assumed to be automatically increased at a rate that remains unchanged between the periodic occasions upon which both the level of one's price and its planned rate of subsequent increase are reconsidered. Thus between these occasions for reoptimization, the rate of price increase continues to be based upon what was judged optimal at an earlier date and thus upon inflation expectations *given the information available at that earlier time.* The role of delays in the diffusion of new information is made more explicit in the Mankiw-Reis model, where wages are assumed to be optimal at any time *conditional upon the individual wage-setter's current information,* but information is assumed to be updated only at random intervals. Incomplete information is also central to the Woodford mode, which assumes that all price-setters constantly receive new information about the current state of aggregate demand, but that private observations at any date are of *only finite precision* (owing to the allocation of only a finite "channel capacity" to the monitoring of such developments). Woodford's analysis also emphasizes the role of higher-order expectations as a source of sluggish adjustment of the aggregate price level. Awareness of the imperfect precision of private observations implies recognition of the even *greater* imprecision of one's knowledge of what *others* may be observing, so that each higher order of expectations is predicted to adjust even more slowly.

Another idea from Phelps's early work that remains central to current concerns is the importance of customer dynamics for pricing behavior, as stressed in Phelps and Winter (1970). In the new Keynesian literature of the past 20 years, the dominant model of pricing behavior has instead come to be monopolistic competition after the fashion of Dixit and Stiglitz (1977); the chapter by Woodford in this volume is an example. In the Dixit-Stiglitz model, all buyers are aware of the complete set of available prices at each point in time, but they distribute their purchases across suppliers because the goods are imperfect substitutes. The market power that results from imperfect substitutability of the differentiated goods is permanent. In the simplest version of this model, the desired markup of price over marginal cost is the same at all times. But once delays in price adjustment are introduced, this sort of model allows for markup variations in response to a variety of types of aggregate disturbances.

The Dixit-Stiglitz model has proven highly tractable and for this reason has been a great success. Nonetheless, many economists would agree that short-run market power is much more widespread in economies such as that of the United States than is any substantial degree of long-run market power. For this reason, the Phelps-Winter idea of "customer markets" may be due for further study. Greenwald and Stiglitz argue forcefully for the importance of the insights that can be obtained from doing so. They stress in particular that the dynamic effects related to the impact of pricing policy on customer retention are far more important in price setting than the static effects (associated with the elasticity of demand) on which conventional theory has focused. The theory may help to explain observed variation in markups, and the endogenous variation in desired markups implied by this theory can be important in amplifying the effects upon economic activity of a variety of types of disturbances. As noted earlier, mechanisms of this kind are prominent in Phelps (1994). Whereas Phelps has emphasized the role of real interest rates, Greenwald and Stiglitz, focusing on imperfections in information that lead to imperfections in capital markets—to credit and equity rationing—highlight the consequences of changes in the *shadow* cost of funds, which can rise markedly in economic downturns.

These chapters are important contributions to the agenda that Phelps has set out in this area over the past three decades. At the same time, they make clear that more work needs to be done. Firms make decisions concerning the *rules* they use and the *information* that they process. They can decide to revise prices more or less frequently. They can have decision rules that use currently available information, for example, related to inventories or sales, and in which there is, accordingly, no lag—though the rules themselves may have to be updated as circumstances change. The modeling of the choice of rules requires one to take into account the risks associated with each. Greenwald and Stiglitz (1989), for instance, have emphasized the greater risks associated with wage and price adjustments—because of the uncertainties associated with knowing the responses of one's competitors—than with quantity adjustments, using models of wage and price setting akin to those of Phelps.

2.2. Imperfect Knowledge, Expectations, and Rationality

Part II continues the exploration of important themes in Phelps's work. The Frydman and Goldberg and Kurz et al. chapters build on Phelps's early insights concerning the role of imperfect knowledge in understanding macroeconomic dynamics. The chapter by Laibson, Repetto, and Tobacman illustrates the remarkable vitality of Phelps's seminal work on hyperbolic intertemporal preferences in explaining savings behavior as well as many other economic phenomena involving intertemporal choice.

Although the chapters presented in Part I rely on various, mostly informational, frictions in their explanations of macroeconomic dynamics, they remain rooted in the rational expectations tradition. In contrast, Frydman and Goldberg and Kurz et al. explore another recurring theme in Phelps's work. They argue that recognition of *imperfect knowledge* as distinct from *incomplete information* appears to be important for understanding macroeconomic behavior. Consequently, in modeling individual expectations, the Frydman and Goldberg chapter abandons the rigid connection between agents' expectations and the economist's structural model that has been the hallmark of the rational expectations hypothesis (REH). While retaining many of the key features of the standard intertemporal equilibrium approach, the Kurz et al. chapter also loosens the connection between expectations and the economist's structural model. This non-REH approach, according expectations a less mechanical and more autonomous role, was already implicit in the Phelps et al. (1970) volume and was the central theme of the Frydman and Phelps (1983) conference volume. As summarized in the introduction (p. 3) to the latter:

> There was no presumption by these authors [Phelps et al., 1970] that an outside investigator could accurately model individual expectations about the "world imagined" on each island. Because individual decisions cannot be derived from the formal maximization framework alone, models of

individual market behavior have to remain "open" in the sense that individual behavior can be analyzed only with some additional assumptions concerning the formation of individual expectations.

The Frydman and Goldberg chapter formulates an alternative model of individual expectations, dubbed *imperfect knowledge expectations* (IKE). In contrast to the usual presumption that departures from the REH are at best "boundedly rational," the chapter argues that IKE are consistent with the postulate of individual rationality in a world of imperfect knowledge. To compare the empirical implications of IKE with those of the REH, Frydman and Goldberg use IKE in a standard monetary model of the exchange rate and show that the model offers surprising promise in explaining hitherto anomalous aspects of the floating-rate experience. In particular, the model provides an explanation of "long swings" in real and nominal exchange rates, and it is consistent with the widespread, though often ignored, evidence concerning the temporal instability of parameters of empirical exchange rate and other macroeconometric models. Although shifts in policy lead to temporal instability of reduced forms under the REH as well (Lucas, 1976), Frydman and Goldberg suggest that it is difficult to reconcile the standard REH with the discontinuous and irregular nature of the temporal instability that appears to take place in the foreign exchange market. This points to the possibility that autonomous changes in expectations might be an important cause of coefficient instability. Since the autonomous nature of expectations introduces indeterminacy into the solution of the model, the chapter analyzes time paths of endogenous variables under various *qualitative* assumptions concerning the updating of individual expectations and discusses some methodological problems arising in the analysis of models with imperfect knowledge expectations.

Kurz et al. model the diversity of individual expectations using an approach dubbed *rational belief equilibrium* (RBE), and applies it to the analysis of the role of monetary policy. In the RBE described in their chapter, real effects of monetary policy arise because agents are assumed to believe in such real effects. The RBE theory assumes that all individual agents form forecasts of the payoff-relevant variables for all future dates, and these forecasts are assumed to encompass all future structural changes in the economy. In contrast to the IKE framework, the RBE theory requires that agents' forecasts be intertemporally correct on average and that the higher moments of the distribution of individual forecasts at all future dates be equal to the empirical distribution of forecasted variables generated by the RBE of the model. This definition of rationality derives from an assumption that, despite the diversity and instability of individual beliefs as well as structural change in the economy allowed for by the theory, there is one overarching "joint system" of exogenous shocks and agents' beliefs that is stationary (Kurz and Motolese, 2001, p. 516). This implies, in turn, that all moments of the *empirical distribution* of the (suitably transformed) data are constant. The RBE theory assumes that the temporal stability of the empirical distribution is common knowledge. It also makes use of all of the traditional assumptions required for the validity of dynamic optimization and standard equilibrium analysis. Since RB equilibria are inherently nonunique, an equilibrium is selected such that the moments generated by the simulated model are the same as the moments (assumed to be constant) of the observed macroeconomic time series.

The seminal paper of Phelps and Pollak (1968) developed an intertemporal framework involving hyperbolic discounting and applied it to the study of inter-generational altruism. Over the last three decades, the Phelps-Pollak framework has been reinterpreted in a variety of contexts involving problems of self-control, that is, conflicts between our preferences regarding the long run and our short-run behavior. (For some examples of contributions to this large literature see Angeletos et al., 2001, and references therein.) In the macroeconomic context Angeletos et al. conclude that "a model of consumption based on a hyperbolic discount function consistently better approximates the data than a model based on an exponential discount function" (p. 64). Moreover, a hyperbolic discounting framework can be used to explain the observed responses of consumption to the predictable changes in income, "matching well-documented empirical patterns of consumption-income co-movement."

Laibson, Repetto, and Tobacman use this form of preferences to provide an explanation of the puzzling co-existence of relatively large voluntary retirement accumulations (suggesting low discount rates) with credit card borrowing (suggest-ing high discount rates). They show that hyperbolic discounting offers a resolution to this puzzle and formulate a model allowing consumers to accumulate highly illiquid assets (e.g., retirement savings) and use high-interest credit card borrowing prior to retirement. They also show that the results of the simulation of a calibrated model incorporating hyperbolic discounting match up well with empirical evi-dence: The hyperbolic consumers save aggressively for retirement, primarily in the form of illiquid assets, while borrowing frequently on their credit cards.

2.3. Determinants of Equilibrium Unemployment

Phelps's concern throughout the 1990s with the real determinants of equilibrium unemployment, the subject of Part III, has been shared by a very active community of scholars, and considerable progress has been made in both the theoretical and empirical analyses of this issue. Much recent theoretical work on unemployment makes use of models of job search and random matching of workers with vacant jobs, which further develop the basic view of the labor market emphasized in Phelps's work of the late 1960s and in the chapters of the Phelps volume (Phelps et al., 1970). An example of current work with an especially close connection to the concerns of that conference is Mortensen's contribution to this volume. In their contributions to the 1970 volume, both Phelps and Mortensen described labor markets in which individual employers have the power to determine their own wage policies, even though there are many competing firms, because of workers' imperfect information about the wages available at other firms. The resulting search frictions make it possible for different firms to pay different wages, though the lower-wage firms will be subject to a higher rate of turnover. (We have already discussed the role of this idea in Phelps's earliest explanation for the existence of a positive equilibrium unemployment rate.) The Mortensen chapter develops an explicit model of search frictions in which a nondegenerate wage distribution exists in equilibrium, with lower-productivity jobs paying lower wages and suffering higher turnover rates (and thus remaining smaller) as a result. It then goes on to test predictions of the model on data on wages and size of labor force for a panel of Danish firms. It argues that the data not only fit the theoretical model, but that they indicate a considerable degree of monopsony power in the Danish labor market.

A particular focus of both Phelps's recent work and other work in a similarly structuralist vein has been the important effects that labor market policies and regulatory policies can have on the equilibrium unemployment rate, which is far from being a constant of nature. The Pissarides chapter in this volume, for example, analyzes the effects of the differing levels of start-up costs for new firms in different countries as a result of complex legal requirements, bureaucratic delays, and so on. A theoretical model is presented in which the number of people who choose to run firms (and hence the size of these firms) is endogenous. Higher start-up costs reduce the equilibrium number of firms and then, given search frictions in the labor market, result in a higher equilibrium unemployment rate. A comparison of measures of start-up costs across the various OECD countries suggests that this factor can explain a certain amount of the observed variation in employment and unemployment rates across countries.

Ljungqvist and Sargent similarly focus on the role of generous unemployment compensation systems in accounting for the intractability of European unemployment over the past two decades. An interesting twist of their argument is that it is not the unemployment benefits alone that guarantee a high equilibrium unemployment rate; after all, they note, unemployment benefits have been generous (in comparison to the United States) in much of western Europe throughout the postwar period, while Europe had *lower* unemployment than the United States during the 1950s and 1960s. Instead, they argue that the unfortunate consequence of the system is the way that the equilibrium unemployment rate *changes* in response to an increase in "economic turbulence." Through a detailed numerical analysis of an equilibrium model with job search, they show how an increase in economic turbulence, of a kind that they argue has in fact occurred since 1980 in both the United States and Europe, can result in a large increase in the number of long-term unemployed workers in the case of a benefits system that allows unemployed workers to collect benefits for an unlimited time at a level tied to their past wage level (which may not be a wage they can realistically expect to earn again under changed economic conditions). In their stress on the role of labor market institutions in determining not only the long-run average rate of unemployment but also the way in which an economy's unemployment rate will be affected by shocks, their analysis is in the spirit of Phelps's structuralist perspective.

Heckman similarly considers the way in which institutions of the European welfare state have interacted with the increased turbulence of the world economy in the past 20 years to generate higher unemployment, with particular reference to the German experience. His wide-ranging review of current knowledge about the effects of labor and product market regulations on equilibrium unemployment considers a broad spectrum of factors, including minimum wages and employment protection legislation as well as the unemployment insurance and company start-up costs stressed by the previous authors. Heckman also stresses the advantages of "decentralized unionism" over centralized wage bargaining in improving labor market flexibility in a way that favors productivity growth and hence ultimately faster growth in average real wages (at the price of some increase in wage inequality in the short run). He argues that what is crucial for adaptation to our new era of rapid change is not getting rid of unions, but rather making unions responsive to local conditions. Finally, Heckman stresses the importance of policies to deal with the human costs of abrupt economic transitions, such as that resulting from German unification, and discusses the ways in which this can be done without interfering unduly with the incentives of the young to acquire the skills that will allow them to use new technologies.

Finally, Nickell et al. offer an econometric analysis of the degree to which variation in labor market institutions across the OECD countries can account for the observed differences across these countries in the evolution of both real wages and unemployment rates. The chapter focuses in particular on the changes in unemployment rates that have been observed since the 1960s, and the extent to which these can be explained by changes in labor market institutions, such as the level of unemployment benefits, the degree of trade union power, the degree of wage "flexibility," and the level of taxes on labor income. Although the chapters in this part differ considerably in style and methodology, taken together they provide a fairly coherent view of an emerging consensus on the sources of structural unemployment of the kind so evidently at the root of the current European unemployment problem.

2.4. Education, Technical Change, and Growth

Part IV includes four contributions on growth, education, population, and vintage effects, which have been strongly influenced by Phelps's work in growth theory, in particular by the Nelson and Phelps (1966) paper on education and technical change.

The Aghion, Howitt, and Violante chapter develops an explanation for the rise in wage inequality based on the idea that technological change is skill biased, not only in the usual sense of enhancing educated workers' productivity in producing goods and services, but also in the sense of raising the reward to adaptability. This argument builds directly upon the idea of Nelson and Phelps (1966) that skills are not only an input to the production of goods and services, but also a factor in the creation and absorption of new technical knowledge. This Nelson-Phelps notion of human capital as a measure of the degree to which labor is adaptable to new technologies is useful in understanding the labor market experience of the United States over the past three decades. The explanation suggested in this chapter is that the arrival of a new "general-purpose technology" and the implied rise in the demand for labor adaptable to the new technological platform produced a surge in the return to adaptability.

Acemoglu revisits the "induced innovation" literature of the 1960s, to which Phelps was a major contributor (Drandakis and Phelps, 1966). This literature offered the first systematic study of the determinants of technical change as well as the first investigation of the relationship between factor prices and technical change. Acemoglu presents a modern reformulation of this literature using tools developed by the endogenous growth literature, and he uses this modern reformulation to shed light on two recent debates: (1) why is technical change often skill biased, and why has it become more skill biased during recent decades?, and (2) what is the role of human capital differences in accounting for income differences across countries? His present contribution to these debates also reiterates some of the leading themes of Nelson and Phelps (1966).

All models of sustained growth are linear in some sense, and the growth literature can be read as the search for the appropriate linear differential equation. Linearity is a "crucial" assumption, in the sense of Solow (1956), and it therefore seems reasonable to ask that this assumption have an intuitive and compelling justification. Jones's chapter proposes that such a justification can be found if the linearity is located in an endogenous fertility equation. It is a fact of nature that the law of motion for population is linear: People reproduce in proportion to their number. By itself, this linearity will not generate per capita growth, but it is nevertheless the first key ingredient of such a model. The second key ingredient is increasing returns to scale. According to this view, the fundamental insight of the idea-based growth literature is a justification for technological progress. Endogenous fertility together with increasing returns generates endogenous growth. This link between population growth and per capita growth has a number of precursors. Two of Phelps's papers (1966a, 1968b) together represent one of the earliest appreciations of this link.

Does it matter whether productivity growth is embodied in new machines or whether it is disembodied and lifts the productivity of all equipment? Phelps (1962) argued that the composition of the sources of growth is irrelevant in the long run. The Benhabib and Hobijn chapter reconsiders the relevance of embodied technological change, both for the long-run equilibrium and for short-run transition dynamics. In particular, it shows that the composition of embodied versus disembodied technical change does affect the elasticity of output with respect to savings, and therefore that it is relevant for analyzing the effects of policies such as investment tax credits. More importantly, it shows that in the short run, the effect of embodied aggregate technology shocks, unlike disembodied ones, produce the hump-shaped impulse responses in output observed in the data. The model also delivers the prediction that investment booms are followed by investment busts, not because of expectational errors but because of the vintage structure of production.

The chapters that make up this volume do not come close to representing the wide range of topics in economics to which Ned Phelps has made notable contributions. But they do, we believe, amply illustrate the continuing relevance of many of the insights first introduced in his work and the continuing importance of the project that he proposed for macroeconomics some 30 years ago.

REFERENCES

Angeletos, G.-M., D. Laibson, A. Repetto, and J. Tabacman (2001), "The Hyperbolic Consumption Model: Calibration, Simulation, and Empirical Evaluation," *Journal of Economic Perspectives* 15:47–68.

Blanchard, O. J. and L. Summers (1985), "Hysteresis and European Unemployemt Problem," in S. Fischer, ed., *NBER Macroeconomics Annual*, p. 1.

Calvo, G. A. (1979)," Quasi-Walrasian Theories of Unemployment," *American Economic Review: Papers and Proceedings* 69:102–7.

——— (1983), "Staggered Prices in a Utility-Maximizing Framework," *Journal of Monetary Economics* 12:383–98.

Cass, D. (1972), "On Capital Overaccumulation in the Aggregative, Neoclassical Model of Economic Growth: A Complete Characterization," *Journal of Economic Theory* 4:200–23.

Dixit, A. and J. E. Stiglitz (1977), "Monopolistic Competition and Optimum Product Diversity," *American Economic Review* 67:297–308.

Drandakis, E. M. and E. S. Phelps (1966), "A Model of Induced Invention, Growth and Distribution," *Economic Journal* 76:823–40.

Fitoussi, J. P. and E. S. Phelps (1986), "Causes of the 1980's Slump in Europe," *Brookings Papers on Economic Activity* 1986(2):487–513; translated and adapted, "Politique économique aux Etats-Unis et croissance du chômage en Europe," *Revue de l'OFCE* 1987(18):123–48.

——— (1988), *The Slump in Europe: Open Economy Theory Reconstructed*, Oxford: Basil Blackwell [Italian translation Bologna: Il Mulino, 1989].

Friedman, M. (1968), "The Role of Monetary Policy," *American Economic Review* 58:1–17.

Frydman, R. and E. S. Phelps, eds. (1983a), *Individual Forecasting and Aggregate Outcomes: "Rational Expectations" Examined*, New York: Cambridge University Press.

——— (1983b), "Introduction," in R. Frydman and E. S. Phelps, eds., *Individual Forecasting and Aggregate Outcomes: "Rational Expectations" Examined*, New York: Cambridge University Press, pp. 1–30.

Greenwald, B. and J. E. Stiglitz (1989), "Toward a Theory of Rigidities," *American Economic Review: Papers and Proceedings* 79:364–69.

Jones, C. (1995), "R&D-Based Models of Economic Growth," *Journal of Political Economy* 103:759–84.

Kurz, M. and M. Motolese (2001), "Endogenous Uncertainty and Market Volatility," *Economic Theory* 17:497–544.

Laibson, D. (1997), "Golden Eggs and Hyperbolic Discounting," *Quarterly Journal of Economics* 62:443–78.

Lucas, R. E., Jr. (1972), "Expectations and the Neutrality of Money," *Journal of Economic Theory* 4:103–24.

——— (1976), "Econometric Policy Evaluation: A Critique," in K. Brunner and A. H. Meltzer, eds., *The Phillips Curve and Labor Markets*, Carnegie-Rochester Conference Series on Public Policy, Vol. 1, Amsterdam: North-Holland, pp. 19–46.

Lucas, R. E. Jr. and E. C. Prescott (1974), " Equilibrium Search and Unemployment," *Journal of Economic Theory* 7:188–209.

Nelson, R. R. and E. S. Phelps (1966), "Investments in Humans, Technological Diffusion and Economic Growth," *American Economic Review: Papers and Proceedings* 56:69–75; reprinted in R. A. Wykstra, ed., *Human Capital Formation and Manpower Development*, New York: The Free Press.

Okun, A. (1981), *Prices and Quantities: A Macroeconomic Analysis*, Washington, D.C.: Brookings Institution.

Phelps, E. S. (1961), "The Golden Rule of Accumulation: A Fable for Growthmen," *American Economic Review* 51:638–43; reprinted in A. K. Sen, ed., *Readings in Economic Growth Theory*, New York: Penguin, 1969.

——— (1962), "The New View of Investment: A Neoclassical Analysis," *Quarterly Journal of Economics* 76:548–67; reprinted in J. E. Stiglitz and H. Uzawa, eds., *Readings in the Theory of Economic Growth*, Cambridge: MIT Press, 1969.

——— (1966a), "Models of Technical Progress and the Golden Rule of Research," *Review of Economic Studies* 33:133–45.

——— (1966b), *Golden Rules of Economic Growth*, New York: W. W. Norton and Amsterdam: North-Holland.

————— (1967), "Phillips Curves, Expectations of Inflation and Optimal Unemployment over Time," *Economica* 34:254–81.

————— (1968a), "Money-Wage Dynamics and Labor-Market Equilibrium," *Journal of Political Economy* 76:678–711; revised version in E. S. Phelps, A. A. Alchain, C. C. Holt, D. T. Mortensen, G. C. Archibald, R. E. Lucas, Jr., L. A. Rapping, S. G. Winter, Jr., J. P. Gould, D. F. Gordon, A. Hynes, D. A. Nichols, P. J. Taubman, and M. Wilkinson, *Microeconomic Foundations of Employment and Inflation Theory*, New York: Norton, pp. 124–66; reprinted in P. G. Korliras and R. S. Thorn, eds., *Modern Macroeconomics*, New York: Harper and Row, 1979.

————— (1968b), "Population Increase," *Canadian Journal of Economics* 35:497–518.

————— (1969), "The New Microeconomics in Inflation and Employment Theory," *American Economic Review: Papers and Proceedings* 59(2):147–60; portions appearing as the Introduction to E. S. Phelps, A. A. Alchain, C. C. Holt, D. T. Mortensen, G. C. Archibald, R. E. Lucas, Jr., L. A. Rapping, S. G. Winter, Jr., J. P. Gould, D. F. Gordon, A. Hynes, D. A. Nichols, P. J. Taubman, and M. Wilkinson, *Microeconomic Foundations of Employment and Inflation Theory*, New York: Norton, pp. 1–23.

————— (1971), "Inflation Expectations and Economic Theory," in N. Swan and D. Wilton, eds., *Inflation and the Canadian Experience*, Kingston, Ontario: Industrial Relation Centre, Queen's University, pp. 31–47.

————— (1972a), *Inflation Policy and Unemployment Theory*, New York: Norton and London: Macmillan.

————— (1972b), "Money, Public Expenditure and the Labor Supply," *Journal of Economic Theory* 5:69–78.

————— (1972c), "The Statistical Theory of Racism and Sexism," *American Economic Review* 62:659–61; reprinted in A. Amsden, ed., *The Economics of Women and Work*, New York: Penguin, 1979.

————— (1978a), "Disinflation without Recession: Adaptive Guideposts and Monetary Policy," *Weltwirtschaftliches Archiv* 114:783–809.

————— (1978b), "Inflation Planning Reconsidered," *Economica* 45:109–23.

————— (1979), "Introduction: Developments in Non-Walrasian Theory," in E. S. Phelps, *Studies in Macroeconomic Theory*, Vol. 1: *Employment and Inflation*, New York: Academic Press, pp. 1–19.

————— (1983), "The Trouble with Rational Expectations and the Problem of Inflation Stabilization," in R. Frydman and E. S. Phelps, eds., *Individual Forecasting and Aggregate Outcomes: "Rational Expectations" Examined*, Cambridge: Cambridge University Press, pp. 31–41.

————— (1994), *Structural Slumps,* Cambridge: Harvard University Press.

Phelps, E. S. and R. A. Pollak (1968), "On Second-best National Savings and Game-equilibrium Growth," *Review of Economic Studies* 35:185–99.

Phelps, E. S. and J. B. Taylor (1977), "Stabilizing Powers of Monetary Policy under Rational Expectations," *Journal of Political Economy* 85:163–90.

Phelps, E. S. and S. G. Winter, Jr. (1970), "Optimal Price Policy under Atomistic Competition," in E. S. Phelps, A. A. Alchain, C. C. Holt, D. T. Mortensen, G. C. Archibald, R. E. Lucas, Jr., L. A. Rapping, S. G. Winter, Jr., J. P. Gould, D. F. Gordon, A. Hynes, D. A. Nichols, P. J. Taubman, and M. Wilkinson, *Microeconomic Foundations of Employment and Inflation Theory*, New York: Norton, pp. 309–37.

Phelps, E. S., A. A. Alchain, C. C. Holt, D. T. Mortensen, G. C. Archibald, R. E. Lucas, Jr., L. A. Rapping, S. G. Winter, Jr., J. P. Gould, D. F. Gordon, A. Hynes, D. A. Nichols, P. J. Taubman, and M. Wilkinson (1970), *Microeconomic Foundations of Employment and Inflation*, New York: Norton.

Rotemberg, J. J. and M. Woodford (1999), "The Cyclical Behavior of Prices and Costs," in J. B. Taylor and M. Woodford, eds., *Handbook of Macroeconomics*, Vol. 1B, Amsterdam: North-Holland, pp. 1051–135.

Sargent, T. J. (1993), *Bounded Rationality in Macroeconomics*, Oxford: Oxford University Press.

———— (1999), *The Conquest of American Inflation,* Princeton: Princeton University Press.

Shapiro, C. and J. E. Stiglitz (1984), "Equilibrium Unemployment as a Discipline Device," *American Economic Review* 74:433–44.

Solow, R. M. (1956), "A Contribution to the Theory of Economic Growth, *Quarterly Journal of Economics* 70:65–94.

Stiglitz, J. E. (1973), "Wage Determination and Unemployment in LDCs," *Quarterly Journal of Economics* 88:194–227.

———— (1984), "Price Rigidities and Market Structure," *American Economic Review* 74(2): 350–55.

Taylor, J. B. (1979), "Staggered Wage Setting in a Macro Model," *American Economic Review* 69:108–13.

———— (1980), "Aggregate Dynamics and Staggered Contracts," *Journal of Political Economy* 88:1–23.

———— (1993), *Macroeconomic Policy in a World Economy,* New York: Norton.

PART I

Information, Wage-Price Dynamics, and Business Fluctuations

—— 1 ——

Imperfect Common Knowledge
and the Effects of Monetary Policy

MICHAEL WOODFORD

1. IMPERFECT INFORMATION AND PRICE ADJUSTMENT

A perennial question in macroeconomic theory asks the reason for the observed real effects of changes in monetary policy. It is not too hard to understand why central-bank actions can affect the volume of *nominal* spending in an economy. But why should variations in nominal expenditure of this sort, not associated with any change in real factors such as tastes or technology, not simply result in proportional variation in nominal wages and prices, without any effect upon the quantities of anything produced or consumed? It has long been observed that wages and prices do not immediately adjust to any extent close to full proportionality with short-run variations in nominal expenditure, but, again, why should not self-interested households and firms act in a way that brings about more rapid adjustment?

A famous answer to this question is that people are not *well enough informed* about changes in market conditions, at least at the time that these changes occur, to be able to react immediately in the way that would most fully serve their own interests. Phelps (1970) proposed the parable of an economy in which goods are produced on separate "islands," each with its own labor market; the parties determining wages and employment on an individual island do so without being able to observe either the wages or production decisions on other islands. As a result of this informational isolation, an increase in nominal expenditure on the goods produced on all of the islands could be misinterpreted on each island as an increase in the relative demand for the particular good produced there, as a result of which wages would not rise enough to prevent an increase in employment and output across all of the islands. Lucas (1972) showed that such an argument for a short-term Phillips-curve trade-off is consistent with "rational expectations" on each island, that is, with expectations given by Bayesian updating conditional upon

I thank Greg Mankiw and Lars Svensson for comments, Charlie Evans for sharing his VAR results, Hong Li for research assistance, and the National Science Foundation for research support through a grant to the NBER.

the market conditions observed on that island, starting from a prior that coincides with the objective ex ante probabilities (according to the model) of different states occurring.

This model of business fluctuations was, for a time, enormously influential and allowed the development of a number of important insights into the consequences for economic policy of endogenizing the expectations on the basis of which wages and prices are determined. However, the practical relevance of the imperfect-information model was soon subjected to powerful criticism. In the Lucas model, equilibrium output differs from potential only insofar as the *average estimate* of current aggregate nominal expenditure differs from the actual value. In terms of the log-linear approximate model introduced by Lucas (1973) and employed extensively in applied work thereafter, one can write

$$y_t = \alpha(q_t - q_{t|t}), \tag{1}$$

where $0 < \alpha < 1$ is a coefficient depending upon the price sensitivity of the supply of an individual good. Here y_t is the deviation of aggregate (log) real GDP from potential, q_t denotes aggregate nominal GDP, and $q_{t|t}$ is the average (across islands) of the expected value of q_t conditional upon information available on that island in period t.

Furthermore, all aggregate disturbances in period t—and hence the volume of aggregate nominal expenditure q_t—become public information (observable on all islands) by date $t + 1$. This implies that

$$E_t[q_{t+1|t+1}(i)] = E_t(q_{t+1})$$

in the case of each island i, where $E_t[\cdot]$ denotes an expectation conditional upon the history of aggregate disturbances through date t, and $q_{t+1|t+1}(i)$ the expectation of q_{t+1} conditional upon the information available on island i in period $t + 1$. When we average over i, it follows that

$$E_t(q_{t+1|t+1}) = E_t(q_{t+1}).$$

Then, taking the expectation of both sides of (1) for period $t + 1$ conditional upon the history of aggregate disturbances through date t, we find that

$$E_t(y_{t+1}) = 0. \tag{2}$$

Equation (2) implies that deviations of output from potential cannot be fore-casted a period earlier by someone aware of the history of aggregate disturbances up to that time. This means that a monetary disturbance in period t or earlier cannot have any effect upon equilibrium output in period $t + 1$ or later. But it follows that such real effects of monetary disturbances as are allowed for by (1) must be highly transitory: They must be present only in the period in which the shock occurs. The model was accordingly criticized as unable to account for the observed *persistence* of business fluctuations.

Of course, the degree to which the prediction of effects that last "one period" only is an empirical embarrassment depends upon how long a "period" is taken to be. In the context of the model, the critical significance of a "period" is the length of time it takes for an aggregate disturbance to become public information. But, many critics argued, the value of the current money supply is published quite quickly, within a few weeks; thus real effects of variations in the money supply should last, according to the theory, for a few weeks at most. Yet statistical analyses of the effects of monetary disturbances indicated effects lasting for many quarters.

Furthermore, the theory implied that monetary disturbances should not have even transitory effects on real activity, except insofar as these result in variations in aggregate nominal expenditure that *could not be forecasted* on the basis of variables that were already public information at the time of the effect on spending. But the VAR literature of the early 1980s (e.g., Sims, 1980) showed that variations in the growth rates of monetary aggregates were largely forecastable in advance by nominal interest rate innovations, and that the monetary disturbances identified by these interest rate surprises had no noticeable effect upon nominal expenditure for at least the first 6 months. This has been confirmed by many subsequent studies. For example, Figure 1 shows the impulse response of nominal GDP to an unexpected

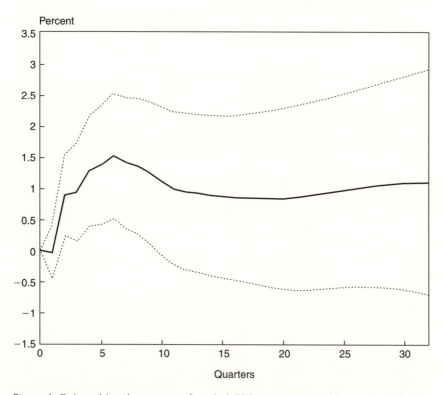

Figure 1. Estimated impulse response of nominal GDP to an unexpected interest rate reduction. (Source: Christiano et al., 2001.)

loosening of monetary policy in quarter zero, according to the identified VAR
model of Christiano et al. (2001). (Here shock is normalized to have a long-run
effect on log nominal GDP of 1 percentage point, and the dotted lines indicate
the ±2 s.e. confidence interval for the response.) Although the federal funds rate
falls sharply in quarter zero (see their paper), there is no appreciable effect upon
nominal GDP until two quarters later.

   Thus, given the estimated effects of monetary disturbances upon nominal
spending—and given the fact that money market interest rates are widely reported
within a day—the Lucas model would predict that there should be *no effect* of
such disturbances upon real activity at all, whether immediate or delayed. Instead,
the same study finds a substantial effect on real GDP, as shown in Figure 2.
Furthermore, the real effects persist for many quarters: The peak effect occurs
only six quarters after the shock, and the output effect is still more than one-third
the size of the peak effect ten quarters after the shock.

   These realizations led to a loss of interest, after the early 1980s, in models of the
effects of monetary disturbances based upon imperfect information and, indeed,
to a loss of interest in monetary models of business fluctuations altogether among
those who found the assumption of noninformational reasons for slow adjustment

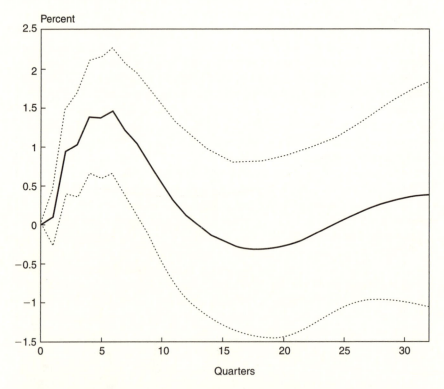

Figure 2. Estimated impulse response of real GDP to an unexpected interest rate reduction. (Source:
Christiano et al., 2001.)

of wages or prices unpalatable. However, this rejection of the Phelpsian insight that information imperfections play a crucial role in the monetary transmission mechanism may have been premature. For the unfortunate predictions just mentioned relate to the specific model presented by Lucas (1972), but not necessarily to alternative versions of the imperfect-information theory.

Rather, persistent effects of monetary disturbances on real activity can be obtained in a model that varies certain of Lucas's assumptions. In particular, one may argue that the Lucas model does not take seriously enough the Phelpsian insight that informational isolation of the separate decision-makers in an economy—captured by the parable of separate "islands"—is an important source of uncertainty on the part of each of them as to what their optimal action should be. For in the Lucas model, the only information that matters to decision-makers, about which they have imperfect information, is the current value of an exogenous aggregate state variable: the current level of nominal GDP (or equivalently in that model, the current money supply). Instead, for the "isolated and apprehensive . . . Pinteresque figures" in an economy of the kind imagined by Phelps (1970, p. 22), an important source of uncertainty is the unknowability of *the minds of others*.

Here I follow Phelps (1983) in considering a model in which the optimal price that any given supplier of goods should charge depends not only upon the state of aggregate demand but also upon the average level of prices charged by *other* suppliers. It then follows that the price set by that supplier depends not only upon its own estimate of current aggregate demand, but also upon its estimate of the average estimate of others, and similarly (because others are understood to face a similar decision) upon its estimate of the average estimate of that average estimate, and so on. The entire infinite hierarchy of progressively higher-order expectations matters (to some extent) for the prices that are set and hence for the resulting level of real activity.

This is important because, as Phelps argues, *higher-order* expectations may be even slower to adjust in response to economic disturbances. Phelps (1983) suggests that rational expectations in the sense of Lucas (1972) constitute a less plausible assumption when the hypothesis must be applied not only to estimates of the current money supply but also to an entire infinite hierarchy of higher-order expectations. Yet here I show that higher-order expectations can indeed be expected to adjust more slowly to disturbances, even under fully rational expectations.[1] The reason is that even when observations allow suppliers to infer that aggregate demand has increased, resulting in a substantial change in their *own* estimate of current conditions, these observations may provide less information about the way in which *the perceptions of others* may have changed and still less about others' perceptions of others' perceptions. Thus, in the model presented here, a monetary disturbance has real effects, not so much because the disturbance passes unnoticed as because its occurrence is not *common knowledge* in the sense of the theory of games.

---

1. Previous illustrations of the way in which additional sources of persistence in economic fluctuations can be created when higher-order expectations matter include Townsend (1983a,b) and Sargent (1991). These applications do not, however, consider the issue of the neutrality of money.

A second important departure from the Lucas (1972) model is to abandon the assumption that monetary disturbances become public information—and hence part of the information set of every agent—with a delay of only one period. Were we to maintain this assumption, it would matter little that in the present model output depends not only upon the discrepancy between q_t and $q_{t|t}$ but on the discrepancy between q_t and higher-order average expectations as well. For if the monetary disturbance at date t is part of every supplier's information set at date $t + 1$ (and this is common knowledge), then any effect of this disturbance on q_{t+1} must increase not only $q_{t+1|t+1}$ but also all higher-order expectations by exactly the same amount. (The argument is exactly the same as the one used in our earlier consideration of the effect on first-order average expectations.) We would again obtain (2), and the criticisms of the Lucas model noted previously would continue to apply.

Hence, it is desirable to relax that assumption. But how can one realistically assume otherwise, given the fact that monetary statistics are reported promptly in widely disseminated media? Here it is crucial to distinguish between *public information*—information that is available *in principle* to anyone who chooses to look it up—and the information of which decision-makers are *actually aware*. Rather than supposing that people are fully aware of all publicly available information—a notion stressed in early definitions of "rational expectations" and of critical importance for early econometric tests of the Lucas model[2]—and that information limitations must therefore depend upon the failure of some private transactions to be made public, I follow Sims (1998, 2001) in supposing that the critical bottleneck is instead the limited capacity of private decision-makers to *pay attention* to all of the information in their environment.[3]

In the model that follows, I assume that each decision-maker acts on the basis of his or her own subjective *perception* of the state of aggregate demand, which I model as observation of the true value with error (a subjective error that is idiosyncratic to the individual observer).[4] That is, all measurements of current conditions are obtained through a "noisy channel" in the communications-theoretic

---

2. Lucas (1977, sec. 9), however, implicitly endorses relaxation of this position when he suggests that it is reasonable to suppose that traders do not bother to track aggregate variables closely: "An optimizing trader will process those prices of most importance to his decision problem most frequently and carefully, those of less importance less so, and most prices not at all. Of the many sources of risk of importance to him, the business cycle and aggregate behavior generally is, for most agents, of no special importance, and there is no reason for traders to specialize their information systems for diagnosing general movements correctly."

3. A similar gap between the information that is publicly available and the information of which decision-makers are actually aware is posited in the independent recent work of Mankiw and Reis (2001). The Mankiw-Reis model is further compared to the present proposal later in Section 4.3.

4. The implications of introducing idiosyncratic errors of this kind in the information available to individual agents has recently been studied in the game-theoretic literature on "global games" (e.g., Morris and Shin, 2001). As in the application here, that literature has stressed that in the presence of strategic complementarities, even a small degree of noise in the private signals can have substantial consequences for aggregate outcomes, owing to the greater uncertainty that is created about higher-order expectations.

sense (e.g., Ziemer and Tranter, 1995). Given the existence of private measurement error, agents will not only fail to immediately notice a disturbance to aggregate demand with complete precision, but they will continue to be uncertain about whether others know that others know that others know . . . about it—even after they can be fairly confident about the accuracy of their *own* estimate of the aggregate state. Thus, it is the existence of a gap between reality and perception that makes the problem of other minds such a significant one for economic dynamics.

Moreover, given the use of a limited "channel capacity" for monitoring current conditions, the amount and accuracy of information that may be made "public" (e.g., on the internet) will not matter. Indeed, in the following model I assume that all aggregate disturbances are "public information," in the sense of being available in principle to anyone who chooses to observe them with sufficient precision and in the sense of being actually observed (albeit with error) by every decision-maker in the entire economy. There is no need for the device of separate markets on different "islands" in order for there to be imperfect common knowledge. (Presumably, Phelps intended the "islands" as a metaphor for this sort of failure of subjective experience to be shared all along—though who can claim to know other minds?) Nor is there any need for a second type of disturbance (the random variations in *relative* demand of the Lucas model) in order to create a nontrivial signal extraction problem. The "channel noise" generated by each decision-maker's own overburdened nervous system suffices for this purpose.

This emphasis upon the limited accuracy of private perceptions is in the spirit of recent interest in weakening the idealized assumptions of rational decision theory in macroeconomics and elsewhere (e.g., Sargent, 1993). Limitations upon the ability of people (and animals) to discriminate accurately among alternative stimuli in their environments are better documented (and admit of more precise measurement) than most other kinds of cognitive limitations, having been the subject of decades of investigation in the branch of psychology known as psychophysics (e.g., Green and Swets, 1966). While it might seem that the introduction of a discrepancy between objective economic data and private perceptions could weaken the predictions of economic theory to the point of making the theory uninteresting, the type of theory proposed here—which assumes that agents correctly understand the characteristics of the noisy channel through which they observe the world and respond optimally to the history of their subjective observations—is still relatively tightly parameterized. The proposed generalization here of a standard neoclassical model adds only a single additional free parameter, which can be interpreted as measuring the rate of information flow in the noisy channel, as in Sims (2001).

Section 2 develops a simple model of pricing decisions in an environment characterized by random variation in nominal spending and imperfect common knowledge of these fluctuations for the reason just discussed. It shows how one can characterize equilibrium output and inflation dynamics in terms of a finite system of difference equations, despite the fact that expectations of arbitrarily high order matter for optimal pricing policy. Section 3 then derives the implications of the model for the real effects of monetary disturbances in the special case where erratic monetary policy causes nominal GDP to follow a random walk with drift, as in the Lucas model. It is shown that not only are deviations of output from potential owing to monetary disturbances not purely transitory, but their degree of persistence may in principle be arbitrarily long. Indeed, arbitrarily long persistence of such real effects is possible (though less empirically plausible) even in the case of quite accurate individual perceptions of the current state of aggregate demand. The dynamics of higher-order expectations are also explicitly characterized, and it is shown that higher-order expectations respond less rapidly to a disturbance, as argued above.

Section 4 then compares imperfect common knowledge as a source of price inertia, and hence of real effects of monetary policy, to the more familiar hypothesis of "sticky prices," in the sense of a failure of prices to be continuously updated in response to changing conditions. In the case of a random walk in nominal GDP, the predicted dynamics of output and inflation are essentially the same in the model developed here and in the familiar Calvo (1983) model of staggered price adjustment: Corresponding to any given assumed average frequency of price adjustment there is a rate of information acquisition that leads to the same equilibrium dynamics in the imperfect-information model, despite continuous adjustment of all prices. However, this equivalence does not hold for more generally stochastic processes for nominal GDP. In the case of positive serial correlation of nominal GDP growth (the more realistic specification as far as actual monetary disturbances are concerned), the predictions of the two models differ, and in a way that suggests that an assumption of incomplete common knowledge of aggregate disturbances may better match the actual dynamics of output and inflation following monetary disturbances. Section 5 concludes the chapter.

2. INCOMPLETE COMMON KNOWLEDGE: A SIMPLE EXAMPLE

Here I illustrate the possibility of a theory of the kind sketched above by deriving a log-linear approximation to a model of optimal price setting under imperfect information. The log-linear approximation is convenient, as in Lucas (1973) and many other papers, in allowing a relatively simple treatment of equilibrium with a signal extraction problem.

2.1. Perceptions of Aggregate Demand and Pricing Behavior

Consider a model of monopolistically competitive goods supply of the kind now standard in the sticky-price literature. The producer of good i chooses the price p_t^i at which the good is offered for sale in order to maximize

$$E\left[\sum_{t=0}^{\infty} \beta^t \Pi(p_t^i; P_t, Y_t)\right],\tag{3}$$

where period t profits are given by

$$\Pi(p; P, Y) = m(Y)\left\{Y(p/P)^{1-\theta} - C[Y(p/P)^{-\theta}; Y]\right\}.\tag{4}$$

Here Y_t is the Dixit-Stiglitz index of real aggregate demand and P_t is the corresponding price index, the evolution of each of which is taken to be independent of firm i's pricing policy. Firm i expects to sell quantity $y_t^i = Y_t(p_t^i/P_t)^{-\theta}$ if it charges price p_t^i, for some $\theta > 1$. Real production costs are given by $C(y_t^i; Y_t)$, where the second argument allows for dependence of factor prices upon aggregate activity. Finally, (4) weights profits in each state by the stochastic discount factor $m(Y_t)$ in that state, so that (3) represents the financial market valuation of the firm's random profit stream (see, e.g., Woodford, 2001). The model here abstracts from all real disturbances.

I assume that the firm can choose its price independently each period, given private information at that time about the aggregate state variables. In this case, the pricing problem is a purely static one each period: choosing p_t^i to maximize $E_t^i \Pi(p_t^i; P_t, Y_t)$, where E_t^i denotes expectation conditional upon i's private information set at date t. The first-order condition for optimal pricing is then

$$E_t^i[\Pi_p(p_t^i; P_t, Y_t)] = 0. \tag{5}$$

In the absence of information limitations, each supplier would choose the same price (which then must equal P_t), so that equilibrium output would have to equal the *natural rate* of output $\bar{Y}$, defined as the level such that $\Pi_p(P; P, \bar{Y}) = 0$. (This is independent of P.)

To simplify the signal extraction issues, I approximate (5) by a log-linear relation, obtained by Taylor series expansion around the full-information equilibrium values $p_t^i/P_t = 1$ and $Y_t = \bar{Y}$.[5] This takes the form

$$p_t(i) = p_{t|t}(i) + \xi y_{t|t}(i), \tag{6}$$

introducing the notation $p_t(i) \equiv \log p_t^i$, $p_t \equiv \log P_t$, $y_t \equiv \log(Y_t/\bar{Y})$, and letting $x_{t+j|t}(i) \equiv E_t^i x_{t+j}$ for any variable x and any horizon $j \geq 0$. Assuming that C is such that $C_y > 0$, $C_{yy} \geq 0$, and $C_{yY} > 0$, one can show that $\xi > 0$. I assume, however, that it satisfies $\xi < 1$, so that the pricing decisions of separate producers are *strategic complements* (again see Woodford, 2001).

Finally, I specify the demand side of the economy by assuming a given stochastic process for aggregate nominal expenditure. Traditional justification for such an assumption is that the central bank determines an exogenous process for the money supply and that there is a constant, or at any rate exogenous, velocity of money. Yet we need not assume anything as specific as this about the monetary transmission mechanism or about the nature of monetary policy. All that matters for the analysis that follows is: (1) that the disturbance driving the nominal GDP process is a

---

5. We abstract here from any sources of real growth, as a result of which the full-information equilibrium level of output, or "natural rate" of output, is constant. Nothing material in the subsequent analysis would be different were we to assume steady trend growth of the natural rate of output. We abstract here from stochastic variation in the natural rate so that producers need *only* form inferences about the monetary disturbances. One advantage of this simplification is that it makes clear the fact that the present model, unlike that of Lucas (1972), does not depend upon the existence of both real and nominal disturbances in order for there to be real effects of nominal disturbances.

monetary policy shock, and (2) that the dynamic response of nominal GDP to such shocks is of a particular form. The assumption of a particular response of nominal GDP under historical policy is something that can be checked against time-series evidence, regardless of how one believes that this response should best be explained. Direct specification of a stochastic process for nominal GDP eliminates the need for further discussion of the details of aggregate demand determination, and for purposes of asking whether our model is consistent with the observed responses of real activity and inflation to monetary disturbances, this degree of detail suffices.[6]

Letting q_t denote the exogenous process $\log(P_t Y_t / \bar{Y})$, and averaging (6) over i, we obtain

$$p_t = \xi q_{t|t} + (1 - \xi) p_{t|t}, \tag{7}$$

introducing the notation $x_{t+j|t} \equiv \int x_{t+j|t}(i) di$. The (log) price level is then a weighted average of the average estimate of current (log) nominal GDP (the exogenous forcing process) and the average estimate of the (log) price level itself.

Iterating (7) allows us to express p_t as a weighted average of the average estimate of q_t, the average estimate of that average estimate, and so on. Introducing the notation

$$x_t^{(k)} \equiv x_{t|t}^{(k-1)} \qquad \text{for each} \quad k \geq 1$$

$$x_t^{(0)} \equiv x_t$$

for higher-order average expectations, we obtain

$$p_t = \sum_{k=1}^{\infty} \xi (1 - \xi)^{k-1} q_t^{(k)}. \tag{8}$$

Thus the (log) price level can be expressed as a weighted average of expectations and higher-order expectations of the current level of (log) nominal GDP, as in Phelps (1983). Since $y_t = q_t - p_t$, it follows that

$$y_t = \sum_{k=1}^{\infty} \xi (1 - \xi)^{k-1} \left(q_t - q_t^{(k)} \right). \tag{9}$$

Thus, output deviates from the natural rate only insofar as the level of current nominal GDP is not common knowledge. However, this equation differs from (1),

---

6. My point here is essentially the same as that of Christiano et al. (1998), who argue that it is possible to test the predictions of their model by computing the predicted responses to a given money growth process, even if they do not believe (and do not assume in their VAR strategy for identifying the effects of monetary policy shocks) that monetary policy is correctly described by an exogenous process for money growth. Of course, if one wanted to ask a question such as what the effect would be of an improvement in suppliers' information, it would be necessary to take a stand on whether or not the nominal GDP process should change. This would depend on how aggregate nominal expenditure is determined.

the implication of the Lucas model, in that higher-order expectations matter, and not simply the average estimate of current nominal GDP.

2.2. Equilibrium Inflation Dynamics

To consider a specific example, suppose that the growth rate of nominal GDP follows a first-order autoregressive process,

$$\Delta q_t = (1 - \rho)g + \rho \Delta q_{t-1} + u_t, \tag{10}$$

where Δ is the first-difference operator, $0 \leq \rho < 1$, and u_t is a zero-mean Gaussian white noise process. Here g represents the long-run average rate of growth of nominal GDP, while the parameter ρ indexes the degree of serial correlation in nominal GDP growth; in the special case where $\rho = 0$, nominal GDP follows a random walk with drift g. The disturbance u_t is assumed to represent a monetary policy shock, which therefore has no effect upon the real determinants of supply costs discussed above.

In the case of full information, the state of the economy at date t would be fully described by the vector

$$X_t \equiv \begin{pmatrix} q_t \\ q_{t-1} \end{pmatrix}.$$

That is to say, knowledge of the current value of X_t would suffice to compute not only the equilibrium values of p_t and y_t but the conditional expectations of their values in all future periods as well. In terms of this vector, the law of motion (10) can equivalently be written

$$X_t = c + AX_{t-1} + au_t, \tag{11}$$

where

$$c \equiv \begin{pmatrix} (1 - \rho)g \\ 0 \end{pmatrix}, \qquad A \equiv \begin{pmatrix} 1 + \rho & -\rho \\ 1 & 0 \end{pmatrix}, \qquad a \equiv \begin{pmatrix} 1 \\ 0 \end{pmatrix}.$$

With incomplete information, however, average expectations and higher-order average expectations $X_t^{(k)}$ will also matter for the determination of prices and output and their future evolution.

Suppose that the only information received by supplier i in period t is the noisy signal

$$z_t(i) = q_t + v_t(i), \tag{12}$$

where $v_t(i)$ is a mean-zero Gaussian white noise error term, distributed independently of both the history of fundamental disturbances (u_{t-j}) and the observation errors of all other suppliers. I suppose that the complete information set of supplier i when setting p_t^i consists of the history of the subjective observations $\{z_t(i)\}$; this means, in particular, that the person making the pricing decision does not actually observe (or does not pay attention to!) the quantity sold at that price.

Suppose, however, that the supplier forms optimal estimates of the aggregate state variables given this imperfect information. Specifically, I shall assume that the supplier forms minimum-mean-squared-error estimates that are updated in real time using a Kalman filter.[7] Let us suppose that the supplier (correctly) believes that the economy's aggregate state evolves according to a law of motion

$$\bar{X}_t = \bar{c} + M\bar{X}_{t-1} + mu_t, \tag{13}$$

for a certain matrix M and vectors $\bar{c}$ and m that we have yet to specify, where

$$\bar{X}_t \equiv \begin{pmatrix} X_t \\ F_t \end{pmatrix}$$

and

$$F_t \equiv \sum_{k=1}^{\infty} \xi (1 - \xi)^{k-1} X_t^{(k)}. \tag{14}$$

Thus, our conjecture is that only a particular linear combination of the higher-order expectations $X_t^{(k)}$ is needed in order to forecast the future evolution of that vector itself. Our interest in forecasting the evolution of this particular linear combination stems from the fact that (8) implies that p_t is equal to the first element of F_t. In terms of our extended state vector, we can write

$$p_t = e_3' \bar{X}_t, \tag{15}$$

introducing the notation e_j to refer to the jth unit vector (i.e., a vector the jth element of which is one, while all other elements are zeros).

In terms of this extended state vector, the observation equation (12) is of the form

$$z_t(i) = e_1' \bar{X}_t + v_t(i). \tag{16}$$

It then follows (see, e.g., Chow, 1975, and Harvey, 1989) that i's optimal estimate of the state vector evolves according to a Kalman filter equation,

$$\bar{X}_{t|t}(i) = \bar{X}_{t|t-1}(i) + k[z_t(i) - e_1' \bar{X}_{t|t-1}], \tag{17}$$

where k is the vector of *Kalman gains* (to be specified), and the forecast prior to the period t observation is given by

---

7. This is optimal if the supplier seeks to maximize a log-quadratic approximation to his or her exact objective function; however, the *exact* objective function implied by the model above would not be log-quadratic.

$$\bar{X}_{t|t-1}(i) = \bar{c} + M\bar{X}_{t-1|t-1}(i). \tag{18}$$

Substituting (18) into (17), we obtain a law of motion for i's estimate of the current state vector. Integrating this over i [and using (16) to observe that the average signal is just $q_t = e_1'\bar{X}_t$], we obtain a law of motion for the *average estimate* of the current state vector,

$$\bar{X}_{t|t} = \bar{X}_{t|t-1} + ke_1'(\bar{X}_t - \bar{X}_{t|t-1})$$
$$= \bar{c} + ke_1'M\bar{X}_{t-1} + (I - ke_1')M\bar{X}_{t-1|t-1} + ke_1'mu_t.$$

Next we observe that (14) implies that

$$F_t = \bar{\xi}\bar{X}_{t|t}, \tag{19}$$

where

$$\bar{\xi} \equiv \begin{pmatrix} \xi & 0 & 1-\xi & 0 \\ 0 & \xi & 0 & 1-\xi \end{pmatrix}.$$

Substituting the above expression for $\bar{X}_{t|t}$, we obtain

$$F_t = \bar{\xi}\bar{c} + \hat{k}e_1'M\bar{X}_{t-1} + (\bar{\xi} - \hat{k}e_1')M\bar{X}_{t-1|t-1} + \hat{k}e_1'mu_t, \tag{20}$$

where $\hat{k} \equiv \bar{\xi}k$.

We now wish to determine whether the laws of motion (11) and (20) for the elements of $\bar{X}_t$ can in fact be expressed in the form (13), as conjectured. We note first that (11) implies that the matrices and vectors in (13) must be of the form

$$\bar{c} = \begin{pmatrix} c \\ d \end{pmatrix}, \qquad M = \begin{pmatrix} A & 0 \\ G & H \end{pmatrix}, \qquad m = \begin{pmatrix} a \\ h \end{pmatrix},$$

where c, A, and a are defined as in (11), and the vectors d and h and the matrices G and H are yet to be determined.

Making these substitutions in (20), we then obtain

$$F_t = \hat{c} + \hat{k}A_1X_{t-1} + [\xi A + (1 - \xi)G - \hat{k}A_1]X_{t-1|t-1} \tag{21}$$
$$+ (1 - \xi)HF_{t-1|t-1} + \hat{k}u_t,$$

where

$$\hat{c} \equiv \xi c + (1 - \xi)d, \tag{22}$$

and A_1 is the first row of A, that is, the row vector $(1 + \rho \quad -\rho)$. Finally, we note that (19) for date $t - 1$ implies that

$$(1 - \xi)F_{t-1|t-1} = F_{t-1} - \xi X_{t-1|t-1}.$$

Using this substitution to eliminate $F_{t-1|t-1}$ from (21), we finally obtain

$$F_t = \hat{c} + \hat{k}A_1 X_{t-1} + H F_{t-1} + [\xi A + (1 - \xi)G - \xi H - \hat{k}A_1] \tag{23}$$
$$X_{t-1|t-1} + \hat{k}u_t.$$

This has the same form as the lower two rows of (13) if it happens that the expression in square brackets is a zero matrix.

In this case, we are able to make the identifications

$$d = \hat{c}, \tag{24}$$

$$G = \hat{k}A_1, \tag{25}$$

$$h = \hat{k}. \tag{26}$$

Given (22), equation (24) requires that $d = c$, and (25) and (26) uniquely identify G and h once we know the value of the gain vector $\hat{k}$. Using solution (25) for G, we observe that the expression in square brackets in (23) is a zero matrix if and only if

$$H = A - \hat{k}A_1. \tag{27}$$

Thus we have a unique solution for H as well. It follows that once we determine the vector of Kalman gains k, and hence the reduced vector $\hat{k}$, we can uniquely identify the coefficients of the law of motion (13) for the state vector $\bar{X}_t$. This then allows us to determine the equilibrium dynamics of p_t and y_t, using (15) and the identity $y_t = q_t - p_t$.

2.3. Optimal Filtering

It remains to determine the vector of Kalman gains k in the Kalman filter equation (17) for the optimal updating of individual suppliers' estimates of the aggregate state vector. Let us define the variance-covariance matrices of *forecast errors* on the part of individual suppliers:

$$\Sigma \equiv \mathrm{var}\left[\bar{X}_t - \bar{X}_{t|t-1}(i)\right],$$
$$V \equiv \mathrm{var}\left[\bar{X}_t - \bar{X}_{t|t}(i)\right].$$

Note that these matrices will be the same for all suppliers i, since the observation errors are assumed to have the same stochastic properties for each of them.

The Kalman gains are then given as usual by[8]

$$k = (\sigma_z^2)^{-1} \Sigma e_1, \tag{28}$$

where

---

8. See, e.g., Chow (1975) or Harvey (1989).

$$\sigma_z^2 \equiv \text{var} \left[z_t(i) - z_{t|t-1}(i) \right] = e_1' \Sigma e_1 + \sigma_v^2. \tag{29}$$

Here $\sigma_v^2 > 0$ is the variance of the individual observation error $v_t(i)$ each period. Relations (28)–(29) then imply that

$$\hat{k} = (e_1' \Sigma e_1 + \sigma_v^2)^{-1} \bar{\xi} \Sigma e_1. \tag{30}$$

Thus once we have determined the matrix Σ, $\hat{k}$ is given by (30), which allows us to solve for the coefficients of the law of motion (13) as above.

The computation of the variance-covariance matrix of forecast errors also follows standard lines. The transition equation (13) and the observation equation (16) imply that the matrices Σ and V satisfy

$$\Sigma = MVM' + \sigma_u^2 \, mm',$$

$$V = \Sigma - (\sigma_z^2)^{-1} \, \Sigma e_1 e_1' \Sigma,$$

where σ_u^2 is the variance of the innovation term u_t in the exogenous process (10). Combining these equations, we obtain the usual stationary *Riccati equation* for Σ:

$$\Sigma = M\Sigma M' - (e_1' \Sigma e_1 + \sigma_v^2)^{-1} \, M\Sigma e_1 e_1' \Sigma M' + \sigma_u^2 \, mm'. \tag{31}$$

The matrix Σ is thus obtained by solving for a fixed point of the nonlinear matrix equation (31). Of course, this equation itself depends upon the elements of M and m, and hence upon the elements of G, H, and h, in addition to parameters of the model. These latter coefficients can in turn be determined as functions of Σ using (25)–(27) and (30). Thus we obtain a larger fixed-point equation to solve for Σ, specified solely in terms of model parameters.

Except in the special case discussed below, this system is too complicated to allow us to obtain further analytical results. Numerical solution for Σ in the case of given parameter values remains possible, however, and in practice proves to be not difficult.

3. THE SIZE AND PERSISTENCE OF THE REAL EFFECTS OF NOMINAL DISTURBANCES

We now turn to the insights that can be obtained regarding the effects of nominal disturbances from the solution of the example described in the previous section. In particular, we shall consider the impulse responses of output and inflation to an innovation u_t implied by the law of motion (13), and how these vary with the model parameters ρ, ξ, and σ_v^2/σ_u^2.[9]

---

9. It should be evident that it is only the *relative* size of the innovation variances that matters for the determination of the Kalman gains k, and hence of the coefficients M and m in the law of motion. It is also only the relative variance that is determined by a particular assumed rate of information flow in the noisy channel through which a supplier monitors current aggregate demand. See Sims (2001) for details of the computation of the rate of information flow.

One question of considerable interest concerns the extent to which an unexpected increase in nominal GDP growth affects real activity, as opposed to simply raising the money prices paid for goods. However, of no less interest is the question of the length of time for which any real effect *persists* following the shock. This is an especially important question given that the inability to explain persistent output effects of monetary policy shocks was one of the more notable of the perceived weaknesses of the first generation of asymmetric-information models.

3.1. The Case of a Random Walk in Nominal Spending

In considering the question of persistence, a useful benchmark is to consider the predicted response to an unexpected permanent increase in the level of nominal GDP. In this case, the subsequent dynamics of prices and output are due solely to the adjustment over time of a discrepancy that has arisen between the level of nominal spending and the existing level of prices and not to any predictable further changes in the level of nominal spending itself. This corresponds to the computation of impulse response functions in a special case of the model of the previous section, the case in which $\rho = 0$, so that the log of nominal GDP follows a random walk with drift.

In this special case, the equations of the previous section can be further simplified. First, we note that in this case, the state vector X_t may be reduced to the single element q_t. The law of motion (11) continues to apply so that now $c = g$, $A = 1$, and $a = 1$ are all scalars. The law of motion for the aggregate state can again be written in the form of (13), where F_t is defined as in (14); but now F_t is a scalar, and the blocks G, H and h of M and m are scalars as well. Equation (19) continues to apply, but now with the definition

$$\bar{\xi} \equiv (\xi \quad 1 - \xi).$$

Equation (26) holds as before, but now $\hat{k}$ is a scalar; equations (25) and (27) reduce to

$$G = \hat{k},$$
$$H = 1 - \hat{k}.$$

Substituting these solutions for the elements of $M(\hat{k})$ and $m(\hat{k})$, we can solve (31) for the matrix $\Sigma(\hat{k})$ in the case of any given reduced Kalman gain $\hat{k}$. The upper-left equation in this system is given by

$$\Sigma_{11} = \Sigma_{11} - (\Sigma_{11} + \sigma_v^2)^{-1}\Sigma_{11}^2 + \sigma_u^2,$$

which involves only Σ_{11} and is independent of $\hat{k}$. It reduces to a quadratic equation in Σ_{11}, which has two real roots, one positive and one negative. Since the variance Σ_{11} must be nonnegative, the positive root is the only relevant solution, and it is given by

$$\Sigma_{11} = \frac{\sigma_u^2}{2} \left\{ 1 + [1 + 4(\sigma_v^2/\sigma_u^2)]^{1/2} \right\}. \tag{32}$$

The lower-left equation in the system (31), in turn, involves only Σ_{21} and Σ_{11}, and given that we have already solved for Σ_{11}, this equation can be solved for Σ_{21}. We obtain

$$\Sigma_{21}(\hat{k}) = \sigma_u^2 \frac{1 + 2(\sigma_v^2/\sigma_u^2) + [1 + 4(\sigma_v^2/\sigma_u^2)]^{1/2}}{(2/\hat{k}) - 1 + [1 + 4(\sigma_v^2/\sigma_u^2)]^{1/2}}. \tag{33}$$

Finally, (30) expresses $\hat{k}$ as a function of Σ, which in fact depends only upon the elements Σ_{11} and Σ_{21}. Substituting expressions (32) and (33) into this relation, we obtain a quadratic equation for $\hat{k}$, namely,

$$(\sigma_v^2/\sigma_u^2)\hat{k}^2 + \xi\hat{k} - \xi = 0. \tag{34}$$

It is easily seen that for any parameters $\xi, \sigma_u^2, \sigma_v^2 > 0$, equation (34) has two real roots, one satisfying

$$0 < \hat{k} < 1, \tag{35}$$

and another that is negative. Substituting our previous solutions for $M(\hat{k})$ and $m(\hat{k})$ into (13), we note that this law of motion implies that

$$q_t - F_t = (1 - \hat{k})(q_{t-1} - F_{t-1}) + (1 - \hat{k})u_t. \tag{36}$$

Equation (36) implies that $q_t - F_t$, which measures the discrepancy between the actual level of nominal spending and a certain average of higher-order expectations regarding current nominal spending, is a *stationary* random variable if and only if $|1 - \hat{k}| < 1$. This requires that $\hat{k} > 0$, and so excludes the negative root of (34). Thus if we are to obtain a solution in which the variances of forecast errors are finite and constant over time, as assumed above, it can correspond only to the root satisfying (35), which is given by

$$\hat{k} = \tfrac{1}{2}\left[-\gamma + (\gamma^2 + 4\gamma)^{1/2}\right], \tag{37}$$

where

$$\gamma \equiv \xi\sigma_u^2/\sigma_v^2 > 0. \tag{38}$$

3.2. Dynamics of Real Activity

Since in this special case, $p_t = F_t$, equation (36) immediately implies that (log) real GDP y_t evolves according to

$$y_t = \nu(y_{t-1} + u_t), \tag{39}$$

where $v = 1 - \hat{k}$ and $\hat{k}$ is given by (37). Since $0 < v < 1$, this describes a stationary process with positive serial correlation. The implied effect of a monetary shock at date t upon current and expected subsequent real activity is given by

$$E_t(y_{t+j}) - E_{t-1}(y_{t+j}) = v^{j+1} u_t,$$

which holds for all $j \geq 0$. Thus the same coefficient v determines both the size of the initial impact upon real activity of a monetary shock (y_t is increased by $v u_t$) and the degree of persistence of such an effect (the effect on output j periods later decays as v^j).

While the model implies that the real effects of a monetary shock die out with time, output is *not* predicted to again equal the natural rate on average in any finite time, as in the Lucas model. Indeed, the degree of persistence of such real effects may be arbitrarily great, for (37) implies that $\hat{k}$ may be an arbitrarily small positive quantity (so that v is arbitrarily close to one), if γ is small enough; and the half-life of output disturbances tends to infinity as v approaches one.

More generally, the degree of persistence is observed to be a monotonically decreasing function of γ, which depends upon both ξ and σ_v^2/σ_u^2. Not surprisingly, this implies that persistence is greater the larger σ_v^2 is relative to σ_u^2, that is, the less the information contained in the individual suppliers' subjective perceptions of the state of nominal GDP. Moreover, if the amount of information is small enough, persistence may be arbitrarily great. This may seem little different from the conclusion in the case of the Lucas model that the output effects of a monetary disturbance may persist for a good while if it takes a long time for changes in the money supply to become public information. But because the bottleneck in our case is assumed to be the inaccuracy of individual subjective perceptions, rather than limitations of the statistics that are publicly available should people bother to pay attention, the mere fact that monetary data quickly enter the public domain does not in itself imply that perceptions of the state of aggregate demand must be accurate.

Even more interestingly, persistence is predicted to be greater as ξ is smaller, which is to say, the greater the extent of "real rigidity" in the sense of Ball and Romer (1990), and hence the greater the degree of strategic complementarity in individual suppliers' pricing decisions.[10] In fact, the model implies that *regardless* of the degree of accuracy of the suppliers' observations of the aggregate state—as long as they are not *perfect*—the degree of persistence of the real effects of a monetary policy shock can be *arbitrarily great,* if the degree of "real rigidity" is sufficiently great (i.e., ξ is sufficiently small)!

This means that substantial real effects of monetary policy, and significant persistence of such effects, do not depend upon private parties being wholly ignorant of the occurrence of the disturbance to monetary policy. If σ_v^2/σ_u^2 is not too large, each individual supplier will have a fairly accurate estimate of current aggregate demand at the time of setting its price, and individual estimates $q_{t|t}(i)$ will quickly adjust by nearly as much as the permanent change in nominal spending that has occurred. Nonetheless, *prices* may be quite slow to adjust, owing

---

10. See Woodford (2001) for further discussion of the interpretation of this parameter and various factors that can make it small in an actual economy.

to continuing uncertainty about *others'* estimates of current aggregate demand and even greater uncertainty about others' estimates of others' estimates. Thus the sluggishness of higher-order expectations stressed by Phelps (1983) can play a critical role in explaining both the size and persistence of the real effects of monetary policy.

3.3. Dynamics of Higher-Order Expectations

This can be shown explicitly through an analysis of the impulse responses of higher-order average expectations following a monetary shock. While we saw earlier that it is not necessary to solve for the complete hierarchy of expectations in order to solve for the equilibrium dynamics of output (only the particular average of higher-order expectations represented by F_t), consideration of the dynamics of expectations at different levels can provide further insight into the reason for the sluggishness of price adjustment in this model.

Similar Kalman-filtering techniques as in the previous section can be used to determine the dynamics of average expectations at each level of the hierarchy. Let $q_t^{(k)}$ denote the average kth-order expectation at date t regarding the current level of (log) nominal GDP, where $q_t^{(0)}$ is defined as q_t, and let us conjecture a law of motion of the form

$$q_t^{(k)} = \sum_{j=0}^{k} \alpha_{kj} q_{t-1}^{(j)} + a_k u_t \tag{40}$$

for each $k \geq 0$, where for $k = 0$ we have $\alpha_{00} = 1$ and $a_0 = 1$. We wish to determine the coefficients α_{kj} and a_k for higher values of k.

Supplier i's estimate of the value of $q_t^{(k)}$ should evolve according to a Kalman filter equation of the form

$$q_{t|t}^{(k)}(i) = q_{t|t-1}^{(k)}(i) + \kappa_{k+1}[z_t(i) - z_{t|t-1}(i)],$$

where the $(k+1)$st-order Kalman gain κ_{k+1} remains to be determined. Substituting the observation equation (12) for $z_t(i)$ and its forecast as before and averaging over i, we obtain

$$q_t^{(k+1)} = q_{t|t-1}^{(k)} + \kappa_{k+1}(q_t^{(0)} - q_{t|t-1}^{(0)}).$$

Then substituting the average forecasts at date $t - 1$ implied by the assumed law of motion (40) and the law of motion itself for $q_t^{(0)}$, we obtain

$$q_t^{(k+1)} = \sum_{j=0}^{k} \alpha_{kj} q_{t-1}^{(j+1)} + \kappa_{k+1}(q_{t-1}^{(0)} - q_{t-1}^{(1)} + u_t).$$

This yields a law of motion for the next higher order of expectations of the desired form (40).

Identifying the coefficients $\alpha_{k+1,j}$ and a_{k+1} with the ones appearing in this last relation, we obtain equations that can be used to solve recursively for these coefficients at each order of expectations. For each $k \geq 1$, we find that

$$\alpha_{k0} = \kappa_k,$$

$$\alpha_{kj} = \kappa_{k-j} - \kappa_{k+1-j} \quad \text{for each} \quad 0 < j < k,$$

$$\alpha_{kk} = 1 - \kappa_1,$$

$$a_k = \kappa_k.$$

Thus once we determine the sequence of Kalman gains κ_k, we know the complete law of motion (40) for all orders of expectations.

The Kalman gains can also be determined using methods such as those employed above. If we let

$$\sigma_{k0} \equiv \text{cov}\left[q_t^{(k)} - q_{t|t-1}^{(k)}(i), \quad q_t - q_{t|t-1}(i) \right],$$

then the usual reasoning implies that the Kalman gains are given by

$$\kappa_{k+1} = (\sigma_z^2)^{-1}\, \sigma_{k0} \tag{41}$$

for each $k \geq 0$.[11] These covariances in turn satisfy a Riccati equation,

$$\sigma_{k0} = \left[1 - (\sigma_z^2)^{-1}\sigma_{00}\right] \sum_{j=0}^{k} \alpha_{kj}\sigma_{j0} + a_k\sigma_u^2, \tag{42}$$

for each $k \geq 0$. Note that once we know the value of σ_{00}, this is a linear equation in the other covariances, and we have already solved for $\sigma_{00} = \Sigma_{11}$ in (32).

Substituting the above solution for the α_{kj} and a_k coefficients as functions of the Kalman gains, and using (41) to replace each covariance σ_{k0} by a multiple of κ_{k+1}, it is possible to rewrite (42) in terms of the Kalman gains alone. We obtain the relation

$$\kappa_{k+1} = \frac{1 - \kappa_1}{1 - (1 - \kappa_1)^2}\left[\sum_{j=1}^{k} \kappa_j\kappa_{k+1-j} - \sum_{j=2}^{k} \kappa_j\kappa_{k+2-j} + \kappa_k\left(\sigma_u^2/\sigma_v^2\right) \right] \tag{43}$$

for each $k \geq 1$. This relation allows us to solve recursively for each of the κ_k, starting from the initial value

$$\kappa_1 = \frac{-1 + [1 + 4(\sigma_v^2/\sigma_u^2)]^{1/2}}{2\sigma_v^2/\sigma_u^2}$$

implied by (41) using (32) for σ_{00}.

---

11. Note that in the case $k = 0$, this equation is equivalent to the first row of (28).

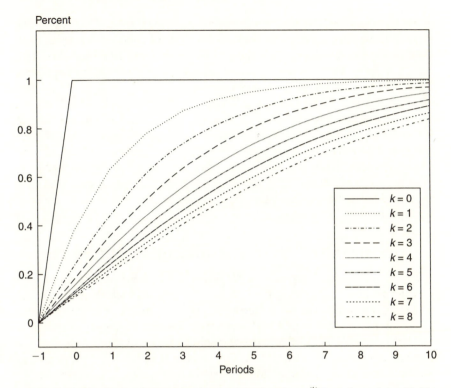

Figure 3. Impulse response functions for higher-order expectations $q_t^{(k)}$ for various values of k. The case $k = 0$ indicates the exogenous disturbance to log nominal GDP itself.

Figure 3 gives a numerical illustration of the implied dynamics of higher-order expectations in response to an immediate, permanent unit increase in nominal spending. The figure shows the impulse responses of $q_t^{(0)}$ (nominal GDP itself), $q_t^{(1)}$ (the average estimate of current nominal GDP), $q_t^{(2)}$ (the average estimate of the average estimate), and so on, up through the eighth-order expectation $q^{(8)}$, in the case of a relative innovation variance $\sigma_v^2/\sigma_u^2 = 4$. One observes that even with this degree of noise in subjective estimates of current nominal spending, the average estimate of current nominal GDP adjusts fairly rapidly following the disturbance: 40 percent of the eventual adjustment occurs in the period of the increase in the nominal GDP itself, and 80 percent has occurred within a further two periods. On the other hand, higher-order expectations adjust much more sluggishly. Eighth-order expectations adjust only a fifth as much as do first-order expectations during the period of the disturbance; even three periods later, they have not yet adjusted by as much as first-order expectations do in the period of the disturbance, and it is only nine periods after the disturbance that they have adjusted by 80 percent of the size of the disturbance.

The extent to which these different orders of average expectations matter for pricing depends, of course, on the degree of strategic complementarity between the pricing decisions of different suppliers. If ξ is near one, then the average price level will adjust at the same rate as the average estimate $q_t^{(1)}$, and the real effects of the disturbance will be modest after the period of the shock and the next period or so.[12] On the other hand, if ξ is small, so that strategic complementarity is great, the sluggishness of higher-order expectations can matter a great deal. Woodford (2001) suggests that $\xi = 0.15$ is an empirically plausible value for the United States. In this case, the impulse response of the average price level would be a weighted average of those shown in Figure 1 (and the responses of still higher-order expectations, not shown), with a weight of only 0.15 on the response of first-order expectations. More than half the weight is put on expectations of order $k > 4$, and more than a quarter of the weight is put on expectations of order $k > 8$, i.e., expectations that adjust more slowly than any that are shown in the figure. Thus the insight of Phelps (1983), that the dependence of aggregate outcomes upon higher-order expectations can be an important source of inertia in the response of prices to nominal disturbances, is borne out.

4. COMPARISON WITH A MODEL OF STICKY PRICES

It may be worth briefly considering the extent to which the predictions of such a model resemble, and differ from, those of a model in which prices do not immediately adjust to nominal disturbances, not because price-setters are unaware of the adjustment that would best serve their interests at any of the times at which they actually consider changing their prices, but simply because they do not continuously reconsider their prices. This familiar hypothesis of "sticky prices" is clearly not entirely unrelated to the hypothesis of incomplete information. In particular, insofar as suppliers behave in the way assumed in models with sticky prices, they surely do so *not* primarily in order to economize on the cost of price changes themselves—literal "menu costs" are in most cases quite small— but rather in order to economize on the cost of *having to make more frequent decisions* about whether their current prices are significantly out of line or not.[13] Moreover, there is obviously a close relationship between the hypothesis that there are substantial costs associated with constant close monitoring of current conditions (the hypothesis explored in this chapter) and the hypothesis that there are substantial costs associated with constant reconsideration of how close one's current prices are to those that are optimal under current conditions.

For this reason, it is interesting to ask how similar or different the implications of the hypothesis of incomplete common knowledge for aggregate dynamics are to those of a model with sticky prices. Here I show that the dynamics of aggregate output and the aggregate price index derived above in the case of a random walk in nominal GDP are indistinguishable from those predicted by a standard sticky-price model, namely, a discrete-time version of the model proposed by Calvo (1983). Thus it need not be possible to distinguish among these models empirically

---

12. If ξ exceeds 1, as is theoretically possible (Woodford, 2001), then prices will adjust even more rapidly than the average expectation of current nominal GDP.

13. Zbaracki et al. (1999) document this in the case of a single industrial firm whose operations they study in detail. They find that the firm's "managerial costs" of price adjustment are many times larger than the physical costs of price changes.

using aggregate data alone. Nonetheless, this does not mean that the models make identical predictions regardless of the nature of monetary policy, as consideration of a more general policy specification will show.

4.1. Dynamics of Real Activity under the Calvo Pricing Model

In the well-known Calvo (1983) model of staggered pricing, the price charged by each supplier is reconsidered only at random intervals of time, with the probability that any given price will be reconsidered within a particular time interval being independent of which price it is, how long ago it was last reconsidered, and the level of the current price (relative either to other prices or to other aspects of current market conditions). In this case (and proceeding directly to a log-linear approximation to the optimal pricing condition), (6) becomes instead

$$p_t(i) = (1 - \alpha\beta) \sum_{j=0}^{\infty} (\alpha\beta)^j E_t(p_{t+j} + \xi y_{t+j}) \tag{44}$$

for any supplier i that reconsiders its price in period t, where $0 < \alpha < 1$ is the probability that any given price is *not* reconsidered during any given period, and $0 < \beta < 1$ is again the discount factor in (3). This says that the price chosen is a weighted average of the prices that would be optimal at the various dates and in the various states of the world in which the price chosen at date t has not yet been revised. Because we now assume full information, subjective expectations at date t are now replaced by an expectation conditional upon the history of disturbances through that date. If instead i does not reconsider its price in period t, then we have simply $p_t(i) = p_{t-1}(i)$.

This model of pricing results (see, e.g., Woodford, 2001) in an aggregate supply relation of the form

$$\Delta p_t = \kappa y_t + \beta E_t \Delta p_{t+1}, \tag{45}$$

where

$$\kappa = \frac{(1 - \alpha)(1 - \alpha\beta)}{\alpha} \xi > 0. \tag{46}$$

This relation is sometimes called the "new Keynesian Phillips curve." Note that it holds regardless of the assumed evolution of nominal spending. Let us first consider the case of a random walk with drift in nominal GDP, as in Section 3.

The rational expectations equilibrium associated with such a policy is then a pair of stochastic processes for the price level and real GDP that are consistent with both (45) and

$$\Delta p_t + \Delta y_t = g + u_t. \tag{47}$$

The unique solution in which inflation and output fluctuations are stationary is given by

$$y_t = v(y_{t-1} + u_t),$$

$$\Delta p_t = g + (1 - v)(u_t + y_{t-1}),$$

where $0 < v < 1$ is given by

$$v = \frac{1 + \beta + \kappa - [(1 + \beta + \kappa)^2 - 4\beta]^{1/2}}{2\beta}. \tag{48}$$

We observe that output fluctuations again follow a law of motion of the form (39), except that now the autoregressive coefficient v depends upon the frequency of price adjustment among other parameters. Thus the impulse responses of both prices and real activity in response to a monetary disturbance are of the same form as in the noisy information model. In fact, for given values of ξ and β, to any value of the variance ratio σ_v^2 / σ_u^2 (or rate of information flow in the model with noisy information) there corresponds a particular value of α (or degree of price stickiness) that results in *identical* dynamics of prices and output. Thus in the case that nominal GDP evolves according to (47), and we treat both α and the variance ratio as free parameters (to be estimated from the dynamics of aggregate output and the aggregate price index), the predictions of the two models are *observationally equivalent.*

In the case that β is near one (a plausible assumption), we can go further, and obtain an equivalence between a particular value of the variance ratio and a particular value of α that holds *regardless of the value of* ξ. When we set β equal to one, (48) reduces to exactly the same expression for v as in the noisy-information model [one minus the right-hand side of (30)], except that γ is equal to κ. Comparing expression (46) for κ (and setting $\beta = 1$) with expression (38) for γ, we see that the value of α required for the sticky-price model to imply the same dynamics as the noisy-information model is the one such that

$$\frac{\alpha}{(1 - \alpha)^2} = \frac{\sigma_v^2}{\sigma_u^2}. \tag{49}$$

In this limiting case, the required value of α is independent of the value of ξ. This means that even if the structure of the economy were to shift in a way that changed the value of ξ, the predictions of the two models would *continue* to be identical.

4.2. Consequences of Persistence in the Growth of Nominal Spending

It would be a mistake to conclude more generally that the noisy-information model is observationally equivalent to the Calvo model of staggered pricing. The models cease to predict the same dynamics of output and inflation if nominal GDP does not follow a random walk with drift. This can be seen by considering the more general stochastic process for nominal GDP [equation (10)] considered earlier, in the case that $\rho > 0$, so that the growth rate of nominal GDP exhibits serial correlation.[14] In this case, we are unable to obtain an analytical solution to the

---

14. It is important to note that this is the case of practical interest, given that variations in nominal GDP growth do exhibit considerable persistence. More to the point, VAR estimates of the effects

Percent

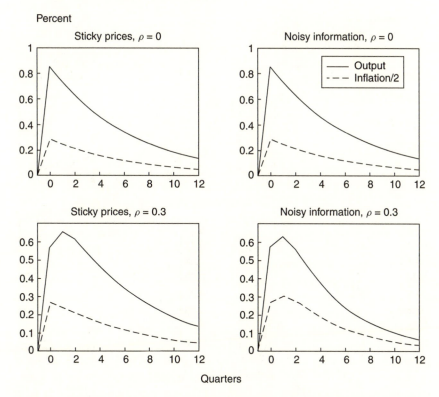

Figure 4. Comparison of impulse response functions predicted by the two models, for the cases $\rho = 0$ and 0.3.

nonlinear equation system (31), and so must resort to numerical solution for particular assumed parameter values.

Figures 4 and 5 plot the impulse responses of output and inflation[15] to an innovation in nominal GDP growth at date zero that eventually raises (log) nominal GDP by one percentage point. (The innovation at date zero is thus of size $u_0 = 1 - \rho$.) The two rows of Figure 4 consider nominal spending processes characterized by $\rho = 0$ and $\rho = 0.3$ respectively, while the two rows of Figure 5 consider the further cases $\rho = 0.6$ and $\rho = 0.9$. The two columns of both figures compare the predictions of two models for each case, the model with Calvo pricing (left column) and the model with noisy information (right column).

In each case, the value of ξ is fixed at 0.15, a value that is argued to be realistic for the U.S. economy in Woodford (2001). The sticky-price model is further calibrated by assuming $\beta = 0.99$, a plausible discount factor if the periods are interpreted as

of monetary policy shocks indicate an effect on nominal GDP that takes many quarters to reach its eventual magnitude, rather than an immediate permanent increase of the kind implied by the random walk specification.

15. In these figures, "inflation" is defined as $4\Delta p_t$, corresponding to an annualized inflation rate if the model "periods" are interpreted as quarters.

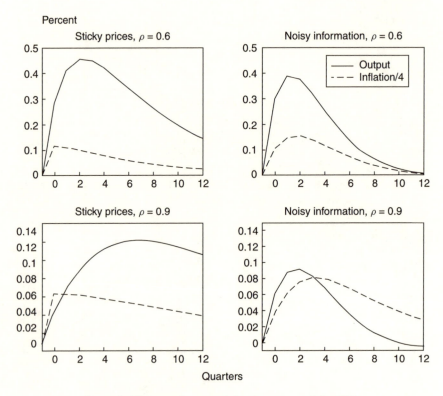

Figure 5. The comparison extended to the cases $\rho = 0.6$ and 0.9.

quarters, and $\alpha = 2/3$, so that one-third of all prices are revised each quarter. This implies an average interval between price changes of 9 months, consistent with the survey evidence of Blinder et al. (1998, table 4.1). The noisy-information model is then calibrated by assuming that $\sigma_v^2/\sigma_u^2 = 6.23$, the value required in order for the predicted inflation and output dynamics of the two models to be identical in the case that $\rho = 0$.[16]

Comparing the two columns, we observe that the predicted impulse responses are the same for both models when $\rho = 0$ (as we have already shown analytically), but that they become progressively more different the larger the value assigned to ρ. Thus the two models are not observationally equivalent in the case of an *arbitrary* monetary policy and will not give the same answers to a question about the consequences of changing the way in which monetary policy is conducted.

Furthermore, the failure of the predictions to agree in the case of substantial persistence in nominal GDP growth is not one that can be remedied by adjusting the value of α in the sticky-price model. The impulse responses predicted by the noisy-information model when $\rho > 0$ are ones that are not consistent with

_____
16. This value differs slightly from the variance ratio of 6 that would be indicated by (49), because β is not exactly equal to one.

the Calvo model for *any* parameter values. This is because relation (45) can be "solved forward" to yield

$$\Delta p_t = \kappa \sum_{j=0}^{\infty} \beta^j E_t y_{t+j}, \tag{50}$$

which implies that the predicted path of inflation is a function solely of expected *subsequent* output gaps. It follows that a monetary disturbance with a *delayed* positive effect on output must increase inflation *earlier*. It is thus not an artifact of the particular parameter values assumed in Figures 2 and 3 that the inflation response is observed to peak sooner than the output response when $\rho > 0$. The noisy-information model can instead generate responses in which inflation peaks *later,* as is especially evident in the case $\rho = 0.9$. Such a response is plainly inconsistent with (50).

Further insight into the difference in the predictions of the two models can be obtained from Figure 6, which plots the impulse response functions for the price level implied by the two models alongside the impulse response for nominal GDP. (The case shown corresponds to the case $\rho = 0.9$ in Figure 5.) A monetary

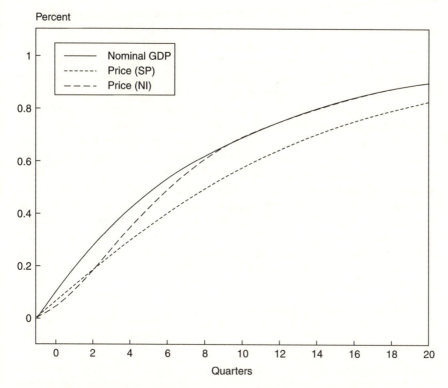

Figure 6. Impulse response function for the price level in the sticky-price model (SP) and the noisy-information model (NI), for the case $\rho = 0.9$.

disturbance results in a gradual increase in the log of nominal GDP, to an eventual level that is higher by one than its level before the shock. The sticky-price model predicts that the average log price of goods will not rise as much as the increase in nominal GDP, and so real output is temporarily increased. But still, by comparison with the noisy-information model, the sticky-price model predicts relatively strong price increases in the time immediately following the shock. The reason is that under the assumption of full information, suppliers who revise their prices soon after the shock can anticipate that further increases in nominal GDP are coming in the next few quarters. Then, because there is a substantial probability that the supplier's price will not be revised again during the time that aggregate demand increases, it is desirable to increase the price *immediately* in order to prevent it from falling too far behind its desired level before the next opportunity for revision arises.

In the noisy-information model, however, there is no such need to "front-load" price increases in the case of a disturbance that is expected to result in persistent above-average growth in nominal spending. Suppliers who suspect that such a shock has occurred will increase prices some, but can *plan to increase prices more later* if their estimate of demand conditions has not changed in the meantime. In the absence of a need to front-load, initial price increases are quite small, owing to uncertainty about whether others are expecting others . . . to expect others to perceive the increase in demand. Rather, a few quarters later price increases are more rapid than in the sticky-price model. Once suppliers can become fairly confident that others expect . . . others to have noticed the surge in spending, the fact that prices were not increased earlier does not prevent them from being rapidly brought into line with the current volume of nominal spending. The result is a surge in inflation that occurs after the peak effect on output.

The Calvo pricing model has in fact come under extensive criticism for implying that the rate of inflation should be a purely "forward-looking" variable, and the relative timing of the output and inflation responses predicted by the noisy-information model are, at least qualitatively, more similar to those indicated by VAR estimates of the effects of monetary policy shocks. The estimated responses generally indicate a stronger effect on inflation in the quarters *after* the peak effect on output; see, for example, the responses in Figure 7, which are again taken from Christiano et al. (2001).[17] The question of how well the precise quantitative predictions of the noisy-information model match empirical evidence of this kind is left for future work.[18] But the model offers some promise of providing a more satisfactory explanation than a standard sticky-price model can.

17. This observation is related to what Mankiw and Reis (2001) call "the acceleration phenomenon," although the evidence that they discuss relates to unconditional correlations between cyclical output and subsequent inflation acceleration rather than to the co-movements of these variables that are associated with identified monetary policy shocks.

18. We cannot address the question here, both because the estimated impulse response of nominal GDP shown in Figure 1 is plainly not consistent with the simple law of motion (10) for any value of ρ and because our theoretical calculations have assumed that nominal GDP is affected only by monetary disturbances, whereas the identified VAR implies otherwise.

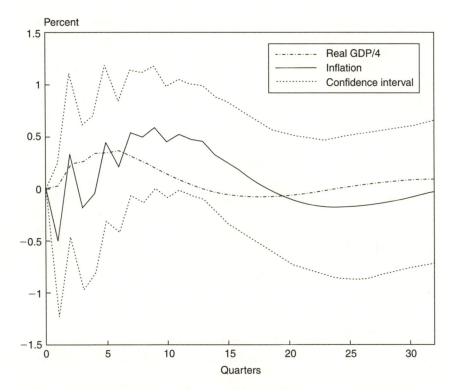

Figure 7. Estimated impulse responses of real GDP and inflation to an unexpected interest rate reduction. (Source: Christiano et al., 2001.)

4.3. Responses to Other Disturbances

The noisy-information model offers qualitatively different predictions from a sticky-price model in another respect as well. We have thus far only considered the predictions of the two models about the effects of a single kind of disturbance, a monetary policy disturbance that affects the path of nominal spending with no effect upon potential output (the constant $\bar{Y}$ above). However, even when the two models predict identical effects of a disturbance of this kind, they need not predict identical effects for other types of disturbances as well.

In general, they will not, for a simple reason: In the sticky-price model, the rate at which prices adjust following a disturbance depends on the rate at which various suppliers choose to reconsider their prices, but this rate, if taken as exogenous as in "time-dependent-pricing" models such as that of Calvo, will be the same *regardless of the type of disturbance* to which the economy must adjust. On the other hand, there is no reason why the rate of *flow of information* about different disturbances must be the same in a noisy-information model. Some variables may be observed with more precision, and others with less, and as a result, prices may succeed better at bringing about an efficient response to some disturbances than to others.

A simple example can easily illustrate the way that this can result in predictions different from those of a sticky-price model. Let us again assume a random walk in nominal GDP, the case in which the two models will (for appropriate parameter values) predict the same responses to a monetary disturbance u_t. But let us now generalize the above model, so that the log of the natural rate of output $(\bar{y}_t)$ follows a random walk with drift—for example, as a result of a random walk with drift in a multiplicative technology factor[19]—that is independent of the random walk in nominal GDP resulting from the actions of the central bank. We can write this process as

$$\bar{y}_t = \bar{g} + \bar{y}_{t-1} + \bar{u}_t,$$

where $\bar{g}$ is the average rate of growth in the natural rate, and $\bar{u}_t$ is a mean-zero iid disturbance, distributed independently of u_t.

The optimal price for any price-setter is still given by (6), if now y_t is interpreted as output *relative* to the time-varying natural rate. Similarly, optimal pricing policy in the sticky-price model continues to be described by (44), under the same reinterpretation. It follows that in the sticky-price model, the relation between inflation and the output gap continues to be described by (45). Equation (47) continues to hold as well, except that the right-hand side becomes

$$(g - \bar{g}) + u_t - \bar{u}_t.$$

Since the composite disturbance $u_t - \bar{u}_t$ is still completely unforecastable at any date prior to t, the stationary rational expectations equilibrium of the sticky-price model takes the same form as before, except with g replaced by $g - \bar{g}$ and u_t replaced by $u_t - \bar{u}_t$. In particular, the equilibrium output gap will evolve according to

$$y_t = v(y_{t-1} + u_t - \bar{u}_t). \tag{51}$$

The predictions of the noisy-information model will instead depend upon what we assume about the observability of the additional disturbance process $\bar{y}_t$. Suppose, for simplicity, that each supplier observes $\bar{y}_t$ *precisely,* while still observing the state of aggregate demand only with noise. In this case, there is again only a single "hidden" state variable to estimate on the basis of the noisy observations. In fact, our previous calculations continue to apply, if we replace p_t throughout by $\tilde{p}_t$, the log of "natural nominal GDP" (i.e., P_t times the natural rate of output). For $\tilde{p}_t$ satisfies the identity $\tilde{p}_t + y_t = q_t$, given our reinterpretation of y_t, and the perfect observability of the natural rate means that (6) may be written equivalently as

$$\tilde{p}_t(i) = \tilde{p}_{t|t}(i) + \xi y_{t|t}(i).$$

With this reinterpretation of the price variable, our derivations go through as before. In particular, the equilibrium output gap will evolve according to

---

19. See Woodford (2001) for an explicit analysis of how the natural rate of output is affected by technology shocks, and other real disturbances, in a model of monopolistic competition of the kind used here.

$$y_t = v(y_{t-1} + u_t).$$

For appropriately chosen parameter values, the coefficient v here may take the same value as in (51). But even in that case, there remains an important difference in the predicted responses to the technology shock. In the sticky-price model, technology shocks produce deviations of output from potential that are exactly as long lasting as those that result from monetary disturbances. In the noisy-information model, on the other hand (under our special assumption about the observability of $\bar{y}_t$), technology shocks have no effect upon the output gap (or upon $\tilde{p}_t$) at all: Whereas prices adjust only slowly to a change in demand conditions (owing to the assumed imperfect common knowledge regarding disturbances of this kind), they adjust immediately to a change in technology (as this is assumed to be common knowledge).

This differing prediction is not just another indication that the two models are not equivalent. It is again potentially of interest as an explanation for one of the more notable embarrassments for the sticky-price model. An extensive empirical literature dating back several decades[20] has found that prices respond more, and more rapidly, to increases in the marginal cost of supply resulting from increases in factor prices than to increases resulting from an increased scale of production as a result of increases in demand. Such a difference is not easily rationalized in terms of a standard sticky-price model. Some have argued that such evidence indicates that prices are set on the basis of considerations other than a constant desired markup over marginal supply cost. The noisy-information model suggests a different, and possibly simpler explanation. Prices are set in proportion to marginal cost, but it must be the supplier's subjective *estimate* of marginal cost; if suppliers are better informed about certain disturbances that affect supply cost than about others, those disturbances will have a larger and more immediate effect on prices.

Of course, I have given no reason why one should assume that suppliers are better informed about variation in the natural rate of output than about variation in aggregate nominal spending. My point is simply that there is no reason why the logic of the noisy-information model should imply that the rate of information flow with regard to different shocks must be the same. Even if one supposes that, on grounds of theoretical parsimony, one should prefer to derive the degree of noise associated with the observation of various disturbances from a single underlying limitation on human information-processing capacity, one should not in general expect that the amount of scarce processing capacity allocated to monitoring different types of disturbances should be the same.

This possibility of explaining the differential responsiveness of prices to different types of disturbances is also an important advantage of the noisy-information model over the model recently proposed by Mankiw and Reis (2001), which is in some ways similar. Mankiw and Reis also argue for a pricing model in which: (1) each supplier's price at any given time is optimal conditional upon that supplier's information set, and (2) in which price adjustment in response to

---

20. See Bils and Chang (1999) for a review of this evidence as well for further evidence for the same conclusion.

a disturbance to aggregate demand is delayed owing to suppliers' not all having complete information about the disturbances that have already occurred. But rather than assuming continuous observation of demand conditions using a noisy channel, as is proposed here, Mankiw and Reis assume that suppliers obtain no new information at all except at random intervals. Yet on the occasions upon which a supplier updates its information, it acquires *complete* information about all disturbances that have occurred up until that time.[21] This is a model in which the relevant cost of information flow is a fixed cost of logging on to the Internet; on the occasions upon which one bears this cost, there is zero additional cost of downloading all of the available news with infinite precision.

A full comparison of these alternative types of incomplete-information models is beyond the scope of the present chapter.[22] However, one disadvantage of the Mankiw-Reis approach is that it suggests that the rate at which suppliers (in aggregate) learn about particular events should be the same for all events, being determined by the single parameter that indicates the frequency of information updates. The noisy-information model, on the other hand, makes it natural that learning about some events should be more rapid than about others.

5. CONCLUSIONS

We have seen that the Phelps-Lucas hypothesis, according to which temporary real effects of purely nominal disturbances result from imperfect information about the nature of these disturbances, deserves more continued interest than is often supposed. When one departs from the assumptions of the Lucas (1972) model in two crucial respects—introducing a monopolistically competitive pricing framework in which the optimal pricing decisions of individual suppliers of goods depend crucially upon the prices that they expect others to set and allowing individual suppliers' subjective perceptions of current conditions to be contaminated by the noise that inevitably results from finite information-processing capacity—it is possible to explain not only real effects of purely nominal disturbances but real effects that may persist for a substantial period of time.

We have shown that a model of this kind offers not only a potential explanation for the kinds of real effects that are usually mentioned as grounds for the assumption of substantial price stickiness, but also some prospect of an explanation of aspects of price dynamics that are not easily reconciled with sticky-price models that assume optimization with full information, subject only to a constraint upon the frequency of price changes. Of course, there is no reason why the best model might not involve *both* sticky prices and noisy information: It may be most realistic to suppose that prices remain fixed for a time but also that when revised they are

---

21. The Mankiw-Reis model is thus an example of what Sims (2001, sec. 8) calls "information-delay RE" modeling, as opposed to "signal extraction RE" modeling, the category to which the present chapter would belong. See Sims for further discussion of the importance of this distinction.

22. Their implications are certainly not equivalent. For example, in the case of a random walk in nominal GDP, the Mankiw-Reis model does not imply inflation and output dynamics that are observationally equivalent to those predicted by the Calvo model, except in the special case that $\xi = 1$.

adjusted on the basis of imperfect subjective perceptions of current conditions. But our preliminary investigation here suggests at least that there is an important cost to abstracting from the information limitations of price-setters.

While the model proposed here seeks to rehabilitate certain aspects of the explanation of the real effects of monetary policy advocated by Phelps and Lucas 30 years ago, acceptance of it would not necessarily lead to all of the conclusions emphasized in the earlier literature. It was widely argued that the Lucas (1972) model implies that there should be little scope for the use of monetary stabilization policy to offset the fluctuations in output relative to potential that would otherwise be caused by other disturbances to the economy: That model implies that monetary policy could have no effect on real activity that was systematically correlated with real disturbances unless the central bank were able to observe and respond to those disturbances, while the private sector could not also observe them and use them to predict the central-bank's response. Successful monetary stabilization policy would then be impossible if the central bank's only information about real disturbances were also available to the general public.

But the interpretation proposed here of the nature of the relevant information limitations undermines this conclusion. If suppliers have an inaccurate estimate of current aggregate conditions not because of the unavailability of good data in the public domain but because of paying insufficient *attention* to the available public-domain data, it is quite possible for the central bank to affect real activity in ways that are correlated with that public information. This should greatly increase the plausible scope of monetary stabilization policy. Analysis of the optimal conduct of policy in the presence of the kind of imperfect common knowledge described here should accordingly be an important topic for further study.

REFERENCES

Ball, L. and D. Romer (1990), "Real Rigidities and the Non-Neutrality of Money," *Review of Economic Studies* 57:183–203.

Bils, M. and Y. Chang (1999), "Understanding How Price Responds to Costs and Production," NBER Working Paper No. 7311.

Blinder, A. S., E. R. D. Canetti, D. E. Lebow, and J. B. Rudd (1998), *Asking About Prices: A New Approach to Understanding Price Stickiness,* New York: Russell Sage Foundation.

Calvo, G. A. (1983), "Staggered Prices in a Utility Maximizing Framework," *Journal of Monetary Economics* 12:383–98.

Chow, G. C. (1975), *Analysis and Control of Dynamic Economic Systems,* New York: Wiley.

Christiano, L. J., M. Eichenbaum, and C. L. Evans (1998), "Modeling Money," NBER Working Paper No. 6371.

———— (2001), "Nominal Rigidities and the Dynamic Effects of a Shock to Monetary Policy," NBER Working Paper No. 8403.

Green, D. M. and J. A. Swets (1966), *Signal Detection Theory and Psychophysics,* New York: Wiley.

Harvey, A. C. (1989), *Forecasting, Structural Time Series Models, and the Kalman Filter,* Cambridge: Cambridge University Press.

Lucas, R. E., Jr. (1972), "Expectations and the Neutrality of Money," *Journal of Economic Theory* 4:103–24.

———— (1973), "Some International Evidence on Output-Inflation Tradeoffs," *American Economic Review* 63:326–34.

———— (1977), "Understanding Business Cycles," *Carnegie-Rochester Conference Series on Public Policy* 5:7–29.

Mankiw, N. G. and R. Reis (2001), "Sticky Information versus Sticky Prices: A Proposal to Replace the New Keynesian Phillips Curve," NBER Working Paper No. 8290.

Morris, S. and H. S. Shin (2001), "Global Games: Theory and Applications," Cowles Foundation Discussion Paper No. 1275R.

Phelps, E. S. (1970), "Introduction: The New Microeconomics in Employment and Inflation Theory," in E. S. Phelps, A. A. Alchian, C. C. Holt, D. T. Mortensen, G. C. Archibald, R. E. Lucas, Jr., L. A. Rapping, S. G. Winter, Jr., J. P. Gould, D. F. Gordon, A. Hynes, D. A. Nichols, P. J. Taubman, and M. Wilkinson, *Microeconomic Foundations of Employment and Inflation Theory,* New York: Norton.

———— (1983), "The Trouble with 'Rational Expectations' and the Problem of Inflation Stabilization," in R. Frydman and E. S. Phelps, eds., *Individual Forecasting and Aggregate Outcomes,* Cambridge: Cambridge University Press.

Sargent, T. J. (1991), "Equilibrium with Signal Extraction from Endogenous Variables," *Journal of Economic Dynamics and Control* 15:245–73.

———— (1993), *Bounded Rationality in Macroeconomics,* Oxford: Oxford University Press.

Sims, C. A. (1980), "Comparison of Interwar and Postwar Business Cycles: Monetarism Reconsidered," *American Economic Review* 70(2):250–57.

———— (1998), "Stickiness," *Carnegie-Rochester Conference Series on Public Policy* 49: 317–56.

———— (2001), "Implications of Rational Inattention," unpublished, Princeton University.

Townsend, R. M. (1983a), "Forecasting the Forecasts of Others," *Journal of Political Economy* 91:546–88.

———— (1983b), "Equilibrium Theory with Learning and Disparate Expectations: Some Issues and Methods," in R. Frydman and E. S. Phelps, eds., *Individual Forecasting and Aggregate Outcomes,* Cambridge: Cambridge University Press.

Woodford, M. (2001), "Optimizing Models with Nominal Rigidities," unpublished, Princeton University.

Zbaracki, M., M. Ritson, D. Levy, S. Dutta, and M. Bergen (1999), "The Managerial and Customer Dimensions of the Cost of Price Adjustment: Direct Evidence from Industrial Markets," unpublished, University of Pennsylvania.

Ziemer, R. E., and W. H. Tranter (1995), *Principles of Communications,* 4th ed., New York: Wiley.

2

Comments on Woodford

LARS E. O. SVENSSON

The general idea of Michael Woodford's chapter is to abandon the Phelps-Lucas model for the Phelps-Woodford model. We know that the Phelps-Lucas idea is that real effects of nominal disturbances arise because of assumed imperfect information about these disturbances. But the standard Lucas formulation of this results in too little persistence of these real effects. Woodford suggests a more elaborate interpretation of the Phelps idea, such that prices depend on "higher-order" estimates of nominal disturbances. If these higher-order estimates are updated more slowly than first-order estimates, more persistent real effects arise. He shows that this idea can generate impulse responses of inflation and output with considerable persistence.

The model has a continuum of firms in monopolistic competition. Each firm i will in equilibrium set its (log) price $p_t(i)$ according to [Woodford's equation (6), hereafter (W6)]

$$p_t(i) = p_{t|t}(i) + \xi y_{t|t}(i), \tag{1}$$

where $p_{t|t}(i)$ denotes the firm's estimate in period t of the (log) price level p_t, $y_{t|t}(i)$ denotes the firm's estimate of the output gap y_t, and ξ $(0 < \xi < 1)$ is a parameter indicating the degree of strategic complementarity between firms' pricing decisions (a lower ξ corresponds to a higher degree of complementarity). Averaging over firms leads to the aggregate price equation

$$p_t = p_{t|t} + \xi y_{t|t}, \tag{1a}$$

where $p_{t|t}$ and $y_{t|t}$ denote average estimates over firms of the price level and the output gap, respectively.

Woodford assumes that monetary policy corresponds to nominal-GDP-growth targeting (adjusted for the growth of potential output). More precisely, he assumes that: (1) (adjusted) nominal GDP growth is exogenous, and (2) nominal GDP (adjusted for potential output) is the crucial variable that firms observe (with noise). This is modeled as nominal GDP (adjusted for potential output), $p_t + y_t$, being equal to an exogenous stochastic process with a unit root q_t:

$$p_t + y_t = q_t. \tag{1b}$$

The process Δq_t can then be interpreted as corresponding to either an exogenous stochastic target for nominal GDP growth or unavoidable deviations from a constant-growth target. Combining this with equation (1a) leads to [(W7) and (W8)]

$$p_t = \xi q_{t|t} + (1 - \xi)p_{t|t} \tag{2}$$

$$= \sum_{k=1}^{\infty} \xi(1 - \xi)^{k-1} q_t^{(k)}, \tag{3}$$

where $q_t^{(k)}$ denotes the k-order estimate of nominal GDP according to the notation $q_t^{(k)} \equiv q_{t|t}^{(k-1)} \equiv \int E_t^i q_t^{(k-1)} di, k \geq 1, q_t^{(0)} \equiv q_t$.

Woodford first assumes that nominal GDP growth follows an AR(1) process [(W6)],

$$\Delta q_t = (1 - \rho)g + \rho \Delta q_{t-1} + u_t, \tag{4}$$

where the parameter ρ fulfills $0 \leq \rho < 1$ and u_t is an iid disturbance. He further assumes that each firm receives a noisy observation of current nominal GDP [(W12)],

$$z_t(i) = q_t + v_t(i), \tag{5}$$

where $v_t(i)$ is an iid measurement error. With impressive analysis, precisely what one would expect from Woodford, he then derives expressions for the equilibrium Kalman filter estimates $q_{t|t}$ and $p_{t|t}$.

In order to get more specific results and to discuss the impulse responses of a permanent increase in nominal GDP, he assumes the special case of q_t being a random walk with drift, $\rho = 0$ and $\Delta q_t = g + u_t$. He can then derive the dynamics for the output gap and the price level, which obey [(W39)]

$$y_t = v(y_{t-1} + u_t), \tag{6}$$

with the price level given by equation (1b). Here the degree of persistence of output, v, fulfills $0 < v = 1 - \hat{k} < 1$, where $\hat{k}$ is the Kalman gain, given by $0 < \hat{k} = [\sqrt{\gamma^2 + 4\gamma} - \gamma]/2 < 1$, where $\gamma = \xi \sigma_u^2 / \sigma_v^2 > 1$. Since v is decreasing in the parameter γ, it follows that an increase in the degree of complementarity (a fall in ξ) and a fall in the signal-to-noise ratio σ_u^2 / σ_v^2 both increase v and thus imply a more persistent output response to nominal GDP disturbances.

Woodford then picks reasonable parameter values and shows that reasonable impulse responses result. In particular, when nominal GDP growth is an AR(1) process, the impulse responses of inflation and output have the attractive and realistic feature that the inflation response peaks later than the output response.

My first comment is that the results are very sensitive to assumptions (1) and (2) noted previously—that nominal GDP is exogenous and the variable that is observed with noise by the firms. Exogenous nominal GDP corresponds to an assumption of successful nominal-GDP-growth targeting. One reason for this assumption is that it allows Woodford to discuss the response to one-time increases in nominal GDP and compare it to that in previous literature, which has often discussed that case. However, no real-world central bank has attempted nominal GDP targeting, and it is of some interest to see to what extent the results depend on the nature of monetary policy that is assumed.

Furthermore, nominal GDP growth (even if not adjusted for potential output) is arguably not the variable that is most easily observed by firms. For one thing, nominal GDP is only published quarterly, with a lag and with considerable noise, as evidenced by substantial later revisions. Media attention also seems to be less on nominal GDP growth than on real GDP growth. Furthermore, the CPI is published monthly in most countries, with a shorter lag and without subsequent revisions (which of course does not mean that the observations contain no noise). Media attention to CPI numbers seems to me to be normally greater than that to nominal GDP (more so for countries where central banks have explicit CPI inflation targets and actual inflation is constantly compared to the target).

A simple way to demonstrate the sensitivity of the results to changes in the above assumptions is to assume a more general "targeting rule," where monetary policy is assumed to achieve the equality of a linear combination of the price level and the output gap, $p_t + \lambda y_t$ for some coefficient $\lambda \geq 0$, with the exogenous unit-root disturbance q_t,

$$p_t + \lambda y_t = q_t. \tag{1c}$$

This exogenous disturbance q_t is then assumed to be observed with noise, as in Woodford's equation (12). When $\lambda = 1$, this would correspond to Woodford's case of nominal-GDP-growth targeting. When $\lambda = 0$, it would correspond to strict inflation targeting, where inflation becomes exogenous and the price level is the variable observed with noise.

Using (1c) in (1a) gives

$$p_t = \tilde{\xi} q_{t|t} + (1 - \tilde{\xi}) p_{t|t}, \tag{1d}$$

which is similar to (2) except that ξ is replaced by $\tilde{\xi} \equiv \xi / \lambda$. Thus, we see that, even if $\xi < 1$, for sufficiently small $\lambda < 1$ we have $\tilde{\xi} > 1$, and for $\lambda \to 0$ we have $\tilde{\xi} \to \infty$. In particular, for $\lambda = \xi < 1$, we have $\tilde{\xi} = 1$ and $p_t = q_{t|t}$. Then, no higher-order estimates of q_t matter, and the degree of persistence ν will be at its minimum. Furthermore, for $\lambda < \xi$, we have $\tilde{\xi} > 1$, and the expression (3) does not converge. For this case, we do not know whether an equilibrium exists and what its properties are if it does.

This simple modification of equation (1) shows that Woodford's results are very sensitive to assumptions about monetary policy and the information used by the firms, and relatively small variations in these assumptions can have large

consequences for the results, leading to doubts about the robustness of those results.
More generally, both (1) and (1c) are drastically simplified assumptions about the
outcome of monetary policy and the information structure of the economy, and
more relevant analysis of the outcome under various kinds of optimizing policy
and alternative information structures is called for.

My second comment refers to the realism of higher-order estimates. The higher-
order estimates are very sophisticated ones. For instance, the second-order estimate
$q_t^{(2)} \equiv q_{t|t|t}$ is given by

$$q_{t|t|t} = \int E_t^i q_{t|t} di.$$

Here, $q_{t|t}$ is the average of firms' (first-order) estimates of nominal GDP, $E_t^i q_{t|t}$
is firm i's estimate of the average of other firms' estimates of nominal GDP
conditional on its specific information, and $q_{t|t|t}$ is the average over all firms of
such firm-specific estimates. Clearly, this is a sophisticated concept, and most
readers probably need to concentrate a bit to grasp its meaning. Moreover, this
is only order two. In Woodford's graphs, one has to go to order four or higher to
find substantial persistence. In this chapter, people are supposed not to be aware
of all the available information, but they are still supposed to be aware of such
sophisticated concepts.

It is possible that people with bounded rationality and limited computational
capacity might apply some simplifications in considering higher-order estimates.
One possible simplification is not to update estimates above a certain order, and
thus to set such estimates equal to a constant. This would increase the persistence
of the real effects of nominal disturbances. Another possible simplification is to
set estimates above a certain order equal to estimates of that certain order. This
would reduce the persistence of the real effects of nominal disturbances. Both
of these alternative simplifications may seem equally plausible a priori, but they
move Woodford's results in opposite directions.

Of course, one would like to see some direct empirical evidence on the relevance
and nature of higher-order estimates. In principle, one could find such evidence.
Some central banks collect survey data on inflation expectations. One could of
course expand such surveys and ask people: (1) What to you think inflation will
be next year? (2) What do you think other people think inflation will be? (3) What
do you think other people think other people think inflation will be? This gets us
to third-order inflation expectations. It remains to be seen whether the answers to
questions (2) and (3) would be different from those to question (1); if not, bad
news for Woodford!

My third comment refers to the existence and possible use of additional information. There is certainly a lot of relevant information available that one has to
assume that people for some reason decide not to use. There is information directly
about the price level p_t (or about industry price indexes). In Woodford's model,
they could be modeled as another signal,

$$z_p(t) = p_t + v_p(t),$$

the result of which would reduce the role of higher-order estimates of q_t and thereby reduce the degree of persistence in the real effects of nominal disturbances.

All over the world, there is a strong trend toward more transparent monetary policy, with inflation-targeting central banks in an increasing number of countries publishing *Inflation Reports* of increasing quality (the trend seems to be stronger outside the United States). These inflation reports publish price indexes, estimates of nominal and real disturbances, the central bank's judgments, and so on, all of which contribute to better and more accessible information. For many central banks, part of the transparent monetary policy is to teach the general public how monetary policy works and to make it aware of what information to look for in order to best predict future monetary-policy actions. Within Woodford's model, this might show up as the measurement error variance falling, which improves the signal-to-noise ratio and reduces the degree of persistence in the real effects of nominal disturbances. More generally, it points to the available information and the awareness of the general public being endogenous to the monetary-policy regime, which poses interesting and important challenges for future research.

In summary, I find the idea of bringing in higher-order estimates very neat and intriguing, but I remain doubtful as to how realistic it is.

3

Sticky Information: A Model of Monetary Nonneutrality and Structural Slumps

N. GREGORY MANKIW AND RICARDO REIS

1. INTRODUCTION

How do employment and inflation respond to real and monetary forces? What frictions cause these macroeconomic variables to deviate from the ideals that would arise in a fully classical world? These questions are at the center of macroeconomic research, as well as at the center of much of Ned Phelps's formidable research career. Early in his career Phelps (1967, 1968), together with Milton Friedman (1968), gave us the natural rate hypothesis, which remains the benchmark for understanding monetary nonneutrality. More recently, Phelps's (1994) work on structural slumps examined the real forces that can cause the natural rate of unemployment to change over time.

This chapter offers a model that weaves these two threads of Phelps's work together. In this model, information is assumed to disseminate slowly throughout the population of wage-setters, and as a result, wages respond slowly to news about changing economic conditions. Our model includes two kinds of relevant information: news about aggregate demand, as determined by monetary policy, and news about equilibrium real wages, as determined by productivity.

We introduce this sticky-information model in Section 2. The model generalizes the one in Mankiw and Reis (2001). In the earlier paper, we applied the assumption of sticky information to the price-setting process in order to understand the dynamic response of the economy to monetary policy. The resulting model has three properties that are consistent with the conventional wisdom of central bankers and the empirical evidence of macroeconometricians. First, disinflations in the model are always contractionary (although announced disinflations are less contractionary than surprise ones). Second, the model predicts that monetary

We thank Laurence Ball and Andrew Caplin for comments. Ricardo Reis is grateful to the Fundacao Ciencia e Tecnologia, Praxis XXI, for financial support and to Jonathan Leape and the Center for Economic Performance at the London School of Economics for their hospitality during part of this research.

policy shocks have their maximum impact on inflation with a substantial delay. Third, given a realistic stochastic process for money growth, the model implies that the change in inflation is positively correlated with the level of economic activity, which is the well-known "accelerationist Phillips curve." The model presented here encompasses the previous model—and thus these results—as a special case.

In Section 3 we offer some new results that come from applying the sticky-information assumption to the labor market and introducing productivity as an additional driving force. We show that disinflations and productivity slowdowns have parallel effects: Both cause employment and output to fall below their classical levels until the information about the new regime works its way through the economy. Thus, the model may help explain why unemployment rose during the productivity slowdown of the 1970s and yet again during the Volcker disinflation of the early 1980s. It may also help explain why the productivity resurgence associated with the "new economy" of the 1990s coincided with falling unemployment. Ball and Moffitt (2001) and Staiger et al. (2001) have recently documented the empirical importance of productivity trends for shifts in the Phillips curve. The sticky-information model presented here offers one interpretation of those findings.

In Section 4 we examine how the economy reacts to a change in trend productivity if the monetary authority responds either by stabilizing employment or by stabilizing inflation. We find that a strict policy of stabilizing inflation causes large fluctuations in employment. We also find that the employment-stabilizing policy keeps both nominal income and the nominal wage on its predetermined path. These results are a warning for the many central banks around the world that have adopted inflation targeting as a policy framework. They suggest that employment would be more stable if the monetary authority used nominal income or the price of labor, rather than the price of goods and services, as its nominal anchor.

In Section 5 we use the model as a lens through which to examine U.S. quarterly time series. According to the model, employment is a function of unexpected movements in inflation and productivity, where expectations are formed at various points in the past. The key parameter that governs this relationship is the one that measures the stickiness of information. When we apply the model and estimate this parameter, we find that the average wage-setter updates his information about once a year. Moreover, the correlation between predicted and actual unemployment is as high as 0.60. Thus, the sticky-information model can be used to explain much of the observed variation in aggregate unemployment as a response to inflation and productivity surprises. One anomaly, however, is that productivity surprises appear to influence unemployment with a lag of several quarters.

This chapter brings together many elements from the literature on inflation-employment dynamics that Phelps helped to spawn. The natural rate hypothesis, imperfect information, infrequent adjustment, and the wage curve all play central roles in the model. Our goal is not to offer a radically new theory but to combine familiar elements in a new way in an attempt to better explain monetary nonneutrality and structural slumps.

2. THE WAGE CURVE MEETS STICKY INFORMATION

The model we offer is designed to explain the dynamics of wages, prices, employment, and output. There are two key elements: the wage curve and the assumption of sticky information.

2.1. The Wage Curve

The starting point is an equation describing the target nominal wage w^*:

$$w_t^* = p_t + \theta_t + \alpha e_t,$$

where p is the price level, θ is labor productivity, and e is employment. All the variables are in logs, and employment is normalized so that it averages zero. This equation resembles the wage curve, as in Phelps (1994) and Blanchflower and Oswald (1995). Some might call it a "pseudo labor supply curve."

The simplest way to motivate this equation is from the standpoint of a union that sets wages. The union has a target for the real wage that depends on its workers' productivity. In addition, high employment makes the union more aggressive, raising the wages they demand.

Another way to view this wage equation is from the standpoint of a firm that sets wages in an efficiency-wage environment. The wage curve describes a "no-shirking condition." Firms pay productive workers more because they have better outside alternatives. In addition, high employment increases shirking among workers because unemployment is a less potent threat. As a result, high employment induces firms to offer higher wages.

2.2. The Sticky Information Assumption

To this standard wage curve, we add the assumption that wage-setters make their decisions based on imperfect information. Every wage-setter sets a new wage every period, but they collect information about the economy and update their decisions slowly over time.

Our assumption about information arrival is analogous to the adjustment assumption in the Calvo (1983) model of price adjustment. That is, adjustment occurs as a Poisson process. In each period, a fraction λ of the wage-setters obtains new information about the state of the economy and recomputes optimal plans based on that new information. Other wage-setters continue to set wages based on old plans and outdated information. Each wage-setter has the same probability of being one of those updating its information, regardless of how long it has been since its last update.[1]

---

1. A natural question is *whose* expectations suffer from the stickiness of information. Under the union interpretation of the wage curve, the expectations are clearly those of the union workers. The answer is less obvious in the efficiency-wage interpretation, according to which the wage curve represents the no-shirking condition. In this case, firms set the wages, but because the firms are trying to induce workers not to shirk, the expectations of the workers are again relevant.

A wage-setter that last updated its information j periods ago sets the wage

$$w_t^j = E_{t-j} w_t^*.$$

The aggregate wage is the average of wages in the economy:

$$w_t = \lambda \sum_{j=0}^{\infty} (1 - \lambda)^j w_t^j.$$

These two equations, together with the wage-curve equation above, fully describe the process of wage setting.

The rest of the model is conventional. The overall price level is determined by the level of wages and labor productivity:

$$p_t = w_t - \theta_t.$$

This equation is both the supply curve in the output market (prices depend on costs) and the demand curve in the labor market (the real wage depends on productivity). The level of output is determined by employment and labor productivity:

$$y_t = e_t + \theta_t.$$

This is the production function. The above five equations together make up the aggregate-supply side of the model.

It is worth noting what happens in the limiting case when information is perfect ($\lambda = 1$). It is straightforward to show that in this case, $e = 0$ and $y = \theta$. That is, under perfect information, employment is constant and output mirrors productivity. In this model, all employment dynamics follow from the assumed stickiness of information.

2.3. The Sticky-Information Phillips Curve

We can solve for the price level as a function of output by combining the previous five equations. The resulting aggregate supply equation is

$$p_t = \left\{ \lambda \sum_{j=0}^{\infty} (1 - \lambda)^j E_{t-j} \left[p_t + \alpha y_t + (1 - \alpha)\theta_t \right] \right\} - \theta_t.$$

With this equation in hand, another special case is apparent. If there are no productivity shocks ($\theta = 0$), the model simplifies to the price adjustment model in Mankiw and Reis (2001). Thus, the results in that paper concerning the dynamic effects of aggregate demand apply here as well.

With some tedious algebra, which we leave to the appendix, this equation for the price level yields the following equation for the inflation rate:

$$\pi_t = [\alpha\lambda/(1-\lambda)]e_t - \Delta\theta_t + \lambda\sum_{j=0}^{\infty}(1-\lambda)^j E_{t-1-j}(\pi_t + \Delta\theta_t + \alpha\Delta e_t),$$

where $\Delta e_t = e_t - e_{t-1}$. We call this the *sticky-information Phillips curve*.

Let us examine each of the determinants of inflation in this model: (1) High employment means higher inflation: This is the conventional short-run Phillips curve. Here it arises because high employment raises target wages, which in turn raises costs and thus the prices charged by firms. (2) Higher productivity growth lowers inflation because it lowers firms' costs of production. (3) Higher expected inflation raises inflation because, by virtue of the sticky-information assumption, past expectations are still affecting current wage increases. (4) Higher expected productivity growth raises inflation because it influences the wages that wage-setters thought were appropriate. (5) Higher expected employment growth also raises inflation because it also influences expected target wages.

2.4. Comparison to a Leading Competitor

This sticky-information Phillips curve is very different from the "new Keynesian Phillips curve," which has become popular in recent years. The latter model, based on the work of Taylor (1980), Rotemberg (1982), and Calvo (1983), implies an expectation-augmented Phillips curve, where current inflation depends on the expectation of next period's inflation. Ignoring productivity shocks for the moment, we can write the new Keynesian Phillips curve as

$$\pi_t = \gamma e_t + E_t\pi_{t+1}.$$

For a notable example of a paper applying this model of inflation dynamics, see Clarida et al. (1999). McCallum (1997) has called this model "the closest thing there is to a standard specification," while Goodfriend and King (1997) said that it is part of a "new neoclassical synthesis" in macroeconomics.

Yet this model has some significant empirical flaws. Mankiw (2001) argues that it is inconsistent with conventional views about the effects of monetary policy. Mankiw and Reis (2001) compare it with a simple version of the sticky-information model and show that the latter yields more plausible dynamics. In particular, according to the new Keynesian Phillips curve, inflation responds immediately and substantially to monetary shocks, whereas according to the sticky-information Phillips curve, the effect of monetary shocks on inflation is delayed and gradual.

The key difference between the models comes from the role of expectations. The new Keynesian Phillips curve gives a prominent role to *current* expectations of *future* inflation. These expectations can adjust quickly in response to changes in monetary policy. By contrast, the sticky-information Phillips curve gives a prominent role to *past* expectations of *current* inflation. These expectations are predetermined and thus cannot change quickly. In this way, the sticky-information model more closely resembles an earlier generation of price-adjustment models proposed by Fischer (1977) and Phelps and Taylor (1977).

3. DISINFLATIONS AND PRODUCTIVITY SLOWDOWNS

We now consider the dynamics of employment and inflation in this sticky-information model. To do this, we have to close the model with a specification for aggregate demand. One approach to doing this would be to add a goods market equilibrium condition (i.e., an IS curve) and a monetary policy reaction function for the interest rate (such as a Taylor rule). This approach has several advantages and might be pursued in future work. However, in this chapter, we adopt an approach that, although perhaps less realistic, is simpler and more transparent. We use a simple money market equilibrium condition:

$$m_t - p_t = \beta y_t.$$

The parameter β is the income elasticity of money demand. More important for our purposes, it determines the elasticity of the aggregate demand curve. The smaller β is, the flatter the aggregate demand curve. The variable m can be viewed narrowly as the money supply or broadly as a summary measure of all variables that shift the aggregate demand for goods and services. Thus, we can refer to m as either money or aggregate demand.

With this equation, we have now fully described the model. For purposes of numerical illustration, we have to choose values for the parameters. We pick $\beta = \frac{1}{2}$. For some of the qualitative results reported below, it is important that $\beta < 1$. We also set $\alpha = 0.1$ and $\lambda = 0.25$. The value of α measures the sensitivity of the target real wage to labor market conditions. In the terminology of Ball and Romer (1990), it measures the degree of "real rigidity." If the period is taken to be a quarter, then $\lambda = 0.25$ means that wage-setters update their information on average once a year. These parameter values strike us as plausible, and we use them for the purposes of illustration. However, in a later section, we use the time-series data to estimate λ, the key parameter measuring the stickiness of information, and find that $\lambda = 0.25$ fits the data well.

Here we look at how this economy responds to a sudden change in regime. In the first case, we assume that the annual rate of growth of money m falls by 2 percentage points, or 0.5 percentage points per quarter. In the second case, we assume that the growth rate of productivity θ falls by this amount. In each case, the change in the exogenous growth rate is assumed to be sudden, unexpected, and permanent.

The appendix explains in detail how we solve for the resulting equilibrium path for the economy, whereas here we present and discuss the solution in more intuitive terms. Figure 1 shows the response to each of these disturbances. The top panel shows the path of employment e, and the bottom shows the response of inflation π. Recall that the natural rate of employment in this model—the level of employment that would prevail if information were perfect—is normalized to zero. Thus, the employment variable measures how far the economy is operating from what might be viewed as its "full employment" level.

Figure 1 shows that employment follows a hump-shaped pattern in response to both disinflations and productivity slowdowns. Employment falls for a while as the impact of the change in regime builds over time. But then the effect on

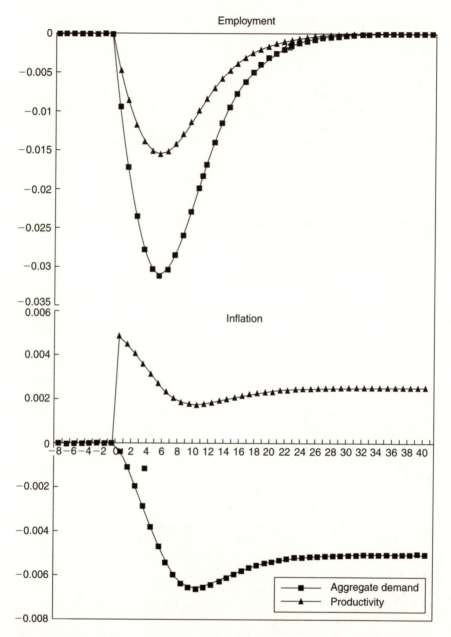

Figure 1. Employment and inflation after a 2 percent fall in the annual growth rate of money or productivity at date 0.

employment dissipates as the information about the change in regime spreads its way throughout the population. For these parameters, the maximum impact on employment occurs at six quarters, although of course this result is sensitive to the parameter values we have chosen.

The two inflation paths in the bottom panel of Figure 1 are quite different from each other. In the case of a slowdown in money growth, inflation declines only gradually. It overshoots the new lower level briefly as agents learn of the new regime and correct their previous mistakes. In the case of a productivity slowdown, inflation immediately spikes up, as firms pass on higher costs to consumers. Inflation gradually declines as wages start reflecting lower productivity growth. After a brief period of overshooting, inflation eventually settles at a new higher level.

The reader might have noticed that the dynamic paths for employment are similar in the case of disinflations and productivity slowdowns. This is not a coincidence. In fact, the appendix proves the following:

PROPOSITION: Productivity has an impact on employment that is exactly $1 - \beta$ times that of aggregate demand.

This naturally leads to:

COROLLARY: If the aggregate demand curve is unit elastic ($\beta = 1$), then productivity has no effect on employment.

The intuition behind the corollary is the following: Adverse news about productivity influences target nominal wages in two ways. They fall because target real wages are lower, and they rise because the price level is higher. If $\beta = 1$ and the path of m is held constant, these two effects exactly cancel. In this special case, wages stay exactly on track to maintain full employment, despite the slow diffusion of information.

4. STABILIZATION POLICY IN THE FACE OF PRODUCTIVITY CHANGE

The outcomes shown in Figure 1 assume that when the economy experiences a productivity slowdown, the monetary authority holds aggregate demand on the same path that it otherwise would have followed. This benchmark is natural, but it need not hold. As employment and inflation fluctuate, the monetary authority may well respond by altering aggregate demand. Here we consider two other natural benchmarks.

One possibility is that the monetary authority may choose a policy to stabilize employment. This means it would adjust aggregate demand m to keep $e = 0$ at all times. Because fluctuations in employment in this model arise because of imperfections in private information and because the monetary authority is assumed to have full information, it might well try to achieve the level of employment and output that private decision-makers would choose on their own if only they were better informed.

Alternatively, the central bank may choose to stabilize inflation. This means it would adjust aggregate demand to maintain a constant inflation rate. This benchmark is interesting in part because many central banks are in fact now committed to inflation targeting as a policy framework (although many such regimes allow temporary deviations from a strict target).

There is also another reason to focus on the employment path that follows under an inflation-stabilizing policy: This path corresponds to what econometricians might measure as the NAIRU (the nonaccelerating inflation rate of unemployment). In this model, the natural rate of employment—that is, the level that would prevail with full information—is assumed constant. Yet the rate of employment associated with nonaccelerating inflation is not constant. To find the level of employment that corresponds to the measured NAIRU, we can solve the model assuming that monetary policy stabilizes inflation.

Figure 2 shows employment and inflation in response to a productivity slowdown under three policies: constant aggregate demand, employment stabilization, and inflation stabilization. The appendix presents the details of solution.

The figure shows that inflation stabilization leads to very large fluctuations in employment. To extinguish the impact on inflation, monetary policy responds to the adverse shift in aggregate supply by contracting aggregate demand. This instability in employment under inflation stabilization can be viewed as a warning to the many central banks around the world that have adopted inflation targeting. In essence, a productivity slowdown in this model looks like a rise in the NAIRU, which is consistent with the empirical results in Ball and Moffitt (2001) and Staiger et al. (2001). Yet the natural rate—the level of employment that would prevail under full information—has not changed. The fall in employment that results from a productivity slowdown is no more desirable in this model than any other downturn. A policy of inflation stabilization not only tolerates the downturn in employment but exacerbates it to keep inflation under control.

Figure 2 also shows that a policy of employment stabilization leads to a permanent rise in the inflation rate. That is, for the central bank to maintain full employment during a productivity slowdown, it has to accommodate the adverse shift in aggregate supply by raising aggregate demand, permitting a higher inflation rate. The rise in inflation needed to stabilize employment equals the magnitude of the slowdown in productivity growth. That is, a slowdown of 2 percent per year requires an increase in the inflation rate of 2 percentage points.

There are other ways to describe the policy of stabilizing employment. It turns out that along the path with stable employment, both nominal income $p + y$ and the nominal wage w equal their previously expected values. Turning this observation around leads to a policy: If the central bank commits to keeping either nominal income or the nominal wage at a constant level (or growing at some constant rate), aggregate demand and inflation in the price of goods and services will automatically respond to a productivity shift by exactly the right amount to maintain full employment.

Overall, this model suggests that inflation targeting may not be the best framework for monetary policy in the face of changing productivity. A better target variable than the price of goods and services is nominal income or the price of labor. Like inflation targeting, targeting nominal income or the nominal wage gives monetary policy a nominal anchor, but it does so in a way that permits greater stability in employment. There is a long tradition suggesting the desirability of nominal income targeting; see Tobin (1980) and Hall and Mankiw (1994) for two

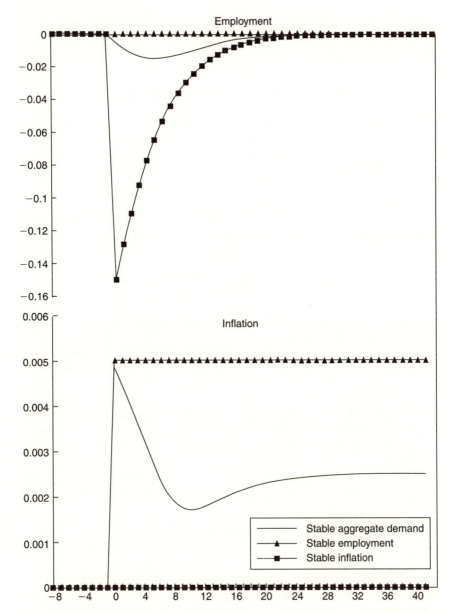

Figure 2. Employment and inflation after a 2 percent fall in the annual growth rate of productivity at date 0, under different policies.

examples. But, as far as we know, the possibility of targeting the price of labor has not received much attention.

One exception is the plan discussed by Phelps (1978). He concludes, "the program envisioned here aims to stabilize wages on a level or rising path, leaving the price level to be buffeted by supply shocks and exchange rate disturbances."

This is precisely the policy suggested by the sticky-information model of wage setting. We agree with Phelps that nominal wage targeting seems like a promising alternative to inflation targeting as a monetary policy rule.[2]

5. AN EMPIRICAL APPLICATION

In the model presented here, inflation and productivity surprises drive employment fluctuations. This section examines this prediction using U.S. time-series data to get a sense of how well the model works and to learn where it has problems matching the world.

5.1. The Approach

We start with the sticky-information Phillips curve presented earlier:

$$\pi_t = [\alpha\lambda/(1-\lambda)]e_t - \Delta\theta_t + \lambda \sum_{j=0}^{\infty}(1-\lambda)^j E_{t-1-j}(\pi_t + \Delta\theta_t + \alpha\Delta e_t).$$

Now we turn this equation around to use it as a theory of employment:

$$e_t = [(1-\lambda)/\alpha\lambda]\left[\pi_t + \Delta\theta_t - \lambda \sum_{j=0}^{\infty}(1-\lambda)^j E_{t-1-j}(\pi_t + \Delta\theta_t + \alpha\Delta e_t)\right],$$

which implicitly expresses employment as a function of inflation, productivity, and the past expectations of these variables. Our goal is to see whether this equation can help explain observed U.S. fluctuations. To do this, we make two auxiliary assumptions.

First, we assume that inflation and productivity growth follow univariate stochastic processes. Their moving average representations can be written as

$$\pi_t = \sum_{j=0}^{\infty}\rho_j\varepsilon_{t-j} \quad \text{and} \quad \Delta\theta_t = \sum_{j=0}^{\infty}\eta_j v_{t-j}.$$

In this case, the expectations of inflation and productivity growth are a function of their past univariate innovations.[3] As the appendix shows, the model can now be solved as

---

2. Aoki (2001) presents a related result: In a world with a sticky-price sector and a flexible-price sector, optimal monetary policy targets inflation in the sticky-price sector. In our model, the labor market is analogous to the sticky-price sector.

3. In reality, expectations may also depend on other information. For example, news about monetary policy may affect expected inflation. But experience suggests that the improvement from multivariate over univariate forecasting is often slight. Future work could improve upon this assumption, but we probably do not go too far wrong in assuming univariate processes for inflation and productivity growth.

$$\alpha e_t = \sum_{j=0}^{\infty} \gamma_j \varepsilon_{t-j} + \sum_{j=0}^{\infty} \Psi_j v_{t-j},$$

where the parameters γ_j and Ψ_j are functions of ρ_j, η_j, and λ. This equation can be used to predict fluctuations in employment, taking as inputs the univariate innovations in inflation and productivity.

Second, we assume that the observed unemployment rate is linearly related to a moving average of e, the employment variable in our model. In particular, the unemployment rate u is assumed to be

$$u_t = \delta_0 - \delta_1 e_t^s,$$

where e_t^s is defined as

$$e_t^s = (e_{t-3} + 2e_{t-2} + 3e_{t-1} + 4e_t + 3e_{t+1} + 2e_{t+2} + e_{t+3})/16.$$

We found that without any smoothing of the predicted employment variable, the model produces too much high-frequency variation in the predicted unemployment rate. This triangular filter smooths out the rapid quarter-to-quarter fluctuations in the predicted series, leaving the business cycle variation and the longer-term trends.[4]

Given these two auxiliary assumptions, we can use the model to produce a predicted path of unemployment for any given set of parameters. The predicted unemployment rate in any period depends on the history of shocks to inflation and productivity.

5.2. Parameter Estimation

The next issue is how to choose the parameters. We estimate the parameters of the univariate processes for inflation and productivity growth as autoregressions using ordinary least squares. We then invert these autoregressions to obtain ρ_j and η_j, the parameters of the moving average representations. The residuals from the autoregressions are the shocks e_t and v_t, which we feed into the model to explain fluctuations in unemployment.

The remaining three parameters are λ, δ_0, and δ_1/α. (The parameters α and δ_1 are not identified separately.) We estimate these parameters using a least-squares procedure; that is, we choose these parameters to minimize the sum of squared deviations between predicted and actual unemployment.

The results from this procedure have a simple interpretation. The estimated δ_0 equals the mean unemployment rate. The estimated δ_1/α ensures that the prediction

---

4. There are two natural hypotheses to explain the high-frequency variation predicted by the model without the filter. (1) Some high-frequency variation in productivity growth and inflation is measurement error. (2) The high-frequency variation in productivity growth and inflation in the data is real, but for some reason, employment responds more sluggishly in the world than it does in our model. Very possibly each explanation has an element of truth.

error is not correlated with the predicted value. These two parameters do not affect the autocorrelations of predicted unemployment or the cross-correlations between predicted and actual. In some sense, these parameters are not interesting: Changing δ_0 and δ_1/α alters the mean and variance of predicted unemployment without altering the dynamics in any other way.

The interesting parameter is λ, which measures the rate of information arrival. Our least-squares procedure picks this parameter to make the model fit the data. In particular, it picks the value for λ that maximizes the correlation between predicted and actual unemployment.

5.3. Data and Results

We use quarterly, seasonally adjusted U.S. data from the first quarter of 1959 to the first quarter of 2001. Inflation is measured by the consumer price index. Productivity growth is the growth of output per hour in the business sector. Unemployment is the civilian unemployment rate.

The univariate autoregressions indicate that inflation and productivity growth follow very different stochastic processes. Productivity growth is indistinguishable from white noise, indicating no persistence. By contrast, inflation is well modeled as an AR(3) with autoregressive parameters 0.37, 0.22, and 0.29. These three coefficients on lagged inflation sum to 0.88, indicating that inflation is borderline nonstationary. We use the white noise specification for productivity growth and the AR(3) parameters for inflation to calculate the moving average parameters and the estimated innovations.[5]

Next we fit the model using the unemployment data. The estimated value of λ, the rate of information arrival, is 0.25. This means that wage setters in the economy update their information on average every four quarters. Figure 3 shows the actual and predicted unemployment rate using this estimate. The correlation between these two series is 0.47.

Figure 4 decomposes the predicted unemployment rate from Figure 3 into two pieces. The top panel shows the piece of predicted unemployment that is driven by inflation innovations. The bottom panel shows the piece of predicted unemployment that is driven by productivity innovations. Actual unemployment is shown in both panels, and all the parameters are held constant at the same values as in Figure 3.

The figure shows that inflation and productivity innovations are both important for explaining unemployment. The correlation of unemployment with the inflation

---

5. When we tried using an estimated AR(3) process for productivity growth, the results were almost the same as those reported here because the estimated autoregressive coefficients were so small. Note that the case we use, according to which the level of productivity follows a random walk, is similar to the specifications commonly used in the real business cycle literature. Exploring alternative processes may be fruitful in future work. If we had assumed a stochastic process with a slowly changing conditional mean (such as an IMA(1,1) process with a large, negative MA parameter), then employment would be related to productivity growth minus a weighted average of past productivity growth. This specification would more closely resemble the one in Ball and Moffitt (2001). See also Grubb et al. (1982, sec. 5) for a related earlier work.

Unemployment (%)

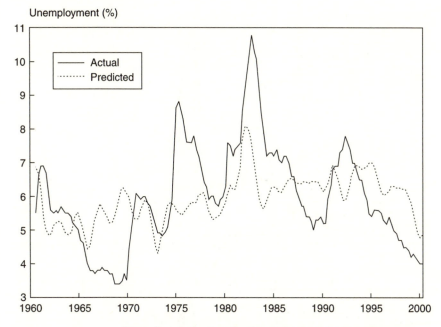

Figure 3. Actual and predicted unemployment.

piece of the predicted series is 0.33. The correlation of unemployment with the productivity piece is 0.17.

Inspection of Figure 4 reveals an anomaly: Unemployment as predicted by productivity innovations moves in advance of actual unemployment. Although this piece of predicted unemployment has a correlation with contemporaneous unemployment of only 0.17, its correlation with unemployment 1 year ahead is 0.48. Productivity appears to take more time to influence unemployment in the world than it does in our model.

As a rough (and, we admit, ad hoc) fix for this lagged response, we add a four-quarter delay to the estimated model. The employment equation then becomes

$$\alpha e_t = \sum_{j=0}^{\infty} \gamma_j \varepsilon_{t-j} + \sum_{j=0}^{\infty} \Psi_j v_{t-j-4}.$$

Otherwise, the model and estimation procedure are the same. The estimate of λ is now 0.26, almost identical to our earlier estimate. The predicted and actual unemployment rates, shown in Figure 5, now have a correlation of 0.60. Adding this lag in the effect of productivity significantly improves the model's fit.

In the end, the empirical verdict on this model is mixed. On the one hand, the model fails to capture some important dynamics in the data. The delay between productivity innovations and unemployment is a puzzle.[6] On the other hand,

---

6. This delay in the response to productivity shocks may be related to the mechanism highlighted in Basu et al. (1998). If prices are sticky in the short run, then a good productivity shock can reduce

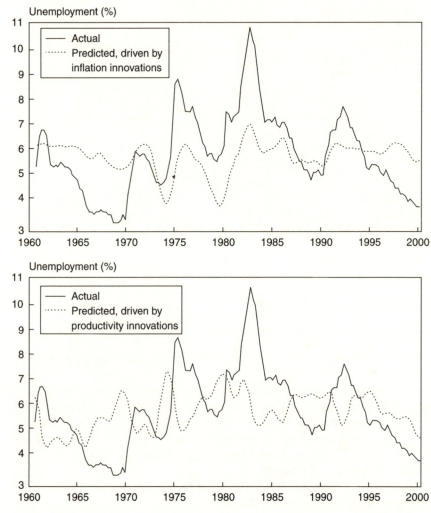

Figure 4. Decomposition of predicted unemployment into inflation- and productivity-driven innovations.

inflation and productivity surprises can account for much of the observed evolution in U.S. unemployment. The simulation in Figure 5 captures many of the main features of the unemployment data, including the big recessions in 1975 and 1982, the rising trend level of unemployment rate during the 1970s and early 1980s, and the declining unemployment rate in the late 1990s.

There are many ways in which this empirical model could be improved. The model excludes many determinants of unemployment, such as changing

employment, because firms need fewer workers to produce the same level of output. Another possibility is that the short-run changes in measured labor productivity are a reflection of labor hoarding over the business cycle rather than exogenous movements in true productivity.

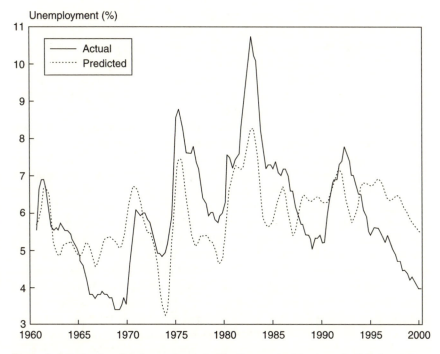

Figure 5. Actual and predicted unemployment with a four-quarter delay to productivity innovations.

demographics, unionization, and minimum wage laws. It also excludes many shocks that might shift the inflation-unemployment relationship, such as exchange rates, food and energy prices, and wage-price controls. The only inputs into these simulations are inflation and productivity surprises. Absent changes in measured productivity, the model interprets all movements in inflation as driven by aggregate demand. Incorporating other sources of unemployment and inflation fluctuations into the model and adding a richer dynamic structure to better explain the link between productivity and employment are tasks we leave for future work.

6. CONCLUSION

Since Friedman (1968) and Phelps (1967, 1968) introduced the natural rate hypothesis in the 1960s, expectations have played a central role in understanding the dynamics of inflation and employment. Early empirical work testing the hypothesis was based on the assumption of adaptive expectations, according to which expected inflation is a weighted average of past inflation. Yet Lucas (1972) and Sargent (1971) forcefully criticized that approach. Since then, economists have most often relied on the assumption of rational expectations.

Over time, however, economists have increasingly realized that while agents may be too smart to form expectations adaptively, they may not be smart enough to form them rationally. Unfortunately, finding a safe haven between the stupidity of adaptive expectations and the hyperintelligence of rational expectations is not easy. Friedman (1979), Summers (1986), and Sargent (1999) have explored the possibility that least-squares learning can help explain how expectations evolve over time. Sims (2001) has suggested modeling agents' limited capacity for processing information. Ball (2000) has proposed that agents form optimal univariate forecasts, but ignore the possible gains from multivariate forecasts. Each of these approaches has some appeal, but each lacks the parsimony that makes rational expectations so compelling.

Like all these efforts, the sticky-information model we have explored here and in our previous paper attempts to model agents that are smart, but not too smart. Our agents form expectations rationally, but they do not do so often. Because of either costs of acquiring information or costs of recomputing optimal plans, information diffuses slowly throughout the population. As a result, expectations conditional on old information continue to influence current behavior.

Recently, many economists have been pursuing "behavioral economics," a research program that tries to incorporate the insights of psychology into economics. The starting point of this work is the observation that people are not quite as rational as the *homo economicus* assumed in standard models. The sticky-information model of inflation-employment dynamics can be viewed as a modest contribution to this literature. The closest antecedent is the work of Gabaix and Laibson (2001), which tries to explain consumption behavior and the equity premium puzzle by assuming that consumers are slow to recognize changes in the values of their portfolios. The sticky-information model we have presented here applies the analogous assumption to the process of wage setting.

From a theoretical standpoint, assuming sticky information is an attempt to have your cake and eat it too. Like many previous efforts, our model tries to describe agents who do not fully understand their environment and gradually learn about it over time. This lack of full understanding motivates our application of Calvo's assumption of Poisson adjustment to the acquisition of information. Whether this approach is the best way to model the imperfections of human behavior is hard to say. But without doubt, it has a major advantage: Once this leap of faith is taken, the powerful tools of rational expectations become available to solve for the resulting equilibrium.

Of course, the validity of this model of inflation-unemployment dynamics is ultimately an empirical question. The model fits some broad stylized facts. In our previous paper, we showed that the model can explain the dynamic response of the economy to monetary policy: It can explain why disinflations are costly, why monetary shocks have a delayed and gradual effect on inflation, and why changes in inflation are positively correlated with the level of economic activity. This chapter has moved the analysis to the labor market and introduced a role for productivity as a driving force. The model can now explain why productivity slowdowns, such as the one that occurred in the 1970s, are associated with rising unemployment (and a rising NAIRU) and why productivity accelerations, such as the one that occurred in the United States in the 1990s, are associated with declining unemployment (and a declining NAIRU). When we applied the model to U.S. time-series data, we found that inflation and productivity surprises account for a sizable fraction of observed unemployment fluctuations.

The model proposed here suggests a possible problem with the policy of inflation targeting that many of the world's central banks adopted during the 1990s. In this model, stabilizing employment in the face of a productivity slowdown requires a rise in the inflation rate of an equal magnitude. The model suggests that a better nominal anchor than the price of goods and services is nominal income or the nominal wage. Targeting inflation in the price of labor, rather than in the price of goods and services, is a policy rule that deserves a closer look.

APPENDIX

This appendix formally justifies some of the claims asserted in the body of the chapter.

The Sticky-Information Phillips Curve

The three equations describing wage setting, together with the demand for labor, lead to

$$p_t = \left[\lambda \sum_{j=0}^{\infty} (1 - \lambda)^j E_{t-j}(p_t + \alpha e_t + \theta_t) \right] - \theta_t. \qquad (A1)$$

Take out the first term to obtain

$$p_t = \lambda[p_t + \alpha e_t + \theta_t] + \left[\lambda \sum_{j=0}^{\infty} (1 - \lambda)^{j+1} E_{t-1-j}(p_t + \alpha e_t + \theta_t) \right] - \theta_t \qquad (A2)$$

and subtract the p_{t-1} version of (A1) from (A2) to obtain, after some rearranging,

$$\pi_t = \lambda(p_t + \alpha e_t + \theta_t) + \left[\lambda \sum_{j=0}^{\infty} (1 - \lambda)^j E_{t-1-j}(\pi_t + \alpha \Delta e_t + \Delta \theta_t) \right]$$

$$- \left[\lambda^2 \sum_{j=0}^{\infty} (1 - \lambda)^j E_{t-1-j}(p_t + \alpha e_t + \theta_t) \right] - \Delta \theta_t, \qquad (A3)$$

where Δ is the first difference operator and the inflation rate is $\pi_t = \Delta p_t$. Multiplying through equation (A2) by λ and rearranging, we get

$$(1 - \lambda)\lambda^2 \sum_{j=0}^{\infty} (1 - \lambda)^j E_{t-1-j}(p_t + \alpha e_t + \theta_t)$$

$$= \lambda\left[(1 - \lambda)p_t - \lambda \alpha e_t + (1 - \lambda)\theta_t\right]. \qquad (A4)$$

Replacing (A4) for the last term in (A3) leads to, after rearranging, the sticky-information Phillips curve:

$$\pi_t = [\alpha\lambda/(1-\lambda)]e_t - \Delta\theta_t + \lambda \sum_{j=0}^{\infty} (1-\lambda)^j E_{t-1-j}(\pi_t + \Delta\theta_t + \alpha\Delta e_t). \quad \text{(A5)}$$

The Response of Employment and Inflation to a Fall in the Growth Rate of Aggregate Demand and Productivity

Replacing for y_t using the aggregate demand equation into the aggregate supply equation, we obtain the law of motion for the price level:

$$p_t = \left\{ \lambda \sum_{j=0}^{\infty} (1-\lambda)^j E_{t-j}[(1-\alpha/\beta)p_t + (\alpha/\beta)m_t + (1-\alpha)\theta_t] \right\} - \theta_t. \quad \text{(A6)}$$

First, say that m_t was growing at the rate 0.005, up to date -1, when it reaches the level 0. Then, unexpectedly, the growth rate falls to 0, so m_t stays at level 0 forever. Formally: $m_t = 0.005(1+t)$ for $t \le -1$ and $m_t = 0$ for $t \ge 0$. Also, set $\theta_t = 0$ for all t. Then, we can break equation (A6) into two components:

$$p_t = \lambda \sum_{j=0}^{t} (1-\lambda)^j E_{t-j}[(1-\alpha/\beta)p_t + (\alpha/\beta)m_t]$$

$$+ \lambda \sum_{j=t+1}^{\infty} (1-\lambda)^j E_{t-j}[(1-\alpha/\beta)p_t + (\alpha/\beta)m_t]. \quad \text{(A7)}$$

In the first summation term are included the agents that set their expectations after the change in m_t. Thus, they set expectations with full information: $E_{t-j}(p_t) = p_t$ and $E_{t-j}(m_t) = 0$. In the second summation term are agents who set expectations prior to the change: $E_{t-j}(p_t) = E_{t-j}(m_t) = 0.005(1+t)$. Thus, (A7) becomes

$$p_t = (1-\alpha/\beta)\left[1 - (1-\lambda)^{t+1}\right] p_t + 0.005(1+t)(1-\lambda)^{t+1}, \quad \text{(A8)}$$

which, after rearranging, gives the solution:

$$p_t = \frac{0.005(1+t)(1-\lambda)^{t+1}}{1 - (1-\alpha/\beta)[1 - (1-\lambda)^{t+1}]}. \quad \text{(A9)}$$

Employment is given by $e_t = -p_t/\beta$ and inflation is $\pi_t = \Delta p_t$.

The fall in productivity is formalized as: $\theta_t = 0.005(1+t)$ for $t \le -1$ and $\theta_t = 0$ for $t \ge 0$, and $m_t = 0$ for all t. Starting again from (A6) we obtain, by very similar steps, the response of prices:

$$p_t = \frac{0.005(1-\beta)(1+t)(1-\lambda)^{t+1}}{1 - (1-\alpha/\beta)[1 - (1-\lambda)^{t+1}]}. \quad \text{(A10)}$$

Inflation and employment follow immediately.

Proof of the Proposition and Corollary

Starting from (A1), replacing for p_t from the aggregate demand equation and for y_t from the production function, we obtain the expectational difference equation for employment as a function of the two exogenous processes, m_t and θ_t:

$$\beta e_t = m_t + (1-\beta)\theta_t - \lambda \sum_{j=0}^{\infty} (1-\lambda)^j E_{t-j}[m_t + (1-\beta)\theta_t + (\alpha-\beta)e_t]. \quad \text{(A11)}$$

If we define the composite disturbance as $m_t + (1-\beta)\theta_t$, employment is driven solely by this term. Shocks to m_t or $(1-\beta)\theta_t$ have exactly the same effect on the equation above and thus on employment. This shows the proposition. The corollary follows from setting $\beta = 1$ in (A11) and noting that θ_t does not enter the stochastic equation determining employment.

Stabilization Policy and Productivity Change

We start with the stable employment policy. From (A11), it follows that if $m_t = -(1-\beta)\theta_t$ then we obtain an expectational difference equation involving only e_t, which has solution $e_t = 0$. This is the policy that stabilizes employment. Given the path for θ_t above, we then have the policy path m_t, and since we know that this ensures $e_t = 0$, then $y_t = \theta_t$ from the production function. The path of prices p_t comes from the aggregate demand equation $p_t = -\theta_t$. A permanent drop in the growth rate of productivity therefore leads to a permanent rise in inflation.

Alternatively, note that combining the wage curve and the labor demand (output supply) equations into the equation for the aggregate wage we obtain

$$w_t = \lambda \sum_{j=0}^{\infty} (1-\lambda)^j E_{t-j}(w_t + \alpha e_t). \quad \text{(A12)}$$

From (A12), having the wage rate equal to some forever known constant ensures that $e_t = 0$. Without loss of generality, we set that constant to zero. The associated policy is $m_t = -(1-\beta)\theta_t$, from using the aggregate demand equation and the production function. Thus, an employment stabilization policy is equivalent to a policy that stabilizes the wage rate in the sense of having w_t deterministic or known to all.

Similarly, we use the labor demand and the production function equations to replace w_t and θ_t in (A12) above and obtain

$$p_t + y_t - e_t = \lambda \sum_{j=0}^{\infty} (1-\lambda)^j E_{t-j}[p_t + y_t + (1-\alpha)e_t]. \quad \text{(A13)}$$

Thus, by the same argument as above, stabilizing nominal income $p_t + y_t$ is equivalent to stabilizing employment.

We now turn our attention to inflation targeting. Without loss of generality we set the target to zero, and the level to zero as well, so the policy aim is to have $p_t = 0$ at all periods. From the law of motion for the price level in (A6) and the set path for prices:

$$\theta_t = \lambda \sum_{j=0}^{\infty} (1 - \lambda)^j E_{t-j}[(\alpha/\beta)m_t + (1 - \alpha)\theta_t]. \qquad \text{(A14)}$$

Given a path for θ_t, the necessary path of policy is given by the solution to this equation. For $t \leq -1$, all agents have full information and $\theta_t = 0.005(1+t)$ so the policy is $m_t = 0.005\beta(1+t)$. For $t \geq 0$, breaking the sum in two components, the first referring to informed agents that set their expectations at or after date 0 and the second to uninformed agents that set their expectations before date 0, we obtain

$$0 = (\alpha/\beta)\left[1 - (1 - \lambda)^{t+1}\right]m_t + 0.005(1 + t)(1 - \lambda)^{t+1}, \qquad \text{(A15)}$$

which, after rearranging, becomes

$$m_t = -\frac{0.005\beta(1 + t)(1 - \lambda)^{t+1}}{\alpha - \alpha(1 - \lambda)^{t+1}}. \qquad \text{(A16)}$$

The path for employment for $t \geq 0$ is $e_t = y_t = m_t/\beta$.

Empirical Implementation

Since the only forces driving employment are inflation and productivity growth, the general solution for employment will be a linear function (with undetermined coefficients) of the shocks to these variables:

$$\alpha e_t = \sum_{j=0}^{\infty} (\gamma_j \varepsilon_{t-j} + \Psi_j v_{t-j}). \qquad \text{(A17)}$$

Using the MA representations for inflation, productivity growth, and employment; plugging these into the equation for employment in the main text; and taking the relevant expectations, we obtain

$$\sum_{j=0}^{\infty} (\gamma_j \varepsilon_{t-j} + \Psi_j v_{t-j}) = [(1 - \lambda)/\lambda]\left\{ \sum_{j=0}^{\infty} (\rho_j \varepsilon_{t-j} + \eta_j v_{t-j}) \right. \qquad \text{(A18)}$$

$$- \left[\lambda \sum_{j=0}^{\infty} (1 - \lambda)^j \sum_{i=j+1}^{\infty} (\rho_i \varepsilon_{t-i} + \eta_i v_{t-i} + \gamma_i \varepsilon_{t-i} + \Psi_i v_{t-i}) \right]$$

$$\left. + \left[\lambda \sum_{j=0}^{\infty} (1 - \lambda)^j \sum_{i=j}^{\infty} (\gamma_i \varepsilon_{t-i-1} + \Psi_i v_{t-i-1}) \right] \right\}.$$

Matching coefficients gives the solution

$$\gamma_0 = [(1-\lambda)/\lambda]\rho_0, \tag{A19}$$

$$\gamma_j = \left\{(1-\lambda)^{t+1}/[1-(1-\lambda)^{t+1}]\right\}\rho_j + \left\{1-\left\{\lambda/[1-(1-\lambda)^{t+1}]\right\}\right\}\gamma_{j-1}, \tag{A20}$$

$$\Psi_0 = [(1-\lambda)/\lambda]\eta_0, \tag{A21}$$

$$\Psi_j = \left\{(1-\lambda)^{t+1}/[1-(1-\lambda)^{t+1}]\right\}\eta_j + \left\{1-\left\{\lambda/[1-(1-\lambda)^{t+1}]\right\}\right\}\Psi_{j-1}. \tag{A22}$$

Given the MA parameters ρ_j and η_j and a series for the shocks ε_t and v_t (all of which we obtain by OLS regressions on the data) we can generate a predicted employment series from (A17), which, after applying the triangular filter in the text, produces a series for smoothed employment: e_t^s. Note then first that, from (A17) and the additive nature of the smoother, $1/\alpha$ factors out of the expressions for e_t^s. Second, that since ρ_j, η_j, ε_t, and v_t are determined by first-stage OLS regressions, the only parameter left determining predicted smooth employment is λ, so that we can write $\alpha e_t^s = g(\lambda)$, where $g(\cdot)$ is the function defined by (A17) and (A19) to (A22). The equation for our predicted unemployment series is

$$\hat{u}_t = \delta_0 - (\delta_1/\alpha)g(\lambda). \tag{A23}$$

We pick parameters by nonlinear least-squares to minimize the sum of squares residuals:

$$\min_{\delta_0, \delta_1/\alpha, \lambda} \sum_{t=1}^{T}(u_t - \hat{u}_t)^2. \tag{A24}$$

Finally, the decomposition of predicted unemployment in Figure 4 follows directly from the two components of (A17).

REFERENCES

Aoki, K. (2001), "Optimal Monetary Policy Responses to Relative-Price Changes," *Journal of Monetary Economics* 48:55–80.

Ball, L. (2000), "Near Rationality and Inflation in Two Monetary Regimes," NBER Working Paper No. 7988.

Ball, L. and R. Moffitt (2001), "Productivity Growth and the Phillips Curve," mimeo, Johns Hopkins University, June.

Ball, L. and D. Romer (1990), "Real Rigidity and the Nonneutrality of Money," *Review of Economic Studies* 57:539–52.

Basu, S., J. G. Fernald, and M. S. Kimball (1998), "Are Productivity Improvements Contractionary?," mimeo, University of Michigan.

Blanchflower, D. G. and A. J. Oswald (1995), "An Introduction to the Wage Curve," *Journal of Economic Perspectives* 9(3):153–67.

Calvo, G. A. (1983), "Staggered Prices in a Utility Maximizing Framework," *Journal of Monetary Economics* 12:383–98.

Clarida, R., M. Gertler, and J. Gali (1999), "The Science of Monetary Policy: A New Keynesian Perspective," *Journal of Economic Literature* 37(4):1661–1707.

Fischer, S. (1977), "Long-term Contracts, Rational Expectations, and the Optimal Money Supply Rule," *Journal of Political Economy* 85:191–205.

Friedman, B. M. (1979), "Optimal Expectations and the Extreme Assumptions of Rational Expectations Macromodels," *Journal of Monetary Economics* 5(1):23–41.

Friedman, M. (1968). "The Role of Monetary Policy," *American Economic Review* 58:1–17.

Gabaix, X. and D. Laibson (2001), "The 6D Bias and the Equity Premium Puzzle," mimeo, MIT and Harvard University.

Goodfriend, M. and R. G. King (1997), "The New Neoclassical Synthesis and the Role of Monetary Policy," *NBER Macroeconomics Annual*, pp. 231–83.

Grubb, D., R. Jackman, and R. Layard (1982), "Causes of the Current Stagflation," *Review of Economic Studies* 49:707–30.

Hall, R. E. and N. G. Mankiw (1994), "Nominal Income Targeting," in N. G. Mankiw, ed., *Monetary Policy*, Chicago: University of Chicago Press.

Lucas, R. E., Jr. (1972), "Econometric Testing of the Natural Rate Hypothesis," in O. Eckstein, ed., *The Econometrics of Price Determination*, Washington D.C.: Board of Governors of the Federal Reserve System.

Mankiw, N. G. (2001), "The Inexorable and Mysterious Tradeoff Between Inflation and Unemployment," *Economic Journal* 111(471):C45–61.

Mankiw, N. G. and R. Reis (2001), "Sticky Information versus Sticky Prices: A Proposal to Replace the New Keynesian Phillips Curve," NBER Working Paper No. 8290 (forthcoming in the *Quarterly Journal of Economics*).

McCallum, B. (1997), "Comment," *NBER Macroeconomics Annual*, pp. 355–59.

Phelps, E. S. (1967), "Phillips Curves, Expectations of Inflation, and Optimal Unemployment over Time," *Economica* 2(3):22–44.

——— (1968), "Money-Wage Dynamics and Labor Market Equilibrium," *Journal of Political Economy* 76(2):678–711.

——— (1978), "Disinflation without Recession: Adaptive Guideposts and Monetary Policy," *Weltwirtschaftsliches Archiv* 114(4):783–809.

——— (1994), *Structural Slumps: The Modern Equilibrium Theory of Unemployment, Interest, and Assets*, Cambridge: Harvard University Press.

Phelps, E. S. and J. B. Taylor (1977), "Stabilizing Powers of Monetary Policy Under Rational Expectations," *The Journal of Political Economy* 85:163–90.

Rotemberg, J. (1982), "Monopolistic Price Adjustment and Aggregate Output," *Review of Economic Studies* 44:517–31.

Sargent, T. J. (1971), "A Note on the Accelerationist Controversy," *Journal of Money, Credit, and Banking* 8(3):721–25.

——— (1999), *The Conquest of American Inflation*, Princeton: Princeton University Press.

Sims, C. (2001), "Implications of Rational Inattention," mimeo, Princeton University.

Staiger, D., J. H. Stock, and M. W. Watson (2001), "Prices, Wages, and the U.S. NAIRU in the 1990s," NBER Working Paper No. 8320.

Summers, L. H. (1986), "Estimating the Long-Run Relationship Between Interest Rates and Inflation: A Response," *Journal of Monetary Economics* 18(1):77–86.

Taylor, J. B. (1980). "Aggregate Dynamics and Staggered Contracts," *Journal of Political Economy* 88:1–22.

Tobin, J. (1980), "Stabilization Policy Ten Years After," *Brookings Papers on Economic Activity* 1:19–72.

— 4 —

A Theory of Rational Inflationary Inertia

GUILLERMO A. CALVO, OYA CELASUN, AND MICHAEL KUMHOF

> If there is such a thing as an economy with a rock-solid inflation rate of 40 per cent,
> plus or minus 2 per cent, per year, institutions would surely adapt, so that prices would
> be announced in catalogs and wage contracts with smooth growth paths paralleling
> the smooth aggregate price path. Nominal rigidity would set in about this price path
> in much the same form as we see around the zero inflation rate in low-inflation
> economies. (Sims, 1988, p. 77)

1. INTRODUCTION

Monetary theory today is dominated by fully microfounded dynamic general
equilibrium models incorporating, in one form or another, the assumption of sticky
prices. A comprehensive survey of this literature is contained in Clarida et al. (1999)
for closed economies and Lane (2001) for open economies. The renewed popularity
of sticky-price monetary economics was motivated by empirical findings that
demonstrated, at least for the U.S. case, that monetary policy has significant real
effects, contrary to the premise of the real business cycle literature. Examples
of that empirical literature include Christiano et al. (1996, 1998) and Leeper et
al. (1996). As surveyed in Taylor (1998), the assumption of sticky prices does a
good job in explaining most, but not all, features of those data. That paper also
documents the micro- and macroeconomic evidence supporting the sticky-price
assumption itself.

The 1990s resurgence of this model class would have been hard to predict from
a 1970s vantage point. At that time, in the wake of the rational expectations revolution, the sticky-price assumption was closely associated with old-style Keynesian
models featuring adaptive expectations, and many economists discarded these
two concepts together. But at that same time a group of researchers started to
build the theoretical foundations for the incorporation of sticky prices into rational
expectations models, and it is to their work that the new generation of models

The authors thank the discussant, Mark Gertler, for helpful comments. They also thank Richard Clarida, Timothy Kehoe, Lars Svensson, John Taylor, and seminar participants at Chicago GSB, Wisconsin, Stanford, the 2001 NBER Summer Institute, the 2001 Latin American Meetings of the Econometric Society, and the 2001 Winter Camp in International Finance in Santiago, Chile.

owes much of its success and respectability. One of the pioneers of this literature was Edmund Phelps, who a decade earlier had made another key contribution to modern monetary theory in the form of the Phelps-Friedman natural rate hypothesis (Phelps, 1967). The first paper to introduce predetermined (one-period ahead) product prices in the context of a rational expectations model was Phelps and Taylor (1977); and Phelps (1978) extended this work to multiperiod staggered contracts, which have become so useful in current work to generate rich and empirically plausible dynamics.

The point of departure for the present chapter is that, despite its undoubted successes, this research strategy has nevertheless left some important puzzles unsolved. Probably the most prominent among them is the failure to generate *endogenous* inflation persistence, an important feature of the data. The models of forward-looking nominal contracts surveyed in Clarida et al. (1999) are only able to generate inflation persistence with the help of serially correlated exogenous shocks, for example, money supply shocks. As pointed out by Taylor (1998), this is not completely satisfactory as the response of inflation to serially uncorrelated money shocks is very persistent. To circumvent these difficulties the literature has thus also relied on less than fully forward-looking pricing behavior, as in Clarida et al. (1999), or on contracting specifications that are not derived from explicit microfoundations, as in Fuhrer and Moore (1995).

Inertia of the inflation rate has been found in a large body of empirical work. For the case of the United States, there is an ongoing debate on the extent to which inflation inertia is attributable to backward-looking pricing behavior. The forward-looking sticky-price model only admits forward-looking inflation terms in estimating equations for inflation dynamics. Fuhrer and Moore (1995) and Fuhrer (1997) document the difficulties of that model in matching the degree of inflation persistence found in the data. Gali and Gertler (1999) and Gali et al. (2001), however, using a different model specification that emphasizes the importance of marginal costs in pricing, estimate that forward-looking terms are significantly more important in inflation dynamics than backward-looking terms. For the case of two high-inflation economies, Mexico and Turkey, Celasun (2000a,b) finds that inflation in the tradables sector exhibits a degree of stickiness similar to the results of Gali and Gertler (1999) for the United States, whereas inflation in the nontradables sector displays a high degree of inertia captured by significant lagged terms in a structural equation for inflation dynamics.

In our view, a very important source of difficulties with the current generation of sticky-price models can be seen much more clearly once one starts to think about price setting in environments with significantly above-zero steady-state inflation, such as many emerging markets. Sticky-price models stipulate that firms/workers cannot continuously adjust their prices/wages, either because of an exogenous arrival process for price-changing opportunities as in Calvo (1983), because of staggered and overlapping contracts of fixed length as in Taylor (1979), or because of exogenous costs of adjusting prices as in Rotemberg (1982).[1] Importantly however,

---

1. The Calvo (1983) specification is used in much of current research owing to its analytical tractability. For examples see Yun (1996), King and Wolman (1996), and Woodford (1996).

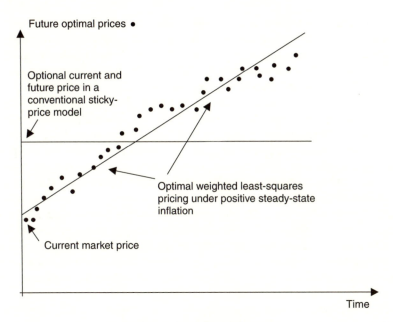

Figure 1. Pricing policies.

at the times when price-setters do reset their prices they choose only a price level. While this may be a sensible assumption in an environment of near-zero steady-state inflation, it is far more questionable under two-digit steady-state inflation rates.

Figure 1 illustrates our argument. If we think of firms as wanting to remain as close as possible to their flexible price optimum at all times but being prevented from doing so by price rigidities, most current models amount to stipulating that firms have to choose their schedule of (logarithms of) future actual prices by fitting a zero-slope regression line through (logarithms of) future optimal prices. The latter, however, rise continuously. The great drawback of this approach is that an increase in steady-state inflation must then give rise to a greater dispersion of relative prices and consequently to lower steady-state output. With significantly nonzero steady-state inflation this real effect is of nontrivial magnitude. Many would consider this type of long-run monetary nonneutrality to be an undesirable feature of the model. In our view, firms in such environments can more usefully be thought of as continuously adjusting their prices according to some pricing rule that is only updated at infrequent intervals, again because of adjustment costs or a Calvo or Taylor staggering rule.[2] In our model we therefore give firms one more choice variable by letting them choose both today's price level and the rate at which they will update prices in the future—a "firm-specific inflation rate." In terms of the regression analogy, it amounts to fitting a weighted least-squares regression line through future optimal prices. In an environment of nonzero steady-state inflation this assumption is much less restrictive than the standard one.

---

2. Taylor (1983) contains evidence for this type of behavior in the U.S. labor market in the 1970s.

An alternative formulation that has been proposed in the literature, starting with Yun (1996), is that price-setting firms choose their current price level and update prices at the *steady-state* inflation rate thereafter, typically in an environment where the steady state itself does not change. This approach, which in steady state is of course identical to ours, avoids the long-run monetary nonneutrality mentioned earlier and as such is certainly very useful. But it may be problematic when thinking about transitions between different steady states, because it amounts to assuming that when the steady state itself changes, all firms, including those that are unable to change their current price level, nevertheless immediately change their updating rule. This means that, unlike in our analysis, changes in monetary policy rules themselves never lead to deviations from steady state. That may still be an appropriate description of firm behavior when the change in the steady-state inflation rate is very large, so that taking the news of this change into account would be a very high priority for price-setters. But when the change in steady-state inflation is moderate our assumption appears more plausible. Future research to endogenize this element of state dependency would evidently be highly desirable. In the meantime, we view our approach and the Yun (1996) approach as complementary.

When firms behave in the fashion we propose and the monetary policy rule changes, the economy contains a large number of firms that have formulated their pricing policies under the previous policy. This gives rise to inflationary inertia, which means that in response to the unexpected announcement of a permanently and credibly lower growth rate of the nominal anchor, the economy cannot immediately move to its new steady state—this can only happen once all firms have changed their pricing policies. The disinflation period is also associated with significant output losses. This is in marked contrast to sticky-price models, for which Ball (1994a) and, in the context of an exchange-rate-based stabilization in a small open economy, Calvo and Vegh (1993) have shown that a permanent and credible reduction in the growth rate of the nominal anchor reduces inflation at a stroke and without output effects. That prediction is not in line with experience even in countries where the monetary authority enjoys a high degree of credibility, as shown by Ball (1994b). Lack of credibility, as in Ball (1995) or Calvo and Vegh (1993), would give rise to inflation persistence, but it is not clear that credibility was always an issue in the episodes where inflation persistence was observed.

The motivation for our theoretical approach was seen most clearly by considering environments with well above zero steady-state inflation. The experiences of many emerging markets are among the best examples of such environments. We therefore choose as the first application of our pricing formulation a model of exchange rate targeting in small open emerging economies. Inflation inertia has in fact been one of the major issues in the application of that policy (Calvo and Vegh, 1999).[3]

In this chapter firms' pricing behavior is modeled as a rule of thumb similar to Calvo (1983). We refer the reader to Calvo et al. (2001) for a fully rigorous

---

3. The question of whether the mechanism we propose is also a good explanation for U.S. inflationary inertia is left for future research, but we certainly consider it a promising candidate. Our theory of price setting is very general and can be embedded in any monetary policy environment.

treatment, including maximizing monopolistically competitive firms. That model is far more complex than the present one and has the important advantage of permitting explicit welfare analysis.[4] But the simpler model in this chapter has qualitatively identical implications for inflation inertia and output losses under disinflations, while being amenable to more elegant analytical characterizations of solutions. It also gives rise to an empirical specification involving excess demand for which data[5] are far easier to obtain than for the more general formulation, which requires real marginal labor cost data.

The rest of the chapter is organized as follows. Section 2 presents the model. Section 3 characterizes the model solution analytically, and Section 4 computes solution paths for a calibrated model economy. Section 5 contains supportive empirical evidence for the case of Mexico. Section 6 concludes the chapter.

2. THE MODEL

Consider a small open economy inhabited by a large number of identical, infinitely lived individuals. The economy trades goods with the rest of the world, and for the prices of these tradables purchasing power parity is assumed to hold. If we normalize the foreign price level to one, this implies that the nominal price of tradables equals the nominal exchange rate E_t. The nominal price level of nontradables is denoted as P_t and the associated inflation rate as $\pi_t = \dot{P}_t/P_t$. The relative price of tradables and nontradables, which will be referred to as the real exchange rate, is $e_t = E_t/P_t$. The economy can also freely borrow from or lend to the rest of the world, and uncovered interest parity is assumed to hold:

$$i_t = r + \varepsilon_t, \tag{1}$$

where r is the exogenous, constant, and positive real international interest rate, $\varepsilon_t = \dot{E}_t/E_t$ is the rate of exchange rate depreciation, and i_t is the nominal interest rate on domestic currency denominated assets. For all nominal price variables, upper-case letters denote price levels and lower-case letters stand for rates of change of prices. The numeraire is tradable goods.

2.1. Households

Households maximize lifetime utility, which depends on their consumption of tradable goods c_t^* and nontradable goods c_t. For simplicity we assume a logarithmically separable form of the utility function for the representative household:

---

4. We compare, in a model with endogenous labor supply, the long-run efficiency gains from a lower steady-state inflation rate to the short-run losses owing to the temporary recession. The efficiency gains arise from the reduction in the monetary distortion to the consumption-leisure choice and are therefore decreasing in the velocity of money. We find that, for the value of velocity calibrated in this chapter and for all lower values, the efficiency gains exceed short-term losses for all interesting values of the remaining parameters.

5. Especially for emerging markets.

$$\max \int_0^\infty \left[\gamma \, \ln(c_t^*) + (1 - \gamma) \, \ln(c_t) \right] e^{-\rho t} \, dt. \tag{2}$$

Households are subject to a cash-in-advance constraint for their purchases of tradables and nontradables:

$$m_t \geq \alpha \left(c_t^* + c_t / e_t \right), \tag{3}$$

where $m_t (M_t)$ are real (nominal) money balances, with $m_t = M_t / E_t$, and α is constant inverse velocity. The opportunity cost of holding one unit of money is equal to the nominal interest rate, which, given our assumption of predetermined positive exchange rate depreciation (see below) and uncovered interest parity, must be greater than zero. The cash-in-advance constraint will therefore be binding at all times. Apart from money, households also hold international bonds denominated in units of tradable goods b_t, with real interest rate r. Households receive a fixed endowment of tradables y^*, an endowment of nontradables y_t, and government lump-sum transfers τ_t. Their period budget constraint is

$$\dot{b}_t = r b_t - \dot{m}_t - \varepsilon_t m_t + y^* + y_t / e_t + \tau_t - c_t^* - c_t / e_t.$$

After imposing the standard no-Ponzi games condition $\lim_{t \to \infty} (b_t + m_t) e^{-rt} \geq 0$, we can write their lifetime budget constraint as

$$b_0 + m_0 + \int_0^\infty \left(y^* + y_t / e_t + \tau_t \right) e^{-rt} dt \geq \int_0^\infty \left(c_t^* + c_t / e_t + i_t m_t \right) e^{-rt} dt. \tag{4}$$

The household maximizes (2) subject to (3) and (4), with (3) binding. The first-order conditions are (4) holding with equality and

$$\gamma / c_t^* = \lambda (1 + \alpha i_t), \tag{5}$$

$$c_t / c_t^* = e_t (1 - \gamma) / \gamma. \tag{6}$$

2.2. Technology and Pricing

Only nontradables-producing firms are assumed to be subject to nominal rigidities whereas purchasing power parity is assumed to hold for tradables. The implication is that all movements in the CPI-based real exchange rate are driven by movements in the relative price of tradables and nontradables e_t. This is directly contrary to the evidence for the United States presented by Engel (1999), who finds that almost all movements in that broad measure of the real exchange rate are accounted for by changes in the relative price of tradables. However, there is substantial empirical evidence showing that in emerging markets the relative price of tradables and nontradables exhibits very large fluctuations (see, e.g., Celasun, 2000a,b, or Mendoza, 2000).

Firms are distributed uniformly along the unit interval. They receive a random price-changing signal that follows an exponential distribution for each individual firm and is therefore independent across time. It is also independent across firms, which allows the application of a law of large numbers, so that there is no aggregate uncertainty. Whenever firms do receive the signal they determine the optimal price schedule, consisting of today's price level V_t and a "firm-specific inflation rate" v_t, to minimize squared deviations from future optimal prices V_s^*. Squared deviations are weighted by the probability that the pricing policy chosen today is still in effect at any future time, that is, by the probability that by such a time another price-changing signal has not been received. This therefore corresponds to a weighted least-squares procedure. In the following derivations we make use of two properties of exponential distributions:

$$\delta \int_t^\infty (s - t)e^{-\delta(s-t)}ds = 1/\delta$$

and

$$\delta \int_t^\infty (s - t)^2 e^{-\delta(s-t)}ds = 2/\delta^2.$$

Firms' price-setting problem is

$$\min_{V_t, v_t} \frac{1}{2}\delta \int_t^\infty \left[V_t + (s - t)v_t - V_s^*\right]^2 e^{-\delta(s-t)}ds. \tag{7}$$

As in Calvo (1983), the optimal price levels at future times s are $V_s^* = P_s + \beta\xi_s$, where P_s is the market price level and ξ_s is a measure of excess demand measured in percentage terms, $\xi_s = [\ln(c_s) - \ln(\bar{y})]$. Here $\bar{y}$ is full-capacity nontradables output. Then, using (6), we have

$$\xi_t = \ln(c_t) - \ln(\bar{y}) = \ln(c_t^*) + \ln(e_t) - \ln(\bar{y}) + \ln[(1 - \gamma)/\gamma]. \tag{8}$$

Note that the real exchange rate is predetermined under predetermined nominal exchange rates and sticky prices. Also, any jumps in $\ln(c_t^*)$ depend only on equation (5) and lifetime resources. This chapter considers only exchange rate policies characterized by piecewise constant depreciation rates ε_t, which by (5) implies $\dot{c}_t^* = 0$ and possibly discrete jumps in tradables consumption. Any jumps in nontradables consumption will therefore be one-for-one with these jumps in tradables consumption, which are exogenous to the nontradables sector. This means that excess demand ξ_t is a predetermined variable. (See Calvo and Vegh, 1994, and Ghezzi, 2001, for similar arguments.) The rate of change of excess demand follows from these arguments as

$$\dot{\xi}_t = \dot{e}_t/e_t = \varepsilon_t - \pi_t. \tag{9}$$

The weighted least-squares normal equations for (7) are

$$V_t + v_t/\delta = \delta \int_t^\infty V_s^* e^{-\delta(s-t)}ds, \tag{10}$$

$$V_t/\delta + 2v_t/\delta^2 = \delta \int_t^\infty V_s^*(s-t)e^{-\delta(s-t)}ds. \tag{11}$$

Equation (10) states that V_t and v_t are to be chosen in such a way that today's price V_t plus the increment in price per unit of time v_t multiplied by the mean duration of the price quotation $1/\delta$ equals the weighted mean of future optimal prices V_s^*. Equation (11) is an orthogonality condition between the regressor, time $s-t$, and the residual $(V_s^* - V_t) - v_t(s-t)$. It states that the slope coefficient v_t is to be chosen in such a way that the mean weighted difference between the optimal price V_s^* and the actual price is minimized. The time derivatives of these equations are

$$\dot{V}_t + \dot{v}_t/\delta = \delta(V_t - V_t^*) + v_t, \tag{12}$$

$$\dot{V}_t + 2\dot{v}_t/\delta = v_t. \tag{13}$$

Combining these expressions and substituting for $V_t^* = P_t + \beta\xi_t$, we can derive the law of motion for firm specific inflation rates v_t as

$$\dot{v}_t = -\delta^2(V_t - P_t - \beta\xi_t). \tag{14}$$

It is clear that v_t is a jump variable. When there is a discrete change in the monetary policy regime it will be optimal for firms receiving a price-changing signal to allow discrete changes in both their current price and their firm-specific inflation rate.

The current price level is the log of the geometric weighted average of all current firm price levels. To derive it one has to take account of the fact that all firms continually adjust their prices, but at different rates:

$$P_t = \delta \int_{-\infty}^t [V_s + (t-s)v_s]e^{-\delta(t-s)}ds. \tag{15}$$

Differentiating this expression with respect to time, one obtains

$$\pi_t = \delta(V_t - P_t) + \delta \int_{-\infty}^t v_s e^{-\delta(t-s)}ds. \tag{16}$$

This makes current inflation a function of past firm-specific inflation rates as well as of changes in the price levels set by current price-setters. Only the former is predetermined, so that π_t is a jump variable. Its rate of change can be computed as follows:

$$\dot{\pi}_t = 2\delta[\delta(V_t - P_t - \beta\xi_t) + v_t] - \delta\pi_t - \delta^2 \int_{-\infty}^t v_s e^{-\delta(t-s)}ds. \tag{17}$$

Using (16) we define a new predetermined variable ψ_t as

$$\psi_t = \pi_t - \delta(V_t - P_t) = \delta \int_{-\infty}^{t} \upsilon_s e^{-\delta(t-s)} ds, \tag{18}$$

with time derivative

$$\dot{\psi}_t = \delta(\upsilon_t - \psi_t). \tag{19}$$

Collecting equations (9), (14), (17), and (19) above, simplifying, and denoting the steady-state rate of exchange rate depreciation by ε_{ss}, one obtains the following system of four differential equations:

$$
\begin{bmatrix} \dot{\psi}_t \\ \dot{\upsilon}_t \\ \dot{\pi}_t \\ \dot{\xi}_t \end{bmatrix} = \begin{bmatrix} -\delta & \delta & 0 & 0 \\ \delta & 0 & -\delta & \beta\delta^2 \\ -3\delta & 2\delta & \delta & -2\beta\delta^2 \\ 0 & 0 & -1 & 0 \end{bmatrix} \begin{bmatrix} \psi_t - \varepsilon_{ss} \\ \upsilon_t - \varepsilon_{ss} \\ \pi_t - \varepsilon_{ss} \\ \xi_t \end{bmatrix} + \begin{bmatrix} 0 \\ 0 \\ 0 \\ \varepsilon_{ss} \end{bmatrix}. \tag{20}
$$

By the above arguments, of these four variables ψ and ξ are predetermined whereas π and υ can jump. The qualitative dynamic behavior of this system will be analyzed in detail in the next section, but before doing so the model is closed with the description of the government and aggregate constraints. This is essential in order to derive the jumps in tradables consumption, which enter the above dynamic system through equation (8).

2.3. Government

The government owns a stock of net foreign assets h_t, issues money M_t, and makes lump-sum transfers τ_t. Its period budget constraint is

$$\dot{h}_t = rh_t + \dot{m}_t + \varepsilon_t m_t - \tau_t.$$

By imposing the transversality condition $\lim_{t \to \infty} (h_t - m_t) e^{-rt} = 0$, one obtains the government's lifetime constraint,

$$h_0 - m_0 + \int_0^{\infty} (i_t m_t - \tau_t) e^{-rt} dt = 0. \tag{21}$$

A *government policy* is defined as a list of time paths $(E_t, \tau_t)_{t=0}^{\infty}$ such that, given the time path $(m_t)_{t=0}^{\infty}$, the constraint (21) holds. In particular, lump-sum redistributions will be assumed to be Ricardian, whereas exchange rate policy is assumed to take one of the following forms:

Permanent Stabilization. The government reduces inflation by a surprise announcement at time 0 of a permanently lower rate of exchange rate depreciation $\varepsilon^l < \varepsilon^h$.

$$\varepsilon_t = \varepsilon^h, \ t \in (-\infty, 0),$$

$$\varepsilon_t = \varepsilon^l, \ t \in [0, \infty). \tag{22}$$

Temporary Stabilization. Under this policy the government also announces a lower rate of exchange rate depreciation, but this is correctly anticipated by the public to be of only limited duration:

$$\varepsilon_t = \varepsilon^h, \ t \in (-\infty, 0),$$

$$\varepsilon_t = \varepsilon^l, \ t \in [0, T), \tag{23}$$

$$\varepsilon_t = \varepsilon^h, \ t \in [T, \infty).$$

2.4. Equilibrium

Let the market clearing level of nontradables output be denoted by $\tilde{y}_t$. An *allocation* is a list of time paths $\left(b_t, h_t, m_t, c_t^*, c_t, y_t^*, y_t, \tilde{y}_t\right)_{t=0}^{\infty}$, and a *price system* is a list of time paths $(P_t, i_t)_{t=0}^{\infty}$. Finally let $f_t = b_t + h_t$, the economy's overall level of net foreign assets. Then equilibrium is defined as follows: *A perfect foresight equilibrium given f_0 is an allocation, a price system, and a government policy such that (a) given the government policy and the price system, the allocation solves the household's problem of maximizing (2) subject to (3) and (4), with (3) binding; (b) given the government policy, the allocation, and the price system satisfy (20); (c) the nontradable goods market clears with output being demand determined, $\tilde{y}_t = c_t \ \forall t$; and (d) perfect foresight with respect to nontradables endowments, $y_t = \tilde{y}_t \ \forall t$.*

Equations (4) and (21) and the definition of equilibrium imply that the following aggregate budget constraint must hold:

$$f_0 + y^*/r = \int_0^{\infty} c_t^* e^{-rt} dt. \tag{24}$$

Combining this constraint with the first-order condition (5), one can derive the path of tradables consumption. This is of course trivial for the permanent policy, where we have

$$c_t^* = y^* + r f_0 \quad \forall t. \tag{25}$$

The temporary policy tradables consumption depends on lifetime income and the entire future path of nominal interest rates. Let $i^h = r + \varepsilon^h$ and $i^l = r + \varepsilon^l$. Then there is a consumption boom for $t \in [0, T)$ and reduced consumption for $t \in (T, \infty)$ by

$$c_t^* = (y^* + r f_0) \left[(1 + \alpha i_t) \left(\frac{1 - e^{-rT}}{1 + \alpha i^l} + \frac{e^{-rT}}{1 + \alpha i^h} \right) \right]^{-1}. \tag{26}$$

3. DYNAMICS OF THE MODEL — ANALYTICAL RESULTS

Consider again the differential equation system (20). It has steady-state values $\psi_{ss} = \upsilon_{ss} = \pi_{ss} = \varepsilon_{ss}$ and $\xi_{ss} = 0$. Its characteristic polynomial has a particularly simple form:

$$\lambda^4 - 2\beta\delta^2\lambda^2 + \beta\delta^4, \tag{27}$$

which has the following roots:

$$\lambda_{1,2} = \pm\delta\sqrt{\beta + i\,[\beta(1-\beta)]^{1/2}},$$
$$\tag{28}$$
$$\lambda_{3,4} = \pm\delta\sqrt{\beta - i\,[\beta(1-\beta)]^{1/2}},$$

where $i = \sqrt{-1}$. If $\beta > 1$ all roots are real. Also, as the expressions under the outer root are then unambiguously positive, exactly two roots are negative. Given two predetermined variables, this implies saddle path stability. If $\beta = 1$ there are repeated real roots, that is, two each of $\pm\sqrt{(\beta\delta^2)}$; and if $\beta < 1$ all roots are necessarily complex. Solving for these roots explicitly, one obtains the following solutions, where $a = \beta^{1/4}$ and $b = \beta^{1/4}(1 - \beta^{1/2})^{1/2}$:

$$\lambda_{1,2} = \delta\,(-a \pm bi) = \delta\theta_{1,2}(\beta),$$
$$\tag{29}$$
$$\lambda_{3,4} = \delta\,(a \pm bi) = \delta\theta_{3,4}(\beta).$$

Two roots have negative real parts and the system is therefore again saddle path stable. In the real-roots case convergence is monotonic whereas in the complex-roots case there will be overshooting. Apart from existence and uniqueness it is possible to establish further analytical results. The following two subsections do so separately for the real- and the complex-roots cases.

3.1. Real Roots

Let an eigenvector associated with a root λ_i of dynamic system (20) be denoted as $(h_\psi^i, h_\upsilon^i, h_\pi^i, h_\xi^i)$. Calvo (1987) and Ghezzi (2001) make use of the fact that a differential equation system of dimension greater than two with two negative real roots can be characterized in terms of its dominant eigenvector. The stable two-dimensional hyperplane of such a system is generated by the eigenvectors associated with the two negative roots. These eigenvectors can be projected onto the two-dimensional space of state variables, for which the initial and final conditions are known. It is then straightforward to show that convergence to the final steady state will be dominated by the "dominant" eigenvector h^d associated with the negative root of smaller absolute value λ_d, for all paths except the one that starts exactly on the nondominant eigenvector h^{nd} associated with the other root λ_{nd}. The intuition is that the motion contributed by the nondominant vector gets driven to zero more quickly because it is associated with a larger negative root.

Let the remaining root-eigenvector pairs be denoted as (λ_3, h^3) and (λ_4, h^4). The solution of system (20), written as $\dot{x}_t = Ax_t + d\varepsilon_{ss}$, then takes the general form

$$(x_t - x_{ss}) = c_d h^d e^{\lambda_d t} + c_{nd} h^{nd} e^{\lambda_{nd} t} + c_3 h^3 e^{\lambda_3 t} + c_4 h^4 e^{\lambda_4 t},$$

where the c_i are arbitrary constants. Saddle path convergence requires $c_3 = c_4 = 0$. Therefore,

$$\frac{\psi_t - \psi_{ss}}{\xi_t - \xi_{ss}} = \frac{c_d h_\psi^d + c_{nd} h_\psi^{nd} e^{(\lambda_{nd} - \lambda_d)t}}{c_d h_\xi^d + c_{nd} h_\xi^{nd} e^{(\lambda_{nd} - \lambda_d)t}},$$

and, because $(\lambda_{nd} - \lambda_d) < 0$,

$$\lim_{t \to \infty} \frac{\psi_t - \psi_{ss}}{\xi_t - \xi_{ss}} = \frac{h_\psi^d}{h_\xi^d}. \tag{30}$$

Appendix A studies the properties of this ratio, which represents the slope of the dominant eigenvector. It is shown to be always negative, whereas the equivalent ratio for the nondominant eigenvector is always positive. This implies a downward-sloping dominant eigenvector ray in ψ-ξ space.

Figure 2 shows the equilibrium paths of ξ and ψ for a permanent (credible), unanticipated stabilization starting from a steady state at full employment ($\xi_0 = 0$) and high inflation ($\psi_0 = \varepsilon^h$). Since solutions are real, variables will change

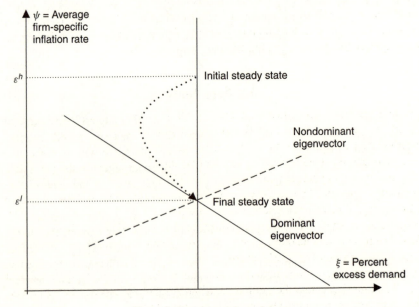

Figure 2. Dynamics under real roots.

direction at most once. Moreover, the equilibrium path will eventually be "absorbed" by the dominant eigenvector ray. Thus, if paths start moving rightward, ξ will first increase and become positive. Since the path cannot hit the nondominant ray if it is to be eventually absorbed by the dominant ray, eventually it would have to cross the full-employment vertical line again and ξ would fall. But since the path eventually mimics the dominant ray it would at some stage have to rise again. Thus, the path would exhibit at least three changes of direction, which is a contradiction. Thus the equilibrium path will have to start going left in Figure 2, as depicted by the arrowed curve.[6] The drop of ξ below zero represents a nontradables recession. By equation (9) the path of ξ provides information about π. As domestic output falls at the beginning of the stabilization, nontradables inflation exceeds exchange rate depreciation. However, when the equilibrium curve turns to the right and domestic output starts to rise again, nontradables inflation undershoots exchange rate depreciation. This is necessary to bring the real exchange rate back to its unchanged equilibrium value. To summarize, in response to an inflation stabilization the model generates slow inflation convergence and a recession.

3.2. Complex Roots

Existing empirical studies of the new Keynesian Phillips curve generally find a very small (<0.1) coefficient for excess demand or real marginal cost. In the original Calvo (1983) model this coefficient equals $\delta^2\beta$. We therefore think that the case of $\beta < 1$, which gives rise to complex roots, is empirically more relevant. The roots in equation (29) show how the nature of convergence depends on the sensitivity of inflation to excess demand β and on the speed of price adjustment δ. A higher δ is associated with faster convergence and with a shorter period of oscillation. As for β, it can be shown that

$$\frac{\partial a}{\partial \beta} > 0,$$

$$\frac{\partial b}{\partial \beta} \begin{array}{c}>\\<\end{array} 0 \text{ for } \beta \begin{array}{c}<\\>\end{array} 0.25. \tag{31}$$

A higher sensitivity to excess demand is therefore also associated with faster convergence. The period of oscillation decreases in β for very low β, but increases for $\beta > 0.25$.

As shown in the left panel of Figure 3, convergence to a new lower-inflation steady state could either be counterclockwise and therefore initially recessionary or clockwise and initially expansionary. We demonstrate that the actual dynamics is counterclockwise by computing the slope of the equilibrium path at its initial point, which is derived in Appendix B, on a very fine grid of 200 million combinations of β and δ, with $\beta \in (0, 1)$ and $\delta \in (0, 2)$ and steps of 10^{-4}. The slope is always positive. Its values as a function of β and for five particular values of δ are

---

6. We cannot rule out an initial rise in ψ.

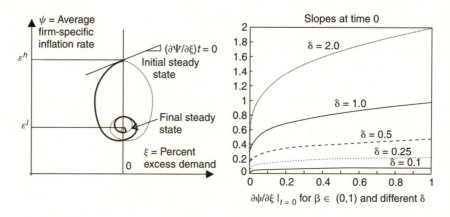

Figure 3. Dynamics under complex roots.

presented in the right panel of Figure 3. This shows that the slope is steeper, that is, less recessionary, for larger β and δ, which is intuitive because larger β and δ are associated by the above argument with faster convergence to the final steady state.

The difference from the real-roots case is that here ψ undershoots the new steady-state inflation rate. At that stage output is increasing. Because the undershooting also implies a stronger undershooting of π there will be stronger real depreciation, and therefore output keeps increasing beyond the full employment level for some time. After that another contractionary phase sets in. Cycles get smaller over time and eventually the steady state is reached. To summarize, in response to an inflation stabilization the model now generates slow inflation convergence with temporary undershooting. This is accompanied by a recession-boom cycle that begins with a recession.

4. DYNAMICS OF THE MODEL —
COMPUTED SOLUTION PATHS

To gain further intuition, particularly for the case of temporary programs, we compute the model's solution paths after calibrating its parameter values with the values shown in Table 1. The time unit for the purpose of calibration of stock-flow ratios is one quarter. The average length of three quarters for price quotations implied by $\delta = 0.75$ is reasonable (see the evidence cited in Obstfeld and Rogoff, 1996, chap. 10). In fact our own subsequent empirical section estimates an even higher δ. It is hard to find direct empirical validation for our choice of β, but combined with our choice of δ it is consistent with typical estimates of the response of inflation to changes in marginal cost (see, e.g., Sbordone, 1998). Consequently all our computations are for the complex-roots case. It should be noted, however, that apart from modest overshooting the behavior of key variables exhibits no major qualitative difference from the real-roots case. The quantitative difference can of course be substantial.

Table 1. Calibrated Parameter Values

Parameter	Value	Description
δ	0.33	Inverse of average contract length in quarters (3)
β	0.5	Sensitivity of inflation to excess demand
ε^h	40% p.a.	Initial exchange-rate depreciation
ε^l	10% p.a.	New, reduced exchange-rate depreciation
T	12/24 quarters	Duration of policy for temporary case
α	0.3	Inverse velocity
γ	0.5	Share of tradables in consumption
r	10% p.a.	Real international interest rate
y^*	1	Tradables endowment
$\bar{y}$	1	Full-employment nontradables output
f_0	0	Initial net foreign assets

The exchange rate target ε^l of 10 percent per annum is very close to many current inflation targets in Latin America. When we compute solution paths for temporary policies we report results for a duration T of 3 and 6 years. Inverse velocity α is set equal to the ratio of the real monetary base to quarterly absorption in Brazil in 1996, a period when that country targeted the nominal exchange rate. A 50 percent share of tradables in consumption γ is empirically reasonable (see De Gregorio et al., 1994). For an emerging economy the real marginal cost of borrowing in international capital markets is given by the real Brady bond yield, which at the time of writing fluctuated between 10 and 15 percent for Brazil and Mexico. After adjusting for U.S. inflation this suggests setting r equal to 10 percent. The tradables endowment y^* is normalized to one, as is full-employment nontradables output. Initial net foreign assets are assumed to be zero. The log-linear specification of the utility index implies an intertemporal elasticity of substitution of one. Empirical estimates of this elasticity are typically below one, as in Reinhart and Vegh (1995). However, see Ogaki and Reinhart (1998) and Eckstein and Leiderman (1992) for examples of estimates closer to one.

4.1. Permanent Policies

Figure 4 shows equilibrium paths for a permanent, that is, perfectly credible, inflation stabilization from 40 to 10 percent per annum. In a conventional sticky-price model this would have no real effects, and inflation would immediately jump to 10 percent. Our results are very different. Inflation π cannot immediately jump to the new lower level as a major component of current inflation is the weighted average of past firm-specific inflation rates ψ, which immediately starts to decline but cannot jump. Combined with the immediately lower exchange rate depreciation this stickiness in nontradables inflation implies that the real exchange rate appreciates very sharply, and this is reflected in a deep nontradables recession, in our particular calibration of around 8 percent. The recession reaches its lowest point at the time nontradables inflation starts to undershoot exchange rate depreciation, thereby starting to depreciate the real exchange rate back to its unchanged equilibrium level. The recession is quite long-lived, lasting for over 2 years.

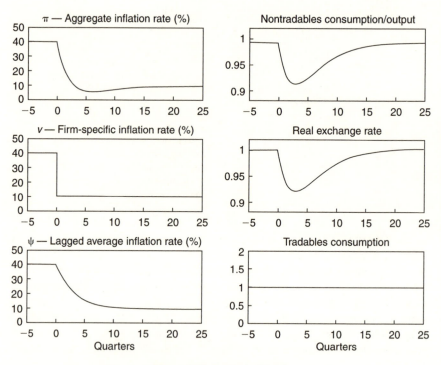

Figure 4. Permanent policies.

4.2. Temporary Policies

As documented by Vegh (1992), emerging market inflation stabilization programs have typically been characterized by early consumption booms as opposed to recessions. One of the most popular explanations, first advanced by Calvo (1986), is lack of credibility modeled as policy temporariness. See Calvo and Vegh (1999) for a survey of this literature. The sticky-price model under policy temporariness has been calibrated by Uribe (1999) in a model with currency substitution and by Kumhof (2000) in a model comparing exchange rate with inflation targeting. Figures 5 and 6 show that, as in those models, we observe a consumption boom in tradables owing to intertemporal substitution, whereas the nontradables sector almost immediately enters a recession owing to real exchange rate appreciation. An important difference is that under sticky inflation the nontradables inflation rate at some stage starts to undershoot exchange rate depreciation and thereby starts to reverse the real appreciation and recession. This recovery phase is nevertheless very short and incomplete when a policy duration of 3 years is assumed, as in Figure 5. The reason is that inflation soon rebounds owing to the anticipation of a reversion to a high-inflation steady state, leading to a renewed real appreciation. When the policy collapses and exchange rate depreciation returns to its high steady state, nontradables inflation takes some time to follow suit. During this time the real exchange rate depreciates, and the recession ends a few quarters later. There

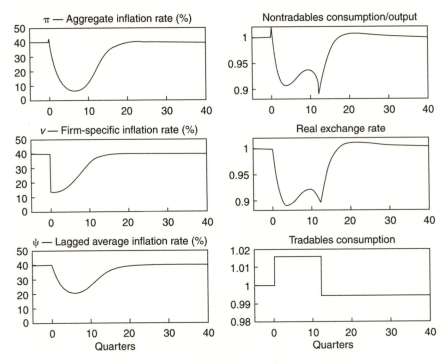

Figure 5. Three-year duration.

is in fact some overshooting of output at that time, which is due to the cyclical nature of the solutions under complex roots.

Figure 6 explores a longer policy duration of 6 years. Here nontradables inflation undershoots for so long that output at some point recovers fully. There is, however, again a late recession when the anticipated reversion to high inflation raises nontradables inflation and appreciates the real exchange rate again.

We should comment briefly on the short initial upward blip in aggregate inflation at time 0 in Figures 5 and 6. This is due to the second, noninertial component of π in equation (16), $\delta(V_t - P_t)$, the initial relative price level chosen by current price-setters. The effect is very small and transient, and is a result of the assumption that we only allow price-setters to perform least squares as opposed to some even better approximation. The intuition is explained in Appendix C.

4.3. General Comments

The model we have proposed exhibits two very commonly observed characteristics of disinflations from moderate inflation levels—inertia of the inflation rate and a significant output sacrifice. However, these characteristics are not observed when initial inflation levels are very high. We have known at least since Sargent (1986) that hyperinflations have been stopped at very low output costs, as suggested by the conventional sticky-price model. Moreover, from Vegh (1992) and others, we know that many of the inflation stabilization episodes in extremely high-inflation

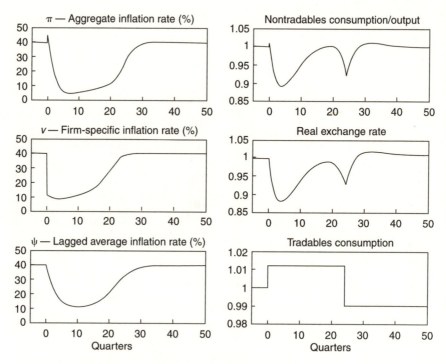

Figure 6. Six-year duration.

emerging markets were characterized by a consumption boom in both tradables and nontradables, not an almost immediate nontradables recession as suggested by our results.

On the other hand, we know from Gordon (1982), Gordon and King (1982), and Ball (1991) that disinflation from moderate levels of initial inflation in industrialized countries has significant output costs. The same may well turn out to be true for those many emerging markets that have now arrived at moderate but still far above zero inflation rates. Our assumption that agents stick to an old price-updating rule in the face of an obviously drastic change such as the end of a hyperinflation or a dramatic stabilization program may in fact not be too appealing. On the other hand, under high but not excessive initial inflation rates and a moderate reduction in targeted inflation, such behavior does seem very plausible. We therefore suggest that the mechanism we propose may be most appropriate to explain moderate disinflations. The final word on this will have to be empirical, but at the very least this chapter has added a new class of models to the tool kit of the monetary economist trying to understand the dynamics of disinflations.

5. EMPIRICAL EVIDENCE

To evaluate whether our pricing specification provides a good description of the data for a typical emerging market, we estimate the implied structural inflation

equation for Mexican nontradables prices. The discrete-time version of our inflation equation (16), derived in Appendix D, is

$$\pi_t = \frac{2(1-\delta)^2}{\delta(2-\delta)}\beta ed_t + \frac{1}{2-\delta}E_t\pi_{t+1} - \frac{1-\delta^2}{2-\delta}v_t \tag{32}$$

$$+ \frac{(2+\delta)(1-\delta)^2}{2-\delta}\sum_{k=1}^{\infty}\delta^{k-1}v_{t-k},$$

where

$$v_t = \frac{(1-\delta)\sum_{k=0}^{\infty}\delta^k[k-\delta/(1-\delta)]E_tV_{t+k}^*}{\delta/(1-\delta)^2}. \tag{33}$$

Here $V_s^* = P_s + \beta ed_s$, P_s is the aggregate price level, ed_s is nontradables excess
demand as a proportion of GDP in period s, and E_t is the expectation operator
with the information set containing all variables known as of the beginning of
period t. The first two right-hand side terms in equation (33) correspond exactly
to the conventional sticky-price new Keynesian Phillips curve. The last two
terms, however, are new, the final one representing the weighted sum of the price
adjustment rates chosen up to time $t - 1$. This term is predetermined and thus
imparts inertia to the inflation process.[7] To obtain a simpler version of this equation
for estimation purposes, we quasi-difference it by deducting $\delta\pi_{t-1}$ from both sides.
The resulting equation is

$$\pi_t = \delta\pi_{t-1} + \frac{2(1-\delta)^2}{\delta(2-\delta)}\beta(ed_t - \delta ed_{t-1}) + \frac{1}{2-\delta}E_t\pi_{t+1} - \frac{\delta}{2-\delta}E_{t-1}\pi_t$$

$$+ \frac{2(1-\delta)^2}{2-\delta}v_{t-1} - \frac{1-\delta^2}{2-\delta}v_t. \tag{34}$$

To deal with the presence of unobservable expectations in equation (34) we
use the "errors-in-variables" approach to estimating rational expectations models
(McCallum, 1976).[8] In this method the expected values are assumed to be equal to
their realized values plus a forecast error that is orthogonal to the set of information
available when the expectation is formed. The terms v_{t-1} and v_t in the equation
are infinite sums of future expected terms from the perspective of periods $t - 1$
and t, respectively. We approximate these sums by their first four terms, assuming
that the weights become insignificant after that. The composite disturbance term
in this estimated equation does not need to be homoscedastic, and as observed

---

7. Note that the weights correspond to the probability that the policies are still in force.

8. Note that the future expected values of the aggregate price level and excess demand enter the
equation through the terms v_{t-1} and v_t.

by Hayashi (1980) it has an MA(4) structure, as four-period ahead expectations enter the equation. To account for the heteroscedasticity and MA(4) structure of the errors, the generalized method of moments of Hansen (1982) is used, allowing for heteroscedastic and MA(4) disturbances.

An important data issue is that excess demand for nontradables, ed_t, is not observed at the quarterly frequency. We make use of the relationship among tradables, nontradables, and the real exchange rate given by the first-order condition (6) to deal with this problem. Linearizing this relationship implies that the demand for nontradables as a proportion of GDP is proportional to the real exchange rate and the demand for tradables as a proportion of GDP[9]:

$$c_t \simeq \alpha_0 + \alpha_1 e_t + \alpha_2 c_t^*.$$

Based on this relationship, we assume that the excess demand for nontradables as a proportion of GDP ed_t is proportional to the deviations of the real exchange rate from trend, $\tilde{e}_t$, and the excess demand for tradables as a proportion of GDP, ed_t^*. Our measure of the latter is the share of the current account in GDP. Then V_t^*, the single-period optimal price, becomes

$$V_t^* = \beta_0 + P_t + \beta_1 \tilde{e}_t + \beta_2 ed_t^*. \tag{35}$$

We use this specification in equation (33). This method does not enable us to identify β, but it does allow us to use a reasonable proxy for the determinants of nontradables pricing, which are otherwise unobserved.

Our sample covers the period 1989:1–1999:1.[10] Given that we have expectational terms dated $t - 1$ as well as t, we use the information set as of period $t - 1$ as the instrument set to ensure consistency. The orthogonality condition that forms the basis of the estimate is

$$E_t \left[\pi_t - \delta \pi_{t-1} - \frac{2(1-\delta)^2}{\delta(2-\delta)} \beta(ed_t - \delta ed_{t-1}) - \frac{1}{2-\delta} E_t \pi_{t+1} + \frac{\delta}{2-\delta} E_{t-1} \pi_t \right.$$
$$\left. - \frac{2(1-\delta)^2}{2-\delta} v_{t-1} + \frac{1-\delta^2}{2-\delta} v_t \middle| I_{t-1} \right] = 0. \tag{36}$$

We assume that I_{t-1} includes the variables dated $t-2$ and earlier. Our instrument set contains the three lags (starting from $t - 2$) of nontradables inflation, the nontradables price level, the deviation of the real exchange rate from trend, the excess demand for tradables, real wages, the nominal deposit interest rate, a constant term

---

9. Note that this linearized relationship holds for any utility function of tradables and nontradables consumption and is not specific to the utility function adopted in Section 2.

10. All our data are from the Bank of Mexico.

Table 2. Estimates of Equation (34), 1988:1–1999:4

	Estimate	Standard error
δ	0.75	0.03
β_1	0.64	0.15
β_2	8.16	5.15
N	42	

and a dummy variable that takes the value one between 1995:1–1995:4 to control for the Tequila crisis. Our estimates are summarized in Table 2.[11]

The parameters δ and β_1 are significant at the 5 percent level, and β_2 at the 1 percent level. The p-value of the test of overidentifying restrictions of Hansen (1982) is 0.979. The contract length implied by $\delta = 0.75$ is four quarters. We find that the parameter estimates are reasonable, and the model fits the data quite well. The composite coefficients on the v_{t-1} and v_t terms are 0.34 (0.03) and 0.10 (0.02) respectively, with standard errors in parentheses. Both are highly significant.

To check the robustness of our specification, we also estimate a modified version that allows for lags of inflation to enter our structural inflation equation (33) and test whether these additional lags enter the equation in a significant manner. This provides a simple test of whether inflation stickiness can be explained by purely forward behavior as we propose or whether lags of inflation introduced by backward-looking pricing behavior are also significant in contributing to inflation stickiness. While this is not a nested model as in Gali and Gertler (1999), which permits backward- and forward-looking firms to coexist, it allows us to test our forward-looking model, under which the lags should not enter the equation significantly. The modified inflation equation is

$$\pi_t = \sum_{i=1}^{n} \varphi_i \pi_{t-i} + \frac{2(1-\delta)^2}{\delta(2-\delta)} \beta \mathrm{ed}_t + \frac{1}{2-\delta} E_t \pi_{t+1} \tag{37}$$

$$- \frac{1-\delta^2}{2-\delta} v_t + \frac{(2+\delta)(1-\delta)^2}{2-\delta} \sum_{k=1}^{\infty} \delta^{k-1} v_{t-k}.$$

The resulting estimating equation becomes

$$\pi_t = \delta \pi_{t-1} + \sum_{i=1}^{n} \varphi_i \pi_{t-i} - \delta \sum_{i=1}^{n} \varphi_i \pi_{t-1-i} + \frac{2(1-\delta)^2}{\delta(2-\delta)} \beta (\mathrm{ed}_t - \delta \mathrm{ed}_{t-1}) \tag{38}$$

$$+ \frac{1}{2-\delta} E_t \pi_{t+1} - \frac{\delta}{2-\delta} E_{t-1} \pi_t + \frac{2(1-\delta)^2}{2-\delta} v_{t-1} - \frac{1-\delta^2}{2-\delta} v_t.$$

---

11. Since our equation is highly nonlinear in δ, our estimates are sensitive to the initial values chosen for that parameter. Therefore we performed a grid search over the admissible range for δ, which is the interval $(0,1)$.

Table 3. Estimates of Equation (38), $n = 1, 2, 3$, 1988:1–1999:4

		Estimate	Standard error
$n = 1$	δ	0.94	0.14
	β_1	4.22	31.2
	β_2	91.52	443.28
	φ_1	0.24	0.18
$n = 2$	δ	0.87	0.16
	β_1	0.57	5.45
	β_2	37.16	74.82
	φ_1	0.61	0.42
	φ_2	0.13	0.19
	$\varphi_1 + \varphi_2$	0.74	0.59
$n = 3$	δ	0.89	0.04
	β_1	0.22	3.41
	β_2	22.22	27.32
	φ_1	0.16	0.13
	φ_2	-0.19	0.15
	φ_3	-0.13	0.07
	$\varphi_1 + \varphi_2 + \varphi_3$	-0.17	0.27

We estimate equation (38) for $n = 1, 2, 3$, and test for the significance of φ_i and $\sum_{i=1}^{n} \varphi_i$ for each case. The results are presented in Table 3 and show that the additional lags do not enter the equations with significantly positive coefficients. Thus, for the Mexican nontradables sector, the pricing specification we propose in the present chapter looks sufficient to capture inflation inertia.

6. CONCLUSION

This chapter has proposed a theory of rational staggered price setting that is able to generate two important empirical features of moderate disinflations—endogenous inflation persistence and output losses in response to disinflations. This represents an important improvement upon the sticky-price models currently used in monetary economics. An attractive feature of this approach is that it addresses this problem while nevertheless remaining firmly within that modeling tradition. It is therefore ideally suited to advance an already large research agenda—an agenda that, like several others in modern macroeconomics, received a crucial early impulse from the pioneering work of Ned Phelps.

APPENDIX A. REAL ROOTS: SLOPE OF THE DOMINANT EIGENVECTOR

System (20) gives rise to the following four conditions on the eigenvector $h^i = (h^i_\psi, h^i_\upsilon, h^i_\pi, h^i_\xi)'$ associated with the root λ_i:

$$-\delta h^i_\psi + \delta h^i_\upsilon = \lambda_i h^i_\psi, \tag{A1a}$$

$$\delta h^i_\psi - \delta h^i_\pi + \beta\delta^2 h^i_\xi = \lambda_i h^i_\upsilon, \tag{A1b}$$

$$-3\delta h^i_\psi + 2\delta h^i_\upsilon + \delta h^i_\pi - 2\beta\delta^2 h^i_\xi = \lambda_i h^i_\pi, \tag{A1c}$$

$$-h^i_\pi = \lambda_i h^i_\xi. \tag{A1d}$$

We normalize eigenvectors by setting $h_\xi = 1$. Equations (A1a, b, and d) and (29) then imply that

$$h^i_\psi = \delta^2 \frac{\lambda_i + \beta\delta}{-\delta^2 + \lambda_i\delta + \lambda_i^2} = \delta\frac{\beta + \theta_i(\beta)}{[\theta_i(\beta)]^2 + \theta_i(\beta) - 1} = \delta f_i(\beta). \tag{A2}$$

PROPOSITION: For $\beta = 1$, h^d_ψ and h^{nd}_ψ equal zero. For $\beta > 1$, h^d_ψ is always negative, and h^{nd}_ψ is always positive.

Proof. The first part of the statement is trivial. We consider $\beta > 1$. For the nondominant root we have $\theta_{nd} = -\left[\beta + (\beta^2 - \beta)^{1/2}\right]^{1/2} < -1$, and one can show trivially that $\theta'_{nd}(\beta) < 0$. The condition for the numerator of $f_{nd}(\beta)$ to equal zero is $\beta^2 = 1 + \beta$, which occurs at $\tilde{\beta} = 0.5(1 + \sqrt{5}) \approx 1.618$. For $\beta > \tilde{\beta}$ the numerator is positive, whereas for $\beta < \tilde{\beta}$ it is negative. It can be verified that the denominator equals zero at the same $\tilde{\beta}$. Also, $\partial(\theta^2_{nd} + \theta_{nd} - 1)/\partial\beta = (2\theta + 1)\theta'_{nd}(\beta) > 0$. Therefore, the denominator flips sign at $\tilde{\beta}$ in the same direction as the numerator. At all $\beta \neq \tilde{\beta}$ it is therefore true that $f_{nd}(\beta) > 0$. That the same is true for $\beta = \tilde{\beta}$ can be verified by L'Hôpital's rule. This means that $h^{nd}_\psi > 0$ for all $\beta > 1$. For the dominant root we have $\theta_d = -\left[\beta - (\beta^2 - \beta)^{1/2}\right]^{1/2}$. One can show that $\theta_d(\beta = 1) = -1$ and $\theta'_d(\beta) > 0$, which implies $\theta_d > -1$. This immediately implies that the numerator of $f_d(\beta)$ is always positive. One can further show by contradiction that $\theta_d < -0.5$. This determines the sign of the derivative of the denominator, which is $\partial(\theta^2_d + \theta_d - 1)/\partial\beta = (2\theta + 1)\theta'_d(\beta) < 0$. Because the denominator evaluated at $\beta = 1$ is -1, it is negative for all $\beta > 1$. It must then be true that $f_d(\beta) < 0$, and therefore $h^d_\psi < 0$, for all $\beta > 1$. QED.

Figure 7 shows the values of f_d and f_{nd} for $\beta \in (1, 5)$.

APPENDIX B. COMPLEX ROOTS:
COUNTERCLOCKWISE DYNAMICS

We determine the slope of the equilibrium path at time zero $\partial\psi_t/\partial\xi_t \mid_{t=0} = \dot{\psi}_t/\dot{\xi}_t \mid_{t=0}$. Consider the root $-a\delta + b\delta i$. The stable solution space is spanned by the real and imaginary parts h^{real} and h^{imag} of the eigenvector associated with this root as follows:

$$x_t - x_{ss} = e^{-a\delta t}\left\{[c_1\cos(b\delta t) + c_2\sin(b\delta t)]h^{\text{real}}\right. \tag{B1}$$

$$\left. + [c_2\cos(b\delta t) - c_1\sin(b\delta t)]h^{\text{imag}}\right\},$$

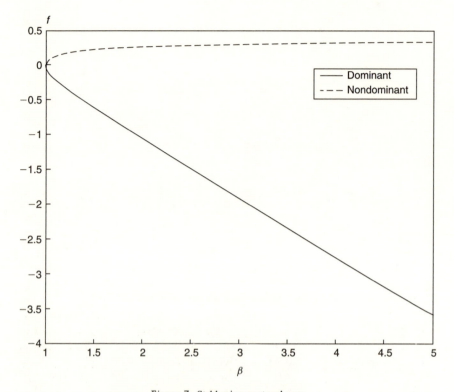

Figure 7. Stable eigenvector slopes.

where c_1 and c_2 are arbitrary constants to be determined by initial conditions,

$$[x_t - x_{ss}] = [(\psi_t - \psi_{ss}), (\upsilon_t - \upsilon_{ss}), (\pi_t - \pi_{ss}), (\xi_t - \xi_{ss})]',$$

$$h^{\text{real}} = [h_\psi^{\text{real}}, h_\upsilon^{\text{real}}, h_\pi^{\text{real}}, h_\xi^{\text{real}}]',$$

and

$$h^{\text{imag}} = [h_\psi^{\text{imag}}, h_\upsilon^{\text{imag}}, h_\pi^{\text{imag}}, h_\xi^{\text{imag}}]'.$$

For ψ and ξ the time derivatives at time zero are

$$\dot{\psi}_0 = -a(\psi_0 - \psi_{ss}) - c_1 b\delta h_\psi^{\text{imag}} + c_2 b\delta h_\psi^{\text{real}}, \tag{B2}$$

$$\dot{\xi}_0 = -c_1 b\delta h_\xi^{\text{imag}} + c_2 b\delta h_\xi^{\text{real}}. \tag{B3}$$

We also have the following initial conditions:

$$\psi_0 - \psi_{ss} = c_1 h_\psi^{\text{real}} + c_2 h_\psi^{\text{imag}}, \tag{B4}$$

$$0 = c_1 h_\xi^{\text{real}} + c_2 h_\xi^{\text{imag}}. \tag{B5}$$

We can only normalize one element of *either* the real *or* the imaginary vector, and choose $h_\xi^{\text{imag}} = 1$. This gives

$$c_2 = -c_1 h_\xi^{\text{real}}, \tag{B6}$$

$$\dot{\xi}_0 = -c_1 b\delta \left[1 + \left(h_\xi^{\text{real}}\right)^2\right]. \tag{B7}$$

Combining (B2), (B4), and (B6), we obtain

$$\dot{\psi}_0 = -c_1 \left[h_\psi^{\text{real}}\left(a\delta + b\delta h_\xi^{\text{real}}\right) + h_\psi^{\text{imag}}\left(b\delta - a\delta h_\xi^{\text{real}}\right)\right]. \tag{B8}$$

The ratio of (B8) and (B7) is therefore

$$\frac{\partial \psi_t}{\partial \xi_t}\Big|_{t=0} = \frac{\dot{\psi}_t}{\dot{\xi}_t}\Big|_{t=0} = \frac{h_\psi^{\text{real}}\left(a + bh_\xi^{\text{real}}\right) + h_\psi^{\text{imag}}\left(b - ah_\xi^{\text{real}}\right)}{b\left[1 + \left(h_\xi^{\text{real}}\right)^2\right]}. \tag{B9}$$

This expression is the basis for the computation results shown in Figure 3.

APPENDIX C. LEAST SQUARES AND THE INITIAL BEHAVIOR OF INFLATION

Figure 8 explains the intuition for the possibility of a small upward jump in inflation after the announcement of a stabilization program. This is due to the fact that current inflation π_t, by equation (16), is a function both of average lagged firm-specific inflation ψ_t, which is predetermined, and of differences between current new prices V_t and the market price level P_t, which can jump. The transition to lower steady-state inflation creates a concave path of future optimal prices during the transition phase. When computing an optimal pricing policy by least squares this will generally require that the intercept V_t lie above the first data point P_t, which gives a small upward push to current inflation.

APPENDIX D. DERIVATION OF ESTIMATING EQUATION (34)

We assume that firms are able to change their pricing policies at discrete intervals, when they receive a random signal. The probability of receiving a price-change signal h periods from now is given by $P(h) = (1 - \delta)\delta^{h-1}$ for $h = 1, 2, \ldots$. The average contract length is given by

$$\sum_{k=1}^{\infty} k(1 - \delta)\delta^{k-1} = \frac{1}{1 - \delta}.$$

Upon receiving a signal in period t, firms choose a pricing policy that applies from period t onward. Specifically, they choose an "intercept" V_t, which is their price level in period t, and a "slope" v_t by which they increment their price every period after t. The intercept and slope parameters chosen by a firm in period t solve the following weighted least-squares problem:

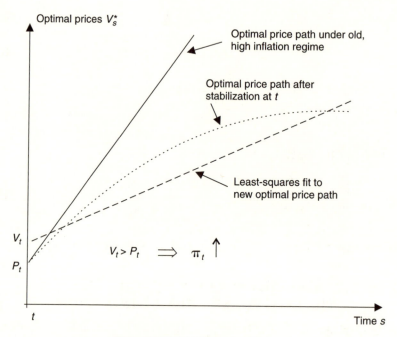

Figure 8. The initial jump in inflation.

$$\min_{V_t, v_t} (1 - \delta) \sum_{k=0}^{\infty} \delta^k \left(E_t V_{t+k}^* - V_t - v_t k \right)^2,$$

where $V_s^* = P_s + \beta \mathrm{ed}_s$, P_s is the aggregate price level, ed_s is the level of excess demand in period s, and E_t is the expectation operator with the information set containing all variables known as of the beginning of period t. The two first-order conditions with respect to V_t and v_t are

$$V_t + \frac{\delta}{1 - \delta} v_t = (1 - \delta) \sum_{k=0}^{\infty} \delta^k E_t V_{t+k}^*, \tag{D1}$$

$$\frac{\delta}{1 - \delta} V_t + \frac{\delta(1 + \delta)}{(1 - \delta)^2} v_t = (1 - \delta) \sum_{k=0}^{\infty} k \delta^k E_t V_{t+k}^*. \tag{D2}$$

Note that the first-order condition with respect to V_t [equation (D1)] specializes to the optimal pricing condition in Calvo (1983) when v_t is constrained to be zero. It implies that today's price V_t plus v_t times the average number of times v_t is expected to be added to the price, $\delta/(1 - \delta)$, equals the weighted mean of future optimal prices. The two first-order conditions can be combined to yield the following expression for v_t:

$$v_t = \frac{(1-\delta)\sum_{k=0}^{\infty}\delta^k[k-\delta/(1-\delta)]E_tV^*_{t+k}}{\delta/(1-\delta)^2}, \tag{D3}$$

which is the weighted least-squares slope coefficient of a regression of all future values of V^* on an intercept and time trend.

The aggregate price level is given by the average of all outstanding firm-specific price levels:

$$P_t = (1-\delta)\sum_{k=0}^{\infty}\delta^k(V_{t-k}+v_{t-k}k)$$

$$= (1-\delta)V_t + \delta(1-\delta)\sum_{k=1}^{\infty}\delta^{k-1}[V_{t-k}+v_{t-k}(k-1)+v_{t-k}]$$

$$= (1-\delta)V_t + \delta P_{t-1} + \delta(1-\delta)\sum_{k=1}^{\infty}\delta^{k-1}v_{t-k}.$$

This expression states that today's price level is determined by two groups of firms. A fraction $1-\delta$ that receive a signal in the current period choose their price to be V_t. The rest, a fraction δ, just increase their prices by the amount that they chose when they last got a signal. Hence, their average price level in period t is $P_{t-1} + (1-\delta)\sum_{k=1}^{\infty}\delta^{k-1}v_{t-k}$.

The inflation rate π_t is given by

$$P_t - P_{t-1} = \pi_t = (1-\delta)(V_t - P_{t-1}) + \delta(1-\delta)\sum_{k=1}^{\infty}\delta^{k-1}v_{t-k}. \tag{D4}$$

Let $\psi_t = \delta(1-\delta)\sum_{k=1}^{\infty}\delta^{k-1}v_{t-k}$. Then using equation (D1), we get

$$\pi_t = (1-\delta)\left[(1-\delta)(P_t+\beta\mathrm{ed}_t)+(1-\delta)\sum_{k=1}^{\infty}\delta^k E_tV^*_{t+k} - \frac{\delta}{1-\delta}v_t - P_{t-1}\right]+\psi_t$$

$$= (1-\delta)\left[\pi_t - \delta P_t + (1-\delta)\beta\mathrm{ed}_t + (1-\delta)\sum_{k=1}^{\infty}\delta^k E_tV^*_{t+k} - \frac{\delta}{1-\delta}v_t\right]+\psi_t,$$

$$\delta\pi_t = (1-\delta)\left[-\delta P_t + (1-\delta)\beta\mathrm{ed}_t + (1-\delta)\sum_{k=1}^{\infty}\delta^k E_tV^*_{t+k} - \frac{\delta}{1-\delta}v_t\right]+\psi_t,$$

$$\delta\pi_t = (1-\delta)^2\beta\mathrm{ed}_t + (1-\delta)\left[-\delta P_t + \delta(1-\delta)\sum_{k=1}^{\infty}\delta^{k-1} E_tV^*_{t+k} - \frac{\delta}{1-\delta}v_t\right]+\psi_t.$$

Note that, by equation (D1),

$$\delta(1-\delta)\sum_{k=1}^{\infty}\delta^{k-1}E_t V_{t+k}^* - \frac{\delta^2}{1-\delta}E_t v_{t+1} = \delta E_t V_{t+1},$$

and therefore

$$\delta\pi_t = (1-\delta)^2\beta \mathrm{ed}_t + (1-\delta)\left[\delta E_t V_{t+1} - \delta P_t + \frac{\delta^2}{1-\delta}E_t v_{t+1} - \frac{\delta}{1-\delta}v_t\right] + \psi_t,$$

$$\delta\pi_t = (1-\delta)^2\beta \mathrm{ed}_t + \delta(1-\delta)(E_t V_{t+1} - P_t) + \delta^2 E_t v_{t+1} - \delta v_t + \psi_t.$$

Also by equation (D4),

$$E_t\pi_{t+1} = (1-\delta)(E_t V_{t+1} - P_t) + \delta(1-\delta)\sum_{k=1}^{\infty}\delta^{k-1}v_{t+1-k}.$$

Then

$$\delta\pi_t = (1-\delta)^2\beta \mathrm{ed}_t + \delta E_t\pi_{t+1} - \delta^2(1-\delta)\sum_{k=1}^{\infty}\delta^{k-1}v_{t+1-k}$$

$$+ \delta^2 E_t v_{t+1} - \delta v_t + \psi_t,$$

$$\pi_t = \frac{(1-\delta)^2}{\delta}\beta \mathrm{ed}_t + E_t\pi_{t+1} - \delta(1-\delta)\sum_{k=1}^{\infty}\delta^{k-1}v_{t+1-k} \qquad (\text{D5})$$

$$+ \delta E_t v_{t+1} - v_t + (1-\delta)\sum_{k=1}^{\infty}\delta^{k-1}v_{t-k},$$

$$= \frac{(1-\delta)^2}{\delta}\beta \mathrm{ed}_t + E_t\pi_{t+1} + \delta(E_t v_{t+1} - v_t) - (1-\delta^2)v_t$$

$$+ (1-\delta)(1-\delta^2)\sum_{k=1}^{\infty}\delta^{k-1}v_{t-k}.$$

By equation (D3),

$$E_t v_{t+1} - v_t = \frac{(1-\delta)^2}{\delta^2}(P_t + \beta \mathrm{ed}_t - V_t). \qquad (\text{D6})$$

Using equations (D4) and (D6), we can write equation (D5) as

$$\pi_t = \frac{(1-\delta)^2}{\delta}\beta \mathrm{ed}_t + E_t\pi_{t+1} + (1+\delta)(1-\delta)^2\sum_{k=1}^{\infty}\delta^{k-1}v_{t-k}$$

$$+ \frac{(1-\delta)^2}{\delta}\left(P_t + \beta \mathrm{ed}_t - \frac{\pi_t}{1-\delta} - P_{t-1} + \delta\sum_{k=1}^{\infty}\delta^{k-1}v_{t-k}\right) - (1-\delta^2)v_t,$$

$$(2 - \delta)\pi_t = \frac{2(1 - \delta)^2}{\delta}\beta e d_t + E_t \pi_{t+1}$$

$$+ (2 + \delta)(1 - \delta)^2 \sum_{k=1}^{\infty} \delta^{k-1} v_{t-k} - (1 - \delta^2) v_t,$$

$$\pi_t = \frac{2(1 - \delta)^2}{\delta(2 - \delta)}\beta e d_t + \frac{1}{2 - \delta} E_t \pi_{t+1}$$

$$+ \frac{(2 + \delta)(1 - \delta)^2}{2 - \delta} \sum_{k=1}^{\infty} \delta^{k-1} v_{t-k} - \frac{1 - \delta^2}{2 - \delta} v_t. \tag{D7}$$

Given that π_{t-1} depends on $v_{t-1}, v_{t-2}, v_{t-3}, \ldots$ we can simplify this equation by quasi-differencing it. We deduct $\delta \pi_{t-1}$ from both sides:

$$\pi_t - \delta \pi_{t-1} = \frac{2(1 - \delta)^2}{\delta(2 - \delta)}\beta (e d_t - \delta e d_{t-1}) + \frac{1}{2 - \delta} E_t \pi_{t+1} \tag{D8}$$

$$- \frac{\delta}{2 - \delta} E_{t-1} \pi_t + \frac{2(1 - \delta)^2}{2 - \delta} v_{t-1} - \frac{(1 - \delta^2)}{2 - \delta} v_t.$$

REFERENCES

Ball, L. (1991), "The Genesis of Inflation and the Costs of Disinflation," *Journal of Money, Credit, and Banking* 23(3):439–52.
——— (1994a), "Credible Disinflation with Staggered Price Setting," *American Economic Review* 84:282–89.
——— (1994b), "What Determines the Sacrifice Ratio?," in N. G. Mankiw, ed., *Monetary Policy,* Chicago: University of Chicago Press.
——— (1995), "Disinflation with Imperfect Credibility," *Journal of Monetary Economics* 35:5–24.
Calvo, G. A. (1983), "Staggered Prices in a Utility-Maximizing Framework," *Journal of Monetary Economics* 12:383–98.
——— (1986), "Temporary Stabilization: Predetermined Exchange Rates," *Journal of Political Economy* 94(6):1319–29.
——— (1987), "Real Exchange Rate Dynamics with Nominal Parities—Structural Change and Overshooting," *Journal of International Economics* 22:141–55.
Calvo, G. A. and C. Vegh (1993), "Exchange Rate Based Stabilization under Imperfect Credibility," in H. Frisch and A. Worgotter, eds., *Open Economy Macroeconomics,* London: Macmillan, pp. 3–28.
——— (1994), "Stabilization Dynamics and Backward-Looking Contracts," *Journal of Development Economics* 43:59–84.
——— (1999), "Inflation Stabilization and BOP Crises in Developing Countries," in J. Taylor and M. Woodford, eds., *Handbook of Macroeconomics,* Amsterdam: North-Holland.
Calvo, G. A., O. Celasun, and M. Kumhof (2001), "Nominal Exchange Rate Anchoring under Inflation Inertia," manuscript, University of Maryland at College Park and Stanford University.
Celasun, O. (2000a), "Real Effects of Exchange Rate Based Stabilization: The Role of Nominal Rigidities," manuscript, University of Maryland at College Park.
——— (2000b), "Are Price Setters Forward Looking? Evidence from Mexico and Turkey," manuscript, University of Maryland at College Park.

Christiano, L. J., M. Eichenbaum, and C. Evans (1996), "The Effects of Monetary Policy Shocks: Evidence from the Flow of Funds," *Review of Economics and Statistics* 78(1): 16–34.

———(1998), "Monetary Policy Shocks: What Have We Learned and to What End?," NBER Working Paper No. 6400.

Clarida, R., J. Gali, and M. Gertler (1999), "The Science of Monetary Policy: A New Keynesian Perspective," *Journal of Economic Literature* 37:1661–1707.

De Gregorio, J., A. Giovannini, and H. C. Wolf (1994), "International Evidence on Tradables and Nontradables Inflation," *European Economic Review* 38:1225–44.

Eckstein, Z. and L. Leiderman (1992), "Seigniorage and the Welfare Cost of Inflation: Evidence from an Intertemporal Model of Money and Consumption," *Journal of Monetary Economics* 29:389–410.

Engel, C. (1999), "Accounting for U.S. Real Exchange Rate Changes," *Journal of Political Economy* 107(3):507–38.

Fuhrer, J. (1997), "The (Un)Importance of Forward Looking Behavior in Price Setting," *Journal of Money, Credit, and Banking* 29:338–50.

Fuhrer, J. and G. Moore (1995), "Inflation Persistence," *Quarterly Journal of Economics* 110:127–59.

Gali, J. and M. Gertler (1999), "Inflation Dynamics: A Structural Econometric Analysis," *Journal of Monetary Economics* 44(2): 195–222.

Gali, J., M. Gertler, and J. D. López-Salido (2001), "Notes on Estimating the Closed Form of the Hybrid New Phillips Curve," manuscript, CREI, NYU, and Bank of Spain.

Ghezzi, P. (2001), "Backward-Looking Indexation, Credibility and Inflation Persistence," *Journal of International Economics* 53(1):127–47.

Gordon, R. J. (1982), "Why Stopping Inflation May Be Costly: Evidence from Fourteen Historical Episodes," in R. E. Hall, ed., *Inflation: Causes and Consequences,* Chicago: University of Chicago Press.

Gordon, R. and S. King (1982), "The Output Costs of Disinflation in Traditional and Vector Autoregressive Models," *Brookings Papers on Economic Activity* 1:205–42.

Hansen, L. P. (1982), "Large Sample Properties of Generalized Method of Moment Estimators," *Econometrica* 50:1029–54.

Hayashi, F. (1980), "Estimation of Macroeconometric Models Under Rational Expectations: A Survey," manuscript, Northwestern University.

King, R. G. and A. L. Wolman (1996), "Inflation Targeting in a St. Louis Model of the 21st Century," *Federal Reserve Bank of St. Louis Review* 78:93–107.

Kumhof, M. (2000), "Inflation Targeting under Limited Fiscal Sustainability," manuscript, Stanford University.

Lane, P. (2001), "The New Open Economy Macroeconomics: A Survey," *Journal of International Economics* 54(2):235–66.

Leeper, E. M., C. Sims, and T. Zha (1996), "What Does Monetary Policy Do?," *Brookings Papers on Economic Activity* 2:1–63.

McCallum, B. (1976), "Rational Expectations and the Natural Rate Hypothesis: Some Consistent Estimates," *Econometrica* 44:43–52.

Mendoza, E. G. (2000), "On the Benefits of Dollarization when Stabilization Policy is not Credible and Financial Markets are Imperfect," manuscript, Duke University.

Obstfeld, M. and K. Rogoff (1996), *Foundations of International Macroeconomics,* Cambridge: MIT Press.

Ogaki, M. and C. M. Reinhart (1998), "Measuring Intertemporal Substitution: The Role of Durable Goods," *Journal of Political Economy* 106(5):1078–98.

Phelps, E. S. (1967), "Phillips Curves, Expectations of Inflation and Optimal Unemployment over Time," *Economica* 34:254–81.

——— (1978), "Disinflation without Recession: Adaptive Guideposts and Monetary Policy," *Weltwirtschaftliches Archiv* 114(4):783–809.

Phelps, E. S. and J. B. Taylor (1977), "Stabilizing Powers of Monetary Policy under Rational Expectations," *Journal of Political Economy* 85(1):163–90.

Reinhart, C. M. and C. A. Vegh (1995), "Nominal Interest Rates, Consumption Booms, and Lack of Credibility: A Quantitative Examination," *Journal of Development Economics* 46(2):357–78.

Rotemberg, J. (1982), "Sticky Prices in the United States," *Journal of Political Economy* 90:1187–1211.

Sargent, T. J. (1986), "The Ends of Four Big Inflations," in T. J. Sargent, ed., *Rational Expectations and Inflation,* New York: Harper & Row.

Sbordone, A. (1998), "Prices and Unit Labor Costs: A New Test of Price Stickiness," manuscript, Rutgers University.

Sims, C. (1988), Comments and Discussion of L. Ball, N. G. Mankiw, and D. Romer, "The New Keynesian Economics and the Output-Inflation Trade-Off," *Brookings Papers on Economic Activity* 1:75–79.

Taylor, J. B. (1979), "Staggered Wage Setting in a Macro Model," *American Economic Review* 69(2):108–13.

——— (1983), "Union Wage Settlements during a Disinflation," *American Economic Review* 73(5):981–93.

——— (1998), "Staggered Price and Wage Setting in Macroeconomics," NBER Working Paper No. 6754.

Uribe, M. (1999), "Comparing the Welfare Costs and Initial Dynamics of Alternative Inflation Stabilization Policies," *Journal of Development Economics* 59:295–318.

Vegh, C. A. (1992), "Stopping High Inflation: An Analytical Overview," *IMF Staff Papers* 39:626–95.

Woodford, M. (1996), "Control of the Public Debt: A Requirement for Price Stability?," NBER Working Paper No. 5684.

Yun, T. (1996), "Nominal Price Rigidity, Money Supply Endogeneity, and Business Cycles," *Journal of Monetary Economics* 37:345–70.

5

Comments on Calvo, Celasun, and Kumhof

MARK GERTLER

1. INTRODUCTION

This chapter is motivated by the following set of observations: First, the evidence across countries and across time suggests that there are significant costs of disinflations in terms of lost output, particularly for countries beginning with moderately high inflation rates (as opposed to those initially experiencing hyperinflations). Second, it is not obvious from this evidence that these disinflation costs are accounted for simply by lack of central-bank credibility. Rather, persistence in inflation appears to be the central factor underlying the short-run output-inflation trade-off. The objective of this chapter, accordingly, is to develop an optimization-based model of inflation and output dynamics that can rationalize these facts.

Providing a cogent account of why disinflations may be costly has been a central topic in macroeconomics for at least the last three or four decades. An important early contribution to the literature is Ned Phelps's classic paper in *Economica*: "Phillips Curves, Expectations of Inflation and Optimal Unemployment Over Time" (Phelps, 1967). It is useful, I think, to place the chapter by Calvo, Celasun, and Kumhof (CCK) in the context of Phelps's original contribution. In Section 2, I summarize the key results in Phelps's seminal paper. In Section 3, I characterize how CCK extend this analysis by drawing upon recent developments in the literature. In Section 4, I discuss some unresolved issues.

2. PHELPS (1967)

As is now a common feature of the relevant contemporary literature, the classic Phelps framework is a neoclassical monetary growth model modified to allow for temporary nominal price stickiness. The following two equations characterize the short-run relation between inflation and output:

$$\pi_t = \lambda \widehat{y}_t + \pi_t^e, \tag{1}$$

$$\pi_{t+1}^e = \alpha \pi_t + (1 - \alpha)\pi_t^e, \tag{2}$$

where π_t is the inflation rate, $\widehat{y}_t$ is the percent difference between real output and its natural (flexible price equilibrium) value, and π_t^e is the expected inflation. In addition, $0 < \alpha < 1$.

Equation (1) is an expectations-augmented Phillips curve, a relation that is quite familiar to us all. Keep in mind, however, that this framework was developed in 1967, when most of the participants at the October 2001 Phelps festschrift were somewhere between diapers and graduate school. Also true in 1967 was that the Phillips curve in most macroeconometric models did not link inflation to expectations in any kind of cogent way. Rather, most models simply linked inflation to excess demand, suggesting a long-run trade-off between inflation and output. In a rather understated manner, as is his tendency, Phelps observes that theory implies that there should be no long-run output-inflation trade-off. To ensure that the model has this feature, he accordingly adds expected inflation to the Phillips curve and restricts the coefficient on this term to be unity. As has now been clear for many years in undergraduate textbooks, this modification ensures the absence of a long-run trade-off.

Closing the model requires an assumption about expectation formation. Phelps appeals to the simple adaptive mechanism popularized by Cagan (1956), as captured by equation (2). To be sure, he states clearly that he views the adaptive expectations hypothesis as a temporary convenience and that he plans eventually to explore the rational expectations hypothesis, which he in fact does in subsequent work with John Taylor (Phelps and Taylor, 1977). In any event, combining equations (1) and (2) leads to

$$\pi_t = \lambda \widehat{y}_t + \alpha \sum_{i=0}^{\infty} (1 - \alpha)^i \pi_{t-i}. \tag{3}$$

Equation (3) relates inflation to excess demand and lagged inflation, with the coefficients on lagged inflation summing to unity. This kind of Phillips curve relation has, of course, been the subject of considerable scrutiny and debate over the years.

Overall, two central insights emerged from the Phelps analysis. First, as I have hinted, is the idea of no long-run output-inflation trade-off. This simple proposition, which later would become known as the Phelps-Friedman natural rate hypothesis, is of course now one of the most basic tenets of modern macroeconomics.

The second major insight, which is perhaps more directly germane to the CCK chapter, is that an optimizing but myopic central bank might lead the economy into a high-inflation trap. Equation (3) implies that inflation responds only with a lag to movements in output, as is consistent with the evidence. As Phelps shows, accordingly, a central bank with a low discount factor may be tempted to reap the near-term gains of pushing output above its natural level at the cost of higher inflation down the road. Once in a regime of high inflation, the central bank may resist disinflating, as the costs of the near-term output loss outweigh the longer term benefits of low inflation. On the other hand, a far-sighted central bank— one with a high discount factor—is likely to resist the temptation to fall into the inflation trap. While his analysis does not contain the formal mechanics of time consistency, Phelps's notion of an inflation trap surely helped lay the groundwork for the important literature on rules versus discretion that would follow.

Phelps's simple model of inflation-output dynamics has strong empirical appeal and for this reason it remains popular today, especially in applied and policy-related work. However, as Phelps recognized, the framework is based on some arbitrary assumptions. Accordingly, the lengthy literature that has followed has focused on trying to improve the microfoundations without sacrificing the empirical appeal. Indeed this is the focus of the CCK chapter, as well as the Mankiw and Reis and Woodford chapters in this volume.

3. CALVO, CESALUN, AND KUMHOF

CCK use an optimization-based approach to derive a system of equations analogous to (1) and (2). As with virtually all of the recent literature, they do not eliminate the arbitrariness altogether, but rather move it to a higher level. In particular, they modify the original Calvo (1983) model of staggered price setting, to have firms choose a pricing policy on a staggered basis, as opposed to a single price. In particular, the pricing policy consists of the pair (p_t^*, π_t^*), where p_t^* is the initial price (in logarithms) set by a firm that adjusts at t, and π_t^* is the percent rate at which the price adjusts each period, as long as the firm is locked into this pricing policy. In particular, under this pricing policy, the price at $t+1$ based on the policy fixed at t, $p_{t,t+i}^*$, is given by

$$p_{t,t+i}^* = p_t^* + \sum_{j=1}^{i} \pi_j^*. \tag{4}$$

In the basic Calvo (1983) framework, of course, $\pi_t^* = 0$. As CCK show, however, firms will prefer the more flexible pricing policy. Allowing firms to lock into a rate of price change, however, introduces costs of disinflation within this framework, similar in spirit to those arising within the Phelps model described above.

To see this, note that by log-linearizing equation (4) and the relevant price index it is possible to obtain the following system of equations:

$$\pi_t = \delta(p_t^* - p_t) + \overline{\pi}_t, \tag{5}$$

$$\overline{\pi}_{t+1} = \theta \pi_t^* + (1 - \theta)\overline{\pi}_t, \tag{6}$$

where p_t is the price level and $\overline{\pi}_t$ is the average of the locked-in rate of price adjustment across firms that cannot adjust their pricing policy. In addition θ is the fraction of firms that readjust their pricing policies each period.

Equation (5) is a relation for inflation that is similar to the expectations-augmented Phillips curve given by equation (1). The first term on the right relates inflation to the gap between the reset price and the price level, $p_t^* - p_t$. This gap is interpretable as a measure of excess demand. The additive term is the average locked-in rate of price adjustment, analogous to, though distinct from, the expected inflation term that enters the traditional Phillips curve. In addition, because the fraction of firms θ adjust their pricing policy each period, $\overline{\pi}_t$ evolves through time following the adaptive rule given by equation (6). This relation, of course, is similar in form to the adaptive expectations mechanism in the Phelps formulation, although the motivation is more explicit.

Overall, by introducing particular assumptions into an explicit staggered price-setting framework, CCK are able to motivate a relation for short-run inflation-output dynamics that has the empirical appeal of the original Phelps model. Combining equations (5) and (6) leads to

$$
\pi_t = \delta(p_t^* - p_t) + \theta \sum_{j=1}^{i} (1 - \theta)^i \pi_{t-i}^*. \tag{7}
$$

Inflation depends on current excess demand, as measured by $p_t^* - p$ and a distributed lag of past locked-in inflation rates. The influence of the lagged locked-in rates implies persistence in inflation and costs of disinflation, much as in the Phelps model.

The optimization-based approach, however, does introduce some additional insights. Both $p_t^* - p_t$ and π_t^* depend not only on current economic conditions, but also on expectations of future economic behavior and, in particular, on the future course of policy. The credibility of government policy will thus affect the mapping between equation (7) and the reduced form that relates inflation to excess demand and lagged inflation rates. For example, if a central bank is prone to accommodate existing inflation, then $\pi_{t-i}^* \simeq \pi_{t-i}$, implying that the reduced form will closely resemble the reduced form of the Phelps model. Inflation persistence and, hence, costs of disinflation will be high in this setting. Conversely, if a central bank has a reputation for not tolerating inflation, then $\pi_{t-i}^* \simeq 0$, implying an absence of inflation persistence, since lagged inflation will not enter the reduced form. In this instance costs of disinflation will be low. This connection between the policy regime and the reduced form behavior of inflation clearly has some empirical appeal. For example, Cogley and Sargent (2001) present evidence to suggest that the Federal Reserve's increased focus on stabilizing inflation over the last several decades has been accompanied by a decline in inflation persistence.

4. SOME UNRESOLVED ISSUES

Let me conclude by noting several key issues that remain unresolved. First, it is not clear what enforces the invariance of the locked-in rate of price adjustment π_t^* to policy shifts, which is of course the critical aspect of the model. One possible interpretation is that it reflects explicit indexing arrangements. In this regard, it might be more desirable to cast the model in terms of wage contracting as opposed to price contracting. Another possibility might be to appeal to sluggish updating of information, as in the Mankiw and Reis and Woodford chapters in this volume.

Second, to explain persistently high inflation it is ultimately necessary to endogenize monetary policy. Within the CCK framework, a central bank that could credibly commit to going to zero inflation at some point in the future, beyond the time at which existing pricing policies expire (say a year or two down the road), could do so in the future without any cost of output loss. Understanding why a central bank cannot makes this commitment is key. Perhaps the original Phelps paper provides some insight.

In sum, this chapter makes a nice contribution to an important literature that Ned Phelps helped pioneer.

REFERENCES

Cagan, P. (1956), "The Monetary Dynamics of Hyperinflation," in Milton Friedman, ed., *Studies in the Quantity Theory of Money*, Chicago: University of Chicago Press, pp. 25–117.

Calvo, G. (1983), "Staggered Price Setting in a Utility Maximizing Framework," *Journal of Monetary Economics* 12(3):383–98.

Cogley, T. and T. J. Sargent (2001), "Evolving Post World War II U.S. Inflation Dynamics," *NBER Macroeconomics Annual* 16:331–73.

Phelps, E. S. (1967), "Phillips Curves, Expectations of Inflation and Optimal Unemployment Over Time," *Economica* 34:254–86.

Phelps, E. S. and J. B. Taylor (1977), "Stabilizing Powers of Monetary Policy Under Rational Expectations," *Journal of Political Economy* 85:163–90.

6

Macroeconomic Fluctuations in an Economy of Phelps-Winter Markets

BRUCE GREENWALD AND JOSEPH STIGLITZ

INTRODUCTION

In a seminal paper Sidney Winter and Edmund Phelps (1970) first examined systematically the evolution over time of markets composed of imperfectly competitive firms with several important real-economy features. First and most significantly, a firm's demand was specified to be the sum of the demands of individual customers (there was no undifferentiated lump of demand). Second, whereas individual customers might respond instantaneously to changes in the firm's price, growth in a firm's customer base would occur only slowly over time as customers compared prices among firms. Third, if a firm's price exceeded the average price of other firms, its customer base would shrink; if its price were to be below average, the firm's customer base would expand. Finally, the number of firms was assumed to be sufficiently large that individual firms would not react strategically to the price behaviors of other firms. Taken together, these assumptions appear to capture the essence of monopolistic competition over time. For that reason, we will refer to markets described by the four basic characteristics outlined above as Phelps-Winter markets as a shorthand for dynamic monopolistically competitive markets. This chapter represents an attempt to describe the macroeconomic implications of an economy of such firms.

In their original paper, Phelps and Winter did examine some of the macro-implications of their basic model. However, they did not focus specifically on two aspects of macroeconomics that have been central to Phelps's subsequent work. The first of these is the significance of capital-financial markets as a source of macroeconomic fluctuations and the critical role played by intertemporal trade-offs. In a Phelps-Winter market, such trade-offs directly affect price-setting policies that have traditionally been regarded as dependent upon short-term factors. Prices

Thanks are due to all the participants in the conference at Columbia University at which the work described in this chapter was presented, but especially to Ned Phelps himself, who was patient and insightful in bringing the original paper to fruition, and to Julio Rotemberg, who was an outstanding discussant under difficult circumstances. Errors and omissions are, of course, the responsibility of the authors.

influence both current demand and revenue and a firm's future customer base. That
customer base is a significant element of the firm's capital stock. Thus, a decision
to raise prices may yield higher immediate revenues and profits, but will do so
at the expense of future customer numbers, demand, and revenue. The extent to
which doing so is appropriate for the firm will depend critically on its current cost
of capital. Yet, in their original paper, Phelps and Winter do not discuss explicitly
the comparative static impact of changes in the rate of interest. (They examine the
effects of wages, demand shifts, and price expectations in detail.) This chapter,
therefore, focuses almost entirely on the effects of the cost of capital shifts—
analyzing both direct changes in the rate of interest and the indirect impact of
demand shocks on the cost of capital owing to informational imperfections in
financial markets.

Second, as is appropriate for a pioneering paper, Phelps and Winter (1970)
concentrate primarily on the partial equilibrium determinants of firm price-setting
policies. In subsequent work, Phelps has been a leader in the literature developing
general equilibrium microfoundation models for macroeconomic phenomena. In
the latter spirit, the model of this chapter examines explicitly the extent to which
the general equilibrium consequence of firm-level behavior mirrors the partial
equilibrium effects.

Finally, this chapter discusses the likely empirical implications of the model and
the role of the key assumption that there are no direct strategic interactions among
firm price-setting policies. A large and valuable literature, most notably Rotemberg
and Woodford (1992), has grown up around the intertemporal dimensions of these
strategic interactions in pricing. Since the implications of that literature often
appear to be markedly at variance with the implications of the Phelps-Winter
model, it is useful to delineate the sets of markets to which the two can be
appropriately (and separately) applied. Properly viewed, the two approaches are
complements, not substitutes.

Beyond this introduction the chapter itself consists of four parts. Section 2
develops a simple variant of the Phelps-Winter model. Section 3 embeds that
model in a general equilibrium macromodel. Section 4 introduces information-
based capital market imperfections to extend the range of business cycle–related
cost-of-capital variations that can be examined. Section 5 considers questions of
the empirical applicability of the Phelps-Winter model, and Section 6 concludes
the chapter.

2. FIRM LEVEL BEHAVIOR

The heart of the Phelps-Winter model is an industry of monopolistically competitive firms that compete for customers. A firm attracts customers based on both its
size (i.e., market presence) and its price relative to that of other firms. Formally,
we assume that the number of customers that the firm attracts in period $t + 1$ is
equal to

$$N_{t+1} = N_t f(p_t, \bar{p}_t), \tag{1}$$

where N_{t+1} and N_t are, respectively, the number of customers attracted by a typical firm in periods $t + 1$ and t, respectively; p_t is the price that the firm charges in period t; and $\bar{p}_t$ is the average price charged by all industry firms in period t. The function f is decreasing in p_t and increasing in $\bar{p}_t$. It should be greater than one if p_t is less than $\bar{p}_t$ (lower than average prices increase a firm's customer base), less than one if $\bar{p}_t$ is lower than p_t (higher than average prices lead to customer losses), and one if $\bar{p}_t$ equals p_t (a stable customer base if $\bar{p}_t$ and p_t are equal).

This formulation subsumes the behavior of both a firm's existing customers and potential customers whether the latter are new market participants or customers of other firms. The rationale for the dependence of future share gains and losses on current customer levels is clear in the case of losses. As customers compare prices among firms, large high-priced firms should lose customers proportionately rapidly. The case for the proportionality of gains to customer size is that firms with many customers should be able to depend on those customers to disseminate favorable price information more widely than comparable information from small firms.

In any single period, we will assume that a firm faces an instantaneous demand function $d(p_t)$ from each customer and that it produces output at a constant unit cost c. Formally, single-period profits are

$$\pi_t = (p_t - c)d(p_t)N_t, \tag{2}$$

where for the moment we assume that there are no fixed costs of being in business and that the technology of production embodies constant returns to scale with a single-factor input—labor. The firm's decision problem is to maximize

$$\sum_t \rho^t \pi_t, \tag{3}$$

where ρ is a firm discount factor and equation (3) is maximized subject to equation (1), which defines the evolution of the firm's customer base N.

The particular value of the constant-returns-to-scale production assumption is that it greatly simplifies this maximization problem. Let T denote the final period of a firm's life. It is immediately clear from (2) and the fact that the firm maximizes only period T profits that

$$p_t^* \equiv \text{Optimal price in period } T$$

is independent of N_T. We can, therefore, denote period T profits by

$$\pi_t^* = N_T v_T(p_T^*),$$

where $v_T = (p_T^* - c)d(p_T^*)$ and p_T^* is the usual single-period monopoly price. The optimization problem in period $T-1$ can now be written as

$$\max N_{T-1}(p_{T-1} - c)d(p_{T-1}) + N_{T-1}f(p_{T-1}, \bar{p}_{T-1})v_T.$$

Again, this is linear in N_{T-1} so that the optimal price p^*_{T-1} is independent of N_{T-1} and the maximum value of the objective function can be written as

$$V_{T-1} = \left[(p^*_{T-1} - c)d(p^*_{T-1} + f(p^*_{T-1}, p_{T-1})v_T \right] \equiv N_{T-1}v_{T-1}.$$

It is then clear, by induction, that the optimal value of p^*_t for any period is independent of N_t, the firm's stock of customers in that period. Thus, assuming that the conditions necessary to ensure convergence of the standard Bellman valuation function are satisfied, we can write the steady-state valuation function as

$$V(N) = Nv = N \left[\max_p (p - c)d(p) + \rho f(p, p)v \right], \tag{4}$$

where v is a value per customer function defined by the equation

$$v = (p^* - c)d(p^*) + pf(p^*) + pf(p^*, p)v, \tag{5}$$

and p^* is the optimal price for the intertemporal maximization problem of equation (4). Solving for v in equation (5), the value per customer (which is independent of N for any t) becomes

$$v = (p^* - c)d(p^*) \left[1/1 - \rho f(p^*, \bar{p}) \right].$$

This end-of-period customer value is very close to $1/(1 - \rho)$ times the single-period valuation of a customer since $f(p^*)$ should, in steady-state equilibrium, be reasonably close to one. (Remember that f includes not just retention of current customers, but recruitment of new ones.)

The steady-state first-order condition for the Phelps-Winter firm can now be written as

$$(p - c)d'(p) + d(p) + pf' \cdot v = 0. \tag{6}$$

Assuming that an interior maximum exists, we can solve this to yield a price markup equation of the familiar constant-cost form

$$p^* = \left(\frac{m + \varepsilon_0}{m + \varepsilon_0 - 1} \right) c, \tag{7}$$

where ε_0 is the individual customer demand elasticity, $m = \varepsilon_R \rho f(p^*) / [1 - \rho f (p^*)]$, and ε_R is the elasticity of customer retention-acquisition with respect to price, that is

$$\varepsilon_R = \partial f / \partial p \cdot p/f. \tag{8}$$

The simple extension embodied in equation (7) of the standard monopolistic markup equation yields a number of immediate consequences for a Phelps-Winter market that have significant macroeconomic implications. The first of these has to do with the importance of interest rates and, by implication, monetary policy. The interest rate directly enters the pricing equation via the m-term and the likely magnitude of this effect is significant. Assume for simplicity that $f(p^*)$ is close to one. Then,

$$m \cong \varepsilon_R(\rho/1 - p) = \varepsilon_R \left(\frac{1}{1 + r - 1} \right) = \varepsilon_R \left(\frac{1}{r} \right),$$

where r is a cost of capital and $\rho = 1/(1+r)$. Thus, the customer retention elasticity aspect of demand behavior gets magnified by the capitalization factor $1/r$ and changes in r will have a large consequent impact on price and markups. Especially if ε_R is large relative to ε_0 to begin with (i.e., current customer demand may be relatively price insensitive, but where-to-shop decisions respond significantly to price differences among firms), a fall in real interest rates may have a decisive effect in decreasing price markups and stimulating input. For example, if the short-run elasticities of both customer demand and customer acquisition are 0.5 (note that in the Phelps-Winter economy inelastic demands are compatible with optimization) and the cost of capital is 10 percent, then the firm's markup over the constant cost c is 22 percent. If the cost of capital declines to 8 percent (and future customers become more valuable) the markup declines to 17 percent. An increase in the cost of capital to 12 percent leads to a markup of 27 percent.

In contrast, shifts in current customer demand, and by implication fiscal policy, may have a far less significant impact on Phelps-Winter firms. An increase in demand that does not change the slope of a demand curve will generally lead to decreasing demand elasticities and higher firm prices. (With no change in demand elasticity there is no change in prices.) However, two points should be made about the resulting shift in output. First, the rise in prices in the Phelps-Winter market will partially offset any initial demand stimulus. Second, if the Phelps-Winter prices are dominated by interfirm competition for customers (i.e., m is much larger in magnitude than ε_0), these changes in consumer demand elasticities may have only minor effects on firm prices. For example, if the initial customer acquisition and demand elasticities are 0.5 and the cost of capital is 10 percent, then a decline in the current customer demand elasticity to 0.25 increases the optimal firm markup from 22 percent by just over 1 percent. The result is almost an order of magnitude smaller than the impact of interest rate changes. Hence, any effect of the initial increase in demand on prices and hence on incentives to enter an industry may be small. These are, however, questions that—in contrast to the relatively straightforward analysis of interest rate changes—require an examination of general equilibrium effects.

3. GENERAL EQUILIBRIUM BEHAVIOR

In specifying a general equilibrium context in which to embed the Phelps-Winter market described above, the emphasis continues to be on keeping things as simple as possible. To begin with, therefore, we assume that the Phelps-Winter firms are fixed in number and identical. Thus, they will charge identical prices and it will be possible to speak unambiguously of the price of the Phelps-Winter good.[1] We denote its price by p, and it is determined by the relationship of equation (7) at the point where $p = \bar{p}$. We assume that the Phelps-Winter good is produced using only labor as an input and that each unit of output produced requires c units of labor input. We further assume that there is a second sector of home production that uses only labor as an input. In this latter sector, we assume that there are constant returns to scale and that each unit of labor produces one unit of output. We designate the output of this sector as the numeraire and assume that opportunities for home production are always used to some extent by households in equilibrium. Thus, the equilibrium level of wages in our economy will always be one, and, in turn, the cost of production in the Phelps-Winter sector is c (i.e., c units of labor at a price of one unit each).

Demand for the Phelps-Winter good is assumed to arise from a utility function that is Cobb-Douglas between the Phelps-Winter good and the good produced by the household sector in each period. Thus, each household spends a fraction w of its income on the Phelps-Winter good, and the amount demanded is, therefore,

$$p \cdot d(p) \cdot H = wyH,$$

with y being household income[2] and H being the number of households (equal to the total number of available customers). Again, scale is immaterial here, so that the number of households H can be ignored. Total income consists of the output of the household sector plus that of the Phelps-Winter sector. The labor used in the latter is

$$l_{pw} = \left(\frac{w \cdot y}{p} \right) \cdot c \equiv \text{Phelps-Winter employment per household.}$$

Since each unit of output requires c units of labor, the labor allocated to household production, assuming each household is endowed with l units of labor, is

$$l_h = l - l_{pw} = l - \left(\frac{w \cdot y}{p} \right) \cdot c \equiv \text{Household labor per household.}$$

Thus, total income consists of the corresponding units of household production plus the revenue per household of the Phelps-Winter sector, namely,

$$y = l - \frac{w \cdot y \cdot c}{p} + \frac{w \cdot y}{p} = l + (1 - c/p) \cdot wy,$$

1. The firms may, however, be of different sizes since, given the specification of the customer acquisition function, any initial distribution of customers will be preserved. Under the circumstances, however, the characteristic of this distribution has no effect on the implications of the model.

2. Given this specification, household demands are unit-elastic for the Phelps-Winter good. However, a well-defined equilibrium markup will still exist since competition among firms for customers serves to increase the effective firm-level demand elasticity.

or

$$y = l \left[\frac{1}{1 - w(1 - c/p)} \right].$$

Output of the Phelps-Winter sector can now be specified by

$$d(p) = \frac{w \cdot y}{p} = \ell \cdot w \left[\frac{1}{p - w(p - c)} \right]. \tag{9}$$

Prices continued to be determined by the markup equation (7). Equation (9) then determines the output level of the Phelps-Winter sector. A higher level of Phelps-Winter prices leads to a lower level of Phelps-Winter output. In both partial and general equilibrium, the Phelps-Winter demand curve is downward sloping.

What has not yet been described, since there is no savings and investment behavior, is how interest rates are determined. However, as specified so far, the model is entirely real and thus one natural specification is the classical one in which monetary policy determines prices and interest rates are determined by real intertemporal trade-offs. The simplest way of closing the model is simply to extend the formulation of household utility so that there is perfect intertemporal substitutability of household good–Phelps-Winter good bundles at a discount rate q. Then

$$r = q \tag{10}$$

closes the model and interest rate shifts can be analyzed directly. Under such conditions, partial equilibrium results become general equilibrium results. However, the identity of interest rate changes with monetary policy no longer applies. Indeed, in most simple variants of these models, fiscal policy through goods market–clearing conditions determines the necessary level of interest rates. Expansionary fiscal policy under these circumstances has distinctly counterproductve effects. Higher public spending requires lower private spending (in the labor good), which requires higher interest rates. The higher interest rates lead to higher prices in the Phelps-Winter sector, which lead to lower not higher output in that sector.[3] It is only in the context of financial market constraints that nonclassical monetary and fiscal policy effects become reasonable, and this leads to the next section of the chapter.

4. IMPERFECT FINANCIAL MARKETS

A fundamental characteristic of firms operating in financial environments with significant information asymmetries is their inability to share risks fully with investors. This is illustrated most simply by examining the process of risk sharing

---

3. Intertemporal demand shocks in equation (10) can be interpreted directly as interest-rate changes. Higher future demand can be interpreted as corresponding to a lower utility discount rate and hence lower current demand.

through sales of equity capital (shares) to outside investors. If a firm's management[4] has better information about its future prospects than investors at large, a decision by management to sell additional stock at its current stock market price should send a negative signal to investors. If the market price is lower than the present value of future returns (from management's informed perspective), the firm faces a relatively high cost of selling equity and will be reluctant to do so. If the market price exceeds the level justified by management's superior information, then a new equity issue represents a relatively cheap source of external financing (from the perspective of existing shareholders). As a result, an equity issue announcement signals (on average) that the firm's stock is overvalued and investors, aware of this, should react negatively to the announcement. The consequent decline in the firm's market value should then inhibit any new issue of equity—as appears to be the case in practice.[5] In the extreme, equity issue markets may dry up completely—a case of complete lemons-related market failure.

The inability of a firm's management to share risks fully by either initial equity sales[6] and/or subsequent sales of seasoned equity means that management should no longer focus on maximizing the expected future value of discounted profits. Consider the case of an owner-manager who for information reasons must continue to hold a significant part of his wealth in his firm's equity (in order to show confidence in its future prospects). In each period, like any householder, he will maximize the expected utility of his terminal wealth (ignoring for simplicity current consumption). The owner's terminal wealth will consist of his share of the terminal value of the firm plus the value of his other investments, the latter being allocated according to the standard principles of optimal portfolio allocation. Thus, assuming again for simplicity that nonfirm wealth goes into risk-free assets, the owner-manager will maximize a linear function of the terminal value of the firm.

The behavior of professional managers is likely to be driven by a similar objective function. If principals are restricted to offering their agent-managers linear payoff schedules, then an agent-manager's compensation will consist of a fixed payment plus a constant times the terminal value of the firm (since that is the most inclusive firm performance measure). Equivalently, if entrenched managers are able for informational reasons to appropriate to themselves a fixed fraction of their firm's value, then management wealth will consist of that fraction of the terminal value of the firm plus any outside wealth that managers have accumulated. If these entrenched managers maximize the expected utility of this terminal wealth, the firm's objective function will again be an expected utility of a linear function of its terminal value. Finally, managers who maximize the expected end-of-period

---

4. Such managers may or may not be owners of the firm. The differences between professional managers and owner-managers is largely immaterial (see discussion below).

5. Equity issue announcements are empirically associated with both immediate price declines (see Asquith and Mullins, 1986, among others) and significant future financial underperformance (see Speiss and Affleck-Graves, 1995). In addition, market sales of equity constitute only a minor source of all equity cash flows, which consist almost entirely of retained earnings (see Mayer, 1990).

6. See Leland and Pyle (1977), who analyze the case of entrepreneurial firms that are owner managed.

value less an expected cost of bankruptcy, which increases linearly with firm size, will behave in a way that closely resembles that of the agent-managers just described (see Greenwald and Stiglitz, 1993).

From many perspectives, therefore, the natural extension of the Phelps-Winter model to a world of imperfect information is to assume that firm decision-makers maximize the expected utility of a linear function of the end-of-period value of the firm. Formally, we will assume that firm decision-makers maximize

$$E\{u[W + N(p - c)d(p) + Nf(p)v \cdot \bar{\mu}]\}. \tag{11}$$

Here most of the variables are those of the perfect-information model, p is the price of the firm's output, N is the number of customers at the beginning of the period, $d(p)$ is the single-period demand, c is a constant cost of production, and $f(p)$ is the customer retention-recruitment function. The variable v designates an expected future value per customer, although it should be noted that this is no longer determined by the simple Bellman equation derived previously. Uncertainty here has been limited for simplicity to this value-per-customer variable. The random variable $\bar{\mu}$ represents a demand-shift parameter whose value, which is only revealed at the end of each operating period, determines the future value of each retained customer. It is assumed to have an expected value of unity (this really just defines the level of v) and constant variance. The variable W is the initial wealth of the firm's decision-makers measured in end-of-period units [i.e., $(1 + r_s)$ units where r_s is a risk-free rate of return].

One important point implicit in the objective function of equation (11) should be noted. It assumes that neither new equity sale nor dividend change decisions can be used to affect the end-of-period firm value. Indeed, dividends are assumed to be zero. This reflects the informational restrictions on equity issue-retention decisions described above.

The first-order condition defining the optimal current price level for the Phelps-Winter firm in an imperfect information environment can now be written

$$N(p - c)d' + Nd(p) + Nf'(p) \cdot v \left\{ 1 + E \frac{u'(\cdot)(\bar{\mu} - 1)}{E[u'(\cdot)]} \right\} = 0. \tag{12}$$

This can be simplified by eliminating N (although now the level of N still enters through the u' terms) and rearranging in the usual markup form. Since the only difference between equation (12) and the equivalent no-uncertainty condition, equation (6), is the term

$$1 + E \frac{u'(\bar{\mu} - 1)}{E[u'(\cdot)]},$$

which substitutes for ρ, the markup equation can be written

$$p^* = \frac{m^* + \varepsilon_0}{m^* + \varepsilon_0 - 1},$$

where

$$m^* = \frac{\varepsilon_g f(p^*)}{1 - (1 + \phi) f(p^*)}$$

and

$$\phi \equiv \frac{E\left[u'(\cdot)(\bar{\mu} - 1)\right]}{E\left[u'(\cdot)\right]},$$

which is a risk-aversion parameter (to which a time-discount factor could be added but has been omitted for simplicity).

The first important point to note about ϕ is that it is less than zero [since high values of $\bar{\mu}$ correspond to low values of $u'(\cdot)$ and $E(\bar{\mu}) = 1$]. Second, its magnitude is increasing in the degree of uncertainty concerning the future ($\bar{\mu}$) and the degree of risk aversion of the firm's decision-maker. Finally, $1 + \phi$ plays a role entirely similar to the discount factor ρ in the certainty case. Thus, since increases in the magnitude of ϕ reduce $1 + \phi$, ϕ itself acts like a cost of capital.

It is now possible to describe two important sources of cyclical price rigidity in the Phelps-Winter economy. First, any increase in uncertainty concerning the value of future customers will materially reduce the present value of customer acquisition. To the extent that customer acquisition plays a critical role in limiting price markups, this will in turn lead to higher price markups and should outweigh any tendency for declining demand to reduce prices. Increased uncertainty as Phelps-Winter firms contemplate a recession will generate higher prices and consequently lower output in the Phelps-Winter segment—precisely the formula for the kind of stagflation experienced during the instabilities of the 1970s and early 1980s.

The second cyclical phenomenon arises when a demand (or supply) shock impairs a firm's financial position. Since imperfect information limits access to external equity markets, any reduction in earnings (assuming dividends are rigid for informational reasons) will lead to a corresponding reduction in a firm's equity capital. If at the same time inventories accumulate, there is a further shift in the firm's balance sheet position from safe cash to risky real assets. For a decision-maker with the objective function of equation (11), this corresponds to a reduction in the original wealth variable W. If the utility function is characterized by decreasing relative risk aversion with respect to wealth, then the decline in W will act to increase the firm decision-maker's effective degree of risk aversion. This will reduce the appeal of risky future investments in customer acquisition and tend to generate higher prices.[7] Again an initial negative demand shock in the Phelps-Winter economy leads to lower output, but to higher not lower prices (i.e., to something like downward price rigidity).

---

7. The magnitudes of these risk-related firm wealth effects may appear to be relatively insignificant. However, in simple models they typically involve output changes that are directly proportional to changes in projected equity levels (see Greenwald and Stiglitz, 1993).

5. EMPIRICAL EVIDENCE

The simple downward price rigidity that characterizes the Phelps-Winter model in both its classical (i.e., interest rate–driven recession) and its imperfect information versions corresponds closely to the history of recessions over the last 50 years in the United States. Table 1 describes price behavior during the contractionary phases of the seven United States recessions identified by the NBER since 1950. In six of the seven cases, the contraction was preceded by a significant acceleration in the rate of inflation (the 1960 contraction is the exception) and this was followed by substantial countervailing monetary policy on the part of the Federal Reserve. At the same time, both the inflation itself and the Federal Reserve's response generated increased macroeconomic uncertainty, which was followed by negative demand shocks. All three of the elements in this sequence—higher interest rates, greater uncertainty, and negative demand shocks—lead to higher Phelps-Winter prices. In four of seven recessions, inflation actually accelerated during the contractionary phase of the cycle. On average there was a slight acceleration in contractionary-period inflation from the prerecession peak. In two further recessions (1957–1958 and 1960–1961) there was only a very slight drop in the rate of inflation and only in the 1953–1954 contraction did the rate of price increase drop significantly. Overall, given the counterintuitive nature of the Phelps-Winter conclusion that contractionary periods should see higher rather than lower prices, this history is strikingly favorable to the model.

Further support for the model comes from the subsequent experience of inflation during recoveries. As firms restore their financial positions, as the macroeconomy stabilizes, and as the Federal Reserve moves toward an expansionary posture, then uncertainty, firm equity positions, and lower interest rates should all tend to drive down the cost of capital. For a Phelps-Winter economy, these forces should lead to intensified competition for customers and lower prices. Table 1 provides striking support for this conclusion. In every single recession in the United States since 1950, the rate of inflation fell between the contractionary and recovery phases of the cycle. On average, rates of inflation were 2.4 percent lower during the recovery phases than during the prior contractions. For the United States, the Phelps-Winter model coincides well with business cycle history.

Table 1. Inflation Behavior in Post-1950 United States Recessions (percent)

Contraction	Contraction inflation	Precontraction inflation	Expansion inflation
July 1953–May 1954	1.3	2.4 (1952)	0.4 (1954–1955)
August 1957–April 1958	2.8	3.3 (1957)	1.9 (1959)
April 1960–February 1961	1.7	1.9 (1959)	1.0 (1961)
December 1969–November 1970	6.0	5.5 (1969)	4.4 (1970)
November 1973–March 1975	11.0	6.2 (1973)	9.1 (1975)
1980–1981	11.9	11.3 (1979)	3.2 (1983)
July 1990–March 1991	5.4	4.8 (1989)	3.0 (1992)
Average	5.7	5.0	3.3

The available microeconomic evidence is difficult to assess for a number of reasons. First, in practice, individual firms follow fairly complicated pricing strategies. Price changes are often implemented in the form of coupons, delivery and financing discounts, special sales, and retail incentives (e.g., frequent flyer promotions), which are designed to discriminate between price-sensitive and price-insensitive customers. Average microlevel price changes may well reflect Phelps-Winter behavior, but this may be difficult to detect in the price data. In addition, the consequences, among both existing and prospective customers, of major price changes may be highly uncertain. For risk-averse firms, optimal pricing strategies will then involve the introduction of such price increases piecemeal over extended periods in order to minimize the risks of major adverse demand changes (see Greenwald and Stiglitz, 1995). Actual price change histories may, therefore, greatly attenuate intended responses to changing capital market and business cycle conditions—although such changes may be detectable in aggregate averages. Finally, the price equations derived previously describe markups above a constant marginal cost and the discussion of price changes has so far tended to ignore cost variations. One reason for doing so is that marginal costs are difficult (if not impossible) to measure in practice. On the other hand, they may well vary over the business cycle in ways that effectively mask the Phelps-Winter phenomena. If marginal costs fall dramatically with capacity utilization during the contractionary phase of an industry cycle, then constant-price rules would correspond to substantially increased markups over marginal costs. The increased markups might reflect purposeful decisions regarding the reduced contraction-period value of customer recruitment. However, the price data by itself might show little or none of this.

The microeconomic evidence regarding the validity of the Phelps-Winter model is, therefore, best looked at indirectly. It is widely recognized in the marketing literature (see Kotler, 1987) that the intensity of price competition embodied in promotion budgets tracks closely with the intensity of advertising competition. Thus, rather than looking at pricing policies, we examine advertising behavior over the course of the business cycle. Aggregate advertising expenditures during the seven recessions of the past 50 years are presented in Table 2.

In five of seven recessions, advertising expenditures fell during the contractionary phase of the business cycle. Average spending during contractions was down about 14 percent from its prior peak. Only in 1953–1954, during the rapid rise in advertising expenditures associated with the introduction of television, and in the very mild recession of 1960–1961 did advertising increase during the contraction. Thus, in general, cyclical downturns appear to have been associated with reduced advertising competition and, by implication, reduced price competition—just as the Phelps-Winter model predicts. During the recovery phase of the business cycle, advertising expenditures rose in five of seven recessions. The exceptions were the 1974–1975 recession (which did see a recovery-related increase in advertising, if 1976 rather than 1975 is treated as the recovery) and the 1990–1991 recession, where as in 1974–1975 advertising was slow to recover. While less striking than the contraction evidence, this too is broadly consistent with the Phelps-Winter model.

Table 2. Cyclical Behavior of Advertising Expenditures ($ millions)

| Contraction | Real advertising expenditures | | Precontraction |
	During contraction	During recovery	
July 1953–May 1954	9,912 (1953–1954)	10,801 (1954–1955)	9,341 (1952–1953)
August 1957–April 1958	12,064 (1957–1958)	12,890 (1958–1959)	12,200 (1956–1957)
April 1960–February 1961	13,220 (1960–1961)	13,443 (1961–1962)	13,172 (1959–1960)
December 1969–November 1970	16,853 (1970)	17,180 (1971)	17,743 (1969)
November 1973–March 1975	17,976 (1974)	17,308 (1975)	18,843 (1973)
1980–1981	65,734 (1980–1981)	72,631 (1982–1983)	67,190 (1979)
July 1990–March 1991	96,615 (1990–1991)	93,192 (1991–1992)	99,435 (1989)
Average	29,315	33,921	33,989

The final test of any model is the appropriateness of the underlying assumptions, and in the Phelps-Winter case, the demand behavior assumed appears to be largely appropriate. The most questionable assumption is that of no direct competitive interactions among firms and even that appears to be true of a wide range of industries. Where many small firms are involved, where there are low or nonexistent barriers to entry and exit, where markets involve a number of global competitors, or where mononpolists are concerned with recruiting customers to their product over time, direct competitive interactions ought not to be a significant factor. Only in the cases of traditional oligopoly should they be of concern, and here, although some consequences of intertemporal decision-making (see Rotemberg and Woodford, 1992) may run counter to those implied by the Phelps-Winter model, this is not always the case. Higher interest rates, for example, reduce the weight of future price discipline–maintaining sanctions and lead to more opportunistic current price behavior. This means lower rather than higher prices. However, negative demand shocks, which reduce the benefits of current opportunistic price reductions, will lead to higher current prices and this behavior is consistent with Phelps-Winter. On balance, therefore, even in situations of direct oligopolistic interactions (barriers to entry and a small number of firms), much of the best existing theory complements rather than contradicts the implications of the Phelps-Winter model.

6. CONCLUSION

We have shown that only a slight extension of the Phelps-Winter model is necessary in order to account for a wide range of observed macroeconomic phenomena. The consideration of intertemporal trade-offs in pricing behavior should play a part in any carefully conceived macroeconomic policy. However, the story does not end here. Phelps-Winter also has important implications in labor markets, where intertemporal worker retention considerations should play an important role in wage-setting decisions. This can account for sticky wages just as the model accounts directly for sticky prices. Like all great papers, Phelps and Winter (1970) poses an almost inexhaustible set of interesting future research questions.

REFERENCES

Asquith, P. and D. Mullins (1986), "Equity Issues and Stock Price Dilution," *Journal of Financial Economics* 13:296–320.

Greenwald, B. and J. Stiglitz (1993), "Financial Market Imperfections and Business Cycles," *Quarterly Journal of Economics* 108:314–39.

———— (1995), "Imperfect Information, Labor Market Adjustments and Unemployment," *American Economic Review* 80:217–21.

Kotler, J. (1987), *Marketing: An Integrated Approach.* New York: Prentice Hall.

Leland, H. and D. Pyle (1977). "Information Asymmetries, Financial Structure and Financial Intermediation," *Journal of Finance* 32:371–87.

Mayer, C. P. (1990), "Financial Systems, Corporate Finance and Economic Development," in R. G. Hubbard, ed., *Asymmetric Information, Corporate Finance and Investment,* Chicago: University of Chicago Press, pp. 216–40.

Phelps, E. and S. Winter (1970), "Optimal Price Policy Under Atomistic Competition," in E. Phelps, A. A. Alchian, C. C. Holt, D. T. Mortensen, G. C. Archibald, R. E. Lucas, Jr., L. A. Rapping, S. G. Winter, Jr., J. P. Gould, D. F. Gordon, A. Hynes, D. A. Nichols, P. J. Taubman, and M. Wilkinson, *Microeconomic Foundations of Employment and Inflation Theory*, New York: Norton, pp. 309–37.

Rotemberg, J. and M. Woodford (1992), "Oligopolistic Pricing and the Effects of Aggregate Demand on Economic Activity," *Journal of Political Economy* 100:107–34.

Speiss, D. and J. Affleck-Graves (1995), "Underperformance in Long Run Stock Returns Following Seasoned Equity Offerings," *Journal of Financial Economics* 38:243–67.

7

General Comments on Part I

ROBERT E. LUCAS, JR.

Of the four parts that make up this volume, this is the one most like the "Phelps volume," the 1970 book more formally known as *Microeconomic Foundations of Inflation and Employment Theory*. The book was in fact co-authored, at Ned Phelps's characteristically generous insistence, and for many years W. W. Norton would send me a royalty check for $12.14, or whatever my one-half of Leonard Rapping's and my share had come to for that year. The book was such a success that one now sees "microfound" used as a verb, as in, "This theory is microfounded." Whether Ned wishes to take responsibility for this usage I cannot say, but I think he ought to if he is to take the credit he deserves for all the good things that came out of this project.

The main theme of the Phelps volume was price rigidity or, as we now say, price stickiness or, as Rapping and I and many others thought of it then, the Phillips curve: the fact that increases in rates of change in dollar-denominated magnitudes—prices or nominal wages—seem to be associated with increases in levels of real variables—employment or GDP. Some contributors attempted to set out individual decision problems in which economic actors would alter their behavior in response to nominal shocks. Others focused on some kind of market equilibrium. Phelps himself had three papers on price stickiness in the volume. One was a revision of his *Journal of Political Economy* paper that introduced the vertical long-run Phillips curve. A second was his joint paper with Sidney Winter, which formulated a model of sellers' price setting under a kind of transient monopolistic competition. A third was his elegant introduction to the volume, in which he introduced an economy of informationally distinct islands, where prices were competitively determined yet "sticky" in the sense of yielding Phillips-like correlations.

Bruce Greenwald's chapter took the Phelps and Winter (1970) paper as its point of departure. He began by reminding us how *hard* that paper was, and still is, and proposed some simplifications that facilitate a more complete analysis. On a rereading occasioned by this celebration, I was also struck by the paper's difficulty, but to me this seemed mainly a reminder of how hard it was to think about price setting in monopolistically competitive markets before Spence (1976) and Dixit and Stiglitz (1977) introduced the symmetric model that everyone now uses. True, in Phelps and Winter a firm's market power is transient, whereas for

Spence-Dixit-Stiglitz it is static and permanent, but I do not know if this distinction is crucial for the macroeconomic issues we were trying to address in the Phelps volume.

In any case, since Blanchard and Kiyotaki (1987) recognized that the Spence-Dixit-Stiglitz model provides a convenient framework for thinking about firms that set nominal prices in a monetary economy, most theoretical discussions of price stickiness have used some version of this model. All of the contributions to this part reflect the way these later contributions helped to advance the agenda that Phelps set out in his contributions to the Phelps volume.

The chapter by Calvo, Celasun, and Kumhof develops a variation on the widely used model of Calvo (1983), in which firms set a nominal price and then have to wait until a Poisson counter goes off before they can change its level. This extremely useful device lets us build any desired amount of persistence into price behavior while adding only one state variable to the model. In the present chapter, the authors modify this model by letting a firm choose *both* a price level *and* a rate of change when its turn to reset prices comes up. In the kind of inflationary economy they want to study, firms will commit to a positive rate of increase. When the government alters monetary policy, then, each firm's price will continue to increase at its preset rate until the opportunity to alter the pricing policy arises again: There is inertia in the inflation *rate*. Calvo, Celasun, and Kumhof do a careful and clear job of analyzing this model. They then work out the model economy's response to a very well specified policy change: a permanent, fully credible, and foreseen reduction in the rate of exchange rate depreciation from 40 percent per year to 10 percent. In this setting, such a disinflation has real consequences.

For me, a high point of the chapter is footnote 4, where the authors write that, for all interesting parameter values, the long-run efficiency gains from a lower steady-state inflation are larger than the short-run losses owing to the temporary recession. The whole point of trying to model price stickiness, I think, is to gain the ability to draw conclusions about trade-offs like this. One needs a genuine economic model to think about the welfare consequences of policy changes at this level, and Calvo, Celasun, and Kumhof have given us one. I think this is exactly why we care about microeconomic foundations, and I view this as a heartening sign of real progress.

The chapter deals with a great economic question, well-posed and seriously analyzed. But does it arrive at the right answer? I am very skeptical. In the simulation carried out in the chapter, firms are locked in to a pricing policy that is completely unsuited to the new policy regime. They understand this new regime fully, but they just cannot act on this knowledge. The situation seems very close to the much more drastic disinflations that Sargent (1986) studied, where he attributed the fact that these disinflations did not trigger even modest recessions to the credibility and permanence of the shift in policy. Since these features are also built into the policy experiment that Calvo, Celasun, and Kumhof study, they should have arrived at the same answer that Sargent did. But they simply ruled out Sargent's answer at the outset. The authors are, of course, fully aware of Sargent's analysis, and they suggest that they chose the size of their hypothetical disinflation—40 percent to 10—in the belief that it is both large enough that inflation inertia could arise and small enough that firms might not reset their price paths without waiting their turns. Maybe this belief is justified, but maybe not. How can one argue usefully about this question?

It seems to me that if we are to have sticky-price models that are helpful in facing this issue, we have to think about menu costs, not just as a background story to make us feel comfortable about assuming price stickiness but as an integral, calibrated component of the models we simulate. Sheshinski and Weiss (1977, 1983) have contributed some useful theory, as have Mankiw (1985), Caplin and Spulber (1987), Caplin and Leahy (1991), and others. The mathematics of menu costs quickly gets hard, I know, but whoever thought successful macroeconomics would be easy? If new Keynesians are going to get beyond matching VARs—the one thing we could do quite well in the 1960s with old Keynesian models—they will have to set their alarms an hour earlier, get in to the office on Saturdays, and do the work that is needed to create a new theory that is consistent with *both* postwar U.S. experience *and* Sargent's evidence.

For me, Sargent's studies of the ends of European inflations define exactly what is hard about the question of price stickiness. The issue is not whether one can see some form of stickiness in the data. Thousands of estimated Phillips curves and other statistical descriptions exhibit correlations that most of us find hard to account for in purely Walrasian terms. But alongside this evidence are equally solid findings of reductions in inflation rates that were associated with modest reductions in production and employment or with no reductions at all. Menu costs that induce firms to stay with a pricing structure until it is clear that a new structure is needed offer one possible route to reconcile such conflicting findings. But then to simulate responses to policy shifts, we need some way of knowing what policy changes will override the fixed cost and trigger reviews of pricing policies and which will not. If this question is not faced, what have we got?

I have focused my discussion of this question on the Calvo, Celasun, and Kumhof chapter only because it gets close enough to an answer that I could not help getting excited. As far as I could tell, Greenwald and Stiglitz do not touch on macroeconomic policy questions at all. Mankiw and Reis write as though estimated trade-offs are as stable as people thought they were in the 1960s. They postulate some equations to describe production and wage and price determination and show that the impulse-response functions generated by these equations are similar to those found in recent U.S. time series. But what questions can we use these equations to answer? Why not just exhibit the appropriate VAR from U.S. data or just present the data themselves?

Woodford offers several ideas, new to me and possibly promising, about ways in which macroeconomic theories might incorporate informational difficulties. He takes the island model of Phelps's introduction and my development (Lucas, 1972) of it as points of departure, describing his approach as similar to mine except for a few changes. But it turns out that to save this particular boat from sinking, we need to throw overboard the islands, rational expectations, utility maximization, cleared competitive markets, and money!

In fact, Woodford does not want to use the Phelps islands, with their competitive markets, as his point of departure at all. Insofar as his chapter gets specific about the economics in his models, he takes off from Phelps and Winter and the monopolistically competitive models they helped to stimulate. The idea of adapting, say, Blanchard and Kiyotaki's setup to incorporate informational imperfections is surely worth developing, but it is only hinted at here and, as Lars Svensson noted in his comments, we will have to wait and see.

Since rational expectations models were first introduced in monetary theory in the 1970s, their central difficulty has been in offering an account of large, persistent real responses to nominal shocks. New frameworks—contracts and monopolistic competition—are introduced, motivated by the inability of earlier theory to resolve this difficulty, but the problem of persistence has proved to be persistent itself. As Chari et al. (2000) have shown most recently, the persistence problem is not going to be resolved simply by replacing competitive market structures with monopolistic competition or nominal contracting, at least if people are given realistic capabilities to write contracts. On the other hand, if we try to avoid the issue and simply assume realistic persistence—as in Calvo (1983)—we run into Sargent's findings.

Ever since the January 1969 conference to which Ned Phelps invited us, the fourteen contributors to the Phelps volume have been apologetic about the fact that we could not resolve these issues. After watching so many of our talented colleagues struggling with them over the 30 years since, maybe we should not feel so bad.

REFERENCES

Blanchard, O. J. and N. Kiyotaki (1987), "Monopolistic Competition and the Effects of Aggregate Demand," *American Economic Review* 77:647–66.

Calvo, G. A. (1983), "Staggered Prices in a Unitility Maximizing Framework," *Journal of Monetary Economics* 12:383–98.

Caplin, A. S. and D. F. Spulber (1987), "Menu Costs and the Neutrality of Money," *Quarterly Journal of Economics* 102:703–26.

Caplin, A. S. and J. Leahy (1991), "State Dependent Pricing and the Dynamics of Money and Output," *Quarterly Journal of Economics* 106:683–708.

Chari, V. V., P. J. Kehoe, and E. R. McGrattan (2000), "Sticky Price Models of the Business Cycle," *Econometrica* 68:1151–80.

Dixit, A. K. and J. E. Stiglitz (1977), "Monopolistic Competition and Optimum Product Diversity," *American Economic Review* 67:293–308.

Lucas, R. E., Jr. (1972), "Expectations and the Neutrality of Money," *Journal of Economic Theory* 4:103–24.

Mankiw, N. G. (1985), "Small Menu Costs and Large Business Cycles: A Macroeconomic Model of Monopoly," *Quarterly Journal of Economics* 100:529–38.

Phelps, E. and S. Winter (1970), "Optimal Price Policy Under Atomistic Competition," in E. S. Phelps, A. A. Alchian, C. C. Holt, D. T. Mortensen, G. C. Archibald, R. E. Lucas, Jr., L. A. Rapping, S. G. Winter, Jr., J. P. Gould, D. F. Gordon, A. Hynes, D. A. Nichols, P. J. Taubman, and M. Wilkinson, *Microeconomic Foundations of Employment and Inflation Theory,* New York: Norton, pp. 309–37.

Phelps, E. S., A. A. Alchian, C. C. Holt, D. T. Mortensen, G. C. Archibald, R. E. Lucas, Jr., L. A. Rapping, S. G. Winter, Jr., J. P. Gould, D. F. Gordon, A. Hynes, D. A. Nichols, P. J. Taubman, and M. Wilkinson (1970), *Microeconomic Foundations of Employment and Inflation Theory*, New York: Norton.

Sargent, T. J. (1986), *Rational Expectations and Inflation*, New York: Harper & Row.

Sheshinski, E. and Y. Weiss (1977), "Inflation and Costs of Price Adjustment," *Review of Economic Studies* 54:287–303.

———— (1983), "Optimum Pricing Policy under Stochastic Inflation," *Review of Economic Studies* 60:513–29.

Spence, M. (1976), "Product Selection, Fixed Costs, and Monopolistic Competition," *Review of Economic Studies* 43:217–35.

PART II

Imperfect Knowledge, Expectations, and Rationality

— 8 —

Imperfect Knowledge Expectations, Uncertainty-Adjusted Uncovered Interest Rate Parity, and Exchange Rate Dynamics

ROMAN FRYDMAN AND MICHAEL D. GOLDBERG

We are merely reminding ourselves that human decisions affecting the future, whether personal or political or economic, cannot depend on strict mathematical expectation, since the basis for making such calculations does not exist; and . . . that our rational selves [are] choosing between alternatives as best as we are able, calculating where we can, but often falling back for our motive on whim or sentiment or chance. (Keynes, 1936, p. 162)

The actors of [our] model[s] have to cope ignorant of the future and even much of the present. Isolated and apprehensive, these Pinteresque figures construct expectations of the state of the economy . . . and maximize relative to that imagined world. (Phelps, 1970, p. 22)

1. INTRODUCTION

The *rational expectations hypothesis* (REH) has become so entrenched in modern economics that the economic analyst need not give a second thought as to how expectations should be modeled. Its popularity among economists as a model of expectations formation does not seem to have been eroded by a substantial

This chapter is a revised and abridged version of the draft presented at the festschrift conference in honor of Edmund S. Phelps, Columbia University, October 5–6, 2001. The authors are grateful to Ned Phelps for generously sharing his numerous ideas and providing unstinting encouragement, and to George Soros for his critical insights on the role of imperfect knowledge in the workings of financial markets. They also thank Andrzej Rapaczynski and Stephen Schulmeister for stimulating discussions on many of the issues raised in this chapter. The authors are pleased to acknowledge helpful comments and reactions to an earlier version of this chapter from participants of the festschrift conference at Columbia, particularly Andy Caplin, Peter Martin, David Papell, Paul Romer, Chris Sims, and Mike Woodford, as well as Katarina Juselius, Jim Ramsey, Niels Thygesen, and colleagues at the University of New Hampshire. The authors are thankful for generous support from the Reginald F. Atkins Chair at the University of New Hampshire and the C. V. Starr Center for Applied Economics at New York University. Responsibility for the ideas and opinions presented in this chapter remains, of course, solely with the authors.

literature arguing that it lacks epistemological and behavioral foundations. The main problem discussed in the literature over the last two decades is that, unless *additional and arguably strong assumptions* concerning agents' knowledge and the coordination of their beliefs are maintained, the REH is *not* tantamount to the basic economic postulate of individual rationality. As Sargent (1993, p. 23) has reminded us quite recently, rather than being a model of individual expectations, "rational expectations is an equilibrium concept that at best describes how the system might eventually behave if the system will ever settle down to a situation in which all of the agents have solved their 'scientific problems.'" Despite such long-standing arguments, the popular belief has persisted that individual rationality *somehow* implies the validity of REH as a model of individual expectations.[1]

Another popular justification for the use of the REH appeals to the positivist standpoint of Friedman (1953): as long as the models using the REH can be shown to deliver rigorous, testable cross-equation restrictions and sharp predictions, the behavioral emptiness of the REH is largely irrelevant. Yet especially in asset markets, the models employing the REH as a model of expectations have encountered considerable difficulties in explaining the observed behavior.

One such class of popular asset market models whose empirical performance *under the REH* has been extremely poor is the monetary class of exchange rate models.[2] In their review of the evidence Dornbusch and Frankel (1988, p. 10) sum up the empirical failure of these models as follows: "Exchange rates are moved largely by factors other than the obvious, observable, macroeconomic fundamentals. Econometrically, most of the "action" is in the error term." Thus, even if one ignores the epistemological and behavioral objections to the REH, the rational expectations versions of the monetary models of the exchange rate have been widely acknowledged to fail on the basis of the strictly positivist (empiricist) criterion.

In this chapter we formulate an alternative model of individual expectations that recognizes the importance of imperfect knowledge and advance the argument that the standard REH assumption appears to be the primary reason for the gross empirical failure of the monetary models of the exchange rate. To this end, we reexamine a modified version of the overshooting model owing to Dornbusch (1976) and Frankel (1979), which has been dubbed the DF model. We show that once the REH is replaced by our alternative model of individual expectations, the DF model offers surprising promise in explaining the hitherto anomalous aspects of the floating-rate experience.[3]

---

1. For a recent discussion of such misconceptions concerning the connection between the REH and individual rationality, see Sargent (1993), Kurz and Motolese (2001), and Evans and Honkapohja (2001) and references therein. For an early discussion of the main problems with the REH, see Frydman (1982, 1983), Frydman and Phelps (1983), and Phelps (1983). See Section 2 for further discussion.

2. For survey articles see Frankel and Rose (1995) and Taylor (1995), and a summary in our Section 7.

3. The DF model has been criticized for its assumptions of exogenous money and income processes and a constant equilibrium real exchange rate, as well as for lacking explicit microfoundations (e.g., see Obstfeld and Rogoff, 1996, chap. 9). It is all the more remarkable that, once the REH is replaced with an alternative, and arguably more plausible, expectational assumption, the DF model appears to be quite useful in explaining exchange rate dynamics.

One important and much overlooked aspect of the empirical record on exchange rates provided a key stimulus in developing our alternative to the REH: There are some subperiods of floating rates during which macroeconomic models explain monthly or quarterly exchange rate movements reasonably well and other subperiods during which their explanatory power completely disappears.[4] As Meese (1986, p. 365) remarks, "the most menacing empirical regularity that confronts exchange rate modelers is the failure of the current generation of empirical exchange rate models to provide stable results across subperiods of the modern floating rate period." Similar observations have been made by Sargent (1999, p. 16) in a more general context of macroeconometric analysis: "[Rational expectations econometrics] left the drift in coefficients unexplained. . . . Yet coefficients continue to drift for macroeconometric models. . . . Thus, the forecasting literature has taken coefficient drift increasingly seriously, but with little help from the rational expectations tradition." Many researchers believe that such coefficient variation is compatible with the REH and, as Lucas (1976) has argued, such variability is simply the consequence of changes in policy rules. However, as we discuss further in this chapter, it seems implausible that the temporal instability of the coefficients of the macroeconometric models is due *solely* to changes in government policy. These arguments, pointing to the possibility that *autonomous* changes in expectations might be an important cause of coefficient instability, have provided an important motivation for our proposed alternative to the REH.

Our approach to modeling individual expectations, dubbed the *imperfect knowledge expectations* (IKE) framework, assumes that in formulating and updating their IKE functions, individual agents will, in general, use qualitative information from the extant *plurality* of economic models, statistical procedures, and publicly available information, as well as subjective assessments and guesses. To model such updating, the IKE framework allows the coefficients of agents' forecast functions to vary over time in both a continuous and discontinuous manner. Moreover, our framework implies that such coefficient variation need not be associated with changes in government policy, that is, the coefficients of forecasting functions can experience structural instability even if the government acts according to a constant policy rule.

Our formulation of IKE functions and their updating involves some indeterminacy. This indeterminacy arises in part because the IKE framework builds on the idea of *theories consistent expectations* (TCE), proposed in Frydman and Phelps (1990) and developed in Goldberg (1991) and Goldberg and Frydman (1993, 1996a). The TCE framework assumes that the extant stock of the *plurality* of economic models provides agents with *qualitative* knowledge about which variables to include in their individual forecast functions and the *signs* of the weights that should be attached to the included variables. Despite its apparent qualitative specificity, the TCE framework does not determine which of the fundamental

---

4. Frankel (1979), for example, found that an overshooting model of the DM/$ exchange rate fitted remarkably well in-sample during the mid-1970s. But when his sample was updated to include the late 1970s and early 1980s, parameter estimates became insignificant or significant and of the wrong sign (Frankel, 1983).

variables from the extant economic models should be included in individual and aggregate forecast functions. Moreover, it does not specify fully the updating of forecast functions, in that only qualitative restrictions are placed on which variables are added and dropped and how weights are updated.

The IKE framework extends the TCE framework by allowing for non-fundamental factors in the individual forecast functions in addition to "theories-consistent" fundamental variables, and as such inherits the indeterminacy of the TCE framework. However, we argue in the following pages that if the economist were to characterize *fully* individual expectations and their updating (i.e., in terms of fixed rules or their generalizations depending on variables or factors observable by other agents), then the resulting formulations would be, in general, inconsistent with the postulate of individual rationality. Consequently, as with TCE, we make use of assumptions implying *qualitative* restrictions *only* in modeling the updating of forecast functions. It is worth noting that the rationality of IKE functions runs counter to the general presumption that expectations based on departures from the REH are at best "boundedly rational," in the sense that they necessarily fall short of "full" rationality.

Beyond the promise to provide reasonable explanations of empirical regularities, especially in asset markets, and its compatibility with the postulate of individual rationality, the IKE framework appears to rest on solid and plausible behavioral foundations. The assumption that agents are endowed with imperfect knowledge appears to be uncontroversial. Moreover, the importance of psychological and sociological factors has been a constant theme in the pre-REH conceptions of the expectations formation process. Knight for example, in his classic book, introduced the distinction between measurable uncertainty—which he called "risk"—and "true uncertainty," which cannot "by any method be reduced to an objective, quantitatively determined probability" (Knight, 1921, p. 321). With his beauty contest example, Keynes underscored the role played by subjective guesses of the average opinion in the formation of individual expectations of asset prices. In modern terms, Keynes's position was that such subjective and psychological factors would preclude the precise modeling of individual expectations by an outside investigator, as well as by other agents. In laying the foundations of modern macroeconomic theory, Phelps argued that there was no presumption that an outside investigator could accurately model each individual's expectations on each island about "the world imagined" (Phelps, 1970, p. 22).

In addition to formulating an alternative expectational framework, we also reconsider the notion of equilibrium in monetary models, that is, uncovered interest rate parity (UIP). As is well known, this condition is difficult to justify on empirical and behavioral grounds (e.g., see Lewis, 1995, and Engel, 1996), which leads us to propose an alternative approach to modeling excess returns and equilibrium in the foreign exchange market. Our approach, which we refer to as uncertainty-adjusted uncovered interest rate parity (UAUIP), is based on a dynamic extension of myopic loss aversion originally proposed in a static context by Kahneman and Tversky (1979) and Benartzi and Thaler (1995).

The remainder of this chapter is structured as follows. In Section 2 we set out the DF model and examine its solution under the REH. In Section 3 we formulate our approach to the modeling of individual expectations in a world of imperfect knowledge and compare it with the REH, standard learning models, and the TCE approach. We show that IKE functions are consistent with individual rationality. In Section 4 we formulate our alternative notion of equilibrium in the foreign exchange market—UAUIP. In Sections 5 and 6 we examine the implications of our monetary model with IKE and UAUIP and show that with imperfect knowledge, the exchange rate can move persistently away from purchasing power parity (PPP) over an extended period of time. We also show, contrary to conventional wisdom, that persistent movements away from PPP do not require the presence of nonfundamental factors; rather such behavior is the consequence of imperfect knowledge.[5] We find that the qualitative assumptions on the updating of expectations needed for persistent movements away from PPP appear to be reasonable from a behavioral standpoint. In Section 7 we argue that in addition to explaining long swings, the monetary model with IKE and UAUIP sheds new light on many of the other puzzles in international finance. We focus on (1) the exchange rate disconnect puzzle, which includes the Meese-Rogoff forecasting puzzle, the Baxter-Stockman puzzle of the neutrality of exchange rate regimes, and the puzzle that empirical exchange rate models fit poorly in sample; (2) the excess returns puzzle; and (3) the PPP puzzle. Section 8 offers some concluding remarks on the implications of IKE for the practice of economics.

2. THE MODEL AND SOLUTION UNDER THE RATIONAL EXPECTATIONS HYPOTHESIS

The DF model consists of equilibrium conditions for the money and foreign exchange markets and an equation describing price adjustment. The model can be expressed as follows:

$$m_r = \gamma p_r + \phi y_r - \lambda i_r, \tag{1}$$

$$E(\dot{s}) - i_r = 0, \tag{2}$$

$$\dot{p}_r = \delta \left[\alpha \left(s - p_r - q_n \right) - \upsilon \left(i_r - i_n \right) \right] + \dot{\bar{p}}_r, \tag{3}$$

where s is the log level of the exchange rate (defined as the domestic currency price of foreign currency); m_r, p_r, and y_r denote log levels of relative (domestic minus foreign) money supplies, goods prices, and incomes, respectively; i_r is the level of relative short-run nominal interest rates; and q_n is the "natural" log level of the real exchange rate, which is assumed to be exogenous to the model and constant.[6] The variable i_n is the "natural" level of relative nominal interest rates,

---

5. In this sense the IKE approach to the foreign exchange market developed in this chapter is similar to the analysis of the boom and bust cycles in Soros (1987, 2000) and long swings in Schulmeister (1983, 1987), which emphasize that such asset price dynamics cannot be understood without imperfect knowledge and substitute qualitative assumptions about exchange rate expectations for the REH.

6. Both Dornbusch (1976) and Frankel (1979) set q_n to be consistent with absolute PPP, i.e., $q_n = 0$. Our assumption of symmetric money demand specifications in no way affects the main conclusions of this chapter and is done for convenience only. See Goldberg (1995, 2000) for the implications of relaxing this assumption in sticky-price monetary models.

which is equal to the steady-state level of the expected relative rate of inflation, π_r, plus the natural level of relative real interest rates, r_n. We assume that r_n is exogenous to the model and constant, and therefore set $r_n = 0$. The overbar denotes the hypothetical value associated with goods market clearing, that is, $\alpha\,(s - p_r - q_n) - v\,(i_r - i_n) = 0$.

Under the usual assumptions that expectations are formed according to the REH, that growth rates for relative money and income levels are constant, and that it is the stable arm that is relevant, the DF model in equations (1)–(3) implies the familiar equation for the expectation of $\dot{s}$:

$$E_{\mathrm{RE}}(\dot{s}) = \theta(\bar{s}_{\mathrm{RE}} - s) + \dot{\bar{s}}_{\mathrm{RE}},\tag{4}$$

where

$$\bar{s}_{\mathrm{RE}} = \frac{1}{\gamma}\,(m_r - \phi y_r) + \frac{\lambda}{\gamma}\pi_r + q_n\tag{5}$$

and $\pi_r = (1/\gamma)(\dot{m}_r - \phi\dot{y}_r)$; θ is the stable root of the system, redefined to be positive. The steady-state value of the exchange rate under RE in equation (5), $\bar{s}_{\mathrm{RE}}$, is the PPP nominal exchange rate associated with goods market clearing.

In this chapter we follow the DF model in using equations (1) and (3) to model money market equilibrium and price adjustment, respectively. But we depart from the basic DF framework in two important ways.

1. First, we replace expectations formed according to the REH with expectation functions consistent with our assumption that agents are endowed with imperfect knowledge. We refer to such expectations as *imperfect knowledge expectations* (IKE).
2. Second, we replace the assumption of risk-neutral agents and UIP in equation (2) with an equilibrium condition that arises from assuming imperfect knowledge and myopically loss-averse agents.

The remainder of this section discusses the main problems with the use of the REH as a model of individual expectations formation. In our view, these problems make the need to develop alternative models of expectations compelling. In the next section we develop our model of expectations formation in a world of imperfect knowledge. In Section 4 we present our alternative specification of equilibrium in the foreign exchange market.

The REH: Individual Rationality, Behavioral Foundations, and Explaining the Dynamics of Exchange Rates. The REH assumes that individual agents form their expectations on the basis of the *particular* (in this case DF) model being analyzed by the economist. Despite its apparent implausibility as a model of individual expectations formation, most economists believe that the REH has solved the problem of modeling expectations that has plagued economics at least since the time of Knight's (1921) important insights on the role of uncertainty in economic behavior. As we noted in the introduction, rather than being a model of individual expectations formation "rational expectations is an equilibrium concept" (Sargent, 1993, p. 23). This point can be alternatively stated as follows:

REMARK 1: *Even if we suppose that the individual agent is endowed with perfect quantitative knowledge of the structural parameters of the RE reduced form of the economist's model, it is not necessarily rational for this individual agent to form his expectations on the basis of such knowledge.*

Thus, the following additional assumptions are necessary for rational agents to form their expectations according to the standard REH in the context of the DF model:

1. "Agents [and the economist] have solved their scientific problems" (Sargent, 1993, p. 23), that is, the economist's model is the "true" model generating the observed time paths of the forecasted variables.
2. Each agent believes that all other agents have also solved their scientific problems (and thus are also endowed with such perfect knowledge) and form their forecasts based on the stable arm of the RE reduced form of the DF model.

Beyond the widespread, and as we have just suggested unfounded, belief that expectations based on the REH are necessarily consistent with individual rationality, many economists find the REH intuitively appealing. Sargent has recently summarized the apparent intuitive appeal of the REH as follows:

The idea of rational expectations is sometimes explained informally by saying that it reflects a process in which individuals are inspecting and altering their forecasting records in ways to eliminate systematic forecast errors. It is also sometimes said that to embody the idea that economists and the agents they are modelling should be placed on equal footing: the agents in the model should be able to forecast and profit-maximize and utility-maximize as well as . . . the econometrician who constructed the model. (Sargent, 1993, p. 21)

Sargent argues, however, that contrary to the general presumption among economists, the REH lacks plausible behavioral foundations. As he put it:

These ways of explaining things are suggestive, but misleading, because they make rational expectations sound less restrictive and more behavioral than it really is. . . . Rational expectations equilibrium . . . typically imputes to the people more knowledge about the system they are operating in than is available to the economists using the model to try to understand their behavior. (Sargent, 1993, p. 21)

Finally, many users of the RE approach would contend that as long as the RE-based models can be shown to deliver rigorous and testable explanations and sharp predictions, "the behavioral emptiness of rational expectations is neither a virtue nor a defect" (Sargent, 1993, p. 24). However, as we noted in the introduction, even if one accepts the Friedman criterion for evaluating models, monetary models under the REH fail on strictly positivist grounds. We show in this chapter that once the

REH is replaced by our IKE framework, the DF model regains surprising potential to explain the hitherto anomalous aspects of the floating rate experience.

3. IMPERFECT KNOWLEDGE AND THE FORMATION OF INDIVIDUAL EXPECTATIONS

In this section we develop an alternative specification of individual expectations formation that recognizes that individual agents, to paraphrase the above quotation from Sargent, have *not* "solved their scientific problems," and thus have to form their expectations on the basis of *imperfect knowledge.*

In order to motivate our formulation of IKE and relate it to other models of individual expectations in the extant literature as well as TCE, we use the following semireduced form equation readily implied by (1)–(3):

$$s = \beta_0 + \beta_1 m_r + \beta_2 y_r + \beta_3 E(\dot{s}) + \beta_4 E(\dot{s}) + \beta_5 \overline{E(\dot{s})}, \tag{6}$$

where the β's are constant coefficients and are given by: $\beta_0 = (q_n - (\upsilon/\alpha)i_n)$, $\beta_1 = 1/\gamma$, $\beta_2 = -\phi/\gamma$, $\beta_3 = (\upsilon/\alpha + \lambda/\gamma)$, $\beta_4 = 1/\delta\alpha$, $\beta_5 = -\beta_4$; $E(\dot{s})$ is the average expectation of the rate of change of the exchange rate, to be referred to as the *average opinion* of $\dot{s}$; $E(\dot{s})$ is the rate of change of the average opinion; and $\overline{E(\dot{s})}$ is the value of $E(\dot{s})$ implied by the model under the assumption of goods market clearing.

Equation (6) can be used to compare different approaches to individual expectations formation. We begin with a brief discussion of the learning models. Except for additional variables capturing the updating of the average opinion, the structure of equation (6) is analogous to the structure of the price equation of a simple cobweb model (and its extensions), which has been analyzed extensively in the recent learning literature.[7] Typically such learning models assume that all agents have *somehow* stumbled upon the economist's model, say the DF model, and *they all* use it in formulating their forecasts. For example, one popular class of learning models assumes that *all* individual agents use the least-squares regressions of s on the fundamental variables of *the economist's model*—in our case m_r, y_r, and π_r—to form and update their forecasts.[8] It should be emphasized that the assumption that all agents learn on the basis of the structure of the *common* model is highly restrictive and it is arguably as implausible as the key assumption of the RE approach that *all* individual agents form their expectations on the basis of the quantitative knowledge of the RE reduced form of the model being analyzed by the economist.[9] Moreover, such least-squares-based forecasts ignore

---

7. For early analysis of learning in the context of the cobweb models, see Frydman (1982) and Bray (1983). For more recent extensive analyses of learning models and references to the literature in the 1980s and 1990s, see Sargent (1999) and Evans and Honkapohja (2001).

8. Analogously, agents could obtain forecasts of $\dot{s}$ and their updates by running regressions based on the discrete-time version of the first derivative of (6). We also note that a similar analysis can be carried out if agents observe only noisy proxies of fundamental variables (see Evans and Honkapohja, 2001).

9. For an early analysis of this problem, see Phelps (1983) and more recently Woodford in this volume. Also see the above quotation from Sargent (1993) and the discussion therein.

the influence of the average opinion on the movement of s, and thus they are based on a misspecified model.

Studies of learning have generally ignored such misspecification on the grounds that if the learning model converges to the RE equilibrium, then the misspecification "vanishes" in the limit. Since convergence obtains only under very special conditions (see Evans and Honkapohja, 2001), this rationale is model specific, thereby limiting the general applicability of learning algorithms based on the common use of the misspecified structure of the model being analyzed by the economist. Furthermore, there is a large and important class of learning algorithms, the so-called "constant-gain algorithms," that has been specifically designed to "escape" convergence to the RE equilibrium (Sargent, 1999; Evans and Honkapohja, 2001). For this class of models, misspecification persists by design.

But even if the learning rule converges to the stable RE equilibrium, would it be *rational* for individual agents to ignore the misspecification of their forecast functions *during the transition to the RE equilibrium*? For example, could an individual agent improve his forecasts, if indeed all other agents use forecasts based on the least-squares regression?[10] We note that if all agents use the least-squares learning rule, then forecast errors will be correlated with the average opinion and its updating in equation (6) makes the exchange rate serially correlated, and this serial correlation can, in general, be exploited by *the individually rational* agents to improve their least-squares forecasts. Thus we are led to the following remark:

REMARK 2: *The key assumption of typical learning models that all agents learn on the basis of a common algorithm and the misspecified structure of the common model being analyzed by the economist is, in general, inconsistent with the postulate of individual rationality.*

The same argument also applies to other learning algorithms based on fixed rules and their extensions. For example, Evans and Honkapohja (2001, p. 359) have noted, in reference to the constant-gain learning algorithms, that "a possible drawback of these approaches is that . . . there are potential regularities in the forecast errors which could be exploited."

In contrast to the REH and the usual learning models discussed previously, the theories consistent expectations (TCE) approach *does not* assume that all agents base their forecasts on the common and specific model being analyzed by the economist. Instead, the TCE approach assumes that individual agents base their forecasts on the *qualitative* knowledge of the *plurality* of extant models relating endogenous variables to the exogenous (and predetermined) variables.[11] Such qualitative knowledge consists of the algebraic signs (but not true values) of the coefficients of explanatory variables that might be useful in forecasting as well as qualitative information about the long-run equilibrium levels of the endogenous variables. The question still remains, however, what is meant by

---

10. The following discussion summarizes the formal analysis in Frydman (1982).

11. The idea of TCE was first proposed in Frydman and Phelps (1990) and developed in the context of the monetary models of the exchange rate in Goldberg (1991) and Goldberg and Frydman (1993, 1996a).

"models"? For example, since s in equation (6) depends on the average opinion and its updating, the so-called infinite-regress problem has to be resolved for the relationship between the endogenous and exogenous (and predetermined) variables, referred to by the TCE approach, to be defined.[12]

In the early development of the TCE approach in the foreign exchange market, Goldberg and Frydman (1993, 1996a) explicitly defined "models" to be the *qualitative* structure of the *RE reduced forms* of the extant *plurality* of models.[13] To the extent that individual agents base their TCE forecasts on different models, TCE forecast errors observed by individual agents will be correlated with the variables used by *other* agents. Thus, rational agents would, in general, attempt to improve their forecasts by adding variables to and modifying weights in their forecast functions.[14] As long as agents attach weights consistent in sign with one of the extant models, the forecast functions resulting from such updating are still consistent with the TCE framework.

Such updating of the TCE functions, however, is not necessarily consistent with the postulate of individual rationality. As is the case for learning models discussed previously, suppose that the updating of TCE forecasts were to be characterized by a systematic rule based on factors observable by an outside investigator or other agents. Such systematic updating of the average opinion would, in general, lead to a systematic pattern in the forecast errors of the individual TCE functions, which would be correlated with the average opinion. Individually rational agents would then attempt to exploit information in their forecast errors, which would imply that they abandon the assumed fixed-updating rule.

Furthermore, if individual agents are assumed to be rational, they will, in general, recognize that the average opinion and its updating play an important role in forecasting the future course of endogenous variables [i.e., equation (6)]. Thus, in addition to fundamentals, the average opinion may also depend on nonfundamental sociological factors such as "market sentiment" as well as other atheoretical and idiosyncratic factors used by agents to proxy the average opinion in their *individually rational* attempts to improve their forecasts. In turn, as we show in Section 6, such forecasting behavior by individual agents implies that the process governing the behavior of the exchange rate is, in general, nonstationary and discontinuous, and this irregular behavior is indeed consistent with the use of subjective assessments and guesses by the individually rational agents in forming their forecasts. The following remark summarizes our discussion of the TCE functions.

---

12. For the seminal discussion of the infinite-regress problem see Keynes (1936). For more recent applications in the context of formal macroeconomic analysis see Phelps (1983) and Woodford in this volume.

13. The rationale for this way of circumventing the infinite-regress problem is that although agents do not know the quantitative structure of the RE reduced forms, the *qualitative* structure of the RE reduced forms is in principle available to them. This interpretation of the TCE was also implicitly adopted in later studies using TCE (see, e.g., Papell, 1997).

14. See Goldberg and Frydman (1996b, 2001) for empirical evidence suggesting that the reduced form of the monetary model depends on different sets of fundamental variables during different subperiods of the floating-rate regime.

REMARK 3: *Based on the foregoing arguments concerning the individual ratio-nality and behavioral plausibility of individual forecast functions, we do not fully characterize individual TCE forecast functions and their updating in terms of fixed rules based on factors observable by an outside investigator and other agents.*

We are now ready to formulate imperfect knowledge expectations (IKE), which we use to replace the REH-based forecast function in the context of the DF model. In general, IKE functions of $\dot{s}$ can take any form. However, to facilitate a comparison with the standard approach and make the analysis tractable, we use the qualitative structure of equation (4) as a simple parameterization of imperfect knowledge expectations of $\dot{s}$. Mirroring the analysis of Dornbusch (1976) for the REH case, we show in Section 5 that imperfect knowledge expectations based on equation (4) are model consistent in a qualitative sense: If individual agents use IKE forecast functions based on (4), then the differential equation describing the actual rate of change in the exchange rate, $\dot{s}$, implied by the model is of the same *qualitative* form.

We define the "medium run" to be the period of time required for prices p_r to converge to their goods market clearing level $\bar{p}_r$ in (3) and denote the medium-run level of the exchange rate by $\bar{s}_{\mathrm{IK}}$.[15] We assume that at each point in time the individual agent i forms an assessment of the medium-run level of the exchange rate, denoted by $\tilde{s}_i$, and the speed with which the exchange rate tends toward this medium-run level, denoted by $\tilde{\theta}_i$. Using the qualitative structure of (4), we can write the general structure of the individual forecast function, $E_i(\dot{s})$, as follows:

$$E_i(\dot{s}) = \tilde{\theta}_i(\tilde{s}_i - s) + \dot{\tilde{s}}_i, \quad i = 1 \ldots N, \tag{7}$$

where N denotes an arbitrarily large number of market participants. To aggregate (7) over all agents, we use weights, w_i, $i = 1 \ldots N$, equal to the proportions of the individual agents' wealth relative to the total wealth invested in the foreign exchange market.[16] This yields the following equation for the average (market) expectation function $E(\dot{s})$:

$$E(\dot{s}) = \tilde{\theta}\,(\tilde{s} - s) + \dot{\tilde{s}}, \tag{8}$$

where $\tilde{s}$ is the market's assessment of $\bar{s}_{\mathrm{IK}}$, and $\tilde{\theta}$ and $\dot{\tilde{s}}$ are weighted averages of individual assessments $\tilde{\theta}_i$ and $\tilde{s}_i$, respectively.[17]

By making progressively less restrictive assumptions on the individual assess-ments of $\tilde{\theta}_i$, $\tilde{s}_i$, and $\dot{\tilde{s}}_i$, we can represent each of the approaches to expectations

---

15. We will make clear below why we do not use the conventional term "long run" in describing goods market clearing levels.

16. In general, the w_i's may vary over time. However, to make the analysis tractable we assume that these weights are constants.

17. While the other aggregate variables are standard weighted averages, the expression for $\tilde{s}$ is given by $\tilde{s} = \sum_i W_i \tilde{s}_i$, where $0 < W_i = w_i \tilde{\theta}_i / \Sigma_i w_i \tilde{\theta}_i < 1$.

formation discussed above, from the REH to IKE, as particular representations of (7) and (8) in the context of the DF model. As already pointed out, these assumptions not only are progressively less restrictive and more plausible from a behavioral standpoint, they are also easier to reconcile with the postulate of individual rationality.

The standard REH approach is tantamount to the assumption that each individual agent uses the quantitative structure of the RE reduced form of the stable arm of the DF model. This implies that $\tilde{\theta}_i = \theta$, $\tilde{s}_i = \tilde{s}_{RE}$ and $\dot{\tilde{s}}_i = \dot{\tilde{s}}_{RE}$ and (7) as well as (8) become the same REH-based forecast function in (4).

Although the standard learning models relax the REH assumption that individual agents know the true values of the parameters, they retain the assumption that all agents learn and form their forecasts on the basis of the structure of the one common model, which in this case is the RE reduced form of the DF model. For example, these models assume that each agent obtains his estimates of $\tilde{s}_i$, $\tilde{s}$, and $\tilde{\theta}_i$ by running regressions based on the RE reduced form of the DF model in (5). As we argued earlier, the assumption that *all* agents use a fixed-learning rule, such as constant-gain or least-squares algorithms, is, in general, inconsistent with the postulate of individual rationality.

To form theories consistent expectations, agents select variables and the signs of the weights from any of the extant economic models of the exchange rate. Thus, the market's TCE assessment $\tilde{s}$ will depend solely on macroeconomic fundamentals, that is,

$$\tilde{s} = \tilde{\beta}'_f X_f, \tag{9}$$

where $\tilde{\beta}'_f$ and X_f denote the aggregates of the vectors of weights and fundamentals used by agents in forming their TCE forecasts.

It should be noted that despite its apparent qualitative specificity, *the TCE framework does not completely restrict the qualitative structure of the forecast function in (9)*. This is because individual agents may focus on only a subset of the extant models in any one time period, implying that the TCE approach does not restrict the aggregate forecast function in (9) to include any specific set of fundamental variables. Furthermore, no restrictions on the signs of the weights in the aggregate function in (9) are implied by the TCE approach in those cases in which the extant models imply conflicting predictions.

To examine the exchange rate dynamics implied by our model we need to address the issue of the updating of expectations. We refer to all forms of updating as *expectations dynamics*, which in our model can take two forms: (1) continuous adjustments of agents' assessments as captured by continuous movements in either $\tilde{\beta}'_f$ or X_f; and (2) discontinuous jumps in $\tilde{\beta}'_f$ and X_f. Differentiation of (9) implies the following expression for the continuous adjustment of $\tilde{s}$:

$$\dot{\tilde{s}} = \tilde{\beta}'_f \dot{X}_f + \dot{\tilde{\beta}}_f X_f. \tag{10}$$

Discontinuous updating of (9) may involve the dropping and adding of variables from and to individual forecast functions as well as discontinuous changes in agents' assessments of the levels and rates of change of the weights. For example, jumps in $\tilde{s}$, denoted by $\Delta\tilde{s}$, can be written as[18]

$$\Delta\tilde{s} = \Delta\tilde{\beta}'_f X_f + \tilde{\beta}'_f \Delta X_f. \tag{11}$$

It is clear from (10) and (11), that

REMARK 4: *The TCE assumption that agents base their forecasts on the qualitative knowledge of the extant models does not, in general, imply any specific rule for the updating of individual or aggregate TCE forecast functions.*

In light of the foregoing remark, we assume the following: *In updating their TCE functions, that is, in adding or dropping fundamental variables and updating weights, individual agents use qualitative information from the extant economic models, statistical procedures, and publicly available information, as well as subjective assessments and guesses concerning the movement of the average opinion. To characterize such updating, we make use of qualitative assumptions only, which we will elaborate upon in Section 6.*

We are now ready to formulate the IKE functions as extensions of the TCE functions. We assume that: *In addition to the TCE component, the IKE functions include atheoretical components based on technical trading and other rules of thumb as well as other subjective assessments concerning the movement of the average opinion.*

Denoting nonfundamental factors (atheoretical components) used by agents by X_{nf} and their weights by $\tilde{\beta}'_{nf}$, we can express the IKE assessment of $\tilde{s}$ as

$$\tilde{s} = \tilde{\beta}'_f X_f + \tilde{\beta}'_{nf} X_{nf}. \tag{12}$$

We note that since (12) allows for nonfundamental factors and variables from the plurality of models and does not restrict the values of the parameters, $\tilde{s}$ in (12) is obviously not an assessment of PPP and $\tilde{s}_{RE}$ in (5). This of course is consistent with the fact that, *even under the REH,* the reduced forms of extant models imply different values of the long-run steady-state level. For example, q_n in (5) could be a constant or a function of some fundamental variables, as in Hooper and Morton (1982). Hence, although the RE benchmark is well determined within the context of a particular model, the REH does not indicate to which RE long-run level agents should subscribe when the plurality of models is recognized.

We also note that although equation (4) has been shown to be useful for forecasting at long horizons (e.g., Mark, 1995; Mark and Sul, 2001), it is well known that it fails at the shorter forecasting horizons (e.g., Messe and Rogoff, 1983). Since movements of the exchange rate away from PPP levels tend to be large and persistent (e.g., Papell and Murray, 2001), there are clearly extended periods of time during which equation (4) would fail at short-term forecasting. Moreover, recent research suggests that nominal exchange rates converge to PPP

---

18. Note that the dropping and adding of variables to forecast functions is captured by jumps in $\tilde{\beta}'_f$ from nonzero to zero and from zero to nonzero values, respectively.

levels much more slowly than goods prices converge toward their steady-state values (Engel and Morley, 2001). This implies that the "medium-run" anchor, $\bar{s}_{IK}$, can be substantially different in general than $\bar{s}_{RE}$ and PPP. As we show in Section 5, the implications of our model under IKE are consistent with this empirical evidence.

4. IMPERFECT KNOWLEDGE EXPECTATIONS, MYOPIC LOSS AVERSION, AND UNCERTAINTY-ADJUSTED UNCOVERED INTEREST RATE PARITY

One of the basic assumptions of the monetary class of models is risk neutrality of agents, which, together with perfect capital mobility, implies the uncovered interest rate parity (UIP) condition in equation (2). As is well known, UIP is difficult to reconcile with the empirical record.[19] In this chapter, therefore, we propose an alternative approach to modeling equilibrium in the foreign exchange market—one that is based on imperfect knowledge expectations, heterogeneity of beliefs, and the prospect theory of Kahneman and Tversky (1979). We follow Benartzi and Thaler (1995) and assume that individual agents are "myopically loss averse": Agents are more sensitive to reductions than to increases in wealth, the effect of the level of wealth is assumed to be of second order, and agents monitor returns on their investments relatively frequently. However, we develop a dynamic version of myopic loss aversion that accounts for the evolution of agents' assessments of losses during episodes of persistent movements of the exchange rate from benchmark levels. Owing to space limitations, we provide in this section only an outline of our approach, which is developed fully in Frydman and Goldberg (2001, 2002).

Uncertainty-Adjusted Uncovered Interest Rate Parity. If individual agents are risk neutral, then their decision to buy or sell foreign exchange depends solely on their assessment of expected returns. Using (8) and (12), we can write the aggregate imperfect knowledge expectation of the excess return on foreign exchange, $E(R)$, as follows:

$$E(R) = \tilde{\theta}\,(\bar{s} - s) + \dot{\bar{s}} - i_r. \tag{13}$$

If borrowing constraints and transactions costs are small enough that the perfect capital mobility assumption applies, then equilibrium in the foreign exchange market requires $E(R)$ to equal zero, that is, it requires UIP. However, if individual agents are loss averse, their decision to buy or sell foreign exchange depends on their assessment of the expected utility of these decisions and, as we show shortly, equilibrium in the foreign exchange market with myopically loss-averse agents occurs at levels of the exchange rate at which UIP *does not* hold.

To formalize myopic loss aversion and the notion of equilibrium in the context of our model of the foreign exchange market, we assume that *at every point in time* an

---

19. See survey articles by Lewis (1995) and Engel (1996).

individual agent assigns nonzero probabilities, denoted by $\tilde{p}_{k,i}$, to a finite number, say K, of potential realizations of R from the set of all potential realizations $\mathcal{R}$.[20] If an individual agent buys (sells) foreign currency, then the potential losses on this speculation are all negative (positive) realizations of R. Thus, we define the set of potential losses and gains from buying or selling foreign currency as follows:

DEFINITION 5: *Let $\mathcal{R}^-$ and $\mathcal{R}^+$ be the sets of negative and positive realizations of R, respectively, so that $\mathcal{R} = \mathcal{R}^- \cup \mathcal{R}^+$. The set of potential losses from buying (selling) the foreign currency $\mathcal{R}_i^{LB}$ ($\mathcal{R}_i^{LS}$) is the subset of negative (positive) values of excess returns in $\mathcal{R}$, that is, $\mathcal{R}_i^{LB} = \mathcal{R}^-$ and $\mathcal{R}_i^{LS} = \mathcal{R}^+$. The complementary sets of potential gains from buying and selling the foreign currency, $\mathcal{R}_i^{GB}$ and $\mathcal{R}_i^{GS}$, respectively, are defined in an analogous manner, so that $\mathcal{R}_i^{GB} = \mathcal{R}^+$ and $\mathcal{R}_i^{GS} = \mathcal{R}^-$.*

To specify a decision rule for buying or selling foreign currency by myopically loss-averse agents, we use the following simple functional form for individual utility, which captures the loss aversion of the individual investor:

$$v_i(R) = \begin{cases} R & \text{if } R \in \mathcal{R}_i^{GB} \text{ or } \mathcal{R}_i^{GS} \\ \lambda_i R & \text{if } R \in \mathcal{R}_i^{LB} \text{ or } \mathcal{R}_i^{LS} \end{cases} \quad \lambda_i > 1, \tag{14}$$

where $v_i(R)$ is the utility function defined over potential gains and losses from buying or selling of foreign currency as given by Definition 5, and λ_i is the coefficient of loss aversion.[21]

Using expression (14) and Definition 5, we follow Benartzi and Thaler (1995) and define the "prospective excess return" of an individual agent facing payoffs $R_k \in \mathcal{R}$ from buying or selling foreign currency as follows:

$$E_i^B[v(R)] = \sum_{k \in K_i^{GB}} \tilde{p}_{k,i} R_k + \lambda_i \sum_{k \in K_i^{LB}} \tilde{p}_{k,i} R_k \equiv G_i^B + \lambda_i L_i^B, \tag{15}$$

$$E_i^S[v(R)] = \sum_{k \in K_i^{GS}} \tilde{p}_{k,i} R_k + \lambda_i \sum_{k \in K_i^{LS}} \tilde{p}_{k,i} R_k \equiv G_i^S + \lambda_i L_i^S, \tag{16}$$

where K_i^{GB} and K_i^{LB} (K_i^{GS} and K_i^{LS}) denote the sets of integers for realizations in the sets $\mathcal{R}_i^{GB}$ and $\mathcal{R}_i^{LB}$ ($\mathcal{R}_i^{GS}$ and $\mathcal{R}_i^{LS}$), respectively, and G_i^B and L_i^B (G_i^S and L_i^S) denote the (truncated) expected gain and loss of an individual agent i who buys (sells) foreign currency.[22]

---

20. If a particular realization $R_k \in R$ is not considered relevant for individual agent i, then the probability assigned by the agent to R_k is equal to zero.

21. This utility function has become the standard in the literature, e.g., see Benarzi and Thaler (1995) and Barberis et al. (2000). The literature has reported λ to be in excess of 2. See Benartzi and Thaler (1995) and references therein.

22. We refer to G_i and L_i as agent i's expected gain and loss, respectively, although strictly speaking G_i and L_i are the average of potential gains and losses based only on the truncated gain and loss parts of the set of individual probabilities, $\tilde{p}_{k,i}$, respectively.

REMARK 6: *We note that if market players are myopically loss averse, then they will attempt to buy foreign currency if $E_i^B[v(R)] > 0$ or sell foreign currency if $E_i^S[v(R)] < 0$. Furthermore, individual agents will not attempt to alter their holdings of the domestic and foreign currency assets if either $E_i^B[v(R)] \leq 0$ or $E_i^S[v(R)] \geq 0$.*

Definition 5 and expressions (15) and (16) readily imply that *only one* of the following four relationships can be satisfied for a given set of values of R_k and probabilities $\tilde{p}_{k,i}$, that is, $E_i^B[v(R)] > 0$, or $E_i^S[v(R)] < 0$, or $E_i^B[v(R)] = 0$ or $E_i^S[v(R)] = 0$. Thus, our decision rule based on the prospective excess return generates an unambiguous decision to sell, buy, or hold foreign currency.

Denoting by I^B and I^S the groups of agents for whom $E_i^B[v(R)] > 0$ (to be referred to as buyers) and $E_i^S[v(R)] < 0$ (to be referred to as sellers), respectively, the aggregate (market) prospective excess return is given by

$$E[v(R)] = \sum_{i \in I^B} w_i E_i^B[v(R)] + \sum_{i \in I^S} w_i E_i^S[v(R)] \equiv E^B[v(R)] + E^S[v(R)] \quad (17)$$

$$\equiv G^B + G^S + \lambda \left(L^B + L^S \right),$$

where G^B, L^B, G^S, and L^S are market averages of G_i^B, L_i^B, G_i^S, and L_i^S, respectively, and $\lambda = \sum \lambda_i [(\Sigma w_i G_i)/G]$, where to simplify the presentation, we assume that the averages of the parameters of loss aversion in the two groups of agents are the same and equal to some $\lambda > 1$.[23]

Given this notation, the aggregate (market) expected excess return is given by

$$E(R) = \sum_{i \in I^B} w_i \left(G_i^B + L_i^B \right) + \sum_{i \in I^S} w_i \left(G_i^S + L_i^S \right) \quad (18)$$

$$\equiv G^B + G^S + L^B + L^S \equiv G + L.$$

We are now ready to replace the UIP equilibrium condition with the following equilibrium condition for the foreign exchange market:

$$E[v(R)] = 0 \quad (19)$$

or equivalently, from (17) and (18),

$$E(R) = E(\dot{s}) - i_r = U, \quad (20)$$

where

$$U = E(R) - E[v(R)] = (1 - \lambda)L^B + (1 - \lambda)L^S \equiv (1 - \lambda)L \equiv U^B + U^S. \quad (21)$$

---

23. We note that an agent will sometimes belong to the group of buyers and at other times belong to the group of sellers, and thus it seems reasonable to suppose that the average λ is very similar for both groups. Also note that positive utility for sellers is represented as negative values of $E^S[v(R)]$.

Condition (19) simply states that equilibrium in the foreign exchange market requires an equality between the expected utilities of buyers from buying foreign currency and sellers from selling foreign currency. Equivalently, condition (20) and the definition of U in (21) imply that in equilibrium the aggregate expected excess return is the (linear transformation of) expected losses aggregated across all agents. Note that the two components of U in equation (21) are opposite in sign, reflecting the fact that losses for buyers and sellers are negative and positive realizations of R, respectively. Also note that U^B and U^S denote the premiums required by loss-averse buyers and sellers for buying and selling foreign currency, respectively. Thus, positive values of the aggregate U represent the *excess* premium required by loss-averse buyers of foreign currency. As we show in Frydman and Goldberg (2001, 2002) and argue subsequently, the market's excess loss aversion as captured by U is related in our model to imperfect knowledge and the associated uncertainty faced by individual agents when forecasting the future excess return. Thus, we refer to U as an aggregate *uncertainty premium* and the equilibrium conditions in (19) or (20) as *uncertainty-adjusted uncovered interest rate parity* (UAUIP).

The equilibrium condition obtained with myopic loss aversion in (19) works in a fashion similar to the case with risk neutrality, although here it is the prospective excess return that matters. Without a loss of generality, suppose that $E[v(R)]$ increases from a point of equilibrium, so that the weight of buyers of foreign currency becomes greater than the weight of sellers of foreign currency, that is, $E^B[v(R)] > -E^S[v(R)]$. This leads to incipient capital flows into foreign exchange and a bidding up of s. From (13), this increase in s leads to a decrease in $E_i(R)$ for all agents and, with a mild assumption on the degree of loss aversion, causes the weight of buyers of foreign exchange, that is, $E^B[v(R)]$, which is positive, to fall and the weight of sellers of foreign exchange, that is, $E^S[v(R)]$, which is negative, to rise.[24] Thus, the increase in s, *ceteris paribus*, leads to a fall in $E[v(R)]$. Equilibrium in the foreign exchange market is reestablished when the increase in s is sufficient to cause once again a balance between the weight of buyers and sellers, that is, when $E[v(R)] = 0$.

To make the equilibrium condition in equation (20) fully operational we have to develop a dynamic model for equilibrium movements in the aggregate uncertainty premium U. Given that changes in U depend on changes in the expected losses of buyers and sellers (i.e., L^B and L^S), we have to reformulate the prospect theory in the context of our model of foreign exchange and specify how changes in L^B and L^S are connected to changes in $\tilde{s}$, $\tilde{s}$, i_r, and s. To accomplish this we make three assumptions.

First, we assume that individual agents view the PPP exchange rate, $\tilde{s}^{PPP}$, as a benchmark level in that they use the gaps between $\tilde{s}$ and $\tilde{s}^{PPP}$ and s and $\tilde{s}^{PPP}$ in assessing the potential losses as follows:

---

24. Assuming that movements in $E_i(R)$ and $E_i[v(R)]$ are positively related implies that revisions of $E_i(R)$ lead to speculation in the direction consistent with the direction of movement of $E_i(R)$. See Goldberg and Frydman (2001) for a more complete discussion.

- *Gap Effect:* An increase in $\widetilde{gap}^{\text{PPP}}$ leads individual buyers (sellers) to revise upward (downward) the absolute value of their assessments of the potential losses, where $\widetilde{gap}^{\text{PPP}} \equiv (1 - a)(\tilde{s} - \tilde{s}^{\text{PPP}}) + a(s - \tilde{s}^{\text{PPP}})$.

Justification for this assumption comes from recognizing that most floating-rate regimes operate informally as wide target zones (e.g., see Fischer, 2001), that is, policy officials become concerned when departures from PPP become "too" large and react by actively intervening in the foreign exchange market (e.g., the coordinated intervention by central banks aimed at bringing down U.S. dollar rates in 1985, yen rates in mid-1995, and the euro/\$ rate in the fall of 2000) and, in some cases, by changing the policy environment (e.g., the Plaza accord in September 1985). Justification also comes from the fact that floating exchange rates have indeed exhibited long swings that revolve around PPP levels.[25] It is important to note that we use PPP as a benchmark for concreteness.[26] For our purposes, what is important is that agents have in mind some long-run benchmark level in the updating of their assessments of potential losses.[27]

Since individual agents are assumed to be myopically loss averse and to understand that their expectations are based on imperfect knowledge, it seems reasonable to assume the following size and trend effects on expected losses (see Frydman and Goldberg, 2001, for a complete analysis):

- *Size Effect:* An increase (decrease) in the absolute value of $E(R)$ leads to an increase (decrease) in the absolute value of agents' assessments of the potential losses.
- *Trend Effect:* If s increases, then buyers (sellers) become more (less) confident in their original decisions to buy (sell) and reduce (increase) their assessments of the potential losses. Conversely for decreases in s.

The foregoing three effects on expected losses, together with two mild distributional assumptions, lead to the following equation for jumps in the equilibrium aggregate uncertainty premium:

$$U^+ = U_0 + \omega \left[\tilde{\theta} \left(\tilde{s}^- - \tilde{s}_0 \right) + \left(\dot{\tilde{s}}^- - \dot{\tilde{s}}_0 \right) - \left(i_r^- - i_{r_0} \right) \right], \tag{22}$$

where a subscript 0 denotes an initial value prior to any jump in $\tilde{s}$, $\dot{\tilde{s}}$, or i_r, a superscript minus sign denotes a value *prior to* the impact effect on s, and U^+ denotes the value of U subsequent to the impact effect on s; ω is an adjustment parameter that depends on the relative magnitudes of the three effects on expected

---

25. For evidence that PPP does serve as a long-run anchor, see the cointegration studies of Frankel and Rose (1995), Juselius (1995), and Papell (1997), among others, as well as the studies on the long-horizon predictability of PPP and monetary fundamentals cited earlier.

26. We note that whether PPP holds in some long-run sense is still an open issue. See Froot and Rogoff (1995) and references therein.

27. Our use of benchmark levels coordinating the market's assessment of potential losses is reminiscent of the role of the "safe" rate of interest in Keynes's (1936) development of liquidity preference.

losses. When a jump in $\tilde{s}$, $\dot{\tilde{s}}$, or i_r causes s to move away from (toward) PPP, then ω is between 0 and 1 (-1 and 0).

To see how the jump model for U works, consider some subperiod of time during which the exchange rate lies above its PPP level and the equilibrium U is positive. A positive aggregate uncertainty premium implies that the level of the exchange rate is less than what is required for UIP to hold, s^{UIP}. This occurs because buyers as a group are unwilling to bid s all the way up to s^{UIP} owing to their greater sensitivity to the potential losses. Suppose that buyers and sellers revise $\tilde{s}$ upward, from $\tilde{s}_0$ to $\tilde{s}^-$, causing an incipient capital flow into foreign currency and a consequent rise in s as the weight of buyers initially dominates. Since the movements of $\tilde{s}$ and s are further away from PPP, buyers (sellers) raise (lower) their assessments of the potential losses, and both of these effects lead to a greater excess of L^B over L^s, causing U to rise as part of the adjustment to equilibrium, that is, ω is between 0 and 1. With a higher equilibrium U, the gap between s and s^{UIP} becomes larger, as buyers relative to sellers require greater compensation for buying foreign exchange. This implies that the jump in s, which is given by the following equation, will be less than one-for-one:

$$s^+ = s_0 + (1 - \omega)\left[(\tilde{s}^- - \tilde{s}_0) + \frac{1}{\bar{\theta}}(\dot{\tilde{s}}^- - \dot{\tilde{s}}_0) - \frac{1}{\bar{\theta}}(i_r^- - i_{r_0})\right]. \quad (23)$$

This result, that the movement of $\tilde{s}$ away from PPP is associated with a less than one-for-one movement in s and a higher equilibrium U, is reminiscent of the assumption of imperfect capital mobility. There is, however, a key difference between the implications of imperfect capital mobility and those of our dynamic model of myopic loss aversion. We show in Frydman and Goldberg (2002) that with the latter, one-time jumps in $E(\dot{s})$ that cause $E(R)$ to switch sign can lead to changes in the sign of the equilibrium U, whereas such sign switching is not possible with imperfect capital mobility alone. This result is important because it is difficult to reconcile standard theories of a risk premium with the frequent sign reversals in expected excess returns that have been observed during floating rate periods (e.g., see Lewis, 1995; Mark and Wu, 1998).

As for equilibrium movements of U arising from continuous movements of $\tilde{s}$ and s, our dynamic model for U can be written as the following log-linear function of $\widetilde{gap}^{\text{PPP}}$:

$$U = \sigma \left|\widetilde{gap}^{\text{PPP}}\right| + d = \sigma\left|(1 - a)(\tilde{s} - \tilde{s}^{\text{PPP}}) + a(s - \tilde{s}^{\text{PPP}})\right| + d, \quad (24)$$

where σ is a slope parameter measuring the sensitivity of the equilibrium U to continuous changes in the absolute value of the PPP gap and d is a constant scaling factor. It is reasonable to assume that $|\sigma| < \bar{\theta}$, which ensures that the impact of a given movement of $\tilde{s}$ influences $E[v(R)]$ in the same direction. We show in the next section that this assumption also ensures stability of the model. In Frydman and Goldberg (2001) and in Section 5 below, we examine the case in which $sign(\sigma) = sign(U)$, that is, a movement of the exchange rate away from PPP is associated with a growing equilibrium uncertainty premium.

5. THE SOLUTION OF THE MODEL WITH CONTINUOUS UPDATING OF IMPERFECT KNOWLEDGE EXPECTATIONS

In this section we begin to explore the implications of our monetary model consisting of equations (1) and (3), imperfect knowledge expectations, as characterized by (8) and (12), and uncertainty-adjusted uncovered interest rate parity, as formalized in equations (20), (22), and (24). The dynamics of the exchange rate also depends on the updating of expectations, which we called in Section 3 *expectations dynamics*. As discussed in Section 3, expectations dynamics, in general, can take two forms in the model: It can involve either one-time jumps in $\tilde{s}$ and/or $\dot{\tilde{s}}$ [see equation (11)] or continuous movements of $\tilde{s}$ over time governed by the rate $\dot{\tilde{s}}$ [see equation (10)]. In this section, we allow *only* for the continuous updating of IKE functions. For simplicity we assume that $\dot{\tilde{s}}$ is a constant. This assumption is relatively mild because we allow for jumps in $\tilde{s}$ and $\dot{\tilde{s}}$ in the next section. We also assume for tractability reasons that $a = 0$ in the definition of the $\widetilde{gap}^{\text{PPP}}$ in equation (24).[28]

In solving the model we make use of the conventional assumptions of constant growth rates for money and income levels. The solution consists of equations describing the time paths of the exchange rate, relative goods prices, relative interest rates, and, by implication, the real exchange rate. The details are given in Frydman and Goldberg (2001). To save space we present here only the solutions for the exchange rate and relative goods prices. Dropping the subscript IK from the goods market–clearing solutions for notational convenience, these solutions are as follows:

$$s(t) = c_1 e^{-\theta t} + \bar{s}, \tag{25}$$

$$p_r(t) = c_{2_j} e^{-\theta t} + \bar{p}_r, \tag{26}$$

where

$$\theta = \frac{\delta[\alpha\gamma + (\tilde{\theta} - \tilde{\sigma})\alpha\lambda + \nu\gamma\tilde{\theta}]}{\lambda\tilde{\theta}}, \tag{27}$$

$$\bar{s} = \bar{s}^* + \frac{(\nu\gamma + \alpha\lambda)(\tilde{\theta} - \tilde{\sigma}D)}{G}(\tilde{s} - \bar{s}^*) + \frac{\nu\gamma}{G}(\dot{\tilde{s}} - \tilde{\pi}_r) + \frac{\nu\gamma}{G}(\dot{\tilde{s}} - \pi^*)$$
$$+ \frac{\tilde{\sigma}D\nu\lambda}{G}(\tilde{\pi}_r - \pi_r^*) + \frac{\tilde{\sigma}D(\nu\gamma + \alpha\lambda)}{G}(\tilde{q}_n - q_n) - \frac{\nu\gamma + \alpha\lambda}{G}d, \tag{28}$$

$$\bar{p} = \bar{p}_r^* + \frac{\alpha\lambda(\tilde{\theta} - \tilde{\sigma}D)}{G}(\tilde{s} - \bar{s}^*) + \frac{\alpha\lambda}{G}(\dot{\tilde{s}} - \pi_r^*) + \frac{\tilde{\theta}\nu\lambda}{G}(\tilde{\pi}_r - \pi_r^*)$$
$$+ \frac{\tilde{\sigma}D\alpha\lambda}{G}(\tilde{q}_n - q_n) - \frac{\alpha\lambda}{G}d, \tag{29}$$

---

28. This assumption greatly simplifies the solution of the model. Using $s - \bar{s}^{\text{PPP}}$ leaves the main results unchanged.

$$G = \alpha\gamma + \alpha\lambda \left(\tilde{\theta} - \tilde{\sigma}D\right) + \tilde{\theta}v\gamma, \tag{30}$$

and the overbar and asterisk denote, respectively, the goods market–clearing level and the level that is obtained in the DF model *under REH*, that is,

$$\bar{s}^* = \frac{1}{\gamma}(m_r - \phi y_r) + \frac{\lambda}{\gamma}\pi_r + q_n, \quad \bar{p}_r^* = \frac{1}{\gamma}(m_r - \phi y_r) + \frac{\lambda}{\gamma}\pi_r$$

and

$$\pi_r^* = \frac{1}{\gamma}(\dot{m}_r - \phi\dot{y}_r),$$

and $-\theta$ is the root of the system. The variable D captures our assumption that the equation for U in (24) contains an absolute-value function: $D = 1$ when $\tilde{s} - \tilde{s}^{\mathrm{PPP}} > 0$ and $D = -1$ when $\tilde{s} - \tilde{s}^{\mathrm{PPP}} < 0$.

The continuous time paths in (25) and (26) are standard in form, in that they depend on two terms: a short-run adjustment term and a corresponding medium-run level.[29] Given that $\tilde{\theta} > \tilde{\sigma}$ (see the preceding section), the root of the system, $-\theta$, is unambiguously negative, implying that the reduced-form time path for the exchange rate in (25) can be rewritten as follows:

$$\dot{s} = \theta\left(\bar{s} - s\right) + \dot{\bar{s}}. \tag{31}$$

Equation (31) shows that if all agents use the functional form of the expectations function in (8), then it is "qualitatively consistent" for them to do so. This leads to the following remark:

REMARK 7: *Imperfect knowledge expectations based on (8) and (12) are model consistent in a qualitative sense, in that the functional form of agents' expectations functions is the same as the functional form of the differential equation describing the actual movement of the exchange rate in equation (31).*

The solution presented in equations (25) through (30) shows that the time paths of s and p_r depend not only on the underlying structural parameters of the economy but also on the assessments of agents, as captured by $\tilde{s}, \dot{\tilde{s}}, \tilde{\pi}_r, \tilde{q}_n, \tilde{\theta},$ and $\tilde{\sigma}$. This general structure allows for the easy comparison of the implications of alternative models of expectations for the time paths of s and p_r. As in Section 2, we will compare the implications of various models of expectations by making progressively less restrictive assumptions on the individual assessments appearing in (25) through (30). As already pointed out, these assumptions not only are

---

29. We use the term medium-run level instead of the more common terms long-run or steady-state level because the equilibrium levels in equations (28) and (29) will jump on impact if agents revise their assessments of $\tilde{s}$ and/or $\dot{\tilde{s}}$ in a discontinuous way. This implies that, in general, the endogenous variables never fully adjust to the medium-run levels. See the next section for a dicussion of the solution allowing for jumps in agents' imperfect knowledge expectations.

progressively less restrictive and more plausible from a behavioral standpoint, they are also easier to reconcile with the postulate of individual rationality.

We begin with the REH. Under the REH and UIP, $\tilde{s} = \tilde{s}^*$, $\dot{\tilde{s}} = \pi_r^* = \tilde{\pi}_r$, $\tilde{q}_n = q_n$, $\tilde{\sigma} = d = 0$, and the medium-run solutions in (28) and (29) collapse to the long-run solutions obtained from the standard DF model in (4). However, as is well known (e.g., see Dornbusch and Frankel, 1988):

REMARK 8: *The time path of the exchange rate implied by the standard DF model under the REH is very difficult to reconcile with the large and persistent movements of the exchange rate away from PPP that have characterized floating-rate regimes.*

We now deal with the implications of the other models of expectations—those based on standard learning algorithms, TCE, and IKE—for large and persistent movements of the exchange rate away from PPP. We first discuss the implications of departing from the REH in general and then examine the three specific cases.

In contrast to the RE solution, equations (28) and (29) reveal that without the REH, the goods market clearing solutions are in general inconsistent with PPP. This can be seen by deriving the goods market–clearing level of the real exchange rate, $\bar{q} = \bar{s} - \bar{p}$, and noting that $\bar{q}$ is in general *not equal* to its PPP level q_n. Furthermore, as we show subsequently, without the REH, the medium-run anchor toward which the exchange rate tends, $\bar{s}$, can itself move persistently either away from or toward PPP levels. This result is summarized in the following proposition:

PROPOSITION 9: *Suppose that agents update their forecast functions in a continuous manner so that jumps in $\tilde{s}$ and $\dot{\tilde{s}}$ do not occur. As long as $\dot{\tilde{s}} \neq \dot{\tilde{s}}^*$, the time path of $\bar{s}$ will involve a persistent movement either away from or toward the time path of the medium-run level of the actual PPP exchange rate, $\bar{s}^{\text{PPP}} = \bar{p}_r + q_n$. If initially the time path of $\bar{s}$ involves a persistent movement toward PPP levels, then eventually the time path of $\bar{s}$ will shoot through the time path of $\bar{s}^{\text{PPP}}$ and begin moving away from PPP levels from the other side.*[30]

The proof of this proposition, presented in Frydman and Goldberg (2001), is based on the following relationship between $\dot{\bar{s}}$ and $\dot{\bar{s}}^{\text{PPP}}$:

$$\dot{\bar{s}} - \dot{\bar{s}}^{\text{PPP}} = \frac{\nu\gamma(\tilde{\theta} - \tilde{\sigma}D)}{G}\left(\dot{\tilde{s}} - \dot{\tilde{s}}^*\right). \tag{32}$$

Equation (32) reveals that the direction of movement of the medium-run anchor, $\bar{s}$, relative to $\bar{s}^{\text{PPP}}$, depends on the relationship between the expectations dynamics, as captured by $\dot{\tilde{s}}$, and the rate of change of RE fundamentals, $\dot{\tilde{s}}^*$. In general, without the REH, $\dot{\tilde{s}} \neq \dot{\tilde{s}}^*$, and given that $\dot{\tilde{s}}$ and $\dot{\tilde{s}}^*$ are both constant with continuous updating, a particular movement of $\bar{s}$ relative to $\bar{s}^{\text{PPP}}$ will persist for as long as updating is

---

30. Note that this and other propositions in this section assume that expectations dynamics involves continuous updating *only*. If expectations dynamics involves jumps, as we show in the next section, then the above solution of the model has to be modified and additional conditions are required to generate persistent movements of the exchange rate away from or toward PPP.

continuous. The movement of $\bar{s}$ either away from or toward PPP (with a shooting through) readily follows.

The economic intuition behind Proposition 9 is as follows. Exchange rate expectations matter for the exchange rate, through the UAUIP condition in (20), leading to medium-run solutions in (22) and (24) that depend on the aggregate expectation $\bar{s}$. With imperfect knowledge, the level of this market expectation is not constrained to be consistent with PPP, as is the case under the REH. In fact, as we point out subsequently, $\bar{s}$ can depend *solely* on macroeconomic fundamentals and yet imply the expectation of a persistent movement of s away from PPP. Moreover, with imperfect knowledge, the rate at which the aggregate expectation changes over time, $\dot{\bar{s}}$, which depends on how agents update their assessments of $\bar{s}$, is not constrained to maintain a constant real exchange rate, as is the case with the REH. In general, the magnitude of $\dot{\bar{s}}$ will imply a persistent movement of $\bar{s}$ either away from or toward PPP levels.

According to equations (25) and (26), the time paths of s and p depend on excess demand terms, in addition to the medium-run anchors $\bar{s}$ and $\bar{p}_r$. Thus, whether the exchange rate moves away from or toward actual PPP levels depends partly on the magnitudes of these excess demand terms. The following proposition, proved in Frydman and Goldberg (2001), shows that whenever $\bar{s}$ moves away from (toward) its PPP level, $\bar{s}^{PPP}$, s moves away from (toward) its PPP level, s^{PPP}, at least after an initial transition period:

PROPOSITION 10: *If the time paths of $s - s^{PPP}$ and $\bar{s} - \bar{s}^{PPP}$ move in the same direction initially, then these time paths will both move monotonically in the same direction for as long as updating is continuous, that is, a persistent movement of $\bar{s}$ either away from or toward $\bar{s}^{PPP}$ will be matched by a similar movement of s either away from or toward s^{PPP}, and if the time path of $\bar{s}$ shoots through its PPP level, then s, too, will shoot through its PPP level and move away from the other side. If the time paths of $s - s^{PPP}$ and $\bar{s} - \bar{s}^{PPP}$ move in opposite directions initially, then these time paths will eventually move in the same direction.*[31]

We now use the foregoing results to examine the implications of the three non-REH-based expectations models for persistent movements of the exchange rate away from PPP. As discussed in Section 3, the standard learning algorithms are, in general, inconsistent with individual rationality. But suppose that the investigator was prepared to sidestep this problem and assume that the so-called "boundedly rational" agents use one of the standard learning algorithms. The question is: Can such learning rules explain long-swings in the exchange rate? If the learning algorithms converge to the RE equilibrium, then in the limit such algorithms encounter the same difficulties as those mentioned above for REH-based expectations in explaining large and persistent movements in s.

During learning, $\bar{s} \neq \bar{s}^*$ in general. According to Proposition 10, a persistent movement of s away from PPP requires that the sign of (the mean of) $\bar{s} - \bar{s}$ remains the same throughout learning. Proposition 10, however, has been established under

---

31. We also prove in Frydman and Goldberg (2001) that analogous conclusions also hold when the time path of $\bar{s}$ intersects the time path of $\bar{s}^{PPP}$, causing a switch in the variable D.

the simplifying assumption that $\tilde{s}$ is constant and thus does not apply to the standard learning models, which in general allow for $\dot{\tilde{s}} \neq 0$. Thus, the question of whether the standard learning models can generate persistent movements of s away from PPP within the context of the DF model remains open. We note, however, that for the standard learning models to provide a reasonable explanation of exchange rate dynamics, they would need to explain not only persistent movements away from PPP for extended time periods but also the turnarounds, persistent countermovements back, and the phenomenon of shooting through. Furthermore, it appears implausible that standard learning models, in which the learning process is aimed at learning the RE equilibrium (and thus the PPP) level, would be consistent with such long-swings behavior of the exchange rate away from PPP.[32]

In contrast to the REH and the doubts concerning standard learning models, the DF model under TCE or IKE and continuous updating readily implies the possibility of large and persistent movements of s away from PPP. Moreover, contrary to the usual presumption, such movements away do not require that agents include nonfundamental factors in their forecast functions. To show this we assume that agents use TCE functions. Since TCE functions are formed on the basis of imperfect knowledge, in general, $\tilde{s} \neq \tilde{s}^*$. Moreover, as long as we do not allow for jumps in $\tilde{s}$, as is the case in this section, the sign of $\tilde{s} - \bar{s}$ necessarily remains *constant*. Since TCE functions are functions of macroeconomic fundamental variables *only*, this argument leads to the following proposition, further discussed and proved in Frydman and Goldberg (2001):

PROPOSITION 11: *A persistent movement of s away from its PPP level can arise even if the exchange rate forecasts of all agents are based solely on macroeconomic fundamental variables.*

Since TCE is a special case of IKE, the foregoing argument also implies the following corollary to Proposition 11, proved in Frydman and Goldberg (2001):

COROLLARY 12: *Suppose that individual agents possess imperfect knowledge expectations and the updating of their IKE functions is continuous (i.e., jumps are ruled out by assumption). Then the exchange rate will, in general, move persistently either away from or toward its PPP level for as long as updating remains continuous; and if the movement is toward PPP, then s will shoot through PPP and move away from the other side.*

Thus, with continuous updating and TCE or IKE, the DF model is consistent with persistent movements of the exchange rate away from PPP, as well as with the shooting through of PPP levels. However, as with the standard learning models, the TCE and IKE frameworks have to explain not only persistent movements away and shooting through, but also the turnarounds and persistent countermovements back. For this we must extend our analysis to allow for discontinuous updating of (i.e., jumps in) individual expectations functions.

---

32. There are other possibilities not considered in this chapter that would preserve the REH, including rational bubbles (e.g., see Blanchard and Watson, 1982), rational learning about shifts in the policy environment (e.g., Lewis, 1989), and sunspots and multiple equilibria (e.g., Farmer, 1999, chap. 10). It is unclear how these other approaches can explain the entire character of the long-swings phenomenon.

6. DISCONTINUOUS UPDATING OF IMPERFECT KNOWLEDGE EXPECTATIONS AND PERSISTENT MOVEMENTS AWAY FROM PURCHASING POWER PARITY

In this section we allow for the updating of forecast functions to involve jumps in $\tilde{s}$ and $\dot{\tilde{s}}$ in addition to continuous movements of $\tilde{s}$ over time. Since the REH and standard learning models do not admit such updating (independently of policy changes), we focus only on the updating of TCE and IKE functions. Extending our analysis to allow for such jumps is important for three reasons. First, from an empirical standpoint, a turnaround in the time path of the exchange rate (i.e., a switch from a persistent movement away to a persistent movement back) requires jumps in expectations functions within the context of our modified monetary model; with only continuous updating and a fixed $\tilde{s}$ and $\tilde{s}^*$, the exchange rate would diverge from PPP without bound.

A second reason for allowing expectations dynamics to involve jumps is that it is reasonable to suppose from a behavioral standpoint that agents update their expectations functions both continuously and discontinuously in a world of imperfect knowledge. Finally, allowing for only continuous updating with a constant $\tilde{s}$ (and thus a fixed rule governing the updating of expectations) suffers from the same problem as the standard learning models: In general, *rational* agents will not follow fixed rules for updating their expectations in a world of imperfect knowledge, that is, agents' expectations dynamics will involve discontinuous jumps in $\tilde{s}$ and $\dot{\tilde{s}}$.

Our analysis allows for discontinuous movements arising from either shifts in the policy environment or from expectational factors that are independent of policy changes. Allowing for the latter is important on both theoretical and empirical grounds. Theoretically, Phelps (1983) (and more recently Woodford in this volume) has pointed out that shifts in policy inevitably bring back the so-called average opinion problem, and agents' attempts to assess the average opinion during transition gives rise to changes in expectations that are at least partly independent of changes in policy rules. Empirically, the record on exchange rate models includes temporal instability of a striking form: Different sets of macroeconomic fundamentals seem to matter for exchange rates during different subperiods of floating.[33] Although shifts in policy lead to temporal instability of reduced forms under the REH (Lucas, 1976), it is difficult to reconcile the standard RE approach with the discontinuous and apparently irregular nature of the temporal instability that seems to appear in the foreign exchange market.[34]

With discontinuous updating, the solutions of the preceding section no longer fully characterize the time paths of the exchange rate and relative goods prices. Instead, these solutions describe a subperiod of time during which expectations

---

33. Meese has observed that "A perusal of the published empirical work reveals that the set of explanatory variables most correlated with exchange rate movements depends on the sample period analyzed" (Meese, 1990, p. 126). For tests of and evidence on such temporal instability see Goldberg and Frydman (1996b, 2001).

34. We should also note that there is considerable controversy over whether the Lucas critique is important on purely empirical grounds (see Ericsson and Irons, 1995, and Linde, 2001, and references therein).

dynamics involves only continuous movements in the parameters of agents' forecasting functions. Each time updating is associated with a jump in $\tilde{s}$ and $\check{s}$, it marks
the beginning of a new subperiod of time characterized by new continuous time
paths for the endogenous variables. Thus, Proposition 11 and Corollary 12 of the
preceding section, which establish that the exchange will move persistently either
away from or toward PPP levels with TCE and IKE, apply only to a particular
subperiod.

Additional conditions on the expectations dynamics leading from one subperiod
to the next are required in order to determine whether a particular movement away
from or toward PPP during one subperiod will continue over successive subperiods.
The TCE and IKE approaches allow, in general, for qualitative assumptions *only*
on the discontinuous updating of expectations. As discussed in Section 3, this
follows from the rationality and behavioral points of view. Moreover, from an
empirical standpoint, the finding that the temporal instability of exchange rate
models occurs at irregular intervals (see Goldberg and Frydman, 1996a,b, 2001)
suggests that discontinuous updating of expectations cannot be captured by a fixed
rule or its generalizations depending on the variables observable by the economist
or other agents.

With qualitative assumptions on expectations dynamics, our model produces
only qualitative implications about the movements of the endogenous variables.
The question we ask is whether there exist reasonable qualitative assumptions on
expectations dynamics that, within the context of our modified monetary model,
lead to exchange rate dynamics matching up with the empirical record. To guide
us in evaluating various qualitative assumptions, we make use of some findings
from the literature on behavioral economics.

A complete analysis of how our monetary model, together with additional qualitative assumptions on expectations dynamics, can produce long swings in the
exchange rate (consisting of persistent movements away, turnarounds, countermovements back, and the phenomenon of shooting through) is clearly beyond
the scope of this chapter. In this section we focus on persistent movements of
the exchange rate away from PPP using a particular example examined fully in
Frydman and Goldberg (2001). Our purpose here is to provide an example and
sketch the potential of our approach for explaining the long-swings phenomenon
more generally. To this end, we state the qualitative conditions on the discontinuous
updating of expectations that are required for persistent movements over successive subperiods and then examine briefly whether these conditions are reasonable
from a behavioral standpoint.

The solution of the model with discontinuous updating can be expressed as the
following piecewise continuous function:

$$z(t) = \sum_j I_j z_j(t), \tag{33}$$

where $z(t)$ is a column vector of the time paths of s and p_r; $z_j(t) = [s_j(t)$
$p_{r_j}(t)]$ is a column vector of continuous time paths for s and p_r over subperiod j,
given by equations (25) and (26), where subperiod j is defined as the time period

$t_j \leq t < t_{j+1}$; and I_j is a 2×2 diagonal matrix, where each element along the diagonal is equal to 1 for all $t_j \leq t < t_{j+1}$ and 0 otherwise. The discontinuous jumps between the pieces or subperiods in (33) arising from jumps in $\tilde{s}$ and/or $\bar{s}$ are given by equation (23).

We are now ready to examine the implications of our model for persistent movements of the exchange rate away from PPP over successive subperiods. Propositions 9 and 10 have already established that s and $\bar{s}$ move either away from or toward PPP in any subperiod j. Without a loss of generality, consider some subperiod j during which both s_j and $\bar{s}_j$ move away from their PPP levels from above, that is, both s_j and $\bar{s}_j$ lie above PPP and both are rising throughout subperiod j. This implies $\tilde{s}_j > \bar{s}^*$according to equation (32).

The length of time that subperiod j will endure and whether successive subperiods will also involve a rising s away from PPP depends on the character of the expectations dynamics leading from one subperiod of time to the next. Since the purpose of this chapter is to provide a simple example rather than a complete analysis of long swings, we make use of one simplifying assumption on the expectations dynamics: namely, subperiod j is assumed to involve an $E(R) > 0$. We show in Frydman and Goldberg (2001) that with this assumption, the qualitative conditions on the discontinuous updating of expectations can be summarized in the following proposition:

PROPOSITION 13: *The persistent movement of the exchange rate away from PPP during subperiod j will be preserved over successive subperiods as long as the jumps in $\tilde{s}$ and $\bar{s}$ either reinforce the movement away or are not "too large." The range over which expectations dynamics are reinforcing or "not too" large increases as the degree of exchange rate pass-through decreases and as the degree to which the PPP gap matters as a benchmark increases.*[35]

Our approach would be incomplete without asking whether these qualitative assumptions on expectations dynamics make sense from an empirical and behavioral standpoint. The answer here depends on how buyers and sellers revise their methods and models over time. As we argued in Section 3, it is reasonable to suppose in a world of imperfect knowledge and loss aversion that the trend in the exchange rate plays an important role for agents' assessments of the potential gains and losses. Thus, if the trend in the exchange rate involves a movement away from PPP from above and the policy environment is unchanged, then there is an inherent bias for expectations dynamics to involve reinforcing changes in $\tilde{s}$ and $\bar{s}$, as the trend effect leads to greater confidence on the part of buyers and less confidence on the part of sellers. But even if expectations dynamics are not reinforcing, the movement of s away from PPP during successive subperiods will be preserved as long as the changes in $\tilde{s}$ and $\bar{s}$ are not too large.

The literature on behavioral economics lends some plausibility to the argument that expectations dynamics tend to involve revisions that are not too large in magnitude. For example, one of the cornerstones of the behavioral model of

---

35. See Frydman and Goldberg (2001) for the definition of jumps that are not too large.

investor sentiment of Shleifer (2000) is a phenomenon well documented by psychologists called conservatism. Psychologists have found that individuals are slow to change their beliefs in the face of new evidence. It is useful to quote directly from Shleifer (2000, p. 127):

> Edwards (1968) benchmarks a subject's reaction to new evidence against that of an idealized rational Bayesian in which the true normative value of a piece of evidence is well defined. In his experiments individuals update their posteriors in the right direction, but by too little relative to the rational Bayesian benchmark. . . . A conventional first approximation to the data would say that it takes anywhere from two to five observations to do one observation's worth of work in inducing the subject to change his opinions.[36]

Although such behavioral evidence buttresses our claim that the DF model with IKE or TCE *can* generate persistent movements of s away from PPP, the model *does not mechanically* imply that expectations will necessarily lead to persistent movements away across subperiods: At any point in time, expectations dynamics could involve "large" nonreinforcing changes in $\bar{s}$ and $\hat{s}$ that cause a countermovement of s back to PPP. Such an event could be tied to an abrupt change in the policy environment (i.e., a decline in $\bar{s}^*$) or an abrupt change in the way market agents interpret the movements of fundamental variables and/or nonfundamental factors. Both possibilities could be triggered for any number of reasons.

However, our assumption that the PPP gap serves as a benchmark for agents in their assessments of the potential gains and losses implies that there exists some level of the gap from PPP beyond which expectations dynamics will tend to involve nonreinforcing changes in $\bar{s}$ and $\hat{s}$ that lead to a countermovement back to PPP over successive subperiods. When precisely such a countermovement will occur is ultimately unforecastable. This assumption that the gap from PPP serves as a benchmark level is reminiscent of Keynes's story behind the relationship between the rate of interest and the speculative motive for holding money: "What matters is not the *absolute* level of r but the degree of its divergence from what is considered a fairly *safe* level of r, having regard to those calculations of probability which are being relied on" (Keynes, 1936, p. 201, italics in original).

The foregoing discussion on the plausibility of the assumptions on the expectations dynamics that lead to movements of s away from PPP over successive subperiods leads to the following conclusion:

CONCLUSION 14: *The qualitative implications of the DF model with IKE (or TCE) and uncertainty-adjusted UIP are consistent with the recurring episodes of persistent movements of the exchange rate away from PPP that have characterized the modern period of floating rates.*

As we noted earlier, we are suggesting neither that long swings will necessarily occur during any time period nor that one can predict such movements of the

---

36. We note that because of imperfect knowledge "the true normative value of a piece of evidence" is *not* so "well defined" in the context of our model. As such, the magnitude of the updating found by Edwards most likely overstates the magnitude of the updating that would occur with IKE.

exchange rate. The ultimate movement of the exchange rate over any time period depends on the particular expectations dynamics prevailing at the time and it is our position that such dynamics is largely unpredictable. However, since the conditions on expectations dynamics that imply persistent movements of the exchange rate away over successive subperiods in Proposition 13 appear to be reasonable on behavioral grounds, episodes of large and persistent departures from PPP should be expected.

The fact that exchange rates do tend to move persistently away from PPP levels and then move persistently back raises the question of why speculators do not place bets so as to cut short any movement away before it goes too far. The answer appears to be twofold. First, in our model with heterogeneous agents there are both buyers and sellers, and if the movement of s is away, then there are market agents (i.e., sellers) who take contrary positions and whose speculation works to cut that movement short. Second, myopic loss aversion works to limit the number of market agents who either increase their contrary positions or switch to such positions from initially being buyers. This is because the evaluation period of most loss-averse agents may be too short for them to incur the risk of exploiting the knowledge that eventually the exchange rate will revert back to its benchmark level of PPP. No myopically loss-averse agent knows precisely when the exchange rate will cease moving away and begin moving back, and such a countermovement may be a long time coming. Any agents contemplating a contrary position must contemplate the possibility of waiting longer than their evaluation periods. If several evaluation periods elapse without the exchange rate turning around, then although the contrary position will eventually turn out to be correct, market agents who take such positions long before the countermovement and who must account for near-term losses will not be around to enjoy their "superior" forecasts.

Why should evaluation periods be relatively short? Benartzi and Thaler (1995), who examine the relative return on stocks and bonds, suggest that the answer is due to corporate governance, that is, portfolio managers are routinely evaluated on a quarterly basis, making it very difficult for portfolio managers to pursue contrary strategies for longer than two or three quarters. In the foreign exchange market, institutional arrangements impose extremely short evaluation periods. It is well known that in managing exchange rate risk, commercial banks place strict position limits on the size of the open positions carried overnight by their traders. Most junior traders are obliged to close all open positions and tally up before retiring for the day.[37] With such short evaluation periods, the knowledge that eventually the exchange rate will move back to PPP will have little significance. As such, the speculative capital forthcoming will sometimes tend to be insufficient to counteract the underlying dynamics working to push the exchange rate away from PPP for extended periods of time.[38]

---

37. See for example Kubarych (1983) and Grabbe (1996).

38. In Frydman et al. (2003) we explore the connection between exploitable profit opportunities at long horizons and corporate governance mechanisms of the trading institutions.

7. IMPERFECT KNOWLEDGE EXPECTATIONS AND EXTANT PUZZLES IN INTERNATIONAL FINANCE

In this section we briefly summarize our earlier work and work in progress on monetary models with IKE and UAUIP and argue that in addition to the long-swings puzzle, this approach sheds new light on many of the other puzzles in international finance. We focus on: (1) the exchange rate disconnect puzzle, which includes the Meese-Rogoff forecasting puzzle, the Baxter-Stockman puzzle of neutrality of exchange rate regimes, and the puzzle that empirical exchange rate models fit poorly in sample; (2) the PPP puzzle; and (3) the excess-returns puzzle.

7.1. The Exchange Rate Disconnect Puzzle

The exchange rate disconnect puzzle arises because researchers have had great difficulty in empirically establishing a connection between exchange rate movements and macroeconomic fundamentals. The evidence comes from a number of sources, including the inability of empirical exchange rate models to fit well when based on in-sample regression analyses (e.g., Frankel, 1983, 1984) or when based on out-of-sample fit (e.g., Meese and Rogoff, 1983) and the empirical regularity that although exchange rates are much more volatile during flexible-rate regimes, this higher volatility is not accompanied by a matching differential in the volatility of macroeconomic fundamentals.

Our monetary model with IKE and uncertainty-adjusted UIP provides a simple explanation of this puzzle. With IKE and expectations dynamics, the parameters of the aggregate forecasting function will be unstable, implying that the parameters of the reduced form relating the exchange rate to a set of macroeconomic fundamentals will be unstable. Thus, with IKE, *no one exchange rate model with fixed coefficients would be expected to fit well over the entire modern period of floating rates.*[39] Yet virtually all of the empirical evidence used to illustrate the disconnection between exchange rates and fundamentals is based on studies that fit one exchange rate model with fixed coefficients over the entire sample period. We show in Goldberg and Frydman (1996b) that when one allows for episodic changes in the parameters of reduced-form exchange rate models as a way to grossly approximate the structural change arising from expectations dynamics, the exchange rate models perform remarkably well. For example, when episodic structural change is incorporated into the analysis, we find that monetary models outperform the random walk model in out-of-sample fit at the shorter forecasting horizons by margins as large as 70 percent in root mean square error.

As for the puzzle of neutrality of exchange rate regimes, it is clear that the expectational problem differs sharply over fixed and floating exchange rate regimes. The idea here is that with IKE, expectations dynamics will be more volatile during

---

39. The evidence that empirical exchange rate models are temporally unstable includes Boughton (1987), Meese and Rogoff (1988), and our earlier work, which shows that empirical exchange rate models are not only unstable but that different sets of macroeconomic fundamentals are significant during different subperiods of floating (see Goldberg and Frydman, 1996a,b, 2001).

flexible-rate regimes than fixed-rate regimes. This implies that the place to look for the unexplained volatility during flexible-rate periods may not be in greater volatility of macroeconomic fundamentals but rather in greater volatility of the parameters of agents' expectations functions.

7.2. The PPP Puzzle

The PPP puzzle, which is closely related to the long-swings puzzle, arises from the fact that RE sticky-price models imply not only persistence in real exchange rates, but that real and nominal exchange rates adjust at the same rate, and yet the half-lives of deviations from PPP are commonly estimated to be between 2.5 and 5 years. Rogoff (1996) states that the half-lives of PPP deviations are "seemingly far too long to be explained by nominal rigidities" (p. 648). In a recent paper, Engel and Morley (2001) offer a refinement to the puzzle, arguing that it is the nominal exchange rate, not goods prices, that slowly adjust toward PPP. Our monetary model with IKE and UAUIP offers a simple explanation of the PPP puzzle and suggests a further refinement to that of Engel and Morley.

As shown in Section 5, the medium-run equilibrium anchors toward which the exchange rate and goods prices both adjust during any subperiod may themselves imply persistent movements away from PPP. In our model, as in the standard DF model, the exchange rate and goods prices adjust to the medium run at the same rate. But with medium-run anchors that involve movements away from PPP, the rate at which the exchange rate and goods prices adjust to the medium run and the rate at which they adjust to PPP are not one and the same. The exchange rate and goods prices may adjust very quickly to their medium-run anchors and yet adjust very slowly to PPP, the latter being determined by the character of the expectations dynamics leading to departures from PPP. Our model suggests that Engel is correct in saying that goods prices adjust more quickly to their equilibrium levels than exchange rates adjust to PPP. However, it is clear that differential speeds of adjustment on the part of the exchange rate and goods prices are not required for this result.

7.3. The Excess Returns Puzzle

The excess returns puzzle arises because of the inability of standard theory to provide empirically compelling explanations of the apparent failure of uncovered interest rate parity. Engel and Morley (2001) surmise that the failure of UIP may be connected to the PPP puzzle and to the differential speeds of adjustment of the exchange rate and goods prices, although they offer no theoretical basis for his conjecture. Our monetary model with IKE and UAUIP provides such a theoretical justification and suggests that both puzzles are indeed intertwined. We showed in Sections 5 and 6 that with IKE, the monetary models can generate persistent movements of the exchange rate away from PPP, and in Section 4, we argued that such dynamics will cause myopically loss-averse agents to require uncertainty premiums on taking open positions in foreign exchange that depend on the gap from PPP. In Frydman and Goldberg (2001), we report some preliminary evidence suggesting that the PPP gap may indeed be an important factor in explaining the behavior of expected excess returns. In Frydman and Goldberg (2002) we examine more closely the ability of our model to explain the behavior of expected excess returns. We show that our model not only offers a reasonable explanation of the time path of expected excess returns, but in particular it offers a simple explanation of the sign reversals that often occur in this variable. The inability of standard theory to explain the frequent sign reversals in expected excess returns is well known (e.g., see Lewis, 1995; Mark and Wu, 1998).

8. THE PRACTICE OF ECONOMICS IN A WORLD OF IMPERFECT KNOWLEDGE

The solution to the problem of modeling expectations offered by the REH is to tie expectations rigidly to the economist's structural model. The epistemological and behavioral foundations of this approach remain problematic and the empirical performance of models using the REH, especially in the asset markets, has been less than satisfactory. In this chapter we suggested that expectations should be accorded a more active role in a world of imperfect knowledge. We showed that if one is prepared to loosen the connection between expectations and the economist's structural model, economics might after all be able to provide plausible explanations of phenomena difficult to explain under the REH.

In this concluding section we compare briefly some of the methodological implications of our approach with the conventional RE approach for the practice of economics, especially in situations in which expectations play a key role. Since a more complete discussion of such a vast topic requires a separate treatment, we mention here only a few of the main issues.

8.1. Free Parameters

We showed in Sections 5 and 6 that the monetary model of the exchange rate generates persistent movements away from PPP under plausible and well-defined assumptions on the *qualitative structure* of agents' forecast functions. In particular, we showed that with imperfect knowledge and the continuous updating of beliefs, the model generated long swings away. Once jumps in expectations were included in the analysis, the model continued to generate long-swings behavior under additional and reasonable qualitative assumptions on the updating of expectations. This ability of the monetary model, with IKE replacing the REH, to explain the empirical record (see Section 7), however, is unlikely to persuade adherents of the RE approach of the view that imperfect knowledge might indeed be the key to understanding exchange rate dynamics as well as movements of other asset prices. The reason is that our analysis introduces "free parameters" arising from agents' expectations into the model. Although the leading proponents of the RE approach have started to consider learning and model misspecification, they make sure that the departures from the REH do not introduce free parameters related to agents' beliefs.[40] As Sargent has recently admonished economists: "remember Lucas's warning to 'beware of theorists bearing free parameters'" (Sargent, 1999, p. 73).

Our approach in this paper is based on the contrary presumption, namely, that economists are unlikely to provide explanations of important aspects of the dynamics of asset prices without according expectations a less mechanical and more autonomous role in their models. Thus, *empirically relevant* models of economic phenomena in which expectations play a key role are very likely to involve free parameters arising from agents' expectations.

8.2. Parameter Drift and Structural Change in Macroeconometric Models: The Role of Expectations

Since the time paths of the endogenous variables under IKE will involve discontinuities and other structural changes, the most immediate implication of our approach is that one should expect empirical models in situations in which expectations are important to be characterized by time-varying parameters that occasionally experience large and discontinuous structural change. In Section 7, we referred to a number of studies that emphasize the importance of structural change in understanding the empirical behavior of exchange rates. Researchers in other areas of macroeconomics are also beginning to recognize the ubiquitous presence of temporal instability of the observed time series and consider the understanding of this instability to be key in explaining important macroeconomic phenomena. In the words of Sargent (1999, p. 17), it is "a smoking gun."

Economists working in the RE tradition (e.g., Sargent and others) have acknowledged the importance of structural change. But, having tied expectations rigidly to the structure of the economist's model and presuming that the parameters of this structure are functions of "deep," largely invariant, parameters of "preferences" and "technology," the RE approach has forced its adherents to consider changes in government policy as the *primary* source of instability of the parameters of the macroeconometric models.

However, the nature of the temporal instability [e.g., that different sets of macroeconomic fundamentals seem to matter for exchange rates during different subperiods of floating (see Section 6)] suggests that changes in government policy are unlikely to be the *sole* source of parameter drift and structural change. Moreover, the characterization of government policy by a fixed rule is also likely itself to involve parameter drift and large and discontinuous structural change

---

40. For example, in his study of U.S. inflation Sargent (1999) introduces learning by the government on the basis of the misspecified model. However, he specifies learning so narrowly and rigidly as to ensure that "as in the rational expectations model, the list [of the parameters of the model] includes no free parameters describing beliefs" (p. 123). More recently, Hansen and Sargent (2001) have expressed genuine concern about the epistemological and behavioral foundations of the REH. Nevertheless, after acknowledging the importance of letting "agents inside the economist's model share his doubts about the model specification" (p. 3), they immediately move on to restrict the set of "misspecified models" sufficiently narrowly so as to preserve the basic features of the RE approach.

as policy officials update their necessarily imperfect views of the world.[41] Thus, structural instability in macroeconometric models is likely to arise from both the instability of government policy and the partly autonomous, continuous and discontinuous, updating of agents' expectations. Consequently:

CONCLUSION 15: *The estimation and use of macroeconometric models should be accompanied by tests for parameter drift and structural change.*

8.3. Confronting Models Using IKE with Empirical Evidence

Since the IKE framework imposes only qualitative restrictions on the structure of agents' forecast functions, confronting such models with empirical evidence raises two questions. First, it might appear that models involving IKE forecast functions can be used to rationalize *any* pattern observed in the data. However, as we showed in Section 6, the model *does not in general* imply long swings in exchange rates. Moreover, the model *does* provide an explanation of long swings under additional qualitative assumptions concerning the updating of agents' expectations (i.e., when changes in expectations are not too great and/or are reinforcing), which are defined in Frydman and Goldberg (2001) in terms of the parameters of the model. Based on findings in the behavioral literature, we also suggested that these conditions on the updating of expectations are indeed reasonable. Also, since IKE functions include TCE functions, which imply particular sets of macroeconomic fundamental variables and the signs of the weights that should be attached to these variables, the testing of variable significance and sign restrictions is possible. Note that such variable and sign restrictions are implied by the TCE framework even with only qualitative assumptions on the updating of expectations and they can be tested against the restrictions implied by the REH. Papell (1997) conducts such an analysis and finds a strong rejection of RE in favor of TCE.

However, more research on the formation and *updating* of agents' expectations is needed to support qualitative expectational assumptions made in analyses using IKE. Since the REH has been so entrenched for so long and has succeeded in convincing the economics profession that it represents *the solution* to the problem of modeling expectations of rational agents, empirical evidence on the formation and updating of individual expectations is at best fragmentary and, to the extent that it exists, has been developed largely by noneconomists.[42] Fortunately this is beginning to change with the work in behavioral economics (e.g., Shleifer, 2000).

The second question involved in confronting the models using IKE with empirical evidence is whether it is possible to distinguish among different structural models using IKE. Although more research is needed to develop or extend existing procedures to address such questions, in principle, if the same qualitative assumptions on the formation and updating of IKE are used with *different* structural models, the *co-movements* of some of the endogenous variables will differ across

---

41. For evidence that some popular "policy rules" are subject to temporal instability see, e.g., Frydman and Rappoport (1987) and more recently Clarida et al. (2000).

42. For an early study in economics see Frankel and Froot (1987).

models. This then would allow us to distinguish among competing model specifications. For example, in Frydman and Goldberg (2001), we show that for a given set of qualitative assumptions on expectations, the time paths of the exchange rate and relative interest rates are negatively related when the degree of exchange rate pass-through is high and can be positively related when the degree of exchange rate pass-through is low. Thus, the co-movement of the exchange rate and relative interest rates can be used to distinguish empirically among the monetary models involving different price-adjustment equations. Incidentally, this way of comparing models empirically—by embedding the same expectational assumptions in different structural models—is analogous to the procedures used in the RE tradition.

Although the qualitative assumptions of IKE (and its predecessor TCE) can be confronted with the data and in principle found to be rejected on empirical evidence, and despite the fact that IKE is clearly a more plausible model of individual expectations on behavioral and rationality grounds, one may still prefer the more restrictive model based on the REH and rely on strictly positivist grounds for model evaluation. But even under such an arguably narrow conception for evaluating economic models and theories, the performance of the monetary models of the exchange rate using the REH is highly unsatisfactory. This, together with the evidence provided in this chapter—that when the REH is replaced with an alternative expectational assumption the monetary models of the exchange provide reasonable empirical explanations—strongly suggests that the REH is one of the primary reasons for the empirical inadequacy of these models. Notwithstanding Sims's (1996) observation that the organization of economics seems to resemble that of "priesthoods and guilds" (p. 107),[43] we do hope that the economics profession is now, at long last, ready to move forward with modeling expectations in a behaviorally and empirically supportable way so we can improve our understanding of the dynamics of asset prices and other important macroeconomic phenomena.

REFERENCES

Barberis, N., M. Huang, and T. Santos (2001), "Prospect Theory and Asset Prices," *Quarterly Journal of Economics* 116:1–53.

Benartzi, S. and R. H. Thaler (1995), "Myopic Loss Aversion and the Equity Premium Puzzle," *Quarterly Journal of Economics* 110:73–92.

Blanchard, O. and M. Watson (1982), "Bubbles, Rational Expectations and Financial Markets," in P. Wachtel, ed., *Crises in the Economic and Financial Structure*, Lexington, Mass.: Lexington Books.

Boughton, J. M. (1987), "Tests of the Performance of Reduced-Form Exchange Rate Models," *Journal of International Economics* 23:41–56.

Bray, M. (1983), in R. Frydman and E. S. Phelps, eds., *Individual Forecasting and Aggregate Outcomes: "Rational Expectations" Examined*, New York: Cambridge University Press.

Clarida, R., M. Gertler, and J. Gali (2000), "Monetary Policy Rules and Macroeconomic Stability: Evidence and Some Theory," *Quarterly Journal of Economics* 115(1):147–80.

---

43. We should perhaps take note that later in his paper Sims says, "As is probably apparent, my own opinion is that whatever the value of economics as rhetoric, that view of economics should remain secondary, with the view of economics as science, in the sense that it is an enterprise that holds theory accountable to data, remaining primary" (Sims, 1996, p. 112).

Dornbusch, R. (1976), "Expectations and Exchange Rate Dynamics," *Journal of Political Economy* 84:1161–74.

Dornbusch, R. and J. A. Frankel (1988), "The Flexible Exchange Rate System: Experience and Alternatives," in S. Borner, ed., *International Finance and Trade*, London: MacMillan.

Edwards, W. (1968), "Conservatism in Human Information Processing," in B. Klinmuntz, ed., *Formal Representation of Human Judgment*, New York: Wiley, pp. 17–52.

Engel, C. A. (1996), "The Forward Discount Anomaly and the Risk Premium: A Survey of Recent Evidence," *Journal of Empirical Finance* 3:123–91.

Engel, C. A. and J. C. Morley (2001), "The Adjustment of Prices and the Adjustment of the Exchange Rate," mimeo, University of Wisconsin and Washington University.

Ericsson, N. R. and J. S. Irons (1995), "The Lucas Critique in Practice: Theory Without Measurement," in K. D. Hoover, ed., *Macroeconomics: Development, Tensions and Prospects*, Boston: Kluwer Academic Publishers, pp. 263–312.

Evans, G. W. and S. Honkapohja (2001), *Learning and Expectations in Macroeconomics*, Princeton: Princeton University Press.

Farmer, R. E. A. (1999), *Macroeconomics of Self-fulfilling Prophecies*, 2nd ed., Cambridge: MIT Press.

Fischer, S. (2001), "Distinguished Lecture on Economics in Government—Exchange Rate Regimes: Is the Bipolar View Correct?," *Journal of Economic Perspectives* 15:3–24.

Frankel, J. A. (1979), "On the Mark: A Theory of Floating Exchange Rate Based on Real Interest Differentials," *American Economic Review* 69:610–22.

——— (1983), "Monetary and Portfolio Balance Models of Exchange Rate Determination," in J. Bhandari and B. Putnam, eds., *Economic Interdependence and Flexible Exchange Rates*, Cambridge: MIT Press.

——— (1984), "Tests of Monetary and Portfolio Balance Models of Exchange Rate Determination," in J. Bilson and R. Marston, eds., *Exchange Rate Theory and Practice*, Chicago: University of Chicago Press.

Frankel J. A. and K. A. Froot (1987), "Using Survey Data to Test Standard Propositions Regarding Exchange Rate Expectations," *American Economic Review* 77:133–53.

Frankel, J. A. and A. K. Rose (1995), "Empirical Research on Nominal Exchange Rates," in G. Grossman and K. Rogoff, eds., *Handbook of International Economics*, Vol. 3, Amsterdam: North-Holland, pp. 1689–729.

Friedman, M. (1953), "The Methodology of Positive Economics," in M. Friedman, ed., *Essays in Positive Economics*, Chicago: University of Chicago Press.

Froot, K. A. and K. Rogoff (1995), "Perspectives on PPP and Long-Run Real Exchange Rates," in G. Grossman and K. Rogoff, eds., *Handbook of International Economics*, Vol. 3, Amsterdam: North-Holland, pp. 1647–88.

Frydman, R. (1982), "Towards an Understanding of Market Processes: Individual Expectations, Learning and Convergence to Rational Expectations Equilibrium," *American Economic Review* 72:652–68.

——— (1983), "Individual Rationality, Decentralization, and the Rational Expectations Hypothesis," in R. Frydman and E. S. Phelps, eds., *Individual Forecasting and Aggregate Outcomes: "Rational Expectations" Examined*, New York: Cambridge University Press.

Frydman, R. and M. Goldberg (2001), "Imperfect Knowledge Expectations, Uncertainty Premia and Exchange Rate Dynamics," paper presented at the Festschrift Conference in Honor of Edmund S. Phelps, October 5–6, www.econ.nyu.edu/user/frydman.

——— (2002), "Imperfect Knowledge Expectations and Myopic Loss Aversion: Shedding New Light on the Excess Returns Puzzle in the Foreign Exchange Market," in preparation.

Frydman, R. and E. S. Phelps (1983), "Introduction," in R. Frydman and E. S. Phelps, eds., *Individual Forecasting and Aggregate Outcomes: "Rational Expectations" Examined*, New York: Cambridge University Press.

————— (1990), "Pluralism of Theories Problems in Post-Rational-Expectations Modeling," paper presented at the 1990 Siena Summer Workshop on "Expectations and Learning," June 20–30.

Frydman, R. and P. Rappoport (1987), "Is the Distinction Between Anticipated and Unanticipated Money Growth Relevant in Explaining Aggregate Output?," *American Economic Review* 77(4):693–703.

Frydman, R., M. Goldberg, P. Kocher, and H. Frisch (2003), "Corporate Control, Myopic Loss Aversion and Long-Horizon Inefficiency in the Foreign Exchange Market," in preparation.

Goldberg, M. D. (1991), "Reconsidering the Basic Relationships Between Exchange Rates, Exchange Rate Expectations and Macroeconomic Fundamentals," Ph.D. dissertation, New York University.

————— (1995), "Symmetry Restrictions and the Semblance of Neutrality in Exchange Rate Models," *Journal of Macroeconomics* 17(4):579–99.

————— (2000), "On Empirical Exchange Rate Models: What Does a Rejection of the Symmetry Restriction on Short-Run Interest Rates Mean?," *Journal of International Money and Finance* 19:673–88.

Goldberg, M. D. and R. Frydman (1993), "Theories Consistent Expectations and Exchange Rate Dynamics," in H. Frisch and A. Wörgöter, eds., *Open-Economy Macroeconomics*, London: Macmillan, chap. 23.

————— (1996a),"Imperfect Knowledge and Behavior in the Foreign Exchange Market," *Economic Journal* 106:869–93.

————— (1996b), "Empirical Exchange Rate Models and Shifts in the Co-Integrating Vector," *Journal of Structural Change and Economic Dynamics* 7:55–78.

————— (2001), "Macroeconomic Fundamentals and the DM/$ Exchange Rate: Temporal Instability and the Monetary Model," *International Journal of Finance and Economics* 6(4):421–35.

Grabbe, J. O. (1996), *International Financial Markets*, Englewood Cliffs, N.J.: Prentice-Hall, chap. 4.

Hansen, L. P. and T. J. Sargent (2001), "Acknowledging Misspecification in Macroeconomic Theory," revised paper prepared for the Society of Economic Dynamics Conference, Costa Rica, June 2000.

Hooper, P. and J. Morton (1982), "Fluctuations in the Dollar: A Model of Nominal and Real Exchange Rate Determination," *Journal of International Money and Finance* 1:39–56.

Juselius, K. (1995), "Do Purchasing Power Parity and Uncovered Interest Rate Parity Hold in the Long-Run?: An Example of Likelihood Inference in a Multivariate Time Series Model," *Journal of Econometrics* 69:211–40

Kahneman, D. and A. Tversky (1979), "Prospect Theory: An Analysis of Decision Under Risk," *Econometrica* 47:263–91.

Keynes, J. M. (1936), *The General Theory of Employment, Interest and Money*, New York: Harcourt, Brace and World.

Knight, F. H. (1921), *Risk, Uncertainty and Profit*, Boston: Houghton Mifflin.

Kubarych, R. M. (1983), *Foreign Exchange Markets in the United States*, New York: New York Federal Reserve Bank.

Kurz, M. and M. Motolese (2001), "Endogenous Uncertainty and Market Volatility," *Economic Theory* 17:497–544.

Lewis, K. (1989), "Can Learning Affect Exchange Rate Behavior?: The Case of the Dollar in the Early 1980s," *Journal of Monetary Economics* 23:79–100.

————— (1995), "Puzzles in International Financial Markets," in G. Grossman and K. Rogoff, eds., *Handbook of International Economics*, Vol. 3, Amsterdam: North-Holland, pp. 1913–17.

Linde, J. (2001), "Testing for the Lucas Critique: A Quantitative Investigation," *American Economic Review* 91(4):986–1005.

Lucas, R. E., Jr. (1976), "Econometric Policy Evaluation: A Critique," in K. Brunner and A. H. Meltzer, eds., *The Phillips Curve and Labor Markets*, Carnegie-Rochester Conference Series on Public Policy, Vol. 1, Amsterdam: North-Holland, pp. 19–46.

Mark, N. (1995), "Exchange Rates and Fundamentals: Evidence on Long-Horizon Predictability," *American Economic Review* 85:201–18.

Mark, N. and D. Sul (2001), "Nominal Exchange Rates and Monetary Fundamentals: Evidence from a Small Post-Bretton Woods Panel," *Journal of International Economics* 53:29–52.

Mark, N. and Y. Wu (1998), "Rethinking Deviations from Uncovered Interest Rate Parity: The Role of Covariance Risk and Noise," *Economic Journal* 108:1686–706.

Meese, R. (1986), "Testing for Bubbles in Exchange Markets: A Case of Sparkling Rates?," *Journal of Political Economy* 94(2):345–73.

——— (1990), "Currency Fluctuations in the Post-Bretton Woods Era," *Journal of Economic Perspectives* 4:117–34.

Meese, R. and K. Rogoff (1983), "Empirical Exchange Rate Models of the Seventies: Do They Fit Out of Sample?," *Journal of International Economics* 14:3–24.

——— (1988), "Was it Real? The Exchange Rate-Interest Differential Relation Over the Modern Floating-Rate Period," *Journal of Finance* 43:933–48.

Obstfeld, M. and K. Rogoff (1996), *Foundations of International Macroeconomics*, Cambridge: MIT Press.

Papell, D. H. (1997), "Cointegration and Exchange Rate Dynamics," *Journal of International Money and Finance* 16(3):445–60.

Papell, D. and C. Murray (2001), "The Purchasing Power Parity Puzzle Is Worse Than You Think: A Note on Long-Run Real Exchange Rate Behavior," mimeo, University of Houston.

Phelps, E. S. (1983), "The Trouble with 'Rational Expectations' and the Problem of Inflation Stabilization," in R. Frydman and E. S. Phelps, eds., *Individual Forecasting and Aggregate Outcomes: "Rational Expectations" Examined*, New York: Cambridge University Press.

Phelps, E. S., A. A. Alchian, C. C. Holt, D. T. Mortensen, G. C. Archibald, R. E. Lucas, Jr., L. A. Rapping, S. G. Winter, Jr., J. P. Gould, D. F. Gordon, A. Hynes, D. A. Nichols, P. J. Taubman, and M. Wilkinson (1970), *Microeconomic Foundations of Employment and Inflation*, New York: Norton.

Rogoff, K. (1996), "The Purchasing Power Puzzle," *Journal of Economic Literature* 34:647–68.

Sargent, T. J. (1993), *Bounded Rationality in Macroeconomics*, Oxford: Oxford University Press.

——— (1999), *Conquest of American Inflation*, Princeton: Princeton University Press.

Schulmeister, S. (1983), "Exchange Rates, Prices and Interest Rates: Reconsidering the Basic Relationships of Exchange Rate Determination," C.V. Starr Center for Applied Economics Working Paper No. 83.

——— (1987), "Currency Speculation and Dollar Fluctuations," *Banca Nazionale del Lavoro Quarterly Review* 167:343–65.

Shleifer, A. (2000), *Inefficient Markets: An Introduction to Behavioral Finance*, Oxford: Oxford University Press.

Sims, C. (1996), "Macroeconomics and Methodology," *Journal of Economic Perspectives* 10(1):105–20.

Soros, G. (1987), *The Alchemy of Finance*, New York: Simon and Schuster.

——— (2000), *Open Society: Reforming Global Capitalism*, New York: Public Affairs.

Taylor, M. (1995), "The Economics of Exchange Rates," *Journal of Economic Literature* 33:13–47.

— 9 —

Comments on Frydman and Goldberg

DAVID H. PAPELL

1. INTRODUCTION

Twenty-five years have passed since the rational expectations hypothesis (REH) became the dominant paradigm of modern macroeconomics. Over that time, criticisms of the REH have centered on two issues: the tension between the REH and individual rationality and the poor empirical performance of models employing the REH to explain the behavior of variables, in particular exchange rates, determined in asset markets. The chapter by Frydman and Goldberg is an ambitious attempt to synthesize and extend this research.

The chapter has two objectives: to develop a theory of expectations consistent with individual rationality and to develop a model consistent with empirical regularities involving exchange rates. In pursuit of the first objective, the concept of imperfect knowledge expectations (IKE), which in turn is an extension of the idea of theories consistent expectations (TCE), is developed and shown to be consistent with rationality of individual agents. Toward the second objective, the concept of uncertainty-adjusted uncovered interest parity (UAUIP) is developed and combined with IKE to provide an alternative to the usual rational expectations (RE) and uncovered interest parity (UIP) solution to the Dornbusch-Frankel (DF) monetary model of exchange rate dynamics. The authors claim that their augmented model sheds new light on the exchange rate disconnect, purchasing power parity (PPP), and excess returns puzzles.

The thrust of my comments is that the chapter is more successful in satisfying the first than the second objective. Moreover, tension between the two objectives is unavoidable. In a world of imperfect knowledge, individual rationality necessitates that the formation of expectations incorporate nonfundamental factors. This implies a degree of indeterminacy that is, by definition, not quantifiable. But if the degree of indeterminacy is not quantifiable, IKE cannot produce restrictions that can be tested against TCE and/or RE. While this has implications for the ability of the augmented model to explain exchange rate dynamics, it also has implications that go far beyond the particular model or empirical puzzle.

2. IMPERFECT KNOWLEDGE EXPECTATIONS AND UNCERTAINTY-ADJUSTED UNCOVERED INTEREST RATE PARITY

Following Dornbusch (1976), models of exchange rate dynamics have typically incorporated both rational expectations and uncovered interest parity. These models produce very strong predictions for real exchange rates that do not stand up well to empirical scrutiny. Frydman and Goldberg develop a theory of real exchange rate dynamics that relaxes both RE and UIP.

Their concept of imperfect knowledge expectations builds upon earlier work on theories consistent expectations, originally proposed in Frydman and Phelps (1990), which they developed further in a series of subsequent papers. The idea of TCE is to model expectations as being *qualitatively* consistent with a *variety* of economic models, while RE would be *quantitatively* consistent with a *single* model. While TCE incorporates imperfect knowledge, it is restricted to imperfect knowledge of the true economic model. The contribution of IKE is to extend the scope of the imperfect knowledge to, as they note in their chapter, "atheoretical components based on technical trading and other rules of thumb as well as other subjective assessments concerning the movement of the average opinion."

IKE is clearly a step forward in consistency with individual rationality. Imperfect knowledge of economic agents clearly extends beyond uncertainty regarding the true model, and the incorporation of atheoretical components makes sense. Moreover, as the authors clearly demonstrate, RE cannot be consistent with individual rationality because agents have to both solve the "scientific" problem (finding the correct model) and take account of the actions of others. This necessarily involves a degree of indeterminacy that goes beyond what can be accounted for by TCE.

IKE is not, however, clearly a step forward in explaining empirical regularities. With TCE, the scope of imperfect knowledge is limited to a variety of models. Using standard econometric techniques, likelihood ratio tests with overidentifying restrictions, one can construct nested tests to compare models with RE and TCE. In Papell (1997), I estimate DF models of exchange rate dynamics with RE and TCE and reject the RE restrictions in favor of the TCE specification. With IKE, the scope of imperfect knowledge is unlimited and nested tests cannot be constructed to compare IKE with either TCE or RE. In the absence of such tests, the concept of IKE is not empirically falsifiable.

The concept of UAUIP uses myopic loss aversion to motivate deviations from UIP. Using the PPP exchange rate as a benchmark level, an equation is derived that relates deviations from UIP to deviations from PPP. This equation is similar to the imperfect capital mobility specification in Frenkel and Rodriguez (1982) although, as noted by the authors, the imperfect capital mobility specification is more restrictive.

3. EXCHANGE RATE DYNAMICS AND THE PURCHASING POWER PARITY PUZZLE

Models of exchange rate dynamics in the DF tradition involve explaining deviations from PPP. The consensus view is that, while PPP holds in the long run for post-1973 real exchange rates, mean reversion is slow. A common measure of the speed of mean reversion is the half-life of PPP deviations, the time it takes for a shock to dissipate by 50 percent. Rogoff (1996) describes a "remarkable consensus" of between 3 and 5 years for half-lives of PPP deviations, "seemingly far too long to be explained by nominal rigidities." He characterizes the "PPP puzzle" as the difficulty in reconciling the high volatility of short-term real exchange rates with extremely slow convergence to PPP.

What do we know about convergence to PPP? Figure 1 depicts the real DM/U.S. $ exchange rate from 1973 to 1998, using quarterly data and national consumer price indexes. The figure is drawn so that an increase represents a real appreciation of the U.S. $ (or depreciation of the DM). It is apparent that the DM/U.S. $ rate cannot be characterized by one convergence experience. While there are long swings in the exchange rate, most notably over the 1980–1987 period, there are also short swings in the early 1970s and 1990s.

What is the magnitude of the PPP puzzle? Murray and Papell (2002) analyze half-lives of PPP deviations over the post–Bretton Woods floating exchange rate period. We estimate augmented Dickey-Fuller regressions for a number of real exchange rates with the U.S. dollar as the numeraire currency:

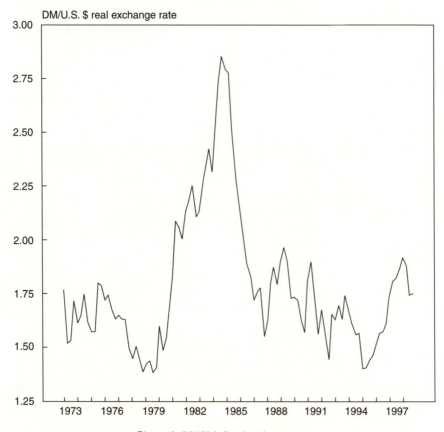

Figure 1. DM/U.S. $ real exchange rate.

$$q_t = c + \alpha q_{t-1} + \sum_{i=1}^{k} \Psi_i \Delta q_{t-1} + u_t, \qquad (1)$$

where q is the (logarithm of the) real exchange rate. An approximate measure of the half-life can be calculated as $\ln(0.5)/\ln(\alpha)$, while an exact measure can be calculated from the impulse response function.

Using approximately median unbiased estimation methods, which correct for the downward bias in least-squares estimates in equation (1), we calculate point estimates and confidence intervals for half-lives of PPP deviations. For the DM/U.S. \$ rate, the point estimate of the half-life calculated from the impulse response function is 3.03 years, just within Rogoff's "consensus." The lower bound of the 95 percent confidence interval, however, is 1.24 years while the upper bound is infinite.[1] These confidence intervals are consistent with almost any type of real exchange rate behavior. Looking at the lower bounds, we see that the fast speed of convergence to PPP is consistent with models based on nominal rigidities. If we look at the upper bounds, the absence of convergence to PPP is consistent with a unit root in the real exchange rate.

The standard DF model with rational expectations does not account for either the varying pattern of long and short swings or the evidence on half-lives of PPP deviations found in the data. What do we learn by augmenting the DF model with IKE and UAUIP? The augmented model can, in principle, account for virtually any pattern of real exchange rate dynamics. One example emphasized by the authors is that by making appropriate case-by-case assumptions regarding revision of expectations, the model can produce both long and short swings. I would also conjecture that, again by making assumptions regarding expectations revision, the model could be consistent with extremely wide confidence intervals for half-lives of PPP deviations.

Does this chapter help "solve" the PPP puzzle? Whereas, in contrast with the DF model with RE and UIP, the augmented model is consistent with a wide variety of movements around PPP, it does not provide a quantifiable explanation for the different experiences. Why was there an 8-year "long" swing in the real exchange rate starting in 1980, followed by a 3-year swing, followed by a 1-year "short" swing? While the model can provide an ex post justification based on factors such as atheoretical components and myopic loss aversion, it cannot provide a falsifiable explanation. Put differently, I cannot see any type of movement around PPP that is inconsistent with the model. Unless restrictions are placed on the scope of the indeterminacy, I am not optimistic that this approach can contribute to our understanding of the PPP and other puzzles in international finance.

4. INDIVIDUAL RATIONALITY
AND EMPIRICAL FALSIFIABILITY

While the objectives of the Frydman and Goldberg chapter are to develop a theory of expectations consistent with individual rationality and to develop a model that

---

1. The estimates for other countries are similar. In particular, they all have an infinite upper bound.

can account for empirical regularities involving exchange rates, these objectives are not weighted equally. The paramount concern of the authors is consistency with individual rationality. Given the primacy of that concern, nonquantifiable factors necessarily enter into agents' expectations functions, leading inexorably to indeterminacy. As the authors write, "*empirically relevant* models of economic phenomena in which expectations play a key role are very likely to involve free parameters arising from agents' expectations."

I do not believe that we should be willing to sacrifice empirical falsifiability on the altar of individual rationality. There is a crucial distinction between TCE, where the indeterminacy is quantifiable and nested tests can be conducted to differentiate between models, and IKE, where the indeterminacy is not quantifiable and nested tests cannot be run. In my view, *nonfalsifiable* models incorporating free parameters arising from agents' *nonquantifiable* expectations cannot be empirically relevant. If inconsistency with individual rationality is the price that must be paid to produce models that can be rejected, then it is a price worth paying.

REFERENCES

Dornbusch, R. (1976), "Expectations and Exchange Rate Dynamics," *Journal of Political Economy* 84:1161–76.

Frenkel, J. and C. Rodriguez (1982), "Exchange Rate Dynamics and the Overshooting Hypothesis," *International Monetary Fund Staff Papers* 29:1–30.

Frydman, R. and E. S. Phelps (1990), "Pluralism of Theories Problems in Post-Rational-Expectations Modeling," paper presented at the 1990 Siena Summer Workshop on Expectations and Learning.

Murray, C. and D. Papell (2002), "The Purchasing Power Parity Persistence Paradigm," *Journal of International Economics* 56:1–19.

Papell, D. (1997), "Cointegration and Exchange Rate Dynamics," *Journal of International Money and Finance* 16:445–60.

Rogoff, K. (1996), "The Purchasing Power Parity Puzzle," *Journal of Economic Literature* 34:647–68.

— 10 —

Endogenous Fluctuations and the Role of Monetary Policy

MORDECAI KURZ WITH HEHUI JIN AND MAURIZIO MOTOLESE

1. INTRODUCTION

Why is monetary policy a desirable social tool and why is public action in this area justified? The controversial nature of these questions arises from the fact that any answers are linked to two related questions: Why does a competitive market economy experience excess fluctuations and why is money nonneutral? Hence, a theory of stabilizing monetary policy has to provide a *unified* explanation as to why our economy experiences fluctuations and why monetary policy can have an impact on these fluctuations.

In a sequence of earlier papers we have argued that most volatility in financial markets is caused by the beliefs of agents (see Kurz and Schneider, 1996; Kurz 1997a,b; Kurz and Beltratti, 1997; Kurz and Motolese, 2001). Using the theory of rational belief equilibrium (RBE) (see Kurz, 1994, 1996, 1997a), we introduced a unified model which explains, simultaneously, a list of financial phenomena regarded as "anomalies." The model's key feature is the heterogeneity of an agent's beliefs. At any time an agent may be a "bull" who is rational but optimistic about future capital gains or a "bear" who is rational but pessimistic about such gains. Phenomena such as the equity premium puzzle are then explained by the fact that pessimistic "bears" who aim to avoid capital losses drive interest rates low and the equity premium high (for a unified treatment see Kurz and Motolese, 2001). The RBE theory was used by Kurz (1997c) to explain the forward discount bias in foreign exchange markets; by Garmaise (1998) to explain the capital structure of firms, and by Wu and Guo (2001) to study speculation and trading volume in asset markets. This chapter initiates our application of the RBE theory to the study

This research was supported by a grant of the Smith Richardson Foundation to the Stanford Institute for Economic Policy Research (SIEPR). We thank Kenneth Judd for constant advice, which was crucial at several points in the development of this work. We thank Peter Hammond, Felix Kubler, and Carsten Nielsen for many insightful conversations regarding the content and methods of this chapter. We also thank Arturo Ricardo Gonzalez de la Mota, Albert Chun, and Peyron Law for detailed comments on an earlier draft and for assistance in preparing the data in the introduction. We are pleased to honor Ned Phelps, whose work has anticipated some of the developments herein.

of endogenous fluctuations in a monetary economy and to an examination of the implied role of monetary policy.

The idea that diverse expectations are important in an equilibrium analysis is not new to economics. Diverse beliefs in financial markets are a central component of Thornton's (1802) view of paper money and financial markets. Expectations are often mentioned in Keynes (1936), although he never developed a formal theory of individual beliefs. Market expectations are central to "cumulative movements" in Pigou (see Pigou, 1941, chap. 6) and expectations are basic to the process of deviations from a stationary equilibrium in the Swedish school (e.g., see Myrdal's view of money in Myrdal, 1939, chap. 3). Also, the concept of "subjective values" based on diverse expectations is a cornerstone of Lindahl's (1939) theory of money and capital. Finally, diverse expectations are generic to an Arrow-Debreu or a Radner equilibrium.

As this work is dedicated to Ned Phelps we observe that he often stressed the importance of expectations. In accord with a Bayesian perspective he saw expectations as subjective models expressing the agent's interpretation of information and needing a dynamic updating that would lead to some concept of equilibrium. Although attracted by the simplicity of the single-belief model, he realized its lack of realism and, more important, its failure to capture the component of volatility induced by the interaction of heterogeneous expectations. More specifically, in evaluating the impact of rational expectations, Frydman and Phelps (1983) stress the importance of diverse beliefs. They justify their position on the ground that any theory with uniform market beliefs of agents is fundamentally nonrobust, saying: "But once the theoretical door is opened to one or more hypotheses of optimality in the expectations formation of the individual agents, the implied behavior of the (otherwise identical) model is often found to be wrenched into directions far from the behavior implied by the rational expectations hypothesis. In short, Pandora's box of disequilibrium behavior is opened up" (p. 26). The theory of rational beliefs (RB) provides an analytical framework and a vocabulary for these ideas. It shows that the interaction of beliefs acts as a propagation mechanism generating volatility endogenously. The component of social risk generated by the distribution of beliefs is called "endogenous uncertainty." Although RB generalize the concept of rational expectations, the RBE theory reveals that, as Frydman and Phelps (1983) conjectured, an economy with diverse beliefs behaves in a drastically different way from an economy with a single, uniform belief.

1.1. On the Diversity of Rational Beliefs

Table 1 presents, as an example, forecasts of GNP growth and inflation made in January 1991 for all of 1991 by participants in the *Blue Chip Economic Indicators*. About half of the forecasters predicted at that time that 1991 would be a recession year and the other half disagreed. The actual growth rate in 1991 was −0.5 percent and the inflation rate 3.6 percent. Now, placing ourselves in January 1991, suppose we make a stationary econometric forecast of GNP growth without nonstationary judgments about the unique conditions prevailing in 1991. We used a model of Stock and Watson (1999a,b, 2001), estimated by employing a combination

Table 1. Blue Chip Forecasts of GNP Growth and Inflation for 1991

Company	Forecasted percent change	
	Real GNP	*GNP price deflator*
Sears Roebuck & Co.	1.6H	4.2
Amhold & S. Bleichroeder	1.2	4.8
Prudential Bache	1.2	3.3L
Chicago Corporation	1.1	4.1
Bostian Economic Research	1.0	4.0
Fairmodel	1.0	3.7
Cahners Economics	0.9	4.3
Wayne Hummer & Co.—Chicago	0.8	4.3
National City Bank of Cleveland	0.7	4.6
Inforum—University of Maryland	0.7	3.8
CRT Government Securities	0.6	4.0
Dun & Bradstreet	0.6	4.0
Conference Board	0.5	4.7
Econoclast	0.5	4.0
First National Bank of Chicago	0.5	3.8
University of Michigan M.Q.E.M.	0.4	4.7
Manufacturers National Bank—Detroit	0.3	4.5
Turning Points (Micrometrics)	0.2	4.3
Brown-Brothers Harriman	0.2	4.0
Dean Witter Reynolds, Inc.	0.1	4.0
LaSalle National Bank	0.1	3.6
Northern Trust Company	0.0	4.3
Evans Economics	0.0	4.0
Morris Cohen & Associates	−0.1	5.0H
Prudential Insurance Co.	−0.1	4.5
Chrysler Corporation	−0.1	4.1
Econoviews International Inc.	−0.1	3.9
U.S. Trust Co.	−0.2	4.3
Reeder Associates (Charles)	−0.3	4.9
Siff, Oakley, Marks Inc.	−0.3	4.8
Morgan Stanley & Co.	−0.3	4.7
Eggert Economic Enterprises, Inc.	−0.3	3.9
CoreStates Financial Corp.	−0.4	4.3
Mortgage Bankers Association of America	−0.4	4.3
Bank of America	−0.4	3.6
E. I. Du Pont de Nemours & Co.	−0.5	4.8
National Association of Home Builders	−0.5	4.5
Metropolitan Life Insurance Co.	−0.5	4.5
Ford Motor Company	−0.6	4.6
Chase Manhattan Bank	−0.6	4.0
U.S. Chamber of Commerce	−0.7	5.0H
Manufacturers Hanover Trust Co.	−0.7	4.4
Bankers Trust Co.	−0.7	4.4
Laurence H. Meyer & Assoc.	−0.7	4.0
Security Pacific National Bank	−0.7	4.0
PNC Financial Corp.	−0.9	4.3
UCLA Business Forecast	−0.9	4.2
Merrill Lynch	−1.1	4.4
Georgia State University	−1.1	3.6
Equitable Life Assurance	−1.2	4.7
Morgan Guaranty Trust Co.	−1.2	3.8
Shawmut National Corp.	−1.3L	4.0

of diffusion indexes and averaged bivariate VAR forecasts and utilizing a large number of U.S. time series. All nonjudgmental stationary forecasts of GNP turned out to be *higher than most of the private forecasts*.

Figure 1 presents the distribution of private forecasts of GDP growth rates in 1990–2001. These forecasts were made in each quarter for GDP growth over the full year *following the year of the forecast*. Hence, in each quarter of a given year the four forecasts were made for the *same year*. For example, in March, June, September, and December of 1994 individual forecasts are for the full year 1995. Figure 1 exhibits the fifth percentile and the ninety-fifth percentile of the forecast distribution in each quarter and the horizontal bars show the realization of GDP growth a year later. For example, the bar in 1999 exhibits the growth rate realized in 2000 and forecasted in each of the four quarters of 1999. The stationary forecasts (not shown) are narrowly distributed just below 3 percent: In some periods private forecasts are above and in other periods they are below the stationary forecasts.

The empirical record thus reveals wide fluctuations of individual forecasts of variables about which there is no private information. Moreover, individual forecasts fluctuate over time around the stationary forecasts, showing no sign of convergence to these nondiscretionary stationary forecasts. So, how does the theory of rational beliefs explain these facts?

An account of the RB theory can be found in Kurz (1997a) or Kurz and Motolese (2001). Here we explain briefly that the RB theory *assumes* that agents do not know the true probability underlying the equilibrium process but that they have a great deal of past data about the observable variables in the economy. Using past data agents compute the empirical distribution and construct from it a probability measure over infinite sequences of observable variables. It can be

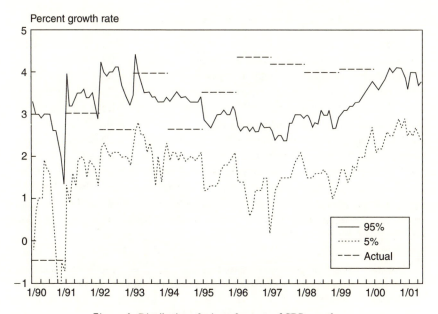

Figure 1. Distribution of private forecasts of GDP growth.

shown that this probability is stationary and hence *agents do not disagree about the stationary forecasts*. Since the true equilibrium process is not known and is likely to be nonstationary, agents who believe the process to be nonstationary construct their own subjective probability models. A *rational belief* is then a probability over infinite sequences of observables, perhaps nonstationary, that *cannot be contradicted by the empirical evidence*. More specifically, if one uses an RB to simulate the data of the economy it will reproduce the known empirical distribution of equilibrium observables. An RB may, at times, exhibit "optimism" or "pessimism" relative to the stationary forecasts, but it would be irrational to forecast *at all dates* above or below the stationary forecasts. That is, rationality requires the RB forecasts to be compatible with the stationary forecasts: The time average of the conditional forecasts must be equal to the conditional stationary forecasts. It is a theorem that nonstationary rational beliefs act as in the data: Conditional upon given observables, the forecasts fluctuate over time around the stationary forecast with no tendency toward convergence. In short, the RB theory proposes that the forecasts in Table 1 and Figure 1 are made by agents who do not believe that the dynamics of the economy is stationary. They use their own models, combining past data with subjective assessment of the unique conditions prevailing in the market at each date.

The purpose of this chapter is to study the implications of RBE for the dynamics of monetary economies, and hence we assume that agents hold rational beliefs rather than rational expectations. We examine to what degree standard results of monetary analysis can be generated by an RBE in comparison with assumptions employed in other monetary models. It would thus be helpful to briefly clarify our assumptions in relation to other current work on economic fluctuations and monetary economics.

1.2. Our Assumptions in Relation to the Literature

i. Technological Shocks and Investments. Traditional real business cycle (RBC) models used the Solow residual as a measure of technological shocks. However, empirical evidence has revealed that this measure depends upon endogenous variables such as capacity utilization (e.g., Greenwood et al., 1988; Burnside et al., 1995; Basu, 1996). Computational limitations preclude us from introducing endogenous capacity utilization and we focus only on the sign and size of productivity shocks. We agree with the critique of most writers (e.g., Summers, 1986; Eichenbaum, 1991) that exogenous technological shocks constitute a small fraction of the Solow residual and negative technological shocks are unjustified.[1] We thus conclude that the observed data of economic fluctuations cannot be explained by an exogenous process of nonnegative productivity shocks with small variance. For examples of alternative approaches within the RBC tradition see Wen (1998a,b) and King and Rebelo (1999).

---

1. In a recent paper Cole and Ohanian (2000) argue that the Great Depression resulted from a cumulative 15 percent negative technological shock to the U.S. economy during 1929–1932. We cannot support such a conclusion.

We assume *a very small variance* of the exogenous technological shocks but explicitly incorporate an investment goods sector, which transforms consumption goods into capital goods ("machines"), to model the uncertainty associated with the outcome of new investments. The output of the investment sector is stochastic, so investment decisions must be based on the assessment of this risk. The investment sector itself is very simple, consisting of two projects that vary in productivity depending upon specified random shocks. We then investigate the impact of the distribution of beliefs on aggregate fluctuations of investments, output, and prices.

ii. Asymmetric Information. In a rational expectations equilibrium (REE) the study of monetary policy focused, at the early stages, on the effects of informational asymmetries. Lucas (1972) argued that money has real effect because people confuse changes in price level with changes in relative prices. By implication, monetary policy has a real effect only when it is unanticipated. Empirical evidence has not supported this conclusion (see, e.g., Mishkin, 1982), revealing that both anticipated as well as unanticipated changes in money have real effects. In an RBE agents hold different conditional probabilities and arrive at different conclusions when they condition on current information. That is, *agents interpret current information differently.* Hence, even fully observed monetary shocks might be interpreted differently by agents, and money nonneutrality is implied (for earlier work, see Motolese, 2000, 2001). Focusing here on the effects of beliefs we thus assume in this chapter *that there is no asymmetric information.*

iii. Sticky Prices, Monopolistic Competition, and Credit. The *dynamic new Keynesian* theory (DNK) has developed an integrated view of monetary equilibrium, built upon two basic assumptions: (1) The market consists of monopolistically competitive firms that are price-setters, and (2) prices are "sticky" owing to the existence of long-term contracts (e.g., Taylor, 1980; Calvo, 1983; Yun, 1996; Clarida et al., 1999; Rotemberg and Woodford, 1999; Woodford, 1999, 2000, 2001a,b). Many authors work with Calvo's (1983) idealization, in which at any date only a fraction of firms are "allowed" to change prices. In such an economy the object of monetary policy is to restore efficiency by countering the negative effect of price rigidity. Although the DNK offers a unified perspective of monetary policy, the model of sticky prices explains very little of the observed volatility in our economy, and we shall thus not adopt any of the assumptions of the DNK. Our RBE is an equilibrium of an economy that is *fully competitive* in which *prices are fully flexible.* In doing so we are not rejecting the proposition that some money nonneutrality is due to wage or price rigidity, and such rigidity has important policy implications. Moreover, some recent versions of the DNK model propose that an important effect of monetary policy operates through its impact on the availability of credit to borrowing firms. Bernanke and Gertler (1989), Carlstrom and Fuerst (1997), and Bernanke et al. (1999) argue that fluctuations in the return to capital and in asset prices alter the collateral available to borrowers, generating an amplification that they call a "financial accelerator." Although we agree that credit is an important component of monetary analysis, the financial accelerator was developed under strong assumptions. We hope to incorporate in our model a credit amplification mechanism that operates under weaker assumptions.

iv. The Rationale for Monetary Policy. Most optimal policy models do not explain why a central bank should follow a stabilization policy. They are typically formulated as reduced-form systems of equations representing the private sector. The central bank then selects *directly* optimal inflation and GNP growth rates so as to minimize a quadratic objective (e.g., Taylor, 1993, 2000). The *implicit* justification for stabilization policy is the view that the private allocation is not Pareto optimal, reflected by fluctuations in the growth rate of GNP and the rate of inflation around their targets. The targets themselves are treated as Pareto-optimal states. Our objectives in this chapter are very limited. We do not characterize optimal monetary policy and only use the "policy" of exogenous variations in money supply. Our modest aim is to study the impact of diverse beliefs in an RBE on the dynamics of a monetary economy. We demonstrate that the distribution of beliefs causes endogenous amplification of fluctuations and argue that Pareto optimality is not an adequate criterion for monetary policy. A preliminary view of stabilization policy is discussed in Section 4.

We thus formulate a monetary model with two infinitely lived agents and study its volatility. We use numerical simulations to demonstrate the theoretical properties of the model but *do not attempt an accurate calibration.* To sum up our conclusions we note first that our investment model is simplistic, incorporating compromises to facilitate computations. Consequently some results are counterfactual and hence the chapter offers only qualitative and conceptual results. With these qualifications stated, this chapter proposes three basic perspectives:

1. The RBE paradigm offers an integrated theory of real and financial volatility with a high volume of trade. Most volatility in an RBE is induced endogenously through the beliefs of agents.
2. Although our RBE assumes *fully competitive* markets in which *prices are fully flexible*, the diverse expectations of agents can explain most of the familiar features of monetary equilibria. This includes money non-neutrality, Phillips curve, and impulse response functions with respect to monetary shocks.
3. Agents with diverse but inconsistent beliefs may induce socially undesirable excess fluctuations even when the allocation is ex ante Pareto-optimal. Central bank policy should aim to reduce the endogenous component of this volatility.

2. THE ECONOMIC ENVIRONMENT

The model economy has four traded goods: a consumption good, a capital good, labor services, and money. Agents can buy existing capital goods on the open market but new capital goods are produced by two alternative activities whose output depends upon a random shock that affects only the investments sector. The decision of how much installed capital goods to buy on the open market and how much to invest in new projects depends upon the beliefs of the agents and upon the price of capital goods. Investments are irreversible: Once produced, capital goods cannot be turned back into consumption goods although they depreciate with use. There are two infinitely lived agents with utility over consumption, labor services, and real money holding. These agents make all the intertemporal decisions in this economy. The income of agents consists of labor income and the income they receive from assets that they trade in competitive markets. The first asset is an ownership unit of real capital goods employed by the firms in the economy. Aggregate supply of such units equals the number of units of capital in the economy. At each date a unit of capital pays a risky dividend and has a risky return consisting of dividends and capital gains. The second asset is a one-period bill that pays a riskless *nominal* return and has a zero net supply. The third asset is fiat money issued by the central bank. Under the money supply policy studied in this chapter a *random* change in the money supply results in a random change in the money holding of an agent. To avoid issues related to public budget constraint, the expected growth rate of money equals the expected growth of output and the model exhibits zero long-run inflation.

Competitive firms in this economy are myopic in outlook. At each date they hire labor services and rent capital from the agents who own the capital goods. They maximize current profits of producing consumer goods given the prices of consumer goods, capital goods, rental on capital, and wage rate. Markets for labor and capital services are competitive. New investments are carried out directly by the two agents utilizing publicly available investment technology, so all intertemporal decisions are made by the agents while firms carry out current production.

2.1. The Technology

The model has two sectors. The production of consumer goods is carried out by competitive firms while the production of capital goods is carried out *directly by the agents* in their own facilities using only consumer goods as inputs. This simple nature of the capital goods sector enables us to use a rather simple notation, as follows: P_t is the price of consumption goods (the "price level") at t; $P_t/P_{t-1} = \pi_t = 1 +$ the rate of inflation at t; K_{t-1} is the real capital stock employed in the production of consumer goods at t; W_t^N is the nominal wage at t; $\tilde{q}_t^s$ is the nominal price at t of a unit of capital goods installed; $q_t^s = \tilde{q}_t^s/P_t$ is the real price of capital goods at t; L_t is the labor input in the production of consumer goods at t; N_t is the input at t, in units of consumption goods, into the production of capital goods; Y_t is the real output of consumer goods at t; and I_t is the real output of new capital goods produced by the investment technology.

2.1.1. Output and Productivity

There are a large number of identical competitive firms, and aggregate output of consumer goods is defined by a standard production function:

$$Y_t = A v_t (K_{t-1})^\sigma (\xi_t L_t)^{1-\sigma} \quad \text{(typically with } A = 1\text{).} \tag{1}$$

The productivity process $\{\xi_t, t = 1, 2, \ldots\}$ is a *deterministic* trend process satisfying

$$\xi_{t+1}/\xi_t = v^*, \tag{1a}$$

whereas random productivity $\{v_{t+1}, t = 1, 2, \ldots\}$ is a Markov process of the form

$$\log(v_{t+1}) = \lambda_v \log(v_t) + \rho_{t+1}^v, \qquad \rho_t^v \sim N\left(0, \sigma_v^2\right) \quad \text{iid.} \tag{1b}$$

Most productivity studies set the quarterly mean rate of technological change at $v^* = 1.0045$, and this is the value we use in all our computations.

The key parameters for the traditional RBC literature are (λ_v, σ_v) set at $\lambda_v = 0.976$, $\sigma_v = 0.0072$ for quarterly data. Empirical evidence suggests that σ_v is a fraction of 0.0072 and for low values of this parameter the RBC model fails to generate volatility (see King and Rebelo, 1999, fig. 8, p. 965). Accordingly, we set these parameters in our model at $\sigma = 0.35$, $\lambda_v = 0.976$, $\sigma_v = 0.002$.

The aggregate capital accumulation equation is defined by

$$K_t = (1 - \delta)K_{t-1} + I_t, \tag{2}$$

where δ is the rate of depreciation and I_t are new units of capital placed into production at $t + 1$ (inputs on these units would have been expanded at t) by the investment goods sector. Most studies set $\delta = 0.025$ and this is the value we use. Define $k_t = K_t/\xi_t$, $i_t = I_t/\xi_t$, $w_t = W_t^N/\xi_t P_t$, and $g_t = Y_t/\xi_t$; hence,

$$g_t = \frac{Y_t}{\xi_t} = Av_t L_t \left(\frac{k_{t-1}}{v^* L_t}\right)^\sigma \tag{3a}$$

and

$$k_t = (1 - \delta)\frac{k_{t-1}}{v^*} + i_t. \tag{3b}$$

Since $q_t^s = \tilde{q}_t^s/P_t$ is the real price of a unit of capital, in equilibrium the real wage rate w_t and the rental rate on capital R_t are defined by the marginal productivity conditions in consumption goods:

$$w_t = Av_t(1 - \sigma)\left(\frac{k_{t-1}}{v^* L_t}\right)^\sigma, \tag{4a}$$

$$R_t = Av_t\sigma\left(\frac{k_{t-1}}{v^* L_t}\right)^{\sigma-1} - \delta q_t^s. \tag{4b}$$

2.1.2. THE INVESTMENT SECTOR

Heterogeneity of investment activities and uncertainty in the productivity of the investment goods sector are central features of our model. Investments embody new technologies, new products, and new processes of production. Such new capacities may or may not be successfully incorporated into the economy. These reflect the fact that most new enterprises fail and a significant number of investments in new technologies do not achieve their goal. Uncertainty in the production of capital goods also incorporates the risk associated with the *diversification* strategy of firms across different product lines or economic sectors. In such cases the risk reflects many different factors. For example, drilling for oil is associated with the direct risk of finding oil. The risk of building a massive network of fiber optics communication is associated with the uncertainty of future demand for such capacities, as has been recently illustrated. Since our model does not have heterogeneous commodities to reflect all these risks, we introduce this uncertainty in the form of *the number of units of realized capital goods that result from an input of one unit of consumption goods.*

Optimal investment decisions depend upon expectations of returns among alternatives. Although we could have introduced a large number of investment activities, simplicity suggests that two activities suffice to exhibit all the essential features. The two constant-returns-to-scale projects transform consumer goods into a random number of units of capital goods depending upon the realized state φ_t. The random output of the two activities is specified in the following way:

TECHNOLOGY I (M):

$$\text{Input: 1 unit of consumption good; Output}_{t+1}^M = \kappa_{t+1}^M = d_1 + \frac{d_2 - d_1}{1 + e^{-\chi^\varphi \varphi_{t+1}}}, \quad (5a)$$

TECHNOLOGY II (S):

$$\text{Input: 1 unit of consumption good; Output}_{t+1}^S = \kappa_{t+1}^S = s_1 + \frac{s_2 - s_1}{1 + e^{-\chi^\varphi \varphi_{t+1}}}, \quad (5b)$$

where the empirical distribution of the shock is $\varphi_t \sim N(0, \sigma_\varphi^2)$ iid. The REE is defined to be the equilibrium under the belief that $\varphi_t \sim N(0, \sigma_\varphi^2)$ is the truth. In an RBE agents know that the long-term frequency of the states is represented by $\varphi_t \sim N(0, \sigma_\varphi^2)$ but they do not know the true process.

We assume that relative to the distribution $\varphi_t \sim N(0, \sigma_\varphi^2)$, it is optimal to fully diversify investments *leading to a perfect hedged position and no aggregate uncertainty.*[2] To clarify this issue consider the case $d_1 = 0.85$, $d_2 = 0.95$, $s_1 = 1.05$, $s_2 = 0.75$, $\chi^\varphi = 3$ used in most of the simulations in this chapter. If an agent invests 1 unit with proportions $I^M = \frac{3}{4}$, $I^S = \frac{1}{4}$ he ensures production of 0.90 units of capital in *all states*. His expected value is also 0.90, so diversification is optimal. When all agents believe that $\varphi_t \sim N(0, \sigma_\varphi^2)$ is the truth, they will have a fully diversified investment portfolio with *no fluctuations in the aggregate level or realized aggregate cost of investments.*

In an economy with diverse beliefs agents do not fully diversify. They believe that the mean value function of $\{\varphi_t, t = 1, 2, 3, \ldots\}$ varies over time (which is true), and they have subjective models about this value. Since the long-term moments of φ_t are $(0, \sigma_\varphi^2)$ with 0 autocorrelation, the rationality of belief conditions require

---

2. Our assumption of the optimality of a perfect hedge is made for convenience only. It is motivated by computational ease since the perturbation method used here enables us to compute the equilibrium using the steady state as a reference point. The case where full diversification is not optimal raises only computational difficulties, not conceptual ones.

the agents' models to be statistically compatible with these facts. However, at each date they do not believe that the mean value is zero, so their optimal investment portfolio will vary depending upon these beliefs.

2.2. The Infinitely Lived Agents

We first introduce the following notation for $k = 1, 2$: C_t^k is the consumption of k at t; $\ell_t^k = 1 - L_t^k$ is the leisure of k at t; K_t^{kd} is the amount of capital stock purchases by k on the open market at t; K_{t-1}^k is the amount of capital owned by k at t and used in production at t; N_t^{kM} is the input (in units of consumption goods) of k in investments technology M at t; N_t^{kS} is the input (in units of consumption goods) of k in investments technology S at t; $N_t^k = N_t^{kM} + N_t^{kS}$ is the total input of agent k in investments technology at t; I_t^k is the total *output of* new investments (in *units of capital goods*) of k at t; B_t^k is the amount of a one-period nominal bill purchased by agent k at t; q_t^b is the price of a one-period bill at t, which is a discount price; M_t^k is the amount of money held by agent k at t; $M_t/M_{t-1} = \varrho_t$ is the random growth rate of money supply when it is a policy instrument; and H_t is the history of all observables up to t.

Before formulating the agents' optimization we need to clarify *the issue of timing*. At date t agent k invests (N_t^{kM}, N_t^{kS}) and at the start of date $t + 1$ the random realization takes place in the investment goods sector, *before* the rate of technical progress is realized. The new capital I_t^k joining production is added to $K_t^d = K_t^{1d} + K_t^{2d}$ to form the capital K_t used in production at date $t + 1$. This implies $I_t^k = \kappa_{t+1}^M N_t^{kM} + \kappa_{t+1}^S N_t^{kS}, k = 1, 2$, which is somewhat odd notation. This odd feature is unavoidable since we compress two random realizations into one date: first of φ_t and then of ν_t, the rate of technological progress. Now, denote the inputs into the investment sector by $N_t = N_t^1 + N_t^2$. Output of new investments at date t is affected by φ_t and is defined by

$$I_{t-1}^k = \kappa_t^M N_{t-1}^{kM} + \kappa_t^S N_{t-1}^{kS}, \qquad k = 1, 2.$$

We thus define I_t^N, the *value* of new investments placed into production at date t, to be

$$I_t^N = \tilde{q}_t^s \left(I_{t-1}^1 + I_{t-1}^2 \right) \quad \text{(while noting that } I_{t-1} = I_{t-1}^1 + I_{t-1}^2 \text{)}$$

and Y_t^N, which is GNP, by $Y_t^N = Y_t - N_t + I_t^N$. Define $g^N = Y_t^N/\xi_t$, $n_t = N_t/\xi_t$, $i_t^N = I_t^N/\xi_t$, and the income identity becomes $g_t^N = g_t - n_t + i_t^N$.

Now, for any probability belief Q^k of agent k, his problem is to maximize the utility

$$\max E_{Q^k} \left\{ \sum_{t=1}^{\infty} \beta_k^{t-1} \frac{1}{1 - \gamma_k} \left\{ \left[C_t^k \left(\ell_t^k \right)^\varsigma \right]^{1-\gamma_k} \right. \right. \tag{6a}$$

$$\left. \left. + \left(M_t^k/P_t \right)^{1-\gamma_k} \right\} \middle| H_t \right\}, \qquad 0 < \beta_k < 1,$$

subject to the budget constraint

$$P_t C_t^k + K_t^{kd} \tilde{q}_t^s + \left(N_t^{kM} + N_t^{kS}\right) P_t + B_t^k q_t^b - \left(1 - \ell_t^k\right) W_t^N \qquad (6b)$$

$$- K_{t-1}^k \left(\tilde{q}_t^s + R_t P_t\right) - B_{t-1}^k + M_t^k - M_{t-1}^k \varrho_t = 0,$$

$$I_{t-1}^k = \kappa_t^M N_{t-1}^{kM} + \kappa_t^S N_{t-1}^{kS}, \qquad N_t^{kM} \geq 0, \qquad N_t^{kS} \geq 0, \qquad (6c)$$

$$K_{t-1}^k = K_{t-1}^{kd} + I_{t-1}^k. \qquad (6d)$$

Note the distinction between K_t^{kd} purchased at t on the open market and K_{t-1}^k used in production at t and owned by the agent at that time. Normalize the problem by $c_t^k = C_t^k/\xi_t$, $b_t^k = B_t^k/P_t\xi_t$, $M_t/P_t\xi_t = m_t$, $M_t^k/P_t\xi_t = m_t^k$, $M_{t-1}^k/P_t\xi_t = m_{t-1}^k/\pi_t v_t$, $n_t^k = N_t^k/\xi_t$, $i_t^k = I_t^k/\xi_t$, $k_t^k = K_t^k/\xi_t$, $K_t^{kd} = K_t^{kd}/\xi_t$. With the use of (5a) and (5b) and $P_{t+1}/P_t = \pi_{t+1}$ the maximization problem becomes

$$\max E_Q \sum_{t=1}^{\infty} \beta_k^{t-1} \frac{1}{1 - \gamma_k} \left\{ \left[c_t^k \xi_t \left(\ell_t^k\right)^\varsigma\right]^{1-\gamma_k} + \left(m_t^k \xi_t\right)^{1-\gamma_k} \right\}, \qquad 0 < \beta_k < 1, \quad (6a')$$

subject to

$$c_t^k = \left(1 - \ell_t^k\right) w_t + \frac{k_{t-1}^k}{v^*} (q_t^s + R_t) + \frac{m_{t-1}^k \varrho_t + b_{t-1}^k}{v^* \pi_t} - k_t^{kd} q_t^s \qquad (6b')$$

$$- \left(n_t^{kM} + n_t^{kS}\right) - b_t^k q_t^b - m_t^k,$$

$$i_{t-1}^k = \kappa_t^M n_{t-1}^{kM} + \kappa_t^S n_{t-1}^{kS}, \qquad n_{t-1}^{kM} \geq 0, \qquad n_{t-1}^{kS} \geq 0, \qquad (6c')$$

$$k_{t-1}^k = k_t^{kd} + i_{t-1}^k. \qquad (6d')$$

To simplify the Euler equations we ignore the inequality constraints in (6c') and handle them only as computational issues raised by the model.[3] Hence, the first-order conditions for labor supply are

$$c_t^k = (1/\varsigma)\ell_t^k w_t. \qquad (7a)$$

Next, the first-order condition with respect to capital purchased on the open market k_t^{kd} is

---

3. An Appendix B on the computational model is not included in this published version. Any interested reader can obtain this appendix by downloading the prepublished version of this chapter, which is posted on the homepage of the first author at http://www.stanford.edu/~mordecai. The prepublished version also contains Appendix A, which provides a short account of the theory of rational beliefs and other technical details not included here.

$$\left(c_t^k\right)^{-\gamma_k}\left[\left(\ell_t^k\right)^\zeta\right]^{1-\gamma_k} q_t^s = \beta_k E_{Q^k}\left(c_{t+1}^k\right)^{-\gamma_k}\left[\left(\ell_{t+1}^k\right)^\zeta\right]^{1-\gamma_k}\left[\frac{q_{t+1}^S + R_{t+1}}{(v^*)^{\gamma_k}}\right]. \quad \text{(7b)}$$

The optimality condition with respect to n_t^{kM} is

$$\left(c_t^k\right)^{-\gamma_k}\left[\left(\ell_t^k\right)^\zeta\right]^{1-\gamma_k} = \beta_k E_{Q^k}\left(c_{t+1}^k\right)^{-\gamma_k}\left[\left(\ell_{t+1}^k\right)^\zeta\right]^{1-\gamma_k}\left[\frac{q_{t+1}^S + R_{t+1}}{(v^*)^{\gamma_k}}\kappa_{t+1}^M\right], \quad \text{(7c)}$$

and the condition with respect to n_t^{kS} is

$$\left(c_t^k\right)^{-\gamma_k}\left[\left(\ell_t^k\right)^\zeta\right]^{1-\gamma_k} = \beta_k E_{Q^k}\left(c_{t+1}^k\right)^{-\gamma_k}\left[\left(\ell_{t+1}^k\right)^\zeta\right]^{1-\gamma_k}\left[\frac{q_{t+1}^S + R_{t+1}}{(v^*)^{\gamma_k}}\kappa_{t+1}^S\right]. \quad \text{(7d)}$$

The first-order condition with respect to b_t^k is

$$\left(c_t^k\right)^{-\gamma_k}\left(\ell_t^k\right)^{\zeta(1-\gamma_k)} q_t^b = \beta_k E_{Q^k}\left(c_{t+1}^k\right)^{-\gamma_k}\left(\ell_{t+1}^k\right)^{\zeta(1-\gamma_k)}\frac{1}{(v^*)^{\gamma_k}\pi_{t+1}}. \quad \text{(7e)}$$

Finally, the optimum with respect to money holdings requires

$$\left(c_t^k\right)^{-\gamma_k}\left(\ell_t^k\right)^{\zeta(1-\gamma_k)} - \left(m_t^k\right)^{-\gamma_k} = \beta_k E_{Q^k}\left[\left(c_{t+1}^k\right)^{-\gamma_k}\left(\ell_{t+1}^k\right)^{\zeta(1-\gamma_k)}\right]\frac{\varrho_{t+1}}{(v^*)^{\gamma_k}\pi_{t+1}}. \quad \text{(7f)}$$

2.3. Monetary Policy

The monetary "policy" in the model is the familiar monetary injection: The central bank increases the money supply by a random amount $(\varrho_{t+1} - 1)M_t$. Hence, M_t^k, which is the date t money holding of agent k, increases to $\varrho_{t+1}M_t^k$ between date t and date $t + 1$. Agents observe the monetary shock and since they observe the real shocks (v_t, φ_t), the exogenous state is fully observed.

Random variations in the money supply do not constitute a serious monetary policy that may be pursued by any central bank. This chapter is a theoretical investigation in which an exogenous money supply is a simple device for studying the effect of beliefs on economic fluctuations. This approach will also enable us to discuss the role that a real monetary policy should play in economic stabilization.

2.4. Equilibrium

For each set of probability beliefs (Q^1, Q^2) of the agents on infinite sequences of observed variables, a monetary equilibrium of the economy is defined by equations: (3a), (3b), (4a), (4b), (6b′), and (7a)–(7f), as well as by the following additional conditions:

Money growth: The money supply satisfies

$$m_t = (\varrho_t/\pi_t v_t)\, m_{t-1}.$$

Market clearing conditions: Given the accounting in (6a)–(6d) we aggregate to establish two equations, one accounting identity, specifying the amount of capital employed at date t:

$$K_{t-1} = K_{t-1}^1 + K_{t-1}^2,$$

and a market clearing condition in the market for installed capital at date t:

$$K_t^{1d} + K_t^{2d} = K_{t-1}(1 - \delta).$$

The dynamics of capital employed is then defined by

$$K_t = K_{t-1}(1 - \delta) + I_t,$$

$$I_{t-1} = I_{t-1}^1 + I_{t-1}^2 = \kappa_t^M \left(N_{t-1}^{1M} + N_{t-1}^{2M} \right) + \kappa_t^S \left(N_{t-1}^{1S} + N_{t-1}^{2S} \right).$$

After normalization we thus have the identities

$$k_t^1 + k_t^2 = k_t \qquad \text{for all } t,$$

$$i_{t-1}^k = \kappa_t^M n_{t-1}^{kM} + \kappa_t^S n_{t-1}^{kS}, \qquad k = 1, 2 \qquad \text{for all } t,$$

and the market clearing conditions

$$k_t = k_{t-1}\left[(1 - \delta)/v^*\right] + i_t \qquad \text{for all } t, \tag{8a}$$

$$k_t^{1d} + k_t^{2d} = k_{t-1}\left[(1 - \delta)/v^*\right] \qquad \text{for all } t, \tag{8b}$$

$$b_t^1 + b_t^2 = 0 \qquad \text{for all } t, \tag{8c}$$

$$\left(1 - \ell_t^1\right) + \left(1 - \ell_t^2\right) = L_t \qquad \text{for all } t, \tag{8d}$$

$$m_t^1 + m_t^2 = m_t \qquad \text{for all } t. \tag{8e}$$

We turn now to the central question of the beliefs of the agents.

3. A RATIONAL BELIEF EQUILIBRIUM

We now construct the RBE and explain the family of rational beliefs that we study. For a detailed account of the method of constructing an RBE see Kurz and Motolese (2001). In Section 3.3 we explain the method of assessment variables, used extensively in this chapter, for describing a rational belief.

3.1. The Equilibrium Map

Our procedure is to construct an RBE for the economy, use perturbation methods to compute it, and study its dynamic properties via simulations. However, to define an RBE we have to specify the beliefs of the agents and this cannot be done without saying something about the empirical distribution implied by that RBE and its induced stationary measure.[4] To break this circularity we start by studying the *structure* of an RBE and use it for a general specification of the *structure* of the stationary measure around which we construct the beliefs of the agents (for details of this approach, see Kurz and Motolese, 2001, sect. 2.4). Such a constructive procedure is possible only when we study a specific family of rational beliefs, which is the case in this chapter. We carry out this procedure in several steps, starting with the equilibrium map.

Recall that in the optimization (6a′)–(6b′) agent k derives optimal decisions by using belief Q_y^k conditional on public information and on y_t^k, the value of his own assessment variable. *We assume that all portfolios and exogenous shocks* $(v_t, \varrho_t, \varphi_t)$ *are observable.* The observables are $x_t = (v_t, \varrho_t, \varphi_t, k_{t-1}^{1d}, n_{t-1}^{1M}, n_{t-1}^{1S}, b_{t-1}^1, k_{t-1}^{2d}, n_{t-1}^{2M}, n_{t-1}^{2S}, b_{t-1}^2, m_{t-1}^1, m_{t-1}^2, q_t^s, q_t^b, \pi_t)$. To simplify we denote lagged endogenous variables $x_{t-1}^E = (k_{t-1}^{1d}, n_{t-1}^{1M}, n_{t-1}^{1S}, b_{t-1}^1, m_{t-1}^1, k_{t-1}^{2d}, n_{t-1}^{2M}, n_{t-1}^{2S}, b_{t-1}^2, m_{t-1}^2)$. Agent k will thus condition on (x_t, y_t^k) and hence optimal decisions are functions of the form

$$k_t^{kd} = k^{kd}\left(v_t, \varrho_t, \varphi_t, x_{t-1}^E, q_t^s, q_t^b, \pi_t, y_t^k\right) \qquad k = 1, 2, \qquad (9a)$$

$$n_t^{kM} = i^{kM}\left(v_t, \varrho_t, \varphi_t, x_{t-1}^E, q_t^s, q_t^b, \pi_t, y_t^k\right) \qquad k = 1, 2, \qquad (9b)$$

$$n_t^{kS} = i^{kS}\left(v_t, \varrho_t, \varphi_t, x_{t-1}^E, q_t^s, q_t^b, \pi_t, y_t^k\right) \qquad k = 1, 2, \qquad (9c)$$

$$b_t^k = b^k\left(v_t, \varrho_t, \varphi_t, x_{t-1}^E, q_t^s, q_t^b, \pi_t, y_t^k\right) \qquad k = 1, 2, \qquad (9d)$$

$$m_t^k = m^k\left(v_t, \varrho_t, \varphi_t, x_{t-1}^E, q_t^s, q_t^b, \pi_t, y_t^k\right) \qquad k = 1, 2, \qquad (9e)$$

$$\ell_t^k = \ell^k\left(v_t, \varrho_t, \varphi_t, x_{t-1}^E, q_t^s, q_t^b, \pi_t, y_t^k\right) \qquad k = 1, 2. \qquad (9f)$$

Market clearing conditions imply that the equilibrium price process $\{(q_t^s, q_t^b, \pi_t), t = 1, 2, \ldots\}$ is thus defined by a map of the form

---

4. The empirical distribution of the observable variables or their moments induce a probability measure over infinite sequences of observables that is central to the theory of rational beliefs. A general definition and construction of this probability measure is explained in Kurz (1997a) or in Appendix A of the prepublished version available at the web address provided in footnote 3. Any statement in the text about "the stationary measure" or "the empirical distribution" is always a reference to this probability measure. Its centrality to the theory arises from the fact that this probability is derived from public information and hence *the stationary measure is known to all agents and agreed upon by all to reflect the empirical distribution of equilibrium quantities.*

$$\begin{pmatrix} q_t^s \\ q_t^b \\ \pi_t \end{pmatrix} = \Phi\left(v_t, \varrho_t, \varphi_t, y_t^1, y_t^2, x_{t-1}^E\right). \qquad (10)$$

Equation (10) reveals that the volatility of equilibrium prices is determined by three factors: exogenous states $(v_t, \varrho_t, \varphi_t)$, lagged endogenous variables x_{t-1}^E, and the states of belief (y_t^1, y_t^2). "Endogenous uncertainty" was defined by Kurz (1974, 1997a) as that component of volatility that is generated by the distribution of beliefs in the market, represented by (y_t^1, y_t^2). In Section 3.3 we explain that an assessment variable y_t^k is a simple mathematical representation of a private state of belief. The term y_t^k is a privately perceived parameter of the agent's belief, *uniquely* defining his conditional probability belief over observables. The states of an agent's belief are restricted by the rationality of belief conditions, and the restrictions applicable to our model are specified later.

The Euler equations and the definition of consumption in (6b')–(6d') show that at any date t agent k has to forecast three categories of variables discussed later: (1) exogenous variables $(v_{t+1}, \varrho_{t+1}, \varphi_{t+1})$ conditional upon information at t and his assessment y_t^k; (2) his own decisions at $t + 1$, $(k_t^{kd}, n_{t+1}^{kM}, n_{t+1}^{kS}, b_{t+1}^k, \ell_{t+1}^k, m_{t+1}^k)$, based on his optimal decision functions and a forecast of his assessment y_{t+1}^k; (3) other endogenous variables, particularly prices $(q_{t+1}^s, q_{t+1}^b, \pi_{t+1})$, conditional upon information at t and his assessment y_t^k. The rationality of belief conditions require that all moments of an agent's subjective model be exactly the same as the moments of the stationary measure derived from the empirical distribution of the observables. Hence, a formulation of the beliefs (or perception models) of agents necessitates our specifying first the general structure of the stationary measure.

3.2. Construction of the Stationary Measure

Our RBE is an equilibrium of a stochastic economy that fluctuates around steady-state values denoted by an asterisk. Since equilibrium quantities satisfy the map (10), the empirical distribution is determined *by the equilibrium map and the long-term behavior of* $(v_t, \varrho_t, \varphi_t, y_t^1, y_t^2)$. Our method of constructing an RBE is to specify first the empirical distribution of $(v_t, \varrho_t, \varphi_t, y_t^1, y_t^2)$. Once this is done, we specify the beliefs of agents and impose the rationality conditions.

The true processes may exhibit nonstationary dynamics. We thus *assume* instead that the stationary measure of exogenous variables $(v_t, \varrho_t, \varphi_t)$ and of states of belief (y_t^1, y_t^2) have the following structure:

$$\log v_{t+1} = \lambda_v \log v_t + \rho_{t+1}^v, \qquad \rho_t^v \sim N\left(0, \sigma_v^2\right) \text{ iid}, \qquad (11a)$$

$$\log \varrho_{t+1} = \log \varrho^* + \lambda_\varrho \left(\log \varrho_t - \log \varrho^*\right) + \rho_{t+1}^\varrho, \qquad \rho_t^\varrho \sim N\left(0, \sigma_\varrho^2\right) \text{ iid}, \qquad (11b)$$

$$\varphi_{t+1} = \rho_{t+1}^\varphi, \qquad \rho_t^\varphi \sim N\left(0, \sigma_\varphi^2\right) \text{ iid}. \qquad (11c)$$

The sequence of states $\{(y_t^1, y_t^2), t = 1, 2, \ldots\}$ is a *realization* of a stochastic process of the form

$$\begin{pmatrix} y_t^1 \\ y_t^2 \end{pmatrix} = \begin{pmatrix} \rho_t^{y^1} \\ \rho_t^{y^2} \end{pmatrix}, \quad \begin{pmatrix} \rho_t^{y^1} \\ \rho_t^{y^2} \end{pmatrix} \sim N \left[\begin{pmatrix} 0 \\ 0 \end{pmatrix}, \begin{pmatrix} \sigma_{y^1}^2, \sigma_{yy} \\ \sigma_{yy}, \sigma_{y^2}^2 \end{pmatrix} \right] \quad \text{iid.} \quad (11d)$$

Equations (11b)–(11d) are *hypothetical*. The assumptions that the investment sector shocks φ_t and the states of belief (y_t^1, y_t^2) *exhibit no long-run persistence* are made for computational simplicity. These assumptions are very strong and their implications will be evaluated later.

We make the following *additional simplifying assumptions:*

A1. $(\rho_t^v, \rho_t^\varrho, \rho_t^\varphi, \rho_t^{y^1}, \rho_t^{y^2})$ are mutually independent.
A2. $\varrho^* = v^*$; hence (v^*, v^*) are the steady-state values of (v_t, ϱ_t) in the riskless economy and the long-term average inflation rate is zero in both REE and RBE.
A3. As discussed earlier $\lambda_v = 0.976$, $\sigma_v = 0.002$.
A4. As monetary shocks and the stochastic investment technology are hypothetical, we specify $\sigma_\varphi = 1$, $\lambda_\varrho = 0.95$, $\sigma_\varrho = 0.0052$. This implies that the standard deviation of monetary shocks over time is 1 percent per quarter.

These assumptions are intended to enable a quantitative evaluation of the workings of our model by postulating persistence in the monetary shocks with a reasonable standard deviation. As for (y_t^1, y_t^2), we assume $\sigma_{y^1} = \sigma_{y^2} = 0.8$ and a correlation coefficient $\rho(y^1, y^2) = 0.95$, hence $\sigma_{yy} = 0.608$.

3.3. The Belief Structure

3.3.1. GENERAL ASSUMPTIONS

a. Properties of Assessment Variables
Assessment variables y_t^k for $k = 1, 2$ are the tools that we use to describe an agent's belief. We briefly review their properties here.

i. Definition. Assessment variables are artificial variables used to describe nonstationarity but without an intrinsic meaning of their own. Thus let X be a space of observables and suppose that we want to describe the nonstationarity of a dynamical system on the space of infinite sequences of observables $[(X)^\infty, \mathcal{B}((X)^\infty)]$, where $\mathcal{B}((X)^\infty)$ is the Borel σ-field of $(X)^\infty$. The conditional stability theorem (see Kurz and Schneider, 1996, and Nielsen, 1996) describes nonstationarity via artificial variables $y_t^k \in Y^k$ with a marginal probability space $[(Y^k)^\infty, \mathcal{B}((Y^k)^\infty), \mu]$. It postulates $(X \times Y^k)$ to be the state space, introduces a universal probability measure Q^k and space $[(X \times Y^k)^\infty, \mathcal{B}((X \times Y^k)^\infty), Q^k]$, and defines the desired nonstationary probability to be $Q_{y^k}^k \equiv Q^k[(\cdot) \mid y^k]$, the conditional probability of Q^k with respect to the sequence y^k. The term Q^k must satisfy the condition that for all $A \in \mathcal{B}((X)^\infty)$ and $B \in \mathcal{B}((Y)^\infty)$,

$$Q^k(A \times B) = \int_B Q^k_{y^k}(A)\mu(dy).$$

The *effective* conditional probability space $[(X)^\infty, \mathcal{B}((X)^\infty), Q^k_{y^k}]$ implies non-stationary dynamics of the observables since probabilities of events in $\mathcal{B}((X)^\infty)$ are not time independent: They change with the parameters y^k_t, which are time dependent. The advantage of using assessment variables is statistical since the stochastic structure above pins down the empirical regularity of y^k_t in relation to observables, and this regularity will be seen to be the basis for the rationality conditions. This approach is common in econometrics, where Y is the set of possible "regimes," y_t identifies the regime at t, and hence the y_t are viewed as "regime variables."

Although the space $[(X \times Y^k)^\infty, \mathcal{B}((X \times Y^k)^\infty), Q^k]$ is defined over a fixed set Y^k, this need not be the case. We could replace $(Y^k)^\infty$ by an infinite number of *different* spaces Y^k_j and define Q over the product space $[(X)^\infty \times \Pi_{j=1}^\infty Y^k_j]$. We can then define the desired nonstationary probability to be $Q^k_{y^k} \equiv Q^k[(\cdot) \mid y^k]$, which is conditional upon a sequence of *different* objects in $\Pi_{j=1}^\infty Y^k_j$. In short, assessment variables of an agent are privately perceived parameters that *the agent himself generates* for a description of his belief. They may be in different spaces at different times and in different spaces across agents so that there is no sense in which they can be compared. The quantity y^j_t is privately perceived by agent j and has meaning only to him; agent $k \neq j$ would not know what y^j_t means even if he could "observe" it.

ii. Economic Interpretation. $Q^k_{y_t}$ is the date t probability belief of future *observables* and y^k_t is used to describe how the agent's forecasts deviate from the stationary forecasts owing to his belief in nonstationarity. There are several issues to note. First, deviation from the stationary forecast is a judgment of "structural breaks" based on limited *recent* data. Such judgments are right or wrong, so in an RBE *rational agents are often wrong*. Second, in a nonstationary environment it is usually not possible to demonstrate with high likelihood that a belief was right, even in retrospect. Third, even if sufficient data become available to determine whether a change of structure had occurred, such information would arrive too late since all important decisions would have already been made.

iii. Statistical Simplicity. Rational agents do not deviate *systematically* from the stationary forecasts and to establish rationality of belief we need a statistical measure of an agent's deviation from these forecasts. Assessment variables provide a simple tool to measure such regularity.

iv. The Infinitely Lived Agent Is a Sequence of Decision-Makers, So Assessment Variables Are Not Subject to Rationality Conditions. An economy with changing technology and products is one in which the commodity space changes, and thus y^k_t at different times describes beliefs about different commodities or technologies. Hence, $y^k_{t_1}$ and $y^k_{t_2}$ for t_1 and t_2 in different time intervals are simply different *objects* making comparisons impossible, so that rationality conditions cannot apply to y_t^k. The problem is that a model with an infinite dimensional commodity space and infinitely varying regimes is analytically untractable. An idealization that makes sense is to assume that the commodity space is fixed[5] and that y_t^k, a private parameter meaningful only to agent k, is *required* to have a consistent meaning through time. But then how do we model the fact that in reality an agent cannot "test" his theory and no rationality conditions should apply to the sequence of y_t^k? The solution is to consider the infinitely lived agent as consisting of *an infinite sequence of members (of a family or organization) each making economic decisions over a relatively short time*. Every decision-maker knows only his own y_t^k, but not those of his predecessors. Hence, even if an agent has data to convince himself that his theory is right or wrong, such data arrive too late to be useful since all important decisions have already been made.

b. Other Assumptions

A5. *Anonymity assumption*: In an economy with two agents the belief of each has an impact on prices. Agents act competitively and ignore the effect of their own beliefs on equilibrium prices.

Agents know that beliefs impact prices and their forecasting models have to forecast the impact of future distribution of beliefs on prices. To explain how this works in our model note that knowing the stationary measure means knowing all long-term conditional distributions given the observed variables. However, given fundamentals $(x_{t-1}^E, v_t, \varrho_t, \varphi_t)$, the variability of endogenous variables is *determined by the variability of the states of belief* (y_t^1, y_t^2). Since states of belief are not observed, their impact is deduced from the long-term distribution of endogenous variables conditional upon $(x_{t-1}^E, v_t, \varrho_t, \varphi_t)$. States of belief account for the higher volatility of the endogenous variables unexplained by $(x_{t-1}^E, v_t, \varrho_t, \varphi_t)$. We have named this component of volatility Endogenous uncertainty and this argument shows that in learning the stationary measure *agents also discover the component of the stationary measure induced by the distribution of beliefs*. For simplicity of computations we make the following assumption:

A6. *Forecasting assumption I*: Agents believe that the endogenous impact of market states of belief on prices and other endogenous variables is the same as the component that is estimated from the stationary measure.

We turn finally to our last simplifying assumption regarding the forecasting of prices in the model.

A7. *Forecasting assumption II*: Agents forecast prices using the map (10) and perceive the impact of states of belief on prices and other endogenous variables via a variable z_t with the same distributional properties as the long-run properties of the unobserved states of belief (y_t^1, y_t^2).

---

5. Hence, one defines commodities by their attributes, such as "transportation equipment" instead of "airplanes" or "communication services" instead of "telephone." Over time, we then experience change in the cost of producing these services and their prices rather than change in the definitions of the products or services themselves.

Assumption A.7 is not entirely compatible with postulates of the RBE theory, which hold that agents do not know equilibrium maps or true probabilities; we make it in order to facilitate the computations of RBE. It amounts to assuming that our RBE are incomplete Radner equilibria (see Radner, 1972) with an expanded state space of unobserved states of beliefs. Markets are incomplete since agents have only two assets to trade market uncertainty.[6]

3.3.2. The Perception Models

Given a stationary measure, true probabilities play absolutely no role in defining equilibrium. What matters is what agents *know* and *how they perceive the future.* We have already selected the basic long-term statistics that agents know, and we now turn to their perceptions. Our strategy is to *specify the agents' beliefs and then rationalize them.* We start with the states of belief. Equation (11d) describes the long-term behavior of the *joint* states of belief but the rationality conditions require marginal distributions of y_t^k to have compatible asymptotic properties. Hence, we postulate that the state of belief of agent k, *on his own,* takes the form

$$y_t^k = \sigma_{z^k} z_t^{y^k}, \tag{12}$$

where $z_t^{y^k}$ is a realization of a normal iid random variable $\tilde{z}_t^{y^k} \sim N(0, 1)$. In the simulations we set the parameter $\sigma_{z^k} = 0.8$ for $k = 1, 2$.

a. Perceived Productivity Shocks and Their Rationality Conditions
The beliefs of agent k is expressed as a stochastic difference equation of the form

$$\log v_{t+1}^k = \lambda_v \log v_t^k + \lambda^{kv}\left(\varrho_t^k\right) y_t^k + \sigma_{z^{kv}}\left(\varrho_t^k\right) \hat{z}_{t+1}^{kv}, \qquad \hat{z}_t^{kv} \sim N(0, 1). \tag{13}$$

The agent believes that λ_v is as in (11a) but the mean value varies with y_t^k. Since the empirical distribution in (11a) exhibits no long-term covariance between productivity shocks, monetary shocks, and states of belief, rationality of belief must conform to that. Hence, rationality requires the statistics of observables generated by (13) and (11a) to be the same when the states of belief y_t^k are treated as unobserved shifts in the mean value function. No rationality conditions are imposed on y_t^k or on the correlation between y_t^k and $\log v_{t+1}^k$.

In (13) agents form beliefs that $\lambda^{kv}(\varrho_t^k)$ and $\sigma_{z^{kv}}(\varrho_t^k)$ depend upon ϱ_t^k. We write ϱ_t^k but rationality requires that for observables, *perception equals realization* so $\varrho_t^k = \varrho_t$. Given this, the basic rationality condition can be stated simply:

The empirical distribution of $\quad \lambda^{kv}(\varrho_t) y_t^k + \sigma_{z^{kv}}(\varrho_t) \hat{z}_{t+1}^{kv} \quad$ is $\quad N(0, \sigma_v^2)$. $\tag{14}$

We use a specific functional form in which monetary shocks impact $\lambda^{kv}(\varrho_t)$ and this function is

---

6. For a discussion of the relationship between an RBE and other equilibrium concepts, including sunspot equilibria, see Kurz and Motolese (2001, sect. 2.2d, pp. 513–7).

$$\lambda^{kv}(\varrho_t) = \frac{\lambda^{kv}}{1 + e^{-\chi^\varrho(\log \varrho_1)}}. \tag{14a}$$

In (14a) the function is increasing in the size of monetary shocks and hence such shocks increase the effect of y_t^k on the perceived mean value of $\log v_{t+1}^k$ in (13). Given our assumptions in this chapter, we show that this belief is rationalized if we require that conditional upon ϱ_t^k, the second empirical moment of $\lambda^{kv}(\varrho_t)y_t^k + \sigma_{z^{kv}}(\varrho_t)\hat{z}_{t+1}^{kv}$ equals σ_v^2 or

$$\left[\lambda^{kv}\left(\varrho_t^k\right)\right]^2 \sigma_{z^k}^2 + \left[\sigma_{z^{kv}}\left(\varrho_t^k\right)\right]^2 = \sigma_v^2. \tag{14b}$$

Condition (14b) pins down the functional form of $\sigma_{z^{kv}}(\varrho_t^k)$.

> LEMMA: Under assumptions A.1–A.4, condition (14b) rationalizes the belief (13) with (14a) and hence the empirical distribution of $\lambda^{kv}(\varrho_t)y_t^k + \sigma_{z^{kv}}(\varrho_t)\hat{z}_{t+1}^{kv}$ is $N(0, \sigma_v^2)$.

PROOF: By (12)–(13) we have that y_t^k is a realization of a $N(0, \sigma_{z^k}^2)$ and $\hat{z}_t^{kv} \sim N(0, 1)$; hence the time averages of y_t^k and of $\hat{z}_t^{kv}$ are both 0. Let $\Upsilon_t^{kv} = \lambda^{kv}(\varrho_t)y_t^k + \sigma_{z^{kv}}(\varrho_t)\hat{z}_{t+1}^{kv}$ and observe that given ϱ_t the empirical distribution of Υ_t^{kv} is normal since it is a linear combination of two independent normal variables. We claim that this distribution is $N(0, \sigma_v^2)$. That is, if we denote the stationary measure by P_m then our claim is that $P_m(\Upsilon_t^{kv} \mid \varrho_t) = N(0, \sigma_v^2)$ *independent of* ϱ_t! To see why this is so note first that

$$E_{P_m}\left(\Upsilon_t^{kv} \mid \varrho_t\right) = \lambda^{kv}(\varrho_t)\left(\lim_{n\to\infty} \frac{1}{n}\sum_{t=1}^n y_t^k\right) + \sigma_{z^{kv}}(\varrho_t)\left(\lim_{n\to\infty} \frac{1}{n}\sum_{t=1}^n \hat{z}_{t+1}^{kv}\right) = 0.$$

Then by (14b)

$$E_{P_m}\left[\left(\Upsilon_t^{kv}\right)^2 \mid \varrho_t\right] = \left[\lambda^{kv}(\varrho_t)\right]^2\left[\lim_{n\to\infty} \frac{1}{n}\sum_{t=1}^n \left(y_t^k\right)^2\right]$$
$$+ \sigma_{z^{kv}}^2(\varrho_t)\left[\lim_{n\to\infty} \frac{1}{n}\sum_{t=1}^n \left(\hat{z}_{t+1}^{kv}\right)^2\right] = \sigma_v^2,$$

and since a normal distribution is characterized by these two moments the claim is proved. But now observe that if we denote the unconditional density of ϱ by $P_m(\varrho)$ we can conclude that

$$P_m\left(\Upsilon_t^{kv}\right) = \int P_m\left(\Upsilon_t^{kv} \mid \varrho_t\right) P_m(\varrho_t)d(\varrho_t)$$
$$= \int \left[N\left(0, \sigma_v^2\right)\right] P_m(\varrho_t)d(\varrho_t) = N\left(0, \sigma_v^2\right).$$

It is useful to specify four implications of the rationality conditions that have been established:

Mean:

The time average of $\quad \lambda^{kv}\left(\varrho_t^k\right) y_t^k + \sigma_{z^{kv}}\left(\varrho_t^k\right) \hat{z}_{t+1}^{kv} \qquad$ is 0. $\qquad$ (15a)

Variance:

The time average of $\quad \left(\lambda^{kv}\left(\varrho_t^k\right) y_t^k + \sigma_{z^{kv}}\left(\varrho_t^k\right) \hat{z}_{t+1}^{kv}\right)^2 \qquad$ is σ_v^2. $\qquad$ (15b)

Serial correlation:

The autocorrelation of $\quad \lambda^{kv}\left(\varrho_t^k\right) y_t^k + \sigma_{z^{kv}}\left(\varrho_t^k\right) \hat{z}_{t+1}^{kv} \qquad$ is 0. $\qquad$ (15c)

Covariance:

The covariance between $\quad \lambda^{kv}\left(\varrho_t^k\right) y_t^k + \sigma_{z^{kv}}\left(\varrho_t^k\right) \hat{z}_{t+1}^{kv} \quad$ and ϱ_t is 0. $\qquad$ (15d)

In the simulations we set the values of $(\lambda^{kv}, \chi^\varrho)$ and (14b) determines the functional form of $\sigma_{z^{kv}}(\varrho_t^k)$. Earlier we explained the choice of $\lambda_v = 0.976$, $\sigma_v = 0.002$ and $\sigma_{z^k} = 0.8$ for $k = 1, 2$. Hence, the feasible range for λ^{kv} is very small. In the simulations we set $\lambda^{kv} = 0.002$ and $\chi^\varrho = 20$ (since $\log \varrho_t^k$ fluctuates mostly between 0.03 and -0.03). This effect is so small that for all practical purposes the reader may assume $\lambda^{kv} = 0$.

b. Perceived Monetary Shocks and Their Rationality Conditions

Analogous to (13), the beliefs of agents about future monetary shocks are expressed by

$$\log \varrho_{t+1}^k = \log v^* + \lambda_\varrho \left(\log \varrho_t^k - \log v^*\right) + \lambda^{k\varrho}\left(\varrho_t^k\right) y_t^k$$
$$+ \sigma_{z^{k\varrho}}\left(\varrho_t^k\right) \hat{z}_{t+1}^{k\varrho}, \quad \hat{z}_t^{k\varrho} \sim N(0, 1). \tag{16}$$

To rationalize this belief we proceed as in (14)–(15) above. The rationality condition is again

The empirical distribution of $\quad \lambda^{k\varrho}\left(\varrho_t^k\right) y_t^k + \sigma_{z^{k\varrho}}\left(\varrho_t^k\right) \hat{z}_{t+1}^{k\varrho} \quad$ is $N\left(0, \sigma_\varrho^2\right)$. (16a)

With $\varrho_t^k = \varrho_t$ the functional form for the effects of monetary shocks on $\lambda^{k\varrho}(\varrho_t)$ is

$$\lambda^{k\varrho}(\varrho_t) = \frac{\lambda^{k\varrho}}{1 + e^{-\chi^\varrho(\log \varrho_t)}}. \tag{16b}$$

In (16b) the function is increasing in the size of monetary shocks and hence such shocks increase the effect of y_t^k on the perceived mean value of $\log \varrho_{t+1}^k$ in (16). Using an argument as in the lemma above, this belief can be rationalized by the condition

$$\left[\lambda^{k\varrho}(\varrho_t)\right]^2 \sigma_{z^k}^2 + \left[\sigma_{z^{k\varrho}}(\varrho_t)\right]^2 = \sigma_\varrho^2. \tag{16c}$$

We have four analogous implications of rationality:

Mean:
The time average of $\quad \lambda^{k\varrho}(\varrho_t)y_t^k + \sigma_{z^{k\varrho}}(\varrho_t)\hat{z}_{t+1}^{k\varrho} \quad$ is 0. $\hfill$ (16d)

Variance:
The time average of $\quad \left(\lambda^{k\varrho}(\varrho_t)y_t^k + \sigma_{z^{k\varrho}}(\varrho_t)\hat{z}_{t+1}^{k\varrho}\right)^2 \quad$ is σ_v^2. $\hfill$ (16e)

Serial correlation:
The autocorrelation of $\quad \lambda^{k\varrho}(\varrho_t)y_t^k + \sigma_{z^{k\varrho}}(\varrho_t)\hat{z}_{t+1}^{k\varrho} \quad$ is 0. $\hfill$ (16f)

Covariance:
The covariance between $\quad \lambda^{k\varrho}(\varrho_t)y_t^k + \sigma_{z^{k\varrho}}(\varrho_t)\hat{z}_{t+1}^{k\varrho} \quad$ and ϱ_t is 0. $\hfill$ (16g)

Equations (16b) and (16c) restrict the value of $\lambda^{k\varrho}$ and $\sigma_{z^{k\varrho}}(\varrho_t^k)$ that the agent can select in (16). We have already selected $\lambda_\varrho = 0.95$, $\sigma_\varrho = 0.0052$, $\sigma_{z^k} = 0.8$, $\chi^\varrho = 20$ and we now add $\lambda^{k\varrho} = 0.01$. Again, this effect is very small and may be disregarded.

c. Perceived Investment Sector Shocks and Their Rationality Conditions

Perceived shocks in the investment sector *are the main propagation mechanism of the model.* If agents believe that the true φ_t process is iid as in (11c), they fully diversify portfolios with $n_t^{kS}/(n_t^{kS}+n_t^{kD}) = \frac{1}{4}$ resulting in a *perfect hedged position* and investment of $0.9(n_t^{kS} + n_t^{kD})$ *independent* of φ_t. In this REE fluctuations in φ_t have no effect. Hence, the reference steady state is a risky economy in which portfolios are perfectly hedged. In an RBE agents do not believe that (11c) is the truth and hence fluctuations occur: When $y_t^k > 0$ the distribution of k's belief moves *in favor of M* and when $y_t^k < 0$ the distribution moves *in favor of S.* We postulate that the agents perceive shifts in the mean value of φ_t in accordance with y_t^k and their beliefs take the form

$$\varphi_{t+1}^k = \lambda^{k\varphi}\left(\varrho_t^k\right)y_t^k + \sigma_{z^{k\varphi}}\left(\varrho_t^k\right)\hat{z}_{t+1}^{k\varphi}, \quad \hat{z}_t^{k\varphi} \sim N(0,1). \tag{17}$$

Note that variations in the values of y_t^k impact the perceived mean of φ_t^k not of $\log(\varphi_t^k)$. As before, the basic rationality condition is

The empirical distribution of $\quad \lambda^{k\varphi}\left(\varrho_t^k\right)y_t^k + \sigma_{z^{k\varphi}}\left(\varrho_t^k\right)\hat{z}_{t+1}^{k\varphi} \quad$ is $N\left(0,\sigma_\varphi^2\right)$. $\hfill$ (17a)

With $\varrho_t^k = \varrho_t$ the functional form for the effects of monetary shocks on $\lambda^{k\varphi}(\varrho_t)$ is

$$\lambda^{k\varphi}(\varrho_t) = \frac{\lambda^{k\varrho}}{1 + e^{-\chi^\varrho(\log \varrho_t)}}. \tag{17b}$$

In (17b) the function is increasing in the size of monetary shocks; such shocks increase the effect of y_t^k on the perceived mean value of φ_{t+1}^k in (17), and this has an important impact. Using an argument as in the lemma above, we can rationalize this belief by the condition

$$\left[\lambda^{k\varrho}(\varrho_t)\right]^2 \sigma_{z^k}^2 + \left[\sigma_{z^{k\varrho}}(\varrho_t)\right]^2 = \sigma_\varrho^2. \tag{17c}$$

This rationalization has four analogous implications to the time average, variance, and serial correlation of $\lambda^{k\varphi}(\varrho_t^k)y_t^k + \sigma_{z^{k\varphi}}(\varrho_t^k)\hat{z}_{t+1}^{k\varphi}$, and to its covariance with ϱ_t, which we do not repeat. Equations (17b) and (17c) determine $\sigma_{z^{k\varphi}}(\varrho_t^k)$ and restrict the feasible values of $\lambda^{k\varphi}$ in (17). As the process is hypothetical we set $\sigma_\varphi^2 = 1$, $\lambda^{k\varphi} = 1$ although these should be estimated from data.

We finally state the implication of assumption A.7, which says that agents use (11d) to forecast the effects of future states of belief. Consistency between (11d) and (12) requires

$$\sigma_{z^k} = \sigma_{y^k} \qquad \text{for } k = 1, 2. \tag{18}$$

3.4. Comments about the Computation Model and the Parameters

We will compute equilibria using a method of perturbation around the steady state of a riskless economy.[7] First, we make some comments to clarify the exposition.

3.4.1. STEADY STATE AND THE INITIAL ASSET DISTRIBUTION

(1) Given the growth context assumed, in order for the model to have a steady state, we assume $\gamma^1 = \gamma^2 = \gamma = 1.5$, $\beta_1 = \beta_2 = \beta = 0.99$, reflecting the quarterly model and $\zeta = 3.5$ to ensure that an agent's labor supply equals 0.2 in steady state. (2) Since the riskless steady state depends upon the initial distribution of assets, we assume the symmetry $\theta_0^1 = \theta_0^2 = \frac{1}{2}$, $b_0^1 = b_0^2 = 0$, $k_0^{kd} = \frac{1}{2}k^{d*}$, $n_0^{kM} = \frac{1}{2}n^{M*}$, $n_0^{kS} = \frac{1}{2}n^{S*}$. (3) It follows from (1) and (2) that the only model heterogeneity is the diversity of agents' beliefs.

3.4.2. ACCURACY OF THE EULER EQUATIONS

The model has nine state and twelve endogenous variables. To compute equilibria we expand policy functions to second-degree polynomials and compute 780 derivatives. This leads to a much higher precision than in most of the literature, based on log-linearization. A solution is acceptable only if the Euler equations are satisfied with a precision of 10^{-3} in the 5 percent neighborhood of the steady-state values of the aggregates (e.g., for values of capital k_t in the interval $0.95k^* \le k_t \le 1.05k^*$) and 10^{-2} in the 10 percent neighborhood of the steady state.

3.4.3. DEFINITION OF AN REE VERSUS AN RBE

Belief parameters of the agents are symmetric and the only asymmetry arises in the investment sector as between the two activities. Parameters are either based

---

7. Details of the computational model are provided in an Appendix B that can be downloaded from the homepage of the first author at http://www.stanford.edu/~mordecai. The appendix covers some additional technical problems associated with the computational procedure.

on *actual econometric estimates* of the corresponding parameters in the economy or are hypothetical. Beliefs are characterized by the following parameters, which are the same for $k = 1, 2$:

$$\sigma_{z^k} = 0.8, \ \lambda^{kv} = 0.002, \ \lambda^{k\varrho} = 0.01, \ \lambda^{k\varphi} = 1, \ \rho_{yy} = 0.95, \ \chi^{\varrho} = 20.$$

An REE is defined as an equilibrium where *agents believe the stationary measure is the truth* and is simply characterized by the conditions, for $k = 1, 2$,

$$\lambda^{kv} = \lambda^{k\varrho} = \lambda^{k\varphi} = 0, \quad \sigma_{z^k}^2 = 0, \quad \sigma_{z^kv}^2 = \sigma_v^2, \quad \sigma_{z^k\varrho}^2 = \sigma_\varrho^2,$$

$$\sigma_{z^k\varphi}^2 = \sigma_\varphi^2, \quad y_t^1 = y_t^2 = 0. \tag{19}$$

3.5. Simulation Results and What We Learn from Them

3.5.1. VOLATILITY CHARACTERISTICS

Table 2 reports standard deviations, first-order autocorrelations, and contemporaneous correlations with output for key variables in the REE and RBE simulations. All variables are log deviations from the model's deterministic trend. All data are HP filtered. We view the REE results as a reference to the volatility that would be generated by small, persistent exogenous productivity shocks. Indeed, with $\sigma_v = 0.002$ such shocks generate only a fraction of the observed volatility. In contrast, the table reveals that the level of volatility generated in the RBE is similar to the level observed in the data. For the United States the standard deviations of the variables are 1.81 for $\log g^N$, 5.30 for $\log i^N$, 1.31 for $\log c$, and 1.79 for $\log L$. These results exhibit the ability of beliefs in the RBE to propagate volatility endogenously in orders of magnitudes observed in the real data.

The two panels in Figure 2 exhibit time series of HP-filtered observations on log (GNP), log (investment). Since the level of volatility of log (GNP) is the same as in the U.S. data, the figure highlights the difference between the volatility generated by the exogenous shocks in comparison with the endogenous component generated by the beliefs of agents.

Table 2 also shows that the RBE fails to exhibit a correlation structure that is present in the real data and would be generated by a larger variance of the productivity shocks. This failure is instructive since it results from our assumptions and provides a deeper understanding of the propagation mechanism of the model. To explain it, we first observe that since agents seek to smooth consumption,

Table 2. Volatility Characteristics

	Standard deviation		Relative standard deviation		First-order autocorrelation		Correlation with GNP	
	REE	RBE	REE	RBE	REE	RBE	REE	RBE
$\log g^N$	0.33	1.80	1.00	1.00	0.72	−0.08	1.00	1.00
$\log i^N$	0.79	9.08	2.39	5.04	0.71	−0.09	0.99	0.91
$\log c$	0.18	1.28	0.55	0.71	0.74	−0.06	0.99	−0.30
$\log L$	0.12	2.04	0.36	1.13	0.71	−0.07	0.98	0.30

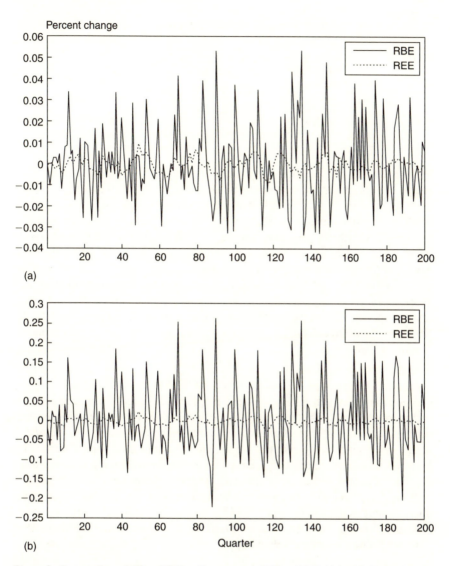

Figure 2. Comparative volatility of GNP and investment in REE and RBE: (a) log (GNP), HP filtered; (b) log (investment), HP filtered.

their investment and consumption plans depend upon *their perception of the persistence of the random shocks*. High persistence in productivity shocks, which leads to persistence in the random component of the wage rate and the return on investments, leads to plans that associate higher investments with higher consumption and hence induce positive correlation among output, consumption, and investments. The fact is that the volatility of the RBE is generated by shocks in the investment goods sector and by the temporal behavior of the states of belief. We assume in (11c) that $\varphi_t = \rho_t^\varphi$, $\rho_t^\varphi \sim N(0, \sigma_\varphi^2)$ iid. In addition, the states of belief exhibit no persistence. Conditioning upon monetary shocks generates some

Table 3. Volume of Trade on Financial Markets

	REE	RBE
Mean TR	0	2.61
σ_{TR}	0	1.74
$\rho(TR_t, TR_{t-1})$	—	0.26
max TR_t	0	11.72
min TR_t	0	0.07

persistence, but the level is small and its effect is of second order. Hence, when agents believe that attractive investment opportunities are present, they perceive them to be temporary, with little persistence. These strong assumptions ensure small or negative serial correlation of the variables, and Table 2 demonstrates this fact. Also, without persistence, perceived high returns on investments provide a strong motive for agents to *substitute consumption for investments* and work harder to finance such projects. This explains the negative correlation between consumption and GNP and the negative correlation between consumption and investments. It also explains the low correlation between hours of work and GNP. For a calibrated RBE to exhibit the correlation structure observed in the data, the RBE would have to exhibit persistence in the rate of return on investments and/or in states of belief.[8]

3.5.2. VOLUME OF TRADE

Our economy has two financial assets: nominal bonds and ownership units in built capital goods. We thus make two observations. First, since the nominal debt instrument is of short duration, it matures each period and has to be traded again. Since bonds are in zero net supply, the volume of their trade is defined by $|q_t^b b_t^k|$. The volume of capital goods traded entails an accounting problem since old units of capital depreciate so the stock owned by agent k at t before trading is $(k_{t-1}^{kd} + i_{t-1}^k)(1 - \delta)/v^*$. The new amount that he buys is k_t^{kd}, so the value of his trade at date t is defined by $q_t^s \{k_t^{kd} - (k_{t-1}^{kd} + i_{t-1}^k)(1 - \delta)/v^*\}$. Owing to growth, a meaningful measure of the volume of trade is the value of trade relative to GNP. Thus we define the relative volume by

$$
TR_t = \frac{1}{GNP_t} \left\{ \left| q_t^s \left[k_t^{1d} - \left(k_{t-1}^{1d} + i_{t-1}^1 \right) \frac{1 - \delta}{v^*} \right] \right| + |q_t^b b_t^1| \right\}. \qquad (20)
$$

Table 3 shows statistics based on 1,000 simulated observations on TR. The RBE generates a dramatic volume of trade and exhibits a large standard deviation of TR. Table 3 reveals that the extreme values are far apart, suggesting sharp variations in volume, which is a result that is consistent with those of Kurz and Motolese's

---

8. To introduce persistence in the states of belief or in the φ_t process we would have to add state variables to a model whose equilibrium is already difficult to compute. We have elected not to do so since we view this work as a theoretical analysis that utilizes computation methods rather than a calibration effort.

(2001) on the dynamics of trade. Finally, the sum of money and bond holdings is large, with an average ratio to GNP of about 12.

3.5.3. MONEY NEUTRALITY AND THE PHILLIPS CURVE

Money is neutral in any REE of the model. An RBE also has an obvious money neutrality property, neutrality *on average,* which means that the average rate of inflation equals the average rate of increase of the money supply minus the average rate of growth of output. In all RBE the mean rate of increase in the money supply is v^*, which is the mean growth rate of output; hence the mean rate of inflation is 0. RBE are, however, generically money nonneutral.

To see that money is not neutral in an RBE we carry out a simple test. We first simulate the equilibrium assuming that both the technological shocks v_t as well as the money shocks ϱ_t are turned off and compute the statistics generated. Next we turn on the monetary shocks at the level of, say, $\sigma_\varrho = 0.05$, and recompute. Table 4 presents comparative results of this experiment. The fact that money injection has real effects is clear and the explanation for why money is not neutral is also simple. Monetary shocks have an effect on expectations of agents and although they observe the rate at which the money supply changes, their demand for money (which depends upon their beliefs) changes but not in the same way. The resulting percentage change in the price level is thus not equal to the percentage change in the money supply.

The analysis of the Phillips curve in an exact general equilibrium context is not a simple matter. It entails a relationship between two endogenous variables, both of which are functions defined by the equilibrium map (10), and this leaves no room for a good instrument to remove the bias. We simulated the model twice: first with $\sigma_\varrho > 0$, $\sigma_v > 0$ and second with $\sigma_\varrho > 0$, $\log v_t = 0$. We used samples of 5,000 observations and estimated the following simple regression model:

$$\log \pi_t = a_0 + a_1 \log g_t^N + a_2 \log \varrho_t + a_3 \log \pi_{t-1} + \vartheta_t$$

keeping in mind that $\log (g_t^N)$ is the log of the deviation of GNP from trend.

ESTIMATION FOR REE
1. With $\sigma_\varrho > 0$, $\sigma_v > 0$:

$$\log \pi_t = -\underset{(0.0001)}{0.003} - \underset{(0.0008)}{0.012} \log g_t^N + \underset{(0.001)}{0.999} \log \varrho_t - \underset{(0.0014)}{0.002} \log \pi_{t-1}$$

$$+ \vartheta_t, \; R^2 = 0.996.$$

Table 4. Money Nonneutrality of RBE (standard deviations in percent)

	$\log (\varrho_t) = 0, \log (v_t) = 0$	$\sigma_p = 0.05, \log (v_t) = 0$
$\log g^N$	1.93	2.05
$\log i^N$	9.38	10.12
$\log c$	1.38	2.18
$\log L$	2.11	3.26

2. With $\sigma_\varrho > 0$, $\log v_t = 0$:

$$\log \pi_t = \underset{(0.003)}{-0.004} + \underset{(0.000)}{0.000} \log g_t^N + \underset{(0.000)}{1.000} \log \varrho_t - \underset{(0.000)}{0.000} \log \pi_{t-1}$$
$$+ \vartheta_t, \, R^2 = 1.000.$$

ESTIMATION FOR RBE

1. With $\sigma_\varrho > 0$, $\sigma_v > 0$:

$$\log \pi_t = \underset{(0.004)}{-0.113} + \underset{(0.021)}{0.774} \log g_t^N + \underset{(0.028)}{1.414} \log \varrho_t - \underset{(0.011)}{0.445} \log \pi_{t-1}$$
$$+ \vartheta_t, \, R^2 = 0.47.$$

2. With $\sigma_\varrho > 0$, $\log v_t = 0$:

$$\log \pi_t = \underset{(0.004)}{-0.319} + \underset{(0.026)}{1.845} \log g_t^N + \underset{(0.022)}{1.419} \log \varrho_t - \underset{(0.008)}{0.468} \log \pi_{t-1}$$
$$+ \vartheta_t, \, R^2 = 0.67.$$

We have tried many different specifications and the conclusions are the same. The REE regressions show money neutrality. As for the RBE, in all regressions the Phillips curve coefficient of $\log g_t^N$ is large and positive.

3.5.4. IMPULSE RESPONSE TO MONETARY SHOCKS

Our final results relate to the impulse response functions of monetary shocks. The study of such functions reveals the manner in which the real effect of monetary shocks works through the RBE. A monetary shock in steady state is different from a productivity shock since a productivity shock forces the economy out of steady state through the *direct* first-order effects it has on output and resource prices. A monetary shock has only a second-order, *indirect* effect on the economy via its impact on parameters such as $\lambda^{kv}(\varrho_t^k)$, $\lambda^{k\varrho}(\varrho_t)$, and $\lambda^{k\varphi}(\varrho_t)$, which are *multiplied* by the states of belief y_t^k. To see the implication recall that every endogenous variable in the economy is represented by a polynomial whose derivatives we evaluate at the steady-state solution of the economy. Hence, the equilibrium is a perturbation of the steady state and the belief parameters (y_t^1, y_t^2) are represented in each polynomial as regular variables. The steady state of an RBE requires us to set $y_t^1 = 0$, $y_t^2 = 0$. Since in any impulse response function all variables are evaluated at steady state, to determine the impact of a monetary shock we evaluate this effect at steady state. An examination of the perception models shows that the impact of a monetary shock works through terms such as

$$\Upsilon_{t+1}^{kv} = \lambda^{kv}\left(\varrho_t^k\right) y_t^k + \sigma_{z^{kv}}\left(\varrho_t^k\right) \hat{z}_{t+1}^{kv}$$

in equations (13), (16), and (17). Indeed, this multiplicative form is the direct result of the rationality conditions: Additive terms would violate rationality. But now the answer is clear: At steady state we set $y_t^k = 0$ and all random variables are also set equal to zero so no monetary shock can have any effect. The conclusion is that a monetary impulse of this RBE at the steady state has only a direct effect on inflation: A change in money supply causes a proportionate change in price level, leaving all real variables unchanged.

The picture changes drastically if we select an alternate state of belief $(y^{1*}, y^{2*}) \neq (0,0)$ and hold it fixed. We now compute the long-term averages of equilibrium variables denoted by x^*, and create a new *hypothetical* steady state (y^{1*}, y^{2*}, x^*) for the economy. In an REE $(y^{1*}, y^{2*}, x^*) = (0, 0, x^*)$ for all (y^{1*}, y^{2*}) since states of belief do not matter. Having defined this steady state, we examine the impulse responses to a monetary shock. The interpretation of these responses is natural: They measure the impact of a monetary shock on real variables around (y^{1*}, y^{2*}, x^*). Since the risky economy is never at the $(y^{1*}, y^{2*}) = (0, 0)$ steady state, the magnitude of the impulse response varies with the point in space at which the economy is evaluated. Hence, the usual steady state with $(y^{1*}, y^{2*}) = (0, 0)$ has no significance and positions away from it better reflect the response of the risky economy to monetary shocks.

Based on the above considerations we selected $(y^{1*} = 0.4, y^{2*} = 0.4)$, which is half a standard deviation of the empirical distribution of (y_t^1, y_t^2), and study the response to an initial monetary shock of log $\varrho_t = 2$ percent. The results are presented in Figure 3. Some comments on these results:

1. *GNP:* This impulse response function exhibits the familiar hump-shaped form, known from empirical work on the effect of monetary shocks and hence is qualitatively in accord with standard results. Keep in mind, however, that this response function is generated entirely endogenously by the structure of market beliefs.

2. *Investment:* This function reveals the impact of the endogenous propagation mechanism of the model. The 2 percent monetary shock alters private expectations and causes a large 0.3 percent burst of investments that slowly decreases in magnitude. It is the size and sharp nature of this burst that explains the impulse response of other variables.

3. *Consumption:* Although the response of consumption exhibits the familiar hump-shaped form, it also has the feature of starting with a *negative* impulse at date 0. This is due to the special features of our model. The monetary shock alters expectations and results in a burst of investments. Owing to lack of persistence in perceived returns on investments, agents reduce present consumption in order to finance investments. After the initial decline, consumption rises, reaches a maximal deviation from trend, and then returns to trend.

4. *Nominal interest rate:* The model has no riskless asset so the impulse response function of the nominal interest rate is relatively simple. A 2 percent monetary shock causes only a 1.8 percent instantaneous inflation at date 0. The burst of investments leads to an increased demand for funds, which pushes real interest rates higher. As the investment effect declines, the full price level adjustment is completed.

5. *Hours:* This function shows the final dimension of the increased demand for investments generated by a monetary shock. As agents perceive

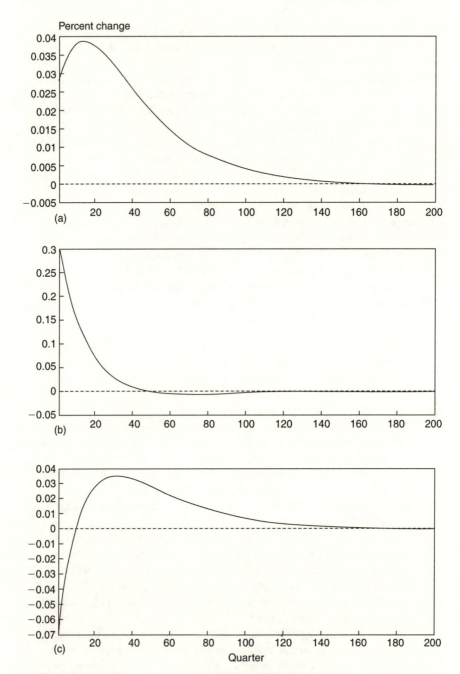

Figure 3. Impulse response to a +2 percent monetary shock: (a) log (GNP); (b) log (investment); (c) log (consumption).

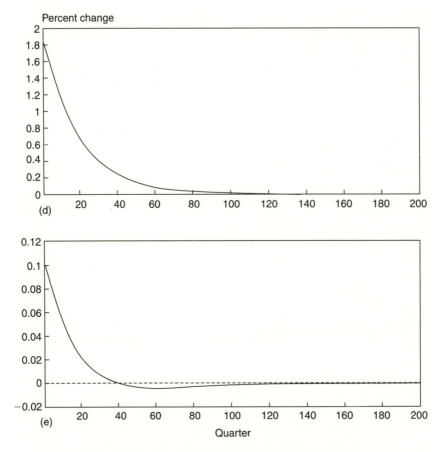

Figure 3. (*Continued*) (d) nominal interest rate; (e) log (hours).

higher rates of return on investments they desire to work more hours to finance such investments, revealing a 0.1 percent rise in hours.

3.5.5. WHY MONETARY SHOCKS HAVE REAL EFFECTS AND POSITIVE SHOCKS INCREASE OUTPUT: A SIMPLE INTUITIVE EXPLANATION

Why do monetary shocks have real effects and why do positive shocks have positive effects on output? These are two *separate* questions that we address separately. The fact that money has a real effect in an RBE is a *generic property arising from the diversity of beliefs*. Monetary shocks have a real effect because agents have diverse forecasts of all variables in the economy. They disagree about the effects of monetary shocks on inflation because they have different forecasts of the rate of return on investments and hence of the demand for money that results from differing investment rates. Also, agents disagree about the distribution of future monetary shocks and hence about the cost of holding money. This argument is not reduced to a sunspot argument saying that money has an effect because agents expect it to have an effect. Agents have different forecasts of the real variables in the economy and once they disagree on the inflation forecast given any monetary shock, monetary shocks have real effects. This is analogous to Lucas's (1972) argument explaining nonneutrality by agents' "confusion" between monetary and real shocks. In an RBE there is no confusion about shocks, only disagreement about forecasting the future, and this is sufficient for money to have real effects (for a similar argument see Motolese, 2000, 2001). Once agents perceive money to have a real effect, it is rational for them to incorporate monetary shocks as a component affecting their own beliefs about all variables in the economy (i.e., for ϱ_t to affect agents' perceptions). We now turn to the second question.

Why do *positive* monetary shocks *increase* output? Given the fact, explained in the previous paragraph, that money has an effect on the belief of agents, the answer to this second question is simple: A positive monetary shock in the model generates optimism among agents about higher rates of return on investments and thus causes them to be willing to engage in more risky investments. When this occurs they increase their inputs into investment projects. For that purpose they work harder and lower their consumption a bit in order to finance the desired investments. In our model these effects are short lived because there is no persistence in either the beliefs or in the investment opportunities. However, the fact that these effects are short lived has nothing to do with the idea of agents being "surprised" by monetary shocks. Our explanation is typical of the mechanism that operates in any RBE model. In future work we hope to modify the model so that this conclusion becomes more transparent.

In the present model the mechanism is a bit complicated because of our assumption that there are two investment opportunities and only one iid random variable to determine their productivity. The result is that whenever agents are optimistic about higher returns in project S they *must* be pessimistic about returns in project M. Hence, it is impossible for them to be optimistic about future returns in both projects. When $y_t^k > 0$ they are optimistic about project M, and they increase investments in M but decrease investments in S. The opposite is true when $y_t^k < 0$. In the model monetary shocks alter the impact of y_t^k on the perceptions of future returns on assets. Hence, in order to stipulate that agents take more risk in response to a monetary shock we require that $\left|\lambda^{k\varphi}(\varrho_t)\right|$ in equation (17c) *increases* with ϱ_t. This achieves the objective because when $\left|\lambda^{k\varphi}(\varrho_t)\right|$ increases with ϱ_t, a larger monetary shock amplifies the impact of y_t^k on forecasted returns on investment. Indeed, it increases the forecasted deviation of φ_{t+1} from 0 and hence increases the expected returns on investments. This, in turn, increases the desire to invest.

But then, one may object, our conclusion regarding the positive effect of monetary shocks hinges on the shocks having the "right" effect on beliefs [via a parameter such as $\lambda^{k\varphi}(\varrho_t)$]. This is entirely true: The positive association will not be present unless parameters such as $\left|\lambda^{k\varphi}(\varrho_t)\right|$ change in the "right" way. But then recall that in an RBE monetary shocks have real effects and all agents recognize this. Once real effects—positive or negative—are present in the economy then, like any endogenous uncertainty, they become part of reality and impact the beliefs of agents. In fact, the idea that actions of the central bank affect agents' expectations is central to modern thinking about monetary policy. Most discussions about credibility of the central bank have to do with the impact of policy on beliefs, and the effect of policy on beliefs is central to the DNK theory discussed earlier (e.g., Woodford, 2001b).

The fact that policy has an impact on beliefs is clear; the only question is the nature of that impact. In this chapter we have not developed a formal theory of this impact. Instead, we assumed that such an effect exists *and have proved that it can be rationalized.* The assumption that parameters such as $\left|\lambda^{k\varphi}(\varrho_t)\right|$ have the right slope is then a condition specifying what it takes for a monetary shock to have a positive effect on output. This discussion also shows that a monetary equilibrium cannot be complete without a full specification of monetary policy.

3.5.6. WHAT HAVE WE LEARNED FROM THE MODEL?
Computational economics is a useful tool for theoretical work in dynamic equilibrium analysis when analytical results are difficult to obtain. Many of our numerical results will change with changes in parameters or specifications. Our model has several unrealistic features that result in no persistence of investment opportunities and no persistence of beliefs. Also, the linear structure of the investment sector is too simplistic and results in low volatility of the price of traded capital goods. Hence, any effort to calibrate the model would require significant model restructuring. However, our objective was to formulate an analytical framework in which the impact of diverse beliefs can be evaluated and, in our view, the present model demonstrated the importance of this economic factor. There are other conclusions that, we believe, can be drawn at this time since *they are generic to any RBE model.* We offer a short summary of these:

1. Diversity of beliefs in an RBE is a propagation mechanism capable of producing volatility of the order of magnitude observed in the data. The mechanism operating in the investment sector applies to other intertemporal decisions such as consumer durables and public investments.
2. The RBE offers an integrated theory of real and financial volatility, where fluctuations in both sectors are *jointly* propagated. It provides a direct explanation for the high volume of trade on financial markets and for the high volatility of aggregate investments.
3. Diverse beliefs in the RBE explain most of the familiar features of monetary equilibria in which money has real effects. This includes money nonneutrality and Phillips curve and impulse response functions with respect to monetary shocks but these have nothing to do with "surprises" of agents. It arises in the RBE owing to the fact that a positive monetary shock reduces the risk premium that agents require in order to engage in risky investments.

A methodological point is also appropriate. We use the "distribution of beliefs" as an *explanatory variable* of market performance. Indeed, the use of the distribution of beliefs as an explanatory variable is central to all work on market volatility in RBE cited in this chapter. It is our view that the distribution of beliefs is as valid an explanatory variable as any information about characteristics of agents or technology used routinely in economic analysis to explain market performance.

For this reason we think that the distribution of beliefs is useful information for the formulation of monetary policy. That is, since an important component of economic fluctuations is endogenous, caused by the beliefs of agents, the conduct of monetary policy could be improved by incorporating information about the distribution of beliefs in the market.

4. WHAT IS THE RATIONALE FOR AND OBJECT OF MONETARY POLICY?

We turn now to a brief discussion of the justification for monetary policy. Owing to the endogenous component of volatility, the level of risk in a market economy is greater than the level induced by exogenous shocks. But if social risk is caused by human conduct, then society may elect to place some limits on individual choice so as to reduce the level of such endogenous volatility. This was a line of thought discussed by Kurz (1997a, pp. ix–x) and explored by Nielsen (1998, 2000). It is a fact that an RBE with complete hedging opportunities is ex ante Pareto-optimal and in that case any effective public policy will make some agents worse off in terms of their *ex ante expected utility.* As a side remark we note that RBE are generically incomplete owing to the lack of observability of the states of beliefs, as is the case with the model economy of this chapter. Nevertheless, the theory of RBE offers an important role for the central bank *regardless of market completeness.* The aim of monetary policy is to reduce the excess endogenous volatility component of economic activity and of the price level. Since a central bank cannot reduce volatility caused by exogenous shocks, the task of reducing the endogenous component is both attainable and socially desirable. However, this task requires some choices.

Investors' freedom of choice is the foundation of all efficiency considerations leading to ex ante Pareto optimality of the allocation in a market economy. However, the price of such freedom is the excessive level of volatility in the market, which is caused by their diverse and often inconsistent beliefs. To support our position that monetary policy is justified in an RBE, we have to argue that the ex post excess volatility of a market economy is undesirable.

The problem of reconciling ex ante and ex post outcomes is not new. It was discussed by Diamond (1967), Drèze (1970), Starr (1973), Mirrlees (1974), Hammond (1981, 1983), Nielsen (1998, 2000), Silvestre (2002), and others. The interest in an ex post concept of optimality was motivated by two considerations. First, researchers held the view that in an uncertain world agents may hold "incorrect" probability beliefs and hence regret their decisions (e.g., Hammond, 1981, p. 236). Also, social preferences over income distribution could be sensitive to ex post outcomes rather than ex ante anticipated distribution of consumptions. Second, diverse and often inconsistent probability beliefs raise difficulties in defining a "representative consumer" who holds a social expected utility.[9] Hammond's (1981,

---

9. Diverse and inconsistent subjective probability beliefs raise difficulties in defining an equilibrium in games with incomplete information and have led to the "Harsanyi doctrine" of a common prior in game theory.

1983) concept of ex post welfare function proposes that society should disregard the probability beliefs of individual agents in favor of the social planner's own consistent probabilities over states.

The RBE theory offers some new elements that enable a different perspective of ex post optimality. In an RBE agents typically hold diverse nonstationary beliefs and society, represented by the central bank, recognizes that when agents hold diverse and inconsistent beliefs *some or all* of them are wrong. Since society does not have better information than private agents, the central bank cannot determine whose beliefs are right. Hence, monetary policy must be symmetric with respect to the diverse beliefs. Over time any agent may hold correct or incorrect beliefs in the form of a subjective joint distribution over observables. Hence, public policy must be optimal in the long run, in the sense that it should be a good policy for any configuration of beliefs that agents may hold over time. The rationality conditions in an RBE imply that the mean belief of any agent over time is exactly the stationary measure,[10] and this probability is also the expected probability belief of an agent on any date. Hence, public policy should be optimal with respect to the stationary measure. That is, it should seek to maximize expected welfare not with respect to the belief of any particular agent but rather with respect to the long-run empirical distribution. Also, agents agree on the stationary measure since it is the probability on sequences deduced from the empirical distribution of observables, and this distribution is known to all. An example will illustrate.

An Example. For simplicity, this example focuses on improving long-run welfare rather than on monetary policy. To that end, consider an infinite horizon economy with a complete market structure (an assumption not satisfied in the RBE above). Within this economy there is a leading sector using a technology that is similar to the one used in the investment sector of the model in Section 3. There are a large number of identical firms each led by an investor-entrepreneur. At each date an investor-entrepreneur uses the publicly available technology to produce output. The constant-returns-to-scale technology employs two agents who live for one period: the investor with an endowment of 1 and a worker who works for the investor and receives 25 percent of the output.

At every date t an investor allocates his endowment between activities M and S, whose technological nature varies over time. However, at all dates uncertainty is represented by two states, L and R. The long-term empirical distribution of the realized states is $\frac{1}{2}$ for L and $\frac{1}{2}$ for R with no serial correlation, and hence the stationary measure is iid with probability of each state being $\frac{1}{2}$. Trading and investments take place in the morning and output and consumption in the afternoon. Investors' beliefs are such that at each t they are certain that either L or R will be realized. They hold rational beliefs so half of the time they are certain L will be realized and half of the time they are certain R will be realized. Beliefs of investors are perfectly correlated. Output possibilities are represented by the

---

10. That is, the mean transition function or joint density over observable variables employed by an agent at different dates is equal to the transition function or joint density over all observable variables in the economy defined by the stationary measure (or, empirical distribution).

following function. If an investor at t places X units in activity S and Y units in activity M subject to $X + Y = 1$, output will be the following random variable:

$$\text{Output}_t \equiv \begin{cases} 2.8X + 1.8Y & \text{if } L \text{ is realized} \\ 2Y & \text{if } R \text{ is realized.} \end{cases}$$

When an investor is certain L will be realized he selects $(X = 1, Y = 0)$; when he is certain R will be realized he selects $(X = 0, Y = 1)$. Since the stationary measure is iid with the probability of L being $\frac{1}{2}$, the empirical distribution of outputs and individual shares of the two participants are:

Proportion of time	Output	Investor's share	Worker's share
25%	2.800	2.100	0.700
25%	0	0	0
25%	2.000	1.500	0.500
25%	1.800	1.350	0.450
Mean:	1.650	1.2375	0.4125

The "proportion of time" entries in the table are probabilities according to the stationary measure. Note that the free market allocation results in outstanding performance 75 percent of the time. However, in 25 percent of the time it has catastrophic consequences, generating significant volatility. Now if society selects $X = \frac{1}{15}$ and $Y = \frac{14}{15}$ at all dates, the following allocation is socially feasible:

Proportion of time	Output	Investor's share	Worker's share
25%	1.867	1.400	0.467
25%	1.867	1.400	0.467
25%	1.867	1.400	0.467
25%	1.867	1.400	0.467
Mean:	1.867	1.400	0.467

Although the first allocation is ex ante Pareto optimal *relative to the beliefs of agents*, the second allocation stochastically dominates the first relative to the stationary measure. A social planner with concave utility will prefer the second allocation if he uses the iid stationary measure.

In our view the second allocation is an appropriate goal for stabilization policy. One may argue that in the free market allocation agents have opportunities to hedge their positions and ensure against all risks, given their beliefs. This is entirely true but fails to address the fact that the first allocation results both in excess fluctuations as well as in a significant loss of social resources in the catastrophic states. Moreover, the bad states, which entail the loss of social resources, are endogenous, man-made, and subject incentives. They are not due to exogenous factors but rather to beliefs and decisions of agents. Because of these lost resources the long-term average consumption is higher in the second allocation than in the first. The example is easily extended to other forms of investment. Thus, the problem of economic volatility is not only one of smoothing consumption. It also entails lost social resources resulting from intertemporal decisions that are optimal relative to the agent's wrong beliefs, but which may not be socially desirable in the long run. Some may regard our example as one of market externalities of beliefs and there is some truth to this label. However, this is merely a terminological resolution. In future work we shall explore these issues in more detail.

REFERENCES

Basu, S. (1996), "Procyclical Productivity: Increasing Returns or Cyclical Utilization?," *The Quarterly Journal of Economics* 111:719–51.

Bernanke, B. S. and M. Gertler (1989), "Agency Cost, Net Worth, and Business Fluctuations," *American Economic Review* 79:14–31.

Bernanke, B. S., M. Gertler, and S. Gilchrist (1999), "The Financial Accelerator in a Quantitative Business Cycle Framework," in J. Taylor and M. Woodford, eds., *The Handbook of Macroeconomics,* Vol. 1C, Amsterdam: North-Holland, chap. 21, pp. 1342–85.

Burnside, C., M. Eichenbaum, and S. T. Rebelo (1995), "Capital Utilization and Returns to Scale," in J. J. Rotemberg and B. S. Bernanke, eds., *NBER Macroeconomics Annual,* Cambridge: MIT Press.

Calvo, G. A. (1983), "Staggered Prices in a Utility-Maximizing Framework," *Journal of Monetary Economics* 12:383–98.

Carlstrom, C. and T. Fuerst (1997), "Agency Cost, Net Worth, and Business Fluctuations: A Computable General Equilibrium Analysis," *American Economic Review* 87:893–910.

Clarida, R., J. Gali, and M. Gertler (1999), "The Science of Monetary Policy: A New Keynesian Perspective," *Journal of Economic Literature* 37:1661–1707.

Cole, H. L. and L. E. Ohanian (2000), "The Great Depression in the United States from a Neoclassical Perspective," *Federal Reserve Bank of Minneapolis Quarterly Review,* 23:2–24.

Diamond, P. A. (1976), "Cardinal Welfare, Individualistic Ethics and Interpersonal Comparisons of Utility: A Comment," *Journal of Political Economy* 75:765–66.

Drèze, J. (1970), "Market Allocation Under Uncertainty," *European Economic Review* 2:133–65.

Eichenbaum, M. (1991), "Real Business-Cycle Theory, Wisdom or Whimsy?" *Journal of Economic Dynamics and Control* 15:607–26.

Frydman, R. and E. S. Phelps (1983), *Individual Forecasting and Aggregate Outcomes: "Rational Expectations" Examined,* Cambridge: Cambridge University Press.

Garmaise, M. J. (1998), "Diversity of Beliefs, Informed Investors and Financial Contracting," Ph.D. dissertation submitted to the Graduate School of Business, Stanford University.

Greenwood, J., Z. Hercowitz, and G. W. Huffman (1988), "Investment, Capacity Utilization, and the Real Business Cycle," *American Economic Review* 78:402–17.

Hammond, P. J. (1981), "Ex-ante and Ex-post Welfare Optimality Under Uncertainty," *Economica* 48:235–50.

———— (1983), "Ex-post Optimality as a Dynamically Consistent Objective for Collective Choice Under Uncertainty," in P. K. Pattanaik and M. Salle, ed., *Social Choice and Welfare,* Amsterdam: North-Holland, chap. 10, pp. 175–205.

Keynes, J. M. (1936), *The General Theory of Employment, Interest and Money.* Reprinted by Harbinger, Harcourt Brace and World, 1964.

King, R. G. and S. T. Rebelo (1999), "Resuscitating Real Business Cycles," in J. Taylor and M. Woodford, eds., *Handbook of Macroeconomics,* Vol. 1B, Amsterdam: North-Holland, chap. 14, pp. 927–1007.

Kurz, M. (1974), "The Kesten-Stigum Model and the Treatment of Uncertainty in Equilibrium Theory," in M. S. Balch, D. L. McFadden, and S. Y. Wu, eds., *Essays on Economic Behavior under Uncertainty*, Amsterdam: North-Holland, pp. 389–99.

————— (1994), "On the Structure and Diversity of Rational Beliefs," *Economic Theory* 4:877–900 (an edited version appears as Chapter 2 of Kurz, M., ed., *Endogenous Economic Fluctuations: Studies in the Theory of Rational Belief*, Berlin and New York: Springer-Verlag).

—————, ed. (1996), Symposium on Rational Beliefs and Endogenous Uncertainty, *Economic Theory* 8:383–553.

—————, ed. (1997a), *Endogenous Economic Fluctuations: Studies in the Theory of Rational Belief*, Studies in Economic Theory, No. 6, Berlin and New York: Springer-Verlag.

————— (1997b), "Asset Prices with Rational Beliefs," in M. Kurz, ed., *Endogenous Economic Fluctuations: Studies in the Theory of Rational Belief*, Berlin and New York: Springer-Verlag, chap 7, pp. 211–50.

————— (1997c), "On the Volatility of Foreign Exchange Rates," in M. Kurz, ed., *Endogenous Economic Fluctuations: Studies in the Theory of Rational Belief*, Berlin and New York: Springer-Verlag, chap. 12, pp. 317–52.

Kurz, M. and A. Beltratti (1997), "The Equity Premium Is No Puzzle," in M. Kurz, ed., *Endogenous Economic Fluctuations: Studies in the Theory of Rational Belief*, chap. 11, pp. 283–316.

Kurz, M. and M. Motolese (2001), "Endogenous Uncertainty and Market Volatility," *Economic Theory* 17:497–544.

Kurz, M. and M. Schneider (1996), "Coordination and Correlation in Markov Rational Belief Equilibria," *Economic Theory* 8:489–520.

Lindahl, E. (1939), *Studies in the Theory of Money and Capital*, London: George Allen and Unwin.

Lucas, R. E., Jr. (1972), "Expectations and the Neutrality of Money," *Journal of Economic Theory* 4:103–24.

Mirrlees, J. A. (1974), "Notes on Welfare Economics, Information and Uncertainty," in M. S. Balch, D. L. McFadden, and S. Y. Wu, eds., *Essays on Economic Behavior under Uncertainty*, Amsterdam: North-Holland, pp. 243–58.

Mishkin, F. (1982), "Does Unanticipated Money Matter? An Econometric Investigation," *Journal of Political Economy* 91:22–51.

Motolese, M. (2000), "Endogenous Uncertainty and the Non-Neutrality of Money," manuscript, Universitá Cattolica di Milano.

————— (2001), "Money Non-Neutrality in a Rational Belief Equilibrium with Financial Assets," *Economic Theory* 18:97–16.

Myrdal, G. (1939), *Monetary Equilibrium*. Reprints of Economic Classics, New York: Augustus M. Kelley, 1962.

Nielsen, K. C. (1996), "Rational Belief Structures and Rational Belief Equilibria," *Economic Theory* 8:339–422.

————— (1998), "Monetary Union versus Floating Exchange Rates under Rational Beliefs: The Role of Exogenous Uncertainty," working paper, University of Copenhagen.

————— (2000), "Stabilizing, Pareto Improving Policies in an OLG Model with Incomplete Markets: The Rational Expectations and Rational Beliefs Case," manuscript, Banco de España.

Pigou, A. C. (1941), *Employment and Equilibrium*, London: Macmillan.

Radner, R. (1972), "Existence of Equilibrium of Plans, Prices and Price Expectations in a Sequence of Markets," *Econometrica* 40:289–303.

Rotemberg, J. J. and M. Woodford (1999), "The Cyclical Behavior of Prices and Cost," NBER Working Paper No. 6909.

Silvestre, J. (2002), "Discrepancies Between Ex-Ante and Ex-Post Efficiency under Subjective Probabilities," 20:413–25.

Starr, R. (1976), "Optimal Production and Allocation Under Uncertainty," *Quarterly Journal of Economics* 87:81–95.

Stock, H. J. and W. M. Watson (1999a), "Diffusion Indexes," Department of Economics, Princeton University.

———— (1999b), "Forecasting Inflation," Department of Economics, Princeton University.

———— (2001), "Forecasting Output and Inflation: The Role of Asset Prices," Department of Economics, Princeton University.

Summers, L. H. (1986), "Some Skeptical Observations on Real Business Cycle Theory," *Federal Reserve Bank of Minneapolis Quarterly Review* 10:23–27.

Taylor, J. B. (1980), "Staggered Contracts," *Carnegie-Rochester Conference Series on Public Policy* 39:195–214.

———— (1993), "Discretion Versus Policy Rules in Practice," *Carnegie-Rochester Conference Series on Public Policy* 39:195–214.

———— , ed. (2000), *Monetary Policy Rules,* Chicago: Chicago University Press.

Thornton, H. (1802), *An Inquiry into the Nature and Effects of the Paper Credit of Great Britain,* Edited with an introduction by F. A. v. Hayek, New York: Augustus K. Kelley, 1962.

Wen, Y. (1998a), "Investment Cycles," *Journal of Economic Dynamics and Control* 22:1139–65.

———— (1998b), "Can a Real Business Cycle Model Pass the Watson Test?," *Journal of Monetary Economics* 42:185–203.

Woodford, M. (1999), "Interest and Prices, Chapter 2: Price-Level Determination Under Interest-Rate Rules," mimeo, Princeton University.

———— (2000), "Interest and Prices, Chapter 4: A Neo-Wicksellian Framework for the Analysis of Monetary Policy," mimeo, Princeton University.

———— (2001a), "Interest and Prices, Chapter 3: Optimizing Models with Nominal Rigidities," mimeo, Princeton University.

———— (2001b), "Inflation Stabilization and Welfare," NBER Working Paper No. 8071.

Wu, H. W. and W. C. Guo (2001), "Speculative Trading with Rational Beliefs and Endogenous Uncertainty," Department of International Business, National Taiwan University Working Paper No. 2001.

Yun, T. (1996), "Nominal Price Rigidity, Money Supply Endogeneity, and Business Cycles," *Journal of Monetary Economics* 37:345–70.

— 11 —

A Debt Puzzle

DAVID LAIBSON, ANDREA REPETTO,
AND JEREMY TOBACMAN

1. INTRODUCTION

At year-end 1998, the Federal Reserve reported that U.S. consumers held approximately $500 billion in credit card debt. This total includes only debt on which consumers pay interest—not the "float."[1] Dividing this debt over 102 million U.S. households yields an average debt of approximately $5,000 per household. Moreover, this average overlooks the fact that many households do not have access to credit. If we restrict attention to the 80 percent of households with credit cards,[2] average debt per household rises to over $6,000. Survey evidence implies that this debt is spread over a large population of debtors. At any given point in time, at least 63 percent of all households with credit cards are borrowing (i.e., paying interest) on those cards.[3] These publicly available credit card statistics match the analysis of Gross and Souleles (1999a, 2002a,b), who have assembled a proprietary data set that contains a representative sample of several hundred thousand credit card accounts from several different credit card issuers.

Credit card borrowing comes at substantial cost. Despite the rise of teaser interest rates and the high level of competition in the credit card industry, the average debt-weighted credit card interest rate has been approximately 16 percent

---

1. The total including the float was $586 billion.

2. Survey of Consumer Finances (SCF), 1995 cross section.

3. The SCF 1995 cross section implies that 63% of households are borrowing at any point in time, but credit card borrowing in the SCF suffers from dramatic underreporting, perhaps because it is stigmatized.

This chapter is a shortened version of NBER Working Paper No. 7879. We have benefited from the insights of Daron Acemoglu, Alberto Alesina, Orazio Attanasio, Robert Barro, Martin Browning, John Campbell, Christopher Carroll, José de Gregorio, Eduardo Engel, Benjamin Friedman, Edward Glaeser, Cristóbal Huneeus, Greg Mankiw, Robert Pollak, Julio Rotemberg, Andrei Schleifer, Nicholas Souleles, Richard Zeckhauser, and Steve Zeldes. Marios Angeletos, Eddie Nikolova, and Stephen Weinberg provided excellent research assistance. Laibson acknowledges financial support from the National Science Foundation (SBR-9510985), the National Institute on Aging (R01-AG-16605), the MacArthur Foundation, and the Olin Foundation; Repetto, from DID-Universidad de Chile, FONDECYT (1990004), and Fundación Andes; and Tobacman, from the National Science Foundation.

in the last 5 years, implying a real interest rate of 14 percent.[4] Within the population of households with cards, average interest payments per year exceed $1,000. This average *includes* households with no interest payments.

This chapter attempts to explain credit card borrowing with a standard life cycle model. Our model has five realistic properties that make credit card borrowing appealing to our simulated consumers.[5] First, our calibrated labor income path follows a trajectory that is upward sloping early in life. Second, our income path has transitory income shocks. Third, we introduce an illiquid asset that attracts substantial investment but is sufficiently illiquid that it cannot be used to smooth transitory income shocks. Fourth, we give consumers the opportunity to declare bankruptcy, making credit card borrowing less costly. Fifth, our simulated households have relatively more dependents early in the life cycle. Despite these institutional features, we are unable to match the actual frequency of credit card borrowing. At any point in time, less than 20 percent of our simulated consumers hold credit card debt.

Our simulated model cannot simultaneously match actual frequencies of credit card borrowing and actual levels of midlife wealth accumulation. Even if one does not count private and public defined-benefit pension wealth, the median U.S. household enters retirement with assets roughly equal to three times annual pre-retirement labor income. Restricting attention to households with heads between the ages of 50 and 59, actual median net wealth per household is $149,401.[6] To match this magnitude of retirement wealth accumulation, we need to calibrate our simulations with low exponential discount rates (≈ 0.05). But, to match actual household credit card borrowing, we need high exponential discount rates (≈ 0.18). Hence, the chapter identifies a life cycle puzzle, which we call the "Debt Puzzle." Consumers do not act consistently, behaving patiently when it comes to retirement accumulation and impatiently in the credit card market.

We argue that the quasi-hyperbolic discount function $(1, \beta\delta, \beta\delta^2, \beta\delta^3, \ldots)$ partially resolves the debt puzzle. This discount function was first analyzed by Phelps and Pollak (1968) in a pathbreaking paper, which has recently spawned a large literature on dynamically inconsistent preferences. Their original application is one of imperfect intergenerational altruism, and the discount factors apply to nonoverlapping generations of a dynasty. Laibson (1997) uses their time preferences to model intrapersonal discounting. Phelps and Pollak's preferences provide an analytically tractable functional form that replicates the qualitative features of generalized hyperbolic discount functions. Such functions predict the intertemporal choices of laboratory subjects (Ainslie, 1992; Loewenstein and Prelec, 1992). Today Phelps

---

4. Board of Governors, Federal Reserve System. This is a debt-weighted interest rate that includes teaser rates.

5. Some of these motives for borrowing are elegantly theoretically analyzed by Brito and Hartley (1995).

6. June 1999 dollars. This number is the mean of the inflation-adjusted medians from the past four SCF surveys. This net wealth calculation includes all real and financial wealth (e.g., home equity and money market accounts) as well as all claims on defined-contribution pension plans [e.g., 401(k)]. The measure does not include Social Security wealth and claims on defined-benefit pension plans.

and Pollak's preferences are often called hyperbolic or quasi-hyperbolic time preferences[7] and have been used to explain a wide range of behavior, including procrastination, contract design, drug addiction, self-deception, retirement timing, and saving (for some examples from this active literature, see Akerlof, 1991; Laibson, 1997; Barro, 1999; O'Donoghue and Rabin, 1999; Benabou and Tirole, 2000; Carrillo and Marriotti, 2000; Krusell and Smith, 2000; Diamond and Koszegi, 2001; Angeletos et al., 2001; Della Vigna and Malmendier, 2001; Harris and Laibson, 2001).

Our simulations show that Phelps and Pollak's quasi-hyperbolic time preferences—hereafter hyperbolic time preferences—predict the patient retirement saving and impatient credit card borrowing exhibited by consumers. Intuition for this result comes from the Euler equation for hyperbolic economies (Harris and Laibson, 2001), which implies that consumers behave as if they have endogenous time preferences. The hyperbolic Euler equation explains why consumers may act like exponential consumers with discount *rates* close to 40 percent, when they are liquidity constrained, and act patiently when accumulating *illiquid* wealth, because illiquid wealth generates utility flows over long horizons. Hence, the hyperbolic model helps explain why the median household borrows aggressively on credit cards *and* accumulates substantial stocks of primarily *illiquid* wealth by retirement.[8]

The rest of the chapter formalizes these claims. In Section 2, we present evidence on the proportion of households borrowing on their credit cards. In Section 3, we present our benchmark model, which can accommodate either exponential or hyperbolic preferences. In Section 4, we provide some analytic approximations that help us evaluate the model's predictions and provide intuition for the simulations that follow. In Section 5, we calibrate the model. In Section 6, we present our simulation results. In Section 7, we present additional simulation results that evaluate the robustness of our conclusions. Section 8 concludes the chapter.

2. CREDIT CARD BORROWING

Eighty percent of households surveyed in the 1995 Survey of Consumer Finances (SCF) reported having a credit card. Of the households with a card, 63 percent reported carrying over a balance the last time that they paid their credit card bill.[9]

---

7. These preferences have also been called present-biased (O'Donoghue and Rabin, 1999) and quasi-geometric (Krusell and Smith, 2000).

8. We do not explain another credit card puzzle that has been documented by Morrison (1998) and Gross and Souleles (1999), who show that a fraction of households (approximately a third) simultaneously carry credit card debt and hold liquid wealth that exceeds 1 month of income. Our model predicts that consumers will carry credit card debt and simultaneously hold illiquid wealth, but explicitly rules out the phenomenon that these authors document. In addition, the model does not explain why consumers carry credit card debt at high interest rates rather than switching to low-interest-rate cards (Ausubel, 1991).

9. Specifically, respondents answer the following question: "After the last payment was made on this account, roughly what was the balance still owed on this account?" The answers to this question are used to determine the incidence and level of credit card borrowing.

The average self-reported unpaid balance was $1,715. The median was $343. This mean and median were both calculated on the population of households with credit cards, including households with zero balances. Table 1 reports these statistics for the entire population and for subgroups conditioned on age and educational status.

An average balance of $1,715 may seem large, but it almost surely reflects dramatic *underreporting* among household respondents to the SCF. The Federal Reserve requires that banks report information on their portfolios of revolving credit loans, excluding loans to businesses. At year-end 1995, the total portfolio of loans was $464 billion. Once the float of no more than $80 billion is removed, the total falls to approximately $384 billion.[10] Dividing among the 81 million U.S. households with credit cards implies an average debt per card-holding household of over $4,500, roughly *three* times as large as the self-reported average from the 1995 SCF. For year-end 1998, the Federal Reserve numbers imply an average debt per card-holding household of over $6,000.

These Federal Reserve numbers match values from a proprietary account-level data set assembled by Gross and Souleles (1999, 2002a,b), which contains several hundred thousand representative credit card account statements provided by several large banks. The Federal Reserve figures and Gross-Souleles figures are reported directly by banks and are hence more reliable than the household survey evidence that is the SCF's raw material. Moreover, the Federal Reserve and Gross-Souleles numbers match each other, reinforcing the conclusion that average debt per card-holding household is approximately $6,000.

Because of the drastic SCF underreporting of the *magnitude* of revolving credit, we focus our analysis on the fraction of households that report carrying over a balance the last time that they paid their credit card bill (e.g., 63% in 1995).[11] We believe that this fraction is probably downward biased, but we believe that this bias is relatively minor when compared to the SCF bias for debt magnitudes. The principal goal of this chapter is to determine if standard economic models can match the observed 63 percent rate of credit card borrowing.

We also analyze the life cycle pattern of the fraction of households borrowing. Figure 1 plots the estimated age-contingent fraction of married households that carry revolving credit. We plot profiles for household heads in three educational categories: no high school diploma (NHS), high school graduate (HS), and college graduate (COLL).[12] To construct these profiles we control for cohort and business cycle effects.[13] Some 72.5 percent of households in the HS group borrow on their credit cards at age 20. The percent borrowing peaks at age 35 at 81.5 percent. This rate is relatively flat between ages 35 and 50, drops to 51.8 percent at age 80, and rises to 64.6 percent by age 90. Households in the NHS group borrow most frequently and COLL households borrow least frequently, but all three groups

---

10. Credit card charges in 1995 totaled approximately $1 trillion. This implies that the interest-free monthly float is bounded above by $(1/12)$ ($1 trillion) = $83 billion.

11. The 1998 SCF reports similar findings.

12. The household's educational status is determined by the educational attainment of the household head.

13. The procedure is described in Laibson et al. (2000).

Table 1. Credit Card Debt[a,b]

Age group	Percent with card	Conditional on having a credit card		
			Balance ($)	
		Percent with debt	Mean	Median
All categories				
20–29	0.72	0.77	1668	746
30–39	0.77	0.76	2114	772
40–49	0.85	0.72	2487	760
50–59	0.84	0.60	1603	343
60–69	0.83	0.43	980	0
70+	0.80	0.27	250	0
All ages	0.80	0.63	1715	343
No high school diploma				
20–29	0.68	0.83	1823	849
30–39	0.66	0.77	2559	943
40–49	0.77	0.84	2988	815
50–59	0.73	0.71	1910	549
60–69	0.71	0.55	1115	129
70+	0.76	0.35	285	0
All ages	0.72	0.68	1832	429
High school graduates				
20–29	0.60	0.84	1885	935
30–39	0.74	0.86	1673	858
40–49	0.81	0.73	2274	772
50–59	0.84	0.72	1424	515
60–69	0.85	0.44	722	0
70+	0.75	0.28	265	0
All ages	0.77	0.70	1537	472
College graduates				
20–29	0.89	0.65	1364	600
30–39	0.92	0.65	2213	532
40–49	0.93	0.64	2340	497
50–59	0.96	0.40	1545	0
60–69	1.00	0.26	1143	0
70+	0.93	0.13	180	0
All ages	0.93	0.53	1767	94

Source: Authors' calculations based on the 1995 Survey of Consumer Finances.

[a] Includes traditional cards such as Visa, Mastercard, Discover, and Optima, and other credit or charge cards such as Diners Club, American Express, store cards, airline cards, car rental cards, and gasoline cards. Excludes business and company cards.

[b] The total credit card debt is constructed on the basis of the responses to the following SCF question: "After the last payments were made on this (these) account(s), roughly what was the balance still owed on this (these) account(s)?"

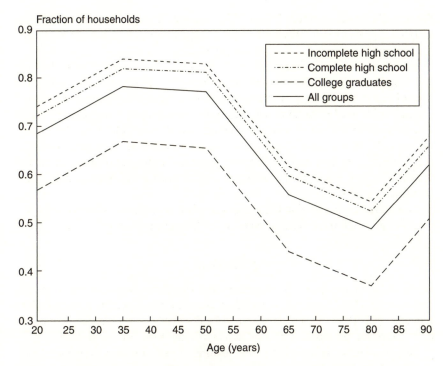

Fraction of households

Incomplete high school
Complete high school
College graduates
All groups

Age (years)

Figure 1. Fraction of households borrowing on their credit cards. Calculated from a regression on a linear spline in age, cohort dummies, the unemployment rate, a marital status dummy, and a set of education dummies. (Source: Survey of Consumer Finances.)

borrow at roughly similar rates. Indeed, the most striking property of the profiles in Figure 1 is the uniformly high rate of borrowing.

The identification strategy used in the previous analysis attributes time trends to age and cohort effects and assumes that the unemployment rate captures business cycle effects. The estimated age profiles are quite sensitive to these identification assumptions. When we replace the cohort dummies with time dummies, we find that the fraction of households borrowing tends to fall over the life cycle. This pattern is reflected in Table 1, which reports the raw data from the 1995 SCF. The sensitivity in the estimated life cycle profiles leads us to be agnostic about the appropriate identification approach. We believe that cohort effects exist—reflecting habits of behavior and social norms fixed at a relatively young age—and we believe that time effects exist—reflecting society-wide changes in technology and borrowing norms. We cannot simultaneously include cohort, age, and time effects in our estimation because these three variables are collinear.[14] We consistently report our cohort-adjusted estimates, as we have greater faith in these results. We urge readers who are skeptical about the identification of age effects to focus on the raw, unadjusted life cycle averages reported in Table 1.

---

14. See Ameriks and Zeldes (2001).

Specifically, unadjusted, 68, 70, and 53 percent of households in the NHS, HS, and COLL groups reported that they were currently borrowing on their credit cards (i.e., paying interest) at the time of the 1995 SCF.

Finally, we are also interested in the relationship between wealth holding and borrowing. Borrowing frequencies in the 1995 SCF tabulated by age and educational status–contingent wealth quartiles are reported in Table 2. Borrowing declines with wealth (holding age fixed), but this decline is surprisingly small among younger cohorts. Among households 40–49 years old in the HS group, for example, 86 percent of those in the bottom wealth quartile reported that they are borrowing on their credit cards, compared to 50 percent of those in the top quartile. By any measure, borrowing is not confined to the bottom half of the wealth distribution.

Using the simulations that follow, we ask whether standard calibrated life cycle models can match these stylized facts on the frequency of credit card borrowing.

3. MODEL

We model the complex set of constraints and stochastic income events that consumers face. Our framework is based on the simulation literature pioneered by Carroll (1992, 1997), Deaton (1991), and Zeldes (1989).[15] We discuss the conceptual features of our model in this section and calibrate the model in Section 5.

Our simulations adopt most of the features of previous life cycle simulation models. We extend the existing literature by enabling households to borrow on credit cards, including a time-varying number of dependent adults and children in the household, allowing the household to invest in a partially illiquid asset, and allowing the household to declare bankruptcy. We divide the presentation of the model into eight domains: (1) demographics, (2) income from transfers and wages, (3) liquid assets and noncollateralized debt, (4) illiquid assets and collateralized debt, (5) budget constraints, (6) bankruptcy, (7) preferences, and (8) equilibrium.

3.1. Demographics

The economy is populated by households that face a time-varying, exogenous hazard rate of survival s_t, where t indexes age. Households live for a maximum of $T + N$ periods, where T and N are exogenous variables that represent, respectively, the maximum length of preretirement life and the maximum length of retirement. If a household is alive at age $20 \leq t \leq T$, then the household is in the workforce. If a household is alive at age $T < t \leq T + N$, then the household is retired. We assume that economic life begins at age 20 and do not model consumption decisions before this date. We assume that household composition—number of adults and nonadults—varies over the life cycle. Households always contain a household head and a spouse, but the number of adult dependents and nonadult dependents varies.

---

15. See also Engen et al. (1994), Gourinchas and Parker (2002), Hubbard et al. (1994), and Laibson et al. (1998).

Table 2. Fraction of Households Borrowing on
Credit Cards across the Distribution of Wealth[a,b]

Age group	Wealth distribution percentile			
	Less than 25	25–50	50–75	Over 75
All categories				
20–29	0.87	0.77	0.70	0.65
30–39	0.86	0.80	0.69	0.51
40–49	0.79	0.76	0.56	0.41
50–59	0.75	0.65	0.40	0.27
60–69	0.55	0.40	0.25	0.18
70+	0.48	0.26	0.11	0.05
Incomplete high school				
20–29	0.91	0.83	0.67	0.82
30–39	0.73	0.82	0.78	0.70
40–49	0.84	0.85	0.80	0.60
50–59	0.83	0.67	0.75	0.45
60–69	0.60	0.51	0.39	0.25
70+	0.57	0.30	0.24	0.10
High school graduates				
20–29	0.89	0.78	0.82	0.73
30–39	0.90	0.83	0.83	0.66
40–49	0.86	0.79	0.74	0.50
50–59	0.79	0.62	0.55	0.40
60–69	0.60	0.42	0.31	0.24
70+	0.47	0.29	0.09	0.14
College graduates				
20–29	0.81	0.65	0.51	0.56
30–39	0.82	0.61	0.55	0.39
40–49	0.71	0.53	0.44	0.20
50–59	0.63	0.38	0.24	0.22
60–69	0.41	0.20	0.09	0.10
70+	0.28	0.07	0.06	0.03

Source: Authors' calculations based on the 1983–1995 Survey of Consumer Finances.

[a] Conditional on having a credit card.

[b] We calculated the fraction of households who are borrowing in each quartile of the wealth distribution contingent on age and education group for every SCF year. The table reports the weighted average across the four SCF years, using the proportion of households with credit cards in a given year/category as weights.

Our population is divided into three education categories: consumers with no high school diploma, high school graduates, and college graduates. We assume that education is exogenous and assign a different working life (T), retirement duration (N), household composition, and labor income process to each education category.

3.2. Income from Transfers and Wages

Let Y_t represent all after-tax income from transfers and wages. Hence, Y_t includes labor income, inheritances, private defined-benefit pensions, and all government transfers. Since we assume that labor is supplied inelastically, Y_t is exogenous. Let $y_t \equiv \ln(Y_t)$. We refer to y_t as "labor income," to simplify exposition. During working life ($20 \leq t \leq T$), $y_t = f^W(t) + u_t + v_t^W$, where $f^W(t)$ is a cubic polynomial in age, u_t is a Markov process, and v_t^W is iid and normally distributed, $N(0, \sigma_{v,W}^2)$. During retirement ($T < t \leq T+N$), $y_t = f^R(t) + v_t^R$, where $f^R(t)$ is linear in age, and v_t^R is iid and normally distributed, $N(0, \sigma_{v,R}^2)$. The parameters of the labor income process vary across education categories.

3.3. Liquid Assets and Noncollateralized Debt

Let X_t represent liquid asset holdings at the beginning of period t, excluding current labor income. Then $X_t + Y_t$ represents total liquid asset holdings at the beginning of period t. To model noncollateralized borrowing—that is, credit card borrowing—we permit X_t to lie below zero, but we introduce a credit limit equal to some fraction of current (average) income. We require $X_t \geq -\lambda \cdot \bar{Y}_t$, where $\bar{Y}_t$ is average income at age t for the appropriate education group.

3.4. Illiquid Assets and Collateralized Debt

Let Z_t represent illiquid asset holdings at age t. The illiquid asset generates two sources of returns: capital gains and consumption flows. We assume that in all periods Z is bounded below by zero, so $Z_t \geq 0$. The household borrows to invest in Z, and we represent such collateralized debt as D, where D is normalized to be positive. Let $I^Z \geq 0$ represent new investments into Z and let $\psi(I^Z)$ represent transaction costs generated by that investment. We assume that each new investment is paid for with a down payment of exactly $\mu \cdot I^Z$, implying that investment of magnitude I^Z generates new debt equal to $(1 - \mu) \cdot I^Z$.

3.5. Dynamic and Static Budget Constraints

Let I_t^X represent net investment into the liquid asset X during period t. Recall that I_t^Z represents net investment into the illiquid asset Z during period t. Let I_t^D represent net repayment of debt D during period t. Hence, the dynamic budget constraints are given by

$$X_{t+1} = R^X \cdot (X_t + I_t^X), \tag{1}$$

$$Z_{t+1} = R^Z \cdot (Z_t + I_t^Z), \tag{2}$$

$$D_{t+1} = R^D \cdot (D_t - I_t^D), \tag{3}$$

where R^X, R^Z, and R^D are the real interest rates, respectively, on liquid wealth, illiquid wealth, and debt. We assume that the interest rate on liquid wealth depends on whether the consumer is borrowing or saving in her liquid accounts. We interpret liquid borrowing as credit card debt:

$$R^X = \begin{cases} R^{CC} & \text{if} \quad X_t + I_t^X < 0 \\ R & \text{if} \quad X_t + I_t^X > 0. \end{cases}$$

Naturally, R^{CC} is the interest rate on credit card debt, and R represents the interest rate on positive stocks of liquid wealth. The within-period budget constraint is

$$C_t = Y_t - I_t^X - I_t^Z - I_t^D - \psi(I_t^Z).$$

For computational tractability, we have made an additional restriction, which eliminates one choice variable. Specifically, we assume that the debt contract is structured so that a proportion $\Delta = 0.10$ of D_t is paid off between periods. Hence, we require that debt repayments I_t^D be set such that

$$D_{t+1} = (1 - \Delta) \cdot D_t + R^D \cdot (1 - \mu) \cdot I_t^Z. \tag{4}$$

Combining equation (4) with equation (3) implies that I_t^D is fully determined by the other variables in the model. Hence, the state variables at the beginning of period t are liquid wealth $(X_t + Y_t)$, illiquid wealth (Z_t), collateralized debt (D_t), and the value of the Markov process (u_t). The nonredundant choice variables are net investment in liquid wealth (I_t^X) and net investment in illiquid wealth (I_t^Z). Consumption is calculated as a residual.

3.6. Bankruptcy

For some of our simulations we will allow households to declare bankruptcy. If a consumer declares bankruptcy in period t, we assume the following consequences: Consumption drops permanently to some level that is proportional to the expected value of permanent income (where permanent income is evaluated at the date bankruptcy is declared), X drops permanently to zero, Z drops permanently to $\min(Z^{\text{Bankruptcy}}, Z_t - D_t)$, and D drops permanently to zero.

3.7. Preferences

We use standard preferences in our benchmark model. The felicity function is characterized by constant relative risk aversion and the discount function is exponential (δ^t).

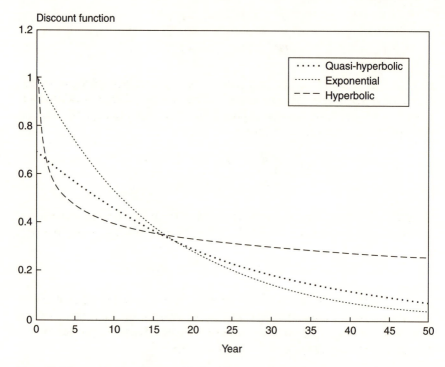

Figure 2. Discount functions. Exponential: δ^t, with $\delta = 0.939$; hyperbolic: $(1+\alpha t)^{-\gamma/\alpha}$, with $\alpha = 4$ and $\gamma = 1$; and quasi-hyperbolic: $\{1, \beta\delta, \beta\delta^2, \beta\delta^3, \ldots\}$, with $\beta = 0.7$ and $\delta = 0.957$. (Source: Authors' calculations.)

We also analyze an alternative model that has hyperbolic discount functions but is otherwise identical to the benchmark model. Hyperbolic time preferences imply that from today's perspective discount rates are higher in the short run than in the long run. Experimental data support this intuition. When researchers use subject choices to estimate the shape of the discount function, the estimates consistently approximate generalized hyperbolas: Events τ periods away are discounted with factor $(1+\alpha\tau)^{-\gamma/\alpha}$, with $\alpha, \gamma > 0$.[16]

Figure 2 graphs the standard exponential discount function (assuming $\delta = 0.944$), the generalized hyperbolic discount function (assuming $\alpha = 4$ and $\gamma = 1$), and the quasi-hyperbolic discount function, which is an analytically convenient approximation of the generalized hyperbola. The quasi-hyperbolic function is a discrete time function with values $(1, \beta\delta, \beta\delta^2, \beta\delta^3, \ldots)$. This discount function was first analyzed by Phelps and Pollak (1968) in a seminal paper on dynamically

---

16. See Loewenstein and Prelec (1992) for an axiomatic derivation of this discount function. See Chung and Herrnstein (1961) for the first use of the hyperbolic discount function. Laboratory experiments have been done with a wide range of real rewards, including money, durable goods, fruit juice, sweets, video rentals, relief from noxious noise, and access to video games. See Ainslie (1992) for a partial review of this literature. See Mulligan (1997) for a critique.

inconsistent preferences.[17] Phelps and Pollak's original application is one of imperfect intergenerational altruism, and the discount factors apply to nonoverlapping generations of a dynasty. Following Laibson (1997) we apply this discount function to an intrapersonal problem. Figure 2 plots the quasi-hyperbolic discount function for the case of $\beta = 0.7$ and $\delta = 0.956$.[18] When $0 < \beta < 1$ the quasi-hyperbolic discount structure mimics the generalized hyperbolic discount function, while maintaining most of the analytical tractability of the exponential discount function.

Quasi-hyperbolic and hyperbolic preferences induce dynamic inconsistency. Consider the discrete-time quasi-hyperbolic function. Note that the discount factor between adjacent periods n and $n + 1$ represents the weight placed on utils at time $n + 1$ relative to the weight placed on utils at time n. From the perspective of self t, the discount factor between periods t and $t + 1$ is $\beta\delta$, but the discount factor that applies between any two later periods is δ. Since we take β to be less than one, this implies a short-term discount rate that is greater than the long-term discount rate. From the perspective of self $t + 1$, $\beta\delta$ is the relevant discount factor between periods $t + 1$ and $t + 2$. Hence, self t and self $t + 1$ disagree about the desired level of patience at time $t + 1$. Because of the dynamic inconsistency, the hyperbolic consumer is involved in a decision that has intrapersonal strategic dimensions. Early selves would like to commit later selves to honor the preferences of those early selves. Later selves do their best to maximize their own interests.

To analyze the decisions of an agent with dynamically inconsistent preferences, we must specify the preferences of all of the temporally distinct selves. We index these selves by their life cycle position, $t \in \{20, 21, ..., T + N - 1, T + N\}$. Self t has instantaneous payoff function

$$u(C_t, Z_t, n_t) = n_t \cdot \frac{\left[(C_t + \gamma Z_t)/n_t\right]^{1-\rho} - 1}{1 - \rho}$$

and continuation payoffs given by

$$\beta \sum_{i=1}^{T+N-t} \delta^i \left(\Pi_{j=1}^{i-1} s_{t+j}\right) \left[s_{t+i} \cdot u(C_{t+i}, Z_{t+i}, n_{t+i}) \right. \tag{5}$$

$$\left. + (1 - s_{t+i}) \cdot B(X_{t+i}, Z_{t+i}, D_{t+i})\right].$$

Here $n_t = (\#\text{ adults}_t) + \kappa(\#\text{ of children}_t)$ is effective household size; ρ is the coefficient of relative risk aversion; γZ_t is the consumption flow generated by Z_t; s_{t+1} is the probability of surviving to age $t + 1$ conditional on living to age t; and $B(\cdot)$ is the payoff in the death state, which reflects a bequest motive. The first expression in the bracketed term in equation (5) represents utility flows realized in period $t + i$ if the household survives to age $t + i$. The second expression in

---

17. See Angeletos et al. (2001) for an introduction to this recent literature.

18. These parameter values represent the calibration for households with a high school graduate head.

the bracketed term represents payoffs realized in period $t + i$ if the household dies between period $t + i - 1$ and $t + i$.

3.8. Equilibrium

When $\beta < 1$ the household has dynamically inconsistent preferences, and hence the consumption problem cannot be treated as a straightforward dynamic optimization. Late selves will not implement the policies that are optimal from the perspective of early selves. Following the work of Strotz (1956), Pollak (1968), and Phelps and Pollak (1968), we model consumption choices as an intrapersonal game. Selves $(20, 21, 22, \ldots, T + N)$ are the players in this game.[19] Taking the strategies of other selves as given, self t picks a strategy for time t that is optimal from its perspective. This strategy is a mapping from the (Markov) state variables $(t, X + Y, Z, D, u)$ to the nonredundant choice variables (I^X, I^Z). An equilibrium is a fixed point in the strategy space, such that all strategies are optimal given the strategies of the other players. We solve for the equilibrium strategies using a numerical backward induction algorithm.

Our choice of the quasi-hyperbolic discount function simplifies the induction algorithm. Let $V_{t,t+1}(X_{t+1} + Y_{t+1}, Z_{t+1}, D_{t+1}, u_{t+1})$ represent the time $t + 1$ continuation payoff function of self t. Then the objective function of self t is

$$u(C_t, Z_t, n_t) + \beta \delta E_t V_{t,t+1}(\Lambda_{t+1}), \tag{6}$$

where Λ_{t+1} represents the vector of state variables: $(X_{t+1} + Y_{t+1}, Z_{t+1}, D_{t+1}, u_{t+1})$. Self t chooses I_t^X and I_t^Z, which jointly define C_t, maximizing this expression. The sequence of continuation payoff functions is defined recursively:

$$V_{t-1,t}(\Lambda_t) = s_t[u(C_t, Z_t, n_t) + \delta E_t V_{t,t+1}(\Lambda_{t+1})] + (1 - s_t)E_t B(\Lambda_t), \tag{7}$$

where s_t is the probability of surviving to age t conditional on being alive at age $t - 1$ and C_t is the consumption chosen by self t. The induction continues in this way. Note that dynamic inconsistency in preferences is reflected in the fact that a β factor appears in equation (6)—reflecting self t's discount factor between periods t and $t + 1$—but does not appear in equation (7), since self $t - 1$ does not use the β factor to discount between periods t and $t + 1$.

Equations (6) and (7) jointly define a functional equation that is not a contraction mapping. Hence, the standard dynamic programming results do not apply to this problem. Specifically, V does not inherit concavity from u, the objective function is not single-peaked, and the policy functions are in general discontinuous and nonmonotonic. We have adopted a numerically efficient solution algorithm—based

---

19. Like Laibson (1997) we assume the horizon is finite, which implies that equilibrium is unique. In their original paper, Phelps and Pollak (1968) assume an infinite horizon, which admits a continuum of equilibria (Krusell and Smith, 2001; Laibson, 1994). Phelps and Pollak avoid this indeterminacy by assuming isoelastic preferences and linear technology and restricting attention to linear Markov policies.

on local grid searches—that iterates our functional equation in the presence of these nonstandard properties.

Our equilibrium concept has a major shortcoming: We adopt the standard economic assumption of unlimited problem-solving sophistication. The consumers in our model solve perfectly a complex backward induction problem when making their consumption and asset allocation choices. We are dissatisfied with this extreme assumption, but view it as a reasonable starting point for analysis.[20]

4. ANALYTIC APPROXIMATIONS

4.1. Exponential Case: $\beta = 1$

Consider a stripped-down version of our benchmark model. Specifically, set $\beta = 1$, assume that labor income is iid, eliminate the illiquid asset, and eliminate time-varying mortality and household size effects. It is possible to use the exponential Euler equation to impute a value for the discount rate, $-\ln(\delta)$. The exponential Euler equation is

$$u'(C_t) = E_t R \delta u'(C_{t+1}).$$

The second-order approximation of this equation is

$$E_t \Delta \ln (C_{t+1}) = \frac{1}{\rho} [r + \ln(\delta)] + \frac{\rho}{2} V_t \left[\Delta \ln (C_{t+1}) \right],$$

which can be rearranged to yield

$$\text{Discount rate} = -\ln(\delta) \tag{8}$$

$$= -\rho E_t \Delta \ln (C_{t+1}) + r + \frac{\rho^2}{2} V_t \left[\Delta \ln (C_{t+1}) \right].$$

To impute the value of the discount rate, we need to evaluate $E_t \Delta \ln (C_{t+1})$, r, ρ, and $V_t \left[\Delta \ln (C_{t+1}) \right]$. We do this for a typical household.

Consider only U.S. households that have access to a line of revolving credit and have a 45-year-old head. Order these households by the expected 1-year rate of consumption growth. Survey data imply that the median household should expect flat consumption between ages 45 and 46.[21] It is reasonable to assume that this median household holds credit card debt, as credit card borrowing peaks in frequency and magnitude for households with 45-year-old heads. Over three-quarters of households with 45-year-old heads and credit cards have credit card

---

20. Another reasonable starting point is the model of "naif" behavior first defined by Strotz (1956) and recently advocated by Akerlof (1991) and O'Donoghue and Rabin (1999). These authors propose that decision-makers with dynamically inconsistent preferences make current choices under the false belief that later selves will act in the interests of the current self.

21. See, e.g., Gourinchas and Parker (2002).

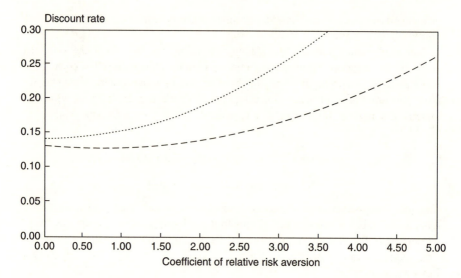

Figure 3. Implied discount rates. Dotted line: $r = 0.14$, $E(\Delta \ln C) = 0$, $V[\Delta \ln C] = 0.025$. Dashed line: $r = 0.13$, $E(\Delta \ln C) = 0.01$, $V[\Delta \ln C] = 0.015$. Figure plots the exponential discount rates and coefficients of relative risk aversion that are consistent with a second-order approximation of the Euler equation, under alternative calibration values for the real interest rate (r), the expected 1 year rate of consumption growth ($E[\Delta \ln C]$), and the conditional variance of consumption growth ($V[\Delta \ln C]$). (Source: Authors' calculations.)

debt.[22] Hence, for our analysis, the appropriate real interest rate is the real credit card borrowing rate, $r = r^{cc} \approx 0.14$.[23] We will consider a range of values for ρ. Finally, the conditional variance of consumption growth can be represented as a proportion of the conditional variance of income growth. When income is a random walk, the conditional variance of consumption growth is approximately equal to that of income growth. We assume that the conditional variance of consumption growth equals 0.025, half the conditional variance of income growth. This assumption is consistent with our calibrated simulation results. The lack of consumption smoothing is also consistent with the fact that the typical household is borrowing in the credit card market, a portfolio decision that suggests low levels of liquid wealth accumulation and hence necessarily imperfect consumption smoothing.

We are now in a position to evaluate $-\ln(\delta)$. Figure 3 plots $-\ln(\delta)$ on the y-axis, against ρ on the x-axis. The dotted line reflects the assumptions described in the previous paragraph. The line is monotonically increasing with a minimum of 0.14 (at $\rho = 0$). For reasons that we describe later, this value turns out to be anomalously high. In anticipation of this problem, we have plotted a second line in Figure 3 (the dashed line), which reflects more aggressive assumptions that lower our envelope of discount rates. Specifically, we raise $E_t \Delta \ln (C_{t+1})$, lower

22. SCF, 1995 cross section.

23. See Section 5 for details on the calibration of interest rates.

r, and lower $V_t\left[\Delta \ln\left(C_{t+1}\right)\right]$ in an effort to make the discount rate $-\ln(\delta)$ as low as possible. For this second line, we set $E_t\Delta \ln\left(C_{t+1}\right) = 0.01$, $r = 0.13$, and $V_t\left[\Delta \ln\left(C_{t+1}\right)\right] = 0.015$. We believe that these assumptions are inappropriate, but they serve to identify a lower bound for the discount rate envelope. This second plotted line begins at a discount rate of 0.13 (at $\rho = 0$), and then falls slightly to a minimum of 0.127 (at $\rho = 0.67$), before rising monotonically thereafter. Hence, whatever assumptions we make, we are unable to generate implied discount rates below 13 percent.

These analytical approximations turn out to match closely the results obtained by numerically simulating the calibrated life cycle model described in the previous section (assuming $\rho = 2$). When we choose the exponential discount rate so our simulations match a credit card borrowing frequency of 0.70 (the empirical frequency for the HS households), we end up selecting an exponential discount rate of 0.179, close to the value predicted by equation (8):

$$-\rho E_t\Delta \ln\left(C_{t+1}\right) + r + \frac{\rho^2}{2}V_t\left[\Delta \ln\left(C_{t+1}\right)\right] = -2\cdot 0 + 0.14 + \frac{2^2}{2}\cdot(0.025)$$
$$= 0.19.$$

Such high discount rates are problematic. Observed household wealth accumulation profiles can only be explained with much *lower* discount rates. For example, the median U.S. household accumulates total preretirement wealth equal to 3.34 times after-tax income.[24] To calibrate lifetime consumption and wealth profiles, most authors have used discount rates that lie below 10 percent. Engen et al. (1994) calibrate their model with a discount rate of 4 percent ($\rho = 3$). Hubbard et al. (1995) calibrate their simulations with a discount rate of 3 percent ($\rho = 3$). Gourinchas and Parker (2001) estimate a discount rate of 4 percent ($\rho = 0.5$). Laibson et al. (1998) estimate two central discount rates: 4 percent ($\rho = 1$) and 6 percent ($\rho = 3$). Engen et al. (1999) calibrate their model with discount rates of 0 and 3 percent ($\rho = 3$).[25]

Hence, these observations suggest a puzzle: Consumers act impatiently in the credit market but patiently when accumulating for retirement. We call this the "debt puzzle."

4.2. Hyperbolic Case: $\beta < 1$

The discussion above only applies to exponential consumers. As Harris and Laibson (2001) have shown, making the discount function hyperbolic generates

---

24. SCF, 1995 survey. Our definition of wealth includes all assets except claims on defined-contribution pension plans. For a detailed list of the assets that we include, see the section on model calibration.

25. All of these papers assume real interest rates (on positive savings) of 1–5 percent. Naturally, substantially higher interest rates would justify substantially higher discount rates, but historical data pin the interest rate down.

an important modification of the Euler equation. To derive this hyperbolic Euler equation,[26] recall that the current self chooses C according to

$$C^* = \arg \max_C u(C) + \beta \delta E_\Omega \left\{ V \left[R \cdot (X + Y - C) + Y_{+1} \right] \right\},$$

where $V(\cdot)$ is the continuation payoff function, and for simplicity the problem is stationary, implying that $V(\cdot)$ does not depend on time. Recall from above that $V(\cdot)$ has the recursive property

$$V(X + Y) \equiv u(C^*) + \delta E_\Omega \left\{ V \left[R \cdot (X + Y - C^*) + Y_{+1} \right] \right\},$$

where Ω represents the current information set. Finally, represent the current self's welfare as

$$W(X + Y) \equiv u(C^*) + \beta \delta E_\Omega \left\{ V \left[R \cdot (X + Y - C^*) + Y_{+1} \right] \right\}.$$

Then the envelope theorem (ET) implies

$$W'(X + Y) = u'(C^*). \tag{ET}$$

Moreover, the first-order condition (FOC) in the current self's problem implies

$$u'(C^*) = R\beta \delta E_\Omega \left\{ V' \left[R \cdot (X + Y - C^*) + Y_{+1} \right] \right\}. \tag{FOC}$$

Finally, $V(\cdot)$ and $W(\cdot)$ are linked by the identity

$$\beta V(X + Y) = W(X + Y) - (1 - \beta) u(C^*) \qquad \text{by definition.}$$

Using these relationships, we find that

$$u'(C_t) = R\beta \delta E_t \left[V'(X_{t+1} + Y_{t+1}) \right] \qquad \text{by the FOC}$$

$$= R\delta E_t \left[W'(X_{t+1} + Y_{t+1}) - (1 - \beta) u'(C_{t+1}) \frac{\partial C_{t+1}}{\partial X_{t+1}} \right] \qquad \text{by definition}$$

$$= R\delta E_t \left[u'(C_{t+1}) - (1 - \beta) u'(C_{t+1}) \frac{\partial C_{t+1}}{\partial X_{t+1}} \right] \qquad \text{by the ET.}$$

Note that the partial derivative of consumption with respect to cash on hand can be equivalently represented as either

$$\frac{\partial C_{t+1}}{\partial X_{t+1}} \quad \text{or} \quad \frac{\partial C_{t+1}}{\partial (X_{t+1} + Y_{t+1})}.$$

---

26. A heuristic derivation follows, which assumes differentiability of the value and consumption functions. For a fully general derivation, see Harris and Laibson (2001).

Rearranging the last equation yields

$$u'(C_t) = E_t R \left[\beta\delta \left(\frac{\partial C_{t+1}}{\partial X_{t+1}} \right) + \delta \left(1 - \frac{\partial C_{t+1}}{\partial X_{t+1}} \right) \right] u'(C_{t+1}).$$

This equation is identical to the exponential case, except that the exponential discount factor δ is replaced by the bracketed term above. This bracketed term, the endogenous effective discount factor, is a weighted average of the short-run discount factor $\beta\delta$ and the long-run discount factor δ. The respective weights are

$$\frac{\partial C_{t+1}}{\partial X_{t+1}},$$

the marginal propensity to consume, and

$$1 - \frac{\partial C_{t+1}}{\partial X_{t+1}}.$$

The effective discount factor is stochastic and endogenous to the model.

When consumers are liquidity constrained, the marginal propensity to consume,

$$\frac{\partial C_{t+1}}{\partial X_{t+1}},$$

is almost one. In this case, the effective discount factor is approximately $\beta\delta$. Assuming that $\beta = 0.7$ and $\delta = 0.95$ (a conservative calibration of the quasi-hyperbolic discount function when each period is 1 year) the effective discount rate will approximately equal $-\ln(0.7 \times 0.95) = 0.41$.

Hyperbolic consumers have an incentive to keep themselves liquidity constrained (Laibson, 1997). By storing wealth in illiquid form, hyperbolic consumers prevent themselves from overspending in the future. Early selves intentionally try to constrain the consumption of future selves. This has the effect of raising the future marginal propensity to consume out of the (constrained) stock of liquid wealth. The high marginal propensity to consume generates high effective discount rates ($\approx$ 0.41), explaining why hyperbolics are frequently willing to borrow on credit cards.

Hyperbolics recognize that illiquid wealth will be spent much more slowly than liquid wealth. Illiquid wealth such as housing generates marginal utility flows for many periods in the future. The consumer discounts utility flows τ periods away with factor $\beta\delta^\tau$. When discounting consumption increments over long horizons, a hyperbolic consumer uses an effective discount rate of

$$\lim_{\tau \to \infty} \left[\ln(\beta\delta^\tau)^{1/\tau} \right] = \lim_{\tau \to \infty} \left[-\frac{1}{\tau} \ln(\beta) - \ln(\delta) \right] = -\ln(\delta).$$

Hence, illiquid wealth accumulation is primarily driven by δ, not β, implying that the consumer accumulates illiquid wealth as if she had a discount rate of $-\ln(\delta) = 0.05$.

With the potential for effective discount rates of 41 percent per year, the model predicts widespread borrowing on credit cards at annual interest rates of 15–20 percent. However, the hyperbolic model simultaneously predicts that most consumers will accumulate large stocks of illiquid wealth, basing accumulation decisions on a relatively low long-run discount rate of 0.05.

5. CALIBRATION OF THE SIMULATION MODEL

5.1. Demographics

We use education group population weights 0.25, 0.50, and 0.25 (no high school, high school, college) that roughly match the actual proportions in the Panel Study of Income Dynamics (PSID).

Consumers live for a maximum of 90 years $(T + N)$, though they do not begin economic life until age 20. The conditional hazard rates of survival are taken from the life tables of the U.S. National Center for Health Statistics (1993). This 1-year survival probability is close to one through age 70, dropping to 96.3 percent by age 80, and 67.6 percent by age 89.

Following Engen et al. (1994), we use the survival rates for a single individual even though the "consumers" in our model are actually multiperson households. Conceptually our model assumes that surviving households always have two nondependent adults (e.g., a head of household and a spouse) and an exogenously age-varying number of dependents—including adult dependents and nonadult dependents.[27]

To calibrate the age-varying number of dependents, we use the PSID and condition on households with a head and a spouse. The measure of children in the household includes all children between 0 and 17. It does not include the head or spouse even if either or both of them is younger than 18. It includes all children whether or not they are actually children of the head or spouse. The number of dependent adults represents the actual number of members 18 years of age and older, excluding head and spouse.

To construct the effective household size, we smooth the observed profiles of dependent children and dependent adults. These smooth profiles are computed, for each educational category, as follows: First, we drop households with heads younger than 20 or older than 90. Second, we restrict the sample to households with a head and a spouse. Finally, we estimate the following nonlinear regression model using nonlinear least squares:

$$x_{it} = \beta_0 \exp(\beta_1 \cdot age_{it} - \beta_2 \cdot age_{it}^2) + \varepsilon_{it}. \tag{9}$$

---

27. Our "single individual" mortality assumption engenders two subtle biases that go in opposite directions. First, our approach may yield *too much* simulated retirement saving because our model implicitly rules out insurance effects that arise when spouses have independent mortality outcomes (in real life an N-person marriage creates a partial annuity which becomes perfect as N goes to infinity). Second, our mortality assumption yields a bias that implies *too little* simulated retirement saving, because widows and widowers have expenses that fall by less than 50 percent when their spouses die.

Note that x_{it} represents either the number of children or the number of dependent adults in household i at date t, and the errors ε_{it} represent iid noise. We picked this particular function because it both captures the shape of the observed profiles and predicts a positive number of children and dependent adults for every age. Estimated coefficients, standard errors, and implied life cycle profiles are reported in Laibson et al. (2000). The life cycle patterns vary across education groups. The profiles are lower and slightly steeper for college-educated households, and the peak in the number of children occurs 2 to 3 years later.

Following Blundell et al. (1994), we define effective household size as the number of adults plus 0.4 times the number of children.[28] We assume that the total number of adults is equal to two (head and spouse) plus the number of predicted dependent adults. As expected, our predicted measure of effective household size exhibits a hump shape pattern. Furthermore, like empirical profiles of consumption (Gourinchas and Parker, 2002), family size peaks in the mid- to late forties.

5.2. Income from Transfers and Wages

We define income as after-tax nonasset income. This includes labor income, bequests, lump-sum windfalls, and government transfers such as AFDC, SSI, workers' compensation, and unemployment insurance. This definition is broader than the one used by Engen and Gale (1993)—who use only labor earnings—and the one used by Hubbard et al. (1994, 1995)—who only add unemployment insurance payments to labor income.

The sample of households is taken from the PSID. We use the family files for the interview years between 1983 and 1990, since these are the only PSID sample years that include bequests and other lump-sum windfalls, as well as federal taxes. We exclude all households whose head is younger than 20 years of age, that report annual income less than $1,000 (in 1990 dollars, deflated by the CPI for urban consumers), or that have any crucial variable missing.[29] To calculate preretirement income we follow the approach of Bernheim et al. (2001), who define a year as preretirement if anyone in the household worked 1500 hours or more in that year or in any subsequent year. A household is retired if no member works more than 500 hours in the current year or in any year in the future.

We estimate the regression equation

$$y_{it} = \text{HSS}_{it} + \text{polynomial}(\text{age}_{it}) + \text{TE}_t + \text{CE}_i + \xi_{it} \qquad (10)$$

by weighted least squares, using the PSID population weights. This equation is estimated twice, once for households in the labor force and once for retired

---

28. There exist other adult equivalence scales. For instance, Attanasio (1999) uses the official OECD scale, which gives weight 1 to the first adult, 0.67 to the following adults, and 0.43 to each child. Using empirical data, Deaton and Muellbauer (1986) estimate that children cost their parents about 30–40 percent of what they spend on themselves.

29. We believe that reported income of less than $1,000 is more likely to reflect a coding or reporting error than to reflect a true report. Recall that our income definition includes all government transfers.

households. Income of household i in period t is determined by a household size effect (HSS_{it}), a polynomial in age, a time effect (TE_t), and a cohort effect (CE_i). The household size effect integrates the influence of three variables: the number of heads in the household (head only or head and spouse), the number of children, and the number of dependent adults. We specify the age polynomial as third degree for our preretirement regression and linear for our postretirement regression. Following Gourinchas and Parker (2002), and to circumvent the problem that age, time, and birth year are perfectly correlated, we assume that the time effect is related to the business cycle and that it can be proxied by the unemployment rate. We use the unemployment rate in the household's state of residence, taken from the Bureau of Labor Statistics. Our cohort effects control for birth year to account for permanent differences in productivity across cohorts. We use 5-year age cohorts, the oldest born in 1910–1914 and the youngest born in 1970–1974. Laibson et al. (2000) report the income regressions for each education group.

We calculate f^W and f^R—the polynomials in the model of the previous section—by setting the cohort and unemployment effects equal to the sample means, setting the number of heads equal to two and the number of dependents—children and adults—equal to the age-varying smoothed profiles estimated in the previous subsection. This allows us to recover variation in expected income over the life cycle for a household that has a typical life cycle evolution in household size, experiences no business cycle effects, and has a typical cohort effect.

To study the stochastic component of preretirement nonasset household income we exploit the panel dimension of the PSID. We model the unexplained part of measured nonasset income (ξ_{it}) as the sum of an individual fixed effect, an AR(1) process, and a purely transitory shock:

$$\xi_{it} = \vartheta_i + u_{it} + v_{it}^W = \vartheta_i + \alpha u_{it-1} + \epsilon_{it} + v_{it}^W.$$

The individual fixed effect is included to account for permanent differences in income that are not captured by the educational categories.

Let $\sigma_{v,W}^2$ be the variance of the transitory shock v^W, and σ_ε^2, the variance of ϵ. Also, let $C_k \equiv E(\Delta \xi_t \Delta \xi_{t-k})$ represent the theoretical autocovariances of $\Delta \xi$. Then,

$$C_0 = \frac{2\sigma_\varepsilon^2}{1+\alpha} + 2\sigma_v^2,$$

$$C_1 = \frac{-\sigma_\varepsilon^2 \cdot (1-\alpha)}{1+\alpha} - \sigma_v^2,$$

$$C_d = \frac{-\alpha^{d-1}\sigma_\varepsilon^2 \cdot (1-\alpha)}{1+\alpha}.$$

We estimate the parameters σ_ε^2, $\sigma_{v,W}^2$, and α using weighted GMM by minimizing the distance between the theoretical and the empirical first seven autocovariances.

The estimated parameters are reported in Laibson et al. (2000). These parameter values are almost identical to the values reported by Hubbard et al. (1994), who estimate an identical after-tax income process.

The transitory noise in retirement income is inferred by estimating $\xi_{it} = \vartheta_i + v_{it}^R$ on retired households, where ϑ_i is a household fixed effect, and v_{it}^R has variance $\sigma_{v,R}^2$.

In the numerical simulations we set the individual effect equal to zero, and we represent u_t (an AR(1) process) with a two-state Markov process to save computational time. The Markov process is symmetric, taking on two states $(-\theta, +\theta)$, with symmetric transition probability p. To make this two-state Markov process match the variance and autocovariance of u_t, we set $\theta = \sqrt{[\sigma_\varepsilon^2/(1-\alpha^2)]}$ and $p = (\alpha + 1)/2$.

To calculate the typical retirement age by education group we look at households that experienced a transition into retirement over the observed period (using the definition in Bernheim et al. 2001). We find that the mean age at which households without a high school diploma (with a high school diploma, with a college degree) begin retirement is 61 (63, 65).

5.3. Liquid Assets and Noncollateralized Debt

We calibrate the credit limit $\lambda \cdot \bar{Y}_t$ using the 1995 SCF. Specifically, for each education group we identify the households with credit cards and for each age t calculate

$$\lambda_t = \sum_h \frac{\theta_{ht} (\text{credit limit})_{ht}}{\bar{Y}_t},$$

where h indexes households, and θ_{ht} is the population weight of household h that is t years old. The age profiles of λ_t are virtually flat, while the levels are quite similar across education groups, with an overall weighted average of almost 24 percent. We selected $\lambda = 0.30$, a number larger than the observed mean, to take into account the fact that the SCF reports the credit limit associated with Visa, Mastercard, Discover, and Optima cards only, and does not include credit limit information on store and other charge cards. It is worth noting that the four listed cards accounted, on average, for about 80 percent of total credit card debt according to the 1995 SCF.

5.4. Illiquid Assets and Collateralized Debt

For our benchmark simulation we assume an extreme form of transaction costs. We set $\psi(I^Z)$ equal to zero when investment I^Z is nonnegative, and equal to infinity when $I^Z < 0$. In other words, purchases of the illiquid asset generate no transaction costs but sales are infinitely costly. Alternatively, one could simply assume that sales costs are sufficiently large to make sales of the illiquid asset unappealing. By making the illiquid asset extremely illiquid we heighten the need for credit card borrowing, since the illiquid asset cannot be used to buffer transitory income shocks. Our simulation code is sufficiently flexible to consider other less extreme assumptions, which we do in Section 7 on robustness.

In our benchmark simulations we allow no collateralized debt, so we set the down payment fraction $\mu = 1$. We explore the parameterization $\mu = 0.10$ in our robustness checks.

5.5. Dynamic and Static Budget Constraints

We set the value of the after-tax real interest rate on liquid savings equal to 3.75 percentage points. This assumes that liquid assets are invested in a diversified portfolio of stocks and bonds (two-thirds stocks and one-third bonds), and that the effective tax rate on real returns is 25 percent.

In our benchmark simulation, we do not allow the household to declare bankruptcy. In this case, we set the real interest rate on credit card loans to 11.75 percentage points, two percentage points *below* the mean debt-weighted real interest rate measured by the Federal Reserve Board. We do this to implicitly capture the effect of bankruptcy. Actual annual bankruptcy rates of 1 percent per year imply that the effective interest rate is one percentage point below the observed interest rate. When bankruptcy is modeled explicitly, we set the real interest rate on credit card loans equal to the Fed figure of 13.75 percent.

We set the real return on illiquid assets to zero, but assume that illiquid assets generate a consumption flow equal to 5 percent of the value of the illiquid asset (i.e., $\gamma = 0.05$). Hence, illiquid assets have the same pretax gross return as liquid assets but generate consumption flows that are by and large not taxed (e.g., housing). Thus the after-tax return on illiquid assets is considerably higher than that on other assets. We explore an even higher rate of return in our robustness checks.

Finally we set the after-tax real interest rate on collateralized debt to 5 percent, so the pretax real interest rate is 6.67 percentage points assuming interest payments on collateralized debt are tax deductible (e.g., housing).

5.6. Bankruptcy

In our benchmark simulations we do not allow bankruptcy and instead lower the credit card interest rate two percentage points to reflect the probability that the debt will not all be repaid. In Section 7, we consider a simulation that explicitly allows households to enter bankruptcy. We describe the assumptions for this case here.

If bankruptcy is declared in period t, we assume the following consequences: Consumption drops permanently to a proportion $\alpha_{\text{Bankruptcy}}$ of the expected value of permanent income (where permanent income is evaluated at the date at which bankruptcy is declared), X drops permanently to zero, Z drops permanently to $\min(Z^{\text{Bankruptcy}}, Z_t - D_t)$, and D_t drops permanently to zero. We set $Z^{\text{Bankruptcy}} = \$100,000$ to reflect state laws that allow bankrupt households to retain partial or full ownership of their primary residence (Repetto, 1998). We found that setting $\alpha_{\text{Bankruptcy}} = 1$ generates simulated bankruptcy rates that approximately match observed bankruptcy rates (on average 0.7 percent of our simulated households enter bankruptcy each year). This match arises because consumers value the flexibility of choosing the timing of consumption. Recall that early-life child rearing and high rates of time preference make it optimal to consume more when young. In our simulations, declaring bankruptcy forces households to give up this flexibility (i.e., they are forced to consume the annuity value of their human and physical wealth). Naturally, this annuity assumption is unrealistic. It simply serves as a calibrated "punishment" for declaring bankruptcy. We know that our assumed punishment has realistic utility consequences because of the associated frequency with which bankruptcy is endogenously chosen by our simulated consumers. In other words, the utility consequence is roughly realistic since our simulated consumers choose bankruptcy as often as real-world consumers.

5.7. Preferences

5.7.1. COEFFICIENT OF RELATIVE RISK AVERSION: ρ

We adopt a utility function with a constant coefficient of relative risk aversion. In our benchmark calibration we set the coefficient of relative risk aversion, ρ, equal to two, a value that lies in the middle of the range of values that are commonly used in the consumption literature (i.e., $\rho \in [0.5, 5]$).[30]

5.7.2. BEQUESTS

We parameterize the bequest payoff function as

$$B(X_t, Z_t, D_t) = (R - 1) \cdot \max \left[0, X_t + \tfrac{2}{3}(Z_t - D_t)\right] \qquad (11)$$

$$\cdot \frac{\alpha^{\text{Bequest}} \cdot u_1(\bar{y}, 0, \bar{n})}{1 - \delta},$$

where $\bar{n}$ is average effective household size over the life cycle, and $\bar{y}$ is average labor income over the life cycle (calculated separately for each educational group). We arbitrarily set $\alpha^{\text{Bequest}} = 1$, but test other values in our section on robustness. We multiply bequeathed illiquid wealth by two-thirds to capture the idea that much of that wealth can only be liquidated with substantial transactions costs (e.g., furniture, automobiles, and to a more limited extent housing). Note that $B(X_t, Z_t, D_t)$ is weakly increasing in X_t and $Z_t - D_t$.

To motivate our specific functional form assumptions, recall that

$$u(C, Z, n) = n \cdot \frac{\left[(C + \gamma Z)/n\right]^{1-\rho} - 1}{1 - \rho},$$

implying that

---

30. See Laibson et al. (1998) for a detailed discussion of calibration of ρ and an argument that ρ is closer to 0.5 than to 5.

$$u_1(\bar{y}, 0, \bar{n}) = (\bar{y}/\bar{n})^{-\rho}.$$

Equation (11) follows from assuming that the bequest recipient's total consumption is approximately equal to $\bar{y}$, the bequest recipient's effective household size is $\bar{n}$, and the bequest recipient consumes bequeathed wealth as an annuity.

5.7.3. TIME PREFERENCES: β

In Section 6 we simulate exponential economies and hyperbolic economies. In these simulations we assume that the economy is either populated exclusively by exponential households (i.e., $\beta = 1$) or exclusively by hyperbolic households, which we model by setting $\beta = 0.7$. Most of the experimental evidence suggests that the 1-year discount rate is at least 30–40 percent.[31] We experiment with β values below 0.7 in Section 7.

5.7.4. TIME PREFERENCES: δ

Having fixed all of the other parameters, we are left with three free parameters in our hyperbolic simulations—$\delta_{\text{hyperbolic}}^{\text{NHS}}$, $\delta_{\text{hyperbolic}}^{\text{HS}}$, $\delta_{\text{hyperbolic}}^{\text{COLL}}$—and three free parameters in our exponential simulations—$\delta_{\text{exponential}}^{\text{NHS}}$, $\delta_{\text{exponential}}^{\text{HS}}$, $\delta_{\text{exponential}}^{\text{COLL}}$. The superscripts NHS, HS, and COLL represent our three educational groups. In our simulations we pick the various δ values so that our simulations replicate the actual level of preretirement wealth holdings. Specifically, we pick δ such that the *simulated* median ratio of total wealth to income for individuals between ages 50 and 59 matches the *actual* median in the data (SCF). When we construct total wealth from the SCF, we include liquid assets (checking accounts, savings accounts, money market accounts, call accounts, CDs, bonds, stocks, mutual funds, cash, minus credit card debt), and illiquid assets (IRAs, defined-contribution pension plans, life insurance, trusts, annuities, vehicles, home equity, real estate, business equity, jewelry/furniture/antiques, home durables, minus education loans). We do not include defined-benefit pension wealth, such as claims on the Social Security system. When we measure total wealth in our simulations, we add: $X + Z + Y/24$, where X represents liquid assets (excluding current labor income), Z represents illiquid assets, and Y represents annual after-tax labor income. The last term is included to reflect average cash inventories used for (continuous) consumption. If labor income is paid in equal monthly installments, $Y/12$, and consumption is smoothly spread over time, then average cash inventories will be $Y/24$.

The SCF data are taken from the 1983, 1989, 1992, and 1995 surveys. We match the mean of the medians across these years. The empirical medians and their means are reported in Table 3. The (mean) median ratio of net wealth to income for individuals between ages 50 and 59 is 2.5 for households whose head has no high school degree, 3.2 for households whose head's highest educational attainment is a high school education, and 4.3 for households whose head has a college degree.

---

31. See Ainslie (1992) for a review.

Table 3. Wealth-Income Ratios[a]

Age group	Means					Medians				
	1983[b]	1989	1992	1995	Average	1983[b]	1989	1992	1995	Average
All categories										
20–29	1.26	3.29	1.07	1.42	1.76	0.45	0.41	0.42	0.52	0.45
30–39	2.97	2.70	2.59	2.38	2.66	1.32	1.27	1.03	1.14	1.19
40–49	5.16	6.69	4.78	4.98	5.40	2.07	2.45	1.87	1.84	2.06
50–59	8.00	8.06	8.82	8.03	8.23,	2.91	3.90	3.87	3.34	3.50
60–69	11.82	19.56	15.30	14.43	15.28	4.07	5.73	5.14	5.13	5.02
70+	13.06	24.08	21.35	24.91	20.85	4.67	7.02	10.13	8.30	7.53
Incomplete high school										
20–29	0.54	1.49	0.78	0.93	0.94	0.22	0.32	0.31	0.42	0.32
30–39	1.87	2.26	1.71	1.65	1.87	0.52	1.27	0.58	0.76	0.78
40–49	3.13	6.64	3.43	4.22	4.35	1.07	2.02	1.53	1.30	1.48
50–59	3.67	6.21	4.44	5.82	5.03	2.29	3.41	2.19	2.16	2.51
60–69	7.19	14.25	9.59	9.73	10.19	2.98	5.00	3.73	3.30	3.75
70+	9.67	24.81	16.56	18.42	17.37	3.75	5.97	9.05	6.95	6.43
High school graduate										
20–29	1.40	2.63	1.10	1.44	1.64	0.46	0.40	0.37	0.47	0.42
30–39	3.08	1.97	2.59	2.22	2.47	1.22	0.86	0.94	1.17	1.05
40–49	3.72	4.11	2.32	3.94	3.52	2.20	2.33	1.22	1.69	1.86
50–59	11.39	7.53	9.18	6.51	8.65	2.78	3.69	3.75	2.74	3.24
60–69	13.10	18.06	15.80	15.35	15.57	4.31	6.53	5.44	6.55	5.71
70+	18.55	21.74	21.79	23.46	21.39	6.08	7.85	10.90	9.25	8.52
College graduate										
20–29	1.31	5.91	1.31	1.97	2.63	0.63	0.82	0.46	0.92	0.71
30–39	3.20	3.72	3.23	3.23	3.34	1.75	1.58	1.44	1.35	1.53
40–49	9.49	8.85	7.34	6.22	7.97	2.33	3.28	2.69	2.42	2.68
50–59	7.90	11.19	12.39	12.12	10.90	3.57	4.78	4.71	4.32	4.34
60–69	21.89	34.40	23.15	21.73	25.29	7.98	8.38	8.49	9.05	8.48
70+	18.08	24.34	32.09	39.35	28.47	11.03	9.85	12.89	14.09	11.97

Sources: Survey of Consumer Finances, Social Security Administration, Congressional Budget Office.

[a] Income is after-tax nonasset income, plus bequests. Taxes include Social Security deductions, and federal income taxes. Social Security deductions were imputed using OASD-HI tax rates and maximum taxable earnings. Federal income taxes were imputed using effective tax rates as reported by the CBO and Pechman.

[b] Bequests are imputed using Laibson et al. (1998) calculations.

The discount rates $(1 - \delta)$ that replicate these wealth-to-income ratios are:

	Exponential consumers	Hyperbolic consumers
High school dropouts	0.088	0.070
High school graduates	0.056	0.044
College graduates	0.055	0.044

Three properties stand out. First, the discount rates generally fall with educational attainment. Since the shape of the labor income profile is roughly similar across educational groups, a relatively high discount rate is needed to replicate the relatively low wealth-to-income ratio of the least-educated households. Second, the discount rates for hyperbolic consumers are lower than the discount rates for exponential consumers. Since hyperbolic consumers have two sources of discounting—β and δ—the hyperbolic δ's must be higher than the exponential δ's. Recall that the hyperbolic and exponential discount functions are calibrated to generate the same amount of preretirement wealth accumulation. In this manner we "equalize" the underlying willingness to save between the exponential and hyperbolic consumers. Third, all of our calibrated long-term discount rates are sensible, falling between 0.04 and 0.09. Note that these discount rates do not include mortality effects which add roughly another 0.01 to the discount rates discussed above.

5.8. Equilibrium

We have developed a numerical backward induction algorithm based on local grid searches that iterates our functional operators [equations (6) and (7)]. The algorithm finds the unique state-contingent equilibrium strategies of the intrapersonal game, which we then use to compute the life cycle consumption and accumulation paths of a population of 5000 simulated households.

6. SIMULATION RESULTS

We begin by presenting our results on the exponential households $(\beta = 1)$. Throughout this section, we focus on households in the HS group and on aggregates, as results for households in the NHS and COLL groups are qualitatively similar to the results for the HS group.

6.1. Exponential Simulation Results

Figure 4 plots the average consumption profile for households whose heads have a high school education (HS group). The average labor income profile is plotted for comparison. Low-frequency consumption-income co-movement is evident in this figure. Our simulations also generate the standard "buffer stock" pattern of high-frequency consumption-income co-movement (Laibson et al., 2000).

Income, consumption ($\times 10^4$)

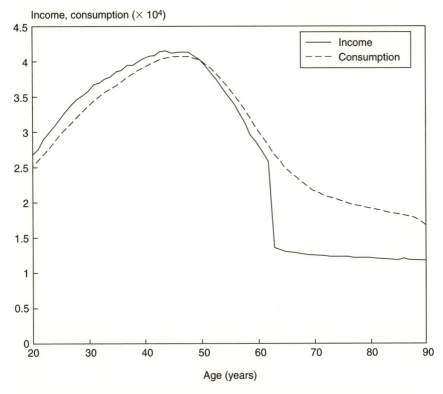

Figure 4. Simulated mean income and consumption of exponential households with heads who are high school graduates. (Source: Authors' simulations.)

Figure 5 plots the mean level of illiquid wealth (Z_t), liquid wealth (X_t), and illiquid plus liquid wealth ($Z_t + X_t$) for simulated households in the HS group. Liquid wealth incorporates the effects of credit card borrowing, and borrowing is sufficiently large to make average liquid wealth negative before age 25. The precautionary motive generates buffer stock saving, which eventually overtakes credit card borrowing in the 30's, pushing average liquid wealth above zero. In midlife the buffer stock vanishes because the consumer can now buffer transitory income shocks by cutting back her substantial investment flow into illiquid assets.

To evaluate the predictive accuracy of the model, we focus on the proportion of households that are borrowing on their credit cards. We focus on this variable since there is no reliable public-use data source for household level credit card borrowing magnitudes (see Section 2). Figure 6 plots the simulated proportion of all households that are borrowing on their credit card,[32] along with the cohort-adjusted

---

32. We calculate population aggregates by taking weighted averages across our three groups of households: NHS, HS, and COLL. These groups, respectively, represent roughly 25, 50, and 25% of the household population, but since we are focusing on households with credit cards, we assume that the percentages are actually 22.6, 48.3, and 29.2%. These proportions are derived from the 1995 SCF,

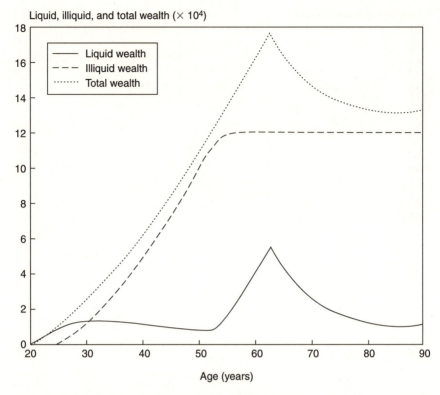

Figure 5. Simulated mean liquid, illiquid, and total wealth for exponential households with heads who are high school graduates. (Source: Authors' simulations.)

empirical estimate. (For the moment ignore the other line in the figure.) It is immediately apparent that these aggregate plots do not match the observed data. On average, 23 percent of the simulated exponential households borrow on their credit card. This proportion is well below 63 percent, the observed fraction of all households that report that they are credit card borrowers in the SCF (1995 cross section; see Table 1). Moreover, the estimated empirical profile lies uniformly above the simulated profile.

Similar results arise for the simulated exponential households in the three educational groups taken individually. In the NHS, HS, and COLL groups, the borrowing frequencies are 22, 20.5, and 28 percent, respectively. These results are particularly puzzling because they reverse the empirical ranking of the educational groups. In the 1995 SCF, the reported frequency is 68 percent for the NHS group, 70 percent for the HS group, and 53 percent for the COLL group.

---

which reports that in the NHS, HS, and COLL groups, respectively, 72, 77, and 93% of households have credit cards. Thus, e.g., we find an NHS population weight of $(.25)(.72)/[(.25)(.72) + (.5)(.77) + (.25)(.93)] = .226$.

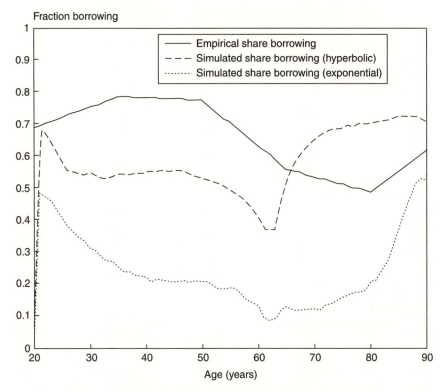

Figure 6. Fraction of exponential and hyperbolic households borrowing on credit cards and the estimated life cycle profile from Figure 1, for all educational groups. (Source: Authors' simulations, and Survey of Consumer Finances.)

We also compare the simulated borrowing frequencies across wealth categories. Table 4 reports the simulated borrowing frequencies across age-contingent wealth quartiles (for both exponential and hyperbolic simulations). These values can be compared to the empirical frequencies in Table 2. It is immediately apparent that the exponential simulations do not match the empirical data. Two tensions arise. First, as already pointed out, the exponential borrowing frequencies are too low. Second, the exponential borrowing frequencies drop off too sharply as wealth rises. For example, for the 40–49-year-olds in the HS group, the quartile-based simulated borrowing frequencies take values of 54, 20, 9, and 2 percent. By contrast, the empirical frequencies take values of 86, 79, 74, and 50 percent. Similar contrasts arise for other age categories and educational groups. Simulated exponential borrowing is too infrequent, and this empirical failure is particularly dramatic among the high-wealth households. Contrary to the data, high-wealth simulated exponential households practically do not borrow at all. This mismatch is most striking at the youngest ages. Simulated exponential consumers between ages 20–29 and 30–39 in their respective top wealth quartiles borrow at an average frequency below 1 percent. This contrasts with empirical borrowing frequencies of

Table 4. Simulated Share Borrowing across the Wealth Distribution[a]

Age group	Wealth quartile			
	0–25	*25–50*	*50–75*	*75+*
Incomplete high school (exponential)				
20–29	1.00	0.34	0.00	0.00
30–39	1.00	0.06	0.01	0.00
40–49	0.68	0.19	0.05	0.00
50–59	0.45	0.20	0.05	0.00
60–69	0.09	0.06	0.05	0.00
70+	0.26	0.30	0.31	0.37
Incomplete high school (hyperbolic)				
20–29	1.00	0.89	0.15	0.13
30–39	1.00	0.68	0.41	0.24
40–49	0.91	0.65	0.49	0.37
50–59	0.75	0.55	0.43	0.31
60–69	0.46	0.43	0.40	0.39
70+	0.72	0.84	0.96	0.98
High school graduates (exponential)				
20–29	1.00	0.25	0.00	0.00
30–39	0.79	0.07	0.02	0.00
40–49	0.54	0.20	0.09	0.02
50–59	0.33	0.17	0.09	0.04
60–69	0.07	0.05	0.04	0.03
70+	0.41	0.33	0.32	0.14
High school graduates (hyperbolic)				
20–29	1.00	0.74	0.17	0.10
30–39	1.00	0.56	0.36	0.19
40–49	0.84	0.60	0.42	0.24
50–59	0.73	0.54	0.44	0.27
60–69	0.56	0.57	0.70	0.45
70+	0.93	0.97	0.98	0.32
College graduates (exponential)				
20–29	1.00	0.98	0.01	0.00
30–39	1.00	0.32	0.01	0.00
40–49	0.70	0.06	0.02	0.03
50–59	0.64	0.14	0.11	0.01
60–69	0.90	0.26	0.02	0.00
70+	0.59	0.10	0.00	0.00
College graduates (hyperbolic)				
20–29	1.00	1.00	0.38	0.03
30–39	1.00	0.90	0.13	0.06
40–49	1.00	0.85	0.24	0.11
50–59	1.00	0.73	0.22	0.00
60–69	1.00	0.57	0.01	0.00
70+	1.00	0.52	0.00	0.00

Source: Authors' simulations.

[a] Fraction of simulated households who borrow in each wealth quartile of an age-education group.

68 percent (ages 20–29, top wealth quartile) and 59 percent (ages 30–39, top wealth quartile).

6.2. Hyperbolic Simulation Results

We now turn to our benchmark hyperbolic simulations. First of all, exponential and hyperbolic consumption time paths are nearly identical (see Laibson et al., 2000, for figures). They differ only in a small hyperbolic consumption boom at the beginning of life, and the relatively steeper decline in hyperbolic consumption during the retirement period.[33]

The life cycle wealth profile of exponential households nearly matches the profile of hyperbolic households. This match arises because of the calibration procedure for $\delta_{exponential}$ and $\delta_{hyperbolic}$, which ensures that simulated consumers of both types have preretirement wealth-to-income ratios that match the data (see Section 5.7). Two properties of the wealth accumulation profiles nevertheless distinguish the hyperbolic households. First, the hyperbolic households borrow more when young, depressing total wealth and even driving it below zero for a substantial portion of the life cycle. Second, hyperbolic households hold more illiquid wealth, which cannot be dissaved in the benchmark model and hence elevates total wealth when old. These comparisons are shown for the high school education group in Figure 7, which plots illiquid wealth for exponentials and hyperbolics, and Figure 8, which plots liquid wealth for exponentials and hyperbolics. Similar exponential-hyperbolic contrasts arise for the simulated households in the NHS and COLL groups.

The relative scarcity of liquid wealth is associated with high levels of credit card borrowing for simulated hyperbolic households. Households in the NHS, HS, and COLL groups borrow at respective frequencies of 60, 58, and 49 percent. These percentages are similar to those in the SCF data: 68, 70, and 53 percent. In both the simulations and the data, the NHS and HS frequencies are approximately equal, and the COLL frequency is noticeably lower.

We now turn to comparisons of population aggregates (aggregating across the three educational groups). Figure 6 plots the proportion of households who are borrowing on their credit cards. For simulated hyperbolic households the aggregate borrowing frequency is 55 percent, compared to 23 percent of the simulated exponential households. Recall that at least 63 percent of actual households are currently borrowing on their credit cards. Figure 6 also plots the estimated cohort-adjusted life cycle profile of borrowing frequencies. This profile lies everywhere above the simulated exponential profile, but either intersects or nearly intersects the hyperbolic profile at ages 21, 66, and 90.

Finally, we compare the simulated borrowing frequencies across wealth categories. Reconsider Tables 2 and 4, which report the empirical and simulated

---

33. Like the exponential simulations, the hyperbolic simulations also exhibit low- and high-frequency co-movement between consumption and income (see Laibson et al., 1998). Hence, the hyperbolic model is consistent with the empirical regularities documented by Carroll (1992, 1997), Gourinchas and Parker (2002), and others.

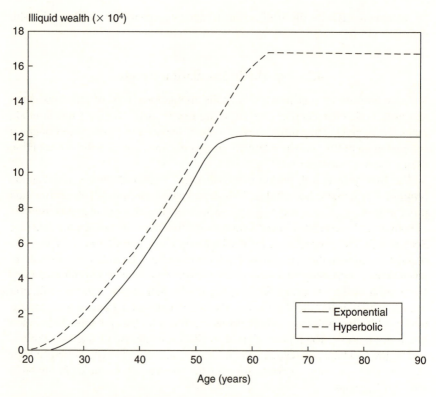

Figure 7. Mean illiquid wealth over the life cycle of exponential and hyperbolic households with heads who are high school graduates. (Source: Authors' simulations.)

borrowing frequencies across age-contingent wealth quartiles. Like the exponential simulations, the hyperbolic simulations also predict too little borrowing by high-wealth households. For example for ages 40–49 in the HS group, the quartile-based hyperbolic borrowing frequencies take the values 84, 60, 42, and 24 percent. The exponential borrowing frequencies take the values 54, 20, 9, and 2 percent. The SCF empirical frequencies take the values 86, 79, 74, and 50 percent. Hence, both the hyperbolic and exponential borrowing frequencies drop off too quickly as wealth rises. Similar patterns arise for other age categories and educational groups.

In summary, the hyperbolic model seems broadly consistent with the empirical data. Hyperbolic consumers borrow at approximately the right average frequency. Moreover, hyperbolics with college educations borrow less frequently than hyperbolics without a college degree. The principal failure of the hyperbolic model is the prediction that high-wealth households will borrow at relatively low frequencies. High-wealth households in the SCF borrow too frequently to match the predictions of either the hyperbolic or the exponential model.

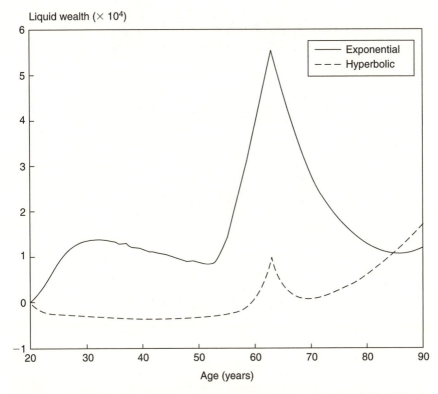

Figure 8. Mean liquid wealth over the life cycle of exponential and hyperbolic households with heads who are high school graduates. (Source: Authors' simulations.)

7. ROBUSTNESS CHECKS

The results reported in the previous section are robust to substantial variation in all of the calibration assumptions. In every variant that we have considered (a fraction of which are reported here), exponential households continue to hold credit card debt far too infrequently.

Table 5 summarizes these results. The first row of the table reports our benchmark simulations (see previous two subsections) for the exponential and hyperbolic households in the HS group. Rows 2–15 report perturbations to these benchmark cases. In each of these rows, the benchmark simulation is perturbed by changing the calibration values of important parameters in the model.

Those perturbed parameters are identified in the first column of Table 5. To simulate behavior with the perturbed parameter values, we replicate the calibration procedure described in Section 5. Specifically, we numerically find the values of $\delta^{HS}_{exponential}$ and $\delta^{HS}_{hyperbolic}$ that generate simulated wealth accumulation that matches the SCF midlife median wealth-to-income ratio. Hence, each row of Table 5 uses a new pair of values of $\delta^{HS}_{exponential}$ and $\delta^{HS}_{hyperbolic}$. Column 2 reports $\delta^{HS}_{exponential}$.

Table 5. Robustness Checks[a]

	Exponential simulations			Hyperbolic simulations		
	Calibrated discount rate	Proportion borrowing	Average debt	Calibrated discount rate	Proportion borrowing	Average debt
1. Benchmarks (with fine partition)	0.056	0.21	$907.54	0.044	0.57	$3,748.28
2. Benchmarks (with coarse partition)	0.056	0.18	$904.99	0.042	0.48	$3,234.01
3. Heavier weight on children ($\kappa = 0.6$)	0.052	0.16	$798.71	0.040	0.43	$3,060.63
4. Reversible investment in Z	0.056	0.17	$890.78	0.042	0.44	$3,109.76
5. Debt-financed purchase of Z	0.059	0.21	$1,075.90	0.049	0.59	$4,036.43
6. Credit card interest rate 9.75%	0.056	0.21	$1,114.58	0.042	0.51	$3,582.20
7. Credit card interest rate 13.75%	0.056	0.15	$716.75	0.042	0.44	$2,923.80
8. Bankruptcy allowed (interest rate 13.75%)	0.056	0.16	$969.90	0.042	0.42	$3,228.59
9. CRRA = 1	0.049	0.15	$553.73	0.036	0.55	$4,038.07
10. CRRA = 3	0.063	0.17	$880.32	0.049	0.38	$2,460.16
11. $\beta = 0.6$	N/A	N/A	N/A	0.038	0.54	$3,891.19
12. $\beta = 0.8$	N/A	N/A	N/A	0.046	0.38	$2,347.36
13. Altruism parameter = 0.5	0.052	0.18	$876.40	0.036	0.52	$3,435.13
14. Illiquid rate of return = 0.06	0.063	0.27	$1,340.07	0.047	0.56	$3,893.96

Source: Authors' simulations.

[a] The table shows the average amount borrowed and the fraction of households borrowing for different calibration assumptions. All education groups are included.

Column 3 shows the simulated percentage of exponential consumers who borrow on their credit card at any point in time. Column 4 reports the average amount of credit card debt held by exponential consumers. Likewise, column 5 reports $\delta_{\text{hyperbolic}}^{\text{HS}}$, column 6 shows the simulated percentage of hyperbolic consumers who borrow on their credit card at any point in time, and column 7 reports the average amount of credit card debt held by hyperbolic consumers.

All of the simulations in rows 2–15 have been implemented with partition jumps of $2,000 for the liquid asset and jumps of $50,000 for the illiquid asset. By contrast, in the benchmark cases (row 1), we use a partition with jumps of $500 for the liquid asset and jumps of $10,000 for the illiquid asset.[34] We adopt a relatively coarse partition in rows 2–15, because many of these simulations are far more complex than the benchmark simulations (e.g., some of the state spaces and action spaces are relatively large in these new runs). Even with the coarse partition, some of these robustness simulations take nearly 2 weeks to execute.

Row 2 matches the benchmark simulation, but adopts the relatively coarse partition. These results provide a check that changing the partition coarseness does not significantly change the original benchmark results. The other reported robustness checks are summarized below:

Row 3: In the benchmark formula for effective household size, children are weighted 40 percent as much as adults. The simulations reported in row 3 change the weighting from 0.4 to 0.6.

Row 4: In the benchmark simulations, disinvestment from the illiquid asset is not permitted. The simulations in row 4 allow such disinvestment and assume disinvestment transaction costs: a fixed cost of $10,000 and a 0.1 proportional cost.

Row 5: In the benchmark simulations the required down payment for the illiquid asset is 100 percent. The simulations in row 5 assume a down payment of 10 percent.

Row 6: In the benchmark simulations the real interest rate on credit card debt is 11.75 percent. The simulations in row 6 assume a credit card interest rate of 9.75 percent.

Row 7: The simulations in row 7 assume a credit card interest rate of 13.75 percent.

Row 8: In the benchmark simulations, bankruptcy is not allowed. The simulations in row 8 allow households to declare bankruptcy and set the credit card interest rate to 13.75 pecent.[35]

Row 9: In the benchmark simulations the coefficient of relative risk aversion ρ is set to 2. The simulations in row 9 assume $\rho = 1$.

---

34. The large partition jumps for the illiquid asset reflect the fact that illiquid assets tend to be lumpier than liquid assets.

35. Since households can declare bankruptcy, we no longer need to set a lower credit card interest rate to account for nonpayment.

Row 10: The simulations reported in row 10 assume $\rho = 3$.

Row 11: In the benchmark hyperbolic simulations, the hyperbolic discount parameter β is set to 0.7. The hyperbolic simulation in row 11 assumes $\beta = 0.6$.

Row 12: The hyperbolic simulation in row 12 assumes $\beta = 0.8$.

Row 13: In the benchmark simulations the altruism parameter α^{Bequest} is set to 1. The simulations in row 13 assume $\alpha^{\text{Bequest}} = 0.5$.

Row 14: In the benchmark simulations the total consumption flow from the illiquid asset γ is 5 percent per year. The simulations in row 14 assume a flow of 6 percent.

Table 5 demonstrates two points. First, the simulation results are not sensitive to our model and calibration assumptions. No reasonable variation in the modeling assumptions drives the simulated exponential borrowing far from the levels in our benchmark simulation. Second, calibrated hyperbolic households always borrow between two and four times as often as their exponential counterparts. This difference arises even though hyperbolic and exponential consumers accumulate identical levels of preretirement wealth.

8. CONCLUSION

Consumers appear to be of two minds. Relatively large voluntary retirement accumulations imply exponential discount rates of only 5 percent. However, frequent credit card borrowing implies exponential discount rates of 18 percent. It does not appear to be possible to calibrate realistic life cycle models to match both observed levels of voluntary retirement savings and the observed frequency of credit card borrowing. We call this apparent paradox the debt puzzle.

We have also suggested a partial resolution to this puzzle. If consumers have hyperbolic discount functions (Phelps and Pollak, 1968), then they may act both patiently *and* impatiently. Our calibrated simulations show that hyperbolic consumers will save aggressively for retirement, primarily in illiquid form, *and* borrow frequently in the credit card market.

REFERENCES

Ainslie, G. (1992), *Picoeconomics,* Cambridge: Cambridge University Press.
Akerlof, G. A. (1991), "Procrastination and Obedience," *American Economic Review, Papers and Proceedings,* pp. 1–19.
Ameriks, J. and S. P. Zeldes (2001), "How Do Household Portfolio Shares Vary with Age?," mimeo, TIAA-CREF Institute.
Angeletos, G.-M., D. Laibson, A. Repetto, J. Tobacman, and S. Weinberg (2001), "The Hyperbolic Consumption Model: Calibration, Simulation, and Empirical Evaluation," *Journal of Economic Perspectives* 15(3):47–68.
Attanasio, O. (1999), "Consumption," in J. Taylor and M. Woodford, eds., *Handbook of Macroeconomics,* Amsterdam: North-Holland.
Ausubel, L. M. (1991), "The Failure of Competition in the Credit Card Market," *American Economic Review* 81(1):50–81.

Barro, R. (1999), "Laibson Meets Ramsey in the Neoclassical Growth Model," *Quarterly Journal of Economics* 114(4):1125–52.

Benabou, R. and J. Tirole (2001), "Willpower and Personal Rules," mimeo, Princeton.

Bernheim, B. D., J. Skinner, and S. Weinberg (2001), "What Accounts for the Variation in Retirement Wealth Among US Households?," *American Economic Review* 91(4):832–57.

Blundell, R., M. Browning, and C. Meghir (1994), "Consumer Demand and the Life-Cycle Allocation of Household Expenditures," *Review of Economic Studies* 61:57–80.

Brito, D. L. and P. R. Hartley (1995), "Consumer Rationality and Credit Cards," *Journal of Political Economy* 103(2):400–33.

Carrillo, J. and T. Mariotti (2000), "Strategic Ignorance as a Self-Disciplining Device," *Review of Economic Studies* 67:529–44.

Carroll, C. D. (1992), "The Buffer Stock Theory of Saving: Some Macroeconomic Evidence," *Brookings Papers on Economic Activity* 1992(2):61–156.

———— (1997), "Buffer-Stock Saving and the Life Cycle/Permanent Income Hypothesis," *Quarterly Journal of Economics* 112:1–57.

Chung, S.-H. and R. J. Herrnstein (1961), "Relative and Absolute Strengths of Response as a Function of Frequency of Reinforcement," *Journal of the Experimental Analysis of Animal Behavior* 4:267–72.

Deaton, A. (1991), "Saving and Liquidity Constraints," *Econometrica* 59:1221–48.

Deaton, A. and J. Muellbauer (1986), "On Measuring Child Costs: With Applications to Poor Countries," *Journal of Political Economy* 94(4):720–44.

DellaVigna, S. and U. Malmendier (2001), "Self-Control in the Market: Evidence from the Health Club Industry," mimeo, Harvard.

Diamond, P. and B. Koszegi (2001), "Quasi-Hyperbolic Discounting and Retirement," mimeo, MIT.

Engen, E. M. and W. G. Gale (1993), "IRAs and Saving: A Life-Cycle Consumption Simulation," mimeo, UCLA.

Engen, E. M., W. G. Gale, and J. K. Scholz (1994), "Do Saving Incentives Work?," *Brookings Papers on Economic Activity* 1994(1):85–180.

Engen, E. M., W. G. Gale, and C. Uccello (1999), "The Adequacy of Retirement Saving," *Brookings Papers on Economic Activity* 1999(2):65–165.

Gourinchas, P.-O. and J. Parker (2002), "Consumption Over the Life-Cycle," *Econometrica* 70(1):47–90.

Gross, D. and N. Souleles (1999), "How Do People Use Credit Cards?," mimeo, Wharton.

———— (2002a), "An Empirical Analysis of Personal Bankruptcy and Delinquency," *Review of Financial Studies* 15(1):319–47.

———— (2002b), "Do Liquidity Constraints and Interest Rates Matter for Consumer Behavior? Evidence from Credit Card Data," *Quarterly Journal of Economics* 117(1):149–86.

Harris, C. and D. Laibson (2001), "Dynamic Choices of Hyperbolic Consumers," *Econometrica* 69(4):935–57.

Hubbard, G., J. Skinner, and S. Zeldes (1994), "The Importance of Precautionary Motives in Explaining Individual and Aggregate Saving," *Carnegie-Rochester Conference Series on Public Policy* 40:59–125.

———— (1995), "Precautionary Saving and Social Insurance," *Journal of Political Economy* 103:360–99.

Krussell, P. and A. Smith (2001), "Consumption and Savings Decisions with Quasi-Geometric Discounting," mimeo, University of Rochester.

Laibson, D. (1997), "Golden Eggs and Hyperbolic Discounting," *Quarterly Journal of Economics* 62(2):443–78.

Laibson, D., A. Repetto, and J. Tobacman (1998), "Self-Control and Saving for Retirement," *Brookings Papers on Economic Activity* 1:91–196.

———— (2000), "A Debt Puzzle," NBER Working Paper No. 7879.

Loewenstein, G. and D. Prelec (1992), "Anomalies in Intertemporal Choice: Evidence and an Interpretation," *Quarterly Journal of Economics* 57:573–98.

Morrison, A. K. (1998), "An Anomaly in Household Consumption and Savings Behavior: The Simultaneous Borrowing and Lending of Liquid Assets," mimeo, Univesity of Chicago.

Mulligan, C. (1997), "A Logical Economist's Argument Against Hyperbolic Discounting." mimeo, University of Chicago.

O'Donoghue, T. and M. Rabin (1999), "Doing It Now or Later," *American Economic Review* 89(1):103–24.

Phelps, E. S. and R. A. Pollak (1968), "On Second-best National Saving and Game-equilibrium Growth," *Review of Economic Studies* 35:185–99.

Pollak, R. (1968), "Consistent Planning," *Review of Economics Studies* 35:201–8.

Repetto, A. (1998), "Personal Bankruptcies and Individual Wealth Accumulation," mimeo, CEA, Universidad de Chile.

Strotz, R. H. (1956), "Myopia and Inconsistency in Dynamic Utility Maximization," *Review of Economic Studies* 23:165–80.

Zeldes, S. P. (1989), "Optimal Consumption with Stochastic Income: Deviations from Certainty Equivalence," *Quarterly Journal of Economics* 104(2):275–98.

12

Comments on Laibson, Repetto, and Tobacman

ROBERT A. POLLAK

How could I not like a paper that builds on an article Ned Phelps and I wrote when we were colleagues at Penn in the late 1960s?

Laibson, Repetto, and Tobacman (hereafter LRT) conclude with a succinct statement of the debt puzzle and their solution:

> Consumers appear to be of two minds. Relatively large voluntary retirement accumulations imply exponential discount rates of only 5 percent However, frequent credit card borrowing implies exponential discount rates of 18 percent. It does not appear to be possible to calibrate realistic life cycle models to match both observed levels of voluntary retirement savings and the observed frequency of credit card borrowing. We call this apparent paradox the debt puzzle.
>
> We have also suggested a partial resolution to this puzzle. If consumers have hyperbolic discount functions (Phelps and Pollak, 1968), then they may act both patiently *and* impatiently. Our calibrated simulations show that hyperbolic consumers will save aggressively for retirement, primarily in illiquid form, *and* borrow frequently in the credit card market.

The authors convince me that the debt puzzle is real, and that hyperbolic discounting provides a plausible resolution for at least part of it.

The chapter contains a great deal of careful and convincing work—simulations with enough moving parts that I can almost resist proposing more. Yet I am not convinced that the authors' "representative household" framework provides the best way to understand the observed patterns of consumption, saving, and borrowing. Before discussing the debt puzzle and arguing for the importance of preference heterogeneity, however, I want to place the discussion of intertemporal allocation and hyperbolic discounting in a broader perspective, focusing on five issues that LRT do not discuss.

1. LRT focus on the lifetime consumption, saving, and borrowing behavior of households. Phelps and Pollak (1968) were concerned with a different intertemporal issue, national saving, and, more specifically, with the time-inconsistency problem implied by the way succeeding generations discount the future. Other

societal intergenerational issues such as global climate change, nuclear waste disposal, and biodiversity may also give rise to social time-inconsistency problems. Portney and Weyant (1999) provide a recent discussion of intergenerational issues in an environmental context, focusing on global climate change.

2. LRT simply assume that households have preferences. Recent work on bargaining and other nonunitary models of the household has abandoned the assumption that households have well-defined preferences. Lundberg and Pollak (1996) survey a literature that assumes that spouses have individual preferences and use bargaining models to analyze the behavior implied by their interactions. Browning (2000) and Lundberg et al. (2003) suggest that if the remaining life expectancies of spouses differ, then their interests in consumption, saving, or the timing of retirement may conflict. I would like to study consumption, saving, and borrowing by relating the behavior of households to the preferences and bargaining power of individuals.

3. LRT assume that preferences are independent of age. Even if preferences can be represented as a weighted sum of one-period utility functions, these one-period utility functions may change systematically with age. We know that young and old buy different baskets of goods and services—the young buy SUVs and the old buy prescription drugs. Age-specific one-period utility functions are the simplest way of accounting for changes in age-specific consumption patterns.

4. LRT assume that one-period utility functions are unaffected by past consumption experience. But consumption experience may affect preferences and, if it does, the intertemporal preference ordering is not separable by periods—indeed, "one-period utility functions" are no longer well-defined. My own early work on habit formation (Pollak, 1970) assumed that households did not recognize the effect of their current consumption on their future behavior. Becker and Murphy (1988) assume that households fully recognize these dynamic effects. Both assumptions cost us intertemporal separability.

5. LRT do not address the welfare issues raised by hyperbolic discounting. For positive analysis, the consistent-planning problem is best described as a game in which the same individual at different ages is treated as a different player. For normative analysis, the "natural" next step is to investigate Pareto-optimal allocations, again treating the same individual at different ages as a different player. But the appropriateness of this treatment for normative analysis is at best uncertain because it raises deep philosophical issues about the meaning of personal identity.

I want to set aside these five issues, focusing instead on preference heterogeneity. Rather than a representative household, I begin with three household types.

Some households are neoclassical grasshoppers who discount the future at relatively high rates and are unlikely to save for retirement—perhaps a third of households at age 50–60 have no retirement savings. Grasshoppers may have substantial credit card balances, but they are not using illiquid retirement saving as a commitment device and they do not present a debt puzzle.

Other households are neoclassical ants who discount the future at relatively low rates. Ants may have substantial illiquid retirement saving, but they are likely to pay off their credit cards every month. Ants are not using illiquid retirement saving as a commitment device, and they do not present a debt puzzle.

Still other households are nonneoclassical Phelps-Pollak-Laibson hyperbolic discounters. At least for some realizations of earnings shocks, hyperbolic discounters have both substantial illiquid retirement savings and substantial credit card debt. These households present a debt puzzle—a puzzle that LRT argue persuasively is resolved by hyperbolic discounting.

What fraction of the households are hyperbolic discounters? What fraction are grasshoppers? Ants? LRT assume that all households have identical preferences, so the only admissible answers to this question are "all" or "none." They show that neither a society composed entirely of grasshoppers nor one composed entirely of ants can account for the debt puzzle. They have persuaded me that some households are hyperbolic discounters who use illiquid retirement saving as a commitment device. They have not convinced me that all households are hyperbolic discounters.

Counting the number of hyperbolic discounters is difficult because we do not observe household preferences. We do observe saving and borrowing patterns, but households with identical preferences that experience different earnings shocks may exhibit different saving and borrowing behavior. Nevertheless, we have no alternative to classifying households on the basis of their observed saving and borrowing behavior.

Following LRT, I have thus far focused on the puzzle involving illiquid retirement saving and credit card debt As they point out, however, another debt puzzle involves liquid saving and credit card debt: about one-third of households "simultaneously carry credit card debt and hold liquid wealth that exceeds 1 month of income" (footnote 8). I am concerned about how households with credit card balances and *liquid* saving fit into the hyperbolic discounting story.

Suppose we partition households into eight cells, depending on whether they have: (a) credit card balances, (b) illiquid saving (let us call it retirement saving), and (c) liquid saving.

I focus on the four cells with positive credit card balances because this is where we must look for evidence of hyperbolic discounting. I have already, at least implicitly, discussed the two cells with credit card balances and no liquid saving:

1. Households with no retirement saving and no liquid saving are grasshoppers; no nonstandard assumptions are required to explain their behavior.

2. Households with retirement saving and no liquid saving are hyperbolic discounters who behave as if they use illiquid retirement saving as a commitment device.

The difficulty, as LRT suggest in their footnote, is with the final two cells in which households have substantial liquid saving: hyperbolic discounting predicts not only positive credit card balances and positive retirement saving but also the absence of substantial liquid saving.

3. Households with no retirement saving and positive liquid saving do not fit the hyperbolic discounting story: Something nonstandard is going on, perhaps something involving mental accounts. But whatever is going on, these households are not using illiquid retirement saving as a commitment device.

4. Households with retirement saving and liquid saving present a problem. Although these households have both credit card balances and retirement saving, I am reluctant to count them as hyperbolic discounters. There are two difficulties.

First, because they have liquid saving as well as retirement saving, they do not appear to be using retirement saving as a commitment device: We know they can save without a commitment device. Second, a satisfactory explanation must account for all three aspects of their saving and borrowing behavior—positive credit card balances, positive retirement saving, and positive liquid saving. Hyperbolic discounting predicts positive credit card balances and positive retirement saving, but it also predicts the absence of liquid saving.

To summarize: Laibson, Repetto, and Tobacman have made an important contribution to our understanding of intertemporal allocation in general and the debt puzzle in particular. Hyperbolic discounting provides a persuasive account of some otherwise anomalous aspects of saving and borrowing behavior. It is not a criticism to say that some parts of the debt puzzle remain puzzling.

REFERENCES

Becker, G. S. and K. M. Murphy (1988), "A Theory of Rational Addiction," *Journal of Political Economy* 96(4):675–700.

Browning, M. (2000), "The Saving Behavior of a Two-Person Household," *Scandinavian Journal of Economics* 102(2):235–25.

Lundberg, S. and R. A. Pollak (1996), "Bargaining and Distribution in Marriage," *Journal of Economic Perspectives* 10(4):139–58.

Lundberg, S., R. Startz, and S. Stillman (2003), "The Retirement-Consumption Puzzle: A Marital Bargaining Approach," *Journal of Public Economics* (forthcoming).

Phelps, E. S. and R. A. Pollak (1968), "On Second-Best National Saving and Game Equilibrium Growth," *Review of Economic Studies* 35(2):185–99.

Pollak, R. A. (1970), "Habit Formation and Dynamic Demand Functions," *Journal of Political Economy* 78(4):745–63.

Portney, P. R. and J. P. Weyant, eds. (1999), *Discounting and Intergenerational Equity,* Washington: Resources for the Future.

13

Reflections on Parts I and II

EDMUND S. PHELPS

It is an honor to be invited to "reflect" on the theory of unemployment and its fluctuation since the birth of "micro-macro," which I was fortunate to start up in the second half of the 1960s. Let me begin with the focus of most of the chapters in this volume—the mechanisms transmitting the *monetary* impact of shocks, real and monetary, to employment and the rest of the "real" economy. I think I had better begin at the beginning, with my early work in this area.

I

What bothered me in the mid-1960s lay at the heart of Keynes's theory of employment: Why would the monetary impact of a real or nominal shock, unobserved and, say, permanent, in shifting up "effective demand" (the IS curve) or shifting down "liquidity preference" (the LM curve), cause an appreciable decrease of unemployment—and possibly a protracted decrease? One might have thought, as many a textbook implied, that the money-price and money-wage levels would quickly rise high enough to forestall such a boom; even Keynes acknowledged the possibility of that outcome when he characterized it as not "general." There was also a particular question on which I later worked a lot: Why might an inflation policy shift by the monetary (or other) authorities cause a transitional recession or boom? But let me focus here on market shocks.

The ideas I hoped would answer this question rested on imperfect information (data costs, coordination obstacles) and, at places, imperfect knowledge (ambiguity, disagreement, uncertainty). Undoubtedly, Robertson, Hayek, and Keynes himself had pointed me that way. To embody these ideas a model would have to have two microeconomic mechanisms not found in the supply-and-demand model or in other existing models. A mechanism was needed to generate positive unemployment as a normal phenomenon even in expectational equilibrium, so that there was room for decreased unemployment in response to the shock. The mechanism needed the further property that if, following the shock, *expectations* of the wage and price increases elsewhere in the economy lagged *behind* the actual increases for reasons of imperfect information, this lag would moderate the increase of wages and cause some of the monetary impact to fall on quantities, not solely on the price and wage levels. (My 1967 paper[1] posited such an effect but it was left intuitive, without an explicit microstory to back it.)

I finally devised two protomodels—the 1968 turnover-training model, or quitting model, of involuntary unemployment and the 1969 "islands model" of voluntary (frictional) unemployment—that had both desired properties.[2]

In the turnover-training model, firms in their effort to combat quitting institute "incentive wages," which drives the wage level above its market-clearing level, and this job rationing generally forces some number to be unemployed. In the islands model, some workers encounter low wage rates and spend the period traveling to another island in hopes of finding better pay. So these models tend to exhibit unemployment even along an expectational-equilibrium path and even in the medium-term steady state. I would comment that *neither* model requires "asymmetric information," in which the two sides in a market (say, employer and worker) do not have the same information. The turnover model does not require that unemployed workers know their quit rates and quit functions better than employers; more likely an employer will know them better. Moreover, if employer and employee do not agree on contracts with no quitting except for cause, the reason may be the *ambiguity* of the information rather than its asymmetry. In the broad list of allowable "causes" that the typical worker would want included, most would be costly or impossible to verify—for example, changed job specifications, poorer working conditions, a decline of the community—so such broad contracts would not be operational and thus not enforceable.

In these models, each period's wage at a firm (or island) depends on *expectations* of the change from the previous period in the economy's general wage level, since the average change is unobservable before the fact; then, with the change in the local wage posted and the actual change in the general wage level reported, quits by employees and hires by firms are decided (or workers rejecting low wages go to other islands). These expectations have to be formed when no one knows the nature or size of the new macro shock and its monetary impact on goods demand at any firm (or island). Hence, the demand increases across firms (islands) brought by the macro shock, coming mixed in with the positive or negative effect of the local micro shocks, cause each firm (or each island's firms) to infer a greater increase or lesser decrease of its *relative* demand price than what is true—that is, to *underestimate* the average money demand-price increase elsewhere.

In the islands model, market-clearing wages are pulled up in general and at average islands the wage rises *relatively* to the average wage level expected to prevail at the other islands; so fewer workers will opt for unemployment in order to try another island. As long as the "expected" wage lags behind the

---

1. *Economica* 34:254–81 (1967).

2. *Journal of Political Economy* 76:678–711 (1968); *American Economic Review: Papers and Proceedings* 59:147–60 (1969).

actual rise, unemployment as well as the money wage will remain below-equilibrium. In the quitting model, the average firm does not expect the general wage level to increase by as much as it calculates it should raise its own wage—that is, the expected general wage level lags behind the actual average wage level; so, wishing to pay more (because quits are now more costly) but not to pay an excessive premium, a firm will not raise its wage as much as it would if it did not underforecast the increase in the economy's average wage; hence expected unit cost underresponds and, as a result, hiring is stimulated. As long as the "expected" wage increase remains less than the actual average wage increase—as long as the average firms believe they are outpaying one another—they will underforecast their quit rates when setting their wage and hence err by choosing a lower wage and hiring more workers than they otherwise would. Thus achievement of the final cumulative wage increase is stretched out, some of the incidence of the shock's monetary impact falls initially on employment, which has to be worked off, and the decline of employment back to the medium-term steady state will be slower than if there were no such underforecasting. (Another explanation of the underresponsiveness of wages competed for attention in the paper: the idea that firms prefer to change their wages in small steps, owing to their uncertainty about the consequences of a raise in their wages.)

A third model, the 1970 customer-market model with Sidney Winter,[3] permitted misexpectations of the average price in a product market with information frictions. If firms' expectations of the average price are too high, the prices they set will be too high—and output too low—for equilibrium.

All three models injected the *ratio* of the *actual* wage (or price) to the *expected* wage (or price) in some behavioral function: expected quitting, migration, or customer flow. *Disequilibrium* (in my terminology) results when the ratio differs from one. These wage-wage and price-price mechanisms differed from Milton Friedman's mechanism, in which a labor force supply curve made employment increasing in the *wage* relative to the *expected price level*. For me, the wage-wage mechanism was more important than Friedman's. It was also a merit that unemployment was central to the story. The shirking models from Samuel Bowles and Guillermo Calvo in the late 1970s provided an additional motive for incentive wages and generated the same wage-wage process.[4]

I thought at the time that, with this expectations mechanism, I had laid a foundation for a largely Keynesian employment theory—one that, unlike money illusion or sheer habit, obeyed the axioms of rational choice. A basic tenet of the microfounded theory—mere effective demand stimulus cannot disequilibrate an economy repeatedly without losing force—did somewhat restrict the original theory, now often termed primitive Keynesianism; but that was not bad, I thought. Moreover, injecting firms' wage and price expectations enriched the theory with a

3. *Microeconomic Foundations of Employment and Inflation Theory,* New York: Norton (1970).

4. Lecture, Columbia University (1979); *American Economic Review: Papers and Proceedings* 69:102–8 (1979).

new causal force to be added to the forces Keynes and Friedman had introduced: animal spirits, mistaken policy, and anticipations of a future shock; and that was good, I thought. The question was the empirical importance of wage-price expectational errors. In the 1968 paper I played it safe in supposing that in each period, before quitting and hiring commence, the new wage level is reported, implying that the expectational error dampens the wage response to the shock but does not fool the workers into underquitting; and such frequent reports updating the wage level would keep a pretty tight lid on errors in the expected wage. But if, with Dale Mortensen, we model the wage reports as lagged, expected wages would have more room to fall behind and the time to affect actual quitting or hiring. More radically, my 1972 inflation policy book suggested that even while participants were getting the changes in the average hourly wage right, they might persistently overestimate their pay *relative* to the pay in some other heterogeneous regions or trades, so the apparent "macro" equilibrium would mask micro errors; and the structure of these errors could shift with the learning that comes with shocks. I had no idea of the twists and turns that subsequent developments would take.

II

Robert Lucas reshaped the embryonic new paradigm when, in his 1972 paper,[5] he adapted my islands story into a *stationary stochastic process* and *endogenized* expectations formation with the premise of rational expectations: each agent's expectations are based on complete *knowledge* of the fundamental parameters of the stochastic processes and his or her information: the local information at the start of the current period and the complete information at the end. Consider a downward disturbance to the demand for money, one exceeding the correctly anticipated trend, which would already have been built into the price level or money supply trend. One implication was that, following this disturbance, production would jump in the first period: More output would be supplied because the higher prices would be mistaken for better *relative* prices—a mechanism paralleling the one in my own islands model. The implications for the subsequent *adjustment process* were strikingly novel: With the issuance of the data at the first period's end, the ex ante expected values of output and relative prices would jump back to their natural levels; if the drop in money demand was judged to be wholly temporary, the expected value of the next period's price level (and hence price-level expectations) would be unchanged from previous expectations; whereas if the drop were tied to a publicly observable event, say, increased military expenditure, the expected price level would increase just enough that the above-normal output resulting if the expenditure continued another period would be exactly counterbalanced by the below-normal output resulting if the expenditure stopped. If the end-of-period data plus background information revealed a permanent shift in money demand (again exceeding the expected trend), the expected price level would jump onto a

---

5. *Journal of Economic Theory* 4:103–24 (1972).

new path.[6] It was obvious to me that this statistical view of things was a profound step and I never doubted that I might at times have to use it. (I had already studied a perfect-foresight model in my 1965 *Fiscal Neutrality*,[7] though expressing misgivings.)

While greatly admiring Lucas's construction I nevertheless saw its vision of the economy as somehow deeply counter to the vision I had but had not managed to articulate—a vision in parts Keynesian, monetarist, and Austrian that I felt also had value. It was not *by itself* the jump back to the natural rate in the expected-value sense that was troubling: A modeler has to simplify somewhere and had Lucas found room for the turnover-training element he might have shown that in the case of a permanent money demand shift, say, the economy *glides* back to a medium-term natural rate along an equilibrium *path* dictated by the unprofitability of firing costly-to-train employees. For me the troubling feature was that expectations were fully realigned *in one fell swoop* as required by essentially nonmonetary equilibrium considerations. The 1973 paper was a challenge to the Keynes-Phillips tenet that the employment adjustment process would tend to be protracted owing to an overly slow adjustment of *wage/price level expectations* or of the wage/price level *itself* (on top of any nonmonetary-equilibrium forces slowing it). As it dispensed with any *causal* role for expectations, it was a shot heard across all of macroeconomics, Keynesian, monetarist, and Austrian alike.

I have had several reactions at one time or another to this challenge and I think I can see all of them in one version or another in the chapters in Parts I and II in this volume. Some of these reactions can be quickly summarized while the issue of a causal role for expectations is best postponed for the last section. Let me focus on the case of a permanent money demand shift, as in the previous section, but suppose in the spirit of the Lucas paper (until notice to the contrary) that it becomes *known* with the issuance of the data. My first response was that equilibration after one period would not happen in an economy with overlapping wage or price "commitments," since only the ones whose turn it was to be reset could jump after the data were in. (It is not the expectations that adjust slowly in this view; it is the wages, which firms do not want to adjust fully as long as the others have not.) Such "staggered" wages were discussed toward the end of my 1968 paper and again in the appendix to its poorer 1970 version (under the same title). I shared the idea with my colleague John Taylor in 1973 and both he and I and later Guillermo Calvo took it up, with much discussion among us and sometimes a joint paper.[8] Columbia became the hotbed of the New Keynesian movement, as Parkin dubbed it. The chapter by Calvo et al. in this volume and that by Greg Mankiw and Ricardo Reis retain this New Keynesian concept while offering ways

---

6. I believe that 100 percent permanency is a limiting case and strictly speaking outside the stationary setup of the 1973 paper. It loosely describes permanence with very high probability.

7. *Fiscal Neutrality toward Economic Growth,* New York: McGraw-Hill (1965).

8. See "Introduction," in *Studies in Macroeconomic Theory,* Vol. 1, New York: Academic Press (1979), pp. 1–19.

to keep the inflation rate from peaking after the surge of employment following a shock, so as to jibe with the data.

Another response, presented in my 1985 textbook,[9] was to propose an alternative formulation in which the "period" is, say, the day, and the data dribble out—one day weekly unemployment claims, another day freight-car loadings, another day the monthly CPI, another the quarterly labor cost index—with no day's statistical releases being fully revealing of what had happened to the economy since the previous release of those series. Even if 30 days' of data releases covered all the variables of the "known" model, by the time any full cycle was completed 29 days of *subsequent* shocks would have occurred, so the early releases in that cycle would have long passed their sell-by dates. (A newspaper column the other day characterized markets as operating "on snippets of information, half-truths, and pure rumor," though I am not going that far.) But I did not attempt to develop this idea into a model. It seems to me that the Mankiw and Reis chapter is pretty close to a development of that idea.

Yet another reaction I have had to the Lucas paper is that, in its usual interpretation at any rate, it asks us to take as known parameters some (occasionally changing) constants that are more naturally taken as *unknowns* to be estimated sequentially by the agents with each period's additional evidence. Take now the case in which the permanent downward shift of money demand, though large, is *not* accompanied by any evidence outside the usual macrodata that would point to such a shift, contrary to the case in the previous two paragraphs. In this new case the agents of the model face an identification problem. Even when, to simplify, the agents have no doubt that the rest of the economy's structure is unchanging, they will not be able to deduce whether the unusually large decrease of money demand inferred from the data is due to a large negative blip of the independently distributed disturbance term (whose expected value always equals zero) or due instead to a downward shift of the constant term in the money demand function. This is, in essence, the famous problem of "permanent or temporary?" To stay within the rational expectations framework we might suppose that the constant term is known to be subject to a linear birth-and-death process, going up one unit or down one unit, as the case may be, according to known probabilities, while the disturbance term has a known variance and can take on the values 1, 0, and -1. Clearly, as agents continually find evidence of lower demand for money they will tend continually to assign lower and lower probability to the possibility that the constant term has remained unchanged. This is what I believe some call rational expectations learning. Thus, the downward shift in money demand drives up employment in the first Lucasian period, and this is followed by an adjustment process in which employment is gradually contracted and the price level gradually pushed up as agents learn about the permanence of the parameter shift. The agents *believe* at each step that the expected value of output in the next period is at the natural level but the *true* expected value is above natural, since the agents' estimates of the constant term are only asymptotically approaching the true value.

---

9. *Political Economy: An Introductory Text,* New York: Norton (1979), pp. 564–5.

This "story" provides yet another rationale for persistence in the expected value of output following a disturbance. It could be the deep foundation below the sort of scenario I was describing in my own island and turnover-training models.

Perhaps this takes us to where many macroeconomists "are" these days: There is unemployment even on *equilibrium* paths, involuntary and voluntary; there is some *staggering* of individual wages or prices; there is *stickiness* in individuals' information sets (in Mankiw's felicitous phrase) since we do not or cannot update all our information all the time; and there is an identification problem that blocks any instant inference of the occasional parameter shift. I regard this present stage as a valuable achievement and I am proud of my role in it. Yet I have come to wonder whether the creation of formal models giving powerful expression to the most tractable of the available ideas, which necessarily abstract from so much, has deflected our attention from some possibly important sources of the big fluctuations and some of the channels through which they work. I have come to feel that some central aspects of Western market economies are underemphasized or even omitted in formal macroeconomics and macroeconomic practice. There is, for example, a huge overemphasis on high-frequency fluctuations and the myriad high-frequency covariances. But some of the chapters in Parts III and IV of this volume serve to right the balance and they will give me an excuse to discuss *medium-term* swings (swings of 5 to 10 years) and *long-term* depressions in economic activity. Here I want to stick to the objects and perspectives of Keynes's theory.

III

What got lost in monetary macroeconomics amid its considerable achievements in modeling imperfect information is the *imperfect knowledge*, or uncertainty in the sense of Knight, that pervades the more entrepreneurial of the market economies. In what I call *modern* economic theory—the theorizing that began in the interwar decades with Knight, Mises, Keynes, Hayek, and M. Polanyi and continued in the postwar decades with Simon, Marschak, Nelson, and Winter, and in the 1990s Frydman and Rapaczynski—core parts of the capitalist market economy are engaged in creating and diffusing knowledge: The ongoing injection of new products, new methods, and new markets entails a *discovery* process of guesswork and sequential investigation by entrepreneurs and venture capitalists. The ensuing stream of such innovations, in creating new opportunities, generates *diffusion* processes of search and evaluation by potential adopters of recent innovations. Moreover, the adoption of innovations requires and stimulates a *learning* process by actual buyers and users. The participants in this economy are all in the business of narrowing gaps in their private knowledge. They cannot know fully the current structure within which they operate—not even the prospective revenue functions and cost functions of their own enterprises and how their own industry has recently changed.

By its nature, then, no one could possibly know the current structure of this nonstationary economy as a whole. Obviously, expectations formation in this capitalist economy is not simply the problem of drawing inferences from local price disturbances using structures of the economy (such as probability distributions of the variables) that are known. An actor in such an economy will always be forming and reforming his or her belief about the structures themselves, which will always have shifted and evolved in ways not anticipated and not governed by known underlying probabilities. If the participants are far behind in this effort, the macroeconomist may need to recognize the degree of their ignorance when modeling their behavior.

For macroeconomics I see two potential ramifications of this ignorance that was so much on the minds of Hayek and Keynes. One is that this sort of economy is not a hospitable environment for rational expectations—although one should not see that proposition as inviting aggressive countercyclical policies. (Even two towering pre–rational expectations figures, Keynes and Friedman, saw no hope of smoothing out sharp fluctuations in investment and employment.) In my paper for the 1983 conference volume on rational expectations I edited with Roman Frydman,[10] I set out what could be seen as another response to the Lucas paper. In my argument I insisted that it was and is a hugely attractive idea to suppose that each actor in an economy uses his or her *model* for the purpose of calculating expectations of the actions of others. But the trouble was that there was no basis for supposing that in an economy of imperfect knowledge all the agents would work with the *same* model, let alone the particular model of the model builder/analyst. (Frydman had shown in a 1982 article that even if all the agents had stumbled onto the same model and it did not have discernible errors that could be exploited for a profit, some agents would depart from it as they try to improve their forecasting.) In general, there will tend to emerge a *pluralism* of economic models finding adherents in any large economy. That would be serious by itself—the modeler would then have to refer to some average model in the population and try to carry on. But another layer of indeterminacy results: Each actor in forming expectations of the upcoming price level and upcoming money supply will want to form expectations of the expectations of the others, since the price level determined by the others will depend upon their expectations. Since each actor has no reason to suppose that the "average expectation" will be determined in the same way as his or her own expectation, that is, through the use of a model like his or her own, this average expectation—which Keynes called average opinion—or, at any rate, the expectations about it come to constitute a causal force in its own right. (Although my 1983 paper was directed at the disinflation problem, the Frydman-Phelps introduction put these ideas in a wider context.)

There is another point concerning the viability of rational expectations in the entrepreneurial economy. Existing rational expectations models describe a finite, stationary sort of economy: There are, so to speak, only so many islands and they are fundamentally alike. The entrepreneurial economy is more like an islands economy where each currently operating entrepreneur is at work exploring and developing an island that is unique and an entrepreneur can move on in hopes of discovering another virgin island that is different. The "state" of such an economy includes each entrepreneur's island-specific plan, which is loosely based on beliefs about some

---

10. *Individual Forecasters and Aggregate Outcomes: Rational Expectations Examined,* Cambridge: Cambridge University Press (1983).

of the island's possibilities and subject to change. So the national economy—the set of islands under development and the plans for them—will be evolving, its structure and its associated correct-expectations path (which cannot be supported in the market owing to differences in expectations) becoming significantly different from decade to decade. This ongoing structural change helps to sustain the diversity of models.

It is obvious, then, that the Lucas model does not apply to an economy in which rational expectations are not attainable, not even rational learning, since there is no stability in the parameters nor in the birth-and-death probabilities of their changes and no common model, and the very state of the economy includes entrepreneurs' visions and plans. The possibility that the medium-run steady-state expectational equilibrium, to which any expectational-equilibrium path would have to lead, has been altered by the real shocks means that the actors in the economy cannot work out the right relative prices; a tendency toward the medium-term natural rate is replaced by a tendency toward some neighborhood of the natural rate. Using models that disagree ensures that they will disagree over the right relative prices to expect, and they cannot all be said to be right. Believing that the others are using models different from their own for such calculations, models possibly differing in unknown ways, people may sometimes expect a slower adjustment of the money-wage and price levels than actually occurs and perhaps sometimes a faster adjustment—but with no likelihood that the average expectation of the price level adjustment will be right on average. To me it seems plausible, perhaps transparent, that actors will place *less weight* on new observations in an economy fraught with uncertainty about its structure than they would if what they did not know was only local information in the other localities. This may be what lay behind Keynes's intuition in his *General Theory*[11] that the market's expectations, while resting on "flimsy" foundations, do not flit from one set of beliefs to another to the extent they would in equilibrium-type models calibrated to the technology and preferences of that marketplace.

At least three chapters in this volume can be seen as entering the world of pluralistic beliefs and correspondingly pluralistic perceptions. Michael Woodford translates to another dimension the premise of my 1983 paper that an agent cannot know that the others are interpreting the public signals observed by all in the same way. In Woodford's chapter, the agent observing a signal has doubts as to whether the others have all observed it too, so the agent has to form his or her expectations of average opinion accordingly. (I would think that the agent may also worry that some others have seen something that he or she has not.) Though not explicit in the chapter, a plausible reason for such doubts is that the agent believes that many others operate with other models and that many of those do not warrant watching for that signal. In Roman Frydman and Michael Goldberg's chapter on the behavior of the foreign exchange market, they argue that recognition of imperfect knowledge and the features of expectations formation that derive from it allow us to understand patterns of exchange rate behavior that had heretofore

---

11. *General Theory of Employment, Interest and Money,* London: Macmillan (1936).

eluded explanation. In their account, the market can swing far from its moving equilibrium zone before finally turning in search of it. Mordecai Kurz's chapter deals with a stock market exhibiting what he calls an "equilibrium" among the diverse beliefs, and he studies the peculiar fluctuations of that sort of market. This is heady stuff.

Perhaps the models just mentioned provide a way of capturing the aforementioned aspects of expectations formation in an entrepreneurial economy. Or perhaps it will have to be done another way. In any case, I suspect that a new stage of major progress in macroeconomics will require us to consider expectations as an independent force in the asset markets of capitalist economies. This new stage, if I am not mistaken, will not see the demise of rational expectations models; it will be as necessary as ever that economists understand the *expectational-equilibrium* motions and steady states of the various models that they and real-life participants adopt. But this does not mean that rational expectations models will suffice. In an economy of imperfect knowledge there will remain phenomena and patterns in the data that will require economists to go on to study the complex expectations formation arising from the pluralism of agents' models. To quote the choreographer Twyla Tharp, the modern is the classical plus *more*.

Although the pluralism of models and expectations of expectations may be the most important ramifications of imperfect knowledge, there are also some ramifications related to Knightian uncertainty. While old uncertainties may be narrowing, new ones break out from time to time. So the degree of objective uncertainty that the world presents, meaning the range or the variance of the possible outcomes' true distribution (which is not known), is variable, and an increase in this uncertainty has the potential for some undesirable effects.

When objective uncertainty increases, there is more room for *subjective* uncertainty, as measured by, say, the variance of people's subjective distribution of outcomes, to increase as well. Plausibly, an increase in the subjective variance of the distribution of various outcomes would act to decrease the value per unit placed by business people on their business assets—customers, new office and factory facilities, and new job-ready employees; and in the sort of Hamiltonian economics of business investment that appears in most of my models, a decrease in the assets' shadow prices would immediately depress businesses' optimal rates of investment in these assets. In their chapter, Bruce Greenwald and Joseph Stiglitz work out the analysis in the case where the business asset is the customer: As businesses respond to the reduced asset value by raising their markups, output and employment contract. Although their model is monetary, presumably an increase of unemployment in my nonmonetary models would result as well.

An increase of (objective) uncertainty also creates more room for a loss of confidence, including notably the confidence of venture capitalists and other financiers in their ability to detect acceptable investment opportunities. Such confidence may drop or it may hold up; either way it is an independent force. If an investor experiences a decline of this confidence, he or she may scale back the search for signs of a good opportunity. If others scale back it is even less urgent to look for an opportunity, as it will be more likely to continue to be there. Investment financing may close down or shrink radically. What is involved here is not a mean-preserving increase in subjective variance but, rather, a variance-preserving decrease in the subjective mean.

An economy marked by Knightian uncertainty is also subject to swings in the confidence of entrepreneurs. Pigou's optimism and Keynes's animal spirits refer to the mean of the subjective distribution of returns believed to be possible outcomes of undertaking a capital project. When there is little uncertainty the subjective mean has little leeway up or down, but when uncertainty is high the subjective mean becomes a potentially important causal force.

Let me try to summarize the daunting—though, I hope, do-able—task before us. The visions exciting Schumpeter's entrepreneurs, the diversity of experience and knowledge in Hayek's theory of discovery, Keynes's role for investors' expectations of other investors' expectations, Knight's focus on uniqueness and novelty, Pigou's confidence or optimism—most if not all of these and possibly other modernist concepts will be needed for a macroeconomics of the entrepreneurial economy, which to varying degree is the kind of economy that many or most Western nations have. The models of order and rational expectations will perhaps always be a sort of base camp playing a necessary role in the assault on the summit. But we cannot scale the summit without the concepts with which to analyze the consequences of the imperfect knowledge that pervades the entrepreneurial economy.

PART III

Determinants of
Equilibrium Unemployment

— 14 —

How Monopsonistic Is the
(Danish) Labor Market?

DALE T. MORTENSEN

1. INTRODUCTION

The existence of wage differences across employers challenges the validity of the "law of one price" in the labor market. Large industry and employer size differentials provide evidence for wage dispersion in the sense that observably identical workers are paid differently.[1] Two main explanations for wage differentials of this form are offered in the literature: Either employers pursue different wage policies and/or high-wage firms attract more able workers.[2] Recent empirical studies by Abowd and Kramarz (2000a,b), based on the analysis of matched employer-worker data for both the United States and France, conclude that the two are roughly equally important as explanations for interindustry differentials and that wage policy differences explain 70 percent of the size differential in both countries.[3]

In this chapter, the empirical implications of employer heterogeneity in labor productivity is explored as the principal source of wage dispersion. Two wage determination hypotheses are considered—the monopsony and the union monopoly

---

1. Papers that provide empirical documentation for this kind of wage dispersion include Kruger and Summers (1988), Katz and Summers (1989), Davis and Haltiwanger (1991), Doms et al. (1997), Abowd et al. (1999), Abowd and Kramarz (2000a,b), and Oi and Idson (1999).

2. Krueger and Summers (1988) emphasized the former explanation, whereas Murphy and Topel (1987) argued that unmeasured differences in individual ability is the principal explanation. Although Dickens and Katz (1987) and Gibbons and Katz (1992) attempted to resolve the debate, their efforts and those of others were hampered by lack of appropriate matched worker-employer data.

3. The conclusions of these studies correct those reported in an earlier article (Abowd et al., 1999) based on the same data. The earlier results are obtained using an approximate method of decomposing worker and employer fixed effects whereas the later papers apply an exact method.

The financial support of NSF #SES-9975207 is gratefully acknowledged. I thank my colleagues on the Danish project, B. J. Christensen, Rasmus Lentz, George Neumann, and Axel Werwatz, for their effort and support. Ken Burdett's and Rob Shimer's insightful comments were also helpful. Finally, I am particularly appreciative of Ned Phelps's encouragement to pursue my intitial interest in this topic many years ago. All remaining errors are mine.

model. The model and cross-firm wage and size distribution data for Denmark are used to explore the plausibility of these two alternatives.

Little is known about cross-firm differences in wages paid. This fact is surprising since the essential elements of a theory of wage policy have appeared in editions of Samuelson's principles of economics textbook since 1951. In the third edition, Samuelson (1955, p. 541) makes the following observations[4]:

> Wage policy of firms. The fact that a firm of any size *must* have a wage policy is additional evidence of labor market imperfections. . . .
>
> But just because competition is not 100 per cent perfect does not mean that it must be zero. The world . . . is a blend of (1) competition and (2) some degree of monopoly power over the wage to be paid. If you try to set your wage too low you will soon learn this. At first nothing much need happen; but eventually you will find your workers quitting a little more rapidly than would otherwise be the case. Recruitment of new people of the same quality will get harder and harder, and you will notice slackening off in the performance and productivity of those who remain on the job.
>
> Availability of labor supply does, therefore, affect the wage you set under realistic conditions of imperfect competition. If you are a very small firm you may even bargain and haggle with prospective workers so as to not pay more than you have to. But if you are of any size at all, you will name a wage for each type of job; then decide how many of the applicants will be taken on.

Subsequently, Phelps (1970) and Mortensen (1970) pursued Samuelson's insights in the "Phelps volume." They argued that every employer faces an inelastic supply of workers as a consequence of search friction because applicants are willing to accept low-wage offers and cannot instantaneously move to higher paying employers. In this environment, a high-paying employer profits by attracting and retaining a larger labor force. Still, a low-paying employer can survive in spite of high turnover. In other words, every employer has some market power even when many competitors populate the market.

The nature of their version of a monopsony labor market equilibrium was not fully spelled out by either Mortensen or Phelps, a critique poignantly made by Rothschild (1973). Later, papers by Butters (1977), Burdett and Judd (1983), and Mortensen (1990) resolved the problem by formulating the model as a noncooperative price-setting game. In addition, they demonstrated that dispersion in wage policy can be the only equilibrium outcome of imperfect wage competition induced under plausible conditions even when all employers are identical. However, persistent cross-firm heterogeneity in productive efficiency is the more likely case and, when present, induces differences in wage policies that reflect differential labor productivity across firms as Burdett and Mortensen (1998) and Bontemps et al. (2000) point out.

Alternatively, wage differences across employers could arise because unions set wages at the firm level. In the version of the monopoly union model considered

---

4. I thank George Neumann for reminding me of this passage.

here, the union wage maximizes the surplus value of those hired under the wage policy. Analogous to the static version of the monopoly wage model, an employer's recruiting effort maximizes the employer's value of the hire flow given the union wage chosen. Of course, the union takes the dependence of recruiting effort into account when setting the monopoly wage.

Does empirical evidence on firm turnover behavior and wage differences support the hypothesis that wage dispersion reflects heterogeneity in firm productivity under one or the other of these wage determination rules? Providing some insights into the answer to this question is the principal purpose of this chapter. The quantitative method used to accomplish this is based on that suggested and applied by Bontemps et al. (2000) and on the empirical model of interfirm flows estimated by Christensen et al. (2001). Either alternative model is regarded as consistent with the data if the observed wage offer distribution could be an equilibrium outcome of the agent's decisions as characterized in the model.

The chapter extends the theory used by Bontemps et al. (2000) in their analysis of French data and applies the general approach that they pioneered to Danish data. Added features include an endogenous worker search effort choice and an employer recruiting effort choice as well as the alternative union monopoly wage determination hypothesis. The data are cross-firm observations drawn from the Danish Integrated Database for Labour Market Research (IDA) developed by Christensen et al. (2001) for their study of job separation flows. For all privately owned employing establishments in Denmark, the IDA observations of interest include the number of employees in November 1994, the number of these who were still employed in the same firm the following November, the number of workers hired during the year by each firm and the prior employment status of each new hire, and the hourly wage paid to each employee during the year. Cross-firm distributions of hourly wage offers, average hourly wages earned, and labor force size are constructed from these observations.

The labor market model underlying the analysis includes the following components. A continuum of workers populate the supply side of the labor market. All are identical, live forever, and act to maximize expected wealth. A continuum of expected wealth-maximizing employers who are differentiated by the productivity of their technology represent the demand side of the market. At a point in time, each worker is either employed or not. A worker looks for a job paying an acceptable wage when unemployed and a higher wage when employed at an endogenously chosen search intensity taking as given the wage offer distribution. Similarly, employers with job vacancies seek workers by investing in recruiting effort. The total resources allocated to search and recruiting investments determine the rates at which workers and employers meet. The fact that this matching process is not instantaneous and costless is the source of friction in the model. Each employer chooses her recruiting policy optimally given the choices made by all other employers and workers. In the monopsony case, each employer sets her wage offer to maximize the value of the flow of workers hired whereas the union wage demand maximizes the net value of employment to the workers hired. In each case, equilibrium is a noncooperative solution to the market game implicit in this description.

Given dispersion in wage offers, both the expected frequency with which a worker locates a higher-paying job and the expected gain in future earnings obtained when one is found decrease with the wage currently earned by an employed worker. As a consequence, one expects search effort by employed workers to decrease with the relative wage earned. Christensen et al. (2001) find supporting evidence for these predictions in Danish IDA data. Indeed, they are able to recover estimates of job turnover parameters and the cost of search effort function. These estimates imply that workers in lower-paying jobs search hard but that search effort diminishes rapidly as the wage earned increases. Furthermore, their empirical model of job separations explains the observed market level relationship between the distribution of wage offers that workers face and the steady-state distribution of wages earned by employed workers. This fact is additional support for the hypothesis that workers flow from lower- to higher-paying jobs at rates that reflect individual rationality.

As Bontemps et al. (2000) argue, one can test whether monopsony is a possible explanation for the wage dispersion observed in the data without observing firm productivity directly. Their argument proceeds as follows. If the distributions of wages offered and wages earned represent outcomes that are consistent with the equilibrium solution to the model, then every observed wage must be optimal, taking the market distributions as given for some level of firm productivity. As a corollary, more productive employers must offer higher wages.

The results presented in this chapter suggest that the monopsony version of the model can be rejected for two reasons. First, the lowest 5 percent of the wage offers observed in the data are not profit maximizing. Second, over the remaining range of the support of the offer distribution, the difference between the value of marginal product and the wage is large and increasing in productivity. Although these results might suggest that more productive employers in the Danish labor market possess considerable monopsony power, the magnitudes implied by the model and the data are implausibly large in the upper reaches of the wage support. For example, the implied difference between marginal productivity and the wage is fifteen times the wage at the ninetieth percentile of the wage distribution.

One can test the alternative hypothesis that each firm's wage is set by a union to maximize the product of the hire flow and the worker's net value of employment. This hypothesis also implies that the wage should increase with employer productivity. For reasonable parameterizations of this model, specifically a quadratic recruiting cost function, the data are fully consistent with the monopoly union hypothesis. Furthermore, the magnitude of the rate at which the wage increases with productivity is plausible. Indeed, the difference between marginal productivity and the wage is zero at the left support of the wage distribution and increases to about 50 percent at the ninetieth percentile.

Finally, the unobserved cross-firm distribution of labor productivity is identified by the observed distributions of wages and firm size when both wage offers and recruiting effort monotonically increase with firm productivity, conditions satisfied by the monopoly union wage rule. The Danish data and the monopoly rule suggest that almost all firms have relatively low productivity but a very few highly productive employers are present in the market who employ a significant fraction of the privately employed labor force.

2. THE LABOR MARKET MODEL

2.1. Worker Search Behavior

In the modeled labor market, all workers are identical, are labor market participants, live forever, and act to maximize expected wealth. Let the unit interval represent the (normalized) set of workers. Suppose that offers arrive at a Poisson frequency proportional to search effort. Specifically, let λs represent the offer arrival rate, where s is search effort and λ is a contact parameter. The worker's value of a job match paying wage w solves

$$r W(w) = \max_{s \geq 0} \left\{ w - c_w(s) + \delta [U - W(w)] \right. \tag{1}$$
$$\left. + \lambda s \int \{\max [W(x), W(w)] - W(w)\} \, dF(x) \right\},$$

where $c_w(s)$ denotes the cost of search effort, δ is the exogenous job destruction rate, and U represents the value of unemployment. The parameter r is the discount rate and $F(w)$ denotes the fraction of offers that pay wage w or less.

Equation (1) is a continuous-time Bellman equation that reflects the optimal search effort and separation choices that the worker makes while employed and the fact that an exogenous transition to unemployment may occur. Specifically, the worker quits to take an outside employment option if and only if it offers a higher value than the current job, the optimal search effort choice maximizes the difference between the expected net gain in value attributable to search and its cost, and the expected future income jumps to the value of unemployment U when the worker transits to unemployment as a consequence of the destruction of the match. Similarly, the value of unemployment solves

$$r U = \max_{s \geq 0} \left\{ b + \lambda s \int \{\max [W(w), U] - U\} \, dF(w) - c_w(s) \right\}, \tag{2}$$

where b is an income flow received when unemployed—the unemployment benefit.

The solution to (1) is increasing in w. Indeed, because

$$W'(w) = \frac{1}{r + \delta + \lambda s(w)[1 - F(w)]} > 0, \tag{3}$$

by the envelope theorem, an employed worker quits to take an alternative job offer if and only if it pays a higher wage. Hence, the rate at which workers quit an employer paying w to take a job elsewhere is $\lambda s(w)[1 - F(w)]$, where optimal search effort is

$$s(w) = \arg \max_{s \geq 0} \left\{ \lambda s \int_w^{\overline{w}} [W(x) - W(w)] \, dF(x) - c_w(s) \right\}.$$

Integration by parts and equation (3) imply the following representation of the first-order condition for an optimal choice:

$$c_w'[s(w)] = \lambda \int_w^{\overline{w}} [W(x) - W(w)] \, dF(x) \qquad (4)$$

$$= \lambda \int_w^{\overline{w}} [W'(x)[1 - F(x)] \, dx$$

$$= \lambda \int_w^{\overline{w}} \frac{[1 - F(x)] \, dx}{r + \delta + \lambda s(x)[1 - F(x)]}.$$

Because the likelihood of finding a better job declines with the wage earned, search intensity declines with an employed worker's current wage, that is, $s'(w) < 0$.

When unemployed, the typical worker accepts an offer only if it is no lower than the reservation wage, denoted as R. As the reservation wage equates the value of employment to the value of unemployed search, acceptance requires that $w \geq R$, where

$$U = W(R). \qquad (5)$$

As a consequence, equations (1), (2), and (5) together imply that the search intensity of an unemployed worker is the same as that of a worker employed at the reservation wage,

$$s_0 = s(R), \qquad (6)$$

and that the reservation wage is equal to the unemployment benefit,

$$R = b. \qquad (7)$$

2.2. Steady-State Conditions

Given that workers flow from lower- to higher-paying employers, the cumulative distribution of wages offered, denoted $F(w)$, and the cumulative distribution of wages paid to employed workers, represented as $G(w)$ in the sequel, are closely linked by steady-state flow conditions. Because all equilibrium wage offers are acceptable, unemployed workers find employment at rate $\lambda s(R)$. Given this fact, the steady-state unemployment rate is

$$u = \frac{\delta}{\delta + \lambda s(R)}, \qquad (8)$$

where δ represents the exogenous job destruction rate.

Because workers employed at wage w quit at rate $\lambda s(w)[1 - F(w)]$, the balance between flows into and out of the set of workers who are employed at wage w or less, required to define the steady-state distribution of wages across employed workers, is

$$\delta G(w) + \lambda[1 - F(w)] \int_{\underline{w}}^{w} s(x)dG(x) = \frac{\lambda s(R)F(w)u}{1-u} = \delta F(w), \quad (9)$$

where the last equality follows from equation (8). The first term on the left-hand side accounts for the fraction of those employed in the wage category who are laid off per period, the second term is the fraction who quit to take higher-paying jobs, and the right-hand side is the flow into the category from unemployment, all expressed as a fraction of employment. In sum, given the exogenous job destruction rate δ, the contact frequency parameter λ, the search effort function $s(w)$, and the wage offer distribution function $F(w)$, the steady-state wage c.d.f. $G(w)$ is the unique solution to the functional equation (9).[5]

The difference between the distribution of wages earned, $G(w)$, and the distribution of wage offers, $F(w)$, represents an *employment selection effect*. According to the on-the-job search theory outlined earlier, the difference is positive because an employed worker is more likely to have found a higher-paying job during her current employment spell, whereas a worker hired from nonemployment earns a random draw from the wage offer distribution. As the steady-state condition relating the wage and offer distribution, equation (9), can be written as

$$\frac{F(w) - G(w)}{1 - F(w)} = \frac{\lambda}{\delta} \int_{\underline{w}}^{w} s(x)dG(x), \quad (10)$$

the theory implies that the horizontal differences between the wage offer and wage earned distribution functions depend on the extent of friction in the market as reflected in the ratio of the offer arrival rate to the job separation rate and the average search effort of the workers earning no more than w.

2.3. Recruiting Effort

Let p represent the value of output per worker employed in a firm of type p and let $\Gamma(p)$ denote the measure of employers with productivity no greater than p. For the moment, let the triple (p, w, v) characterize an employer where w represents per period wage paid and v denotes recruiting effort per period as reflected in, say, the number of workers contacted per period.

A specification of the relationship between recruiting effort and a firm's hire flow requires that one account for the endogenous search effort choices of the workers. Here I assume that the probability that the particular worker is contacted by an employer is proportional to that worker's relative search effort. Because an unemployed worker accepts a wage no less than R but an employed worker accepts only if currently paid less than the wage offered, the probability that a randomly contacted worker will accept is

---

5. By differentiating both sides of (9) with respect to w and then substituting from equation (9) to eliminate the integral, one obtains a first-order differential equation in $G(w)$. The solution of interest is the particular solution associated with the initial condition $G(\underline{w}) = 0$.

$$
h(w) = \begin{cases} \dfrac{us(R) + (1-u)\int_{\underline{w}}^{w} s(z)dG(z)}{us(R) + (1-u)\int_{\underline{w}}^{\overline{w}} s(z)dG(z)} & \text{if} \quad w \geq R \\[6pt] 0 & \text{otherwise.} \end{cases} \tag{11}
$$

The sampling assumption underlying (11) captures the following idea: Employers contact workers by advertising in newspapers, on line, and through employment agencies. A particular worker is contacted at a relative frequency that depends on the worker's awareness as reflected in the time and effort that he or she spends searching. Finally, all unemployed workers accept offers above their common reservation wage and employed workers accept only if the wage offer exceeds the wage currently earned.

An employer's expected profit flow per worker contacted is the product of the hire probability per worker contacted and the value of filling a job vacancy, that is,

$$
\Pi(p, w) = h(w)J(p, w),
$$

where $J(p, w)$ denotes the expected present value of the future profit flow generated by a job-worker match given the employer's productivity p and wage w. Because an employed worker quits when aware of a higher outside offer, the employer's value of continuing the match solves the Bellman equation

$$
rJ(p, w) = p - w - \delta J(p, w) - \lambda s(w)[1 - F(w)]J(p, w).
$$

Equivalently,

$$
J(p, w) = \frac{p - w}{r + d(w)}, \tag{12}
$$

where

$$
d(w) = \delta + \lambda s(w)[1 - F(w)] \tag{13}
$$

represents the job separation rate for an employer paying wage w. Hence, expected profit per worker contacted can be written as

$$
\Pi(p, w) = \begin{cases} \dfrac{h(w)(p - w)}{r + d(w)} & \text{if} \quad w \geq R \\[6pt] 0 & \text{otherwise.} \end{cases} \tag{14}
$$

In other words, expected profit per worker contacted is the product of the acceptance probability, and the present value of the profit flow discounted by the sum of the interest rate and the match separation rate.

The optimal recruiting policy maximizes the employer's total expected profit flow, that is,

$$v(p, w) = \arg\max_{v \geq 0} \left[\Pi(p, w)v - c_f(v) \right], \tag{15}$$

where v denotes the number of workers contacted and $c_f(v)$ is the cost of recruiting. Hence, any interior solution for the optimal number of workers contacted, $v(p)$, equates the marginal cost and expected profit per contact, that is,

$$c_f'[v(p, w)] = \Pi(p, w). \tag{16}$$

As equation (14) implies that expected profit increases with employer productivity, recruiting effort increases with productivity given the wage from (16) and the second-order condition, $c_f''(v) > 0$.

2.4. Wage Determination

2.4.1. Monopsony Wage Rule

By definition, the monopsony wage maximizes the total expected profit attributable to recruiting effort, the right-hand side of equation (15). As a corollary, it maximizes expected profit per contact, that is,

$$w(p) = \arg\max_{w \geq R} \Pi(p, w). \tag{17}$$

As one can easily demonstrate, the necessary second-order condition and the fact that the expected profit increases with firm productivity implies that the wage policy function defined by (17) is strictly increasing for any interior maximum, that is, $w'(p) > 0$. Furthermore, equation (16) and the envelope theorem require that recruiting effort expressed as a function of firm productivity, $v[p, w(p)]$, be strictly increasing.

As more productive employers offer a higher wage and invest more in recruiting effort in the monopsony case, they attract workers more quickly and retain them more easily. Consequently, the relationship between size and productivity is increasing. Formally, an employer's average expected labor force size over the long run is

$$n(p) = \frac{h[w(p)]v[p, w(p)]}{d[w(p)]}. \tag{18}$$

2.4.2. Monopoly Wage Rule

The monopoly union model is a natural alternative hypothesis. By analogy with the monopsony case, the local union chooses the wage to maximize the product of the hire flow, $h(w)v(p, w)$, and each hired worker's surplus value of employment in the firm, $W(w) - U$, that is,

$$w(p) = \arg\max_{w \geq R} \{h(w)v(p, w)[W(w) - U]\}. \tag{19}$$

Given the wage chosen, the firm selects the contact frequency v to maximize profit as specified above. Since the solution $v(p, w)$ is increasing in p, the optimal monopoly wage also increases with p by the second-order condition, that is, $w'(p) > 0$ in this case as well.

The fact that $w(p)$ does not maximize expected employer profit, $\Pi(p, w)$, in the monopoly case implies that the net effect of productivity on the number of workers contacted is unclear. However, because equations (14) and (15) require that

$$c'_f\{v[p, w(p)]\} = \frac{h[w(p)][p - w(p)]}{r + d[w(p)]}, \tag{20}$$

$0 < w'(p) \le 1$ is a sufficient condition for $v[p, w(p)]$ to be increasing in productivity p.

2.5. Labor Market Equilibrium

As already noted, the search effort behavior of the workers determines the steady-state relationship between the distribution of wages offered and wages earned represented by equation (9). The employer wage and recruiting policy functions determine the wage offer distribution and the contact or offer frequency per worker. Specifically, the total number of employer contacts made per worker is

$$\lambda = \int_{\underline{p}}^{\overline{p}} v[x, w(x)]d\Gamma(x) \tag{21}$$

under either wage-setting hypothesis. Since the wage increases with productivity is both cases, the fraction of offers that pay a wage no greater than $w(p)$ can be expressed as

$$F[w(p)] = \frac{\displaystyle\int_{\underline{p}}^{p} v(x)d\Gamma(x)}{\displaystyle\int_{\underline{p}}^{\overline{p}} v(x)d\Gamma(x)} = \frac{\displaystyle\int_{\underline{p}}^{p} v(x)d\Gamma(x)}{\lambda}. \tag{22}$$

In other words, the steady state and these aggregation conditions imply that a search strategy $s: (\underline{w}, \overline{w}) \to \Re_+$, a wage function $w: (\underline{p}, \overline{p}) \to \Re_+$, and a recruiting strategy $v: (\underline{p}, \overline{p}) \times (\underline{w}, \overline{w}) \to \Re_+$ determine the contact frequency λ, the cumulative distribution of wages offered $F: (\underline{w}, \overline{w}) \to \Re_+$, and the cumulative distribution of wages earned $G: (\underline{w}, \overline{w}) \to \Re_+$. Equations (4), (16), (17), and (19) imply that the optimal strategies of the market participants under either wage determination rule depend only on the agents' expectations regarding these market outcomes. A *rational expectations labor market equilibrium*, then, is a fixed point of the map implicitly defined by these relationships from the space of search, recruiting, and wage functions to itself.

3. EMPIRICAL INFERENCE

In this section, information about the distributions of wages offered and wages earned found in the Danish Integrated Database for Labor Market Research (IDA) is used to test for consistency with each wage determination model. Following the method suggested and applied by Bontemps et al. (2000), I ask whether these distributions could have been generated as equilibrium market outcomes under either or both wage determination rules. Formally, the test is whether the necessary second-order condition for the optimal choice of the wage is satisfied.

3.1. The Data

The distributional information used here is from data drawn from the IDA by Christensen et al. (2001) for their study of on-the-job search behavior as an explanation for observed differences in worker separation rates across employers. For the 113,525 privately owned firms, the observations of interest include an hourly firm wage w, defined as the average hourly wage paid to all employees during the year beginning in November 1994 expressed in Danish crowns (DKK), the number of workers hired by the firm who were not previously employed during the year, and the size of the firm's labor force, n, in that month. The observed wage c.d.f., $G(w)$, is the fraction of workers employed by a firm paying an average hourly wage of w or less. An unbiased estimate of the observed wage offer c.d.f., $F(w)$, is the fraction of workers hired from nonemployment by all firms paying the average wage w or less. The size distribution, $Q(n)$, is the observed size c.d.f.

The constructed wage and offer cumulative distribution functions for the complete sample are illustrated in Figure 1. As search on-the-job theory implies, the wage distribution, denoted as G in the figure, stochastically dominates the offer distribution, represented by F. In other words, the positive employment effect characterized by equation (10) exists uniformly on the common support of the wage and offer distributions. The distribution of firm size as characterized by its relative frequency distribution is illustrated in Figure 2. Note that almost all firms are small. Indeed, 26.5 percent employ a single wage earner and 62 percent have four or fewer. Only 9 percent of the firms have more than twenty employees and a mere 3 percent have more than fifty workers. Still, there are a few very large firms. The obvious skew in the distribution is reflected in the fact that the median size lies between two and three employees whereas the average is 13.2.

3.2. The Search Effort Strategy

Christensen et al. (2001) use observations on worker separations at the firm level to estimate the arrival rate and job destruction parameters, λ and δ, respectively, and the search effort function $s(w)$ implied by a power function specification of the cost of search. Specifically, they assume a cost-of-search effort function of the form

$$c_w(s) = \frac{c_0 s^{1+1/\gamma}}{1 + 1/\gamma}. \tag{23}$$

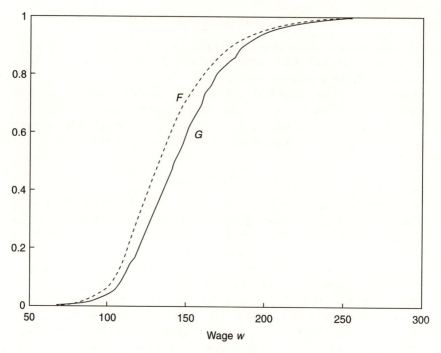

Figure 1. Offer (F) and wage (G) distribution functions.

In this case, the first-order condition, equation (4), can be rewritten as

$$\lambda s(w) = \left\{ \frac{\lambda^2}{c_0} \int_w^{\overline{w}} \frac{[1 - F(x)]dx}{r + \delta + \lambda s(x)[1 - F(x)]} \right\}^\gamma. \tag{24}$$

In other words, for any vector of parameters $(c_0, \delta, \lambda, \gamma)$, the product of the arrival rate and the optimal search effort function, $\lambda s(w)$, is the unique solution to this functional equation.

Estimates of the parameters are obtained by finding those values that maximize the likelihood of the observed number of separations experienced by each firm during the year beginning in November 1994. Since the duration of a job spell in a firm paying wage w is exponential with a parameter equal to the separation rate $d(w) = \delta + \lambda s(w)[1 - F(w)]$, the number of workers who stay with the firm is binomially distributed with "sample size" equal to firm size n and "probability of success" equal to $e^{-d(w)}$. Under the assumption that the parameters are identical across firms, the maximum likelihood estimates conditional on the interest rate r and offer distribution F are

$$(c_0, \delta, \lambda, \gamma) = \arg\max \sum_i \left[\ln \binom{n_i}{x_i} - d(w_i)x_i \right.$$

$$\left. + (n_i - x_i)\ln(1 - e^{-d(w_i)}) \right], \tag{25}$$

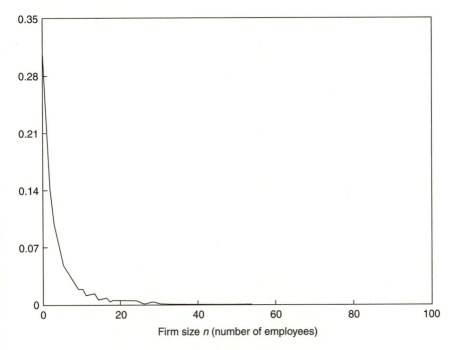

Figure 2. Firm size density $[q(n) = Q'(n)]$.

where $d(w)$ is the function specified in equation (13), w_i represents the average wage paid, n_i is the size, and x_i is the number of stayers for firm i. Since c_0 and λ^2 are not separately identified, search effort at the lowest wage $s(\underline{w})$ is normalized to equal unity.

Given the offer c.d.f. $F(w)$ observed in the data and an annual interest rate r equal to 4.9 percent per annum, the estimates of the remaining parameters are $\delta = 0.2872$, $\lambda = 0.5933$, and $\gamma = 1.1054$.[6] (Because the sample size is very large, the precision of the estimates is virtually certain to the third significant digit.) As an out-of-sample test, the authors show that the distribution of wages implied by the observed offer distribution, these estimates, and the steady-state condition [equation (9)] is very close to the actual wage c.d.f. $G(w)$ observed.

The arrival rate and job destruction rate parameter estimates reflect relatively high turnover in the Danish labor market. The implied average duration of a job spell in the highest-paying job, equal to $1/\delta$, is about 3.5 years, whereas expected duration in the lowest-paying job is only $1/(\delta + \lambda) = 1.15$ years. Given the cost function specification in equation (23), the fact that the estimate of the elasticity of search effort with respect to the return to search, γ, is close to unity suggests that the cost-of-search function is reasonably approximated by a quadratic.

___

6. These estimates are slightly different from those reported in Christiansen et al. (2001) because they were obtained using a different bin width for the construction of the wage and offer c.d.f.'s, F and G. Otherwise, the estimates were obtained using the same procedure.

3.3. The Wage Function

In the language of Bontemps et al. (2000), the observed wage and offer distributions are said to be *admissible* only if the first-order condition for an optimal wage choice implicitly defines an increasing relationship between wage and productivity over the common support of the two distributions. In other words, the distributions are admissible only if they can be rationalized as possible outcomes under the wage determination hypothesis assumed. In this section, I show that the distributions are not consistent with the monopsony model but are consistent with the monopoly union model.

Equations (14) and (17) imply that the first-order condition for an interior optimal wage choice in the monopsony case is

$$\frac{\Pi_w(w, p)}{\Pi(w, p)} = \frac{h'(w)}{h(w)} - \frac{d'(w)}{r + d(w)} - \frac{1}{p - w} = 0.$$

The necessary second-order condition requires that the solution to the equation, the wage policy function $w(p)$, increase with p over the support of the productivity distribution. Since the inverse of the wage policy function can be written as

$$p(w) = w \left(1 + \frac{1}{wh'(w)/h(w) - wd'(w)/[r + d(w)]} \right), \qquad (26)$$

one can simply check whether it is monotonically increasing over the support of the wage distribution given the acceptance probability function $h(w)$ and separation function $d(w)$ implied by the estimates obtained by Christensen et al. (2001).

In the case of monopoly, the first-order condition for the bargaining outcome defined by equation (19) can be written as

$$\frac{h'(w)}{h(w)} + \frac{W'(w)}{W(w) - U} + \frac{1}{\alpha[v(p, w)]} \frac{\Pi_w(w, p)}{\Pi(w, p)} = 0$$

given (14) and (16), where

$$\alpha(v) = \frac{c_f''(v)v}{c_f'(v)} \qquad (27)$$

is the elasticity of the marginal cost of recruiting function. Solving this expression for p yields

$$p = w \left\{ 1 + \left\{ \frac{wh'(w)}{h(w)} - \frac{wd'(w)}{r + d(w)} + \alpha[v(p, w)] \left[\frac{wh'(w)}{h(w)} \right. \right. \right. \qquad (28)$$

$$\left. \left. \left. + \frac{(r + \delta)w}{[r + d(w)]\left\{w - b + c_s'[s(w)]s(w) - c_s[s(w)] - c_s'[s(b)]s(b) + c_s[s(b)]\right\}} \right]^{-1} \right\} \right\}$$

from equations (1), (2), and (4).

Note that the two solutions are related. Indeed, if the recruiting cost function were linear, that is, $\alpha = 0$, the monopsony and monopoly wage choices would be the same. However, if the hires flow is invariant with respect to profit in the sense that $\alpha = \infty$, then the union sets the wage equal to the value of the marginal product p. In the general case, the monopoly wage lies somewhere between these two extremes.

3.4. Results

The results reported below are obtained as follows: The separation function $d(w)$ and the search cost function $c_f(s)$ are computed using equations (13) and (23), where δ, λ, γ, and $s(w)$ are the Christensen et al. estimates; $F(w)$ is the solution to the steady-state equation (9); and $G(w)$ is a smooth approximation to the observed wage distribution. The curve of the estimated separation rate function is illustrated in Figure 3. The fact that the elasticity is quite large in the lower half of the wage support but then tends to zero as the wage tends to the upper support constitutes the most interesting features of the curve. These characteristics reflect the fact that search effort while employed falls and approaches zero well before the upper support is reached.

The acceptance probability function $h(w)$ is computed using equation (11) and the offer c.d.f. $F(w)$ derived from the steady-state condition (9) given $G(w)$ after assigning a value to the unemployment rate u. Under a strict interpretation of

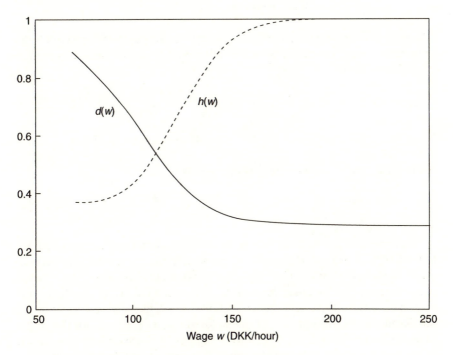

Figure 3. Separation $d(w)$ and acceptance $h(w)$ rates.

the theory, the steady-state condition for unemployment, equation (8), and the separation parameters determine the unemployment rate. However, the estimates $\delta = 0.2872$ and $\lambda = 0.5933$ and the normalization $s(\underline{w}) = 1$ imply a steady-state unemployment rate equal to 32.6 percent, far larger than the 12.2 percent unemployment rate recorded for Denmark in the relevant year, 1995.

The Christensen et al. (2001) estimate of δ seems to be excessive as an estimate of the annual transition rate from employment to unemployment. For example, Rosholm and Svarer (2000) derive an estimate equal to 0.099 per annum using panel data on Danish worker labor market event histories for the 1980s. One possible explanation for the difference is that the Christensen et al. (2001) estimate should be interpreted as the intercept of the separation function rather than as the employment-to-unemployment transition rate, especially since the worker's destination state is not used in the estimation procedure. Indeed, this reasoning suggests that $\delta = \delta_0 + \delta_1$, where $\delta_0 = 0.099$ represents the transition rate to unemployment and δ_1 is that part of the job-to-job transition rate that is unrelated to wage differences.

Interestingly, the steady-state condition (9) continues to hold given the alternative interpretation of δ. To prove the assertion, let $\delta = \delta_0 + \delta_1$, where δ_0 is regarded as the rate of transition from employment to nonemployment and δ_1 is the intercept of the job-to-job transition rate function. Under the assumption that workers who move between jobs for nonwage reasons earn a random wage offer and all wage offers are acceptable, the flow of workers to jobs that pay w or less is

$$s(R)\lambda F(w)u + \delta_1 F(w)(1 - u),$$

where the first term is the inflow from nonemployment and the second term is the inflow from employment. Equating the inflow to the outflow yields an equation equivalent to (14):

$$\delta G(w) + \lambda[1 - F(w)] \int_{\underline{w}}^{w} s(x) dG(x) = \frac{s(R)\lambda F(w)u + \delta_1 F(w)(1 - u)}{1 - u}$$

$$= (\delta_0 + \delta_1)F(w) = \delta F(w),$$

because the steady-state unemployment rate now solves

$$u = \frac{\delta_0}{\delta_0 + \lambda s(R)}. \tag{29}$$

Under the alternative interpretation, the implied steady-state unemployed fraction is $0.099/(0.099 + 0.5933) = 0.143$ given $s(R) = s(\underline{w})$, a number that is near the 12.2 percent unemployment rate actually experienced in the relevant year. A possible reason for the remaining difference between the two is that the lowest wage paid $\underline{w}$ actually exceeds the reservation wage R, in which case equation (4) implies that the search intensity of an employed worker $s(R)$ exceeds that of the same worker when employed at the lowest wage, $s(\underline{w})$. Since the inferences drawn in the sequel are essentially the same for either unemployed fraction, I choose to use the actual unemployed fraction in the relevant year, $u = 0.122$, in equation (11). The associated acceptance probability function $h(w)$ is illustrated in Figure 3. Note that the probability is also highly elastic at low wages but tends to unity in the upper ranges of the support of the wage distribution.

3.4.1. THE MONOPSONY CASE

In the monopsony case, the curve of the wage function $w(p)$ implied by equation (26) and the computed separation and acceptance rate functions illustrated in Figure 3 is shown in Figure 4. The curve itself is obtained by computing $p(w)$ for a series of wage values in the support of the wage distribution and then plotting each wage rate against the associated computed value of $p(w)$. As clearly illustrated in the figure, the wage does increase with productivity for all rates above 100 DKK/hour. The fact that the curve for wage rates below that critical value has a negative slope implies that any wage on the segment minimizes rather than maximizes expected profit per worker contacted at the associated value of productivity. Contrary to the model, none of the observed wage rates in this region of the support can be profit maximizing. About 5 percent of all wage offers fall in the region. Although it is possible that this inconsistency can be attributed to sampling and measurement error, the large sample size used in the derivation suggests otherwise.

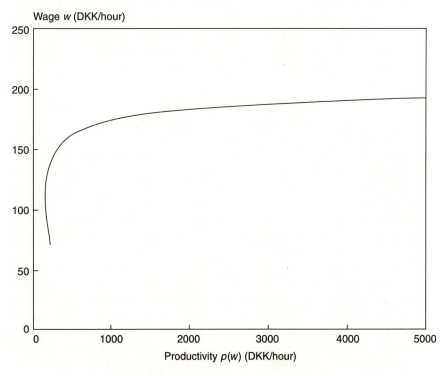

Figure 4. Inferred wage function: monopsony case.

Over the remaining range, the wage increases rapidly with productivity initially but then the rate of increase falls dramatically. Monopsony rents, as measured by profit per hour divided by the hourly wage, $(p - w)/w$, are large even at relatively low wage rates For example, at the lowest admissible wage, $w = 100$ DKK/hour, this measure of monopsony rent is 50 percent. At the median wage earned, equal to 144 DKK/hour, the ratio equals roughly 80 percent of the wage. Finally, at the ninetieth percentile, $w = 186$ DKK, the implied value of p is 2,720 DKK/hour. In this case, marginal productivity is almost fifteen times the wage! These results for the upper tail of the wage distribution, although consistent with the model, are hardly plausible.

The reason inferred monopsony rents are large is reflected in equation (26) and the shapes of $h(w)$ and $d(w)$ shown in Figure 3. The first-order condition for an optimal choice, equation (26), implies that the monopsony rent measure $(p - w)/w$ is approximately equal to the sum of the elasticities of the separation rate function and the acceptance probability function. Both $h(w)$ and $d(w)$ are relatively elastic at low wages but converge to constants as the wage tends to the upper support. In other words, a small wage differential in the lower reaches of the support has a substantial impact on an employer's ability to both attract and retain workers but the same differential in the upper reaches has little effect on either. Clearly, the reason for the differences in the response of the separation rate function $d(w)$ at different wage levels is that well-paid workers have less incentive to invest in search than low-paid workers. For the same reason, an employer is more likely to contact a lower- than a higher-paid worker given the assumption that contact rates reflect search intensity. This fact and the concentration of employment in relatively low-paying jobs combine to explain the observed variation in the elasticity of the acceptance probability $h(w)$.

3.4.2. The Monopoly Union Case

In the monopoly union case, equation (28) implies that the shape of the wage policy function depends on but is not solely determined by the elasticities of the separation and acceptance functions. The elasticity of the product of the acceptance probability and the net value of employment, $h(w)[W(w) - U]$, is also a factor in this case. Although we do not have direct evidence concerning the magnitude of the elasticity of the marginal cost of the recruiting function, $\alpha = 1$ would obtain if the cost of the recruiting function $c_f(v)$ were quadratic. The implied wage policy function in that case is illustrated in Figure 5. In the figure, the 45° ray, represented by the dotted line, is included as a visual aid.

With a quadratic recruiting cost function, the wage and offer distributions are fully admissible in the sense that the wage paid is a strictly monotonically increasing function of employer productivity over its support as required by the theory. Furthermore, the quantitative inferences are far more reasonable than for the monopsony case. The difference between a worker's product and the wage paid is zero initially but then increases with employer productivity at a more plausible rate. For example, at the tenth percentile of the wage distribution, a wage equal to 111 DKK/hour, the ratio of gross profit to the wage, $(p - w)/w$, is about 12.5 percent. At the median wage of 144 DKK/hour gross profit divided by the wage is

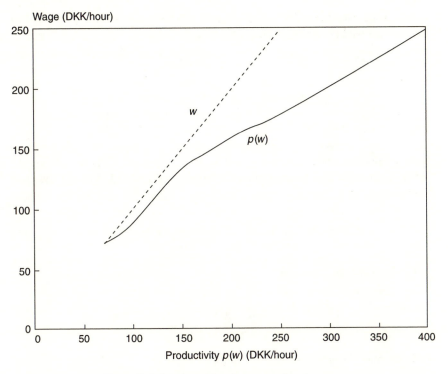

Figure 5. Inferred wage function: monopoly union case.

19.1 percent, whereas at the ninetieth percentile, 187 DKK/hour, the ratio equals 43.7 percent. In short, the monopoly union solution provides a consistent and plausible explanation of the wage offer distribution data.

3.5. The Distribution of Firm Productivity

Provided that firm size $n(p)$ is monotonic in firm productivity p, one can use information contained in the firm size distribution $Q(n)$ and the wage distribution $G(w)$ to infer both the size-wage relation and the distribution of productivity across firms. Equations (18) and (20) and the fact that the wage function $w(p)$ has a slope less than unity imply that firm size $n(p)$ is monotonically increasing in firm productivity when wages are determined by the union monopoly model. It follows that the fraction of workers employed at a wage no greater than $w = w(p)$ is the fraction of workers employed by firms with productivity no greater than p. Formally,

$$G[w(p)] = \frac{\displaystyle\int_{\underline{p}}^{p} n(x)d\Gamma(x)}{\displaystyle\int_{\underline{p}}^{\overline{p}} n(x)d\Gamma(x)}. \tag{30}$$

For the same reason, the fraction of firms of size no greater than $n(p)$ is equal to the measure with productivity no greater than p, that is,

$$Q[n(p)] = \Gamma(p) = \frac{\int_{\underline{p}}^{p} d\Gamma(x)}{\int_{\underline{p}}^{\overline{p}} d\Gamma(x)}. \tag{31}$$

By first differentiating these two equations with respect to p and then using the result to eliminate $\Gamma'(p)$, one obtains the following ordinary differential equation in $n(p)$:

$$G'[w(p)]w'(p) = \frac{n(p)\Gamma'(p)}{En} = n(p)Q'[n(p)]n'(p), \tag{32}$$

where, by a change in variable,

$$En = \int_{\underline{p}}^{\overline{p}} n(x)\Gamma'(x)dx = \int_{n(\underline{p})}^{n(\overline{p})} nQ'(n)dn \tag{33}$$

is the mean of the size distribution. Equivalently,

$$N'(w) = \frac{G'(w)}{N(w)Q'[N(w)]}, \tag{34}$$

where by definition

$$N(w) \equiv n[p(w)] \tag{35}$$

is firm size expressed as a function of the wage paid rather than productivity.

As all the terms on the right-hand side of (34) are observable, the function $N(w)$ can be computed as the particular solution to the ordinary differential equation associated with the initial condition $N(\underline{w}) = 1$, the lower support of the observed firm size distribution. The results of the calculation, which are necessarily increasing, are plotted in Figure 6. Initially, firm size $N(w)$ increases at an increasing rate but then reverses its curvature and flattens out at high levels. It is of interest to note that this relationship together with the observed size and wage distributions used to compute it imply that about half of the employed, those paid more than the median wage, work for the largest 1 percent of the firms, that is, those firms with 118 or more employees.

Given $N(w)$, equation (34) also provides the means needed to compute the distribution of productivity across employers implied by the model and the observed wage and firm size distributions. The implied density function evaluated at any wage is

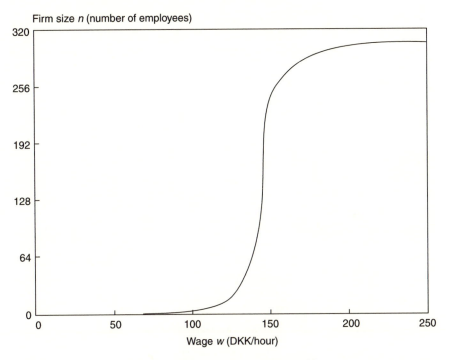

Figure 6. Firm size $N(w)$ versus wage paid.

$$\Gamma'[p(w)] = \frac{Enq[N(w)]N'(w)}{p'(w)}, \tag{36}$$

where $q(n) = Q'(n)$ is the size density. The density is plotted in Figure 7 for the monopoly union case. Although skewed, the inferred density resembles that of a log normal more than a Pareto. A simple computation using the inferred inverse of the wage function $p(w)$ yields the fact that the productivity of 99 percent of the firms ranges between 70 and 176 DKK/hour. However, only half of the privately employed Danish work force is employed by these firms. By implication, there are a very few highly productive, large, profitable, and well-paying firms in Denmark.

4. CONCLUSIONS

As a consequence of friction, search theory implies that workers accept any wage offer above some reservation value when unemployed and then seek a higher-paying job once employed at an intensity that reflects expected potential gain in future income. Given this strategy, employers with different labor productivities coexist in the market although the more productive employers find it optimal to acquire and retain larger labor forces by offering higher wages and by investing more in recruiting effort. I find that Danish data on labor turnover at the firm

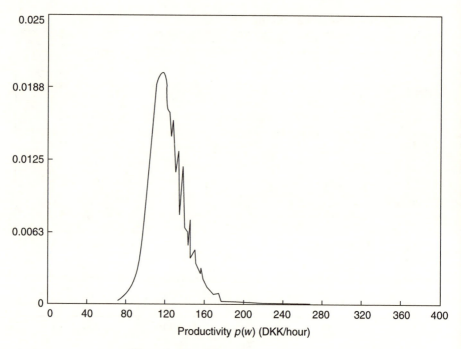

Figure 7. Inferred productivity density $\Gamma'(p)$.

level and the observed distributions of wages offered and wages earned reported in the IDA are not consistent with this explanation of wage dispersion. However, the alternative joint hypothesis that the wage paid by each firm is set by a local monopoly union and that productivity is disperse across firms can explain the observed offer and wage distribution data.

Christensen et al. (2001) demonstrate that firm separation behavior observed in the IDA supports the proposition that employed workers search at intensities that reflect the expected gain in future income attributable to search effort. Furthermore, the estimated separation function and the observed wage offer distribution imply a steady-state distribution of wages earned that is virtually identical to that observed in the data. In this chapter, I show that the estimated separation function and the acceptance probability implied by the parameters of the separation function and the wage distribution observed in the data are consistent with the hypothesis that the wage is set to maximize the product of the hire flow and the typical worker's net value of employment in the firm. Finally, the wage and size distributions found in the Danish data and the union wage model imply that the labor productivity of almost all employers is relatively low but that a few employers are very productive, large, and high paying.

Of course, there are numerous caveats, but these suggest fruitful avenues for future research. To verify the principal conclusions of this chapter, one needs actual observations on employer productivity. To the extent that firm level productivity measures exist for the Danish data, they are available only for the largest 9 percent of all private firms, those with twenty or more employees. Still, my co-authors from the separations project reported in Christensen et al. (2001) and I are currently in the process of determining the extent to which observed cross-firm differences in these measures explain observed differences in hire rates and wage offers.

Allowing for worker heterogeneity, both in the model and in the empirical analysis, is another needed extension. One should note, however, that doing so is potentially important only to the extent that worker characteristics, say, individual ability, and employer productivity are correlated since differences in the average wage paid across employers reflect only differences in employer wage policy if employer and worker characteristics are orthogonal. Of course, matching theory suggests that a positive association should exist given worker and employer complementarity in the production process. Although search theories of matching heterogeneous partnerships are in their infancy, their empirical estimation with matched worker-employer data should soon be feasible.

REFERENCES

Abowd, J. and F. Kramarz (2000a), "Inter-industry and Firm-size Wage Differentials in the United States," Cornell University Working Paper.

———— (2000b), "The Structure of Compensation in France and in the United States," Cornell University Working Paper.

Abowd, J., F. Kramarz, and D. Margolis (1999), "High Wage Workers and High Wage Firms," *Econometrica* 67:251–334.

Bontemps, C., J.-M. Robin, and G. J. van den Berg (2000), "Equilibrium Search with Continuous Productivity Dispersion: Theory and Non-Parametric Estimation," *International Economic Review* 41:305–58.

Burdett, K. and K. Judd (1983), "Equilibrium Price Dispersion," *Econometrica* 51:955–70.

Burdett, K. and D. T. Mortensen (1998), "Wage Differentials, Employer Size, and Unemployment," *International Economic Review* 39:257–73.

Butters, G. R. (1977), "Equilibrium Distributions of Sales and Advertising Prices," *Review of Economic Studies* 44:465–91.

Christensen, B. J., R. Lentz, D. T. Mortensen, G. R. Neumann, and A. Werwatz (2001), "On the Job Search and the Wage Distribution," Northwestern University Working Paper.

Davis, S. J., and J. Haltiwanger (1991), "Wage Dispersion within and between Manufacturing Plants," *Brookings Papers on Economic Activity: Microeconomics* 1991:115–80.

Dickens, W. T. and L. Katz (1987), "Inter-Industry Wage Differences and Industry Characteristics," in K. Land and J. S. Leonard, eds., *Unemployment and the Structure of the Labor Market*, Oxford: Blackwell.

Doms, M., T. Dunne and K. R. Troske (1997), "Workers, Wages, and Technology," *Quarterly Journal of Economics* 112:252–90.

Gibbons, R. and L. Katz (1992), "Does Unmeasured Ability Explain Inter-Industry Wage Differentials?," *Review of Economic Studies* 59:515–35.

Katz, L. F. and L. H. Summers (1989), "Industry Rents: Evidence and Implications," *Brookings Papers on Economic Activity: Microeconomics* 1989:209–75.

Kruger, A. B., and L. H. Summers (1988), "Efficiency Wages and the Inter-Industry Wage Structure," *Econometrica* 56:259–94.

Mortensen, D. T. (1970), "A Theory of Wage and Employment Dynamics," in E. S. Phelps, A. A. Alchian, C. C. Holt, D. T. Mortensen, G. C. Archibald, R. E. Lucas, Jr., L. A. Rapping, S. G. Winter, Jr., J. P. Gould, D. F. Gordon, A. Hynes, D. A. Nichols, P. J. Taubman, and M. Wilkinson, eds., *Microeconomic Foundations of Employment and Inflation Theory*, New York: Norton, pp. 167–211.

———— (1990), "Equilibrium Wage Distributions: A Synthesis," in J. Hartog, G. Ridder, and J. Theeuwes, eds., *Panel Data and Labor Market Studies*. Amsterdam: North-Holland.

———— (2000) "Equilibrium Unemployment with Wage Posting: Burdett-Mortensen Meet Pissarides," in H. Bunzel, B. J. Christensen, P. Jensen, N. M. Kiefer, and D. T. Mortensen, eds., *Panel Data and Structural Labour Market Model,* Amsterdam: Elsevier.

Murphy, K. M. and R. Topel (1987), "Unemployment, Risk, and Earnings: Testing for Equalizing Wage Differences in the Labor Market," in K. Land and J. S. Leonard, eds., *Unemployment and the Structure of the Labor Market*, Oxford: Blackwell.

Oi, W. Y. and T. L. Idson (1999), "Firm Size and Wages," in O. Ashenfelter and D. Card, eds., *Handbook of Labor Economics,* Vol. 3B, Amsterdam: Elsevier, pp. 2165–214.

Phelps, E. S. (1970), "Money Wage Dynamics and Market Equilibrium," in E. S. Phelps, A. A. Alchian, C. C. Holt, D. T. Mortensen, G. C. Archibald, R. E. Lucas, Jr., L. A. Rapping, S. G. Winter, Jr., J. P. Gould, D. F. Gordon, A. Hynes, D. A. Nichols, P. J. Taubman, and M. Wilkinson, *Microeconomic Foundations of Employment and Inflation Theory,* New York: Norton, pp. 124–66.

Rosholm, M., and M. Svarer (2000), "Wage, Training, Turnover in a Search-Matching Model," CLS Working Paper No. WP1999 003.

Rothschild, M. (1973), "Models of Market Organization with Imperfect Information: A Survey," *Journal of Political Economy* 81:1283–308.

Samuelson, P. A. (1955), *Economics: An Introductory Analysis*, 3rd edn., New York: McGraw-Hill.

— 15 —

Company Start-Up Costs and Employment

CHRISTOPHER A. PISSARIDES

1. INTRODUCTION

This chapter is a contribution to the literature that explains cross-country differences in employment or unemployment rates in terms of structural models of the economy. Edmund Phelps contributed to this literature in 1994 with his important book *Structural Slumps*.[1] My focus in this chapter is on a factor that has been neglected in previous studies—the regulation of new company start-ups.

With the increasing interdependence of the world's industrial economies, differences in the performance of labor markets are more likely the outcome of different institutional structures than of different experiences with macroeconomic or policy shocks. Recent evidence has revealed large differences in the regulatory environment for company start-ups across countries, even within the OECD.[2] The important quantifiable variables in this framework are currently policy related: the legal rules and regulations that a new entrepreneur has to comply with before starting his or her new company. But other factors, for example, those related to the availability of finance and the stigma attached to bankruptcy, are also important ingredients of this institutional structure.

Company start-up costs influence overall employment patterns through the birth (and perhaps death) of new firms, so a prerequisite for their importance is that company births should account for a nontrivial fraction of total net job creation. Although there is controversy about the precise role of small firms in the job generation process, a consensus view is emerging that over the last 30 years small firms have become more important job creators than used to be the case. This change is partly due to the shift from manufacturing to services, where there is a higher concentration of small firms, but other factors may be present too. It has even been claimed that most of the gap in net job creation between Europe and the Unites States is in the small-business sector (OECD, 1987). Moreover, most net job creation in that sector is done by new entrants rather than by expansions

---

1. Earlier seminal contributions include the books by Bruno and Sachs (1985) and Layard et al. (1991). For more recent contributions see Blanchard (1999) and Blanchard and Wolfers (2000).

2. For preliminary results with OECD data see Fonseca et al. (2001). For a different and more comprehensive set of data, covering seventy-five countries, see Djankov et al. (2000).

of existing firms.[3] Thus, the channels through which start-up costs can influence aggregate performance appear well established in the labor markets of Europe and North America.

Although I discuss some preliminary empirical work with aggregate OECD data, my primary objective in this chapter is to discuss the theory underlying the connection between start-up costs and employment performance. Detailed empirical testing is postponed to future work. I strip the model of many important elements that careful empirical study has to take into account in order to focus on the key links between start-up costs and employment. The model that I use builds on another of Phelps's seminal contributions—search equilibrium—but uses the more recent framework developed in my own book (Pissarides, 2000) and the ideas about entrepreneurship used by Lucas (1978) in his "span-of-control" model.

In order to find a role for start-up costs in the determination of employment there has to be a precise definition of the firm and the incentives that entrepreneurs have for creating firms. I define a firm as a collection of jobs, each one occupied by a worker or vacant, managed by an entrepreneur. The entrepreneur is both the owner and the manager of the firm. The overall cost of managing a firm depends on the number of jobs managed and on a parameter specific to the manager that summarizes the agent's "managerial skill" or "entrepreneurship." Agents choose whether to become entrepreneurs or workers by maximizing expected lifetime income. I show that the choice of career is determined by a cut-off managerial ability, with more-able managers choosing to set up their own firms and create jobs. Employment is determined by an aggregate matching function that matches the posted jobs with the agents who choose to become workers.

In contrast to Lucas's (1978) model, managerial skill in my model does not influence the firm's total factor productivity. More-able managers in my model spend fewer resources on managing their firm but produce the same output for each job that they own as less-able managers. This property enables the derivation of a conventional search and matching equilibrium conditional on the numbers of managers and workers. I do not consider the role of capital and savings, although their introduction should not be difficult, given existing results in search theory.

Section 2 describes the theoretical framework and the key assumption about managers and workers. Section 3 derives the decentralized search equilibrium without start-up costs. Section 4 introduces three different kinds of start-up costs and studies their roles in the determination of employment. Section 5 presents some preliminary evidence from seventeen OECD countries supporting the link between start-up costs and employment.

2. THE ECONOMY

The economy consists of a continuum of infinitely lived individuals in the unit interval. Each individual can be either a worker or a manager. Managers establish a firm that they own, create jobs, and recruit workers. A manager can manage many

---

3. See the special issue of *Business Economics*, July 1994, for extensive discussion of the role of small firms in the U.S. economy.

jobs at the same time but a worker can only occupy one job at a time. A firm is a collection of jobs headed by a single manager.[4]

All agents have linear utility functions and capital markets are perfect and characterized by a safe interest rate r. Agents decide to become workers or managers by maximizing utility under rational expectations over their horizon. They are identical in all respects except for their managerial ability, or "entrepreneurship." Managerial ability is summarized in a function that gives the cost of managing jobs. The cost of managing α jobs is given by $xg(\alpha)$, with $x \in [x_0, \infty)$ and $g(\alpha)$ increasing and convex. The parameter x is specific to each individual and has known distribution $F(x)$ over the population. Good managers have a low x and poor managers have a high x. Managerial ability influences only the cost of management. It does not influence the productivity of the worker or manager.

When a firm is first created, the manager posts α job vacancies and workers arrive according to the parameters of a matching technology. The number α is chosen optimally to maximize profit, so in general it will depend on x. Because a firm is owned and headed by a single manager, we can identify firms with managers and with the parameter x. We can therefore refer to firm x or manager x. When the firm is mature some of its $\alpha(x)$ jobs will be occupied and some vacant. We refer to the occupied jobs as employment in firm x and denote it by $n(x)$. Posted vacancies in firm x are then given by $\alpha(x) - n(x) \geq 0$. The cost of managing a job is the same irrespective of whether it is vacant or filled, an assumption that can easily be relaxed.

Each occupied job produces a constant flow of output y and continues producing this output until the worker leaves. In the simple version of the model in this chapter I assume that there are no productivity shocks and that the only reason for an interruption of production is an exogenous process that separates workers from jobs. The separation process could be interpreted as exogenous death and replacement of the worker or manager, with only trivial modifications to the argument. I simplify the exposition by assuming that there is no death and replacement; all agents have infinite horizons but they are separated at a constant Poisson rate λ. After separation the job is readvertised as a vacancy and the worker becomes unemployed to search for another job. Unemployed workers enjoy income flow b but job vacancies produce and cost nothing (with the exception of their management costs).

The allocation of jobs to workers is modeled as in the simplest case analyzed in Pissarides (2000, chap. 1), with an important modification necessitated by the introduction of managers. Suppose at some time t entrepreneurs have created and are managing a total of $n + v$ jobs, with n of them occupied by workers and v of them vacant. There are $n + u$ workers in this market, one in each occupied job and u unemployed. The v vacant jobs and u unemployed workers engage in a process of search and matching governed by an aggregate matching function

---

4. Although I do not refer explicitly to self-employment, the model can easily be extended to deal with it. For example, a self-employed individual can be interpreted as a firm that yields some output with no workers apart from the manager. I simplify the exposition by assuming that although managers are never unemployed, the firm cannot yield output without workers.

with constant returns to scale. It is shown in Pissarides (2000, chap. 1) that under these assumptions the arrival process can be summarized by a single parameter, the *tightness* of the market $\theta \equiv v/u$, such that workers arrive to jobs according to a Poisson rate $q(\theta)$, which has elasticity in the interval $(-1, 0)$, and jobs arrive to unemployed workers according to a related Poisson rate $\theta q(\theta)$, with elasticity in the interval $(0, 1)$ and with

$$\lim_{\theta \to \infty} q(\theta) = \lim_{\theta \to 0} \theta q(\theta) = 0, \tag{1}$$

$$\lim_{\theta \to 0} q(\theta) = \lim_{\theta \to \infty} \theta q(\theta) = \infty. \tag{2}$$

3. DECENTRALIZED SEARCH EQUILIBRIUM

There are several ways in which a decentralized search equilibrium can be specified and solved. The key properties of a search equilibrium, which were noted by Phelps in his two seminal contributions in search theory (Phelps et al., 1970; Phelps 1972), are first, that search frictions introduce monopoly rents, and second, in the decentralized solution the dependence of the aggregate arrival rates on individual actions are ignored. The former implies that we need a monopoly solution to wage determination and the latter that there are congestion externalities that are likely to be ignored in the individual optimization problems. In this chapter I study the decentralized equilibrium when wages split the monopoly rents from each job between the worker and the manager according to the arbitrary constant $\beta \in (0, 1)$, with β denoting the share of the worker in each job. This solution to wage determination is different from the "wage-posting" solution adopted by Phelps (1970, 1994) (and more recently by Burdett and Mortensen, 1998, among others). It can be derived from the solution to the static Nash bargain, when the bargain takes place between isolated pairs of managers and workers, but I do not explore its foundations here and treat β as an arbitrary constant.

3.1. Managers and Workers

If an individual decides to become a worker, she can search for a job offered by a manager. If she becomes an entrepreneur, she can create α jobs and post vacancies waiting for workers to arrive. Individuals decide whether to become managers or workers by maximizing income over an infinite horizon, with a constant discount rate r.

Let U be the present discounted value (PDV) of income of the searching worker and V the expected PDV of profit income from a vacant job. Both U and V are independent of the individual's managerial ability x. The cost of managing α jobs is $xg(\alpha)$, irrespective of whether they are occupied or vacant. Therefore, with infinite horizon, in the steady state the total management cost paid by an x individual who creates α jobs is $xg(\alpha)/r$. By creating one more job a manager can enjoy additional income over the infinite horizon of V for an additional lifetime management cost of $xg'(\alpha)/r$. Therefore, the optimal α satisfies

$$xg'[\alpha(x)] = rV. \tag{3}$$

The marginal cost of managing a job is equal to the "permanent income" generated by a new job vacancy, the marginal revenue from the posting of one more job vacancy. It is constant across firms because V is independent of the manager's ability. This immediately gives the distribution of jobs across managers in terms of the marginal cost of management and the distribution of abilities. If two managers have ability x and x', respectively, and create α and α' jobs, respectively, they satisfy $xg'(\alpha) = x'g'(\alpha')$. For example, if $g(\alpha) = \gamma\alpha^2/2$, $\alpha' = \alpha x/x'$.

If an x individual becomes an entrepreneur and creates $\alpha(x)$ jobs, her initial net expected payoff is $\alpha(x)V - xg[\alpha(x)]/r$. If she becomes a worker, her initial payoff is U. Therefore, individuals whose x satisfies the following inequality become entrepreneurs:

$$\max_{\alpha}[\alpha V - xg(\alpha)/r] \geq U. \tag{4}$$

As expected, the maximization condition is (3). Agents who become entrepreneurs will post the maximum number of jobs immediately.

Individuals who have been entrepreneurs for a while will have some jobs filled and some vacant. Because of the obvious property that filled jobs do not have lower expected payoffs than vacant jobs, no agent who satisfies inequality (4) will drop out of entrepreneurship and become a worker after some jobs are filled. Similarly, individuals who do not satisfy (4), and are therefore workers, will eventually find jobs. Because the expected returns from employment are at least as high as the expected returns from unemployment, if (4) is not satisfied for an unemployed worker it will not be satisfied for an employed worker. Therefore, (4) is a general condition for the allocation of agents between entrepreneurship and worker status.

The functions V and U are both independent of x by assumption, so (4) satisfies the reservation property: there is a reservation managerial ability R, such that an x individual becomes an entrepreneur if $x \leq R$; otherwise she becomes a worker. The reservation ability satisfies

$$R = \frac{\alpha(R)rV - rU}{g[\alpha(R)]} \tag{5}$$

with $Rg'[\alpha(R)] = rV$. Conditions (4) and (5) state the property that the income flow from the α jobs, $\alpha(x)rV$, has to cover their management cost and the manager's loss of the expected returns from search.

3.2. Expected Payoffs

The expected payoffs to workers and job owners are derived as in conventional search models. The PDV of income of a posted vacancy V satisfies

$$rV = q(\theta)(J - V), \tag{6}$$

where J are the expected returns from an occupied job, which satisfy

$$rJ = y - w - \lambda(J - V). \tag{7}$$

The job switches between employment and vacancy according to the transition rates $q(\theta)$ and λ. When it is vacant it produces and costs nothing but when it is filled it produces y, yielding net income $y - w$ to the manager and w to the worker. Management costs can be ignored in these calculations because they are the same for both vacancies and filled jobs.

The unemployed worker's PDV of income, U, satisfies

$$rU = b + \theta q(\theta)(W - U), \tag{8}$$

where W denotes the expected returns from holding a job and satisfies

$$rW = w - \lambda(W - U). \tag{9}$$

The worker moves from unemployment to employment and back at rates $\theta q(\theta)$ and λ, respectively, with income in unemployment given by b and in employment by w.

Wages share the surplus from the job match according to the fixed parameter $\beta \in (0, 1)$. Total surplus is given by $J - V + W - U$, with $J - V$ going to the owner of the job and $W - U$ going to the worker. Therefore wages solve

$$(1 - \beta)(W - U) = \beta(J - V). \tag{10}$$

From (8), (10), and (6), we obtain

$$rU = b + \frac{\beta\theta}{1 - \beta}rV. \tag{11}$$

Adding up the value equations (6)–(9) and making use of the sharing rule (10) to substitute out $W - U$ and $J - V$ in terms of the surplus from the job, we obtain the following expression for the surplus:

$$J - V + W - U = \frac{y - b}{(1 - \beta)q(\theta) + r + \lambda + \beta\theta q(\theta)}. \tag{12}$$

Equations (6), (10), and (12) yield

$$rV = \frac{(1 - \beta)q(\theta)(y - b)}{(1 - \beta)q(\theta) + r + \lambda + \beta\theta q(\theta)}. \tag{13}$$

We can therefore write $V = V(\theta)$, with $V'(\theta) < 0$. This is an important property: Intuitively, the larger the number of jobs posted by all firms for each unemployed worker, the less the expected profit of each firm from posting one more vacancy. The reason for this result is the congestion externality caused by the posting of vacancies because production is not characterized by diminishing returns to the number of jobs. However, the implications for equilibrium are similar. At the aggregate level, the marginal profit from one more job falls as the number of jobs increases.

Now given (13), (11) implies that $U = U(\theta)$ with $U'(\theta) > 0$. Workers are made better off when more jobs are posted for each unemployed worker. Once again, the reason for this result is the search externality associated with these models.

Note finally that although we cannot say in general whether the PDV of income is higher or lower for a worker or her manager, it follows immediately from the value equations that for as long as $y > b$, a necessary condition for a nontrivial equilibrium is $J \geq V$ and $W \geq U$; that is, both managers and workers are better off when they are producing than when they are searching. These inequalities confirm that if the career choice condition (4) is satisfied for unemployed agents then it is certainly satisfied for employed agents.

3.3. Equilibrium

An equilibrium is defined as a reservation managerial ability R; a market tightness θ; and distributions of jobs, employment, and wages $[\alpha(x), n(x), w(x)]$ across managers, given the distribution of abilities $F(x)$. The equilibrium satisfies the value equations (6)–(9), the wage sharing rule (10), the career choice rule (4), the marginal job entry rule (3), and the equation for the evolution of employment in each firm,

$$\dot{n}(x) = [\alpha(x) - n(x)]\theta q(\theta) - \lambda n(x). \tag{14}$$

I illustrate the solution with the help of Figure 1.

The results in (11) and (13) imply that the equilibrium R, which satisfies (5), is a monotonically decreasing function of aggregate tightness, θ. When tightness is higher, managers find it more difficult to recruit workers, so fewer individuals decide to start their own companies and more become workers. This relationship is shown in (R, θ) space as a downward-sloping curve labeled "entrepreneurship" (see Figure 1). The limits to this curve are derived as follows.

If $\theta = 0$, equations (13) and (1) and (2) imply $rV = y - b$ and (11) implies $rU = b$. Therefore, from (5) we derive $Rg[\alpha(R)] = \alpha(R)(y - b) - b$, where $Rg'[\alpha(R)] = y - b$. This gives the maximum feasible value of R. It also follows from (4) that for any choice of $\alpha(x)$, in a feasible equilibrium $\alpha(x)V(\theta) \geq U(\theta) + xg[\alpha(x)] > 0$. Thus we define $\tilde{\theta}$ by $V(\tilde{\theta}) = 0$ and θ_0 by $\alpha(x_0)V(\theta_0) = U(\theta_0) + x_0 g[\alpha(x_0)]$, where x_0 is the ability of the best manager. Equilibrium is nontrivial only for values of θ that satisfy $\theta \leq \theta_0 < \tilde{\theta}$, where $\tilde{\theta}$ is the equilibrium value of tightness in models that derive the demand for labor from a zero-profit condition on the value of a new vacancy (as in Pissarides, 2000; of course, if there are management costs in these models, the zero-profit condition would have to take them into account). The value θ_0 is the tightness level at which finding a new worker is so difficult that only the most able manager in the market will choose to become an employer (see Figure 1).

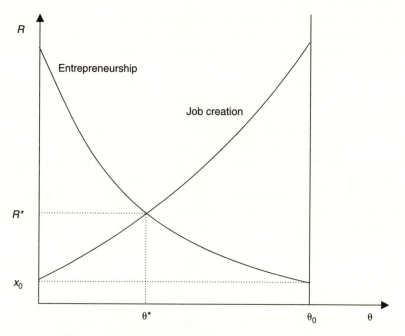

Figure 1. Equilibrium entrepreneurship and labor market tightness.

In order to derive a second equilibrium relationship between θ and R, consider the definition of θ as the ratio of aggregate vacancies to unemployment. With each firm owner creating $\alpha(x)$ jobs, aggregate vacancies for any aggregate employment level n measure $\int_{x_0}^{R} \alpha(x) dF(x) - n$. With all agents with managerial ability at least as good as R becoming managers, unemployment is $1 - F(R) - n$, where $1 - F(R)$ is the total number of workers in the economy and n is their employment level. Hence,

$$\theta = \frac{\displaystyle\int_{x_0}^{R} \alpha(x) dF(x) - n}{1 - F(R) - n}. \tag{15}$$

The evolution of aggregate employment is given by aggregating over x in (14). In the steady state, employment in each firm satisfies

$$n(x) = \frac{q(\theta)}{q(\theta) + \lambda} \alpha(x). \tag{16}$$

Aggregating over x we obtain one expression for aggregate employment in the steady state:

$$n = \frac{q(\theta)}{q(\theta) + \lambda} \int_{x_0}^{R} \alpha(x) dF(x). \tag{17}$$

A second expression for steady-state employment can be derived by focusing on worker flows. The flow of unemployed workers into employment is $\theta q(\theta)[1 - F(R) - n]$ and the flow of employed workers into unemployment is λn. Equating the two flows gives steady-state employment

$$n = \frac{\theta q(\theta)}{\theta q(\theta) + \lambda}[1 - F(R)]. \tag{18}$$

Substitution from (18) and (17) into (15) yields

$$\frac{\theta q(\theta) + \theta \lambda}{\theta q(\theta) + \lambda} = \frac{\displaystyle\int_{x_0}^{R} \alpha(x)dF(x)}{1 - F(R)}. \tag{19}$$

Now, from (3) and (13) each $\alpha(x)$ is a function of x and $V(\theta)$, with

$$\frac{\partial \alpha(x)}{\partial \theta} = \frac{\partial \alpha(x)}{\partial V}\frac{\partial V}{\partial \theta} < 0 \qquad \forall x. \tag{20}$$

Total differentiation of (19) therefore gives $d\theta/dR > 0$: At higher R there are more managers and fewer workers, so more jobs are created and posted for each job seeker. We refer to this curve in (R, θ) space as job creation. As $R \to x_0$, $\theta \to 0$, giving the shape of the curve shown in Figure 1.

Obtaining equilibrium is now straightforward. The equilibrium R and θ are unique and are shown by the intersection of the two curves in Figure 1. With R and θ known, V and U can be obtained from (11) and (13), and (3) then gives $\alpha(x)$ for each firm x. With knowledge of $\alpha(x)$, employment in each firm is obtained from (16). To obtain wages, note that the value equation (7) can be rearranged to yield

$$J - V = \frac{y - w - rV}{r + \lambda} \tag{21}$$

and the one for W, equation (9), yields

$$W - U = \frac{w - rU}{r + \lambda}. \tag{22}$$

Substitution into the sharing rule (10) gives

$$w = (1 - \beta)rU + \beta(y - rV), \tag{23}$$

which can be solved for wages. It is noteworthy that wages are common across all jobs and managers: Better managers do not pay more, despite the decentralized sharing rule and the frictions that do not eliminate monopoly rents.

4. THE ROLE OF START-UP COSTS

In the equilibrium derived in the preceding section agents can become managers and set up a firm without any fixed costs or waiting time. Evidence, however, points to large start-up costs, partly in the form of legal procedures that have to be satisfied before a business firm can open its doors, partly in terms of a waiting time for the permit to arrive, and partly in the form of a fee that has to be paid to the authorities. Our framework is ideally suited to the introduction of costs of this kind. Although in the simple version of the model that I describe here all costs have a similar impact on the equilibrium allocation of agents and job creation, I consider separately the role of three distinct costs.

First, an agent who decides to become an entrepreneur has to start legal procedures for the creation of her company. Next, a permit giving the license to start operating comes with some randomness. Finally, when the permit arrives, the entrepreneur has to pay a fee to the authorities to receive the registration documents. I assume that permits arrive stochastically, at a rate $a > 0$. The expected waiting time for a new company is $1/a$. This rate is influenced mainly by policy, although in many countries it is possible to speed up the procedure by paying "bribes" (see Djankov et al., 2000). During the waiting time, the entrepreneur has to give up her worker status and pay some out-of-pocket costs to go through the necessary procedures. I represent these costs as a flow $c \geq 0$, paid until the permit arrives. When the permit arrives, a fee $s \geq 0$ is paid and the company starts operation.

A new company headed by an individual of ability x starts operations with $\alpha(x)$ posted vacancies, which satisfy the marginal condition (3). The value of the firm at start-up is $\alpha(x)V(\theta) - xg[\alpha(x)]$, which I denote for simplicity by $S(x, \theta)$, S_x, $S_\theta < 0$. The introduction of the start-up costs does not alter this value for given θ and x, so its solution is known from the preceding analysis.

Let the entrepreneur's optimal PDV of income when the decision is made to apply for a new company be Q. With discount rate r and the stationary policy variables a, c, and s, this value satisfies the Bellman equation,

$$rQ = -c + a[S(x, \theta) - s - Q]. \tag{24}$$

The entrepreneur pays c per period until a permit arrives, which changes her state from Q to S, for a fee s. Solving (24) for Q gives

$$Q(a, c, s, \theta; x) = \frac{a}{r+a} S(x, \theta) - \frac{c + as}{r+a}. \tag{25}$$

Given knowledge of $S(x, \theta)$, $Q(\cdot)$ is immediately obtained from (25) because r, a, c, and s are all parameters.

Equation (25) implies that for given x and θ, the value of applying for a new firm falls in the costs c and s and rises in the arrival rate of the permit a (and so falls in the expected waiting time $1/a$). An x individual will apply for a new company if $Q(a, c, s, \theta; x) \geq U(\theta)$. Because $Q(\cdot)$ falls monotonically in x, a reservation rule similar to the one in (5) is again satisfied. At the optimal R,

$$\frac{a}{r+a} S(R, \theta) - \frac{c+as}{r+a} = U(\theta). \tag{26}$$

Equation (26) can be represented in (R, θ) space as a downward-sloping curve similar to the entrepreneurship curve of Figure 1, but now shifts down in the costs c and s and in the expected delay $1/a$. The start-up costs do not influence any of the other expressions in the derivation of equilibrium because workers arrive and wage determination takes place after the company is set up and the costs paid.

The influence of start-up costs can be derived with the help of Figure 2. Start-up costs shift the entrepreneurship curve down and so reduce the fraction of the population that becomes entrepreneurs. Employment falls for two reasons. First, because entrepreneurs have higher employment rates than workers, the shift from managers to workers reduces employment. We refer to this as the *composition* effect of start-up costs. Overall employment is given by the sum of the number of managers and the aggregate employment of workers:

$$F(R) + n = \frac{\lambda F(R) + \theta q(\theta)}{\lambda + \theta q(\theta)}. \tag{27}$$

The composition effect is shown by a lower $F(R)$.

Second, with fewer entrepreneurs, job creation is lower, so fewer workers find jobs. We refer to this as the *job creation* effect of start-up costs. It is shown in (27) by a lower $\theta q(\theta)$.

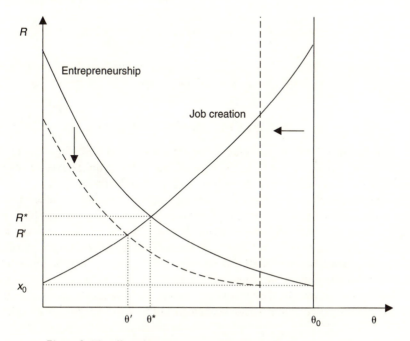

Figure 2. The effect of start-up costs on entrepreneurship and job creation.

Start-up costs reduce market tightness and so through (13) increase the expected profit from a new vacancy. This is an equilibrium response to the costs: New entrepreneurs have to pay the start-up costs and so need higher expected profit from new jobs to compensate for them. The costs are borne by workers in the form of higher unemployment, lower wages, and lower PDV of income of both employed and unemployed persons, implied by (11) and (23).

However, the number of jobs in each existing firm increases because of the increase in the expected profit per job, as implied by (3) and (20). Start-up costs protect the incumbents, who now make more profit per job and create more jobs. But the market as a whole suffers, because the number of entrepreneurs now falls and there is less aggregate job creation. This is what Djankov et al. (2000) call the "grabbing-hand" view of regulation. Following Stigler's analysis of regulation, they argue that one of the reasons for regulation is to make entry more difficult and create rents for incumbents. Their second version of the grabbing-hand, what they call the "tollbooth view" of entry costs, is also satisfied by the model. According to this version the reason for start-up costs is for the politicians to collect revenue, which is represented in the model by the two cost variables c and s.[5]

Our model can also be used to analyze the impact of bribes. It is asserted by many (see again Djankov et al., 2000) that entrepreneurs can pay bribes to speed up the arrival of permits for business start-ups. Let the bribe be a payment p, made when the permit arrives (the analysis is similar if it is paid during the waiting period with no guarantee of a faster arrival). The bribe speeds up arrival by increasing the arrival rate a: let $a = a(p)$, where $a'(p) > 0$. Then (24) changes to

$$rQ = \max_p \{-c + a(p)[S(x, \theta) - s - p - Q]\}. \tag{28}$$

The optimal bribe increases in the expected payoff $S(x, \theta)$ and the recurring cost c but decreases in the fee s under standard restrictions.

5. SOME PRELIMINARY EVIDENCE

Several factors related to policy have been identified as contributing to country differences in employment or unemployment rates. The problem that has to be confronted when considering the influence of company start-up costs is how to distinguish the influence of those costs from that of other related variables, given that a country that has a lot of regulation in company start-ups is also likely to have a lot of regulation elsewhere. My modest objective in this section is to look at some partial correlations between start-up costs and employment performance and at the relation between start-up costs and another much-researched regulation candidate, employment protection legislation.

Table 1 reports two sources of data for start-up costs for major countries of the OECD. The first two columns show data gathered by Logotech for the European

---

5. Their first, Pigovian view, that regulation gives consumers a "helping hand" by ensuring that only good entrepreneurs start up is not in the model. They do not find evidence for it.

Table 1. Company Start-Up Costs, 1997–1998

Country	Procedures (1)	Weeks (2)	Index (3)	Procedures (4)	Days (5)	Cost (6)
Australia	6.5	1	2.47	3	3	0.021
Austria	10	8	7.03	12	154	0.454
Belgium	7	6	5.12	8	42	0.010
Denmark	2	1	1.11	5	21	0.014
Finland	7	6	5.12	4	32	0.012
France	16	6	7.85	16	66	0.197
Germany	10	16	11.03	7	90	0.085
Greece	28	6.5	11.73	13	53	0.480
Ireland	15	3	6.04	4	25	0.114
Italy	25	10	12.57	11	121	0.247
Japan	14	3	5.74	11	50	0.114
Luxembourg	5	2	2.51			
Netherlands	9	12	8.73	8	68	0.190
Portugal	10	8	7.03	12	99	0.313
Spain	17	23.5	16.90	11	83	0.127
Sweden	7	3	3.62	4	17	0.025
United Kingdom	4	1	1.71	7	11	0.006
United States	3.5	1.5	1.81	4	7	0.010

Source: Djankov et al. (2000).

Notes: Columns (1) and (4) give the number of procedures that a new company has to go through before starting operations. Column (1) is from Fonseca et al. (2001) and column (4) from Djankov et al. (2000). Columns (2) and (5) give the average length of time, in weeks and business days, respectively, needed to complete these procedures. Sources as above. Column (3) combines the first two measures according to the formula (number of weeks + number of procedures/average procedures per week)/2. The average is computed as the ratio of the sum of procedures to the sum of weeks, so the index has the sample mean of weeks. Column (6) gives the expected financial cost as a percent of GDP per capita in 1997.

Commission and reported by Fonseca et al. (2001). Column (1) gives the number of procedures needed to register a company. A procedure is anything that has to be done in an office outside the company's premises, such as filling in a form and submitting it for obtaining a VAT number. Column (2) gives the average number of weeks that lapse between the first application for a start-up and the first legal trading day. Column 3 combines these series into a single index. In order to compile the index, we first calculate how many procedures are on average completed within a week in the sample as a whole. We then divide the actual number of procedures that a country requires by the average and obtain a series that has the dimension of weeks but is a linear transformation of the number of procedures. Our index is the average of the actual number of weeks needed and the constructed series, so it is an index that adjusts the original series for weeks up or down according to whether the country requires more or fewer procedures than the sample average.

Columns 4–6 report data compiled by Djankov et al. (2000). Again, the first two columns show the number of procedures and the expected waiting time, in business days. Column 6 gives the expected cost as a percent of GDP per capita in 1997.

Although there are differences between the two data sources, the correlations are high. Table 2 reports correlation coefficients. The correlation between the

Table 2. Correlations

	Employment	Unemployment	Procedures 1	Procedures 2	Index
Unemployment	−0.82				
Procedures 1	−0.81	0.56			
Procedures 2	−0.49	0.28	0.64		
Index	−0.80	0.70	0.77	0.59	
EPL	−0.60	0.47	0.70	0.76	0.75

Notes: Employment is defined as the ratio of employment to population of working age in 1998; unemployment is the standardized unemployment rate in 1998; procedures 1 is the series shown in column (1) of Table 1; procedures 2 is shown in column (4) of Table 1; index is the index of start-up costs shown in column (6) of Table 1; and EPL is the OECD's index of employment protection legislation in the late 1990s.

two series for procedures is 0.64, which is almost identical to the correlation between the two series for waiting times (not reported in the table). The table also shows the correlations between the start-up series and the OECD's index for employment protection legislation, which is representative of labor market regulation. The correlation is positive and over 0.70 with all measures of start-up costs, indicating that countries with a lot of regulation of company start-ups also have a lot of labor regulation.

The correlations between employment-to-population ratios and the measures for start-up costs are better than the respective correlations with unemployment. The series compiled by Fonseca et al. (2001) gives better correlations, which are in turn better than the correlations between employment and employment protection. Figure 3 shows the correlation between the index for start-up costs and the employment-to-population ratio (which is about the same as the one with the

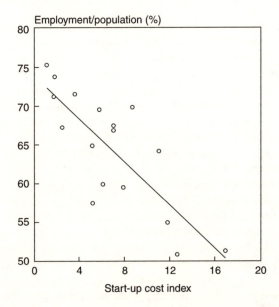

Figure 3. Start-up costs and employment (OECD countries, 1998).

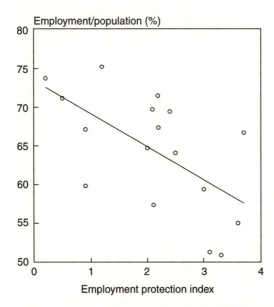

Figure 4. Employment protection legislation and employment (OECD countries, 1998).

number of procedures). The correlation is better than the one between employment and employment protection shown in Figure 4 (0.80 versus 0.60). Figures 5 and 6 show the partial correlations between unemployment and the respective measures of regulation. Again, although the fit is not as good as for employment, it is better with our index of start-up costs than with employment protection legislation.

Despite the correlation between start-up costs and employment protection, the partial correlations give encouraging results about the likely importance of start-up costs in the explanation of OECD employment. With only seventeen observations not much more can be said at this stage. However, a simple regression of employment rates on the start-up index (or the number of procedures) and employment protection gives a significant result for start-up costs (t-statistic -3.25) but not for EPL (t-statistic -0.02), with an R^2 of 0.64. If the dependent variable is unemployment, the t-statistic on start-up costs is 2.75 and on employment protection -0.46, with $R^2 = 0.49$. It is intended to test formally the propositions of this chapter in future work.

6. CONCLUSIONS

The motivation for this chapter is very much the same as in Phelps's (1994) book *Structural Slumps*: The factors that can explain the differences in labor market performance across the OECD are "structural," and should be sought in the institutional structures of the countries. The factor discussed here is one neglected by previous studies—the regulatory framework for the establishment of new companies. I have shown how the costs that governments impose on new entrepreneurs can give rise to differences in equilibrium employment rates within a fairly standard

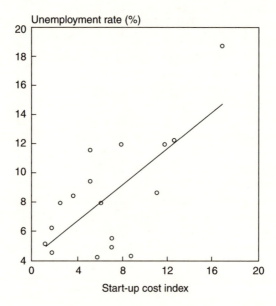

Figure 5. Start-up costs and unemployment (OECD countries, 1998).

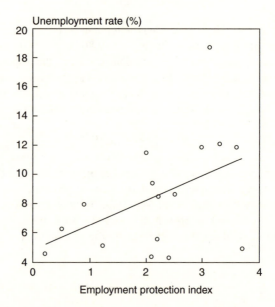

Figure 6. Unemployment and employment protection legislation (OECD countries, 1998).

model of equilibrium search with career choice. A preliminary examination of the data shows that there are large differences across the OECD in company start-up costs and that these costs are strongly correlated with employment performance. Of course, although lower costs of entering an activity in the labor market are obviously better than higher costs, this chapter has nothing to say about the welfare aspects of regulation in business start-ups. Regulation is exogenous in the model and its implications for the labor market are the trivial ones of imposing some entry costs on new entrepreneurs. My purpose was to examine the extent to which the different entry costs imposed by governments across essentially similar economies have implications for the observed differences in labor market performance. Fewer costs are not necessarily better than more costs along all their dimensions. For example, in models with imperfect information about the manager's ability or her motivation, high start-up costs may play the useful role of screening out poor managers.

The next step in this research is a more general model of employment determination that can distinguish between the regulation of entry and other types of regulations. I have made a beginning in this chapter by looking at labor regulation in the form of employment protection legislation. Although the correlation between start-up costs and employment protection measures is positive and high, start-up costs appear to be better correlated with employment performance than is employment protection. The welfare features of different aspects of regulation and start-up costs also have to be examined before policy recommendations can be made.

REFERENCES

Blanchard, O. J. (1999), "European Unemployment: The Role of Shocks and Institutions," Baffi Lecture, Rome.

Blanchard, O. J. and J. Wolfers (2000), "The Role of Shocks and Institutions in the Rise of European Unemployment: The Aggregate Evidence," *Economic Journal* 110:C1–33.

Bruno, M. and J. D. Sachs (1985), *Economics of Worldwide Stagflation*, Cambridge: Harvard University Press.

Burdett, K. and D. T. Mortensen (1998), "Wage Differentials, Employer Size, and Unemployment," *International Economic Review* 39:257–73.

Djankov, S., R. La Porta, F. Lopez-de-Silanes, and A. Shleifer (2000), "The Regulation of Entry," Harvard Institute of Economic Research, Discussion Paper No. 1904.

Fonseca, R., P. Lopez-Garcia, and C. A. Pissarides (2001), "Entrepreneurship, Start-up Costs and Employment," *European Economic Review* 45:692–705.

Layard, R., S. Nickell, and R. Jackman (1991), *Unemployment: Macroeconomic Performance of the Labour Market*, Oxford: Oxford University Press.

Lucas, R. E. (1978), "On the Size Distribution of Business Firms," *Bell Journal of Economics* 9:508–23.

OECD (1987), Economic Outlook, Paris.

Phelps, E. S. (1972), *Inflation Policy and Unemployment Theory: The Cost-Benefit Approach to Monetary Planning*, New York: Norton.

———— (1994), *Structural Slumps*, Cambridge: Harvard University Press.

Phelps, E. S., A. A. Alchian, C. D. Holt, D. T. Mortensen, G. C. Archibald, R. E. Lucas, Jr., L. A. Rapping, S. G. Winter, Jr., J. P. Gould, D. F. Gordon, A. Hynes, D. A. Nichols, P. J. Taubman, and M. Wilkinson (1970), *Microeconomic Foundations of Employment and Inflation Theory*, New York: Norton.

Pissarides, C. A. (2000), *Equilibrium Unemployment Theory*, 2nd ed., Cambridge: MIT Press.

— 16 —

European Unemployment:
From a Worker's Perspective

LARS LJUNGQVIST AND THOMAS J. SARGENT

1. INTRODUCTION

This chapter summarizes and extends our supply side explanation of two striking patterns in unemployment for Europe and the rest of the OECD (see Figure 1 and Table 1).[1] First, average unemployment performances for Europe were similar to the rest of the OECD during the 1960s and 1970s, but since the 1980s unemployment in Europe has persistently exceeded the average unemployment rate in the OECD by around two percentage points. Several European countries in fact saw their unemployment rates double between those periods. Second, since the 1980s, the average *duration* of unemployment spells in Europe has greatly exceeded that in the rest of the OECD. We attribute these patterns to the incentive effects on labor supply of the far more generous unemployment compensation arrangements in Europe.[2]

Our explanation of the broad patterns is in terms of how shocks and institutions shape workers' incentives to supply labor: random *shocks* that end workers' jobs and diminish their human capital when jobs end and public *institutions* that subsidize unemployed workers. We confront the observation that unemployment compensation arrangements have been more generous in Europe *throughout* the post–World War II period, during the first part of which European unemployment

---

1. This chapter builds on Ljungqvist and Sargent (1998), which contains a rigorous description of our model.

2. The notion of unemployment compensation should be interpreted broadly in our framework. The welfare states have various programs assisting individuals out of work. For example, totally disabled persons in the Netherlands in the 1980s were entitled to 70% (80% prior to 1984) of last earned gross wage until the age of 65—after which they moved into the state pension system. At the end of 1990, disability benefits were paid to 14% of the Dutch labor force and 80% of them were reported to be totally disabled (see OECD, 1992b).

We are grateful to Cristina De Nardi, Juha Seppälä, and Christopher Sleet for excellent research assistance. Ljungqvist's research was supported by a grant from the Bank of Sweden Tercentenary Foundation. Sargent's research was supported by a grant to the National Bureau of Economic Research from the National Science Foundation.

Unemployment rate

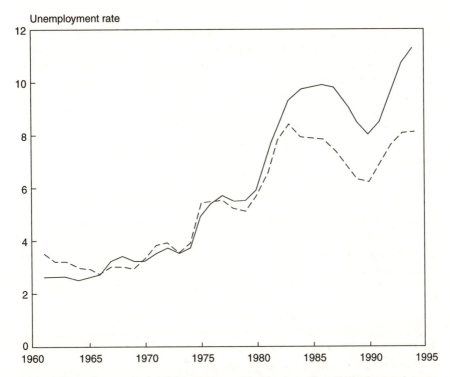

Figure 1. Unemployment rate in OECD as a percent of the labor force. The solid line is unemployment in the European OECD countries and the dashed line is unemployment in the total OECD. (Source: Data for 1961–1977 are from OECD [1984a], and data for 1978–1994 are from OECD [1995].)

was *not* higher than for the rest of the OECD. We attribute the rise in unemployment in Europe after 1980 to a change in the environment that raised the value of adaptability by workers who are forced to change jobs by changing conditions. During the more tranquil times prior to 1980, there was a lesser role for adaptability, so that a generous unemployment compensation system could coexist with low unemployment rates. However, when the required adaptability increased after 1980, that generous unemployment compensation system propelled European economies into persistently high unemployment.[3]

---

3. In contrast to our labor supply explanation, early theories of European unemployment focused on a shortfall in the demand for labor owing to insufficient aggregate demand (Blanchard et al., 1986), trade union behavior driven by insider-outsider conflicts (Blanchard and Summers, 1986; Lindbeck and Snower, 1988), hiring and firing costs (Bentolila and Bertola, 1990), and capital shortages (Malinvaud, 1994). Our analysis will instead bear out the assertion by Layard et al. (1991, p. 62) that the "unconditional payment of benefits for an indefinite period is clearly a major cause of high European unemployment." However, our model differs sharply from their framework, which emphasizes hysteresis and nominal inertia in wage and price setting. Independently of our work, Bertola and Ichino (1995) pursued the same idea that increased economic turbulence might explain the outbreak of high European unemployment but once again their mechanism hinged on rigid wages

Long-term unemployment is the heart of the European unemployment problem. According to Table 1, workers unemployed for 1 year or more today constitute about half of all unemployment in the European OECD countries. This stands in sharp contrast to earlier decades that saw much less long-term unemployment as well as a shorter duration of unemployment. Sinfield's (1968) study established that, except for Belgium, long-term unemployment was not much of a problem in Europe in the 1960s. Defining "long-term" as 6 months or more, Sinfield concluded that long-term unemployment typically affected 0.5 percent of a country's labor force. In countries such as former West Germany and the Scandinavian countries, it was less than 0.2 percent.

2. A SEARCH MODEL OF UNEMPLOYMENT

To study the level and duration of unemployment, we use a "lake and streams" model (see Figure 6 in Section 4 for an example with several lakes). We posit enough lakes and streams, that is, *states,* to capture what we see as important aspects of the situation confronting European workers. We begin with John McCall's simple two-lake, two-streams (two-state) model and then describe the way we extend it.

The McCall Worker. A simple version of McCall's (1970) search model sees workers moving between the two states of being employed and being unemployed. Each state defines a "lake." The flows between them define "streams." At the beginning of each period that he is unemployed, a worker receives one offer to work at a job with a fixed wage drawn from a time-invariant cumulative distribution function $F(w)$. He can take or leave the offer, with no opportunity to recall rejected offers. Successive draws from F are independent. At the beginning of each period that he is employed, the worker is exposed to a probability $\lambda \in (0, 1)$ of being cast into unemployment during that period. If he lives forever and sets reservation wage $\overline{w}$ for accepting wage offers, he spends a fraction

$$U = \frac{1/[1 - F(\overline{w})]}{1/\lambda + 1/[1 - F(\overline{w})]} \tag{1}$$

of his life unemployed. In this two-state model, workers have average spells of employment of $1/\lambda$ and average spells of unemployment of $1/[1 - F(\overline{w})]$. If the economy is populated by a fixed large number of ex ante identical such workers who make independent draws from the wage offer distribution F and the Bernoulli job-extinguishing distribution with parameter λ, then U is also the aggregate unemployment rate in every period. Thus, equation (1) justifies an analysis of the unemployment rate, such as the one of Layard et al. (1991) described in

---

and high firing costs that reduced labor demand. Since then, there have been several studies focusing on the interaction between a change in the economic environment and welfare-state institutions, and some of those have emphasized negative labor supply effects of generous benefits, e.g., Mortensen and Pissarides's (1999) model of skill-biased technology shocks. However, these models commonly fail to produce long-term unemployment or falling hazard rates of individual unemployed workers, features that we think are crucial for understanding high European unemployment.

Table 1. Unemployment and Long-Term Unemployment in OECD

	Unemployment (%)			Long-term unemployment of 6 months and over (% of total unemployment)			Long-term unemployment of 1 year and over (% of total unemployment)			
	1974–1979[a]	1980–1989[a]	1995[b]	1979[c]	1989[d]	1995[e]	1970[f]	1979[c]	1989[d]	1995[e]
Belgium	6.3	10.8	13.0	74.9	87.5	77.7	...	58.0	76.3	62.4
France	4.5	9.0	11.6	55.1	63.7	68.9	22.0	30.3	43.9	45.6
Germany[g]	3.2	5.9	9.4	39.9	66.7	65.4	8.8	19.9	49.0	48.3
Netherlands	4.9	9.7	7.1	49.3	66.1	74.4	12.2	27.1	49.9	43.2
Spain	5.2	17.5	22.9	51.6	72.7	72.2	...	27.5	58.5	56.5
Sweden	1.9	2.5	7.7	19.6	18.4	35.2	...	6.8	6.5	15.7
United Kingdom	5.0	10.0	8.2	39.7	57.2	60.7	17.6	24.5	40.8	43.5
United States	6.7	7.2	5.6	8.8	9.9	17.3	...	4.2	5.7	9.7
OECD Europe	4.7	9.2	10.3	...	...	...	...	31.5	52.8	...
Total OECD	4.9	7.3	7.6	...	...	...	...	26.6	33.7	...

[a] Unemployment in 1974–1979 and 1980–1989 is from OECD, Employment Outlook (1991), Table 2.7.

[b] Unemployment in 1995 is from OECD, Employment Outlook (1996), Table 1.3.

[c] Long-term unemployment in 1979 is from OECD, Employment Outlook (1984b), Table H; except for the OECD aggregate figures, which are averages for 1979 and 1980 from OECD, Employment Outlook (1991), Table 2.7.

[d] Long-term unemployment in 1989 is from OECD, Employment Outlook (1992a), Table N; except for the OECD aggregate figures that are from OECD, Employment Outlook (1991), Table 2.7.

[e] Long-term unemployment in 1995 is from OECD, Employment Outlook (1996), Table Q.

[f] Long-term unemployment in 1970 is from OECD, Employment Outlook (1983), Table 24.

[g] Except for year 1995, data refer to former West Germany only.

Section 3.1, in terms of an entry rate into unemployment λ and a mean duration of unemployment $1/[1 - F(\overline{w})]$. Given the wage distribution F, both the level and duration of unemployment are influenced by the reservation wage $\overline{w}$.

McCall theorized about how workers choose $\overline{w}$. He derived a Bellman equation for the reservation wage $\overline{w}$, above which all wage offers are accepted. For the present setting with firing probability λ, the reservation wage $\overline{w}$ satisfies

$$\frac{\overline{w} + \beta\lambda Q}{1 - \beta(1 - \lambda)} = b + \beta Q,$$

where b is the level of unemployment compensation, β is a discount factor, and Q is the optimal value of the expected discounted income of an unemployed worker who is about to draw a wage offer. The worker accepts all wage offers above $\overline{w}$ and rejects all those below it. In turning down a wage offer, the worker preserves the opportunity to look for a better job. McCall thus showed how the reservation wage is influenced by the distributions F and λ, as well as by any unemployment compensation to which the unemployed worker might be entitled.

When coupled with the above equation for U, McCall's theory of $\overline{w}$ completes what Lucas called a "prototype (at least) of a theory of unemployment" (Lucas, 1987, p. 56). Lucas praised McCall's model for the way it invites criticism:

> in so criticizing McCall's model, we are . . . really thinking about what it is like to be unemployed. . . . Questioning a McCall worker is like having a conversation with an out-of-work friend: "Maybe you are setting your sights too high," or "Why did you quit your old job before you had a new one lined up?" This is real social science: an attempt to model, to *understand,* human behavior by visualizing the situations people find themselves in, the options they face and the pros and cons as they themselves see them. (Lucas, 1987, p. 57)

We seek conversations with two McCall workers: one who lives under Europe's generous unemployment compensation system and another his American clone who experiences identical shocks but confronts the opportunities offered by stingy unemployment compensation arrangements. We extend McCall's model to enable us to have these conversations.

At every moment in the basic McCall model, all employed workers are alike and all unemployed workers are alike. To explain the observations on European unemployment, Ljungqvist and Sargent (1998) extended the basic model to make employed and unemployed workers heterogeneous with respect both to their skills and to the unemployment compensation to which they are entitled. We use that heterogeneity to model how Europe's generous systems of unemployment compensation influence the level and the duration of unemployment.

3. EMPIRICAL PATTERNS TO BE LINKED

This section sketches some evidence about the structure of recent European unemployment and the relative generosity of European unemployment compensation. It then turns to evidence that we interpret as indicating that the environment confronting workers has become more turbulent in the last couple of decades, exposing them to larger probable losses of valuable skills on those occasions when their jobs terminate.

3.1. Decomposition of Unemployment

As equation (1) indicated, an unemployment rate can be analyzed in terms of an inflow rate and an average duration of unemployment. As summarized by Layard et al. (1991), the rise in European unemployment is caused mainly by an increase in the duration of unemployment, whereas the inflow rate has been roughly constant. This phenomenon is illustrated in Figure 2 for Great Britain [panel (b)], whereas the United States [panel (a)] shows no trend in either the average duration or the inflow rate. Layard et al. continue with the observation that the average duration of unemployment does not capture the huge variation in the length of spells of

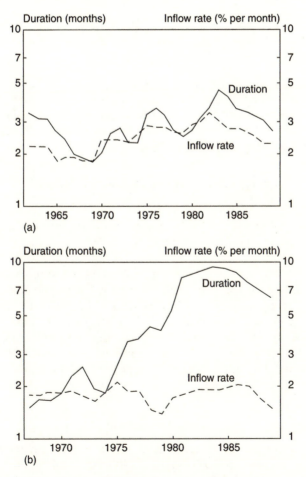

Figure 2. Inflow rates and duration of unemployment: (a) United States and (b) Great Britain, males. (Reproduction of Layard et al., fig. 3 [1991, p. 225].)

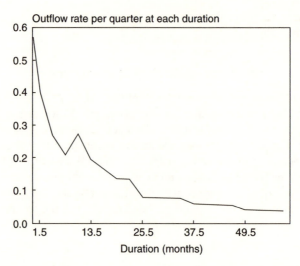

Figure 3. Outflow rates per quarter for different durations of unemployment: Great Britain, males, 1985. (Reproduction of Layard et al., fig. 4, panel c [1991, p. 226].)

unemployment. Figure 3 reproduces their data for the outflow rates for different durations of male unemployment in Great Britain in 1985. The outflow or "hazard" rate is the proportion of survivors of each duration that leave unemployment in the subsequent quarter. The figure shows starkly how the outflow rate in Great Britain is much lower at the longer durations.

3.2. Generosity of Unemployment Benefits

It is difficult to provide a summary measure of a country's "replacement rate," that is, the proportion of lost income from work that is replaced by unemployment compensation and related welfare benefits. The benefits come not only from different programs, such as housing benefits, but also depend on specific personal and family characteristics of the unemployed. The OECD has launched a project to gather relevant data and construct replacement rates comparable across countries. Martin (1996) reports the OECD's computations of the welfare benefits available to the average 40-year-old worker with a long employment. Table 2 shows net unemployment benefit replacement rates, depending on family status, after tax and housing benefits. The United States stands out in the table with hardly any benefits after the first year of unemployment, whereas the European countries have replacement rates around 70 percent even in the 5th year out of work.

3.3. Turbulence

It is a widely held notion that the economic environment has become more turbulent in the two last decades. OECD (1994, pp. 29–30) sums it up as follows:

> In the stable post–World War II economic environment, standards of living in most OECD countries grew rapidly, narrowing the gap with the area's highest

Table 2. Net Unemployment Benefit Replacement Rates[a] in 1994 for
Single-Earner Households by Duration Categories and Family Circumstances

	Single			With dependent spouse		
	1st year	*2nd and 3rd years*	*4th and 5th years*	*1st year*	*2nd and 3rd years*	*4th and 5th years*
Belgium	79	55	55	70	64	64
France	79	63	61	80	62	60
Germany	66	63	63	74	72	72
Netherlands	79	78	73	90	88	85
Spain	69	54	32	70	55	39
Sweden[b]	81	76	75	81	100	101
United Kingdom[b]	64	64	64	75	74	74
United States	34	9	9	38	14	14

Source: Martin (1996, table 2).

[a] Benefit entitlement on a net-of-tax and housing benefit basis as a percentage of net-of-tax earnings.

[b] Data for Sweden and the United Kingdom refer to 1995.

per capita income country, the United States. The OECD area's terms of trade evolved favourably; trade and payments systems were progressively liberalised, without major problems; GDP and international trade grew strongly.

In the 1970s, the economic environment became turbulent. The two oil price rises, in 1973/74 and 1979/80, imparted major terms-of-trade shocks, each of the order of 2 per cent of OECD-area GDP, and each sending large relative price changes through all OECD economies. Exchange rate became volatile after the breakdown of the Bretton Woods system of fixed exchange rates. Then there came, mainly in the 1980s, waves of financial-market liberalisation and product market deregulation which greatly enhanced the potential efficiency of OECD economies, and also accelerated the pace of change. All these developments challenged the capacity of economies and societies to adapt. At the same time, the need to adapt was heightened by pervasive technological change, especially as the new information technologies appeared; and by the trend towards globalisation.

The sense of turbulence relevant for us must manifest itself in terms of greater volatility of workers' earnings. Gottschalk and Moffitt (1994) provide empirical evidence of such an increase. For the two periods 1970–1978 and 1979–1987, they summarized U.S. earnings distributions in ways that led them to conclude that both the "permanent" and "transitory" components of the distributions had spread out from one subperiod to the next. In particular, using data from the Michigan Panel Study on Income Dynamics (PSID), they computed an individual's average earnings for each subperiod to arrive at an estimate of the individual's permanent earnings. Figure 4a shows the distribution of those earnings in the two subperiods. They also computed the variance of an individual's income fluctuations, or transitory earnings, around his or her permanent earnings. The distribution of the standard deviations of transitory earnings in the two subperiods is depicted in Figure 4b. As can be seen, the dispersion of *both* permanent earnings and the standard deviations of transitory earnings increased in 1979–1987 compared to

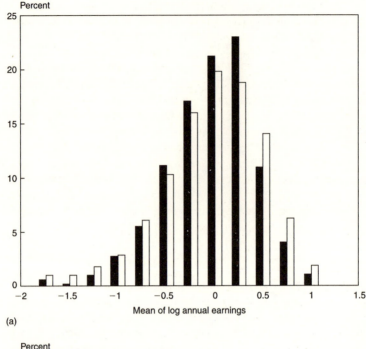

(a)

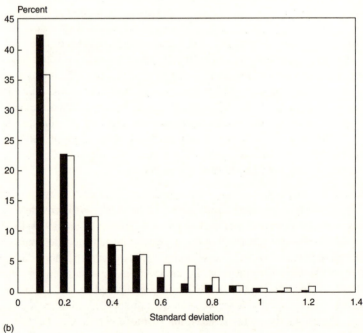

(b)

Figure 4. (a) Distribution of permanent earnings, 1970–1978 (black bars) and 1979–1987 (white bars). (b) Distribution of standard deviations of individuals' transitory earnings, 1970–1978 (black bars) and 1979–1987 (white bars). (Reproduction of Gottschalk and Moffitt, figs. 2 and 4 [1994].)

1970–1978. Gottschalk and Moffitt and their discussants (see Katz, 1994; Dickens, 1994) interpreted these statistics in terms of how the increase in the dispersion of earnings observed during the 1980s in the United States was accompanied by an increase in the intertemporal volatility of an individual's earnings.[4]

We want to interpret the volatility of earnings studied by Gottschalk and Moffitt partly in terms of the destruction of a worker's human capital that occurs at the time of a job termination. A study that provides evidence of that destruction in the United States is by Jacobson et al. (1993), who found that long-tenured displaced workers experienced large and enduring earnings losses. In their Pennsylvania sample from the 1980s, a displaced worker experienced the following typical pattern: a sharp drop in earnings in the quarter a job was left, followed by a rapid recovery during the next couple of years toward an eventual level of about 25 percent less than earned at the predisplacement job. Figure 5 reproduces Figure 1 from Jacobson et al., which dramatically displays the pattern by showing the disparate expected earnings patterns of long-tenured workers who were displaced in the first quarter of 1982 compared to workers who remained employed throughout the period.

Evidence in the style of Jacobson et al. is especially relevant to us because we model economic turbulence in terms of the risk of losing skills at the time of a layoff. The next section describes a search model of the labor market with such a skill technology and the assumption that unemployment benefits are determined by workers' past earnings. In Ljungqvist and Sargent (1998), we showed that our model of increased turbulence can produce outcomes for earnings processes that mimic the findings of both Gottschalk and Moffitt and Jacobson et al.[5] In this chapter, we take a more personal approach and study the life histories of two workers who are identical in all respects except for the institutions governing unemployment compensation under which they live (Section 5). In addition, simulations presented in Section 6 show that a generous replacement rate for unemployment makes the unemployment rate, the mean duration of unemployment, and the incidence of long-term unemployment very sensitive to the amount of economic turbulence.

4. A MULTISTATE MODEL OF A EUROPEAN McCALL WORKER

We have added three features to the basic McCall search model[6]:

1. In period $t+1$, an unemployed worker receives an offer drawn from c.d.f. F with a probability $\pi(s_t)$ that depends on a variable search intensity s_t chosen at time t at a cost $c(s_t)$.

---

4. More evidence was analyzed by Blundell and Preston (1998) and Meghir and Pistaferri (2001). From data on British households' consumption and income for 1968–1992, together with the restrictions implied by consumption-smoothing models, Blundell and Preston found "strong growth in transitory inequality toward the end of this period" as well as rising permanent components of income inequality. For U.S. data from the PSID, Meghir and Pistaferri found rising volatility of innovations for much of the period from 1969 to 1990 and somewhat of a decline late in their sample.

5. See Figures 14 and 15 of Ljungqvist and Sargent (1998).

6. Like McCall's model, ours assumes that the wage offer completely characterizes the job.

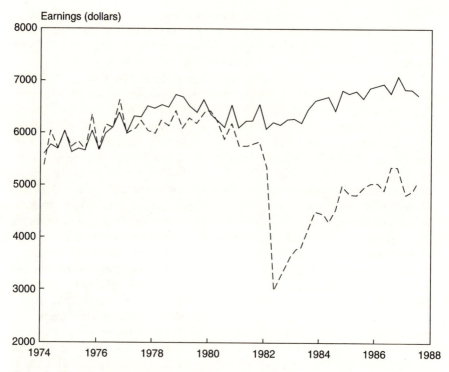

Figure 5. Quarterly earnings of high-attachment workers separating in the first quarter of 1982 and workers staying through 1986. The solid line refers to stayers, the dashed line, to separators. (Reproduction of Jacobson et al., fig. 1 [1993]. We have omitted the last observation of Jacobson et al. because it is based on too small a sample.)

2. The worker's earnings on a job are the product of his initial wage draw w and his level of skill h_t. Skill accumulates or depreciates stochastically at rates depending on whether the worker is employed or unemployed. In particular, we assume that work experience makes skills accumulate whereas unemployment makes them depreciate.
3. Unemployment compensation is based upon the unemployed worker's last earnings on a job.

To represent turbulence, we allow for the possibility that a worker instantaneously loses some skills at the time of being laid off. Such a loss reflects the fact that some skills are job specific and that those skills become obsolete especially quickly in times of industry restructuring. We capture economic turbulence in our analysis by changing the amount of instantaneous skill losses. A more turbulent economic environment in our model is tantamount to making workers face bigger risks of skill loss at times of layoff. Regardless of any such skill loss, laid-off workers are entitled to unemployment compensation as a fraction of their lost earnings.

4.1. Details of Environment

There is a continuum of workers with geometrically distributed life spans, indexed on the unit interval with births equaling deaths. An unemployed worker in period t chooses a search intensity $s_t \geq 0$ at a disutility $c(s_t)$ increasing in s_t. Search may or may not generate a wage offer in the next period. With probability $\pi(s_t)$, the unemployed worker receives one wage offer from the distribution $F(w) = \text{Prob}(w_{t+1} \leq w)$. With probability $1 - \pi(s_t)$, the worker receives no offer in period $t + 1$. We assume $\pi(s_t) \in (0, 1)$, and that it is increasing in s_t. Accepting a wage offer w_{t+1} means that the worker earns that wage (per unit of skill) for each period he is alive, not laid off, and has not quit his job. The probability of being laid off at the beginning of a period is $\lambda \in (0, 1)$. In addition, all workers are subjected to a probability of $\alpha \in (0, 1)$ of dying between periods.

Employed and unemployed workers experience stochastic accumulation or deterioration of skills. There is a finite number of skill levels with transition probabilities from skill level h to h' denoted by $\mu_u(h, h')$ and $\mu_e(h, h')$ for an unemployed and an employed worker, respectively. That is, an unemployed worker with skill level h faces a probability $\mu_u(h, h')$ that his skill level at the beginning of the next period is h', contingent on not dying. Similarly, $\mu_e(h, h')$ is the probability that an employed worker with skill level h sees his skill level change to h' at the beginning of the next period, contingent on not dying and not being laid off. In the event of a layoff, the transition probability is given by $\mu_l(h, h')$. After this initial period of a layoff, the stochastic skill level of the unemployed worker is again governed by the transition probability $\mu_u(h, h')$. All newborn workers begin with the lowest skill level.

A worker observes his new skill level at the beginning of a period before deciding to accept a new wage offer, choose a search intensity, or quit a job. The objective of each worker is to maximize the expected value

$$E_t \sum_{i=0}^{\infty} \beta^i (1 - \alpha)^i y_{t+i},$$

where E_t is the expectation operator conditioned on information at time t, β is the subjective discount factor, and $1 - \alpha$ is the probability of surviving between two consecutive periods; y_{t+i} is the worker's after-tax income from employment and unemployment compensation at time $t + i$ net of disutility of searching.[7]

Workers who were laid off are entitled to unemployment compensation benefits that are a function of their last earnings. Let $b(I)$ be the unemployment compensation to an unemployed worker whose last earnings were I. Unemployment compensation is terminated if the worker turns down a job offer with earnings that are deemed to be "suitable" by the government in view of that individual's past earnings. Let $I_g(I)$ be the government-determined "suitable earnings" of an

---

7. We have abstracted from the benefits of risk sharing that government policies can provide when capital markets are incomplete. Adding such considerations would modify but not change the flavor of our results.

unemployed worker whose last earnings were I. Newborn workers and workers who have quit their previous job are not entitled to unemployment compensation. Income from both employment and unemployment compensation are subject to a flat income tax of τ. The government policy functions $b(I)$ and $I_g(I)$ and the tax parameter τ must be set so that income taxes cover the expenditures on unemployment compensation in an equilibrium.

Let $V(w, h)$ be the value of the optimization problem for an employed worker with wage w and skill level h at the beginning of a period. The value associated with being unemployed and eligible for unemployment compensation benefits is given by $V_b(I, h)$, which is both a function of the unemployed worker's past earnings I and his current skill level h. In the case of an unemployed worker who is not entitled to unemployment compensation, the corresponding value is denoted by $V_0(h)$ and depends only on the worker's current skill level. The Bellman equations can then be written as follows:

$$V(w, h) = \max_{accept, reject} \left\{ (1 - \tau)wh + (1 - \alpha)\beta \left[(1 - \lambda) \sum_{h'} \mu_e(h, h')V(w, h') \right. \right.$$

$$\left. \left. + \lambda \sum_{h'} \mu_l(h, h')V_b(wh, h') \right], V_0(h) \right\}, \tag{2}$$

$$V_b(I, h) = \max_s \left\{ -c(s) + (1 - \tau)b(I) + (1 - \alpha)\beta \sum_{h'} \mu_u(h, h') \right.$$

$$\left[[1 - \pi(s)]V_b(I, h') + \pi(s)\left(\int_{w \geq I_g(I)/h'} V(w, h')dF(w) \right. \right.$$

$$+ \int_{w < I_g(I)/h'} \max_{accept, reject} \left\{ (1 - \tau)wh' \right.$$

$$+ (1 - \alpha)\beta \left[(1 - \lambda) \sum_{h''} \mu_e(h', h'')V(w, h'') \right.$$

$$\left. \left. \left. \left. + \lambda \sum_{h''} \mu_l(h', h'')V_b(wh', h'') \right], V_b(I, h') \right\} dF(w) \right) \right] \right\}, \tag{3}$$

$$V_0(h) = \max_s \left\{ -c(s) + (1 - \alpha)\beta \sum_{h'} \mu_u(h, h') \left[[1 - \pi(s)]V_0(h') \right. \right.$$

$$\left. \left. + \pi(s) \int V(w, h')dF(w) \right] \right\}. \tag{4}$$

Associated with the solution of equations (2)–(4) are two functions, $\bar{s}_b(I, h)$ and $\bar{w}_b(I, h)$, giving an optimal search intensity and a reservation wage of an unemployed worker with last earnings I and current skill level h, who is eligible for unemployment compensation benefits, and two functions, $\bar{s}_0(h)$ and $\bar{w}_0(h)$, giving an optimal search intensity and a reservation wage of an unemployed worker with skill level h, who is not entitled to unemployment compensation. The reservation wage of an employed worker will be the same as for an unemployed worker without benefits, $\overline{w}_0(h)$, since anyone who quits his job is not eligible for unemployment compensation.

4.2. Stationary Equilibria

We will study stationary equilibria, or steady states, for our economy. A steady state is defined in a standard way, as a set of government policy parameters, optimal policies $[\overline{s}_0(h), \overline{w}_0(h), \overline{s}_b(I, h), \overline{w}_b(I, h)]$ and associated time-invariant employment and unemployment distributions and total unemployment compensation payments that satisfy workers' optimality conditions and the government's budget constraint. We compute a steady state as a fixed point in the tax rate τ. For a fixed tax rate τ, we solve the workers' optimization problem and use the implied search intensities and reservation wages to deduce stationary employment and unemployment distributions and compensation. A balanced government budget defines a fixed point in τ, which is associated with a stationary equilibrium.[8] After finding a stationary equilibrium, we compute various quantities such as GNP per capita, average productivity of employed workers, average skill level, average duration of unemployment, and measures of long-term unemployment.

4.3. Lakes and Streams

As with the basic McCall model described above, we can imagine the labor market as a set of lakes connected by inlet and outlet streams. Figure 6 depicts an example with two possible skill levels. The volume of water in each lake represents the number of people in a particular labor market state (e.g., employed, unemployed and having quit a previous job, unemployed and having been laid off from a previous job, unemployed because of having just entered the labor force), and the flows between lakes represent rates of hiring, firing, and quitting. The system is in a stationary equilibrium when all lake levels are constant over time, which means that inflows just balance outflows for each lake. The rates of inflow and outflow are evidently the critical determinants of the lake levels. The individual search model lends itself to becoming a model of these inflow and outflow rates if we simply reinterpret the probability of job acceptance as determining the *rate* of flow from a state of unemployment to a state of employment.

4.4. Skill Dynamics

Two sets of parameters mainly drive our results—those giving the skill technology and the unemployment compensation scheme.[9] There are twenty-one skill levels

---

8. The iterative procedure picks the lowest possible τ consistent with a stationary equilibrium. We choose to focus on this, the least distortionary, tax rate and ignore any higher tax rates that might be consistent with other steady states.

9. For a detailed discussion of all parameter values in our model, see Ljungqvist and Sargent (1998).

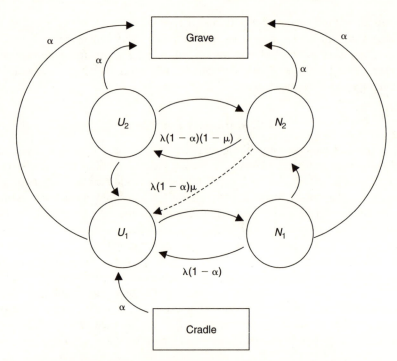

Figure 6. Employment flows and reservoirs in a model with birth/death probability α, layoff probability λ, quitting, and decisions to accept or refuse offers. Here U_1 and U_2 denote pools of unemployed workers of low and high human capital, respectively; N_1 and N_2 measure employed workers of low and high human capital, respectively. The dotted line flowing from the high-skill pool of employed people N_2 to the low-skill pool of unemployed people U_1 depicts the stochastic depreciation of skills that we use to represent turbulence; conditional on being laid off, the skilled worker's skill level drops from high to low with probaiblity μ. A flow of quitters has been omitted from the graph. Employed workers who gain human capital may choose to quit to seek better-paying jobs.

in our model that evenly span the range $[1, 2]$. Newborn workers are endowed with the lowest skill level, equal to one, and work experience can result at most in twice that level of skill. The evolution of skills while employed is as follows. After each 2-week period of employment not followed by a layoff, the worker has a one in ten chance to increase skills by one level; otherwise, the skill level remains unchanged. Employed workers who have reached the highest skill level retain those skills until becoming unemployed. It will take a worker who is continuously employed, on average, about 7 years and 8 months to reach the highest skill level. We assume the stochastic depreciation of skills during unemployment to be twice as fast as the accumulation of skills. That is, after each 2-week period of unemployment, there is a one in five risk that the worker's skills decrease by one level; otherwise, they remain unchanged. Once the lowest skill level is reached through depreciation, the worker remains at that level until becoming employed.

In a period of being laid off, we assume that the worker draws a new skill level from one of the distributions in Figure 7. The range of each distribution

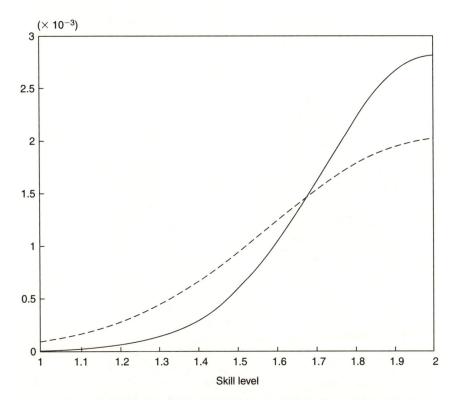

Figure 7. The probability distribution of a worker's skills immediately after a layoff. The range starts at the lowest skill level of 1 and ends at the worker's skill level before the layoff. The graph is drawn for a worker who had attained the highest skill level of 2 before the layoff. The solid line and dashed line refer to different degrees of economic turbulence indexed by variance .02 and .04, respectively.

starts at the lowest possible skill level equal to one, and ends at the worker's skill level before the layoff. In other words, the worker stands to lose some skills immediately; occasionally workers draw a significantly lower skill level, one from the left-hand tail of the distribution. The two distributions in Figure 7 refer to two different degrees of economic turbulence. The distribution indexed by variance .04 corresponds to a more turbulent economic environment since there is a higher probability for large skill losses; that is, the left-hand tail is fatter compared to the distribution indexed by variance .02.

Concerning the unemployment compensation scheme, we examine the outcome for two economies, one with unemployment insurance and one without. The economy with unemployment insurance is called the welfare state (WS), and has both a 70 percent replacement rate and a 70 percent "suitable earnings" criterion. That is, laid-off workers receive unemployment benefits equal to 70 percent of lost earnings as long as they do not turn down jobs with earnings greater than or equal to those benefits. The economy with no unemployment insurance is called the laissez-faire (LF) economy.

5. "CONVERSATIONS" WITH TWO WORKERS

We now follow the lives of one worker in the WS economy and another in the LF economy. The economic environment is taken to be the more turbulent one indexed by variance .04 in Figure 7. The two workers confront identical realizations of individual shocks. Thus, both workers die after 40 years in the labor market. For each 2-week period during those 40 years, we draw random realizations of layoff/continuing employment, conditional on employment in the previous period; skill changes (bounded by the permissible skill range [1, 2]), conditional on layoff in the current period; continuing employment or unemployment in the previous period; and a search outcome with or without a wage offer, conditional on unemployment in the previous period and chosen search intensity. The two workers share these 40-year-long sequences of potential shocks. That is, if both workers were employed in the previous period, they share the same layoff shock in the current period. If they are not laid off, both either retain their skills or gain one skill level depending on another common shock in the current period (the exception being a worker who has already reached the highest skill level). Similarly, if both workers were unemployed in the previous period, both either retain their skills or lose one skill level depending on a common shock in the current period (the exception being a worker who has already reached the lowest skill level). If the workers are laid off in the same period, they face the same draw from the distribution indexed by variance .04 in Figure 7 but their realized absolute skill levels depend on their particular right-hand end points (i.e., skill levels just before the layoff). Moreover, if the two workers find jobs in the same period, they will be offered the same wage per unit of skill. The likelihood of generating a wage offer will naturally depend on their search intensities chosen in the previous period.

Since our two workers share the same sequences of potential shocks, they would also experience the same lives if they made the same decisions at all points in time. Our assumption of maximizing behavior implies that they *would* make the same decisions if they lived in the same environment, in particular, under the same tax and benefit rules. But the two workers are unlikely to make identical decisions because they live with different institutional arrangements in the WS economy and the LF economy. Figures 8a and b show what occurs for our particular random draw of shocks. It happens that the two workers do actually make the same decisions during the first $27\frac{1}{2}$ years in the labor force. After entering the labor market, they both find and accept a job after 3 months of unemployment. However, their first job lasts less than a year and they experience another spell of unemployment. This time the worker in the WS economy receives unemployment compensation equal to 70 percent of his lost earnings (not shown in Figure 8, which only depicts labor earnings). The workers' second job lasts 4 years and they accumulate considerable skills before being laid off again and thereby losing some of these skills. Their third job has a very attractive wage per unit of skill and, in a little more than 6 years, they have attained the highest skill level and their labor income is at the top of the earnings distribution.[10]

---

10. Wages per unit of skill are confined to the unit interval and the highest skill level is equal to two, which means that maximum earnings are two.

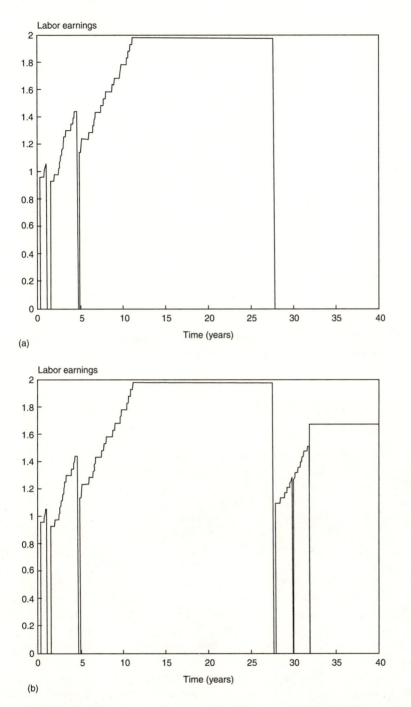

Figure 8. (a) Simulated labor earnings of a worker in the WS economy. (b) Simulated labor earnings of a worker in the LF economy.

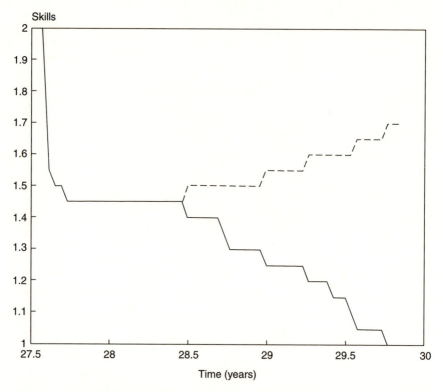

Figure 9. Simulated skills of a worker in the WS economy (solid line) and one in the LF economy (dashed line).

When the two workers are laid off from their long-tenure job in their 27th year in the labor market, their fates diverge dramatically in Figure 8. The worker in the WS economy never again posts any labor earnings, whereas the worker in the LF economy returns to work after 4 months of unemployment, though at substantially lower earnings. The question is, what goes wrong in the welfare state regime in that unfortunate 27th year? Figure 9 reveals that the workers experience a large loss (about 25%) of skills at the time of the layoff. A year after the layoff, the worker in the LF economy starts to rebuild skills in his new job, whereas the unemployed worker in the WS economy continues losing skills. A factor contributing to the inability of the worker in the WS economy to find an acceptable job can be found in Figure 10. The worker sets much higher "reservation earnings" for an acceptable job as compared to the worker in the LF economy. Given a replacement rate of 70 percent, the worker in the WS economy is more choosy than his colleague in the LF economy.

In the next couple of years, the worker in the WS economy starts lowering his reservation earnings in Figure 10, so it might seem surprising that he continues to have trouble finding a job. But the reservation earnings are set in relation to the unemployed worker's skills, which are also depreciating over time. It is therefore more informative to focus on the "reservation wage" per unit of skill in Figure 11.

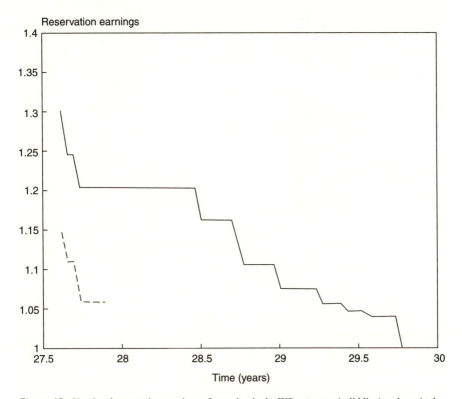

Figure 10. Simulated reservation earnings of a worker in the WS economy (solid line) and one in the LF economy (dashed line).

As can be seen, the worker in the WS economy is not becoming less choosy over time but *more*. The unemployed worker demands higher and higher reservation wages per unit of skill before being willing to surrender benefits that amount to 70 percent of past earnings. In other words, the worker is looking for a better and better "match" in the labor market, or wage per unit of skill, to compensate for his depreciating skills. The generous unemployment benefits make him compare any potential job with his past high earnings. Of course, the worker in our model is well aware of the low probability of finding such high wage offers, so it becomes rational for him to invest less in job search. Figure 12 shows a falling search intensity over time for the worker in the WS economy. After about 2 years of unemployment and fruitless job search, the worker becomes totally disillusioned and withdraws from labor market participation by setting his search intensity equal to zero (but he continues to receive benefits in our model).

6. AGGREGATE OUTCOMES

The simulations of two workers' lives illustrate the economic forces at work in our model. We can gain further insights by exploring the aggregate implications of alternative degrees of economic turbulence. Table 3 reports the steady states for the

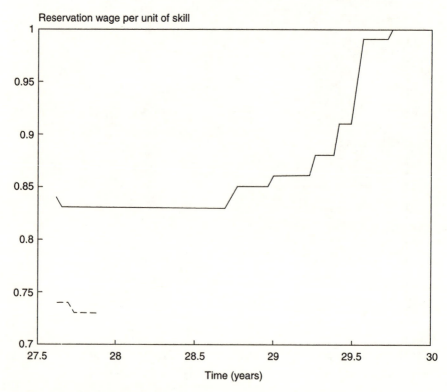

Figure 11. Simulated reservation wage per unit of skill of a worker in the WS economy (solid line) and of one in the LF economy (dashed line).

WS economy and the LF economy when turbulence is indexed by variance .02 and .04, respectively. The unemployment responds to increased economic turbulence in strikingly different ways in the two economies. When moving from low to high turbulence, the unemployment rate remains roughly constant in the LF economy but doubles in the WS economy. This outcome is consistent with our theory that increased economic turbulence in the 1980s contributed to high unemployment in the European welfare states, while leaving the U.S. unemployment rate unchanged, as in Table 1. Moreover, a decomposition of our artificial unemployment data into inflow rates and average duration of unemployment spells produces the same pattern as in Figure 2, provided that we once again let the United States approximate a LF economy and Great Britain represent a WS economy. In our analysis, the inflow rate remains practically constant across different degrees of economic turbulence because we keep the layoff rate λ unchanged. The parameter λ is chosen so that the monthly layoff rate is just above 1.8 percent. According to Table 3, the average duration of unemployment remains around $2\frac{1}{2}$ months in the LF economy for both degrees of economic turbulence. In contrast, the most turbulent economic environment produces an average duration of about 8 months in the WS economy, which is significantly higher than the 3 months in less turbulent times.

The worse employment performance of the WS economy arises from the increasing incidence of long-term unemployment. The fractions of long-term

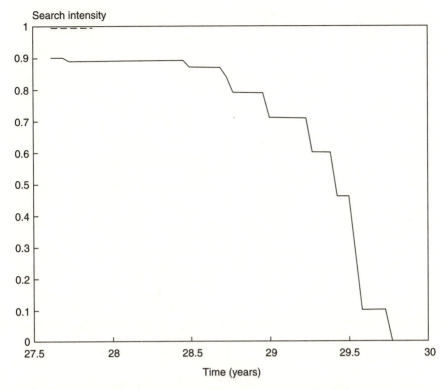

Figure 12. Simulated search intensity of a worker in the WS economy (solid line) and of one in the LF economy (dashed line).

Table 3. Equilibrium Outcomes for the WS Economy and the LF Economy with Different Degrees of Economic Turbulence

	Degree of economic turbulence			
	.02		.04	
	WS	LF	WS	LF
Tax rate (%)	3.88	n.a.	11.69	n.a.
Unemployment rate (%)	7.13	5.81	14.87	5.73
Average duration of unemployment (weeks)	13.7	10.6	31.8	10.7
Percentage of unemployed at a point in time with spells so far ≥ 6 months	18.2	8.2	63.1	8.5
Percentage of unemployed at a point in time with spells so far ≥ 12 months	5.8	0.6	55.6	0.6

unemployed explode in the WS economy when economic turbulence increases in Table 3. The percentage of currently unemployed workers with spells to date of 6 months or more rises from 18.2 to 63.1 percent. Concerning the percentage of unemployed workers with spells to date of 1 year or more, we find the corresponding increase in the WS economy to be from 5.8 to 55.6 percent. In the LF

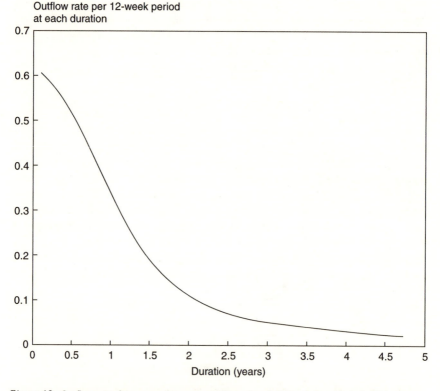

Figure 13. Outflow rates from unemployment per 12-week period at each duration in the WS economy
with economic turbulence indexed by variance of .04.

economy, the small numbers of long-term unemployed stay virtually unchanged
in response to increased economic turbulence.

The problem of long-term unemployment in the WS economy can also be
studied in terms of hazard rates. Given the highest degree of economic turbulence
indexed by variance .04, Figure 13 depicts the outflow rate from unemployment
for the WS economy. This figure corresponds to our Figure 3, which we borrowed
from Layard et al. (1991). Figure 13 from our artificial economy does a good job of
emulating the pattern in the Layard et al. figure. Most unemployed workers leave
unemployment during the first year of a spell. Thereafter, a significantly lower
outflow rate tends to produce very long unemployment spells for the remaining
unemployed.

We conclude that moving from a turbulence indexed by variance .02 to .04 can
account quite well for the unemployment experience of Europe (the WS economy)
and the United States (the LF economy) in the decades before and after 1980,
respectively. The question then becomes what the empirical support is for our
parameterization of the degree of economic turbulence. Since there are no data
on human capital losses at layoffs, we will have to rely on indirect evidence such
as observations on labor earnings. As mentioned above, we have shown earlier
that our parameterization does in fact produce outcomes for earnings processes

that mimic studies in the United States of both increased turbulence between the 1970s and the 1980s, and earnings losses of displaced workers.[11] If anything, our artificial earnings data suggest that the mechanism generating high long-term unemployment in our model operates at much lower levels of economic turbulence than those observed in the United States.

7. CONCLUSIONS AND EXTENSIONS

Having been encouraged by the way our model matches some of the facts about European unemployment, we are now refining it to capture more (see Ljungqvist and Sargent, 2002). In particular, we want to understand: (1) how Europe's unemployment was actually *lower* than America's during the 1950s and 1960s; and (2) how it is *older* workers who are now especially drawn into long-term unemployment in Europe. To understand these facts, we proceed in the spirit of Lucas's conversation with a McCall worker and add some more realistic features to the worker's environment. First, we add a worker's age as part of the description of his state. To control the dimension of the state, we add a small number of discrete ages and posit an exogenous stochastic aging process.[12] Second, in the spirit of Ljungqvist and Sargent (1995), instead of being constant during the worker's tenure on a job, we posit that the wage process while employed is a stochastic one. Stochastic "job reclassifications" confront the employed worker with the decision of staying or quitting. Third, we impose a tax on job destruction, a feature that several writers have emphasized in discussions of European unemployment.[13] These three features are overlaid on the model described above.

The interaction of a stochastic on-the-job wage with layoff costs is the key to explaining how unemployment was lower in Europe in the less turbulent environment of the 1950s and 1960s. The model predicts that Europe (modeled as having high unemployment compensation and a high job destruction tax) had a lower unemployment rate than a laissez faire country would have had in that period: With low turbulence, the model predicts that Europe would have lower job destruction rates and longer job tenures than would a country under laissez faire. That lower unemployment might have been purchased at an efficiency cost by making workers stay too long in jobs that had gone sour. An increase in turbulence in the extended model has broader effects than those analyzed in this chapter, prompting older workers especially to choose extended periods of unemployment. Thus, we expect to gain further insights from our extended McCall model.

REFERENCES

Bentolila, S. and G. Bertola (1990), "Firing Costs and Labour Demand: How Bad is Euro-sclerosis?," *Review of Economic Studies* 57:381–402.

---

11. See Ljungqvist and Sargent (1998) for details.

12. The additional dimension of age adds lakes to the counterpart of Figure 6.

13. See Ljungqvist (2001) for a critical evaluation of how layoff costs work in several models of the labor market.

Bertola, G. and A. Ichino (1995), "Wage Inequality and Unemployment: United States vs. Europe," in B. S. Bernanke and J. J. Rotemberg, eds., *NBER Macroeconomics Annual*, Cambridge: MIT Press.

Blanchard, O., R. Dornbusch, J. Drèze, H. Giersch, R. Layard, and M. Monti (1986), "Employment and Growth in Europe: A Two-Handed Approach," in O. Blanchard, R. Dornbusch, and R. Layard, eds., *Restoring Europe's Prosperity: Macroeconomic Papers from the Centre for European Policy Studies,* Cambridge: MIT Press.

Blanchard, O. J. and L. H. Summers (1986), "Hysteresis and the European Unemployment Problem," in S. Fischer, ed., *NBER Macroeconomics Annual,* Cambridge: MIT Press.

Blundell, R. and I. Preston (1998), "Consumption Inequality and Income Uncertainty," *Quarterly Journal of Economics* 113:603–40.

Dickens, W. T. (1994), "Comments and Discussion," *Brookings Papers on Economic Activity* 2:262–69.

Gottschalk, P. and R. Moffitt (1994), "The Growth of Earnings Instability in the U.S. Labor Market," *Brookings Papers on Economic Activity* 2:217–72.

Jacobson, L. S., R. J. LaLonde, and D. G. Sullivan (1993), "Earnings Losses of Displaced Workers," *The American Economic Review* 83:685–709.

Katz, L. F. (1994), "Comments and Discussion," *Brookings Papers on Economic Activity* 2:255–61.

Layard, R., S. Nickell, and R. Jackman (1991), *Unemployment: Macroeconomic Performance and the Labour Market,* Oxford: Oxford University Press.

Lindbeck, A. and D. J. Snower (1988), *The Insider-Outsider Theory of Unemployment,* Cambridge: MIT Press.

Ljungqvist, L. (2001), "How Do Layoff Costs Affect Employment?," mimeo, Stockholm School of Economics, forthcoming in *Economic Journal.*

Ljungqvist, L. and T. J. Sargent (1995), "Welfare States and Unemployment," *Economic Theory* 6:143–60.

———— (1998), "The European Unemployment Dilemma," *Journal of Political Economy* 106(3):514–50.

———— (2002), "The European Employment Experience," mimeo, Stockholm School of Economics and Stanford University.

Lucas, R. E., Jr. (1987), *Models of Business Cycles,* Oxford and New York: Basil Blackwell.

Malinvaud, E. (1994), *Diagnosing Unemployment,* Cambridge: Cambridge University Press.

Martin, J. P. (1996), "Measures of Replacement Rates for the Purpose of International Comparisons: A Note," *OECD Economic Studies* 26:99–115.

McCall, J. J. (1970), "Economics of Information and Job Search," *Quarterly Journal of Economics* 84:113–26.

Meghir, C. and L. Pistaferri (2001), "Income Variance Dynamics and Heterogeneity," mimeo, WP01/07, Institute for Fiscal Studies, University College, London.

Mortensen, D. T. and C. A. Pissarides (1999), "Unemployment Responses to 'Skill-Biased' Technology Shocks: The Role of Labour Market Policy," *Economic Journal* 109:242–65.

OECD (1983), *Employment Outlook,* Paris.

———— (1984a), *Labour Force Statistics,* Paris.

———— (1984b), *Employment Outlook,* Paris.

———— (1991), *Employment Outlook,* Paris.

———— (1992a), *Employment Outlook,* Paris.

———— (1992b), *OECD Economic Surveys—The Netherlands,* Paris.

———— (1994), *The OECD Jobs Study: Facts, Analysis, Strategies,* Paris.

———— (1995), *Employment Outlook,* Paris.

———— (1996), *Employment Outlook,* Paris.

Sinfield, A. (1968), *The Long-Term Unemployed: A Comparative Survey,* Employment of Special Groups, No. 5, Paris: OECD.

Comments on Ljungqvist and Sargent

OLIVIER J. BLANCHARD

Discussions in a festschrift are like Japanese haikus. They must follow strict rules. In particular, they must have three parts (although—in contrast to haikus, and perhaps not for the best—each part can have more than five or seven syllables): The first part must show how the paper being discussed derives from the seminal work of the honoree. The second must argue that the paper being discussed shows how fruitful the approach has been. The third, which is required to establish the credibility of the first two, must pick a small bone of contention. I find all three very easy to achieve in this case.

1. ON THE GENERAL THEME AND THE FILIATION

The proposition that explaining the evolution of unemployment at anything lower than business cycle frequencies requires looking at shocks, institutions, and their interactions is a theme that I have made mine over the past few years. But it is a theme directly traceable to Ned's *Structural Slumps* (Phelps, 1994).

In that book, Ned took issue with the then prevailing Keynesian explanations for European unemployment. He argued that a model that ignored nominal rigidities could actually go a long way in explaining what had happened. He emphasized the role of shocks, insisting in particular on the role of real interest rates on both the demand and the supply of goods. He emphasized the roles of labor and goods market imperfections and of labor market institutions in creating and amplifying the effects of shocks on output and unemployment.

As a combatant initially on the opposite side, and one involved in many (intellectual) skirmishes with Ned over the years, I would submit that he has won the war. With the passage of time and the accumulation of research, viewing the evolution of European unemployment as largely an equilibrium phenomenon— as movements in the natural rate, or as Phelps calls it, the structural rate of unemployment, rather than as movements of the actual rate away from the natural rate—appears increasingly plausible. Movements in aggregate demand surely played a role in affecting the timing of the increase in unemployment, but the basic forces for the ups and the more recent downs must be found elsewhere.

Ned has not won all the battles. The set of relevant shocks, and the relevant market imperfections, may not be exactly those he relied on in *Structural Slumps*.

Whether fiscal policy has played the prominent role attributed to it in his analysis appears doubtful. Whether movements in markups reflect profit maximization by firms investing in consumers and how much changes in the real interest rate can affect the markup are still highly contentious issues. Whether the determination of real wages is best explained by an efficiency wage model, or by the type of bargaining captured in flow/matching models, or by models of collective bargaining is also far from established. Still, one finds many Phelpsian themes in current research. Take for example two of the themes of the Ljungqvist and Sargent chapter (LS in what follows): the description of the labor market as a decentralized market with search, a vision first articulated in the "Phelps volume" (1970); and hysteresis, the lasting effects of the loss of human capital coming from being unemployed, a theme first developed in Phelps's 1972 book. The legacy is impressive.

2. ON THE SPECIFIC MECHANISM IN LJUNGQVIST AND SARGENT

The notion that evolutions of unemployment across European countries over the last 30 years are best explained by the interaction of shocks and institutions is an appealing one. It offers the potential for reconciling largely similar shocks and mostly stable labor market institutions with the heterogeneity of unemployment experiences across countries.

In that context, the story developed by LS, in their chapter in this volume and in the work on which they built, is extremely appealing: Europe had institutions designed for quiet times. Times have changed, becoming more turbulent, requiring faster and higher reallocation of resources over time. The old institutions now stand in the way; in particular they are generating higher unemployment.

The story sounds highly plausible. It is yet another incarnation of the old trade-off between distribution and efficiency, between the welfare state and output maximization. Tell the story to noneconomists, to business people, and they will not only understand it, but also nod in approval.

The model itself is splendid and extremely rich in its implications. If anybody wanted proof that the stochastic dynamic programming methods introduced and developed by Sargent and others over the last two decades constitute a marvelous tool, this chapter provides it.

It allows for a smooth integration of a rich microeconomic story—the stories of the unemployed—and its macroeconomic implications: longer duration and a higher unemployment rate. LS are right to use the term "conversations": Some of the realized paths followed by the unemployed in their model sound like stories straight out of Studs Terkel's oral history of the Great Depression (Terkel, 1970). How the unemployed look for jobs, how some of them have bad luck, how they lose heart and give up searching, and how some of them, in the end, become unemployable.

Moreover, the value is clearly more than just in the story telling. Much is learned from calibration, from finding the assumptions and the parameters that give rise to the right stories. More importantly, the microtexture is rich enough to be confronted directly with microeconomic data. While LS do not do it, it is easy to see how one could take this model to panel data on workers and see how it fits. We have the data sets to do so, and I am sure it will soon be done.

3. WHY I REMAIN SKEPTICAL: TURBULENCE

At the center of the LS story is an increase in turbulence. Again, a priori, this seems very plausible. After all, we all know how globalization, financial market deregulation, the dictatorship of pension funds, and higher product market competition are all forcing firms to act more quickly, discontinue old product lines, reallocate production across countries, and so on.

However, there is a catch: We may all know it, but the data just do not show it. . . .

This puzzle showed up early on, when European unemployment was just rising in the late 1970s. Increased turbulence already seemed to be a plausible candidate. But it turned out that the measures of reallocation we could construct, typically measures based on the standard deviation of rates of change of employment, either across sectors or across regions, showed no trend increase. The evidence as of the early 1980s is well summarized in Table 16-15 in Layard and Johnson (1986). That table gives measures by industry or by region for a number of countries: Half of the standard deviations are higher in 1979 than they were in 1960 and half are lower. In all cases, the changes are small. I could not locate a full update of this table for the 1980s and 1990s, but the series I have seen for a few countries yield the same conclusion: no apparent increase.

One may reasonably argue that these measures are too raw. Perhaps, the increase in reallocation is taking place mostly within industries or regions, rather than across them. In that respect, measures of job flows based on plant-level data along the lines of the work by Davis et al. (1996) are clearly preferable. The problem is that they typically do not go back far enough in time. But to the extent that they do, they also show little sign of increased turbulence.

Figure 1, for the United States, is based on the data constructed by Davis et al. (1996) for the period 1972 to 1993 (and downloaded from their web site). The lower line shows the evolution of job destruction (the sum of all employment changes at plants with decreasing employment divided by total employment); the upper line shows the evolution of job reallocation, defined as the sum of job destruction and job creation. If anything, the two lines appear to decline over time.

Figure 2 puts together evidence for France, based on two studies, one by Nocke (1994) for data from 1985 to 1990 and the other by Duhautois (1999) for data from 1990 to 1996. (The juxtaposition of the two series, constructed using slightly different data and methodologies, implies that there may be an artificial break in the series between 1990 and 1991.) The two lines are defined in the same way as in Figure 1. The conclusion is the same as for the United States: At least starting from when data are available, namely, 1985, there is no evidence of an increase in turbulence.

I have focused on turbulence because this is how the LS chapter sells itself. But the specific mechanism in the model is actually a bit different. It is better described

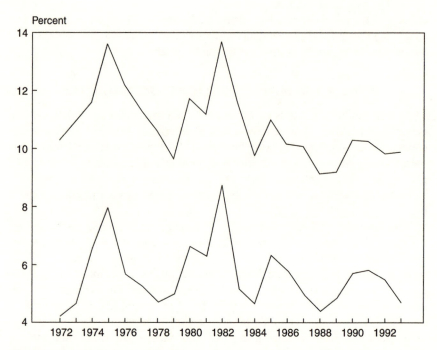

Figure 1. Job destruction and job reallocation, United States: Averages of quarterly rates, 1973 to 1993 (Davis et al., 1996).

as an increase in on-the-job learning and—more importantly for the results—an increase in off-the-job forgetting (the loss of skills by the unemployed). What is central to the results is the fact that when a worker becomes unemployed, the wage he can hope to get is now substantially lower than the wage he had in his previous job. Because unemployment benefits are indexed to the wage he received, this leads the worker to choose a high reservation wage relative to the distribution of wages he now faces. The larger the drop between the old wage and the new mean wage, the longer the unemployment duration, the higher the aggregate unemployment rate.

Turbulence can indeed plausibly generate a larger gap between the old and the new mean wage. But so can many other factors, which may or may not be directly related to turbulence. For example, stronger learning by doing, and so a steeper increase in the marginal product of a worker on a given job, will have the same effect, as will a steeper wage profile relative to the marginal product profile, reflecting higher bonding by workers. All these mechanisms can lead to a larger gap between the wage in the last job and the mean of the distribution faced by the unemployed worker, and so to the results in the chapter.

All of these explanations have one thing in common. They should be reflected in a steeper wage profile as a function of time on a job; and, here, the evidence—at least the evidence that I know of—is far from supportive. In France, for example, a study by Kramarz et al. (1996), which estimates Mincerian wage equations for 1986 and 1992, finds a significant reduction in the effect of time on the job on the

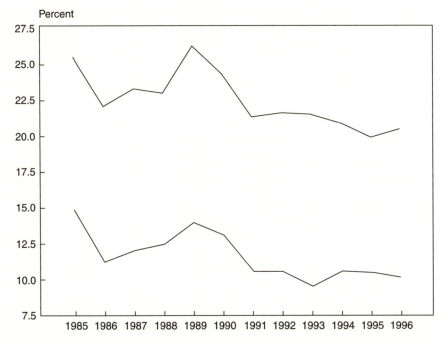

Figure 2. Job destruction and job reallocation, France: Annual rates, 1985 to 1996 (break in 1990–1991).

wage between the two dates. Interestingly, the reduction appears to hold across skill levels. The years 1986 and 1992 may be too close in time for us to draw strong conclusions about trends. But, at a minimum, the results do not appear very supportive of that central component of the LS story.

So where do we stand? Maybe our gut feelings are right: There is more turbulence, and the problem is with our measures, not with the facts. Maybe the story needs to be changed a bit. My own take on this is that European labor market institutions indeed lead to much longer unemployment duration and lower flows than in the United States, even at a given rate of unemployment. In that context, the same adverse shocks lead to very different individual unemployment experiences, along the lines of the chapter. Durations can become so long in Europe as to lead the long-term unemployed to drop out altogether. The story is a bit different from that of LS. But it is in the same spirit, and the tools they have developed can prove very useful there as well.

REFERENCES

Davis, S. J., J. Haltiwanger, and S. Schub (1996), *Job Creation and Destruction*, Cambridge: MIT Press.

Duhautois, R. (1999), "Evolution des Flux d'Emplois en France entre 1990 et 1996; Une Etude Empirique à Partir du Fichier des 'Benefices Réels Normaux,'" INSEE, G9915.

Kramarz, F., S. Lollivier, and L. Pelé (1996), "Wage Inequalities and Firm-Specific Compensation Policies in France," *Annales d'Economie et de Statistique* 41/42:375–86.

Layard, R. and G. Johnson (1986), "The Natural Rate of Unemployment: Explanation and Policy," in O. Ashenfelter and R. Layard, eds., *Handbook of Labor Economics,* Vol. 2, Amsterdam: North-Holland, pp. 921–99.

Nocke, V. (1994), "Gross Job Creation and Gross Job Destruction: An Empirical Study with French Data," mimeo, Bonn University.

Phelps, E. S. (1972), *Inflation Policy and Unemployment Theory*, New York: Norton.

———— (1994), *Structural Slumps: The Modern Equilibrium Theory of Unemployment, Interest, and Assets*, Cambridge: Harvard University Press.

Phelps, E. S., A. A. Alchian, C. C. Holt, D. T. Mortensen, G. C. Archibald, R. E. Lucas, Jr., L. A. Rapping, S. G. Winter, Jr., J. P. Gould, D. F. Gordon, A. Hynes, D. A. Nichols, P. J. Taubman, and M. Wilkinson (1970), *Microeconomic Foundations of Employment and Inflation Theory*, New York: Norton.

Terkel, S. (1970), *An Oral History of the Great Depression in America*, New York: Pantheon.

— 18 —

Flexibility and Job Creation: Lessons for Germany

JAMES J. HECKMAN

I know from life and from history that . . . often, the outward and visible material signs and symbols of happiness and success only show themselves when the process of decline has set in. The outer manifestations take time like the light of the star up there, which may in reality be already quenched when it looks to be shining brightest. (Thomas Buddenbrooks to his sister Tony in *Buddenbrooks*, Part 7, Chapter 6)

1. INTRODUCTION

The German economy lacks the robustness and vitality it possessed in the Erhard era. It is still a strong economy, competitive in medium-high technology trade, but it could be stronger. Unemployment is high, employment growth is low, and its competitive position in world trade is weak in areas of high technology, such as computers, communication technology, and biotechnology.

Germany's poor competitive position in high technology is a symptom of two interrelated factors. First, weak incentives to invest in skill (human capital) and venture capital, produced by the current level of regulation, taxation, and bureaucratization. Second, the inability of the German system to respond to change rapidly. The new economy of the twenty-first century is characterized by variability and the need for flexible responses. This variability creates opportunity, but only for those able to respond quickly and with efficiency. It creates a demand for highly skilled labor and venture capital to respond to the new opportunities. The social system in Germany impedes rapid responses and hence thwarts the German economy from making use of the opportunities created by the new economy.

I thank Christina Gathmann of the University of Chicago for her comments and insights into the Germany economy. Pedro Carneiro provided additional useful comments, as did Bernard Salanie. Thomas Bauer of IZA, Horst Siebert of the University of Kiel, Joachim Wagner of the University of Lüneburg, Rainer Winkelmann of IZA, and Klaus Zimmermann of IZA all provided very helpful information, for which I am grateful. This chapter was first presented as a lecture at the Daimler-Chrysler Center, Berlin, sponsored by Chancen für Alle, on July 3, 2001.

To understand the problems that beset the German economy and their possible solutions, it is important to understand their causes more clearly and to distinguish the short- from the long-run problems. In my view, it is the incentives in place that have long-run consequences that are the most worrisome because they affect the way Germany will perform in the next generation. By the miracle of compound interest, high growth rates produce high wealth levels for future generations while low growth rates produce low wealth levels. Germans should be worried about these rates, although most political discussions focus only on the short-run targets.

The immediate problem facing Germany and much of Europe is that of high unemployment rates. Thirty years ago, the German unemployment rate was the envy of the world. It was one-fifth of that in the United States, which was the same then as it is today. Thirty years later, the German unemployment rate is roughly twice that of the United States. More generally, European unemployment has increased to extraordinarily high levels over the past 20 years. Something has changed and that something is not specific to Germany, but is common to many countries in Europe. Understanding that common factor, or set of factors, is the topic of a lot of recent research in economics. Despite appearances to the contrary, there is more agreement among economists than might first meet the eye. Contrary to public perception, professional economists who study European unemployment and the German economy agree on the basic forces underlying the high persistent unemployment in Germany and much of Europe.

There is a substantial body of empirical evidence pointing to the fact that incentives matter and that firms, individuals, and nations respond to them. Germans who remember the rigid incentives of the former East German economy do not have to be reminded that weak incentives can stifle productivity, investment, and effort. Less dramatically, incentives in Western economies to collect unemployment or disability benefits have been shown to have substantial effects in inducing people not to work and to go into beneficiary status. All economists looking at the empirical evidence accept this and the further point that the work disincentive effects of these programs are large. Disincentives imposed on firms such as minimum wages, union-imposed wage floors, or entry regulations have substantial effects especially when the minimums are binding. Studies from France, Latin America, and Puerto Rico, where minimum wages are often a substantial fraction of average wages, as they are in Germany, have shown substantial disemployment effects of wage floors. Yet in the public discussion of employment creation these disemployment effects are minimized or ignored entirely.

Incentives motivate economic life. It is important to understand how the modern welfare state affects these incentives in order to understand why welfare states perform the way they do.

When the American economy is compared to the German and other European economies, it is not hard to reach the conclusion that it is something about incentives in the welfare state that gives rise to the differential performance of these two types of economies. This chapter is about those incentives, how they affect economic performance, and how incentives might be changed to improve that performance. I want to consider the economic consequences of these incentives in both the short and the long run. Elections are won on short-term performance, so politicians focus on short-run problems. However, as a detached scholar, I want to direct attention to the long-run issues: Nations prosper or founder on their long-run performance.

I make four main points and present empirical evidence to back them up, using references listed at the end of the chapter.

1. The incentives in European and German welfare states distort resource allocation and impair efficiency. The best estimates of the welfare cost of government activity—what economists call deadweight burden—is 40 pfennigs for each mark raised by government activity, and some would place the cost even higher. These costs arise from the distortions in economic activity induced by the fiscal system. Much more than the direct cost of taxation is involved.

Centralized bargaining and regulation of business entry, banking practices, and employment all contribute to the burden. The levels of these disincentives are higher in Europe than in America, and this contributes to higher unemployment, lower employment growth, and a lower level of effort in the society. Such disincentive effects are much discussed in academic circles but they seem never to make their way into popular discussions of policy issues.

The benefit of the current system is alleged to be the universal social insurance it provides. According to this argument, the efficiency cost of taxation and regulation is to be set against the benefit of greater equity and security (Agell, 1999). A closer look at how the system works in Germany and many other European countries shows that it produces security and even wage gains for protected insiders at the cost of inequity, job loss, and income losses for outsiders who are only partially protected by social insurance. Far from promoting social justice at the price of efficiency, it provides security for some at the cost of exclusion for others.

2. The inefficiency and distortions created by the modern welfare state cannot explain the growth in European and German unemployment over the past 20 years. The edifice of the welfare state was in place 30 years ago, and arguably the incentives then were *less* favorable to employment at that time than they are now (Ljungqvist and Sargent, 1998; Blanchard and Wolfers, 2000). A vast empirical literature over the past 25 years has documented the distortions created by the welfare state. Many European governments reduced the worst of those incentive features in response to this literature but typically only by modest amounts. The reforms in Europe and Germany only partly close the incentive gap with America.

What is it then that accounts for the rise in European unemployment? This is the second major topic of this chapter. A growing body of evidence points to the fact that the world economy is more variable and less predictable today than it was 30 years ago when the modern European welfare state with its high levels of taxation and regulation was established. This variability is associated with the entry of many countries into world trade; with the creation of new financial markets and markets for goods; and with the explosion in technology, especially in computers, information technology, and biotechnology. This variability is associated with the onset of skill-biased technical change proceeding at an uneven and unpredictable pace that is still transforming the workplace and making traditional methods of production and management obsolete. Many empirical studies have shown that

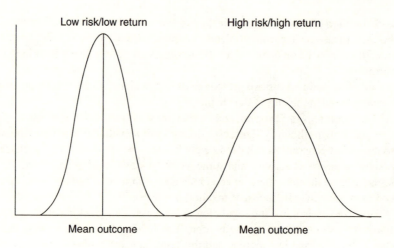

Figure 1. Two alternative social orders.

skill-biased technology is at work in advanced countries as well as Third World economies. These developments contribute to enormous increases in productivity in many industries and create new trading opportunities. At the same time, they lead to more variability and unpredictability in economic life. This variability is a source of wealth for those who can adapt to it. Figure 1 contrasts the distribution of outcomes in the less variable old economy with the distribution of outcomes in the new world economy.

The manifestations of the new variability are legion: rising wage inequality in markets favoring skilled workers in freely functioning labor markets, the large-scale increase in merger activity, and patenting that occurred in the early 1980s at the time of the rising wage inequality and the growth in volatility in trade and in some financial markets. The world has become more open and more fluid and at the same time many traditional methods and organizations have become obsolete.

We live in an era of creative destruction. The new order grows out of the old by destroying the old ways of producing goods and trading. This is an era of greater risk and greater return. The modern welfare state even at its newly "reformed" level is maladapted to this new world economy because it discourages risk taking and efficient adaptation by providing "social insurance" to preserve the status quo at precisely the time when many old economic practices are no longer productive. This explains why so many of the piecemeal reforms implemented in many welfare states around the world have apparently failed and have been associated with rising unemployment. These reforms would have promoted employment and reduced unemployment in a former era. In this modern era of change they do not go nearly far enough to make the reformed economies flexible enough to respond to the new and changing world economy. The world has been changing too fast for European politicians and policy makers to keep up, and Europe will now have to run to keep in place.

An economic order that was well adapted to the more stable and predictable economic environment of the 1950s and 1960s has become dysfunctional in the late twentieth and early twenty-first centuries. The problem of unemployment in Germany is not due solely to the fact that the cost of labor is too high, although that is a problem (Bertola, 2000). It is also due to the inability of the economy to adapt to change and to exploit the opportunities and challenges of the new economy. The opportunity cost of security and preservation of the status quo—whether it is the status quo technology, the status quo trading partner, or the status quo job—has risen greatly in recent times.

3. The opening up of world trade and the increased competitiveness that flows from it means that now, more than ever before, uniformity in the prices of traded goods dictates labor market outcomes. Benefits given to workers are costs to firms and must be paid for in terms of lower wages or less employment. Something has to give in costs because market prices are set internationally and, increasingly, capital markets are uniform around the world. Thus nonwage mandates to workers nominally paid by firms must be borne by the workers themselves. Higher wages achieved by unions or by minimum wage statutes must lead to substitution against labor—fewer jobs—if firms are to remain competitive.

4. Hallmark features of the new economy are diversity, heterogeneity of opportunities, and value of local knowledge. One feature of the dynamics of the new order is that many idiosyncratic opportunities arise as potential trading partners and potential production partners seek each other out.

The old economics focused on stable technologies where broad aggregates such as capital and labor were assumed to be homogeneous. The economics of the modern era focuses on models of matching and sorting of heterogeneous individuals into trading and production units in the face of uncertainty about the suitability of any particular trading or production arrangement. This is a new model of the economy that features the unique and the relation specific. It is a model of marriage that emphasizes the value of partners that know each other in making the decisions to produce or trade and the value of divorce when circumstances change.

It is a model of the gains to trade among idiosyncratic individuals. The new model emphasizes the value of local knowledge and the benefit of exploiting local knowledge about particular possibilities and circumstances that are not widely known. The new economy emphasizes that one person's gain is not another person's loss and that economic efficiency is enhanced by allowing those equipped with local knowledge to act on it.

A striking example of the benefits of local knowledge is the reform of British unionism. When the locus of bargaining was shifted from the national and industry level to the firm level, the face of British unionism changed for the better (Pencavel, 2000). Firms and workers in Britain are now allowed to respond to the local opportunities and conditions that characterize their particular situation and can more freely adapt to those conditions than they could when national wage setting arrangements were in place. National or industry bargaining diverted the attention of workers away from the economic realities of their own productive situation and toward the redistributive possibilities that flow from the application of uniform rules across diverse industrial or national units. Not only does the implementation of local bargaining exploit local information and hence promote productivity but it also inhibits the application of monopoly and rent seeking that occurs when bargaining units become more expansive. Unionism per se is not a cause of inefficiency. Rather it is monopoly unionism using its power to redistribute resources and divert productive activity that leads to great harm.

In addressing these issues, I distinguish between long- and short-run problems and separate long-run solutions from short-run solutions that may be of no value, or even harmful, in the long run.

2. GERMAN UNEMPLOYMENT AND WAGES

The facts about German unemployment are well known. Unemployment is high and has been rising over the past 20 years (Bertola, 2001; Bean, 1994; Nickell, 1997). Lower than American employment 30 years ago, it is now much higher. See Figures 2a and 2b, which compare OECD Europe with North American overall unemployment rates. Figure 3 charts the temporal evolution of the German unemployment rate, which has been in the middle of the OECD pack. German unemployment, like most European unemployment, is largely made up of individuals suffering long spells. The unemployed are essentially removed from the labor market (see Figure 4). American unemployment is typically of much shorter duration and is associated with people changing jobs as opportunities appear and dissolve.

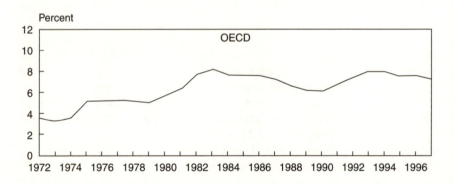

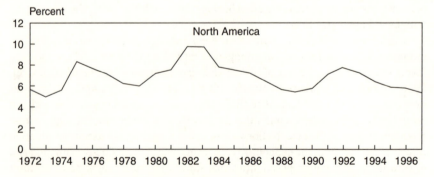

Figure 2a. Standardized unemployment rates in OECD countries. (Source: Scarpetta, 1998.)

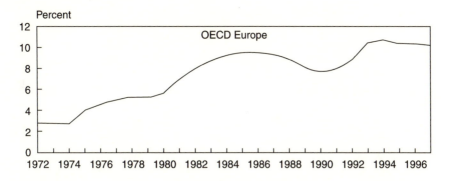

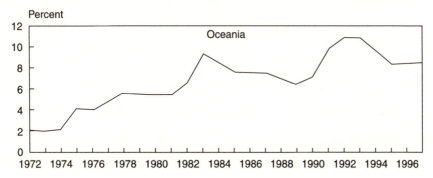

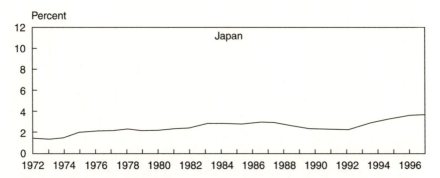

Figure 2b. Standardized unemployment rates in OECD countries. (Source: Scarpetta, 1998.)

The rise in the unemployment rate in Germany is not due to an increase in employment or labor force participation rates. Prime age male employment rates are similar in the United States and in much of Europe. Overall employment rates in Europe and Germany are lower, a topic to which I return later. Unemployment rates are low among German youth (see Figure 5).

European unemployment is structural, not cyclical (Bertola, 2001) (see Figure 6). By this I mean that European—and German—employment is not amenable to the classical demand management policies of macroeconomics, although a few diehard Keynesians still push that line. The factors at work that produce higher

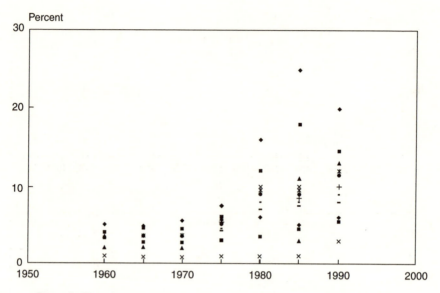

Figure 3. Unemployment rate, E15 countries. (Source: Blanchard and Wolfers, 2000.)

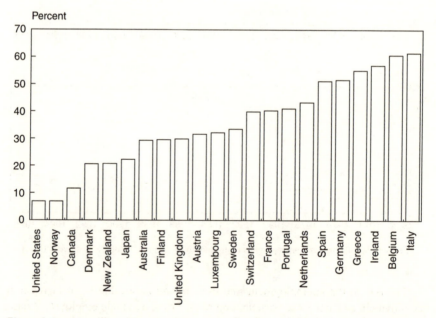

Figure 4. Long-term unemployment as a percentage of total unemployment (12 months and over) in 1999. (Source: OECD, 2000.)

levels of German unemployment are due to the economic fundamentals of incentives, technology, and labor supply.

One structural feature unique to Germany is the problem of the integration of East Germany. It is in fact remarkable that German unemployment rates are only in the middle of the European pack given the special circumstances of the

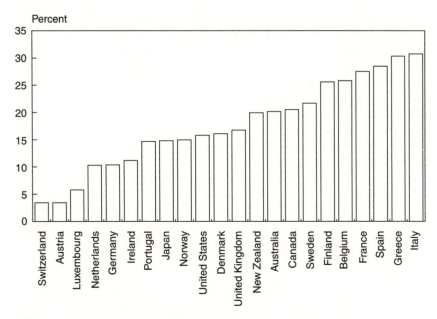

Figure 5. Youth unemployment in 1999. The ratio refers to unemployed persons aged 15 to 24 years divided by the labor force of the same age group. (Source: OECD, 2000.)

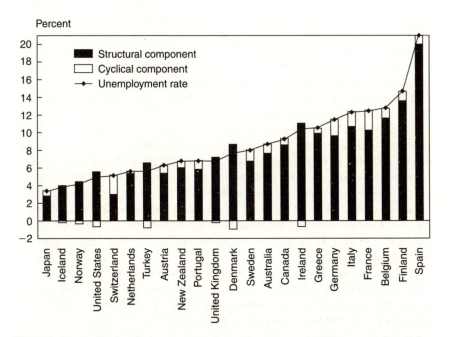

Figure 6. Structural and cyclical components of unemployment rates in 1997 (percent of total labor force). (Source: Scarpetta, 1998.)

East German case. Arguably, Germany would have one of the lower European unemployment rates were it not for the integration.

It is well documented that East German labor productivity was substantially lower than that in West Germany, and this difference was not due solely to differences in the technology between the two regimes. It is widely acknowledged that mandated wage parities between the regions contributed to unemployment and disemployment in the East and that they still play a substantial role in inhibiting employment growth in the former East German regions. These parities coupled with the work disincentives in the social insurance system account for the 2:1 ratio of East-West unemployment rates.

In understanding the problems of the East, it is important to account for the cohort-specific nature of the problem. In the eastern regions, there are substantial numbers of middle-age workers educated and trained to work with an obsolete technology who cannot adapt to the new technology. Adapting these workers to the new social order is prohibitively expensive, although in 1989 official German policy was predicated on the belief that it was easy to retrain such workers.

One very well-established finding from the empirical literature in economics (Heckman, 2000; Heckman et al., 1999) is that publicly supported job-training programs for displaced adult workers are ineffective. The economics of skill investment reveal that it is more efficient to invest in the young and the able than to invest in the middle-aged and the less able, where the returns to training have consistently been shown to be negligible.[1] Competent empirical studies of these retraining programs for displaced Easterners have shown them to be failures (see Eicher and Lechner, 2000). In the short run, these policies reduce unemployment by making the unemployed persons trainees. In the long run, they are ineffective. Collecting the revenue to pay for these programs distorts the economy and diverts resources away from more socially useful opportunities.

This evidence, as well as the evidence from around the world, suggests that the East German problem is a cohort-specific one. A whole cohort of older workers caught up in the change is not well adapted to the modern technology, and training programs will not absorb them into the productive mainstream. Their children can be educated to be productive workers but they themselves cannot be. Two strategies for coping with this problem are: (1) to subsidize their employment and attach the workers to the economy with dignity by reducing the costs of these workers to firms while giving them an acceptable wage, or (2) to put them on the dole. Current overstated wage parities have forced option (2) onto the eastern Germany economy. These parities and the whole issue of wage subsidies should be examined carefully.

In designing any such subsidies, it is necessary to make them cohort specific. They are a short-run solution to a short-run problem. The fathers and mothers should be subsidized but the children should be educated. If the children are subsidized, they will have no incentive to acquire skills.

----

1. They have fewer incentives to invest in new skills because of their shorter working lives and because it takes skill to produce skill (Heckman, 2000).

The East German case is a dramatic example of a more general observation that characterizes markets in transition around the world. When new technology and opportunities become available, as they did in East Germany or in Argentina when it opened its markets to the new economy, it is the younger, more-educated, and more-able workers who benefit from the transition and the older, less-able, and less-educated workers who suffer the most. In Argentina, educated workers who would have been company presidents under the old regime were unemployed under the new one. The economic fundamentals suggest lower wages for such workers. A more humane social policy would pay them higher wages but subsidize firms for employing them. Economic policy must recognize the problem of the transition as an important feature of modern economies undergoing change.

The same forces are at work in all economies although in a less dramatic fashion. In the face of changes in technology and trading opportunities, it is the younger, the more educated, and the more able who benefit the most. The middle-aged and the older workers are at a disadvantage. Unless their wages adjust, they become unemployable.

This observation serves to explain why unemployment in Europe has increased across education and skill categories, especially among more experienced workers. As a consequence of rigidity in wages across the skill categories, these workers have become less employable. Economic policy should promote wage flexibility if it seeks to improve the employability of these workers. It should also reduce incentives to be unemployed from high-income replacement rates.Wage subsidies for the cohorts of workers caught up in the transition represent one option for improving their employment without reducing their standard of living (Snower, 1994; Phelps, 1997). Germans and other Europeans abhor the route of wage flexibility followed by the American economy, arguing that equity or social justice is as important, if not more important, than economic efficiency.

I do not want to tell Germans how to run their economy. Nor do I want to argue that European values placed on equality are inappropriate. However, I cannot help but note that the popular emphasis on "equity" and "social justice" is usually made in a factual void about the true costs of redistribution, which groups are targeted for social justice and which groups are excluded. It is certainly true that there is less inequality in earnings among workers in Germany and Europe than in the United States and in other economies with less rigid markets (see Table 1). At the same time, it is important to recognize that these statistics exclude the long-term unemployed, who constitute more than half of the unemployed in Germany. Accordingly, comparisons of income inequality between the United States and Germany exclude people with zero earnings and bias the comparisons, although this does not eliminate the gap in U.S.-German inequality. The long-term unemployed and the long-term dropouts are excluded from the accounting system of "social justice."

Implicit in many popular discussions of income inequality is the crude belief that one person's gain is another person's loss, that is, that the economic problem is a matter of dividing a fixed pie. In fact, the welfare state, at the level it currently operates in Germany, reduces the total social pie by discouraging production. It makes the size of the pie for the next generation smaller than it would otherwise be by discouraging investment in skills, technology, and knowledge. It discourages

Table 1. Comparisons of Levels of Income Inequality: The Gap between Low- and High-Income Individuals

	Low (P10)	Length of bars represents the gap between high- and low-income individuals	High (P90)	Ratio of high to low (decile ratio)	Gini coefficient
Finland (1991)	58		158	2.74	0.227
Sweden (1992)	57		159	2.78	0.229
Belgium (1992)	58		163	2.79	0.230
Norway (1991)	56		158	2.80	0.230
Denmark (1992)	54		155	2.86	0.239
Austria (1987)	56		163	2.89	0.227
Luxembourg (1985)	59		174	2.95	0.238
Germany (1984)	57		171	3.01	0.249
The Netherlands (1991)	57		173	3.05	0.268
Italy (1991)	56		176	3.14	0.255
Switzerland (1982)	54		185	3.43	0.311
France (1984)	55		193	3.48	0.294
Canada (1991)	47		183	3.90	0.285
Spain (1990)	49		198	4.02	0.306
Israel (1992)	50		205	4.12	0.305
Ireland (1987)	50		209	4.23	0.328
Australia (1989/1990)	45		193	4.30	0.308
United Kingdom (1991)	44		206	4.67	0.335
United States (1991)	36		208	5.78	0.350
	53		180	3.52	0.274

Source: Gottschalk and Sneeding (1997).

Note: Numbers given are percent of median in each nation and Gini coefficient.

venture capital by taxing the proceeds of good investments and by regulating capital markets.

Going back to Figure 1, we see that the welfare state reduces the dispersion of social outcomes by reducing the level of social outcomes. How sizable is the cost in lost output? This is the crucial empirical question that is never asked or answered in public discussions. How much of the rise in German unemployment and the slow growth in output is due to institutions of the welfare state?

3. THE CAUSES OF JOBLESSNESS

In order to answer the question of what causes joblessness, it is useful to review the sharp contrast in the institutional features of German (and European) labor and product markets with those of American and other less regulated markets. The familiar picture that emerges is that European markets are much more regulated, wage setting is much more centralized and less adaptable to local conditions, and the replacement rate (the percentage of earnings an unemployed worker can claim) is much higher in Europe than in the United States (see Figures 7, 8, and 9, respectively). The level of payroll taxation is substantially higher in Europe than in the United States (see Table 2). The tax wedge between what a firm pays per unit labor and what the worker receives is much greater in Europe than in the United States.

A large body of evidence suggests that at the current levels of incentives, the German welfare state reduces employment, raises unemployment, retards flexibility and creates a two-tier system, with a protected enclave surrounded by a partially protected group of unskilled, uneducated, and marginal workers (Siebert, 1997).

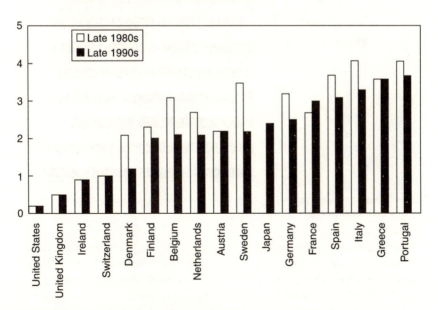

Figure 7. Strictness of employment protection. The scores can range from 0 to 6, with higher values representing stricter regulation. (Source: OECD, 2000.)

Unionized workers as
a share of nonfarm
labor force: 1995

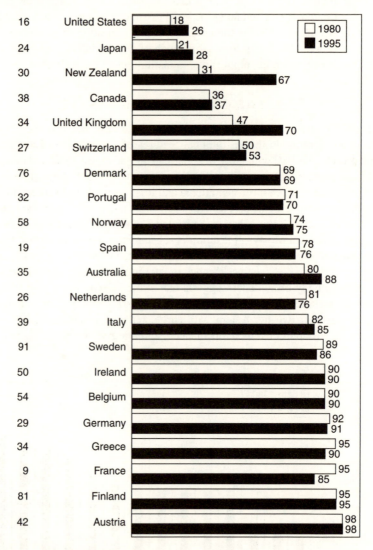

16	United States
24	Japan
30	New Zealand
38	Canada
34	United Kingdom
27	Switzerland
76	Denmark
32	Portugal
58	Norway
19	Spain
35	Australia
26	Netherlands
39	Italy
91	Sweden
50	Ireland
54	Belgium
29	Germany
34	Greece
9	France
81	Finland
42	Austria

Figure 8. Percent of employees whose wages are set by collective bargaining (contracts: 1980 and 1995). (Source: Bierhanzl and Gwartney, 1998.)

The high level of centralized wage bargaining thwarts the ability of workers and firms to act on local conditions and to bargain flexibly. Pencavel (1996) documents that the application of three principles—(1) decentralization of bargaining to the enterprise level; (2) removal of government intervention from the bargaining process; (3) local determination of the terms over which to bargain—promotes productivity and links payments to productivity in the workplace and not to politics.

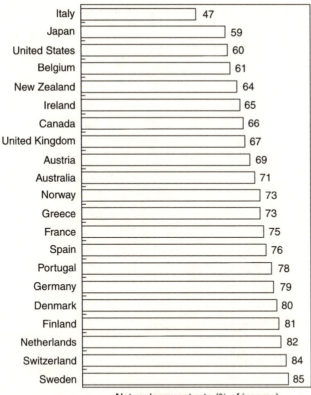

Net replacement rate (% of income)
(including housing benefits)

Figure 9. Net initial replacement rate for an unemployed married worker with two children (1995). These data are for a 40-year-old worker (with spouse and two children) employed continuously since age 18. (Source: OECD, 1997a [table 9], 1997b.)

Studies of reforms of union systems in Great Britain, New Zealand, and Chile reveal that application of these principles to previously centralized wage-setting environments promoted productivity and raised wages in the aggregate.[2]

Detailed econometric studies by Nickell et al. (1992), Gregg et al. (1993), and Machin and Stewart (1996) demonstrate that substantial productivity growth occurred after decentralized unionism began to govern economic relations. The issue on the table is not about getting rid of unions; substantial productivity gains were registered at union plants when decentralized unionism was introduced. The issue is about making wage setting responsive to local conditions and to adapt to opportunities that appear. It has been shown that locally responsive unions facilitate plant-wide response to technical change (Levine, 1995). Decentralization improves adaptability, and the new economy places a premium on adaptability.

---

2. While wage inequality rose in Great Britain during this period, so did real wages, and at a much faster rate than in the United States.

Table 2. Tax Wedge and Social Security Contributions (in percent of gross wages)[a]

	Total tax wedge		Employers' social security contribution rate	
	1985	1994	1985	1994
Australia	22.9	23.5	0.0	0.0
Austria	40.3	39.7	18.6	19.1
Belgium	54.2	53.5	28.8	25.8
Canada	26.9	31.4	4.7	6.2
Denmark	47.8	45.2	2.8	0.0
Finland	38.0	39.4	5.7	3.6
France	43.4	43.6	27.5	26.2
Germany	44.5	48.3	14.5	16.3
Greece	31.4	. . .	17.9	21.6
Iceland	16.5	22.9	2.1	2.8
Ireland	42.4	38.4	10.9	10.9
Italy	50.0	49.9	29.9	31.5
Japan	21.6	21.6	6.8	7.0
Luxembourg	38.4	35.1	13.3	13.0
Mexico	. . .	26.5	15.2	16.2
Netherlands	49.9	45.6	19.2	7.3
New Zealand	27.9	24.3	0.0	0.0
Norway	41.8	36.9	13.5	11.3
Portugal	30.7	34.3	16.7	19.7
Spain	36.6	38.8	23.8	24.0
Sweden	50.9	46.8	24.0	23.2
Switzerland	28.8	28.7	9.4	9.3
Turkey	37.0	35.7	8.3	6.7
United Kingdom	37.8	33.3	9.5	9.3
United States	33.6	31.2	6.6	7.1

Source: Scarpetta (1998).

[a] Total tax wedges include income taxes, employer and employee social security contributions, but not indirect taxes. Tax rates refer to one earner without dependents and take into account standard tax relief.

It is sometimes argued that centralized bargaining is beneficial and that unions can act in an enlightened way to correct any spillovers created by the action of local wage agreements. In theory, this is possible and experience with recent Dutch wage setting, until recently, illustrates that in a small country with few unions, it may be possible to make centralized bargaining work. However, as Pencavel demonstrates, the monopoly power created by centralization is too tempting not to use and the track record on centralized bargaining is poor, especially in large economies such as that of Germany.

Germany does not have a governmentally mandated minimum wage although union wage floors effectively operate as wage minimums. One measure of the effectiveness of a minimum wage is the ratio of the minimum to the average wage. This ratio is much higher in Germany, and continental Europe more generally, than it is in the United States or Great Britain (see Table 3). The higher this ratio, the more binding these minimums are on the operations of firms.

The French ratio is below that of Germany but much higher than that of the United States or Great Britain. A series of important papers by John Abowd

Table 3. Minimum to Average Wage in Latin America and the Industrialized Countries

Bolivia (1995)	0.21	Columbia (1995)	0.54
Brazil (1995)	0.24	Costa Rica (1995)	0.54
Argentina (1995)	0.26	Denmark (1994)	0.54
Chile (1994)	0.30	Germany (1991)	0.55
Spain (1994)	0.32	Ireland (1993)	0.55
Mexico (1994)	0.36	Netherlands	0.55
Peru (1996)	0.36	Luxembourg	0.56
United States (1993)	0.39	Belgium (1992)	0.60
United Kingdom (1993)	0.40	Honduras (1996)	0.61
Panama (1995)	0.43	Austria (1993)	0.62
Portugal (1995)	0.45	Greece (1995)	0.62
France (1995)	0.50	Paraguay (1995)	0.64
Finland (1993)	0.52	El Salvador (1995)	0.69
Sweden (1996)	0.52	Italy (1991)	0.71
Switzerland (1995)	0.52	Venezuela	0.88

Source: LAC countries; authors' calculations based on household surveys. Industrial countries: Dolado et al. (1996).

(e.g., Abowd et al., 1997, 1999) and various co-authors documents the substantial disemployment effects of French minimum wages. Minimum wage effects are weak only when minimum wages do not bind. A widely cited study by Card and Krueger (1995) that claimed to find no disemployment effects of minimum wages has been challenged in the professional journals. Even if correct for the small wage changes studied in the United States, this study is irrelevant for Europe, which has much higher effective—and binding—minimums. Machin et al. (2002) demonstrate how New Deal minimum-wage increases substantially reduced employment in the home care sector in England.

Some indirect evidence of the importance of the disemployment effects of the minimum wage is implicit in Figure 5. The lower rate of youth unemployment in Germany compared to that of many other countries is frequently attributed to the apprenticeship system. It is certainly true that a system that encourages youth to both work and learn promotes their immediate employment. A closer look at this system reveals that during the apprenticeship period, firms can pay apprentices wages that are substantially below the minimum wage. When the apprenticeship period ends, union-mandated minimum wages apply. It is no accident, then, that Germany is one of the few countries in the world to have a higher rate of unemployment among young adults (in their early 20s) not covered by the minimum-wage exemption than among teenage youth (Heckman et al., 1994). Reducing minimum wages substantially promotes employment in economies such as that of Germany, where minimum wages are high.

German replacement rates of the earnings of the unemployed by social insurance are substantial (see Figure 9). It is very well documented that higher levels of unemployment compensation induce greater rates of unemployment (see the evidence summarized in Layard and Nickell, 1999). As the generosity of benefits increases, so does the incentive not to work. Germans, like all people, respond to these incentives.

German levels of labor market regulation are high compared to those in the United States. Employment protection laws protect the status quo and make

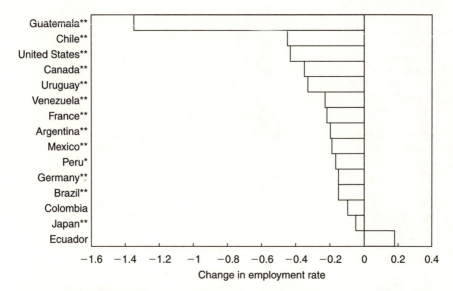

Figure 10. Unemployment response to GDP growth. * or ** indicates the coefficient is significant at the 5 or 1 percent level, respectively. Only countries for which unemployment data are available for at least 10 years are included. (Source: Inter-American Development Bank, 1996.)

it difficult for firms to respond flexibly to changing market conditions and to improved technologies. Thus it is no accident that the unemployment-GDP growth relationship is weak in Germany compared to that of countries with more flexible labor markets. Figure 10 compares the change in the unemployment rate in response to GDP growth across a variety of countries. In economies where it is costly to fire workers, job growth in response to GDP growth is diminished since firms account for the possibility that the economy might turn sour in the future and employment protection laws make it difficult to fire redundant labor. Hence, they hire fewer workers to avoid having to pay the costs of possibly having to fire them. The other side of the coin, however, is that employment protection laws make slowdowns in GDP growth less costly in terms of unemployment. It protects the insiders against job loss.

The United States has a very flexible labor market compared to Germany. Nonetheless, substantial changes have recently been made to the "employment at will" doctrine that gave freedom to the employer to fire employees without any cost. This has moved the American system of severance pay closer to that of Europe. Union work rules impose some restrictions on U.S. firms, and the portion of the costs of unemployment insurance borne by the firm make work force reduction costly.

In the 1980s, many state judiciaries in the United States adopted "wrongful termination" doctrines. These doctrines impose substantial costs of employment termination on employers that are similar in character to severance cost payments in the German system. In what appears to be a natural experiment, it is possible to examine the consequences of these doctrines on employment. The effectiveness and comprehensive nature of the law vary from state to state.

While the *direct* legal costs of the new doctrines are relatively low, on average the whole process adds uncertainty to the employment process and some settlements are high ($177,000 in U.S. 1998 dollars). Firms now play a lottery with the court system. Despite small average costs, the response of firms to the potential of experiencing a very visible wrongful termination case has been dramatic. Elaborate procedures have been established at all stages of the hiring and discharge process. Firms now institute more elaborate screening and review procedures when hiring and firing workers.

These costs have a potent negative effect on employment in states that adopt "wrongful termination" laws. Dertouzos and Karoly (1992) examine the employment consequences of these costs. The most severe systems, which in my view are lower bounds for the German case, suggest that employment declines by 5 percent in states with the most comprehensive employment protection legislation.

Employment protection laws *in theory* need not have any adverse effects on employment. The argument is that if a firm were mandated to offer a benefit such as job security to its workers, the latter would be willing to accept lower wages to obtain the benefit. The composition of the pay package would be affected even if the total level of compensation is not. For this argument to have any practical significance, wages have to be downward flexible. Yet Table 3 suggests that they are not. Binding minimum wages, whether imposed by national laws as in France or by union minimums as in Germany, prevent the necessary wage adjustments.

Evidence of the impact of employment protection legislation on employment and wage inequality suggests the following. Countries with more severe employment regulation legislation have lower employment rates (Figure 11) and less wage inequality among workers (Figure 12). Those who keep jobs stay at them longer (Figure 13). There is little effect of this legislation on the employment of prime age males (Figure 14).

The picture that emerges from this evidence is that the employment protection laws (EPL) create a protected enclave of insiders who experience less unemployment and wage fluctuations than the excluded outsiders. Social justice applies to this enclave but not to the entire society. Given that the long-term unemployed are excluded from the statistics on income inequality, international comparisons of income inequality such as those in Table 1 dramatically understate the inequality inherent in the European welfare state.

4. RESTRICTIONS IN OTHER MARKETS

When considering Germany's employment problems, the natural first impulse is to look at the institutions governing the labor market. Yet economists since the time of Alfred Marshall have recognized that the structure of the product and the capital markets affect the performance of the labor market.

The German product market is highly regulated, although it is far from the most regulated product market in Europe (see Figure 15). Product market regulation goes hand in glove with labor market regulation (see Figure 16) (Nicoletti and Scarpetta, 2001; Scarpetta, 1998). Inducing competition in the product market is one way

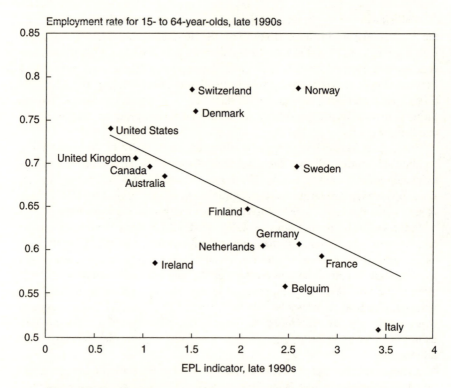

Figure 11. Overall employment and labor market regulation. (Source: Bertola, 2001.)

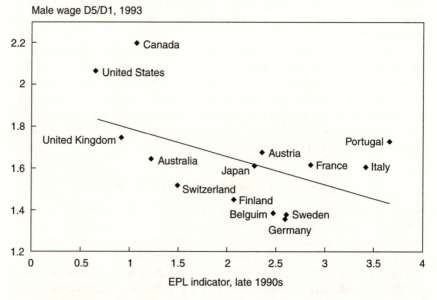

Figure 12. Employment protection legislation and wage inequality. (Source: Bertola, 2001.)

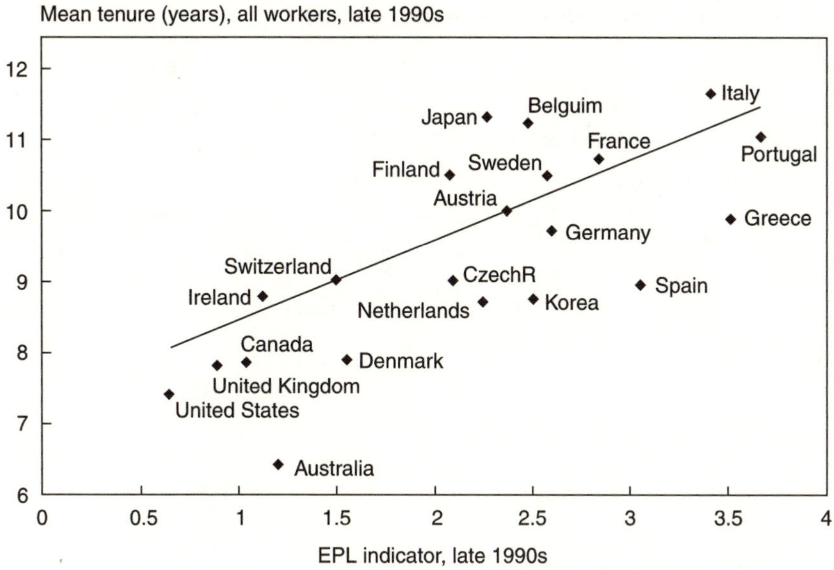

Mean tenure (years), all workers, late 1990s

Figure 13. Employment protection legislation and length of tenure. (Source: Bertola, 2001.)

of curbing excess union power. Price-taking firms offer fewer opportunities for rent-seeking unions.

Regulation of the product market retards the responsiveness of the German economy to new trade and technology opportunities and inhibits job creation (Djankov et al., 2000). Table 4 compares the regulatory environment in Germany with that of the rest of the world. Compared to the United States, German firms are required to go through more procedures (seven versus four) and take a longer time (90 versus 7 days), and the process costs roughly ten times more in Germany than in the United States. By inhibiting entry and retarding flexibility, product market regulation reduces the demand for labor and the growth of jobs. This unfriendly regulatory environment also retards investment and risk taking. It inhibits German adaptation to the new economy. As an example, consider the relationship between Internet usage and EPL (see Figure 17). The more stringent the employment protection or business regulation laws, the less the use of the Internet (see Samaniego, 2001), which accounts for the lesser use of the Internet in Germany (see Figure 18).

This unfriendly environment also helps to explain why, in recent years, the share of foreign direct investment in Germany has been so low (see Figure 19) and why German investment in venture capital is low (see Figure 20). It also accounts for why Germans have found investment abroad so attractive.

Reforms in the product market and in capital markets will promote flexibility and will facilitate reforms in the labor market. That is a lesson learned during many successful economic reforms around the world.

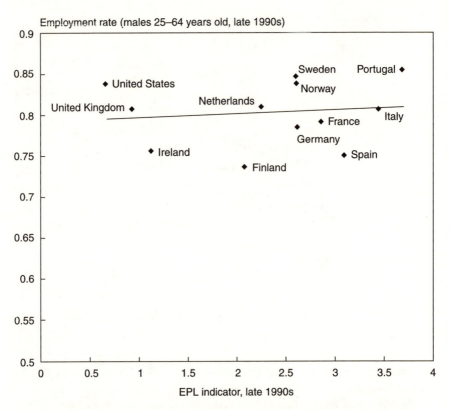

Figure 14. Male adult employment and labor market regulation. (Source: Bertola, 2001.)

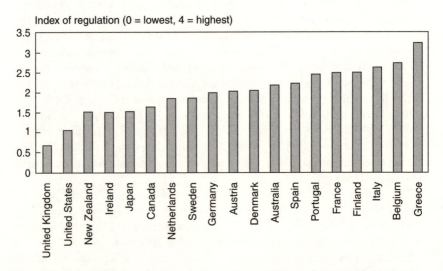

Figure 15. Overall indicator of product market regulation. Factor analysis is applied to summary indicators of state control, barriers to entrepreneurial acitvity, and barriers to trade and investment. (Source: Nicoletti and Scarpetta, 2001.)

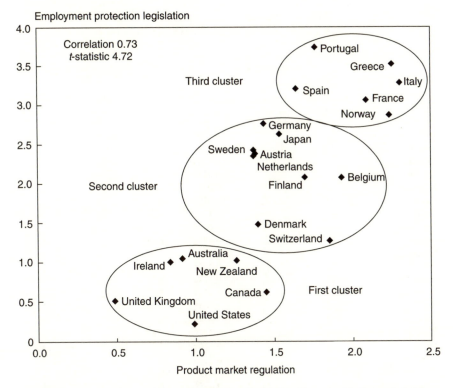

Figure 16. Product market regulation and employment legislation. The scale of indicators is 0–6 from least to most restrictive. (Source: Nicoletti and Scarpetta, 2001.)

5. THE LONG-RUN CONSEQUENCES OF REGULATION AND THE WELFARE STATE FOR GERMANY

Product market and labor market regulation not only impede the flexibility of the German economy but also threaten its future vitality. These long-run effects are rarely debated in public because they operate in a subtle fashion and do not show up on the front pages of newspapers.

Trade is the engine of German economic power. Germany retains its strong competitive position in medium-high technology (e.g., traditional manufacturing). But it does not have comparative advantage in the cutting edge technologies of computers, information technology, and biotechnology (see Figure 21). The technology intensity of German exports is low by international standards (see Figure 22). The highly regulated capital markets have prevented German venture capital from flowing into these cutting-edge areas of world trade and technology (Siebert and Stolpe, 2001). As a consequence, German supremacy in trade in future world markets is at risk.

The high tax rates inherent in the German system and the rigidity of the educational system discourage skill formation. Since knowledge is created by educated people, the failure of German institutions of higher learning to train more

Table 4. Regulation of Business Formation and
Protection of Investors in Advanced OECD Countries

	Business formation			Protection of investors (higher = better)		
	Number of procedures required	Days to get approval	Cost/GDP per capita	Rule of law	Antidirector rights	Creditor rights
Australia	3	3	0.0209	10	4	1
Austria	12	154	0.4545	10	2	3
Belgium	8	42	0.1001	10	0	2
Canada	2	2	0.0140	10	4	1
Denmark	5	21	0.0136	10	3	3
Finland	4	32	0.0199	10	2	1
France	16	66	0.1970	8.98	2	0
Germany	7	90	0.0851	9.23	1	3
Greece	13	53	0.4799	6.18	1	1
Ireland	4	25	0.1145	7.80	3	1
Italy	11	121	0.2474	8.33	0	2
Japan	11	50	0.1144	8.98	3	2
Netherlands	8	77	0.3031	10	2	2
New Zealand	3	17	0.0042	10	4	3
Norway	6	24	0.0249	10	3	2
Portugal	12	99	0.3129	8.68	2	1
Spain	11	83	0.1269	7.80	2	2
Sweden	4	17	0.0254	10	2	2
Switzerland	12	88	0.1336	10	1	1
United Kingdom	7	11	0.0056	8.57	4	4
United States	4	7	0.0096	10	5	1

Source: Freeman (2001).

students and to develop flexible arrangements with industry bodes ill for the future of German technology.

6. SUMMING UP

The Germany economy labors under the burden of heavy regulation and weak incentives. The German welfare state has succeeded in raising the wages and benefits of protected insiders but at the cost of low employment growth, low productivity growth in the manufacturing sector, and higher unit labor costs (see Figures 23–26). These factors threaten the long-term competitive position of German industry in world trade and inhibit Germany from investing in the technologies of the future.

In analyzing German employment problems, I have stressed the importance of distinguishing long-run from short-run problems and long-run from short-run solutions. German unemployment is a structural problem. Some aspects of German unemployment will fade as older cohorts of workers trained under the East German system retire and are replaced by more educated workers adapted to the new system.

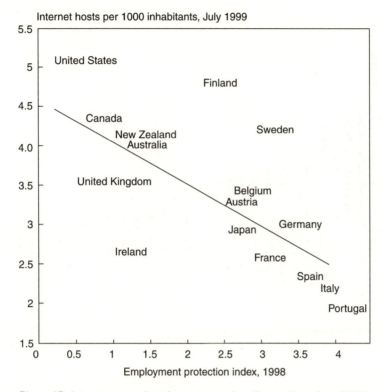

Internet hosts per 1000 inhabitants, July 1999

Employment protection index, 1998

Figure 17. Internet usage and employment protection. (Source: Samaniego, 2001.)

Apart from this short-run feature a substantial portion of German unemployment is a symptom of the deeper problem that incentives to innovate, to acquire skills, and to take risks have been thwarted by the welfare state. The costs of preserving the status quo have increased in the new world economy that is characterized by many new opportunities in technology and trade. The winners in world trade in the next generation will be those countries that can respond flexibly with educated work forces.

I opened this chapter with a quotation from Thomas Mann's *Buddenbrooks.* In closing, let me explain its relevance. The German economy is, in many ways, still in robust health. Germany remains a major factor in the world economy. Germans have begun to shift toward making markets more flexible, unemployment benefits lower, and bargaining more decentralized. These reforms have only been partial in character and are not substantial enough to successfully adapt the German economy to the economy of the future.

In pursuit of social justice—which in actuality is a defense of a protected enclave of workers and firms—Germany has muted incentives to invest in ideas, skills, and new technology. These muted incentives portend a second-rate German economy in the future. While Germany is not yet Thomas Mann's dead star, sending forth its light, it will be a dying star if it fails to adapt to the new world economic order.

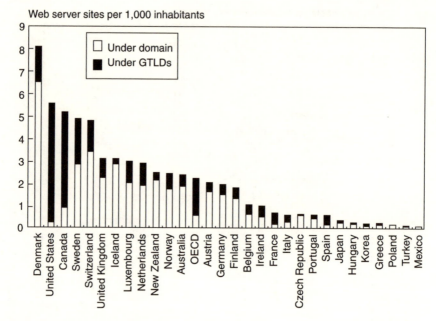

Figure 18. Web server sites per 1,000 inhabitants, July 1998 (including: com, net, org). (Source: OECD from Netcraft Data, www.netcraft.co.uk.)

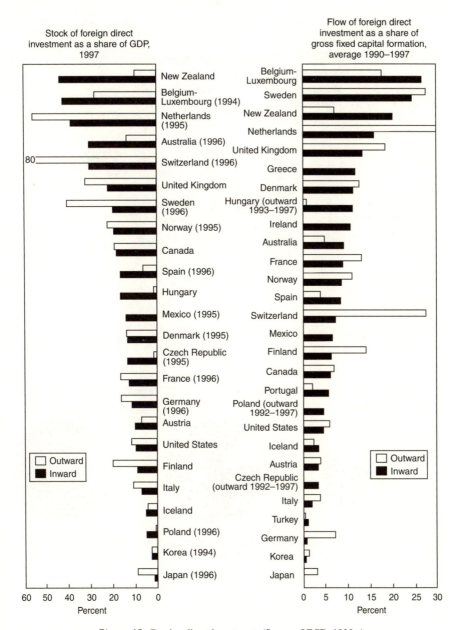

Figure 19. Foreign direct investment. (Source: OECD, 1999a.)

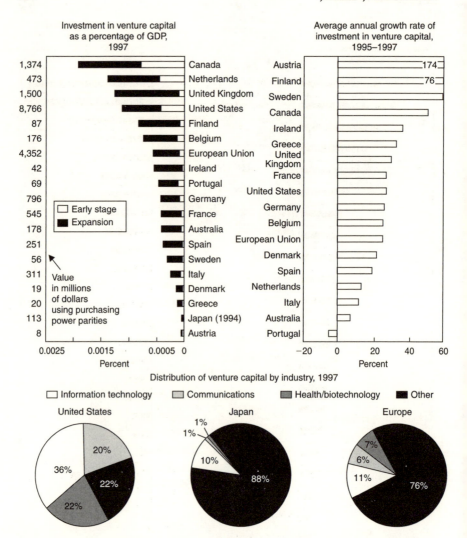

Figure 20. Venture capital. (Source: OECD, based on data from European Venture Capital Association; MITI [Japan]; CVCA [Canada]; NVCA [United States].)

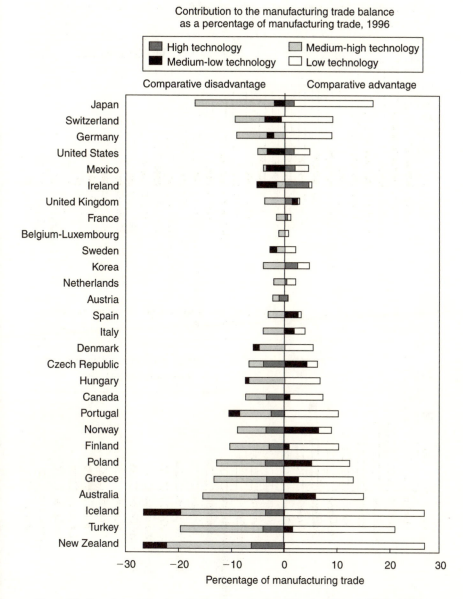

Figure 21. Revealed comparative advantage by technology intensity. (Source: OECD, 1999b.)

Share of high- and medium-high-technology industries in manufacturing exports, 1996

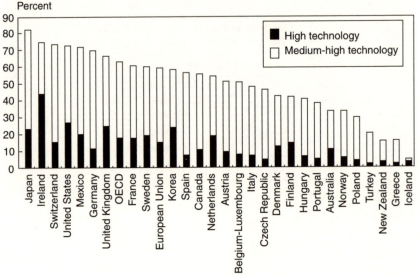

Annual growth rate of exports in high- and medium-high-technology industries, 1990–1996

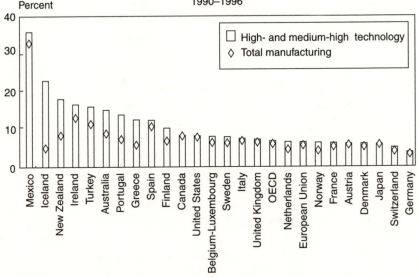

Figure 22. Exports by technology intensity. (Source: OECD, 1999b.)

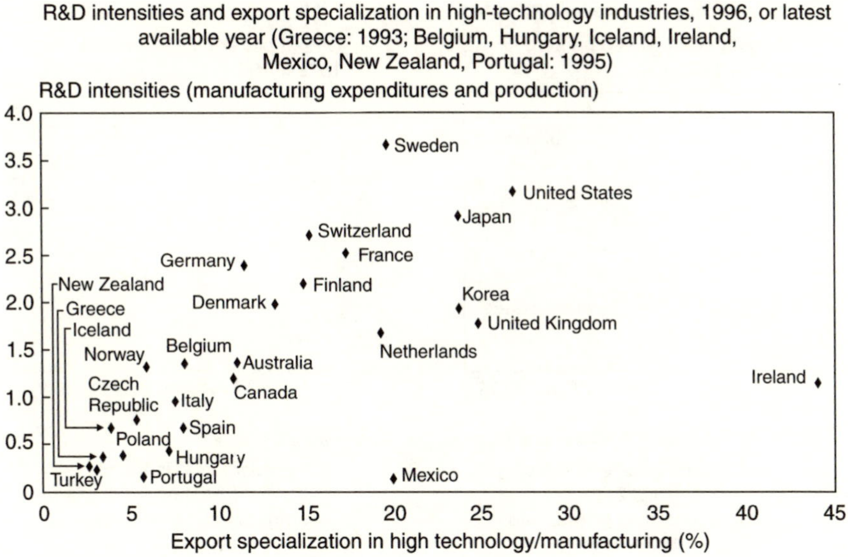

R&D intensities and export specialization in high-technology industries, 1996, or latest available year (Greece: 1993; Belgium, Hungary, Iceland, Ireland, Mexico, New Zealand, Portugal: 1995)
R&D intensities (manufacturing expenditures and production)
Sweden
United States
Japan
Switzerland
France
Germany
Finland
Denmark
Korea
United Kingdom
Netherlands
Ireland
New Zealand
Greece
Iceland
Norway
Belgium
Australia
Canada
Czech Republic
Italy
Spain
Poland
Hungary
Turkey
Portugal
Mexico
Export specialization in high technology/manufacturing (%)

Figure 22. (*Continued*)

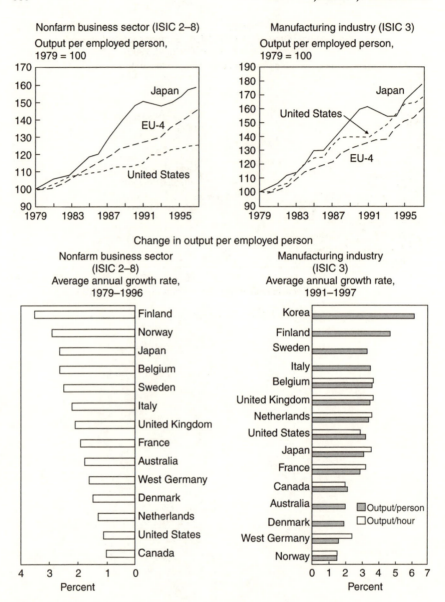

Figure 23. Productivity growth. (Sources: OECD and U.S. Bureau of Labor Statistics.)

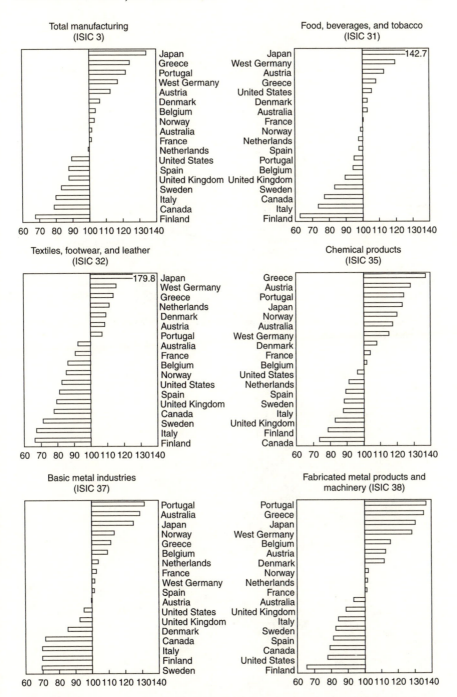

Figure 24. Unit labor costs. Relative trade-weighted unit labor costs by industry, 1996 (1990 = 100, U.S. dollar basis). (Source: OECD, STAN, and Bilateral Trade databases, May 1999.)

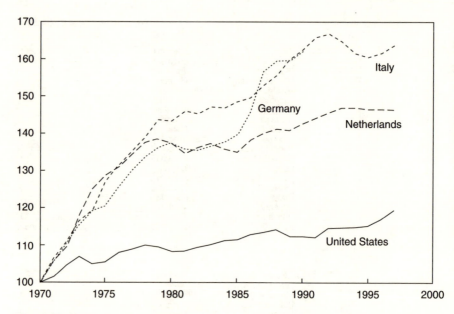

Figure 25. Real total compensation per employee in the United States, Germany, Italy, and The Netherlands. (Source: Bertola, 2000.)

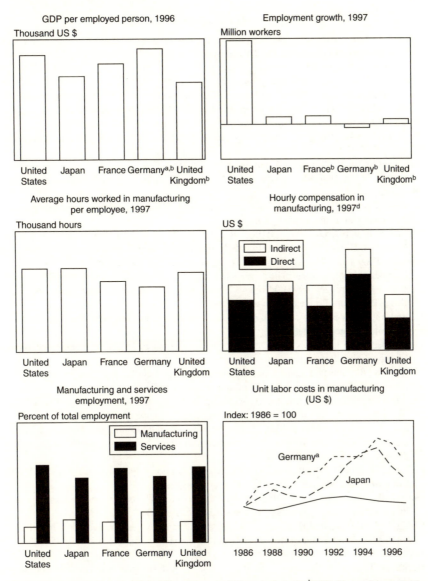

Figure 26. Dimensions of comparative performance. [a]Western area only. [b]1996. [c]Latest data available. [d]Labor costs for production workers. Hourly direct pay includes pay for time worked, pay for time not worked, bonuses, and the cost of any payments in kind. Hourly indirect pay includes employer expenditures for legally required insurance programs and contractual and private benefit plans plus taxes on, minus subsidies of, payrolls or employment. (Source: Central Intelligence Agency, 1999.)

REFERENCES

Abowd, J., F, Kramarz, T. Lemieux, and D. Margolis (1997), "Minimum Wages and Youth Employment in France and The United States," National Bureau of Economic Research Working Paper No. 6111.

Abowd, J., F. Kramarz, and D. Margolis (1999), "Minimum Wages and Employment in France and the United States," National Bureau of Economic Research Working Paper No. 6996.

Agell, J. (1999), "On The Benefits from Rigid Labor Markets: Norms, Market Failures, and Social Insurance," *Economic Journal* 109(453):143–64.

Bean, C. (1994), "European Unemployment: A Survey," *Journal of Economic Literature* 32(2):573–619.

Bertola, G. (2000), "Europe's Unemployment Problems," in *Economics of the European Union: Policy Analysis*, M. Artis and F. Nixson, eds., 2nd ed., Oxford: Oxford University Press.

——— (2001), "Aggregate and Disaggregated Aspects of Employment and Unemployment," European University Working Paper.

Bierhanzl, E. and J. Gwartney (1998), "Regulations, Unions and Labor Markets in OECD Countries: Higher Unionization Equals Higher Employment," *Regulation* 21(3):40–53.

Blanchard, O. and J. Wolfers (2000), "The Role of Shocks and Institutions in the Rise of European Unemployment: The Aggregate Evidence," *Economic Journal* 110(462):C1–33.

Card, D. and A. Krueger (1995), *Myth and Measurement: The New Economics of the Minimum Wage*, Princeton: Princeton University Press.

Central Intelligence Agency (1999), *Handbook of International Statistics*, Washington, D.C.: Central Intelligence Agency.

Dertouzos, J. and L. Karoly (1992), *Labor Market Responses to Employer Liability*, Santa Monica, Calif.: Rand Corporation, Institute for Civil Justice.

Djankov, S., R. Laporta, F. Lopez, and A. Shleifer (2000), "Regulation of Entry," unpublished manuscript, Harvard University, Department of Economics.

Dolado, J. F., Kramarz, S. Machin, A. Manning, D. Margolis, and C. Teulings (1996), "The Economic Impact of Minimum Wages in Europe," *Economic Policy* 23:317–57.

Eicher, M. and M. Lechner (2000), "Public Sector Sponsored Continuous Vocational Training in East Germany: Institutional Arrangements, Participants and Results of Empirical Studies," IZA Working Paper No. 76.

Freeman, R. (2001), "Institutional Differences and Economic Performance Among OECD Countries," unpublished manuscript, Harvard University.

Gottschalk, P. and T. M. Sneeding (1997), "Cross-Natural Comparisons of Earnings and Income Inequality," *Journal of Economic Literature* 34(2):633–87.

Gregg, P., S. Machin, and D. Metcalf (1993), "Signals and Cycles? Productivity Growth and Change in Union Status in British Companies," *Economic Journal* 103(419):854–907.

Heckman, J. (2000), "Policies to Foster Human Capital," *Research in Economics* 54(1):3–56.

Heckman, J., R. Roselius, and J. Smith (1994), "U.S. Education and Training Policy: A Reevaluation of the Underlying Assumptions behind the New Consensus," in A. Levenson and L. C. Solomon, eds., *Labor Markets, Employment Policy and Job Creation*, Santa Monica, Calif.: Milken Institute for Job and Capital Formation.

Heckman, J., R. LaLonde, and J. Smith (1999), "The Economics and Econometrics of Active Labor Market Programs," in *Handbook of Labor Economics*, Vol. 3, O. Ashenfelter and D. Card, eds., Amsterdam: Elsevier, pp. 1865–2097.

Inter-American Development Bank (1996), "Economic and Social Progress in Latin America, 1996 Report, Special Section: Making Social Services Work," Washington, D.C.: Johns Hopkins University Press.

Layard, R. and S. Nickell (1999), "Labor Market Institutions and Economic Performance," in *Handbook of Labor Economics*, Vol. 3C, O. Ashenfelter and D. Card, eds., Amsterdam: North-Holland, pp. 3029–84.

Levine, D. (1995), *Reinventing the Workplace. How Business and Employees Can Both Win*, Washington, D.C.: Brookings Institution.

Ljungqvist, L. and T. Sargent (1998), "The European Unemployment Dilemma," *Journal of Political Economy* 106(3):514–50.

Machin, S. and M. Stewart (1996), "Trade Unions and Financial Performance," *Oxford Economic Papers* 48:213–41.

Machin, S., A. Manning, and L. Rahman (2002), "Where the Minimum Wage Bites Hard: The Introduction of the UK National Minimum Wage to a Low-Wage Sector," University College London, Department of Economics Working Paper.

Mann, T. (1924), *Buddenbrooks*, translated by H. T. Lowe-Porter, New York: Knopf.

Nickell, S. (1997), "Unemployment and Labor Market Rigidities: Europe vs. North America," *Journal of Economic Perspectives* 11(3):55–74.

Nickell, S. and J. Van Ours (2000), "The Netherlands and the United Kingdom: A European Unemployment Miracle?," *Economic Policy* 30:137–80.

Nickell, S., S. Wadwahni, and M. Wall (1992), "Productivity Growth in U.K. Companies: 1975–1986," *European Economic Review* 36:1055–91.

Nicoletti, G. and S. Scarpetta (2001), "Interactions Between Product and Labor Market Regulations: Do They Affect Employment? Evidence from OECD Countries," Banco Portugal Conference, June 3–4, Cascais, Portugal.

OECD (1997a), *Job Strategy: Making Working Pay*, Paris.

—— (1997b), *Database on Taxation and Benefit Entitlements*, Paris.

—— (1999a), *International Direct Investment Database and IMF*, Paris.

—— (1999b), *Main Industrial Indicators and R&D Database*, Paris.

—— (2000), Economic Outlook, Paris.

Pencavel, J. (1996), "Selected International Experience Concerning the Legal Framework for Collective Bargaining and Unionism," unpublished manuscript, Stanford University.

—— (2000), "The Surprising Retreat of Union Britain," unpublished manuscript, Stanford University.

Phelps, E. (1997), *Rewarding Work: How to Restore Participation and Support Free Enterprise*, Cambridge: Harvard University Press.

Samaniego, R. (2001), "Does Employment Protection Inhibit Technology Diffusion?," Unpublished Manuscript, University of Pennsylvania, Department of Economics.

Scarpetta, S. (1998), "Labor Market Reforms and Unemployment: Lessons from the Experience of the OECD Countries," IADB Working Paper No. 382, Washington, D.C.

Siebert, H. (1997), "Labor Market Rigidities: At the Root of Unemployment in Europe," *Journal of Economic Perspectives* 11(3):37–54.

Siebert, H. and M. Stolpe (2001), "Technology and Economic Performance in Germany," Kiel Working Paper No. 1035.

Snower, D. (1994), "Converting Unemployment Benefits into Employment Subsidies," *American Economic Review* 84(2):65–70.

— 19 —

The Beveridge Curve, Unemployment, and Wages in the OECD from the 1960s to the 1990s

STEPHEN NICKELL, LUCA NUNZIATA,
WOLFGANG OCHEL, AND GLENDA QUINTINI

The main message transmitted by the Beveridge curves for France and Germany goes squarely against the cliché that high and persistent unemployment is entirely or mainly a matter of worsening functioning of the labour market. It is precisely in France and Germany that there is no sign of a major unfavourable shift of the Beveridge curve during the period of rising unemployment. (Solow, 2000, p. 5)

Explanations (of high unemployment) based solely on institutions also run however into a major empirical problem: many of these institutions were already present when unemployment was low. . . . . Thus, while labour market institutions can potentially explain cross country differences today, they do not appear able to explain the general evolution of unemployment over time. (Blanchard and Wolfers, 2000, p. C2)

Despite conventional wisdom, high unemployment does not appear to be primarily the result of things like overly generous benefits, trade union power, taxes, or wage "inflexibility." (Oswald, 1997, p. 1)

1. INTRODUCTION

It is widely accepted, not least because of the pioneering work of Phelps, that labor market rigidities are an important part of the explanation for the high levels of unemployment that are still to be found in many OECD countries. However,

We thank the ESRC Centre for Economic Performance; CES ifo, Munich; and the Bank of England External MPC Unit for help in the preparation of this chapter. We are also grateful to the Leverhulme Trust Programme on the Labour Market Consequences of Structural and Technological Change and CES ifo, Munich, for financial assistance. Finally our thanks are due to Michèle Belot, Olivier Blanchard, Guiseppe Nicoletti, Andrew Oswald, Jan Van Ours, and Justin Wolfers for help with our data, as well as for useful comments on a draft of the manuscript.

this view is not universally accepted and, as the above quotations indicate, serious problems remain. One such problem, emphasized by Blanchard and Wolfers (2000), may be summarized as follows: Labor market rigidities cannot explain why European unemployment is so much higher than U.S. unemployment because the institutions generating these rigidities were much the same in the 1960s as they are today, and in the 1960s unemployment was much higher in the United States than in Europe.

Before going any further, it is worth looking at the actual numbers reported in Table 1, which confirm that the United States indeed had the highest unemployment in the OECD in the early 1960s but the picture today is not quite as clear-cut as is commonly thought. In fact, many of the smaller European countries have unemployment rates that are in the same ballpark as that in the United States, although none have reached the extraordinarily low unemployment rates that ruled in the early 1960s.

Our purpose in what follows is to shed some further light on the patterns of unemployment seen in the OECD from the 1960s to the 1990s. In particular, we want to focus on the problem noted earlier and, more generally, on the challenges

Table 1. Unemployment (Standardized Rate)

Country	Unemployment (%)							
	1960–1964	1965–1972	1973–1979	1980–1987	1988–1995	1996–1999	2000	2001 June/December
Australia	2.5	1.9	4.6	7.7	8.7	8.7	6.6	6.7
Austria	1.6	1.4	1.4	3.1	3.6	4.3	3.4	4.0
Belgium	2.3	2.3	5.8	11.2	8.4	9.4	7.0	7.0
Canada	5.5	4.7	6.9	9.7	9.5	8.7	6.8	7.5
Denmark	2.2	1.7	4.1	7.0	8.1	5.5	4.7	4.4
Finland	1.4	2.4	4.1	5.1	9.9	12.2	9.8	9.2
France	1.5	2.3	4.3	8.9	10.5	11.9	9.5	9.2
Germany (W)	0.8	0.8	2.9	6.1	5.6	7.1	6.4	6.6
Ireland	5.1	5.3	7.3	13.8	14.7	8.9	4.2	4.1
Italy	3.5	4.2	4.5	6.7	8.1	10.0	9.0	8.3
Japan	1.4	1.3	1.8	2.5	2.5	3.9	4.7	5.4
Netherlands	0.9	1.7	4.7	10.0	7.2	4.7	2.8	2.2
New Zealand	0.0	0.3	0.7	4.7	8.1	6.8	6.0	5.6
Norway	2.2	1.7	1.8	2.4	5.2	3.9	3.5	3.6
Portugal	2.3	2.5	5.5	7.8	5.4	5.9	4.2	4.2
Spain	2.4	2.7	4.9	17.6	19.6	19.4	14.1	13.0
Sweden	1.2	1.6	1.6	2.3	5.1	8.7	5.9	5.0
Switzerland	0.2	0.0	0.8	1.8	2.8	3.7	2.6	2.6
United Kingdom	2.6	3.1	4.8	10.5	8.8	6.9	5.4	5.2
United States	5.5	4.3	6.4	7.6	6.1	4.8	4.0	5.5

Notes: As far as possible, these numbers correspond to the OECD standardized rates and conform to the ILO definition. The exception here is Italy, where we use the U.S. Bureau of Labor Statistics "unemployment rates on U.S. concepts." With the exception of Italy, these rates are similar to the OECD standardized rates. For earlier years we use the data reported in Layard et al. (1991, table A3). For later years we use *OECD Employment Outlook* (2000) and *U.K. Employment Trends*, published by the U.K. Department of Education and Employment.

set out in our introductory quotes. Our aim is to see how far it is possible to defend the proposition that the dramatic long-term shifts in unemployment seen in the OECD countries over the period from the 1960s to the 1990s can be explained simply by changes in labor market institutions in the same period. The institutions concerned will be the usual suspects set out in the Oswald (1997) quote, namely, generous benefits, trade union power, taxes, and wage "inflexibility." Our strategy is very straightforward. We analyze shifts in the Beveridge curve, real wages, and unemployment over time and explain these shifts by institutional changes and macroeconomic shocks. We focus on the time-series variation in the data and eschew the extensive use of interactions, which differentiates our analysis from those of Blanchard and Wolfers (2000), Belot and Van Ours (2000), and Fitoussi et al. (2000). Are we successful in our main aim? We feel that we probably deserve a B grade. The story that emerges is reasonably consistent but not totally decisive. Experts on individual countries probably feel that we have not produced wholly persuasive explanations of the unemployment shifts in each country and we make no attempt to provide a country-by-country story. Furthermore, we have not faced up to the problem of the endogeneity of the institutional shifts. In certain cases these may be important but, overall, we do not feel that this problem seriously distorts our results. In any event, the absence of suitable instruments precludes our dealing with the issue.

The remainder of the chapter is set out as follows. In the next section we briefly discuss our theoretical framework and then, in Section 3, we look at the various institutions and discuss our data. In Section 4 we lay out our empirical strategy and in Section 5 we present our results. We finish in Section 6 with a summary and conclusions.

2. THEORETICAL BACKGROUND

There are innumerable detailed theories of unemployment in the long run. These may be divided into two broad groups—those based on flow models and those based on stock models. Pissarides (1990) and Mortensen and Pissarides (1999) provide good surveys of the former model type. Blanchard and Katz (1999) present a general template for the latter models. Fundamentally, all the models have the same broad implications. First, unemployment in both the short and the long run is determined by real demand. Second, over the long term, real demand and unemployment generally tend toward the level consistent with stable inflation, which we term the equilibrium level. Various possible mechanisms may be at work here. For example, many OECD countries now set monetary policy on the basis of an inflation target that naturally moves real demand and unemployment toward the equilibrium defined above.[1] Third, the equilibrium level of unemployment

---

1. It is, of course, possible to make macroeconomic policy mistakes that have the effect of keeping real demand and unemployment away from their equilibrium level for long periods. Japan in the 1990s is arguably an example. There is no reason to believe that equilibrium unemployment in Japan was rising in the 1990s and so unemployment persisted above its equilibrium level. This is, of course, consistent with the emergence of negative inflation over the same period.

is affected first by any variable that influences the ease with which unemployed individuals can be matched to available job vacancies, and second by any variable that tends to raise wages in a direct fashion despite excess supply in the labor market. There may be variables common to both sets. Finally, both groups of variables will tend to impact on real wages in the same direction as they influence equilibrium unemployment, essentially because the direction of equilibrium labor demand, which is negatively related to wages, has to be opposite that of equilibrium unemployment.

Before going on to consider these variables in more detail, it is worth noting that the first group of variables just referred to will tend to impact on the position of the Beveridge curve (UV locus), whereas the second will not do so in any direct fashion. However, this division is not quite as clear-cut as might appear at first sight (see later). What we can say, nevertheless, is that any variable that shifts the Beveridge curve to the right will increase equilibrium unemployment. So a shift of the Beveridge curve is a sufficient but not necessary sign that equilibrium unemployment has changed.

We turn now to consider a series of variables that we might expect to influence equilibrium unemployment either because of their impact on the effectiveness with which the unemployed are matched to available jobs or because of their direct effect on wages. The *unemployment benefit system* directly affects the readiness of the unemployed to fill vacancies. Aspects of the system that are clearly important are the level of benefits, their coverage, the length of time for which they are available, and the strictness with which the system is operated. Related to unemployment benefits is the availability of other resources to those without jobs. These include the returns on nonhuman wealth that may be increasing in the *real interest rate* (see Phelps, 1994, for an extensive discussion). *Employment protection laws* may tend to make firms more cautious about filling vacancies, which slows the speed at which the unemployed move into work. This obviously reduces the efficiency of job matching. However, the mechanism here is not clear-cut. For example, the introduction of employment laws often leads to an increased professionalization of the personnel function within firms, as was the case in Great Britain in the 1970s (see Daniel and Stilgoe, 1978). This can increase the efficiency of job matching. Thus, in terms of outflows from unemployment, the impact of employment protection laws can go either way. By contrast, it seems clear that such laws will tend to reduce involuntary separations and hence lower inflows into unemployment.[2] So the overall impact on the Beveridge curve is an empirical question. Furthermore, employment law may also have a direct impact on pay since

---

2. Note that the steady-state Beveridge curve is based on the matching function $M = \varepsilon m(cU, V)$, where M is the number of matches or hires from unemployment, U is unemployment, V is vacancies, ε is matching efficiency, and c is the search effectiveness of the unemployed. The function is increasing in both arguments and is often assumed to have constant returns. If sN is the flow into unemployment, where s is the exogenous exit rate from employment into unemployment and N is employment, then in steady state we have $sN = M$ and hence $s = \varepsilon m(cU/N, V/N)$, which is the Beveridge curve. If employment protection laws become more stringent, s tends to fall and ε may fall if firms are more cautious about hiring or may rise if the personnel function becomes more efficient. Since a fall in s shifts the Beveridge curve to the left and a fall in ε shifts it to the right, the overall effect is indeterminate.

it raises the job security of the current employees, encouraging them to demand higher pay increases.

Anything that makes it easier to match the unemployed to the available vacancies will shift the Beveridge curve to the left and reduce equilibrium unemployment. Factors that operate in this way include the reduction of *barriers to mobility,* which may be geographical or occupational. Furthermore, numerous government policies are concerned with increasing the ability and willingness of the unemployed to take jobs. These are grouped under the heading of *active labor market policies.*

Turning now to those factors that have a direct impact on wages, the obvious place to start is the institutional structure of wage determination. Within every country there is a variety of structures. In some sectors wages are determined more or less competitively but in others they are bargained between employers and trade unions at the level of the establishment, firm, or even industry. The overall outcome depends on *union power* in wage bargains, *union coverage,* and the degree of *coordination* of wage bargains. Generally, greater union power and coverage can be expected to exert upward pressure on wages, hence raising equilibrium unemployment, but this can be offset if union wage setting across the economy is coordinated. Superficially it may be argued that wage-setting institutions impact directly on wages without influencing the efficiency of job matching or the separation rate into unemployment, that is, without influencing the position of the Beveridge curve. However, if we use a model of the Beveridge curve that endogenizes the rate of separation into unemployment or the rate of job destruction (see, e.g., Mortensen and Pissarides, 1994), this no longer applies. For example, if union power raises the share of the matching surplus going to wages, this will tend to raise the rate of job destruction and shift the Beveridge curve to the right. The same thing will also happen if factors such as the coordination of wage bargaining reduce the extent to which wages at the firm level can fluctuate to offset idiosyncratic shocks and stabilize employment at the firm level. Thus while coordination can reduce overall wage pressure, which tends to lower equilibrium unemployment, it may raise the rate of idiosyncratic job shifts, which will tend to shift the Beveridge curve to the right and have an offsetting effect.

The final group of variables that directly impacts on wages falls under the heading of *real wage resistance.* The idea here is that workers attempt to sustain recent rates of real wage growth when the rate consistent with stable employment shifts unexpectedly. For example, if there is an adverse *shift in the terms of trade,* real consumption wages must fall if employment is not to decline. If workers persist in attempting to bargain for rates of real wage growth that take no account of the movement in the terms of trade, this will tend to raise unemployment. Exactly the same argument applies if there is an unexpected *fall in trend productivity growth* or an increase in *labor taxes.* For example, if labor taxes (payroll tax rates plus income tax rates plus consumption tax rates) go up, the real post-tax consumption wage must fall if real labor costs per employee facing firms are not to rise. Any resistance to this fall will lead to a rise in unemployment. This argument suggests that increases in real import prices, falls in trend productivity growth, or rises in the labor tax rate may lead to a temporary increase in unemployment.

However, some argue that these effects can be permanent. For example, Mortensen and Pissarides (1999) use their standard flow model of equilibrium unemployment to analyze various economic policies, including changes in payroll taxes, and they find enormous effects. For example, in one simulation, with a benefit replacement ratio of 0.4, a rise in the payroll tax rate from 15 to 25 percent is enough to raise equilibrium unemployment permanently by over 6 percentage points. The reason labor taxes have a big impact in this case is because Mortensen and Pissarides introduce into their model a value of leisure that is independent of the consumption wage. This fixing of an important element of the individual reservation wage implies that labor supply and willingness to work will increase permanently if the real consumption wage goes up. This will induce *permanent* reductions in equilibrium unemployment if labor taxes fall or productivity rises. Ultimately, this is an empirical question but it may be argued that in a satisfactory model, the value of leisure, and the individual reservation wage more generally, should, in the long run, move proportionally to the consumption wage and the general level of productivity. If this adjustment is made in the Mortensen-Pissarides model, the impact of payroll taxes on equilibrium unemployment disappears.

To summarize, the variables that we might expect to influence equilibrium unemployment include the unemployment benefit system, the real interest rate, employment protection laws, barriers to labor mobility, active labor market policies, union structures and the extent of coordination in wage bargaining, labor taxes, terms of trade changes, and shifts in trend productivity growth. Given the inverse relationship between equilibrium unemployment and equilibrium employment, the impact of any of these variables on unemployment should be reflected by a *ceteris paribus* impact in the same direction on real wages, which are, of course, inversely related to employment.

3. FACTORS INFLUENCING UNEMPLOYMENT IN THE OECD FROM THE 1960s TO THE 1990s

Our purpose is to investigate the effect of changes in labor market "institutions" on the Beveridge curve, real wages, and equilibrium unemployment in the OECD from the 1960s to the 1990s. In order to undertake this task, we require long time series for the appropriate countries. In this section, we describe the information we possess and also indicate the gaps in our knowledge. The variables we consider relate, in turn, to the benefit system, the system of wage determination, employment protection, labor taxes, and barriers to labor mobility.

3.1. The Unemployment Benefit System

There are four aspects of the unemployment benefit system for which there are good theoretical and empirical reasons to believe that they will influence equilibrium unemployment. These are, in turn, the level of benefits,[3] the duration

---

3. A good general reference is Holmlund (1998). A useful survey of microstudies can be found in OECD (1994, chap. 8). Microevidence from policy changes is contained in Hunt (1995), Harkman

of entitlement,[4] the coverage of the system,[5] and the strictness with which the system is operated.[6] Of these, only the first two are available as time series for the OECD countries. The OECD has collected systematic data on the unemployment benefit replacement ratio for three different family types (single, with dependent spouse, with spouse at work) in three different duration categories (1st year, 2nd and 3rd years, 4th and 5th years) from 1961 to 1995 (every other year) (see OECD, 1994, table 8.1, for the 1991 data). From this we derive a measure of the benefit replacement ratio, equal to the average over family types in the 1st-year duration category and a measure of benefit duration equal to [0.6(2nd- and 3rd-year replacement ratio) + 0.4(4th- and 5th-year replacement ratio)] ÷ (1st-year replacement ratio). So our measure of benefit duration is the level of benefit in the later years of the spell normalized on the benefit in the first year of the spell. A summary of these data is presented in Tables 2 and 3.

It is unfortunate that we have no comprehensive time-series data on the coverage of the system or on the strictness with which it is administered. This is particularly true in the case of the latter because the evidence we possess appears to indicate that this is of crucial importance in determining the extent to which a generous level of benefit will actually influence unemployment. For example, Denmark, which has very generous unemployment benefits (see Tables 2 and 3), totally reformed the operation of its benefit system through the 1990s with a view to tightening the criteria for benefit receipt and the enforcement of these criteria via a comprehensive system of sanctions. The Danish Ministry of Labor is convinced that this process has played a major role in allowing Danish unemployment to fall dramatically since the early 1990s without generating inflationary pressure (see Danish Ministry of Finance, 1999, chap. 2).

A further aspect of the structure of the benefit system for which we do not have detailed data back to the 1960s are those policies grouped under the heading of active labor market policies (ALMP). The purpose of these is to provide active assistance to the unemployed that will improve their chances of obtaining work. Multicountry studies basically using cross-section information indicate that ALMPs do have a negative impact on unemployment (e.g., Scarpetta, 1996; Nickell, 1997; Elmeskov et al., 1998). This broad-brush evidence is backed up by

---

(1997), and Carling et al. (1999) and from experiments in Meyer (1995). Cross-country macroevidence is available in Scarpetta (1996), Elmeskov et al. (1998), and Nickell and Layard (1999). The average of their results indicates a 1.11 percentage point rise in equilibrium unemployment for every 10 percentage point rise in the benefit replacement ratio.

4. There is fairly clear microevidence that shorter benefit entitlement leads to shorter unemployment duration (see Ham and Rea, 1987; Katz and Meyer, 1990; Carling et al., 1996).

5. Variations in the coverage of unemployment benefits are large (see OECD, 1994a, table 8.4) and there is a strong positive correlation between coverage and the level of benefit (OECD, 1994, p. 190). Bover et al. (1998) present strong evidence for Spain and Portugal that the covered exit unemployment more slowly than the uncovered.

6. There is strong evidence that the strictness with which the benefit system is operated, at given levels of benefit, is a very important determinant of unemployment duration. Microevidence for the Netherlands can be found in Abbring et al. (1999) and Van Den Berg et al. (1999). Cross-country evidence is available in Danish Ministry of Finance (1999, chap. 2) and in OECD (2000, chap. 4).

Table 2. Unemployment Benefit Replacement Ratios, 1960–1995

Country	Replacement ratios				
	1960–1964	1965–1972	1973–1979	1980–1987	1988–1995
Australia	0.18	0.15	0.23	0.23	0.26
Austria	0.15	0.17	0.30	0.34	0.34
Belgium	0.37	0.40	0.55	0.50	0.48
Canada	0.39	0.43	0.59	0.57	0.58
Denmark	0.25	0.35	0.55	0.67	0.64
Finland	0.13	0.18	0.29	0.38	0.53
France	0.48	0.51	0.56	0.61	0.58
Germany (W)	0.43	0.41	0.39	0.38	0.37
Ireland	0.21	0.24	0.44	0.50	0.40
Italy	0.09	0.06	0.04	0.02	0.26
Japan	0.36	0.38	0.31	0.29	0.30
Netherlands	0.39	0.64	0.65	0.67	0.70
New Zealand	0.37	0.30	0.27	0.30	0.29
Norway	0.12	0.13	0.28	0.56	0.62
Portugal	—	—	0.17	0.44	0.65
Spain	0.35	0.48	0.62	0.75	0.68
Sweden	0.11	0.16	0.57	0.70	0.72
Switzerland	0.04	0.02	0.21	0.48	0.61
United Kingdom	0.27	0.36	0.34	0.26	0.22
United States	0.22	0.23	0.28	0.30	0.26

Source: OECD. Based on the replacement ratio in the first year of an unemployment spell averaged over three family types. See OECD (1994a, table 8.1) for an example.

Table 3. Unemployment Benefit Duration Index, 1960–1995

Country	Index				
	1960–1964	1965–1972	1973–1979	1980–1987	1988–1995
Australia	1.02	1.02	1.02	1.02	1.02
Austria	0	0	0.69	0.75	0.74
Belgium	1.0	0.96	0.78	0.79	0.77
Canada	0.33	0.31	0.20	0.25	0.22
Denmark	0.63	0.66	0.66	0.62	0.84
Finland	0	0.14	0.72	0.61	0.53
France	0.28	0.23	0.19	0.37	0.49
Germany	0.57	0.57	0.61	0.61	0.61
Ireland	0.68	0.78	0.39	0.40	0.39
Italy	0	0	0	0	0.13
Japan	0	0	0	0	0
Netherlands	0.12	0.35	0.53	0.66	0.57
New Zealand	1.02	1.02	1.02	1.04	1.04
Norway	0	0.07	0.45	0.49	0.50
Portugal	—	—	0	0.11	0.35
Spain	0	0	0.01	0.21	0.27
Sweden	0	0	0.04	0.05	0.04
Switzerland	0	0	0	0	0.18
United Kingdom	0.87	0.59	0.54	0.71	0.70
United States	0.12	0.17	0.19	0.17	0.18

Source: OECD. Based on [0.06(replacement ratio in 2nd and 3rd years of a spell) + 0.04(replacement ratio in 4th and 5th years of a spell)] ÷ (replacement ratio in 1st year of a spell).

numbers of microeconometric studies (see Katz, 1998, or Martin, 2000, for useful surveys) that show that under some circumstances active labor market policies are effective. In particular, job search assistance tends to have consistently positive outcomes but other types of measures such as employment subsidies and labor market training must be well designed if they are to have a significant impact (see again Martin, 2000, for a detailed analysis).

3.2. Systems of Wage Determination

In most countries in the OECD, most workers have their wages set by collective bargaining between employers and trade unions at the plant, firm, industry, or aggregate level. This is important for our purposes because there is some evidence that trade union power in wage setting has a significant impact on unemployment.[7] Unfortunately, we do not have complete data on collective bargaining coverage (the proportion of employees covered by collective agreements) but the data presented in Table 4 give a reasonable picture. Across most of Continental Europe, including Scandinavia but excluding Switzerland, coverage is both high and stable. As we shall see, this is either because most people belong to trade unions or because union agreements are extended by law to cover nonmembers in the same sector. In Switzerland and in the OECD countries outside of Continental Europe and Scandinavia, coverage is generally much lower with the exception of Australia. In the United Kingdom, the United States, and New Zealand, coverage has declined with the fall in union density, as there are no extension laws.

In Table 5, we present the percentage of employees who are union members. Across most of Scandinavia, membership tends to be high. By contrast, in much of Continental Europe and in Australia, union density tends to be less than 50 percent and is gradually declining. In these countries there is, consequently, a wide and widening gap between density and coverage, which it is the job of the extension laws to fill. This situation is at its most stark in France, which has the lowest union density in the OECD at around 10 percent but one of the highest levels of coverage (around 95 percent). Apart from these regions, both density and coverage tend to be relatively low and both are declining at greater or lesser rates. The absence of complete coverage data means that we have to rely on the density variable to capture the impact of unionization on unemployment. As should be clear, this is only half the story, so we must treat any results we find in this area with some caution.

The other aspect of wage bargaining that appears to have a significant impact on wages and unemployment is the extent to which bargaining is coordinated.[8,9]

---

7. See the discussion in Nickell and Layard (1999, sect. 8) and Booth et al. (2000, particularly around table 6.2) for positive evidence.

8. See the discussion in Nickell and Layard (1999, sect. 8), Booth et al. (2000, particularly around table 6.1), and OECD (1997, chap. 3).

9. One aspect of wage determination that we do not analyze in this chapter is minimum wages. This is for two reasons. First, the balance of the evidence suggests that minimum wages are generally low enough not to have much of an impact on employment except for young people. Second, only around

Table 4. Collective Bargaining Coverage

Country	Coverage (%)							
	1960	1965	1970	1975	1980	1985	1990	1994
Austria[a]	n.a.	n.a.	n.a.	n.a.	n.a.	n.a.	99	99
Belgium[b]	80	80	80	85	90	90	90	90
Denmark[c]	67	68	68	70	72	74	69	69
Finland[d]	95	95	95	95	95	95	95	95
France[e]	n.a.	n.a.	n.a.	n.a.	85	n.a.	92	95
Germany[f]	90	90	90	90	91	90	90	92
Ireland[g]	n.a.	n.a.	n.a.	n.a.	n.a.	n.a.	n.a.	n.a.
Italy[h]	91	90	88	85	85	85	83	82
Netherlands[i]	100	n.a.	n.a.	n.a.	76	80	n.a.	85
Norway[j]	65	65	65	65	70	70	70	70
Portugal[k]	n.a.	n.a.	n.a.	n.a.	70	n.a.	79	71
Spain[l]	n.a.	n.a.	n.a.	n.a.	68	70	76	78
Sweden[m]	n.a.	n.a.	n.a.	n.a.	n.a.	n.a.	86	89
Switzerland[n]	n.a.	n.a.	n.a.	n.a.	n.a.	n.a.	53	53
United Kingdom[o]	67	67	68	72	70	64	54	40
Canada[p]	35	33	36	39	40	39	38	36
United States[q]	29	27	27	24	21	21	18	17
Japan[r]	n.a.	n.a.	n.a.	n.a.	28	n.a.	23	21
Australia[s]	85	85	85	85	85	85	80	80
New Zealand[t]	n.a.	n.a.	n.a.	n.a.	n.a.	n.a.	67	31

Source: These data were collected by one of the authors (W. Ochel) from the country experts noted below. We are most grateful for all their assistance. Further details may be found in Ochel (2000b).

[a] Traxler et al. (2001): National Labour Relations in International Markets, Oxford.

[b] Estimates by J. Rombouts; OECD (1997) for 1990 and 1994.

[c] Estimates by St. Scheuer; 1985 figures are survey based; OECD (1997) for 1990 and 1994.

[d] Estimates by J. Kiander; OECD (1997) for 1990 and 1994.

[e] OECD (1997) for 1980, 1990, and 1995; estimate by J.-L. Dayan for 1997.

[f] Estimates by L. Clasen; OECD (1997) for 1980, 1990, and 1994.

[g] —

[h] Estimates by T. Boeri, P. Garibaldi, and M. Macis; OECD (1997) for 1980, 1990, and 1994.

[i] Estimate by J. Visser for 1960; survey by Van den Toren for 1985; OECD (1997) for 1980 and 1994.

[j] Estimates by K. Nergaard.

[k] OECD (1997) for 1980, 1990, and 1994.

[l] Estimates by J. F Jimeno for 1980 and 1985; OECD (1997) for 1990 and 1994.

[m] OECD (1997) for 1990 and 1994.

[n] OECD (1997) for 1990 and 1994.

[o] Estimates by W. Brown based on Millward et al. (1992), Milner (1995), and Cully and Woodland (1998).

[p] Estimates by M. Thompson; OECD (1997) for 1990 and 1994.

[q] Estimates by W. Ochel for 1960 to 1980; Current Population Survey for 1985, 1990, 1994, and 1999.

[r] OECD (1997) for 1980, 1990, and 1994.

[s] Estimates by R. D. Lansbury; OECD (1997) for 1990 and 1994.

[t] OECD (1997) for 1990 and 1994.

---

half the OECD countries had statutory minimum wages over the period 1960–1995. Of course, trade unions may enforce "minimum wages" but this is only a minor part of their activities, and these are already accounted for in our analysis of density, coverage, and coordination.

Table 5. Union Density

Country	1960–1964	1965–1972	1973–1979	1980–1987	1988–1995	Extension laws in place[a]
			Density (%)			
Australia	48	45	49	49	43	✓
Austria	59	57	52	51	45	✓
Belgium	40	42	52	52	52	✓
Canada	27	29	35	37	36	X
Denmark	60	61	71	79	76	X
Finland	35	47	66	69	76	✓
France	20	21	21	16	10	✓
Germany (W)	34	32	35	34	31	✓
Ireland	47	51	56	56	51	X
Italy	25	32	48	45	40	✓
Japan	33	33	30	27	24	X
Netherlands	41	38	37	30	24	✓
New Zealand	36	35	38	37	35	X
Norway	52	51	52	55	56	X
Portugal	61	61	61	57	34	✓
Spain	9	9	9	11	16	✓
Sweden	64	66	76	83	84	X
Switzerland	35	32	32	29	25	✓[b]
United Kingdom	44	47	55	53	42	X
Unites States	27	26	25	20	16	X

Source: See Data Appendix.

Notes: (i) Union density = union members as a percentage of employees. In both Spain and Portugal, union membership in the 1960s and 1970s does not have the same implications as elsewhere because there was pervasive government intervention in wage determination during most of this period. (ii) [a]Effectively, bargained wages extended to nonunion firms typically at the behest of one party to the bargain. [b]Extension only at the behest of both parties to a bargain. See OECD. For details, see OECD (1994a, table 5.11).

Roughly speaking, the evidence suggests that if bargaining is highly coordinated, it will completely offset the adverse effects of unionism on employment (see, e.g., Nickell and Layard, 1999). Coordination refers to mechanisms whereby the aggregate employment implications of wage determination are taken into account when wage bargains are struck. This may be achieved if wage bargaining is highly centralized, as in Austria, or if there are institutions, such as employers' federations, that can assist bargainers to act in concert even when bargaining itself ostensibly occurs at the level of the firm or industry, as in Germany or Japan (see Soskice, 1991). It is worth noting that coordination is not, therefore, the same as centralization, which refers simply to the level at which bargaining takes place (plant, firm, industry, or economy-wide). In Table 6, we present coordination indexes for the OECD from the 1960s. The first index (coordination 1) basically ignores transient changes, whereas the second (coordination 2) tries to capture the various detailed nuances of the variations in the institutional structure. Notable changes are the increases in coordination in Ireland and the Netherlands toward the end of the period and the declines in coordination in Australia, New Zealand, and Sweden. Coordination also declines in the United Kingdom over the same period, but this simply reflects the sharp decline of unionism overall.

Table 6. Coordination Indexes (Range 1–3)

Country	Index									
	1960–1964		1965–1972		1973–1979		1980–1987		1988–1995	
	1	2	1	2	1	2	1	2	1	2
Australia	2.25	2	2.25	2	2.25	2.36	2.25	2.31	1.92	1.63
Austria	3	2.5	3	2.5	3	2.5	3	2.5	3	2.42
Belgium	2	2	2	2	2	2.1	2	2.55	2	2
Canada	1	1	1	1	1	1.63	1	1.08	1	1
Denmark	2.5	3	2.5	3	2.5	2.96	2.4	2.54	2.26	2.42
Finland	2.25	1.5	2.25	1.69	2.25	2	2.25	2	2.25	2.38
France	1.75	2	1.75	2	1.75	2	1.84	2	1.98	1.92
Germany (W)	3	2.5	3	2.5	3	2.5	3	2.5	3	2.5
Ireland	2	2	2	2.38	2	2.91	2	2.08	3	2.75
Italy	1.5	1.94	1.5	1.73	1.5	2	1.5	1.81	1.4	1.95
Japan	3	2.5	3	2.5	3	2.5	3	2.5	3	2.5
Netherlands	2	3	2	2.56	2	2	2	2.38	2	3
New Zealand	1.5	2.5	1.5	2.5	1.5	2.5	1.32	2.32	1	1.25
Norway	2.5	3	2.5	3	2.5	2.96	2.5	2.72	2.5	2.84
Portugal	1.75	3	1.75	3	1.75	2.56	1.84	1.58	2	1.88
Spain	2	3	2	3	2	2.64	2	2.3	2	2
Sweden	2.5	3	2.5	3	2.5	3	2.41	2.53	2.15	1.94
Switzerland	2.25	2	2.25	2	2.25	2	2.25	2	2.25	1.63
United Kingdom	1.5	1.56	1.5	1.77	1.5	1.77	1.41	1.08	1.15	1
Unites States	1	1	1	1	1	1	1	1	1	1

Notes: The first series (1) only moves in response to major changes; the second series (2) attempts to capture all the nuances. Coordination 1 was provided by Michèle Belot, to whom we owe many thanks (see Belot and Van Ours, 2000, for details). Coordination 2 is the work of one of the authors, W. Ochel. Coordination 1 appears in all the subsequent regressions.

3.3. Employment Protection

Employment protection laws are thought by many to be a key factor in engendering labor market inflexibility. Despite this, evidence that they have a decisive impact on overall rates of unemployment is mixed, at best.[10] In Table 7, we present details of an employment protection index for the OECD countries. Features to note are the wide variation in the index across countries and the fact that in some countries the basic legislation was not introduced until the 1970s.

3.4. Labor Taxes

The important labor taxes are those that form part of the wedge between the real product wage (labor costs per employee normalized on the output price) and the real consumption wage (after-tax pay normalized on the consumer price index).

---

10. The results presented by Bentolila and Bertola (1990), Lazear (1990), Addison and Grosso (1996), Elmeskov et al. (1998), and Nickell and Layard (1999) do not add up to anything very decisive, although there is a clear positive relationship between employment protection and long-term unemployment.

Table 7. Employment Protection (Index, 0–2)

Country	Index				
	1960–1964	1965–1972	1973–1979	1980–1987	1988–1995
Australia	0.50	0.50	0.50	0.50	0.50
Austria	0.65	0.65	0.84	1.27	1.30
Belgium	0.72	1.24	1.55	1.55	1.35
Canada	0.30	0.30	0.30	0.30	0.30
Denmark	0.90	0.98	1.10	1.10	0.90
Finland	1.20	1.20	1.20	1.20	1.13
France	0.37	0.68	1.21	1.30	1.41
Germany (W)	0.45	1.05	1.65	1.65	1.52
Ireland	0.02	0.19	0.45	0.50	0.52
Italy	1.92	1.99	2.00	2.00	1.89
Japan	1.40	1.40	1.40	1.40	1.40
Netherlands	1.35	1.35	1.35	1.35	1.28
New Zealand	0.80	0.80	0.80	0.80	0.80
Norway	1.55	1.55	1.55	1.55	1.46
Portugal	0.00	0.43	1.59	1.94	1.93
Spain	2.00	2.00	1.99	1.91	1.74
Sweden	0.00	0.23	1.46	1.80	1.53
Switzerland	0.55	0.55	0.55	0.55	0.55
United Kingdom	0.16	0.21	0.33	0.35	0.35
United States	0.10	0.10	0.10	0.10	0.10

Note: These data are based on an interpolation of the variable used by Blanchard and Wolfers (2000), to whom we are most grateful. This variable is based on the series used by Lazear (1990) and that provided by the OECD for the late 1980s and 1990s. Since the Lazear index and the OECD index are not strictly comparable, the overall series is not completely reliable.

These are payroll, income, and consumption taxes. Their combined impact on unemployment remains a subject of some debate despite the large number of empirical investigations. Indeed some studies indicate that employment taxes have no long-run impact on unemployment whatever, whereas others present results that imply that they can explain more or less all the rise in unemployment in most countries during the period 1960–1985.[11] In Table 8 we present the total tax rate on labor for the OECD countries. All countries exhibit a substantial increase over the period from the 1960s to the 1990s, although there are wide variations across countries. These mainly reflect the extent to which health, higher education, and pensions are publicly provided along with the all-round generosity of the social security system.

3.5. Barriers to Labor Mobility

Oswald (1997) proposes that barriers to geographical mobility, as reflected in the rate of owner occupation of the housing stock, play a key role in determining unemployment. He finds that changes in unemployment are positively correlated

---

11. A good example of a study in this latter group is Daveri and Tabellini (2000), while one in the former group is OECD (1990, annex 6). Extensive discussions may be found in Nickell and Layard (1999, sect. 6), Disney (2000), and Pissarides (1998).

Table 8. Total Taxes on Labor
(Payroll Tax Rate + Income Tax Rate + Consumption Tax Rate)

Country	*Total tax rate (%)*				
	1960–1964	*1965–1972*	*1973–1979*	*1980–1987*	*1988–1995*
Australia	28	31	36	39	—
Austria	47	52	55	58	59
Belgium	38	43	44	46	50
Canada	31	39	41	42	50
Denmark	32	46	53	59	60
Finland	38	46	55	58	64
France	55	57	60	64	67
Germany (W)	42	44	48	50	52
Ireland	23	30	30	37	41
Italy	57	56	54	56	67
Japan	25	25	26	32	33
Netherlands	45	54	57	55	47
New Zealand	—	—	29	30	—
Norway	—	52	61	65	61
Portugal	20	25	26	33	40
Spain	19	23	29	40	46
Sweden	41	54	68	77	78
Switzerland	30	31	35	36	35
United Kingdom	34	43	45	51	47
United States	34	37	42	44	45

Note: These data are based on the London School of Economics, Centre for Economic Performance OECD dataset.

with changes in owner occupation rates across countries, U.S. states, and U.K. regions. He also presents U.K. evidence that owner occupation represents a significant mobility barrier relative to private renting. However, Gregg et al. (2000) find that while unemployment is significantly negatively related to unemployment both across U.K. regions and across time in a regional fixed-effects model, this relationship becomes significantly positive once other relevant regional characteristics are included. We propose to include owner occupation as a variable in our investigation and the data are shown in Table 9. It must be borne in mind, however, that these data are heavily interpolated, so the results should be treated with caution.

4. THE BASIC EMPIRICAL STRATEGY

Our aim is to explain the different patterns of unemployment exhibited across the OECD in the period from the 1960s to the 1990s. Our approach is to see how far we can get with a very simple empirical model. We have already discussed those factors that can be expected to influence equilibrium unemployment in the long run. Then, since we are, in practice, explaining actual unemployment, we must also include in our model those factors that might explain the short-run deviations of unemployment from its equilibrium level. Following the discussion in Hoon and Phelps (1992) or Phelps (1994) we note that these factors include aggregate demand shocks, productivity shocks, and wage shocks. More specifically, we include the following (see Data Appendix for details):

Table 9. Mobility: Owner Occupation

Country	Occupation (%)				
	1960–1964	1965–1972	1973–1979	1980–1987	1988–1995
Australia	64	66	69	71	70
Austria	39	41	45	50	55
Belgium	51	54	57	60	62
Canada	65	61	61	62	61
Denmark	44	48	51	52	51
Finland	57	59	60	63	67
France	42	44	49	52	54
Germany (W)	30	35	38	39	38
Ireland	62	69	74	77	78
Italy	46	49	55	62	67
Japan	69	61	61	62	61
Netherlands	30	34	39	43	44
New Zealand	69	68	69	70	71
Norway	53	53	57	59	59
Portugal	—	—	—	—	—
Spain	54	62	69	75	78
Sweden	36	35	39	41	42
Switzerland	33	29	29	30	30
United Kingdom	43	48	53	60	68
United States	64	65	67	67	64

Note: These numbers are based on data supplied by Andrew Oswald, to whom we are most grateful. For most countries, the original data are generated by the population census, which takes place relatively infrequently. They are then linearly interpolated.

1. Money supply shocks, specifically changes in the rate of growth of the nominal money stock (i.e., the second difference of the log money supply).
2. Productivity shocks, measured by *changes* in total factor productivity (TFP) growth or deviations of TFP growth from trend.
3. Labor demand shocks, measured by the residuals from a simple labor demand model.
4. Real import price shocks, measured by proportional changes in real import prices weighted by the trade share.
5. The (ex post) real interest rate.

With the exception of the real interest rate, these variables are genuine "shocks" in the sense that they are typically stationary and tend to revert to their mean quite rapidly. Nevertheless, their impact may persist for some time, since we also include the lagged dependent variable in our model to capture endogenous persistence.

Some further specific points are worth noting. The first of these is the role of productivity shocks and real import shocks in capturing real wage resistance. As we noted in Section 2, increases in real import prices or declines in trend productivity growth will lead to temporary increases in unemployment (and in real product wages *relative to trend productivity*) if real consumption wages do not adjust appropriately. Second, we include the real interest rate because some have accorded it a significant role in the determination of unemployment even in the long run (e.g., Phelps, 1994, or Blanchard and Wolfers, 2000). Third, we are not simply looking at unemployment but we also try and explain real product wages (real labor costs) and shifts in the Beveridge curve in order to see if we can obtain a consistent picture.

Our focus is on the time-series variation in the cross-country data, so all our models include country dummies as well as time dummies. We are by no means the first to undertake this task but what we are attempting is perhaps a little different from what has gone before. There have been a number of previous studies but a representative picture may be garnered from Layard et al. (1991, chap. 9, pp. 430–37), Belot and Van Ours (2000), Blanchard and Wolfers (2000), and Fitoussi et al. (2000), all of which use panel models with country dummies.[12] The first and the last two of these focus specifically on the way in which institutions interact with variables that are either shocks or factors that may influence unemployment in the longer term. Layard et al. (1991) present a dynamic model of unemployment based on annual data, where unemployment depends on wage pressure (simply a dummy that takes the value one from 1970), the benefit replacement ratio, real import price changes, and monetary shocks. Their impact on unemployment depends on time-invariant institutions, with different sets of institutions affecting the degree of unemployment persistence (captured by the lagged dependent variable), the impact of wage pressure variables including the replacement rate and import prices, and the effect of monetary shocks. The model generally explains the data better than individual country autoregressions with trends.

Blanchard and Wolfers (2000) also focus on the interaction between institutional variables and shocks, using 5-year averages of the data to concentrate on long-run effects. The shock variables consist of the level of TFP growth, the real interest rate, and labor demand shifts (essentially the log of labor's share purged of the impact of factor prices). These shocks differ from those used here because, over the length of the sample (35 years), they are not mean reverting. For example, annual TFP growth is as much as 3 percentage points higher in the 1960s than in the 1990s in many countries. Interacting these shocks with institutions fits the data well.

Fitoussi et al. (2000) proceed in a slightly different way. First, they interact their baseline variables with country dummies and then investigate the cross-sectional relationship between these and labor market institutions. The baseline variables include nonwage support relative to labor productivity (income from private wealth plus social spending), the real price of oil and two factors in common with Blanchard and Wolfers (2000), the real rate of interest and productivity growth.[13] The explanation of unemployment shifts in all three papers (Layard et al., 1991; Blanchard and Wolfers, 2000; Fitoussi et al., 2000) has the same fundamental structure. They depend on long-run changes in a set of baseline variables, with

---

12. This distinguishes these studies from those that focus on the cross-country variation in the data by using cross sections or random-effects panel data models (e.g., Scarpetta, 1996; Nickell, 1997; Elmeskov et al., 1998).

13. In fact they differ a little because in the Fitoussi et al. (2000) paper, the real rate of interest is a world average and productivity growth refers to labor productivity.

the impact of these long-run shifts being much bigger and longer lasting in some countries than in others because of institutional differences. The extent to which these explanations are persuasive depends on whether the stories associated with the baseline variables are convincing. For example, the notion that a fall in trend productivity growth or a rise in the real price of oil leads to a permanent rise in the equilibrium unemployment rate is one that many find unappealing.

Belot and Van Ours (2000) are closer in spirit to our analysis. They rely on "institutional" shifts to explain the changes in unemployment. They typically include large numbers of interactions among institutions, many of which are highly significant [see, e.g., their table 6, equation (8)]. This has a sound theoretical foundation (see, e.g., Coe and Snower, 1997) and undoubtedly helps greatly with the explanatory power of the model. However, the model is static so that the within-country persistence of unemployment is excluded.

In the light of what has gone before, we propose to see how much the institutional information described in Section 3 can explain if it is taken more or less straight, that is, with only a minimum number of interactions and with the addition of some mean reverting shocks. The results of our investigation are presented next.

5. SHIFTS IN THE BEVERIDGE CURVE, REAL WAGES, AND UNEMPLOYMENT

In this section we set out our results concerning (1) shifts in the Beveridge curve, (2) real labor costs, and (3) unemployment. We also look briefly at employment rates for the benefit of those who prefer to use this measure.[14]

5.1. Shifts in the Beveridge Curve

In Figure 1 we present plots of the unemployment rate against the vacancy rate for all our countries except Ireland and Italy, where vacancy data are unavailable. For completeness, in France we also show a plot using a labor shortage index in place of the vacancy rate.

Recall that if the economy fluctuates with a stationary Beveridge curve, we expect to see the UV dots cycling anticlockwise around a fixed downward-sloping line. If the steady-state Beveridge curve is also moving then these cycles will shift either rightward or leftward. Furthermore, if the steady-state curve is moving very fast, the cycles will not be clearly visible. From a look at the pictures, two points

---

14. Some investigators prefer to use the employment or nonemployment rate as opposed to the unemployment rate when considering labor market performance. The nonemployed consist of five main groups, the unemployed, those in full-time education, the sick and disabled, the early retired, and those at home looking after dependents. While the unemployed are, by definition, seeking work, in practice individuals from all these categories can and do enter employment, although the rate of entry into employment is typically much greater for the unemployed than for those in any other category. Nevertheless, the distinction between the unemployed and the remainder is not clear-cut and this partly explains why some analysts prefer to focus on nonemployment rather than unemployment. However, in our opinion, the disparate nature of the nonemployed makes results based on the nonemployment rate less easy to interpret.

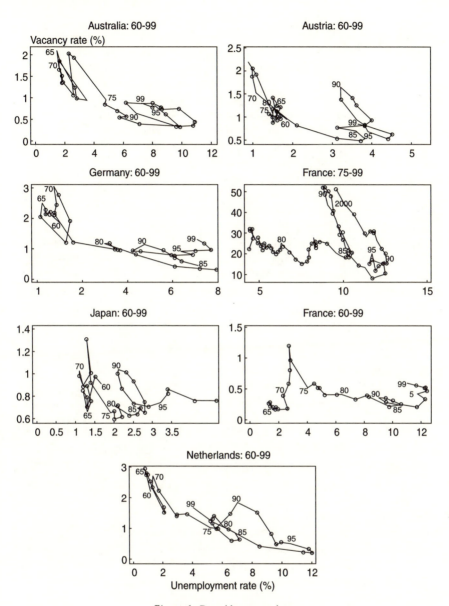

Figure 1. Beveridge curve plots.

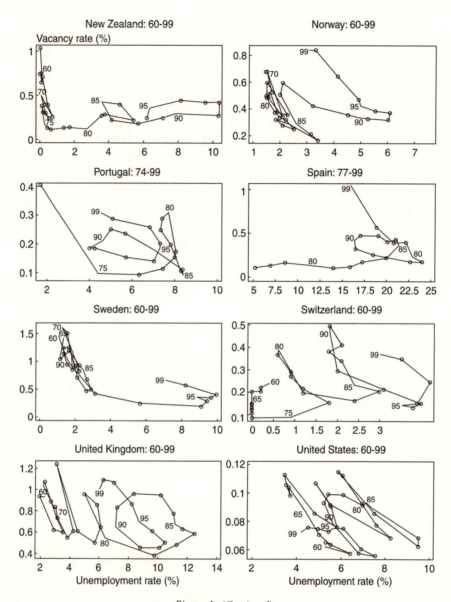

Figure 1. (*Continued*)

stand out. First, for every country except Norway and Sweden, the Beveridge curve shifted to the right from the 1960s to the mid-1980s. Of course, the distance moved varies a lot from country to country but the movement is clear in all cases. Second, after the mid-1980s, the countries fall into two groups: those for which the Beveridge curve carries on moving to the right with no serious hint of a turnaround and those for which it starts moving back to the left. The former group definitely includes Belgium, Finland, France, Germany, Japan, Norway, Spain,

Sweden, and Switzerland. The latter group definitely includes Canada, Denmark, Netherlands, the United Kingdom and the United States; Australia, Austria, New Zealand, and Portugal are harder to place although all are probably showing some recent improvement (leftward move).

These reasonably clear-cut movements in the Beveridge curve provide evidence that some factors of the type discussed in previous sections have raised equilibrium unemployment in most countries over the period from the 1960s to the mid-1980s and, from then on, they have caused a fallback in some of these countries and a continuing rise in others. In order to pin these things down a bit further, we estimate a pooled, cross-country Beveridge curve, although note that the panel is not balanced. From footnote 2, we see that the steady-state Beveridge curve can be written as

$$s = \varepsilon m(cu, v), \tag{1}$$

where s is the exit rate from employment into unemployment, u is the unemployment rate, v is the vacancy rate, ε is the level of matching efficiency, and c is the level of search intensity. Noting that ε and c depend on some institutional variables z, we estimate a dynamic (non-steady-state) version of (1) that has the form

$$\ln u_{it} = \alpha_i + \alpha_t + \beta_1 \ln u_{it-1} + \beta_2 \ln v_{it} + \beta_3 \ln s_{it} + \sum_j \gamma_j z_{jt} + \varepsilon_{it}.$$

A representative equation is shown in Table 10. Note that this curve is estimated *given the inflow rate* s. In order to analyze the overall Beveridge curve shifts, we also have to account for any exogenous movements in s, and we do this later. The picture generated by the results is that, given the inflow rate, increasing benefit duration shifts the curve to the right as does the owner occupation rate. These results might have been expected. However, the strictness of employment protection law shifts the Beveridge curve to the left. This is, perhaps, surprising although, as we have already noted, it could come about if the introduction of employment legislation raises the efficiency of the personnel function in firms. Variables that directly impact on wages do not seem to have any impact on the Beveridge curve with the possible exception of union density, which tends to shift it to the right.

Turning now to an explanation of the inflow rate into unemployment, we report our results in Table 11. Notable among them are the fact that the impact of the owner occupation rate (i.e., mobility barriers) is only weakly positive, whereas that of employment protection is negative as expected. Of the variables that impact directly on wage determination, union density turns out to be strongly positive. This is consistent with the role of union power in the Mortensen and Pissarides (1994) model of job destruction, where unions raise the destruction rate by increasing the share of the matching surplus going to wages.

Combining the Beveridge curve and inflow rate equation, we find that once we include the impact of these variables on the inflow rate the duration of benefits, union density, and owner occupation all tend to shift the Beveridge curve to the

Table 10. Beveridge Curve, 1961–1995

Independent variables	Dependent variable: $\ln u_{it}$
$\ln u_{it-1}$	0.61(21.1)
$\ln v_{it}$	−0.23(10.7)
ln (inflow rate)$_{it}$	0.23(7.6)
Benefit replacement rate$_{it}$	0.03(0.2)
Benefit duration$_{it}$	0.22(2.1)
Employment protection$_{it}$	−0.19(3.0)
Owner occupation rate$_{it}$	1.03(2.5)
Employment tax rate$_{it}$	−0.11(0.4)
Coordination$_{it}$	−0.02(0.2)
Union density$_{it}$	0.48(1.9)
Country dummies	✓
Time dummies	✓
N	15
NT	324
$\bar{R}^2$	0.97

Notes: (i) For most countries, the inflow rate is proxied by the number of unemployed with duration less than 1 month divided by employment, so it approximates the monthly inflow rate. (ii) The benefit replacement rate, union density, employment tax rate, and the owner occupation rate are proportions (range 0–1); benefit duration is effectively a proportion (range 0–1.1, see Table 3); employment protection and coordination are indexes (ranges 0–2 and 1–3). (iii) This equation is estimated by OLS. If we instrument $\ln v_{it}$ using $\ln v_{it-1}$, $\ln v_{it-2}$, labor demand shock$_{it}$ as external instruments, the coefficients and t ratios barely change.

Table 11. Inflow Rate into Unemployment, 1962–1995

Independent variables	Dependent variable: $\ln$ *(inflow rate)*$_{it}$ *(%)*
Employment protection$_{it}$	−0.45(3.5)
Owner occupation rate$_{it}$	0.93(1.1)
Employment tax rate$_{it}$	0.70(1.1)
Coordination$_{it}$	0.46(1.8)
Union density$_{it}$	2.41(5.3)
Country dummies	✓
Time dummies	✓
N	15
NT	324
$\bar{R}^2$	0.88

Notes: (i) Inflow rate approximates the monthly inflow normalized on employment. (ii) The owner occupation rate, the employment tax rate, and union density are proportions (range 0–1); employment protection and coordination are indexes (ranges 0–2 and 1–3, respectively).

right, whereas stricter employment protection shifts it to the left. These should translate directly into effects on equilibrium unemployment. However, we should bear in mind that variables such as union density, coordination, and employment protection may also have a direct effect on wages and hence further effects on equilibrium unemployment. Indeed, we might expect employment protection to impact on unemployment via its direct wage effect in the opposite direction to the

Beveridge curve effects. So our next step is to go directly to the impact of our variables on unemployment and wages.

5.2. Explaining Real Wages

The idea here is to add to the overall picture by seeing if the impact of the institutions on real wages is consistent with their impact on unemployment. Broadly speaking, the institutional variables can influence wages directly by raising the bargaining power of workers, or they can operate by modifying the effect of unemployment on wages. For example, trade unions may reduce the impact of unemployment on wages by insulating the existing work force from the rigors of the external labor market. Either raising wages directly or reducing the (absolute) value of the unemployment coefficient will lead to an increase in equilibrium unemployment.[15] Furthermore, it is worth noting that in most standard models, institutions that shift the Beveridge curve also tend to impact on wages as well as on equilibrium unemployment.

In Table 12, we present some real wage equations (or wage curves), where the dependent variable is the log of real labor costs per employee (i.e., real wages including payroll taxes normalized on the GDP deflator at factor cost). The unemployment term uses the level rather than the log of unemployment because in some countries, such as Germany, New Zealand, and Switzerland, unemployment in the 1960s was very close to zero, which would tend to distort the equation in log form.[16] Apart from the standard institutional variables, we also include trend productivity growth and both TFP and import price shocks to capture temporary real wage resistance effects.

Each equation has country dummies, time dummies, and country-specific trends to control for the various types of unobservables and a lagged dependent variable to capture the sluggish responsiveness of wages. Most of the variables in the model have a unit root so we report a standard cointegration test that confirms that our equation explains real wages in the long run. All the equations have a sensible basic structure with a strong negative unemployment effect. Coordination increases the *absolute* impact of unemployment and both union density and the benefit replacement ratio reduce it. The overall impact of both employment protection and employment taxes is to raise real wages but the latter effect is modified in economies where wage bargaining is coordinated, which is consistent with the findings of Daveri and Tabellini (2000).

---

15. For example, ignoring nominal inertia and short-run dynamics, suppose the wage equation has the form $w - p = \alpha_0 - \alpha_1(z)u + \alpha_2(z)$, where $\alpha_1' < 0$, $\alpha_2' > 0$, and z are institutional factors that tend to raise wages and unemployment. Then if the price equation/labor demand function has the form $\rho - w = \beta_0 - \beta_1 u$, equilibrium unemployment satisfies $u^* = [\alpha_0 + \beta_0 + \alpha_2(z)]/[\beta_1 + \alpha_1(z)]$. So z can increase equilibrium unemployment via either α_1 or α_2 or both of them.

16. If we use the log form, then the impact of the increase in unemployment from the 1960s to the 1990s for those countries with negligible unemployment in the 1960s is massively greater than that for the average country. For example, in log form, the rise in unemployment in Switzerland from 1960–1964 to 1996–1999 (0.2 to 3.7%) has a negative impact on wages that is nearly 300 percent larger than that in Italy, where unemployment rose from 3.5 to 10%. This differential seems somewhat implausible.

Table 12. Explaining OECD Real Labor Cost Per Worker, 1961–1995

Independent variables	Dependent variable: ln (real labor cost per worker)$_{it}$	
	1	2
ln (real labor cost per worker)$_{it-1}$	0.70(30.3)	0.70(30.1)
u_{it}	−0.50(7.1)	−0.47(6.8)
Coordination$_{it}$ × u_{it}	−0.19(2.7)	−0.20(2.7)
Union density$_{it}$ × u_{it}	0.41(2.1)	0.47(2.5)
Benefit replacement ratio$_{it}$ × u_{it}	0.44(2.1)	0.35(1.7)
Employment protection$_{it}$	0.023(4.8)	0.018(3.4)
Benefit replacement ratio$_{it}$	0.037(3.1)	0.037(3.0)
Coordination$_{it}$	−0.026(2.6)	−0.024(2.3)
Δ union density$_{it}$	0.20(2.7)	0.18(2.3)
Total employment tax rate$_{it}$	0.12(3.9)	0.11(3.6)
Coordination$_{it}$ × total employment tax rate$_{it}$	−0.14(4.3)	−0.13(3.9)
Proportion owner occupied$_{it}$		0.14(1.8)
Trend productivity$_{it}$	0.47(12.6)	0.50(12.1)
TFP shock$_{it}$	−0.38(4.0)	−0.43(4.5)
Real import price shock$_{it}$	0.36(6.9)	0.37(7.1)
Time dummies	✓	✓
Country dummies	✓	✓
Country-specific trends	✓	✓
N	20	19
NT	572	553

Notes: Estimation: Generalized least squares allowing for heteroscedastic errors and country-specific first-order serial correlation. Each equation contains country dummies, time dummies, and country-specific trends.

Variables: The unemployment rate, benefit replacement ratio, union density, employment tax rate, and owner occupation rate are proportions (range 0–1), benefit duration has a range (0–1.1), employment protection and coordination are indexes (ranges 0–2 and 1–3).

Tests: (a) *Poolability*: the large sample version of the Roy (1957), Zellner (1962), and Baltagi (1995) test for common slopes is $\chi^2(171) = 99.8$, so the null of common slopes is not rejected. (b) *Heteroscedasticity*: with our two-way error component model, the error has the form $\alpha_i + \alpha_t + \varepsilon_{it}$. The null we consider is that ε_{it} is homoscedastic. Using a groupwise likelihood ratio test, we reject the null [$\chi^2(19) = 4592.7$] so we allow for heteroscedasticity. (c) *Serial correlation*: assuming a structure of the form $\varepsilon_{it} = \mathcal{P}\varepsilon_{it-1} + v_{it}$, the null $\mathcal{P} = 0$ is rejected using an LM test [$\chi^2(1) = 31.5$]. So we allow for first-order autoregressive errors with country-specific values of $\mathcal{P}$. (d) *Cointegration*: For most of the variables, the null of a unit root cannot be rejected (except for the shock variables). To test for cointegration, we use the Maddala and Wu (1996) test. Under this test, using Dickey-Fuller tests for individual countries, the null of no cointegration is rejected [$\chi^2(40) = 96.3$]. This test relies on no cross-country correlation. Our use of time dummies should capture much of the residual cross-correlation in the data.

Other: When interactions are included, the variables are set as deviations from the mean, so the interactions take the value zero at the sample mean.

The benefit replacement ratio has a direct impact on wages but benefit duration has no effect and is omitted. We also investigated the interaction between the two on the basis that higher benefits will have a bigger effect if duration is longer. This interaction effect was positive but insignificant. Looking at real wage resistance effects, we find that a TFP shock has a negative effect on real wages (given trend productivity) and an import price shock has a positive effect. Both these are consistent with the real wage resistance story. Finally, we find in column 2 that the impact of owner occupation on wages is positive and close to significance. Our next step is to see how these results tie in with those generated by an unemployment model.

5.3. Explaining Unemployment

The basic idea here is to explain unemployment by (1) those factors that impact on equilibrium unemployment and (2) those shocks that cause unemployment to deviate from equilibrium unemployment. These would include demand shocks, productivity and other labor demand shocks, and wage shocks (see Nickell, 1990, Layard et al., 1991, pp. 370–74, for a simple derivation). In Table 13, we present the basic equations corresponding to the two wage equations in Table 12. As with the latter, each equation has country dummies, time dummies, and country-specific trends as well as a lagged dependent variable. Again, a standard cointegration test confirms that our equation explains unemployment in the long run despite the rather high value of the coefficient on the lagged dependent variable. This reflects a high level of persistence and/or the inability of the included variables to capture fully what is going on. Recall that we are eschewing the use of shock variables that last for any length of time, so we are relying heavily on our institutional variables.

Looking further at how well we are doing, we see in Table 14 that with the exception of Portugal, the time dummies and the country-specific time trends are not close to significance, so they are not making a great contribution to the overall fit. So how well does our model fit the data? Given the high level of the lagged dependent variable coefficient, we feel that presenting a dynamic simulation for each country is a more revealing measure of fit than the country-specific R^2 (which would probably be 1 for every country), and these are presented in Figure 2. Overall, the equation appears to do quite well, particularly for those countries with big changes in unemployment. However, for countries with minimal changes such as Austria, Japan, and Switzerland, the model is not great.

How do the institution effects compare with those in the wage equation? First, just as in the wage equation, both employment protection and employment taxes have a positive effect, with the latter being modified in economies with coordinated wage bargaining. Our tax effects are not nearly as large as those of Daveri and Tabellini (2000) with a 10 percentage point increase in the total employment tax rate leading to around a 1 percentage point rise in unemployment in the long run at average levels of coordination (see column 1).

As may have been expected from the wage equation, benefit levels have an important impact on unemployment as does benefit duration and their interaction, something that did not show up in the wage equation. Furthermore, despite the fact that union density reduces the unemployment effect in the wage equation, we can find no significant effect on unemployment although we do find a positive rate-of-change effect. There is a positive role for owner occupation but, as in the wage equation, it is not very significant. Finally, the impacts of the import price and TFP shocks seem sensible and consistent with those in the wage equation. However, whereas money supply shocks do not have any effect, the real interest rate does have some positive impact.

Table 13. Explaining OECD Unemployment, 1961–1992

Independent variables	Dependent variable: u_{it} (%)	
	1	2
u_{it-1}	0.86(48.5)	0.87(47.6)
Employment protection$_{it}$	0.15(0.9)	0.15(0.9)
Benefit replacement ratio$_{it}$	2.21(5.4)	2.20(5.2)
Benefit duration$_{it}$	0.47(2.5)	0.40(2.1)
Benefit duration $_{it}$ × benefit replacement ratio$_{it}$	3.75(4.0)	3.07(3.2)
Δ union density$_{it}$	6.99(3.2)	5.97(2.6)
Coordination$_{it}$	−1.01(3.5)	−0.90(3.0)
Coordination$_{it}$ × union density$_{it}$	−6.98(6.1)	−7.48(6.5)
Total employment tax rate$_{it}$	1.51(1.7)	1.59(1.8)
Coordination$_{it}$ × total employment tax rate$_{it}$	−3.46(3.3)	−3.63(3.4)
Owner occupied$_{it}$		3.02(1.2)
Labor demand shock$_{it}$	−23.6(10.4)	−24.9(10.6)
TFP shock$_{it}$	−17.9(14.1)	−17.5(3.3)
Real import price shock$_{it}$	5.82(3.3)	5.00(2.8)
Money supply shock$_{it}$	0.23(0.9)	0.24(1.0)
Real interest rate$_{it}$	1.81(1.6)	2.54(2.1)
Time dummies	✓	✓
Country dummies	✓	✓
Country-specific trends	✓	✓
N	20	19
NT	600	579

Notes: *Estimation:* Generalized least squares allowing for heteroscedastic errors and country-specific first-order serial correlation. Each equation contains country dummies, time dummies, and country-specific trends.

Variables: The benefit replacement ratio, union density, employment tax rate, and the owner occupation rate are proportions (range 0–1), benefit duration has a range (0–1.1), and employment protection, coordination are indexes (ranges 0–2, 1–3).

Tests: These are the same as for the labor costs regressions (see notes to Table 12). (a) *Poolability:* $\chi^2(190) = 87.7$, so the null of common slopes is not rejected. (b) *Heteroscedasticity:* the null of homoscedasticity is rejected [$\chi^2(19) = 843.9$], so we allow for heteroscedasticity. (c) *Serial correlation:* the null of no serial correlation is rejected [$\chi^2(1) = 77.3$], so we allow for first-order autoregressive errors with country-specific values of the relevant parameter. (d) *Cointegration:* Maddala-Wu test, $\chi^2 = 75.9$, so the null of no cointegration is rejected.

Thus, it appears that, overall, changing labor market institutions provide a reasonably satisfactory explanation of the broad pattern of unemployment shifts in the OECD countries and their impact on unemployment is broadly consistent with their impact on real wages. With better data, for example, on union coverage or the administration of the benefit system, we could probably generate a more complete explanation, in particular one that does not rely on such a high level of endogenous persistence to fit the data. To see how well the model is performing from another angle, we present in Figure 3 a dynamic simulation of the model fixing all the institutions from the start.

In the following countries, changing institutions explain a significant part of the overall change in unemployment since the 1960s: Australia, Belgium, Denmark, Finland, France, Italy, Netherlands, Norway, Spain, Switzerland, and the United

Table 14. Time Dummies and Time Trends (units: percentage points)

Time dummies					
1966	0.07(0.3)	1976	0.69(0.6)	1986	0.62(0.3)
1967	0.02(0.1)	1977	0.61(0.5)	1987	0.79(0.4)
1968	0.11(0.3)	1978	0.72(0.5)	1988	0.56(0.3)
1969	−0.06(0.1)	1979	0.59(0.4)	1989	0.53(0.2)
1970	0.11(0.2)	1980	0.55(0.4)	1990	0.98(0.4)
1971	0.37(0.6)	1981	1.14(0.7)	1991	1.33(0.5)
1972	0.50(0.7)	1982	1.41(0.8)	1992	1.62(0.6)
1973	0.28(0.3)	1983	1.21(0.7)	1993	1.55(0.6)
1974	0.08(0.1)	1984	0.69(0.4)	1994	1.14(0.4)
1975	0.92(0.9)	1985	0.52(0.3)	1995	0.58(0.2)

Time trends			
Australia	−0.054(0.5)	Japan	−0.059(0.6)
Austria	−0.059(0.6)	Netherlands	−0.045(0.5)
Belgium	−0.022(0.2)	New Zealand	0.003(0.0)
Canada	−0.072(0.8)	Norway	−0.067(0.7)
Denmark	−0.078(0.8)	Portugal	−0.107(1.1)
Finland	0.017(0.2)	Spain	0.042(0.4)
France	−0.019(0.2)	Sweden	−0.078(0.8)
Germany (W)	−0.006(0.1)	Switzerland	−0.041(0.4)
Ireland	0.022(0.2)	United Kingdom	−0.007(0.1)
Italy	−0.015(0.2)	United States	−0.026(0.3)

Note: Taken from regression reported in column 1 of Table 13; *t* ratios in brackets.

Kingdom. They explain too much in Austria, Portugal, and Sweden. They explain very little in Germany, New Zealand, and the United States, although in the last there is very little to explain.

Thus, given the dramatic rise in European unemployment from the 1960s to the 1980s and early 1990s, how much of an overall explanation do our institutional variables provide? Consider the period from the 1960s to 1990–1995. Over this period, the unemployment rate in Europe, as captured by the European OECD countries considered here,[17] rose by around 6.8 percentage points. How much of this increase is explained by our institutional variables? Based on the dynamic simulations keeping institutions fixed at their 1960s values shown in Figure 3, the answer is around 55 percent.[18] Given that the period 1990–1995 was one of deep

---

17. So we are excluding Greece and Eastern Europe.

18. When accounting for the rise in unemployment using a dynamic equation such as the first column in Table 13, it is vital that adequate account be taken of the lagged dependent variable. The dynamic simulation method used here is probably the best, but one can also work directly from the equation by noting that changes in unemployment in country i between two periods can be estimated by using the fact that

$$\Delta u_i = \alpha \Delta u_{i-1} + \sum_j \beta_j \Delta z_{ij} + \sum_k \gamma_k \Delta x_{ik},$$

where the z variables are the institutions and the x variables are all the rest. Thus one might imagine at first sight that $\sum_j \beta_j \Delta z_{ij}$ is the contribution of the institutions. This, however, would be a grave mistake. To approximate the correct answer most easily, assume that the impact of institutions on Δu_i

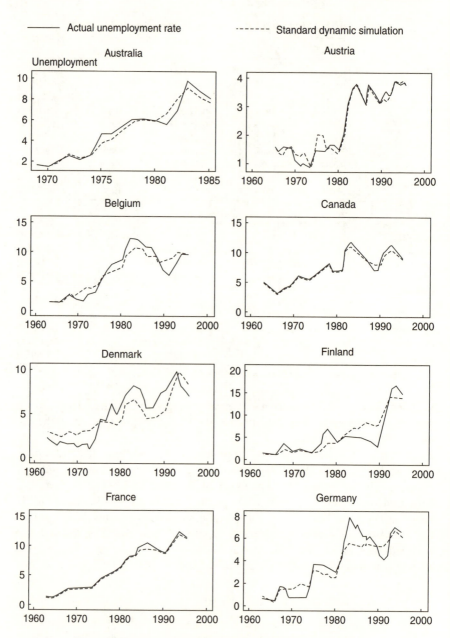

Figure 2. A dynamic simulation of the baseline unemployment model.

is the same as their impact on Δu_{i-1} (e.g., their impact on the change from 1965 to 1992 is the same as their impact on the change from 1964 to 1991, something that will only be approximately correct). Then under this assumption, we see that the contribution of institutions is $\sum \beta_j \Delta z_{ij}/(1-\alpha)$. In our case, where $\alpha = 0.86$, this means that $\sum \beta_j \Delta z_{ij}$ understates the contribution of institutions by a multiple of 7! Of course, using the dynamic simulation method gives the correct answer immediately.

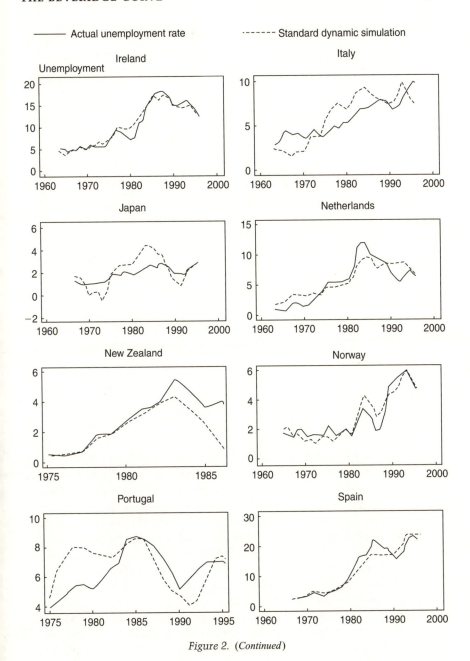

Figure 2. (*Continued*)

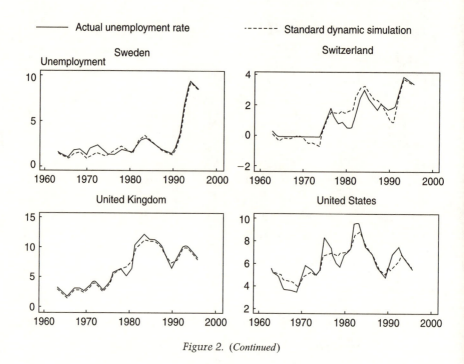

Figure 2. (*Continued*)

recession in much of Europe, this level of explanation is highly significant. Indeed, if we exclude Germany, where institutional changes explain nothing, changes in labor market institutions account for 63 percent of the rise in unemployment in the remainder of Europe. So what proportions of this latter figure are contributed by the different types of institutions? Changes in the benefit system are the most important, contributing 39 percent. Increases in labor taxes generate 26 percent, shifts in the union variables are responsible for 19 percent, and movements in employment protection law contribute 16 percent. So the combination of benefits and taxes are responsible for two-thirds of that part of the long-term rise in European unemployment that our institutions explain.

Finally, to round things off, we present in Table 15 a set of equations explaining the employment/population ratio that matches the unemployment equations in Table 13. The broad picture is very similar although the institutional effects are generally smaller, which is consistent with the fact that the nonemployed are a far more heterogeneous group than the unemployed, and their behavior is influenced by a much wider variety of factors, such as the benefits available to the sick, disabled, and early retired; the availability of subsidized child care; and so on. One factor that is different, however, is the strong negative impact of owner occupation, which contrasts with its small effect on unemployment.

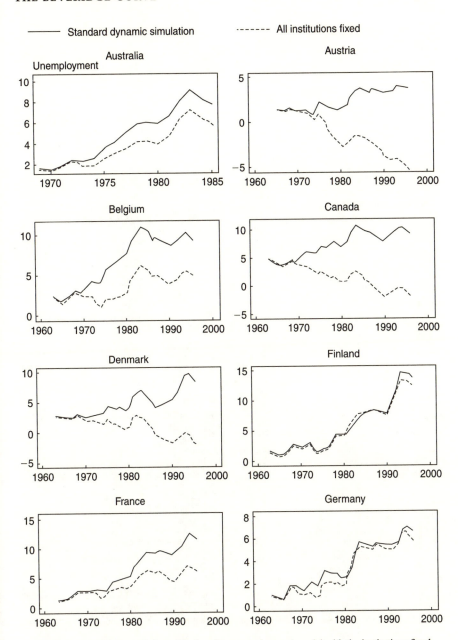

Figure 3. A dynamic simulation of the baseline unemployment model with the institutions fixed.

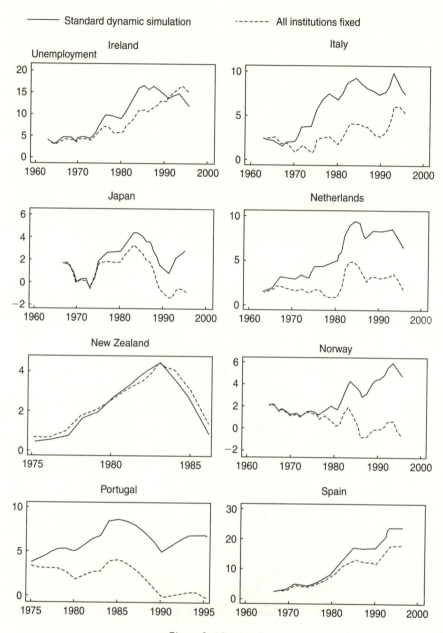

Figure 3. (*Continued*)

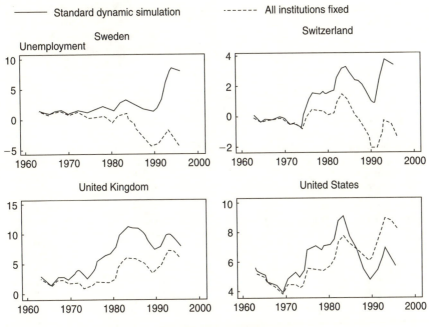

Figure 3. (*Continued*)

6. SUMMARY AND CONCLUSIONS

We have undertaken an empirical analysis of unemployment patterns in the OECD countries from the 1960s to the 1990s. This has involved a detailed study of shifts in the Beveridge curves and real wages as well as unemployment in twenty countries. The aim has been to see if these shifts can be explained by changes in those labor market institutions that might be expected to impact on equilibrium unemployment. In this context, it is important to recall that unemployment is always determined by aggregate demand. As a consequence we are effectively trying to understand the long-term shifts in both unemployment *and* aggregate demand (relative to potential output). We emphasize this because it is sometimes thought that the fact that unemployment is determined by aggregate demand factors is somehow inconsistent with the notion that unemployment is influenced by labor market institutions. This is wholly incorrect.

Our results indicate the following. First, the Beveridge curves of all the countries except Norway and Sweden shifted to the right from the 1960s to the early/mid-1980s.[19] At this point, the countries divide into two distinct groups: those where Beveridge curves continued to shift out and those where they started to shift back. Second, we find evidence that these movements in the Beveridge curves may be partly explained by changes in labor market institutions, particularly those that

---

19. Italy and Ireland are missing here because no vacancy data are available.

Table 15. Explaining OECD Employment/Population Ratios, 1961–1995

Independent variables	Dependent variable = employment population$_{it}$ (%)	
	1	2
Employment population$_{it-1}$	0.91(65.6)	0.92(66.3)
Employment protection$_{it}$	0.07(0.3)	0.14(0.7)
Benefit replacement ratio$_{it}$	−2.07(4.5)	−1.94(4.2)
Benefit duration$_{it}$	0.14(0.5)	0.13(0.4)
Benefit duration$_{it}$ × benefit replacement ratio$_{it}$	−4.16(4.0)	−2.79(2.7)
Δ union density$_{it}$	−11.59(4.3)	−8.85(3.1)
Coordination$_{it}$	1.64(7.0)	1.18(4.7)
Coordination$_{it}$ × union density$_{it}$	2.72(2.2)	4.50(3.6)
Total employment tax rate$_{it}$	−2.45(2.4)	−2.10(2.1)
Coordination$_{it}$ × total employment tax rate$_{it}$	3.85(3.1)	3.86(3.1)
Owner occupied$_{it}$		−13.34(4.7)
Labor demand shock$_{it}$	65.18(21.3)	67.02(21.9)
TFP shock$_{it}$	16.80(10.5)	16.94(10.3)
Real import price shock$_{it}$	−2.22(1.2)	−2.23(1.3)
Money supply shock$_{it}$	−0.14(0.3)	−0.14(0.4)
Real interest rate$_{it}$	−3.65(2.7)	−3.61(2.6)
Time dummies	✓	✓
Country dummies	✓	✓
Country-specific trends	✓	✓
N	20	20
NT	600	579

Notes: Estimation: Generalized least squares allowing for heteroscedastic errors and country-specific first-order serial correlation. Each equation contains country dummies, time dummies, and country-specific trends.

Variables: The benefit replacement ratio, union density, employment tax rate, and owner occupation rate are proportions (range 0–1), benefit duration has a range (0–1.1), employment protection, coordination are indices.

are important for search and matching efficiency. Third, labor market institutions impact on real labor costs in a fashion that is broadly consistent with their impact on unemployment. Finally, broad movements in unemployment across the OECD can be explained by shifts in labor market institutions. To be more precise, changes in labor market institutions explain around 55 percent of the rise in European unemployment from the 1960s to the first half of the 1990s, much of the remainder being due to the deep recession that ruled in the latter period.

DATA APPENDIX

The countries in the sample are: Australia, Austria, Belgium, Canada, Denmark, Finland, France, Germany, Ireland, Italy, Japan, Netherlands, New Zealand, Norway, Portugal, Spain, Sweden, Switzerland, United Kingdom, United States. Where possible, the data refer to West Germany throughout. The latest version of these data (mostly 1960–1992) can be found attached to D.P.502 at http://cep.lse.ac.uk/papers/.

Benefit Replacement Rate. Benefit entitlement before tax as a percentage of previous earnings before tax. Data are averages over replacement rates at two earnings levels (average and two-thirds of average earnings) and three family types (single, with dependent spouse, with spouse at work). They refer to the first year of unemployment. Source: OECD (Database on Unemployment Benefit Entitlements and Replacement Rates). The original data are for every second year and have been linearly interpolated.

Benefit Duration Index. ($0.6 \times$ replacement rate in 2nd/3rd year of an unemployment spell $+ 0.4 \times$ replacement rate in 4th/5th year of an unemployment spell) $\div$ (replacement rate in 1st year of an unemployment spell). Replacement rate defined as above. Source: OECD (1994b).

Trade Union Density. This variable is constructed as the ratio of total reported union members (less retired and unemployed members), from Ebbinghaus and Visser (2000).

Coordination Index (1–3). This captures the degree of consensus between the actors in collective bargaining: 1 low, 3 high. There are two series: (1) Based on interpolations of OECD data (OECD, 1994, 1997) and data made available by Michèle Belot, described in Belot and Van Ours (2000). (2) Based on data reported in Windmüller (1987), OECD (1994b, 1997), Traxler (1996), Bamber and Lansbury (1998), Ferner and Hyman (1998), Traxler and Kittel (1999), Wallerstein (1999). For full details, see Ochel (2000b). The first series is used in all the regressions reported in the paper.

Employment Protection Index (0–2). This captures the strictness of employment protection laws: 0 low, 2 high. Made available by Olivier Blanchard. Based on the series used by Lazear (1990) and that reported in OECD (1999). The series is an interpolation of 5-year averages.

Labor Taxes. This consists of the payroll tax rate plus the income tax rate plus the consumption tax rate. These are taken from the CEP-OECD Dataset (Centre for Economic Performance, London School of Economics) and are based mainly on OECD National Accounts.

1. Payroll tax rate $= EC/(IE - EC)$, $EC = EPP + ESS$. EPP = employers' private pensions and welfare plans contributions, ESS = employers' social security contributions, IE = compensations of employees.
2. Income tax rate $= (WC + IT)/HCR$. WC = employees' social security contributions, IT = income taxes, HCR = households' current receipts.
3. Consumption tax rate $= (TX - SB)/CC$. TX = indirect taxes, SB = subsidies, CC = private final consumption expenditure.

Owner Occupation Rate. Refers to the percentage of the housing stock classified as owner occupied. The data were supplied by Andrew Oswald and have been heavily interpolated. Not available for Portugal.

Unemployment Rate. Where possible, these correspond to OECD standardized unemployment rates and conform to the ILO definition. For Italy: the data correspond to "unemployment rates on U.S. concepts" from the U.S. Bureau of Labor Statistics. For earlier years, we use data reported in Layard et al. (1991, table A3). For later years we use OECD (2000, table A) and *U.K. Employment Trends*, table C51.

Vacancy Rate. This is defined as the number of registered vacancies divided by employment. The latter is total civilian employment (OECD Labour Force Statistics). The former refers to the number of registered vacancies, to be found in OECD Main Economic Indicators. In Canada and the United States, the vacancy data come in the form of a "help wanted" advertising index.

Inflow Rate. This variable is the monthly inflow into unemployment divided by employment (total civilian employment). In the United Kingdom, the data refer to the actual inflow into claimant status (*U.K. Employment Trends*) and we use the male rate because of the large variations over time in the benefit eligibility of unemployed women. In the remaining countries where data are available we use the number of unemployed with duration less than 1 month (or 4 weeks).

Real Labor Cost per Worker. The real wage adjusted to include payroll taxes. This is defined by the compensation of employees divided by employment and normalized on the GDP deflator. Source: OECD, National Accounts and Main Economic Indicators.

Real Import Prices. Defined as the import price deflator normalized on the GDP deflator. Source: OECD, National Accounts and Main Economic Indicators. The real import price shock is the change in the log of real import prices times the share of imports in GDP (OECD Main Economic Indicators).

Trend Productivity. Based on the Hodrick-Prescott trend of (log real GDP–log employment).

Real Interest Rate. Long-term nominal interest rate less the current rate of inflation from the OECD Economic Outlook Database.

Total Factor Productivity (TFP). Based on the Solow residual for each country, smoothed using a Hodrick-Prescott (HP) filter (see Nickell and Nunziata, 2000, for more detail). There are two versions of the TFP shock. (1) Three-year moving average of Δ^2 (so low residual), which is used in the labor cost equations in Table 12. (2) The cyclical component of TFP, that is, the deviation of the Solow residual from its HP filter trend. This is used in the unemployment and employment equations (Tables 13 and 15).

Labor Demand Shock. Residuals from country-specific employment equations, each being a regression of employment on lags of employment and real wages.

Money Supply Shock. Δ^2 ln (money supply) from OECD Economic Outlook Database.

Employment Population Ratio. Total civilian employment normalized on the working age population (15–64 years), from CEP OECD dataset, updated.

REFERENCES

Abbring, J. H., G. J. Van Den Berg, and J. C. Van Ours (1999), "The Effect of Unemployment Insurance Sanctions on the Transition Rate from Unemployment to Employment," Tinbergen Institute, University of Amsterdam.

Addison, J. T. and J-L. Grosso (1996), "Job Security Provisions and Unemployment: Revised Estimates," *Industrial Relations* 35:585–603.

Baltagi, B. (1995), *Econometric Analysis of Panel Data.* New York: Wiley.

Bamber, G. J. and R. D. Lansbury, eds. (1998), *International and Comparative Employment Relations: A Study of Industrialised Market Economies*, London and New Delhi: Thousand Oaks.

Belot, M. and J. C. Van Ours (2000), "Does the Recent Success of Some OECD Countries in Lowering their Unemployment Rates Lie in the Clever Design of their Labour Market Reforms?," IZA Discussion Paper No. 147.

Bentolila, S. and G. Bertola (1990), "Firing Costs and Labour Demand: How Bad is Eurosclerosis?," *Review of Economic Studies* 57:381–402.

Blanchard, O. and L. Katz (1999), "What We Know and Do Not Know about the Natural Rate of Unemployment," *Journal of Economic Perspectives* 11(1):51–72.

Blanchard, O. and J. Wolfers (2000), "The Role of Shocks and Institutions in the Rise of European Unemployment: The Aggregate Evidence," *The Economic Journal* 110:C1–33.

Booth, A., M. Burda, L. Calmfors, D. Checchi, R. Naylor, and J. Visser (2000), "What Do Unions Do in Europe?," Report for the Fondazione Rodolfo DeBenedetti, Milan.

Bover, O., P. Garcia-Perea, and P. Portugal (1998), "A Comparative Study of the Portuguese and Spanish Labour Markets," mimeo, Banco de Espana.

Carling, K., P-A. Edin, A. Herkman, and B. Holmlund (1996), "Unemployment Duration, Unemployment Benefits and Labor Market Programs in Sweden," *Journal of Public Economics* 59:313–34.

Carling, K., B. Holmlund, and A. Vejsiu (1999), "Do Benefit Cuts Boost Job Findings? Swedish Evidence from the 1990s," Swedish Office of Labour Market Policy Evaluation Working Paper 1999:8.

Coe, D. T. and D. J. Snower (1997), "Policy Complementarities: The Case for Fundamental Labour Market Reform," CEPR Discussion Paper No. 1585.

Cully, M. and S. Woodland (1998), "Trade Union Membership and Resulting Labour Market Trends," in *Labour Market Trends*, Office of National Statistics, London.

Daniel, W. W. and E. Stilgoe (1978), *The Impact of Employment Protection Laws*, London: Policy Studies Institute.

Danish Ministry of Finance (1999), *The Danish Economy: Medium Term Economic Survey,* Copenhagen: Ministry of Finance.

Daveri, F. and G. Tabellini (2000), "Unemployment, Growth and Taxation in Industrial Countries," *Economic Policy* 30:49–90.

Disney, R. (2000), "Fiscal Policy and Employment 1: A Survey of Macroeconomic Models, Methods and Findings," mimeo, IMF.

Ebbinghaus, B. and J. Visser (2000), *Trade Unions in Western Europe*, London: Macmillan.

Elmeskov, J., J. P. Martin, and S. Scarpetta (1998), "Key Lessons for Labour Market Reforms: Evidence from OECD Countries' Experiences," *Swedish Economic Policy Review* 5(2): 205–52.

Ferner, A. and R. Hyman, eds. (1998), *Changing Industrial Relations in Europe*, 2nd ed., Oxford: Malden.

Fitoussi, J-P., D. Jestaz, E. S. Phelps, and G. Zoega (2000), "Roots of the Recent Recoveries: Labor Reforms or Private Sector Forces?," *Brookings Papers on Economic Activity* 1: 237–91.

Gregg, P., S. Machin, and A. Manning (2000), "Mobility and Joblessness," mimeo, London School of Economics, Centre for Economic Performance.

Ham, J. and S. Rea (1987), "Unemployment Insurance and Male Unemployment Duration in Canada," *Journal of Labor Economics* 5:325–53.

Harkman, A. (1997), "Unemployment Compensation and Unemployment Duration—What was the Effect of the Cut in the Replacement Rate from 90 to 80 percent?," in A. Harkman, F. Jansson, K. Kallberg, and L. Öhrn, eds., *Unemployment Insurance and the Functioning of the Labour Market*, The Swedish National Labour Market Board, Stockholm.

Holmlund, B. (1998) "Unemployment Insurance in Theory and Practice," *The Scandinavian Journal of Economics* 100(1):113–41.

Hoon, H. T. and E. S. Phelps (1992), "Macroeconomic Shocks in a Dynamized Model of the Natural Rate of Unemployment," *American Economic Review* 82:889–900.

Hunt, J. (1995), "The Effect of Unemployment Compensation on Unemployment Duration in Germany," *Journal of Labor Economics* 13:88–120.

Katz, L. F. (1998), "Wage Subsidies for the Disadvantaged," in R. Freeman and P. Gottschalk, eds., *Generating Jobs*, New York: Russell Sage Foundation.

Katz, L. and B. Meyer (1990), "The Impact of Potential Duration of Unemployment Benefits on the Duration of Unemployment," *Journal of Public Economics* 41:45–72.

Layard, R., S. Nickell, and R. Jackman (1991), *Unemployment: Macroeconomic Performance and the Labour Market*, Oxford: Oxford University Press.

Lazear, E. P. (1990), "Job Security Provisions and Employment," *Quarterly Journal of Economics* 105:699–726.

Maddala, G. S. and S. Wu (1996), "A Comparative Study of Unit Root Tests with Panel Data and a New Simple Test: Evidence from Simulations and the Bootstrap," mimeo, Ohio State University.

Martin, J. (2000), "What Works among Active Labour Market Policies? Evidence from OECD Countries," *OECD Economic Studies* No. 30, Paris: OECD, pp. 79–112.

Meyer, B. (1995), "Lessons from the US Unemployment Insurance Experiments," *Journal of Economic Literature* 33:91–131.

Millward, N., D. Smart, and W. Hawes (1992), *Workplace Industrial Relations in Transition,* Aldershot: Gower Press.

Milner, S. (1995), "The Coverage of Collective Pay-setting Institutions in Britain, 1895–1990," *British Journal of Industrial Relations* 33(1):71–91.

Mortensen, D. T. and C. A. Pissarides (1994), "Job Creation and Job Destruction in the Theory of Unemployment," *Review of Economic Studies* 61:397–415.

———— (1999), "New Developments in Models of Search in the Labor Market," in O. Ashenfelter and D. Card, eds., *Handbook of Labor Market*, Amsterdam: North-Holland.

Nickell, S. J. (1990), "Unemployment: A Survey," *Economic Journal* 100:391–439.

———— (1997), "Unemployment and Labour Market Rigidities: Europe versus North America," *Journal of Economic Perspectives* 11(3):55–74.

Nickell, S. J. and R. Layard (1999), "Labour Market Institutions and Economic Performance," in O. Ashenfelter and D. Card, eds., *Handbook of Labor Economics*, Vol. 3, Amsterdam: North-Holland.

Nickell, S. J. and L. Nunziata (2000), "Employment Patterns in OECD Countries," CEP Discussion Paper 448, London School of Economics.

Ochel, W. (2000a), "Collective Bargaining Coverage", Ifo Institute for Economic Research, Munich.

————— (2000b), "Collective Bargaining (Centralization and Co-ordination)," Ifo Institute, Munich.

OECD (1990), *Employment Outlook*, Paris.

————— (1994a), *The OECD Jobs Study, Evidence and Explanations, Vols. I and II*, Paris.

————— (1994b), *Employment Outlook*, Paris.

————— (1997), *Employment Outlook*, Paris.

————— (1999), *Employment Outlook*, Paris.

————— (2000), *Employment Outlook*, Paris.

Oswald, A. (1997), "The Missing Piece of the Unemployment Puzzle," Inaugural Lecture, University of Warwick.

Phelps, E. S. (1994), *Structural Slumps: The Modern Equilibrium Theory of Unemployment, Interest and Assets*, Cambridge: Harvard University Press.

Pissarides, C. A. (1990), *Equilibrium Unemployment Theory*, Oxford: Blackwell.

————— (1998), "The Impact of Employment Tax Cuts on Unemployment and Wages: The Role of Unemployment Benefits and Tax Structure," *European Economic Review* 47:155–83.

Roy, S. (1957), *Some Aspects of Multivariate Analysis*, New York: Wiley.

Scarpetta, S. (1996), "Assessing the Role of Labour Market Policies and Institutional Settings on Unemployment: A Cross Country Study," *OECD Economic Studies* 26:43–98.

Solow, R. (2000), "Unemployment in the United States and in Europe: A Contrast and the Reasons," *CES ifo Munich Forum*, Spring.

Soskice, D. (1991), "Wage Determination: The Changing Role of Institutions in Advanced Industrialised Countries," *Oxford Review of Economic Policy* 6:36–61.

Traxler, F. (1996), Collective Bargaining and Industrial Change: A Case of Disorganization? A Comparative Analysis of Eighteen OECD Countries, *European Sociological Review* 12(3): 271–87.

Traxler, F. and B. Kittel (2000), "The Bargaining System and Performance: A Comparison of 18 OECD Countries," *Comparative Political Studies* 33:1154–90.

Van Den Berg, G., B. Van Der Klaauw, and J. C. Van Ours (1999), "Punitive Sanctions and the Transition Rate from Welfare to Work," Tinbergen Institute, University of Amsterdam.

Visser, J. (1996), "Unionisation Trends: The OECD Countries Union Membership File," University of Amsterdam, Centre for Research of European Societies and Labour Relations.

Windmüller, J. P. (1987), *Collective Bargaining in Market Economics: A Reappraisal*, Geneva: ILO.

Zellner, A. (1962), "An Efficient Method of Estimating Seemingly Unrelated Regression and Tests for Aggregation Bias," *Journal of the American Statistical Association* 57:500–9.

— 20 —

Comments on Nickell, Nunziata, Ochel, and Quintini

JEAN-PAUL FITOUSSI

1. INTRODUCTION

Stephen Nickell and his co-authors have contributed a very useful and comprehensive chapter. It extends the framework developed earlier by Layard, Nickell, and a number of co-authors to reexamine the evolution of unemployment over the last four decades in twenty OECD countries. The aim of the chapter "is to see how far it is possible to defend the proposition that the dramatic long-term shifts in unemployment seen in the OECD countries over the period from the 1960s to the 1990s can be explained simply by changes in labor market institutions in the same period."

The influence of institutions, especially labor market institutions, on labor market performances has been a debated question at least since the 1920s. I remember a paper by Jacques Rueff published in 1931, whose title was self-explanatory: "Unemployment Insurance, Cause of Persistent Unemployment," in which the author was trying to explain the increase in unemployment in the United Kingdom in the 1920s. Simple correlations convinced him that there was no other cause for the evolution of unemployment in that country than the generosity of the unemployment insurance system. Of course we have made a lot of technical progress in dealing with data since then, but that the question is still debated today shows that almost a century of hard and rigorous research has been unable to settle the debate. Stephen Nickell and his associates recognize this point from the outset, quoting economists of different persuasions and admitting that their chapter deserves a B grade because "the story that emerges from their research is reasonably consistent but not totally decisive."

This kind of honesty has become sufficiently rare in scientific research to be emphasized and applauded, as what they are saying about their chapter applies to almost all the papers I have read (or written) on the same issues.

The theoretical background of their chapter can be summarized as follows: "The equilibrium level of unemployment is affected first by any variable that influences the ease with which unemployed individuals can be matched to available job vacancies, and second, by any variable that tends to raise wages in a direct fashion despite excess supply in the labor market." These variables include, among others, the unemployment benefit system, the real interest rate, employment protection, active labor market policy, union structures, the extent of coordination in wage bargaining, and labor taxes. The strategy then followed by the authors is both systematic and rigorous; they proceed by steps looking at the effect of institutions on the Beveridge curve first, the real wage second, and unemployment third. Their findings at least with respect to the qualitative effect of institutions on the labor market are consistent in the three steps. I will not quarrel with the empirical methodology they use nor with the fact that they use reduced-form equations rather than an articulated structural model. But I will try first to find out how much of the variation in unemployment owing to institutions their equations actually explain before turning to more general arguments about the institutional explanation of unemployment and looking at other suspects.

2. WHAT PERCENTAGE OF THE INCREASE IN UNEMPLOYMENT IS EXPLAINED BY INSTITUTIONS?

Nickell and his co-authors focus on time-series variation in the cross-country data. Their typical equations include various institutions plus shocks as independent variables. Their strategy is thus different from the one followed by Blanchard and Wolfers (2000) or Fitoussi et al. (2000) in that they are not looking at the interaction between shocks and institutions.

There are two reasons why the interaction strategy seems more appealing. First unemployment rates in the OECD countries rose roughly in unison from the mid-1970s to the mid-1980s. Thus all the favored candidates to explain the phenomenon are OECD-wide shocks. Second labor market institutions may have played a role mainly in propagating these shocks rather than originating them. (See Krugman, 1994, on this point.) The welfare state had its origins well before the rise in unemployment at the beginning of the 1970s when Europe was enjoying low unemployment and generally good labor market performance. Moreover, a better understanding of the early shocks that drove unemployment to new heights in previous decades in Europe can possibly help save some institutions that, by making up for failures in insurance markets and training, may be worth keeping.

Finally, the institutions reflect a social contract that arises from a democratic process. In this process there are winners and losers so structural reform is unlikely to lead to a Pareto-improving outcome, even one supported by a majority of the electorate (see Cohen and Saint-Paul, 1997). Former research showed that it was hard to explain change in unemployment by change in institutions (see Fitoussi et al., 2000). Only two variables appeared to be significant: an increase in union coordination tends to reduce unemployment and an increase in union coverage increases it. Moreover, the significance of these two variables stems from a fall in union coordination in Finland (which experienced a rise in unemployment) and a fall in union coverage in the United Kingdom (which had a fall in unemployment). Other countries did not have a change in either the coordination or coverage of unions.

These are the reasons why it is important to estimate first the baseline equation for each country separately, without imposing any cross-country restrictions. It is important to do so because once we start constraining coefficients to take the same value across countries, the possibility arises that a significant relationship for some of the countries will create the illusion of a sample-wide relation. That is, if the equation fits for one group of countries but not for another the panel estimation may yield significant results owing only to the inclusion of the first group.

That being said and knowing that the parameters of the equations should be different among countries, I have nevertheless tried to sort out the explanatory power of the different kind of institutions in their equations, as if the coefficients were the same for all countries. For that I used the data generously provided by Stephen Nickell. I have added, for each equation, the result for the European Union as a whole to have a middle ground between the results of the individual equations and the sample-wide relation of the chapter. The result is shown in Tables 1 and 2, which detail the Beveridge curve and the unemployment equations.[1]

What is striking is the weak, to say the least, explanatory power of the institutional variables, especially those considered as being the more important, namely, the benefit replacement rate and employment protection in the Beveridge curve. The authors recognize that the latter may have ambiguous effects: The fact that firms are more cautious about hiring because of strong labor protection may increase the efficiency of the matching process. But what they do not recognize is that the same may be said for the workers. The fact that unemployment benefit allows the unemployed to search for a job better suited to their skills and expectations may also increase the efficiency of the matching process. Certainly labor productivity could be greater if the worker has the feeling that his job corresponds better to his desire.

The picture that emerges from this admittedly crude exercise is not as clear-cut as some would like us to believe. Despite common beliefs, it does not seem that institutions are playing such an important role in explaining the rise of unemployment.

3. INSTITUTIONS AND ECONOMIC PERFORMANCES

Two general remarks are in order. Until now, there has been no convincing evidence that labor market institutions are responsible for the high level of unemployment in Continental Europe or for the disappointing macroeconomic performances of Europe during the 1990s. Economic outcomes are more easily explained by the big shocks that OECD countries have suffered: changing trend in productivity growth, the oil shocks, and the important increase in the real rate of interest. Moreover, structural reforms in the countries that implemented them do not appear to have played an important role either (see Fitoussi et al., 2000).

---

1. I am not sure that I have used the same units as the authors. For example, they may have used proportion variables rather than percentage variables. If that is the case, the coefficients of some institutional variables should have been even lower and my point would be strengthened. Second, the coefficient of the lagged unemployment variable in their equations is quite high (0.86). That means that the stationary form of their equations (when unemployment is constant) should have their coefficients multiplied by about 7. Where the coefficient of the lagged variable is 0.99, the multiplier would have been 100! But if such a long-term equilibrium reasoning may be applied to a theoretical structural model, I would have strong reservations about applying it to an empirical reduced-form equation, especially when this form is used by the authors to simulate the evolution of unemployment in different countries.

Table 1. Beveridge Curve, 1961–1995[a]

Country	$\Delta \log U_t$	log vacancy	log inflow	Benefit replacement (E)	Benefit duration (F)	Employment protection index (EP) (G)	Owner occupation (H)	Tax rate (I)	Coordination (J)	Union density (K)	Total (columns E to K %)
Belgium	2.65	-2.94	na	0.12	-1.91	-4.51	4.27	-0.50	0.00	2.17	**-0.35**
France	6.00	-1.35	3.84	0.05	0.77	-3.29	2.06	-0.22	-0.08	-0.80	**-1.51**
Germany (W)	6.00	2.25	6.32	-0.03	0.15	-3.39	1.37	-0.18	0.00	-0.24	**-2.32**
Italy	1.31	na	na	0.39	2.18	0.43	**16.46**	-0.84	0.15	5.48	**24.25**
Netherlands	7.00	1.97	-1.63	0.13	1.41	0.19	2.06	-0.03	0.00	-1.17	**2.60**
Spain	7.17	na	3.19	0.14	0.83	0.69	3.45	-0.41	0.00	0.47	**5.16**
European Union	4.36	2.88	2.45	0.06	0.51	-3.11	3.59	-0.27	0.00	-0.06	**0.71**
United Kingdom	2.38	1.81	0.42	-0.06	-1.57	-1.51	**10.80**	-0.60	0.29	-0.40	**6.94**
Canada	0.73	0.37	**20.40**	0.78	-3.33	0.00	-5.67	-2.87	0.00	5.94	**-5.14**
United States	0.11	**-35.09**	**-9.91**	1.10	**12.10**	0.00	0.00	**-11.09**	0.00	**-48.40**	**-46.29**

Note: This is an extension of Table 10 in Chapter 19. $\log U_t = 0.61 \log U_{t-1} - 0.23 \log \text{vacancy} + 0.23 \log \text{inflow rate} + 0.03 \text{ benefit replacement rate} + 0.22 \text{ benefit duration} - 0.19 \text{ EP} + 1.03 \text{ owner occupation rate} - 0.11 \text{ tax rate} - 0.02 \text{ coordination} + 0.48 \text{ union density}$. Contribution of each variable to the increase in the log of the unemployment rate depends on the country or group of countries (%).

[a] Boldface entries indicate the factors that have a sizable effect.

Table 2. Unemployment Equations[a]

Country	ΔU_t	Benefit replacement (C)	Benefit duration (D)	Employment protection index (EP) (E)	Benefit duration × benefit replacement (F)	Coordination union density (G)	Tax rate (H)	Coordination (I)	Union density (J)	Coordination tax rate (K)	Total (columns C to K %)
Belgium	6.10	3.99	-1.77	1.55	-0.02	**-27.46**	2.97	0.00	**13.75**	**-13.61**	**-20.62**
France	9.00	2.46	1.10	1.73	6.24	**11.79**	2.01	-2.58	-7.77	**-14.00**	**0.98**
Germany (W)	4.80	-2.76	0.39	3.34	-1.52	**13.09**	3.15	0.00	-4.37	**-21.63**	**-10.30**
Italy	4.60	**8.17**	1.33	-0.10	2.76	**-28.07**	3.28	2.20	**22.79**	-6.24	**6.11**
Netherlands	6.30	**10.87**	3.36	-0.17	**20.96**	**37.67**	0.48	0.00	**-18.86**	-2.20	**52.12**
Spain	17.20	4.24	0.74	-0.23	4.00	-5.68	2.37	0.00	2.84	-10.86	**-2.58**
European Union	7.41	2.52	0.64	1.45	3.74	1.32	2.20	0.07	-0.55	-10.86	**0.52**
United Kingdom	6.20	-1.78	-1.29	0.46	-4.89	**19.93**	3.17	5.70	-2.25	-1.70	**17.33**
Canada	4.00	**10.50**	-1.29	0.00	-0.10	**-15.71**	7.17	0.00	**15.73**	**-16.44**	-0.14
United States	0.60	**14.73**	4.70	0.00	**12.75**	**127.97**	**27.68**	0.00	**-128.15**	**-63.43**	**-3.75**

Note: This is an extension of Table 13 in Chapter 19. $U_t = 0.68\,U_{t-1} + 2.21$ benefit replacement rate $+ 0.47$ benefit duration $+ 0.15$ EP $+ 3.75$ benefit duration × benefit replacement ratio $- 6.98$ coordination union density $+ 1.51$ tax rate $- 1.01$ coordination $+ 6.99$ union density $- 3.46$ coordination tax rate $+$ etc. All variables are significant at the 5% level, except the EP and the tax rate. Contribution of institutions to the increase in the unemployment rate depends on the country or group of countries (%) (applied to 1960–1995, following the data given in Table 1).

[a] Boldface entries indicate the factors that have a sizable effect.

There is thus a gap between the usual recommendations and the weaknesses of the evidence to support them. At best empirical studies are able to explain second order of importance effects of institutions on unemployment, as shown by two recent studies conducted independently on the subject (see Fitoussi and Passet, 2000; Freeman, 2000). In market democracies, the institutional structure is not a powerful factor in explaining economic performances. Capitalism is sufficiently robust to accommodate rather different institutional settings. If we had followed conventional wisdom in each decade we would have recommended that every country in the world adopt the French institutional model in the 1960s, the Japanese one in the 1970s, the German one in the 1980s, and the U.S. one in the 1990s. The nationality of the winning model of the present decade (the 2000s) is still unknown.

This first remark led me to think that if we believe in the results of such studies we should revise our criteria for the evaluation of social policy. In our countries social policy is not a simple appendix to economic policy because it is consubstantial with democracy. But the criteria used to evaluate policies or reforms are usually efficiency criteria. About 20 years ago Dan Usher (1981) proposed using another criterion: Is such or such social reform likely to reinforce democracy or weaken it? The diversity of the institutional framework in OECD countries shows that institutions are the outcome of a political process anchored in the specific history, culture, and anthropology of the country rather than a way to increase efficiency. If, for example, the labor contract that emerged after World War II was open ended and of indefinite duration despite the cultural diversity of the countries concerned, this may simply have been because after a war, the solidarity between social groups had to be reassessed.

My second remark is that there is a strong presumption that institutions are endogenous. Nickell and his collaborators recognize that they have not faced up to the problem of the endogeneity of the institutional shifts. Structural measures are usually taken to cope with a problem—but not necessarily those measures that economists would recommend. Rising unemployment in Europe in a period during which stabilization policies were aimed at disinflation and at maintaining monetary parities has led to structural activism to alleviate the pain of the unemployed. For example, in France there is a clear causal relation between restrictive policies, mounting unemployment, and the 1997 law on the reduction of working time—the 35-hour week.

In a co-authored paper (Creel et al., 1999), we have shown that countries with higher unemployment growth in the 1980s have in the 1990s increased the degree of employment protection and expenses on active labor market policies and have exhibited a lower union density (see Figure 1). Some active labor market policies have also had the (unintended?) effect of putting the blame almost entirely on the workers, who are considered as being inclined to adopt a passive behavior when confronted with unemployment and an egoistical behavior when they are insiders. What is striking is that in Europe the advocates of orthodox macroeconomic policies (the stability pact and the single objective for monetary policy) are recommending incredibly interventionist structural policies that are in a way more limiting of the freedom of people than any kind of classical demand policy.

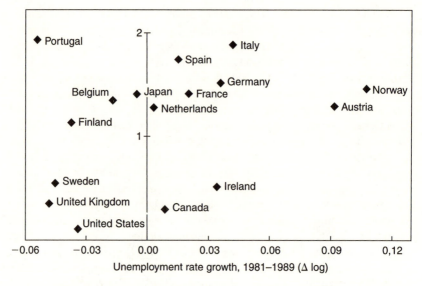

Figure 1. Employment protection (1988–1995) and unemployment (1981–1989).

4. ON OTHER SUSPECTS

We had better think twice before recommending that governments change such an essential thing as the social contract on the basis of weak, uncertain, and even contradictory evidence, especially when we know that in some countries (those in which the Beveridge curve has shifted to the right) monetary policy has been restrictive to an extent unseen since the 1930s for nearly 5 years. Figures 2 and 3 illustrate the point very clearly.[2]

That we have not yet been able to produce neat econometric results about the influence of monetary policy on unemployment—but see Creel and Fitoussi (2001)—implies that more work is needed. The difficulty lies in the fact that no single variable has a claim to even approximately represent monetary policy because of the importance of endogenous reactions of monetary policy to economic disturbances. But even without neat econometric results, how can we believe that the course of unemployment in Europe has been unaffected by the fact that the short-term real rate of interest has been higher than 5 percent in a period (1991–1995) in which the rate of growth was about 1 percent?

We usually compare the U.S. and European economies as if they were operating under the same normal conditions in the 1990s. But it does not need more than a modicum of historical sensitivity to understand that during this period Europe experimented with huge structural changes that amount to enormous investments in

---

2. In the graphs, the monetary policy gap is the difference between the actual short-term interest rate and the rate of interest computed from the Taylor rule (cf. Creel and Fitoussi, 2001).

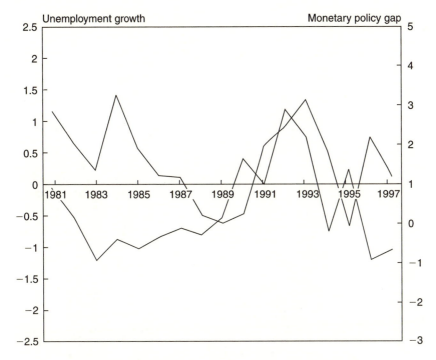

Figure 2. Unemployment growth and monetary policy gap (France).

intangible assets: German unification, the single market, and the euro. During most of this period monetary policy was following an objective other than stabilization.

As a consequence, growth receded and unemployment increased. But by now these structural changes should have enhanced potential growth in the euro area, in a measure that is certainly sizable even if difficult to estimate. There is no doubt that the single market together with the birth of the euro has increased the intensity of competition, as there is no doubt that the move toward privatization and deregulation in the product market has improved the conditions of competition in the whole area. On the other hand, owing to a long period of mass unemployment, real wage resistance seems to have completely disappeared and the flexibility of the labor market has noticeably increased, with or without structural reforms.

In addition the single currency has markedly decreased the cost of stabilization in European economies. For a large country, fluctuations in the exchange rate have minor consequences for internal stability. It is primarily the medium-size countries that are really confronted with the dilemma of choosing between internal and external equilibrium. That means that for the future, Europe will not be burdened by an excessive cost of stabilization as it was in the past. That is a far-reaching structural change that implies that the conditions for future growth are much more favorable. The structural reforms that are forcefully advocated on the labor markets appear in comparison to be of second-order importance—and they probably are.

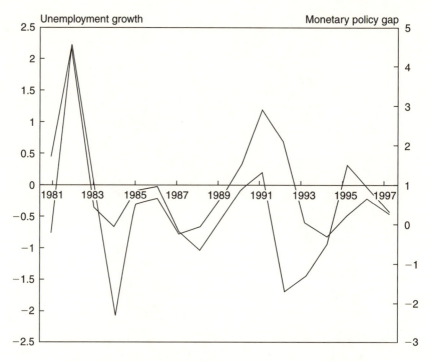

Figure 3. Unemployment growth and monetary policy gap (United States).

REFERENCES

Blanchard, O. J. and J. Wolfers (2000), "The Role of Shocks and Institutions in the Use of European Unemployment: The Aggregate Evidence," Harry Johnson Lecture, *Economic Journal* 110:1–33.

Cohen, D. and G. Saint-Paul (1997), "French Unemployment: A Translatlantic Perspective," *Economic Policy* 25:267–91.

Creel, J. and J.-P. Fitoussi (2001), "Unemployment in OECD Countries: Does Economic Policy Matter?," Conference American Economic Association of Policy Modelling for European and Global Issues, Brussels, July 6.

Creel, J., J.-P. Fitoussi, and C. Fuss (1999), "Explaining Successful Anti-unemployment Policies," Paper Presented at the XII World Congress of the International Economic Association, Buenos Aires, August 23–27.

Fitoussi, J.-P. and O. Passet (2000), "Réduction du chômage: les réussites en Europe," *Conseil d'Analyse Economique* 23, La Documentation française.

Fitoussi, J.-P., D. Jestaz, E. S.Phelps, and G. Zoega (2000), "Roots of the Recent Recoveries: Labor Reforms Sound Public Finance or Private Sector Forces?," *Brookings Papers on Economic Activity* 2001(1):237–309.

Freeman, R. B. (2000), "Single Peaked vs. Diversified Capitalism: The Relation between Economic Institutions and Outcomes," NBER Working Paper No. 7556.

Krugman, P. R. (1994), "Competitiveness: A Dangerous Obsession," *Foreign Affairs* 73(2): 28–44.

Rueff, J. (1931), "L'assurance chômage, cause du chômage permanent," *Revue d'Econonomie Politique* 45:211–51.

Usher, D. (1981), *The Economic Prerequisite to Democracy*, Oxford: Blackwell.

PART IV

Education, Technical Change, and Growth

Wage Inequality and Technological Change: A Nelson-Phelps Approach

PHILIPPE AGHION, PETER HOWITT, AND
GIANLUCA VIOLANTE

1. INTRODUCTION

The sharp increase in wage inequality evident since the early 1980s in developed countries, especially in the United States and Great Britain, has led to intense debates among economists. The rapidly growing literature on the subject reflects substantial progress in narrowing down the search for robust explanations, in particular by emphasizing the primary role of (skill-biased) technological progress; yet this literature leaves some important puzzles open to further inquiry.

The first puzzle concerns the evolution of wage inequality *between* educational groups. Although the relative supply of college-educated workers has increased noticeably within the past 30 years, the wage ratio between college graduates and high school graduates rose substantially in countries such as the United States and Great Britain between the early 1980s and the mid-1990s. In the United States, for example, Autor et al. (1998) show that the ratio of "college equivalents" (defined as the number of workers with a college degree plus half the number of workers with some college education) to "noncollege equivalents" (defined as the complementary set of workers) increased at an average rate of 3.05 percent between 1970 and 1995, up from an average rate of 2.35 percent between 1940 and 1970. In parallel to these movements in relative supply, the ratio between the average weekly wages of college and high school graduates went up by more than 25 percent during the period 1970–1995, although it had fallen by 0.11 percent a year on average during the previous period.

The second puzzle is that wage inequality has also increased sharply *within* educational and age groups. In particular Machin (1996a) finds that the *residual* standard deviation in hourly earnings increased by 23 percent in Great Britain and by 14 percent in the United States over the period between 1979 and 1993. Equally intriguing is the fact that the rise in within-group wage inequality began *before* the rise in between-group inequality and accounts for a substantial fraction of the overall increase in income inequality (Katz and Autor, 2000).

The third puzzle is that the increase in within-group inequality has affected mainly the *temporary* component of income, whereas the increase in between-group inequality has affected mainly the *permanent* component of income (Blundell and Preston, 1999).

In this chapter we develop an explanation for these puzzles that is based on the idea that technological change is skill biased, not only in the usual sense of enhancing educated workers' productivity in producing goods and services under given technological conditions but also in the sense of raising the reward for adaptability. This argument builds directly upon the idea of Nelson and Phelps (1966) that skills are not just an input to the production of goods and services but also a factor in the creation and absorption of new technological knowledge.[1]

The chapter is organized as follows. In Section 2 we review and discuss the principal existing explanations for the increase in wage inequality. In Section 3 we develop our own explanation, which combines adaptability considerations and the idea that an important driving force behind the evolution of the wage structure is the arrival of new "general-purpose technologies." Finally, Section 4 concludes the chapter by noting a few potential extensions and policy implications of our approach.

2. ALTERNATIVE EXPLANATIONS FOR RISING WAGE INEQUALITY

2.1. Trade

One possible explanation for rising wage inequality, inspired by the Heckscher-Ohlin theory, is that the observed upsurge is a direct consequence of *trade liberalization*. In a nutshell, a globalization boom should drive up the demand for skilled labor in developed countries, where skilled labor is cheap relative to developing countries, and it should drive down the relative demand for unskilled labor, which is relatively expensive in developed countries. Unfortunately, this trade liberalization explanation is not supported by the evidence. First, as argued by Krugman and others, how could trade liberalization have such a big impact on wage inequality in a country such as the United States where trade with non-OECD countries represents no more than 2 percent of the GDP? Second, this explanation would imply a fall in prices of less skill-intensive goods relative to those of more skill-intensive goods in developed countries, but empirical studies find little evidence of this in the United States or Europe during the 1980s. A third implication of the trade explanation is that labor should be reallocated from low-skill to high-skill industries or from those sectors in developed countries that are most exposed to international competition to the other sectors. However, Berman et al. (1994) for the United States and Machin (1996b) for Great Britain found that only a minor part (about 20%) of the shift away from manual/blue-collar workers to nonmanual/white collars was

---

1. While our explanation of the facts is similar to that of Galor and Moav, it differs in placing emphasis on the *generality* of technological change as well as its pace, in generating a steady-state increase in within-group wage inequality that is not just transitional, and in basing the explanation of within-group inequality on luck rather than on ability.

due to between-industry changes, the remaining 70 or 80 percent being entirely attributable to within-industry shifts. Finally, the Heckscher-Ohlin theory would predict that the ratio of skilled to unskilled employment should have gone down in skill-intensive industries in developed economies, which did not happen.

2.2. Institutions

A second explanation would link wage inequality to institutional change. The primary candidate is the *deunionization* trend experienced by the United States and Great Britain since the Reagan-Thatcher period. According to Machin (1997), in the latter, union density among male workers fell from 54 percent in 1980 to 38 percent in 1990; in the former the percentage of private-sector workers that are unionized fell from 24 percent in 1980 to less than 12 percent in 1990. The argument is simply that unionization is often positively correlated with wage compression,[2] so that deunionization should naturally lead to an increase in wage inequality.[3] DiNardo et al. (1996) and Card (1996) examine the effects of deunionization on the wage distribution and find that it can explain a significant part of the rise in *male* inequality. However, the attempt to attribute the increase in wage inequality to deunionization has at least three important shortcomings: First, "timing" considerations: In Great Britain the rise in wage inequality started in the mid-1970s but union density kept increasing until 1980; on the other hand, in the United States, deunionization began in the 1950s at a time when wage inequality was relatively stable. Second, these empirical studies find no impact of deunionization on the rise of female inequality. Third, most of the impact of deunionization on inequality takes place through a declining middle region of the wage distribution, so deunionization fails to explain the fall in the lower deciles and the sharp surge in the upper deciles.[4]

Changes in direct government intervention in setting the minimum wage is another potential candidate: The nominal minimum wage was fixed at $3.35 an hour for all of the 1980s, so in real terms it has declined over the whole period. DiNardo et al. (1996) and Lee (1999) examine empirically the role of the declining minimum wage and conclude that whereas one can detect large effects in the 50-10 wage differential for males, neither rising inequality for women nor the increase in the male college–high school premium can be attributed to changes in minimum-wage regulations.

---

2. For example, Freeman (1993) showed that the standard deviation of within-firm log wages in the United States was 25% lower in unionized firms compared to nonunionized firms.

3. For example, Card (1996).

4. Although deunionization (organizational change) and trade liberalization do not fully explain the recent evolution in wage inequality, nevertheless we believe that these factors can become more significant when analyzed in relation to skill-biased technical change (see, e.g., Aghion et al., 2001, on deunionization and skill-biased technical change and Acemoglu, 1999, on trade liberalization and skill-biased technical change).

2.3. Technology

A number of empirical studies have pointed to a significant impact of *skill-biased technical change* (SBTC) on the evolution of wage inequality. For example, using R&D expenditures and computer purchases as measures of technical progress, Berman et al. (1994) found that these two factors could account for as much as 70 percent of the move away from production to nonproduction labor over the period 1979–1987. Murphy and Welch (1992) find that the share of college labor has increased substantially in all sectors since the mid-1970s, which, together with the observed increase in the college premium, provides further evidence of skill-biased technical change. More recently, based on the data reported in Autor et al. (1998) and assuming an elasticity of substitution of 1.4 between skilled and unskilled labor, Acemoglu (2000) estimates that the relative productivity of college graduates increased from 0.157 in 1980 up to 0.470 in 1990 (whereas this relative productivity had risen at a lower rate prior to the early 1980s). Krusell et al. (2000) argued that skill-biased technical change can be interpreted as an increased growth in the stock of capital equipment since capital and skills are complementary in the aggregate production function.

This is only a starting point, however, as we still need to understand why we observed an *accelerated* increase in wage inequality following a sharp increase in the supply of skilled workers in the early 1970s. The existing literature provides two main answers to this puzzle.

On the one hand, Katz and Murphy (1992) argue that the observed accelerated increase in the college premium during the 1980s was the combined result of: (1) secular skill-biased technical change at a constant pace over the past 50 years; (2) the temporary fall in the college premium caused by the baby boom–driven increase in the relative supply of skilled labor in the early 1970s (before moving back to its secular path, the college premium was bound to increase at an accelerated rate).

An alternative view is that there has been a true *acceleration* in the pace of skill-biased technical change since the 1970s. This view was first put forward by Krusell et al. (2000), who pointed to the increased rate of decline in the relative price of production equipment goods since the mid-1970s,[5] which they interpreted as an increase in the pace of capital-embodied technological progress. However, the "acceleration view" begs two questions: First, what caused the increased rate of capital-embodied technological progress? Second, how do we reconcile a technological acceleration with the fact that measured total factor productivity growth was much slower in the two decades following 1975 than during the previous two decades?

Acemoglu (1998, 2000) provided the first compelling explanation for the rise in the pace of skill-biased technological change: His main idea is that the increased relative supply of college-educated workers in the 1970s was responsible for a shift in the *direction* of technological change, which became more skill biased

---

5. See McHugh and Lane (1987) and Gordon (1990).

than before because of a "market size" effect. That is, suppose that final output is produced by two kinds of intermediate product—one that requires college graduates to operate it (a "skill-intensive product") and one that can be operated by high school graduates—and technological progress comes from innovations that improve the quality of intermediate products. An R&D firm must direct its efforts toward improving one kind of intermediate product or the other. This choice will be governed by profitability considerations. When the relative supply of college graduates rises, the relative profitability of improving the skill-intensive product will also increase, provided that the elasticity of substitution between the two kinds of intermediate products in the final-goods sector is sufficiently large.

The result is a manifestation of the increasing returns to scale that typically prevail in an economy with endogenous technology, under which an increase in supply of some good or service can lead to an increase in its relative price. It is reinforced by an additional mechanism that is exemplified by the "robot model" of Aghion and Howitt (1998, chap. 9), in which technological change is always presumed to be skill biased, taking the form of improved intermediate products that substitute for unskilled labor. Whereas Acemoglu takes as given the overall level of innovation in the economy, Aghion and Howitt take into account that an increase in the supply of college graduates will increase the overall innovation rate, given that R&D is a skill-intensive activity. Thus an increase in the relative supply of skilled workers will speed up the pace of skill-biased technological change, thus raising the rate at which the skill premium rises and leading to a long-run increase in the skill premium.

This market size explanation is quite appealing, especially since it appears to fit the evidence of a wage premium first decreasing (during the early 1970s) and then sharply increasing (starting in the late 1970s), following the increase in relative skilled-labor supply in the late 1960s. On the other hand, this explanation raises two issues, which we should like to discuss briefly.

ISSUE 1: *Historical Perspective.* The above story can account for the dynamic pattern followed by the skill premium in the United States after the baby boom increase in skilled-labor supply in the early 1970s, but it does not explain why the rise in wage inequality occurred around this time in contrast with other historical episodes in which similar increases in the supply of educated labor were not followed by any noticeable increase in wage inequality. For example, in a relatively recent paper Goldin and Katz (1999) show that in spite of a substantial increase in the relative supply of educated labor between 1900 and 1920 following the so-called "high school movement," the wage ratio between white collars and blue collars fell continuously during the first half of the century and especially during the 1920s and the 1940s. Moreover, even though they mention a "strong association between changes in the use of purchase in electricity and shifts in employment toward more educated labor," they report no sharp widening of the wage distribution prior to the 1970s. Obviously, any explanation of the recent patterns in wage inequality really has to integrate the distinguishing features of previous episodes during the past 20 years if it is to be taken as comprehensive. This does not invalidate the importance of *market size* effects, but it does suggest that any explanation that relies primarily upon those effects may not be fully satisfactory from a historical point of view.

ISSUE 2: *Productivity Slowdown.* In a highly influential paper, Jones (1995) points out that OECD countries have experienced substantial increases in the average duration of schooling and in R&D levels during the past 50 years, yet there has been no apparent payoff in terms of faster growth; if anything, measured *productivity growth slowed*, especially between the mid-1970s and the early 1980s.[6] These findings appear to be at odds with R&D-based models of growth that predict that the innovation rate should significantly increase when the supply of skilled labor s increases.[7] The Acemoglu model is actually more subtle in the sense that it predicts a change in the direction—not the speed—of technological change. Yet the growth rate, as derived from the above model, should still increase following a (discontinuous) increase in relative skilled-labor supply, which is still at variance with the Jones-style evidence, at least up until the mid-1990s. To reconcile the market size explanation with this evidence, Acemoglu (2000) invokes the existence of decreasing returns in R&D aimed at skill-biased technical progress. Now, even if individual researchers experience decreasing returns in their R&D activities, it is not clear why the *whole* economy should: The exception would be if individual innovations were more like secondary discoveries induced by an economy-wide fundamental breakthrough, which becomes more and more incremental over time.

An alternative way to reconcile the acceleration theory with the evidence on measured productivity is to argue that the recent wave of technological change marked the birth of a new technological paradigm. A natural explanation for the aggregate productivity slowdown is that it takes some time before producers and developers economy-wide become fully acquainted with the new technological platform. This brings us naturally to the notion of *general-purpose technology*,[8] which we develop in the next section.

---

6. For example, the annual growth rate in the United States has declined by 1.8% on average since the 1970s. The decline has been most pronounced in the service sector, and more generally the productivity slowdown appears to be mainly attributable to a decline in *disembodied* productivity growth. Indeed, since the early 1970s the rate of *embodied* technical progress has accelerated (see McHugh and Lane, 1987; Greenwood and Yorukoglu, 1997; Comin, 1999), and the bulk of this acceleration, e.g., as measured by the decline in the quality-adjusted price of equipment goods, appears to be attributable to computers and other information-processing goods. This, again, points to the important role played by the new information technologies and their diffusion during the past 20 years.

7. Howitt (1999) provides a response to Jones, according to which a combination of product proliferation, capital deepening, and diminishing returns to the production of ideas can be invoked to reconcile R&D-based models with the fact that productivity growth did not increase until the late 1990s. But something more is needed to reconcile the above arguments with the fact that productivity growth actually appeared to fall.

8. See Bresnahan and Trajtenberg (1995), and the papers in the Helpman (1998) volume.

3. GENERAL-PURPOSE TECHNOLOGIES
AND THE PREMIUM TO ADAPTABILITY

In this section we sketch a pair of models that show in more detail how the Nelson-Phelps idea of skill as a measure of adaptability to technological change together with the notion of general-purpose technology (GPT) can help to account for several observed facts concerning rising wage inequality both between and within educational groups. The key to both of these models is the idea that how quickly a worker can adapt to working with a new technology is partly a matter of education and partly a matter of luck.[9]

In the long run, we assume that everyone will adapt to a given technology. Our reason for making this assumption is that in the long run technological progress automates skills. Ballpoint pens are easier to use than straight pens, modern photocopiers take less skill than lithograph machines, operating a car skillfully requires less training than riding a horse skillfully, electronic calculators are less demanding than mental addition, and so forth. Even the ability of fast-food clerks to read is being replaced by computer graphics. Thus in the long run we assume there is no skill bias to technological change. In the short run, however, some people catch on faster than others, and they earn a premium for their adaptability. The introduction of a new GPT can enhance this premium in several ways, as we explain in what follows.

3.1. Between-Group Inequality

Our first model is a simplified version of the one involving social learning presented in Aghion and Howitt (1998, chap. 9). In this model, the way a firm or sector typically learns to use a new technology is not to discover everything on its own but to learn from the experience of others in similar situations. In order for a firm to begin experimenting with a new technology it must first find another firm that has used the technology successfully in solving problems similar to the ones it faces itself; it can then use the other firm's experience as a "template" for its own experimentation. For a long time, improvements in knowledge will take place slowly because there are so few successful firms from which to draw a template; but eventually a point will be reached when enough other firms are using the new technology that experimentation snowballs. This quickly raises the demand for skilled labor and thereby raises the skill premium.

We begin by assuming that there are two technologies that can be used in any sector—an old technology and a new one that has just arrived in the form of a GPT. Aggregate final output is produced by labor according to

---

9. Gould et al. (2001) also emphasize the interplay between education and random adaptability in explaining between- and within-group inequality. In their model, less-able and therefore less-educated workers acquire technology-specific skills through on-the-job training, whereas more-able workers acquire general skills through education; within-group inequality among low-ability workers then results primarily from the random obsolescence of existing technologies, whereas within-group inequality among the high-ability workers results from changes in the ability composition among them.

$$y = \left[\int_0^1 A(i)^\alpha x(i)^\alpha di \right]^{1/\alpha},$$

where $A(i) = 1$ in sectors where the old GPT is still used, and $A(i) = \gamma > 1$ in sectors that have successfully innovated, while $x(i)$ is the flow of intermediate good i currently used in the production of final output. Manufacturing labor produces intermediate goods using a one-for-one technology, so that $x(i)$ also denotes the labor demand flow in sector i. The total labor force L is divided into skilled and unskilled workers. Whereas old sectors are indifferent between skilled and unskilled workers, experimentation with and implementation of the new GPT can be done only by skilled labor.

For simplicity, we assume that the supply of skilled workers is monotonically increasing over time, partly as a result of schooling and/or training investments and partly as a result of the technology becoming more familiar:

$$L_s(t) = L - (1 - s)Le^{-\beta t},$$

where $s < 1$ is the initial fraction of skilled workers and β is a positive number measuring the speed of skill acquisition. Those sL workers who are skilled initially learn to use the new GPT as soon as it arrives. The rest learn randomly with a Poisson arrival rate β. Thus in the long run everyone will be skilled in using the new GPT. All that differs across individuals are the rates at which they learn.

In each sector i, moving from the old to the new GPT requires two steps. First, as indicated above, a firm in that sector must acquire a template on which to base experimentation; second, the firm must succeed in its experimentation with the new GPT. Let n_0 denote the fraction of sectors that have not yet acquired a template, n_1 the fraction of sectors that are currently experimenting on the new GPT, and $n_2 = 1 - n_0 - n_1$ the fraction that have completed the transition to the new GPT.

Let $\lambda(n_2)$ denote the Poisson arrival rate of templates for the new GPT in a given sector and suppose that it is increasing in n_2, to reflect the social learning process by which firms acquire their templates. A special case is given by

$$\lambda(n_2) = \begin{cases} \lambda_0 & \text{if } n_2 < \bar{n}, \\ \lambda_0 + \Delta & \text{if } n_2 \geq \bar{n}. \end{cases}$$

Now, suppose that for a templated firm to succeed in implementing the new GPT, it must employ at least H units of skilled labor per period. We can think of this labor as being used in R&D or in an experimental start-up firm. In any case it is not producing current output. Instead, it allows the sector to access a Poisson process that will deliver a workable implementation of the new GPT with an arrival rate of λ_1. Thus the flow of new sectors that can implement the new GPT will be the number of experimenting sectors n_1 times the success rate per sector per unit of time λ_1.

The evolution over time of the two variables n_1 and n_2 is then given by the autonomous system of ordinary differential equations:

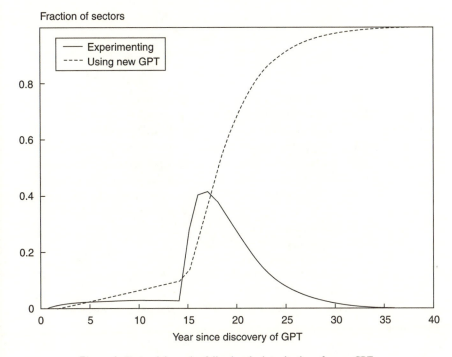

Fraction of sectors

Figure 1. Sectoral dynamics following the introduction of a new GPT.

$$\dot{n}_1 = \lambda(n_2)(1 - n_1 - n_2) - \lambda_1 n_1,$$

$$\dot{n}_2 = \lambda_1 n_1,$$

with initial condition $n_1(0) = 0$, $n_2(0) = 0$. The time path of n_0 is given automatically by the identity $n_0 \equiv 1 - n_1 - n_2$.

Figure 1 depicts the kind of dynamic pattern followed by n_1 and n_2 when λ_0 is small and Δ is sufficiently large.[10] Not surprisingly, the time path of n_2 follows a logistic curve, accelerating at first and then slowing down as n_2 approaches one, with the maximal growth rate occurring somewhere in the middle. Likewise, the path of n_1 must peak somewhere in the middle of the transition, because it starts and ends at zero.

The transition process from the old to the new GPT can be divided into two subperiods. First, in the early phase of transition (i.e., when t is low) the number of sectors using the new GPT is too small to absorb the whole skilled-labor force, which in turn implies that a positive fraction of skilled workers will have to be employed by the old sectors at the same wage as their unskilled peers. Thus, during the early phase of transition the labor market will remain unsegmented, with the

---

10. The figure represents the case in which $\lambda_0 = 0.01$, $\lambda_1 = 0.3$, $\Delta = 0.5$, and $\pi = 0.1$.

real wage being the same for skilled and unskilled labor and determined by the labor market–clearing equation:

$$(1 - n_2)x_O + n_2 x_N + n_1 H = L,$$

where x_O, x_N, and H denote the labor demands, respectively, by an old manufacturing sector, a sector using the new GPT, and an experimenting sector.[11]

In the later phase of transition, however, where the fraction of new sectors has grown sufficiently large that it can absorb all of the skilled labor force, the labor market may become segmented, with skilled workers being employed exclusively (and at a higher wage) by new sectors while unskilled workers remain in old sectors. Let w_u and w_s denote the real wages paid, respectively, to unskilled and skilled workers. We now have $w_s > w_u$, since the two real wages are determined by two separate labor market–clearing conditions. The skilled wage is determined by the market-clearing equation for skilled labor:

$$L_s = n_1 H + n_2 x_N,$$

while w_u is obtained from the market-clearing equation for unskilled labor, namely,[12]

$$L - L_s = (1 - n_2)x_O.$$

Figure 2 depicts the time path of real wages, assuming a relatively high cost H of experimentation.[13] The skill premium, measured here by the ratio w_s/w_u, starts increasing about when the diffusion of the new GPT across sectors accelerates, as a result of the increased demand for skilled labor in production and experimentation. The premium keeps increasing, although more slowly, during the remaining part

---

11. For any sector i, profit maximization by the local monopolist in such a sector gives

$$x_i = \arg \max_x [p_i(x)x - wx]$$

where

$$p_i(x) = \frac{\partial y}{\partial x_i} = [A(i)]^\alpha x^{\alpha-1} y^{1-\alpha}.$$

The first-order condition for this maximization, respectively for $A(i) = 1$ and $A(i) = \gamma$, yields

$$x_O = (w/\alpha)^{1/(\alpha-1)} y; \qquad x_N = (w/\gamma^\alpha \alpha)^{1/(\alpha-1)} y.$$

12. Substituting for x_O and x_N in these two labor market–clearing equations, we get

$$w_s = \gamma^\alpha \alpha \left(\frac{n_2 y}{L_s - n_1 H}\right)^{1-\alpha}, \qquad w_u = \alpha \left[\frac{(1-n_2)y}{L - L_s}\right]^{1-\alpha}.$$

13. In addition to the parameter values specified in footnote 10, Figure 2 is plotted with $\gamma = 1.5$, $\alpha = 0.5$, $L = 10$, $H = 6$, $\beta = 0.05$, and $s = 0.25$.

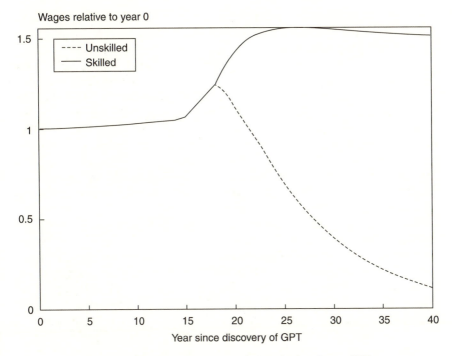

Wages relative to year 0

Figure 2. Wage inequality following the introduction of a new GPT.

of the transition process. Since everyone ends up earning the same (skilled) wage, standard measures of inequality first rise and then fall.[14]

This explanation of increased inequality between skill groups is also consistent with the observed dynamic pattern of the skill premium in the United States or Great Britain since 1970, namely, a reduction of the wage premium during the early 1970s, followed by a sharp increase in that premium between the late 1970s and the mid-1990s. In particular, a one-time increase in skilled-labor supply occurring during the acceleration phase in the diffusion of new information technologies

---

14. This simple model of GPT diffusion and between-group wage inequality can be extended easily to accommodate the existence of productivity spillovers among sectors that currently adopt the new GPT. For example, in line with other multisector models of endogenous growth (e.g., see Aghion and Howitt, 1998, chap. 3) we could assume that the productivity γ of a sector that has just adopted the new GPT depends positively upon the current flow of adoptions, e.g., according to

$$\gamma = \gamma_0 + \lambda(n_2)\sigma,$$

where σ is a positive number that reflects the extent of the cross-sector spillovers. In such an extension of the above GPT model, the speed of technological change as measured by the derivative $d\gamma/dt$ will increase during the acceleration phase in the GPT diffusion; this, in turn, will only magnify the increase in skill premium during that phase. That the speed of technological change should increase when a new GPT hits the economy is a plausible assumption, which we also make in the next section when discussing the effects of GPT diffusion on within-group inequality.

would also result in a short-run reduction followed by a medium-term increase in the skill premium. This mechanism provides an explanation for the first puzzle we mentioned in our introduction.

With regard to the comparison between the recent period and the early 1900s (the *historical-perspective* issue), the spread of the electric dynamo did not result in a comparable increase in the skill premium because that earlier GPT was not nearly as skill biased as recent information technologies, even in the transitional sense used in the Nelson-Phelps framework. For example, whereas workers operating steam engines needed to know how to maintain and repair their own engines, the maintenance of new electrical machinery only required firms to hire a limited number of skilled workers specialized in that task. Thus the appearance of bottle-necks that segment the labor market in our story may have been less of a factor in accounting for wage movements in the earlier example.

The clustering of experimentation that results from social learning also makes this story easy to reconcile with the *productivity-slowdown* issue. Figure 3 shows the time path of GDP, relative to its initial value, assuming the same parameter values as in Figures 1 and 2. GDP falls at the beginning of the acceleration phase in the diffusion of the new GPT, as a result of the diversion of labor away from the production of goods (which is measured in GDP) and into the production of technological change (which is not measured in GDP), before growing again at a later stage in the diffusion process. The explanation also appears to be consistent with the observed deceleration of between-group wage inequality during the late

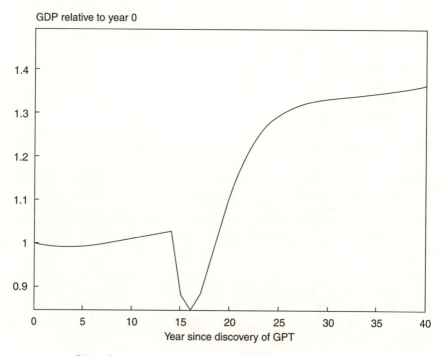

Figure 3. Aggregate output following the introduction of a new GPT.

1990s; one may indeed interpret this embryonic trend reversal as reflecting the fact that the diffusion of new communication and information technologies is now entering a mature phase. Perhaps we are now beyond the experimentation phase and ready to start reaping the benefits of a GPT that is getting more familiar and more user friendly.

3.2. Within-Group Inequality

Existing explanations for the rise in residual wage inequality[15] are based on the idea that whatever raises the demand for observed skills also raises the demand for unobserved skills, which are generally treated as one form or another of innate ability. As mentioned above, this explanation is at odds with recent econometric work, for example, by Blundell and Preston (1999), which shows that the within-group component of wage inequality in the United States and Great Britain is mainly *transitory,* whereas the between-group component accounts for most of the observed increase in the variance of permanent income. These explanations also fail to explain why the rise in within-group inequality has been accompanied by a corresponding rise in individual wage instability (see Gottschalk and Moffitt, 1994). In the remaining part of this section, we argue, using the Nelson-Phelps framework, that the diffusion of a new general-purpose technology can account for the evolution of within-group wage inequality in a way that is consistent with these and other puzzling facts.

The basis of this argument is the model of Aghion et al. (2001),[16] which is built on prior work of Violante (1996, 2002). That model, like that of the preceding section, involves differential rates of adaptability, which in this case are entirely random, among a group of ex ante identical workers with the same educational background. The diffusion of a new GPT raises (within-group) inequality for two reasons. First, the rise in the speed of technical change associated with the new GPT increases the market premium to those workers who are lucky enough to adapt quickly to new versions of the technology. Second, to the extent that the new GPT generates a wave of secondary innovations that are closely related to one another, its diffusion especially benefits workers who are lucky enough to adapt quickly several times and so can profit from transferring recently acquired knowledge to the task of working with the latest innovations.

3.2.1. BASIC FRAMEWORK

We construct an infinite-horizon discrete-time model with sequential productivity-improving innovations in a one-good economy. A new technology arrives each

---

15. See Acemoglu (1998), Rubinstein and Tsiddon (1999), and Galor and Moav (2000) for models of within-group inequality based on differences in innate ability.

16. The model in this subsection is a stripped-down version of the framework developed by Aghion et al. (2001). In that paper, we assume an overlapping-generations structure and capital-embodied technological progress. We also allow for two dimensions of generality of the GPT—not just the transferability of skills τ but also the compatibility of capital across successive technologies.

period. At any date t some fraction of workers can work with technology t, which has just arrived. The rest are all able to work with technology $t - 1$, which arrived last period. Thus no one will find it profitable to employ a technology that is more than one period old.

a. Production Relations
Aggregate output using each technology is given by the same Cobb-Douglas production kernel. Thus the economy's GDP on each date t is

$$Y_t = K_{0t}^\alpha (A_t x_{0t})^{1-\alpha} + K_{1t}^\alpha (A_{t-1} x_{1t})^{1-\alpha}, \qquad 0 < \alpha < 1,$$

where x_{0t} and K_{0t} are the labor and capital inputs working with technology t (i.e., in "sector 0"), x_{1t} and K_{1t} are the inputs working with technology $t - 1$ (in sector 1), and A_t is the (labor-augmenting) productivity parameter of technology t. Each new technology is $(1 + \gamma)$ times more productive than the previous one, so

$$A_t = (1 + \gamma) A_{t-1} \qquad \forall t.$$

Capital is perfectly mobile between sectors. Therefore in a competitive equilibrium the marginal product of capital must be the same in each sector:

$$\partial Y_t / \partial K_{0t} = \partial Y_t / \partial K_{1t},$$

which can be written, using the Cobb-Douglas production function, as

$$\alpha (K_{0t} / A_t x_{0t})^{\alpha-1} = \alpha (K_{1t} / A_{t-1} x_{1t})^{\alpha-1}.$$

This capital market equilibrium condition implies that the capital stock per efficiency unit of labor must be the same in each sector:

$$K_{0t} / A_t x_{0t} = K_{1t} / A_{t-1} x_{1t} \equiv k_t.$$

As the capital stock per efficiency unit is the same in each sector, the marginal product of labor will be higher in sector 0 (where it works with the new technology) than in sector 1 (where it works with the old technology) by the growth factor $1+\gamma$. That is,

$$\partial Y_t / \partial x_{0t} = (1 - \alpha) (K_{0t} / A_t x_{0t})^\alpha A_t \qquad = (1 - \alpha) k_t^\alpha A_t,$$

$$\partial Y_t / \partial x_{1t} = (1 - \alpha) (K_{1t} / A_{t-1} x_{1t})^\alpha A_{t-1} = (1 - \alpha) k_t^\alpha A_t / (1 + \gamma).$$

b. Adaptation, Learning, and Transferability
At each date t a given fraction σ_t of all workers is randomly given the capacity to adapt to (i.e., to work with) the new technology in that period. In equilibrium they will all take advantage of this opportunity by working in sector 0.[17]

---

17. As we shall see, to work in sector 1 would give the worker a lower current wage, because $\gamma > \eta$. If we suppose, as seems reasonable, that the probability of being adaptable next period is not enhanced

Table 1. Labor Units Supplied by Each Worker

	Working this period in sector	
	0	1
Worked last period in sector 0	$1 + \tau\eta$	1
Worked last period in sector 1	$1 + \eta$	$1 + \eta$

Experience with a technology produces learning by doing that enhances the productivity of a worker who remains working with the same technology as last period by the factor $1 + \eta$. In order to ensure that workers in equilibrium always choose to work with the most recent technology when they are able to adapt, we assume that

$$0 < \eta < \gamma.$$

If the worker switches to working with a technology that is one period newer, then some of this learning by doing can be transferred, and the worker's productivity is thus enhanced by the factor $1 + \tau\eta$, where τ is a parameter measuring the generality of the technology, with

$$0 < \tau < 1.$$

We assume, however, that learning cannot be transferred if the worker switches to working with a technology that is more than one period newer. That is, skills acquired by experience eventually (in this case after two periods) become obsolete. Moreover, we assume that once a technology is one period old, the benefits of learning by doing with that technology can be shared by all who work with it, even those who did not work with it last period. That is, eventually the skills involved in working with a particular technology become publicly available.

It follows from this description of adaptability, learning, and transferability that different workers will supply different amounts of labor input depending upon their work experience. Suppose, as a normalization, that a worker having no previous experience with a technology the same as, or one period older than, the one he or she is currently working with supplies one unit of labor input. Then the amount supplied by each worker will be given by Table 1.

Thus every worker employed this period in sector 1, working with the old technology, supplies $1 + \eta$ units of labor input no matter where he or she was employed last period, because all such workers benefit equally from the learning by doing of those who worked on the technology last period when it was new. Workers who go from the old sector 1 last period to the new sector 0 this period are skipping a technology so, in accordance with our assumption that learning by doing becomes obsolete in two technological generations, they supply only the

---

by working in sector 1 this period, then working in sector 1 would also yield a lower continuation value, since it would require the worker to give up the possibility of transferring knowledge to the leading edge if he or she were to be adaptable next period.

basic one unit of labor input. Workers who go from sector 0 to sector 0 are able to adapt to the latest technology two periods in a row, and they are able to supply $1 + \tau\eta$ units of labor input because they can transfer the fraction τ of their learning by doing from last period's leading-edge technology to this period's.

3.2.2. Equilibrium Within-Group Wage Inequality

In a competitive labor market each worker will receive a wage equal to his or her supply of labor input, as given by Table 1, times the marginal product of labor in his or her sector (sector 0 if the worker is lucky, in the sense of being able to adapt to the latest technology, or sector 1 if unlucky). Thus there will be three different wages observed at each date t:

$$w_{0t}^0 = (\partial Y_t / \partial x_{0t})(1 + \tau\eta) = (1 - \alpha) k_t^\alpha A_t (1 + \tau\eta),$$

$$w_{0t}^1 = (\partial Y_t / \partial x_{0t}) \qquad\qquad = (1 - \alpha) k_t^\alpha A_t,$$

$$w_{1t} = (\partial Y_t / \partial x_{1t})(1 + \eta) = (1 - \alpha) k_t^\alpha A_t (1 + \eta) / (1 + \gamma),$$

where w_{0t}^i denotes the wage of someone working with the new technology (in sector 0) who worked in sector i last period, and w_{1t} is the wage of everyone working with the old technology (in sector 1).

The three wage rates are listed above in decreasing order of size. Thus the highest wage w_{0t}^0 will be earned by those workers who have been lucky enough to be adaptable two periods in a row, while the lowest wage w_{1t} will be earned by those who are unlucky this period. Our measure of inequality is the ratio R between the maximum and minimum wage:

$$R_\omega = w_{0t}^0 / w_{1t} = (1 + \tau\eta)(1 + \gamma) / (1 + \eta) > 1.$$

It follows that this measure of within-group wage inequality increases with both the rate of technical progress as parameterized by γ and the transferability of knowledge as parameterized by τ. Both variables, in turn, are likely to have increased during the acceleration phase in the diffusion of new communication and information technologies. As noted earlier, McHugh and Lane (1987), Gordon (1990), Greenwood and Yorukoglu (1997), and Krusell et al. (2000) show that there has been an acceleration in the rate of technical change since the mid-1970s, as measured, for example, by the decline in the quality-adjusted price of equipment goods; likewise, the "general nature" of the technological wave in communication and information implies that the acceleration phase of that wave was probably accompanied by an increased similarity between successive vintages, which in turn should have increased the degree of skill transferability across technologies.

The implied surge in inequality is purely "residual" as workers are ex ante equal. Furthermore, the model's residual wage inequality is linked to the stochastic nature of workers' adaptability to the newest vintage more than to innate ability. Thus the model predicts that the diffusion of a new GPT should affect primarily the transitory component of income, since individual luck in adapting quickly to a new sector will obviously vary over time, in line with the empirical work of Gottschalk and Moffitt (1994) and Blundell and Preston (1999).

4. CONCLUDING REMARKS

In this chapter we have argued that the notion of human capital shaped by Nelson and Phelps (1966), as labor *adaptable* to the new technologies, is crucial in understanding the labor market experience of the U.S. economy during the past three decades. The arrival of a new general-purpose technology and the implied rise in the demand for labor adaptable to the new technological platform produced a surge in the return to adaptability.

Insofar as formal education is correlated with adaptability, this mechanism can explain the dynamics of the educational premium, as argued in Section 3.1. The approach based on the notion of adapting to major technological change can shed light not only on the observed evolution of the college premium but also on the increase in residual wage inequality, as argued in Section 3.2. Moreover, if the economy comprises several educational groups of workers, with more educated workers being more able to transfer recently acquired knowledge to the newest vintages, then a fall in the education premium could easily be accompanied by a rise in residual inequality, as appears to have been the case in the United States during the mid and late 1970s and also possibly in the late 1990s. For example, an increase in the relative supply of educated labor that would occur when an information revolution hits the economy might temporarily reduce the education premium, but meanwhile the continuing increase in the speed of embodied technical progress and in the transferability of recently acquired knowledge induced by the new GPT would continue to sustain a rise in within-group inequality. The alternative theories of within-group inequality based upon market size effects and unobserved innate ability do not seem to provide equally convincing explanations for these divergent patterns of between-group and within-group inequality.

What policy lessons can we learn from the labor market experience of the past 30 years? Rapid and major technical change transmits benefits to the whole society in the long run. However, in the short run it can create large redistributions. Adaptability is the key skill that allows workers to reap the benefits of technological improvements from the early start and prevents situations of skill obsolescence and prolonged exclusion from the labor market.[18] This makes the case for the creation of a more favorable institutional environment for the acquisition of general skills for the young (formal education) and for retraining programs later in life (continuous learning) for those workers whose jobs are made obsolete by technological progress.

REFERENCES

Acemoglu, D. (1998), "Why Do Technologies Complement Skills? Direct Technical Change and Wage Inequality," *Quarterly Journal of Economics* 113:1055–90.
——— (1999), "Patterns of Skill-Premia," mimeo, MIT.
——— (2000), "Technical Change, Inequality, and the Labour Market," mimeo, MIT.
Acemoglu, D., P. Aghion, and G. Violante (2000), "Deunionization, Technical Change, and Inequality," mimeo, University College London.

---

18. Murphy and Topel (1997) document the rise in nonparticipation and long-term unemployment among prime-aged males in the United States and argues that this phenomenon is strictly linked to the surge in wage inequality.

Aghion, P. and P. Howitt (1998), *Endogenous Growth Theory*, Cambridge: MIT Press.

Aghion, P., P. Howitt, and G. Violante (2001), "General Purpose Technology and Wage Inequality," mimeo, University College London.

Autor, D., L. Katz, and A. Krueger (1998), "Computing Inequality: Have Computers Changed the Labour Market?," *Quarterly Journal of Economics* 113:1169–1214.

Berman, E., J. Bound, and Z. Griliches (1994), "Changes in Demand for Skilled Labour Within US Manufacturing: Evidence from the Annual Survey of Manufactures," *Quarterly Journal of Economics* 109(2):367–97.

Blundell, R. and I. Preston (1999), "Inequality and Uncertainty: Short-Run Uncertainty and Permanent Inequality in the US and Britain," mimeo, University College London.

Bresnahan, T. F. and M. Trajtenberg (1995), "General Purpose Technologies: Engines of Growth?," *Journal of Econometrics* 65:83–108.

Card, D. (1996), "The Effects of Unions on the Structure of Wages: A Longitudinal Analysis," *Econometrica* 64:957–79.

Comin, D. (1999), "An Uncertainty-Driven Theory of the Productivity Slowdown: Manufacturing," mimeo, Harvard.

DiNardo J., N. Fortin, and T. Lemieux (1996), "Labor Market Institutions and the Distribution of Wages, 1973–1992: A Semi-parametric Approach," *Econometrica* 64:1001–44.

Freeman, R. B. (1993), "How Much Has Deunionization Contributed to the Rise in Male Earnings Inequality?," in S. Danziger and P. Gottschalk, eds., *Uneven Tides: Rising Inequality in America*, New York: Russell Sage Foundation, pp. 133–63.

Galor, O. and O. Moav (2000), "Ability Biased Technological Transition, Wage Inequality Within and Across Groups, and Economic Growth," *Quarterly Journal of Economics* 115:469–97.

Galor, O. and D. Tsiddon (1997), "Technological Progress, Mobility, and Economic Growth," *American Economic Review* 87:363–82.

Goldin, C. and L. Katz (1999), "The Returns to Skill across the Twentieth Century United States," mimeo, Harvard.

Gordon, R. J. (1990), *The Measurement of Durable Good Prices*, NBER Monograph Series, Chicago: University of Chicago Press.

Gottschalk, P. and R. Moffitt (1994), "The Growth of Earnings Instability in the U.S. Labour Market," *Brookings Papers on Economic Activity* 2:217–72.

Gould, E., O. Moav, and B. Weinberg (2001), "Precautionary Demand for Education, Inequality, and Technological Progress," *Journal of Economic Growth* 6:285–315.

Greenwood, J. and M. Yorukoglu (1997), "1974," *Carnegie-Rochester Series on Public Policy* 46:49–95.

Helpman, E., ed. (1998), *General Purpose Technologies and Economic Growth*, Cambridge: MIT Press.

Howitt, P. (1999), "Steady Endogenous Growth with Population and R&D Inputs Growing," *Journal of Political Economy* 107:715–30.

Jones, C. (1995), "R&D Based Models of Economic Growth," *Journal of Political Economy* 103:759–84.

Katz, L. and D. Autor (2000), "Changes in the Wage Structure and Earnings Inequality," in O. Ashenfelter and D. Card, eds., *The Handbook of Labour Economics,* Vol. 3, Amsterdam: Elsevier.

Katz, L. and K. Murphy (1992), "Changes in Relative Wages: Supply and Demand Factors," *Quarterly Journal of Economics* 107:35–78.

Krusell, P., L. Ohanian, J.-V. Ríos-Rull, and G. Violante (2000), "Capital-Skill Complementarity and Inequality," *Econometrica* 68(5):1029–54.

Lee, D. (1999), "Wage Inequality in the U.S. During the 1980s: Rising Dispersion or Falling Minimum Wage?," *Quarterly Journal of Economics* 114:977–1023.

Machin, S. (1996a), "Wage Inequality in the UK," *Oxford Review of Economic Policy* 12(1):47–64.

———— (1996b), "Changes in the Relative Demand for Skills," in *Acquiring Skills, Market Failures, their Symptoms and Policy Responses,* A. L. Booth and D. J. Snower, eds., Cambridge: Cambridge University Press.

———— (1997), "The Decline of Labour Market Institutions and the Rise in Wage Inequality in Britain," *European Economic Review* 41(3–5):647–57.

McHugh, R. and J. Lane (1987), "The Role of Embodied Technical Change in the Decline of Labor Productivity," *Southern Economic Journal* 53:915–24.

Murphy, K. and R. Topel (1997), "Unemployment and Nonemployment," *American Economic Review Papers and Proceedings* 87:295–300.

Murphy, K. and F. Welch (1992), "The Structure of Wages," *Quarterly Journal of Economics* 107:255–85.

Nelson, R. and E. Phelps (1966), "Investment in Humans, Technological Diffusion, and Economic Growth," *American Economic Review* 61:69–75.

Rubinstein, Y. and D. Tsiddon (1999), "Coping with Technological Progress: The Role of Ability in Making Inequality so Persistent," mimeo, Hebrew University.

Violante, G. L. (1996), "Equipment Investment and Skill Dynamics: A Solution to the Wage Dispersion Puzzle?," mimeo, University College London.

———— (2001), "Technological Acceleration, Skill Transferability and the Rise in Residual Inequality," *Quarterly Journal of Economics* 117:297–338.

22

Comments on Aghion,
Howitt, and Violante

ROBERT E. HALL

This very interesting chapter deals with the most important distributional issue in the United States in recent decades—the dramatic widening of the differnece in wages between successful and less successful groups. There are many ways to identify the successful groups, including the following:

- The better educated, especially those who have graduated from college.
- Those who work at desks rather than with their hands.
- Those who solve problems.

The authors' model contains six features to deal with this issue:

1. It distinguishes young workers from old.
2. It incorporates learning by doing—old workers are $1 + \eta$ more productive than young ones on this account.
3. It includes technical progress embodied in capital at rate γ.
4. It recognizes that old workers lose a fraction $1 - \tau$ of their efficiency if they upgrade to use the new technology.
5. It permits the old capital to be retooled so that its efficiency is κ units of new capital embodying the new technology.
6. It hypothesizes that a fraction σ of workers are capable of upgrading their skills.

I focus on what I take to be the central case, where retooling of capital occurs. Taking the wage of young workers to be 1, we find that the wage of an old worker on capital embodying the old technology is $[(1 + \eta)/(1 + \gamma)]\kappa^{\alpha/(1-\alpha)}$, and the wage of an old worker on capital embodying the new technology is $1 + \tau\eta$. Old workers on old technology gain the full benefit of learning by doing, η, but forego the benefit of technical progress, γ, and suffer capital depletion from upgrading, $\kappa^{\alpha/(1-\alpha)}$. That is, workers who do not upgrade cooperate with less capital and hence earn less when the kind of capital they know how to use is converted to the new technology that they do not know how to use.

The upgraded old workers are generally at the top of the wage distribution: They earn the benefit of the new technology (and avoid the depression captured by the $1 + \gamma$ in the denominator of the relative wage formula for old workers on old technology). Both young workers and old workers using old technology are at the bottom of the wage distribution. The latter are ahead by the learning-by-doing factor $1 + \eta$ but suffer the absence of technical progress (the $1 + \gamma$ in the denominator) and the effect of capital depletion from capital upgrading.

The chapter builds the case that both workers and capital have become more adaptable (τ and κ have increased). The result has been a widening of the wage distribution, as the wage of old workers using new technology rises because their upgrading losses are smaller, and the wage of old workers using old technology falls because the capital depletion effect is greater.

The time period here is half a work lifetime or about 20 years. Rates of technical progress over 20-year periods are substantial—γ is something like 20 or 30 percent. I think that adaptability to new technologies is an important ingredient in wage differentials. All else held constant, people who use computers, e.g., earn substantially more than those who do not. Among older macroeconomists, those who have mastered the Dixit-Spence-Stiglitz apparatus, Abreu-Pearce-Stacchetti dynamic contracting, the universal stochastic discounter, and max-min control theory earn more than those whose toolboxes have remained unchanged since 1970.

Education is a determinant of adaptability, it seems. People who learn to work within multiple problem-solving systems when they are young are better at mastering new technology later. Childhood exposure to Latin makes one better at learning the Oracle database.

I find the capital-depletion part of the story to be less convincing than the labor-upgrading part. The issue is whether older workers are capital-starved because they only know how to use 8088 PCs with 256 K of memory and DOS 1.0, but these machines are not available because they have been upgraded with Windows XP. In fact, those old computers were thrown away a long time ago. As a practical matter, almost no equipment survives over a period of 20 years. Typical depreciation rates are 15 percent per year, and $0.85^{20} = 0.04$. Only 4 percent of capital survives from one period to the next in the model. Workers who can use only 20-year-old capital are almost completely capital-starved anyway, so an increase in retooling starvation has almost no effect.

There is a distinct and important limit to the explanatory power of models such as this one that rely on skill bias in technical change. We know the rate of growth of the Solow residual, and we know that that rate is a weighted average of the rates of labor-augmenting technical change for the two kinds of labor. The amount of skill bias needed to explain the movements of relative wages in the past 20 years turns out to imply *negative* rates of growth of the efficiency of less skilled labor. I regard this implication as implausible. Rather than attribute all movements of relative wages as arising from skill bias, I believe we need to consider other sources (Hall, 2000). I learned much from studying this interesting chapter. I believe that it shows the way to better understanding of important movements in the wage distribution.

REFERENCE

Hall, R. E. (2000), "e-Capital: The Link between the Labor Market and the Stock Market in the 1990s," *Brookings Papers on Economic Activity* 2000(2):73–118.

—— 23 ——

Factor Prices and Technical Change: From Induced Innovations to Recent Debates

DARON ACEMOGLU

1. INTRODUCTION

In many ways, one can see the "induced innovations" literature of the 1960s as the harbinger of the endogenous growth literature of the 1980s and 1990s. Whereas the endogenous growth literature studies the process of growth at the aggregate, the induced innovations literature attempted to understand what type of innovations the economy would generate and the relationship between factor prices and technical change. Although it was Hicks in *The Theory of Wages* (1932) who first discussed the issue of induced innovation,[1] the important advances were made during the 1960s by Kennedy (1964), Samuelson (1965), and Drandakis and Phelps (1966), who studied the link between factor prices and technical change.

However, during the 1960s the economics profession did not possess all the tools necessary for a systematic study of these issues. In particular, when firms choose technology in addition to capital and labor, the notion of competitive equilibrium has to be modified or refined, either by introducing technological externalities (Romer, 1986; Lucas, 1988) or by introducing monopolistic competition (Romer, 1990; Grossman and Helpman, 1991; Aghion and Howitt, 1992).[2] The absence of the appropriate tools forced this literature to take a number of shortcuts and ultimately to rely on heuristic arguments rather than fully microfounded models.

In this chapter, I briefly survey the approach taken and the problems faced by the induced innovations literature and then recast the results of this literature in terms of

---

. In particular, Hicks argued that technical change would attempt to replace the more expensive factor. He wrote, "A change in the relative prices of the factors of production is itself a spur to invention, and to invention of a particular kind—directed to economizing the use of a factor which has become relatively expensive" (p. 124).

2. In addition, see the work by Segerstrom et al. (1990), Jones (1995), Stokey (1995), and Young (1998), and the survey in Aghion and Howitt (1998).

thank Nancy Stokey, Jaume Ventura, and participants at the festschrift conference for their comments and Rubén Segura-Cayuela for excellent research assistance.

models of endogenous technology (or directed technical change) based on my own recent work (e.g., Acemoglu, 1998, 1999, 2001; Acemoglu and Zilibotti, 2001, as well as Kiley, 1999). This modeling exercise not only formalizes the contribution of the induced innovations literature but also highlights a new economic force that did not feature in this literature. In particular, like Hicks, the induced innovations literature emphasized relative prices as the key determinant of which factors new technologies would save on. In models of endogenous technology, as emphasized by Romer (1990), there is a market size effect because new technologies, once developed, can be used by many firms and workers. This market size effect also features in the analysis of the direction and bias of technical change: There will be greater incentives to develop technologies for more abundant factors. The market size effect not only is of theoretical interest, but also turns out to play an important role in a number of recent debates.

In the second part of the chapter, I discuss how the directed technical change model, the modern reformulation of its induced innovations literature, sheds light on two recent debates. The first relates to the question of why the demand for skills increased throughout the twentieth century, and has even accelerated over the past 30 years. The second concerns the role of human capital in economic development. I argue that a model of directed technical change provides an explanation for both why we should expect technical change to be skill biased in general and why this skill bias may have accelerated over recent decades. I also show that this model points out an interesting interaction between human capital and technology, and via this channel, it suggests why human capital differences may be more important in explaining differences in income per capita across countries than standard models imply.

These two debates are interesting not only because they have been active areas of recent research, but also because they relate to another of Phelps's important contributions: Nelson and Phelps (1966) postulated that human capital is essential for the adoption of new technologies. This view has at least two important implications: First, the demand for skills will increase as new technologies are introduced, and second, economies with high human capital will effectively possess better technologies. These insights are relevant for the two debates mentioned previously, as they provide a theory for why technical change may be skill biased and why human capital differences can be essential in accounting for differences in income per capita across countries. Nelson and Phelps developed this insight in a reduced form model. Interestingly, the directed technical model change provides a framework to derive related results from a more microfounded model. But these results differ in interesting and empirically testable ways from the predictions of the Nelson-Phelps approach.

The rest of this chapter is organized as follows. In Section 2 I briefly survey the induced innovations approach of the 1960s. In Section 3 I outline a simple model of directed technical change based on my own research, especially Acemoglu (2001). I show how this framework captures many of the insights of the induced innovations literature in a microfounded model, and without encountering some of the problems that this earlier literature faced. In Section 4 I use the directed technical change model to investigate when and why the demand for skills will increase. In Section 5 I discuss the role of human capital in accounting for differences in income and output per worker across countries, and then I use the directed technical change model to highlight how the interaction between technology and skills can lead to large differences in income per capita across countries. Section 6 concludes the chapter.

2. A SIMPLE INDUCED INNOVATION MODEL

In this section, I outline a version of the model considered by Drandakis and Phelps (1966), which in turn builds on Kennedy (1964). The economy is populated by a mass of consumers with constant savings rate θ.

All firms have access to a constant elasticity of substitution (CES)–constant returns-to-scale production function,

$$Y = \left[\gamma \, (N_L L)^{(\sigma-1)/\sigma} + (1 - \gamma) \, (N_K K)^{(\sigma-1)/\sigma} \right]^{\sigma/(\sigma-1)}, \tag{1}$$

where L is labor, which is assumed constant throughout the chapter, K is capital, and N_L and N_K are labor- and capital-augmenting technology terms, which are controlled by each individual firm; σ is the elasticity of substitution between labor and capital.[3] For simplicity, there is no depreciation of capital. Although firms hire the profit-maximizing amount of labor and capital, they choose their technologies to maximize the current rate of cost reduction for given factor proportions (see Kennedy, 1964, p. 543; Drandakis and Phelps, 1966, p. 824). This is equivalent to maximizing the instantaneous rate of output growth, R, taking K and L as given. To calculate this rate of output growth, simply take logs and differentiate (1) with respect to time, holding K and L constant. This gives

$$R = s \left(\dot{N}_L / N_L \right) + (1 - s) \left(\dot{N}_K / N_K \right), \tag{2}$$

where s is the share of labor in GDP.

In maximizing R, firms face a constraint first introduced by Kennedy (1964), which I refer to as the "innovation possibilities frontier."[4] This frontier is of central importance for the arguments of the induced innovations literature, as it specifies the technologically determined constraints on how labor-augmenting and capital-augmenting technical change can be traded off. Let me for now take a general form,

$$\dot{N}_L / N_L = \Gamma \left(\dot{N}_K / N_K \right), \tag{3}$$

where Γ is a strictly decreasing, differentiable and concave function. This frontier captures the intuitive notion that firms (or the economy) have to trade off a

---

3. I choose the CES form to simplify the discussion.

4. Kennedy (1964) called this the "innovation possibility function," whereas Drandakis and Phelps (1966) called it the "invention possibility frontier."

higher rate of labor-augmenting technical change for a lower rate of capital-augmenting technical change. As a result, the innovation possibilities frontier traces a downward-sloping locus as shown in Figure 1.

The solution to maximizing (2) subject to (3) takes a simple form satisfying the first-order condition

$$(1 - s) + s\Gamma' \left(\dot{N}_K/N_K\right) = 0. \tag{4}$$

Diagrammatically, this solution is drawn in Figure 1 as the tangency of the counters for the instantaneous rate of output growth, (2), and of the innovation facilities frontier, (3), as shown by point A. Comparative statics are straightforward. A greater share of labor in GDP, s, makes labor-augmenting technology more valuable and increases $\dot{N}_L/N_L$ and reduces $\dot{N}_K/N_K$. Put differently, technical change, very much as Hicks conjectured, tries to replace the expensive factor. A greater s corresponds to labor being more expensive and, as a result, technical change becomes more labor-augmenting. This is the first important insight of the induced innovations literature, which I highlight for future reference:

RESULT 1: There will be greater technical change augmenting the factor that is more "expensive."

Next note that the growth rate of output is given by

$$\frac{\dot{Y}}{Y} = \frac{\gamma \left(\dot{N}_L/N_L\right) (N_L L)^{(\sigma-1)/\sigma} + (1 - \gamma) \left[\theta(Y/K) + \left(\dot{N}_K/N_K\right)\right] (N_K K)^{(\sigma-1)/\sigma}}{\gamma (N_L L)^{(\sigma-1)/\sigma} + (1 - \gamma) (N_K K)^{(\sigma-1)/\sigma}},$$

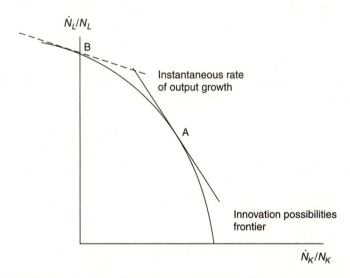

Figure 1. Equilibrium in the induced innovations model. Point B corresponds to the equilibrium with capital accumulation.

where I have replaced $\dot{K}/K$ by $\theta(Y/K)$ using the constant saving rule. Let us now look for an equilibrium satisfying the Kaldor facts that the output-to-capital ratio Y/K is constant and output grows at a constant rate. This necessarily implies that $\dot{N}_K/N_K = 0$ and $\dot{N}_L/N_L = \theta(Y/K) = \dot{Y}/Y$. Therefore, technical change has to be purely labor augmenting (or the tangency point has to be at B as drawn in Figure 1). Moreover, the fact that $\dot{N}_K/N_K = 0$ immediately pins down the equilibrium labor share from (4) as[5]

$$(1 - s) + s\Gamma'(0) = 0.$$

Intuitively, there are two ways of performing capital-like tasks in this economy: accumulate more capital or increase the productivity of capital. In contrast, there is only one way of increasing the productivity of labor—via technical change.[6] In equilibrium, all technical change is directed to labor, while capital accumulation increases the supply of capital-like tasks. Therefore, this model gives us not only a theory of the type of technical change, but also a theory of factor shares. This gives a second major result:

RESULT 2: Induced innovations and capital accumulation determine equilibrium factor shares, ensure that all technical change will be labor augmenting, and imply a constant share of labor in GDP in the long run.

Finally, Drandakis and Phelps (1966) also addressed the question of whether the economy would tend to this long-run equilibrium. They showed that as long as the elasticity of substitution (between labor and capital) is less than 1, the economy is stable. Intuitively, a greater share of labor in GDP encourages more labor-augmenting technical change as shown by the first-order condition (4). When the elasticity of substitution is greater than 1, this labor-augmenting technical change increases the share of labor even further, destabilizing the system. In contrast, when the elasticity of substitution is less than 1, the share of labor falls and the economy converges to the steady state. This leads to the third major result of the induced innovations literature:

RESULT 3: As long as the elasticity of substitution between capital and labor is less than 1, the economy converges to the steady state with constant factor shares.

Overall, the induced innovations literature provided the first systematic study of the determinants of technical change and of the relationship between factor prices and technical change. Moreover, this literature obtained a number of important results that are summarized in Results 1–3.

However, there are also some problems with the approach that this literature takes, the most important of which lies in the assumption that firms simply

---

5. This equation also indirectly determines the capital-output ratio to satisfy the requirement that $\dot{N}_L/N_L = \theta(Y/K)$.

6. Interestingly, Hicks (1932) also anticipated this result. He wrote, "The general tendency to a more rapid increase in capital than labor which has marked European history during the last few centuries has naturally provided a stimulus to labor-saving invention" (p. 125).

maximize (2). Why can we not have profit-maximizing firms instead? The answer relates to the problems that Romer (1986) had to confront in order to construct a model of long-run growth. If aggregate technology has increasing-returns-type characteristics, a competitive equilibrium with complete markets does not exist. In this context, profit-maximizing firms would solve

$$
\max_{K,L,N_K,N_L} \int \exp(-rt) \left\{ \left[\gamma\, (N_L L)^{(\sigma-1)/\sigma} + (1-\gamma)\, (N_K K)^{(\sigma-1)/\sigma} \right]^{\sigma/(\sigma-1)} \right. \\
\left. - wL - rK \right\} dt,
$$

subject to (3), and taking the factor prices w and r as given. But this problem does not have an interior solution, since the production function exhibits increasing returns to scale. Therefore, to go beyond the heuristics of maximizing the instantaneous rate of cost reduction, we need a microfounded model of innovation.[7]

3. A MODEL OF DIRECTED TECHNICAL CHANGE

How do we incorporate profit-maximizing firms in an economy with increasing returns and maintain the flavor of a competitive/decentralized equilibrium?[8] Romer (1986) and Lucas (1988) achieved this by introducing technological externalities. In these models investments (in either physical or human capital) increase the productivity of other firms in the economy, and because individual firms do not internalize this effect, they are subject to constant "private returns" (in the sense that when they double all factors, their profits double, while total output may increase by more). As a result, despite increasing returns at the aggregate level, a competitive equilibrium continues to exist. Romer (1990), Grossman and Helpman (1991), and Aghion and Howitt (1992) developed a different formulation by introducing monopolistic competition and an explicit discussion of endogenous technical change. In these models final good producers (users of technology) are competitive, but suppliers of technology command market power. As a result, when these monopolistic producers double their inputs, total output increases more than twofold, but their profits only double because of the decline in the prices they face. Here I build on this class of models and extend them to discuss the central issues of the induced innovations literature—the possibility of innovations benefiting factors differentially.

3.1. Basics

Consider an economy that admits a representative consumer with logarithmic preferences

$$
\int_0^\infty \ln C e^{-\rho t} dt, \tag{5}
$$

---

7. See Salter (1966) and Nordhaus (1973) for some of the early criticisms.

8. The material here borrows liberally from Acemoglu (2001). I omit many of the details and opt for a heuristic presentation to save space and minimize repetition.

where C is constant, ρ is the rate of time preference, and the budget constraint is

$$C + I \leq Y \equiv \left[\gamma Y_L^{(\varepsilon-1)/\varepsilon} + (1-\gamma) Y_Z^{(\varepsilon-1)/\varepsilon} \right]^{\varepsilon/(\varepsilon-1)}, \tag{6}$$

where I denotes investment. I also impose the usual no–Ponzi game condition, requiring that the lifetime budget constraint of the representative consumer be satisfied. The production function in (6) implies that consumption and investment goods are "produced" from an output of two other (intermediate) goods, a labor-intensive good Y_L and a good that uses another factor Z, Y_Z (or, alternatively, utility is defined over a CES aggregate of Y_L and Y_Z). I am being deliberately vague about the other factor of production, Z, as I want to think of it as skilled workers or capital in different applications.

The two intermediate goods have the following production functions:

$$Y_L = \frac{1}{1-\beta} \left[\int_0^{N_L} x_L(j)^{1-\beta} dj \right] L^\beta \text{ and } Y_Z = \frac{1}{1-\beta} \left[\int_0^{N_Z} x_Z(j)^{1-\beta} dj \right] Z^\beta, \tag{7}$$

where $\beta \in (0, 1)$. The labor-intensive good is produced from labor and a range of labor-complementary machines. The term $x_L(j)$ denotes the amount of the jth labor-complementary (labor-augmenting) machine used in production. The range of machines that can be used with labor is denoted by N_L. The production function for the other intermediate uses Z-complementary machines and is explained similarly. It is important that these two sets of machines are different, enabling me to model the fact that some technologies will be augmenting labor, while others will increase the productivity of Z.

Although, for given N_L and N_Z, the production functions in (7) exhibit constant returns to scale, when N_L and N_Z are chosen by the firms in the economy, there will be increasing returns in the aggregate.

I assume that machines in both sectors are supplied by profit-maximizing "technology monopolists." Each monopolist will set a rental price $\chi_L(j)$ or $\chi_Z(j)$ for the machine it supplies to the market in order to maximize its profits. For simplicity, I assume that all machines depreciate fully after use and that the marginal cost of production is the same for all machines and equal to ψ in terms of the final good.

First suppose that N_L and N_Z are given. Then an equilibrium consists of machine prices $\chi_L(j)$ or $\chi_Z(j)$ that maximize the profits of technology monopolists, machine demands from the two intermediate goods sectors $x_L(j)$ or $x_Z(j)$ that maximize intermediate good producers' profits, and factor and product prices w_L, w_Z, p_L, and p_Z that clear markets.

Characterization of this equilibrium is straightforward. Since the product markets for the two intermediates are competitive, product prices satisfy

$$p \equiv \frac{p_Z}{p_L} = \frac{1-\gamma}{\gamma} \left(\frac{Y_Z}{Y_L} \right)^{-1/\varepsilon}. \tag{8}$$

The greater the supply of Y_Z relative to Y_L, the lower its relative price p.

Firms in the labor-intensive sector solve the following maximization problem:

$$\max_{L,[x_L(j)]} p_L Y_L - w_L L - \int_0^{N_L} \chi_L(j) x_L(j) dj, \tag{9}$$

taking the price of their product, p_L, and the rental prices of the machines, $\chi_L(j)$, as well as the range of machines, N_L, as given. The maximization problem facing firms in the Z sector is similar. The first-order conditions for these firms give machine demands as

$$x_L(j) = [p_L/\chi_L(j)]^{1/\beta} L \quad \text{and} \quad x_Z(j) = [p_Z/\chi_Z(j)]^{1/\beta} Z. \tag{10}$$

The important point that emerges from these expressions is that a greater level of employment of a factor raises the demand for machines complementing that factor, because it creates a greater market size for the machines. This observation underlies the market size effect that was emphasized in the introduction.

The profits of a monopolist supplying labor-intensive machines j can be written as $\pi_L(j) = [\chi_L(j) - \psi]x_L(j)$. Since the demand curve for machines facing the monopolist, (10), is isoelastic, the profit-maximizing price will be a constant markup over marginal cost: $\chi_L(j) = \psi/(1 - \beta)$. To simplify the algebra, I normalize the marginal cost to $\psi \equiv 1 - \beta$. This implies that in equilibrium all machine prices will be given by $\chi_L(j) = \chi_Z(j) = 1$.

Using this price, machine demands given by (10), and the assumption of competitive factor markets, we can also calculate relative factor rewards as

$$\frac{w_Z}{w_L} = \left(\frac{1-\gamma}{\gamma}\right)^{\varepsilon/\sigma} \left(\frac{N_Z}{N_L}\right)^{(\sigma-1)/\sigma} \left(\frac{Z}{L}\right)^{-1/\sigma}, \tag{11}$$

where

$$\sigma \equiv \varepsilon - (\varepsilon - 1)(1 - \beta).$$

Inspection of (11) immediately shows that σ is the elasticity of substitution between factors, which in turn is derived from the elasticity of substitution between the goods in consumers' utility function ε.

For a given state of technology as captured by N_Z/N_L, the relative factor reward w_Z/w_L is decreasing in the relative factor supply Z/L. This is the usual substitution effect: The more abundant factor is substituted for the less abundant one, and its relative marginal product falls.

To determine the direction of technical change, we need to calculate the profitability of different types of innovations. Using the profit-maximizing machine prices, $\chi_L(j) = \chi_Z(j) = 1$, and machine demands given by (10), we find the monopoly profits to be

$$\pi_L = \beta p_L^{1/\beta} L \quad \text{and} \quad \pi_Z = \beta p_Z^{1/\beta} Z. \tag{12}$$

Then, the discounted net present value of technology monopolists is given by standard Bellman equations:

$$r V_L = \pi_L + \dot{V}_L \qquad \text{and} \qquad r V_Z = \pi_Z + \dot{V}_Z, \tag{13}$$

where r is the interest rate. These value functions have a familiar intuitive explanation, equating the discounted value, $r V_L$ or $r V_Z$, to the flow returns, which consist of profits, π_L or π_Z, and the appreciation of the asset at hand, $\dot{V}_L$ or $\dot{V}_Z$.

In steady state, the prices, p_L or p_Z, and the interest rate will be constant, r, so $\dot{V}_L = \dot{V}_Z = 0$ and

$$V_L = \beta p_L^{1/\beta} L / r \qquad \text{and} \qquad V_Z = \beta p_Z^{1/\beta} Z / r. \tag{14}$$

The greater V_Z is relative to V_L, the greater the incentives to develop Z-complementary machines N_Z rather than labor-complementary machines N_L. Equation (14) highlights two effects on the direction of technical change:

1. The price effect: there will be greater incentives to invent technologies producing more expensive goods (V_Z and V_L are increasing in p_Z and p_L).
2. The market size effect: a larger market for the technology leads to more innovation. The market size effect encourages innovation for the more abundant factor. (V_L and V_Z are increasing in Z and L, the total supplies of the factors combined with these technologies.)

The price effect is the analog of Result 1 of the induced innovations literature, showing that there will be more technical change directed toward more "expensive" factors [note that $w_L = \beta N_L p_L^{1/\beta} / (1 - \beta)$ and $w_Z = \beta N_Z p_Z^{1/\beta} / (1 - \beta)$]. In addition, this model introduces a new force—the market size effect—which will play an important role in the applications to be described and is essential for a new result discussed subsequently—that an increase in the supply of a factor induces technical change biased toward that factor.

3.2. The Innovation Possibilities Frontier

Instead of equation (3), which specified an innovation possibilities frontier trading off the two types of innovations, we now need a frontier that transforms actual resources into either of the two types of innovations. This frontier will embed a specific form of (3). In addition, we have to be careful in the choice of the form of the innovation possibilities frontier, since, as is well known in the endogenous growth literature, many specifications will not enable long-run growth. In particular, when scarce factors are used for R&D, sustained growth requires that these factors become more and more productive over time, owing, for example, to spillovers from past research.[9]

Here I assume that R&D is carried out by scientists and that there is a constant supply of scientists equal to S. With only one sector, sustained growth requires $\dot{N}/N$ to be proportional to S: that is, current research benefits from the stock of

---

9. See Acemoglu (1998, 2001) for models of directed technical change where R&D uses final output and there are no spillovers.

past innovations N. With two sectors, instead, there is a variety of specifications, with possible interactions between the two sectors. In particular, each sector can benefit either from its own stock of past innovations or from a combination of its own stock and the stock of the other sector.

To clarify the issues, it is useful to first introduce the concept of "state dependence." The degree of state dependence relates to how future relative costs of innovation are affected by the current composition of R&D. When current R&D in a sector benefits more from its own stock of past innovations than from past innovations complementing the other factor, I refer to the innovation possibilities frontier as "state dependent." A flexible formulation is

$$\dot{N}_L = \eta_L N_L^{(1+\delta)/2} N_Z^{(1+\delta)/2} S_L \quad \text{and} \quad \dot{N}_Z = \eta_Z N_L^{(1+\delta)/2} N_Z^{(1+\delta)/2} S_Z, \quad (15)$$

where $\delta \in (0, 1)$ measures the degree of state dependence: When $\delta = 0$, there is no state dependence since both N_L and N_Z create symmetric spillovers for current research in the two sectors. In contrast, when $\delta = 1$, there is an extreme degree of state dependence because an increase in the stock of labor-complementary machines today makes future labor-complementary innovations cheaper, but has no effect on the cost of Z-complementary innovations.[10]

To find the steady-state equilibrium of this economy, we need to equate the relative profitability of Z-augmenting technical change to its relative cost. The relative profitability is V_Z/V_L given by (14), while the relative cost is

$$\left(\partial \dot{N}_Z / \partial S_Z\right) / \left(\partial \dot{N}_L / \partial S_L\right) = \eta_Z N_Z^\delta / \eta_L N_L^\delta.$$

The steady-state equilibrium condition is then

$$\eta_L N_L^\delta \pi_L = \eta_Z N_Z^\delta \pi_Z. \quad (16)$$

Now solving condition (16) together with (12), we obtain the equilibrium relative technology as

$$\frac{N_Z}{N_L} = \left(\frac{\eta_Z}{\eta_L}\right)^{\sigma/(1-\delta\sigma)} \left(\frac{1-\gamma}{\gamma}\right)^{\varepsilon/(1-\delta\sigma)} \left(\frac{Z}{L}\right)^{(\sigma-1)/(1-\delta\sigma)}. \quad (17)$$

In Acemoglu (2001), I show that the equilibrium will be stable as long as $\sigma < \delta^{-1}$, and here I simply assume that this condition is satisfied, so $1 - \delta\sigma > 0$.

A number of important results follow from equation (17). First, the relative degree of Z-augmenting technology depends simply on the relative supply of Z. This captures both the price and the market size effects emphasized previously, since in equilibrium prices are also determined by relative supplies [from equation (8)]. Second, in the case when the elasticity of substitution between the two factors

---

10. With existing data it is not possible to determine the extent of state dependence. In Acemoglu (2001), I argued that results from the patent citations literature (e.g., Thajtenberg et al., 1992) suggest that there is at least some degree of state dependence in the innovation process.

is greater than 1, that is, $\sigma > 1$, an increase in the relative supply of Z increases N_Z/N_L. That is, greater Z/L leads to Z-augmenting technical change. This is a consequence of the market size effect. Greater relative supply of Z creates more demand for machines complementing this factor. This in turn further increases the productivity of Z.

One way to illustrate the implications of the market size effect is to compare the constant-technology relative demand curve for Z, which keeps N_Z/N_L constant [equation (11)], to the endogenous-technology relative demand, where N_Z/N_L is given by (17). For this purpose, substitute (17) into (11) to obtain the endogenous-technology relative demand:

$$\frac{w_Z}{w_L} = \left(\frac{\eta_Z}{\eta_L}\right)^{(\sigma-1)/(1-\delta\sigma)} \left(\frac{1-\gamma}{\gamma}\right)^{[(1-\delta)\varepsilon]/(1-\delta\sigma)} \left(\frac{Z}{L}\right)^{(\sigma-2+\delta)/(1-\delta\sigma)}. \quad (18)$$

Figure 2 draws the endogenous-technology relative demand curve given by (18), ET_1, together with the constant-technology demand curve, CT. It is straightforward to verify that with $\sigma > 1$, ET_1 is flatter than CT—the increase in Z/L raises N_Z/N_L and the relative demand for Z. This is because, as pointed out previously, changes in technology increase the demand for the factor that has become more abundant.

Now contrast the previous case to the one where the elasticity of substitution, σ, is less than 1. With $\sigma < 1$, an increase in the relative supply of Z now reduces N_Z/N_L, making technology more labor-augmenting, wherein the price effect dominates the market size effect, and new technologies are directed at the factor that has become more scarce. Interestingly, however, the endogenous-technology relative demand curve is still flatter, as drawn in Figure 2 [again simply compare (18) to (11)]. Why is this? Because when $\sigma < 1$, a decline in N_Z/N_L

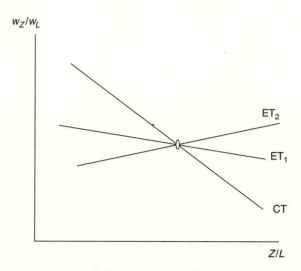

Figure 2. Constant-technology (CT) and endogenous-technology relative demand curves (ET_1 and ET_2).

is actually *biased* toward Z [see equation (11), and the discussion in Acemoglu, 2001]. So irrespective of the elasticity of substitution (as long as it is not equal to 1, i.e., as long as we are not in the Cobb-Douglas case), the long-run relative demand curve is flatter than the short-run relative demand curve. At some level, this is an application of the LeChatelier principle, which states that factor demands become flatter when all other factors adjust (here these other factors correspond to "technology").

But there is more to this framework than the LeChatelier principle. Somewhat surprisingly, the relative demand curve can be upward sloping, as shown by ET_2 in Figure 2. This happens when

$$\sigma > 2 - \delta. \tag{19}$$

Intuitively, the increase in the relative supply of Z raises the demand for Z-complementary innovations, causing Z-biased technical change. This biased technical change increases the marginal product of Z more than that of labor, and despite the substitution effect, the relative reward for the factor that has become more abundant increases. Inspection of (19) shows that this can only happen when $\sigma > 1$. That is, the market size effect has to be strong enough for an upward-sloping relative demand curve. The possibility of an upward-sloping relative demand curve for skills is of interest not only to show the strength of directed technical change, but also because it will play an important role in the first application of this framework below.

So we now have a microfounded framework that can be used to study the direction of technical change and to determine toward which factors new technologies will be biased. This framework also leads to an analog of Result 1 of the induced innovations literature. Does it also capture the insights of the induced innovations literature related to the behavior of the shares of capital and labor in GDP? To answer this question, let us look at the implications of directed technical change for factor shares. Multiplying both sides of equation (18) by Z/L, we obtain relative factor shares as

$$\frac{s_Z}{s_L} \equiv \frac{w_Z Z}{w_L L} = \left(\frac{\eta_Z}{\eta_L}\right)^{(\sigma-1)/(1-\delta\sigma)} \left(\frac{1-\gamma}{\gamma}\right)^{[(1-\delta)\varepsilon]/(1-\delta\sigma)} \left(\frac{Z}{L}\right)^{(\sigma-1+\delta-\delta\sigma)/(1-\delta\sigma)}. \tag{20}$$

This equation shows that there is no reason to expect endogenous technical change to keep factor shares constant. In fact, generally as Z/L changes (e.g., owing to capital accumulation as in the simple induced innovation model of Section 2), s_Z/s_L will change.

However, factor shares *will be* constant in an interesting, and perhaps empirically relevant, special case where there is full state dependence in the innovation possibilities frontier, that is, when $\delta = 1$ in terms of equation (15). In this special case, the accumulation equations take the familiar-looking simple form

$$\dot{N}_L/N_L = \eta_L s_L \quad \text{and} \quad \dot{N}_Z/N_Z = \eta_Z s_Z. \tag{21}$$

That is, research effort devoted to one sector leads to proportional improvements in that sector and has no effect on the other sector. Using this formulation of the innovation possibilities frontier and multiplying both sides of (11) by Z/L, we now have

$$s_Z/s_L = \eta_L/\eta_Z. \tag{22}$$

Hence, in this case, directed technical change works to stabilize factor shares. This formulation of the innovation possibilities frontier therefore leads to the second major result, Result 2, of the induced innovations literature, but with a microfounded model where firms maximize profits and with the caveat that this result only obtains for a specific formulation of the innovation possibilities frontier.

Now imagine that Z stands for capital as in the canonical model of the induced innovations literature. Capital accumulation is given by the optimal consumption decision of the representative consumer. Hence, we have the Euler equation

$$\dot{C}/C = r - \rho, \tag{23}$$

where r is the interest rate, and capital accumulation is given by

$$\dot{Z} = Y - C. \tag{24}$$

In steady state, equation (22) ensures that factor shares are constant. In addition, capital accumulation, which follows from (24), implies that there will be labor-augmenting technical change. This can be seen by first noting that the relative share of capital is given by

$$\frac{s_Z}{s_L} = \left(\frac{1-\gamma}{\gamma}\right)^{\varepsilon/\sigma} \left(\frac{N_Z}{N_L}\frac{Z}{L}\right)^{(\sigma-1)/\sigma}.$$

Inspection of this equation shows that this relative factor share can only remain constant if N_L/N_Z is growing at the same rate as capital for workers, Z/L. So technical change has to be labor augmenting. In fact, the result here is stronger than this: In steady state the interest rate has to remain constant in the long run, so N_Z has to remain constant (see Acemoglu, 1999).[11] This model then predicts that the share of capital should stay constant along the steady-state equilibrium, and technical change should be purely labor augmenting.[12]

---

11. Briefly, the interest rate is $r = \beta N_Z p_Z^{1/\beta}/(1-\beta)$, and to ensure balanced growth, the interest rate has to be constant. Along the balance growth path, p_Z is constant, so N_Z has to remain constant.

12. The reader may note one difference between the reasoning for constant factor shares in the induced innovations model and my model. In the induced innovations model, the constancy of the factor shares follows from the requirement that there has to be steady capital accumulation. Otherwise, equation (4) is consistent with different factor shares. In contrast, in my model equation (22) implies that "any technology equilibrium" has to give constant factor shares. Capital accumulation can then be introduced into this framework, as discussed briefly above and much more in detail in Acemoglu (1999), and leads to the conclusion that all technical change has to be labor augmenting.

Is this steady-state equilibrium stable? Recall that in this framework stability requires $\sigma < \delta^{-1}$. In addition, to ensure the constancy of factor shares in the long run, we now have $\delta = 1$. Therefore, as in Drandakis and Phelps (1966), stability requires the elasticity of substitution to be less than 1. The intuition is also similar to that in the induced innovations literature: when $s_Z/s_L > \eta_L/\eta_Z$, the share of the Z factor is sufficiently large that all firms want to undertake Z-augmenting technical change. If the introduction of new technologies increases s_Z/s_L further, the economy will diverge away from steady state. Therefore, for the steady state to be stable, we need Z-augmenting technical change to reduce the relative factor share of Z. This requires the two factors to be gross complements, that is, $\sigma < 1$ (see Acemoglu, 1999, for details). Therefore, Result 3 of the induced innovations literature also follows from this more microfounded framework.

I next discuss how the directed technical change model, the modern reformulation of the induced innovation literature, sheds new light on two recent debates.

4. DEBATE 1: WHY IS TECHNICAL CHANGE SKILL BIASED?

4.1. Skill-Biased Technical Change

The general consensus among labor and macro economists is that technical change has been skill biased over the past 60 years, and most probably throughout the twentieth century.

Figure 3 summarizes the most powerful argument for why we should think that technical change has been favoring skilled workers over unskilled workers. It plots a measure of the relative supply of skills (the number of college equivalent workers divided by noncollege equivalents) and a measure of the return to skills (the college premium).[13] It shows that over the past 60 years, the U.S. relative supply of skills has increased rapidly and that, in the meantime, the college premium has also increased. If technical change had not been biased toward skilled workers (and presuming that skilled and unskilled workers are imperfect substitutes), we would expect a large decline in the returns to skills. On the contrary, over this time period, returns to skills, as proxied by the college premium, appear to have increased. The figure also shows that despite the rapid increase in the supply of skills, the college premium has been increasing very rapidly over the recent decades. Most economists attribute this pattern to an acceleration in the skill bias of new technologies.

Why has technical change been skill biased throughout the twentieth century? Further, why has it become more skill biased over the recent decades? There are

---

13. The samples are constructed as in Katz and Autor (2000). I thank David Autor for providing me with data from this study. Data from 1939, 1949, and 1959 come from 1940, 1950, and 1960 censuses. The rest of the data come from 1964–1997 March CPSs. The college premium is the coefficient on workers with a college degree or more relative to high school graduates in a log weekly wage regression. The relative supply of skills is calculated from a sample that includes all workers between the ages of 18 and 65. It is defined as the ratio of college equivalents to noncollege equivalents, calculated as in Autor et al. (1998) using weeks worked as weights.

College wage premium

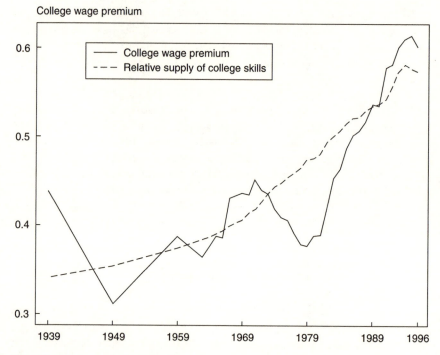

Figure 3. Relative supply and relative demand for college skills in the U.S. labor market 1939–1996. (Source: Author's calculations from Census and Current Population Surveys data.)

two popular explanations. In the first, technical change is sometimes skill biased, but there is no theory for when we should expect more skill bias. This approach can obviously account for the patterns we observe, since it has enough degrees of freedom, and for this reason, it is not particularly attractive. Moreover, according to this explanation the pattern whereby technical change appears to have become more skill-biased during the past 25 years, precisely when the supply of skills has increased very rapidly, has to be viewed as a coincidence.

The second explanation, interestingly, builds on another seminal paper by Phelps (Nelson and Phelps, 1966), in which it was suggested that human capital and skills are important for the absorption and use of new technologies. (I outline a simple version of the Nelson-Phelps model in the appendix.) According to this view, the demand for skills increased during the twentieth century, because there were more (or more high-tech) new technologies, and perhaps because the rate of technical change increased during the past 30 years. This explanation also has some drawbacks. First, the original Nelson-Phelps model and its modern reformulations (e.g., Greenwood and Yorukoglu, 1997; Aghion et al., 2000; Galor and Maov, 2000) are very "reduced form": the adoption and use of new technologies is simply assumed to be skill intensive. Yet, one can imagine new technologies simplifying previously complex tasks, such as scanners. Second, there are many historical examples of skill-replacing technologies, such as weaving machines, the factory system, the interchangeable parts technology, and the assembly line. So the presumption that new technologies always increase the demand for skills is not entirely compelling.

I next show that an approach based on directed technical change provides an explanation for why technical change was skill biased over the past century and has become more skill biased over the past 30 years, without assuming that technical change is always and everywhere skill biased.

4.2. Directed Technical Change and Skill Bias

Consider the model of Section 3, with Z interpreted as the number of skilled workers, and L as the number of unskilled workers.[14] Then, equation (17) gives the degree of skill bias of technology and leads to a number of interesting implications.

First, an increase in the relative supply of skills will encourage the development of skill-biased technologies. Throughout the twentieth century, the relative supply of skills increased very rapidly, both in the United States and in most other OECD economies. Therefore, the framework here suggests that this increase in the supply of skills should have induced new technologies to become more and more skill biased.

Second, with the same reasoning, when the supply of skills accelerates, we expect the degree of skill bias of new technologies to accelerate. Moreover, recall that when condition (19) is satisfied, equation (18) traces an upward-sloping long-run relative demand curve for skills. Therefore, the induced skill bias of new technologies can be sufficiently pronounced that the skill premium increases in response to a large increase in the supply of skills. In fact, this model, together with condition (19), provides an attractive explanation for the behavior of the college premium over the past 30 years, shown in Figure 3. Because technology is slow to change (i.e., because N_Z and N_L are state variables), it is reasonable to expect the first response of the college premium to a large increase in supplies to be along the constant-technology demand curve. That is, in response to the increase in the supply of skills, returns to skills will initially decline. Then once technology starts adjusting, the economy will move to the upward-sloping long-run relative demand curve, and returns to skills will increase sharply. Figure 4 draws this case diagrammatically.

Therefore, this theory can explain the secular skill bias of technical change, why technical change has become more skill-biased during recent decades, and also why in response to the large increase in the supply of skills of the 1970s, the college premium first fell and then began to increase sharply in the 1980s.[15]

---

14. This material builds on Acemoglu (1998).

15. This framework also suggests a reason why many technologies developed during the early nineteenth century may have been skill-replacing. This is because there was a large increase in the supply of unskilled labor in British cities during that time. See Acemoglu (2001) for a more detailed discussion.

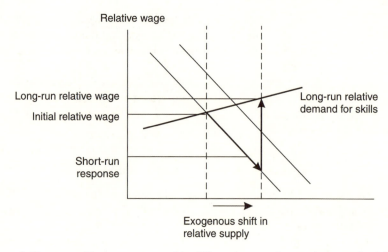

Figure 4. Short-run and long-run response of the skill premium to an increase in the supply of skills.

5. DEBATE 2: THE ROLE OF HUMAN CAPITAL IN CROSS-COUNTRY INCOME DIFFERENCES

5.1. Human Capital and Income Differences

There are large differences in human capital across countries. For example, while the average years of schooling of the population in 1985 was just under 12 in the United States and New Zealand, it was less than 2 years in much of sub-Saharan Africa. Can these differences in educational attainment (more generally, human capital) be the proximate or the ultimate cause of the large differences in income per capita across countries? A number of economists, including Lucas (1988), Azariadis and Drazen (1990), Becker et al. (1990), Stokey (1991), and Mankiw et al. (1992), have emphasized the role of human capital in cross-country differences in income levels and growth rates.

Can these effects be quantitatively large? The recent literature on decomposing differences in income per capita or output per worker across countries into different components concludes that the answer is no. Both Klenow and Rodriguez-Clare (1997) and Hall and Jones (1999) find that differences in human capital, or even differences in physical capital, can account for only a fraction of the differences across countries, with the rest due to differences in efficiency of factor use (or "technology").

Let me reiterate this point somewhat differently. Figure 5 plots the logarithm of output per worker relative to the United States for 103 countries against average years of schooling in 1985. The figure shows a strong correlation between output per worker and schooling. In fact, the bivariate regression line plotted in Figure 5 has a slope coefficient of 0.29 (standard error 0.02) and an R-square of 65 percent.[16]

---

16. Data on output per worker are from Summers and Heston (1991), with the Hall and Jones (1999) correction. Education data are from Barro and Lee (1993).

log output per worker relative to the United States

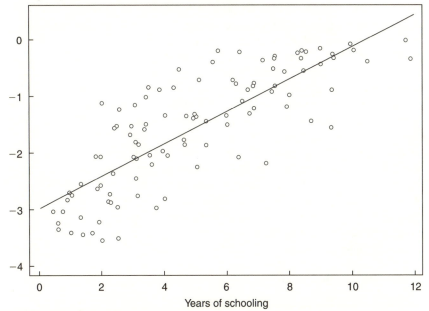

Figure 5. The relation between schooling and output per worker.

So in a regression sense, it appears that there could be a lot in the differences in human capital. However, a simple calculation suggests that it is difficult to rationalize educational attainment raising income as steeply as suggested by Figure 5.

To see this, note that the "private" return to schooling—the increase in individual earnings resulting from an additional year of schooling—is about 6–10 percent (e.g., Card, 1999). In the absence of human capital externalities, the contribution of a 1-year increase in average schooling to total output would be of roughly the same magnitude.[17] But then differences in schooling can explain little of the cross-country variation in income. More specifically, the difference in average schooling between the top and bottom deciles of the world education distribution in 1985 is less than 8 years. With the returns to schooling around 10 percent, we would expect the top decile countries to produce about twice as much per worker as the bottom decile countries. In practice, the output per worker gap between these deciles is approximately a factor of 15.

So how can we justify human capital differences playing a more important role in the world distribution of income? There are a number of possible avenues. First, formal schooling is only one component of human capital, and differences in formal schooling may be understating the true differences in human capital. This could be because workers acquire much more on-the-job training in some countries than

---

17. If capital were in scarce supply, it would be lower.

in others or because the quality of schooling varies substantially across countries. There is undoubtedly much truth to both of these points, but it appears unlikely that they can make up the whole story. For example, workers who migrate to the United States from other countries quickly converge to the earning levels similar to those of U.S. workers with similar schooling, suggesting that quality differences are not the major factor behind the differences in income across countries. Moreover, even without controlling for education, these workers earn not much less than U.S. workers (certainly nothing comparable to the output gaps we observe across countries), so differences in output across countries must have to do more with physical capital or technology differences (see Hendricks, 2002).[18]

Second, perhaps the above calculation understates the importance of human capital because it ignores human capital externalities. After all, it is quite plausible that the whole society benefits indirectly from the greater human capital investment of a worker. In fact, externalities were the centerpiece of Lucas's (1988) paper, which argued for the importance of human capital differences and has been a major building block for many of the papers in the endogenous growth literature.

How large do human capital externalities have to be to justify a strong "causal" effect of human capital differences on income differences consistent with the bivariate relationship shown in Figure 5? A back-of-the-envelope calculation suggests that in order to justify the magnitudes implied by Figure 5, human capital externalities have to be very large. The slope of the line in Figure 5 (0.29) is consistent with (total or social) returns to education of approximately 34 percent $[\exp(0.29) - 1 \simeq 0.34]$. Or alternatively, the comparison of the top and bottom decile countries implies returns on the order of 40 percent. To rationalize Figure 5, we therefore need human capital externalities of 25–30 percent on top of the 6–10 percent private returns. In other words, external returns created by education have to be of the order of three to four times the private returns—very large human capital externalities indeed!

What is the evidence? There have been a number of studies attempting to estimate human capital externalities by exploiting differences in average schooling across cities or states in the United States (e.g., Rauch, 1993). However, these studies face serious identification problems. Cities with more average schooling may also have higher wages for a variety of other reasons. To solve this problem, one has to find "quasi-exogenous" differences in schooling across labor markets. In Acemoglu and Angrist (2000), we attempted to do this by looking at variations in compulsory attendance laws and child labor laws in U.S. states between 1920 and 1960. It turns out that these laws were quite important earlier in the century in determining educational attainment, especially high school graduation rates. For example, we found that a person growing up in a state with strict child labor laws was 5 percent more likely to graduate from high school than a person growing up in a state with the most permissive child labor laws. Moreover, these differences in laws do translate into substantial differences in average schooling across states.

---

18. These results have to be interpreted with some caution, since it may be workers with relatively high observed or unobserved skills who migrate to the United States.

These laws therefore provide an attractive source of variation to identify human capital externalities.

So how high are human capital externalities? Contrary to my expectations, we found very small human capital externalities, often not significantly different from 0. Our baseline estimates are around 1 or 2 percent (in other words, they imply plausible externalities of the order of 20 percent of the private returns). These are magnitudes far short of what is required for human capital to be a major ultimate or proximate cause of the differences in income per capita.

Are we then to conclude that human capital differences across countries are more of a symptom than the cause of the differences in income? This may be the correct conclusion, but it is too early to jump to it, since there is one more line of attack: Human capital differences can affect the type of technologies that a country adopts and how effectively these technologies are utilized. At an intuitive level, human capital differences have a much larger effect on income when they interact with technology choices. This is the insight that comes out of Nelson and Phelps (1966), which is discussed in the appendix, and also follows from the modern reformulation of the induced innovations literature discussed in Section 3 (see Section 5.2).[19]

Can human capital play a much more important role in accounting for cross-country income differences when it interacts with technology? Although existing evidence does not enable us to answer this question, there are a few pieces of evidence that suggest that there might be something there. First, Benhabib and Spiegel (1994) present cross-country regression evidence consistent with this view. Second, there is microevidence consistent with the notion that human capital facilitates the absorption and use of new and more productive technologies (e.g., Foster and Rosenzweig, 1996). Third, in Acemoglu and Zilibotti (2001), we undertook a simple calibration of a model with skill-technology mismatch and found that it can account for a large fraction of the actual differences in income per capita with the differences in human capital across countries.

Finally, a quick look at the cross-country data shows that there is a strong correlation between "technology" and human capital, especially, a measure of the relative supply of high human capital workers. For example, Figure 6 plots the total factor productivity (TFP) measure (relative to the United States) calculated by Hall and Jones (1999) from a cross-country levels accounting exercise against the ratio of college to noncollege workers in the population in 1985 (from Barro and Lee, 1993). This correlation might of course reflect the effect of some other factors on both variables, for example, institutional differences across countries as emphasized by Hall and Jones (1999) and Acemoglu et al. (2001), or the effect of higher (exogenous) productivity on human capital investments. Nevertheless, it suggests that a more careful look at the relationship between human capital and technology is required. This chapter, naturally, is not the right forum for this, so here instead I will simply develop an alternative approach to analyze the interaction between human capital and technology based on the insights of the directed technical change/induced innovations literature.

---

19. This point is developed in Acemoglu and Zilibotti (2001).

log TFP from Hall and Jones

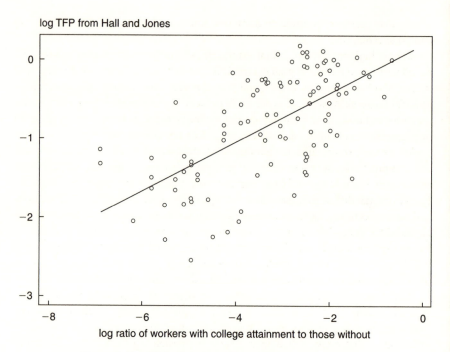

log ratio of workers with college attainment to those without

Figure 6. The relation between college education and productivity.

5.2. Directed Technical Change, Appropriate Technology, and Human Capital

The notion of directed technical change implies that new technologies in the United States or in the OECD countries, which are often used by less developed countries (LDCs), will be designed to work best with the conditions and factor supplies in these technologically more advanced nations. Because these nations are more abundant in human capital, the frontier technologies they develop will typically require highly skilled workers. Lack of skilled personnel in LDCs will then create a technology-skill mismatch, making it difficult for these countries to benefit from frontier technologies. In other words, these technologies will be, at least to some degree, "inappropriate" to the LDCs' needs. This insight follows from an application of the directed technical change model, but is also related to the insights of Nelson and Phelps (1966).

To develop these ideas more formally, consider the model of Section 3 applied to a world economy. A technology leader that I refer to as the North, for example, the United States, produces the technologies N_Z and N_L, while the other countries, the South or the LDCs, simply copy these. For simplicity, I take all of the LDCs to be identical, with L' unskilled workers and Z' skilled workers. A key characteristic of the LDCs is that they have fewer skilled workers than the North, that is,

$$Z'/L' < Z/L.$$

Assume that LDCs can copy new machine varieties invented in the North, without paying royalties to Northern technology monopolists because of lack of intellectual property rights. This assumption implies that the relevant markets for the technology monopolists will be given by the factor supplies in the North. I also assume that the cost of producing machines in the LDCs may be higher, $\kappa^{-\beta/(1-\beta)}$ rather than $\psi \equiv (1 - \beta)$ as in the North. This cost differential may result from the fact that firms in the LDCs do not have access to the same knowledge base as the technology monopolists in the North. I also assume that there is free entry to copying Northern machines. This implies that all machines will sell at marginal cost in the LDCs, that is, at the price $\kappa^{-\beta/(1-\beta)}$. It is natural to think of κ as less than 1, so that machines are more expensive in the South than in the North. Finally, there is no international trade.

Using the above expressions, we obtain the output levels of the two final goods in the North as

$$Y_L = \frac{1}{1 - \beta}(p_L)^{(1-\beta)/\beta} N_L L$$

and

$$Y_Z = \frac{1}{1 - \beta}(p_Z)^{(1-\beta)/\beta} N_Z Z,$$

while in the LDCs, we have

$$Y'_L = \frac{1}{1 - \beta}(p'_L)^{(1-\beta)/\beta} \kappa N_L L'$$

and

$$Y'_Z = \frac{1}{1 - \beta}(p'_Z)^{(1-\beta)/\beta} \kappa N_Z Z',$$

where p''s denote prices in the LDCs, which differ from those in the North because factor proportions are different and there is no international trade. The parameter κ features in these equations since machine costs are different in the South. Note also that the technology terms, N_L and N_Z, are the same as in the North, since these technologies are copied from the North.

The ratio of aggregate income in the South to that in the North can be written as

$$\frac{Y'}{Y} = \kappa \left[\frac{\gamma \left[(p'_L)^{(1-\beta)/\beta} N_L L' \right]^{(\varepsilon-1)/\varepsilon} + (1 - \gamma) \left[(p'_Z)^{(1-\beta)/\beta} N_Z Z' \right]^{(\varepsilon-1)/\varepsilon}}{\gamma \left(p_L^{(1-\beta)/\beta} N_L L \right)^{(\varepsilon-1)/\varepsilon} + (1 - \gamma) \left(p_Z^{(1-\beta)/\beta} N_Z Z \right)^{(\varepsilon-1)/\varepsilon}} \right]^{\varepsilon/(\varepsilon-1)}. \quad (25)$$

Simple differentiation and algebra show that (see Acemoglu, 2001)

$$\frac{\partial Y'/Y}{\partial N_Z/N_L} \propto \left(\frac{N_Z}{N_L}\right)^{-1/\sigma} \left[\left(\frac{Z'}{L'}\right)^{(\sigma-1)/\sigma} - \left(\frac{Z}{L}\right)^{(\sigma-1)/\sigma}\right]. \qquad (26)$$

Since $Z'/L' < Z/L$, this expression implies that when $\sigma > 1$, that is, when the two factors are gross substitutes, an increase in N_Z/N_L raises the income gap between the LDCs and the North (i.e., reduces Y'/Y). This implies that as technologies produced by the North become more and more directed toward skilled workers, there will be a tendency for the income gap between the North and the South to increase. Intuitively, these new technologies are less and less appropriate to the needs of the LDCs, which do not have a sufficient number of skilled workers to make best use of these technologies.[20]

What are the implications of directed technical change for income differences across countries? Equation (26) shows that a greater skill bias of technology will increase the income gap between rich and poor countries (among countries with different levels of skill abundance). Directed technical change implies that technologies developed in the United States or the OECD will cater to their own needs, so typically be more skill-biased than they would have been otherwise. As a result, directed technical change will increase the income gap across countries.

To gain further insight, consider a special case with $\sigma = 2$ (the case that was derived as an equilibrium of a more detailed model with many sectors in Acemoglu and Zilibotti, 2001), and suppose that $\delta = 0$ in terms of equation (15). In general, equation (25) is complicated because domestic prices in the North and the South differ depending on domestic factor supplies and world technology. However, in the case with $\sigma = 2$, equation (25) simplifies to

$$\frac{Y'}{Y} = \kappa \left[\frac{\gamma^{\varepsilon/2}(L')^{1/2} + (1-\gamma)^{\varepsilon/2}\left[(N_Z/N_L)Z'\right]^{1/2}}{\gamma^{\varepsilon/2}(L)^{1/2} + (1-\gamma)^{\varepsilon/2}\left[(N_Z/N_L)Z\right]^{1/2}}\right]^2. \qquad (27)$$

This expression shows explicitly that the extent to which a less developed country can take advantage of new technologies depends on the number of skilled workers. A country with few skilled workers will have difficulty adapting to the world technology, especially when this technology is highly biased toward skilled workers, that is, when N_Z/N_L is high. To develop this point further, note that when $\sigma = 2$ and $\delta = 0$, the endogenous technology equation (17) implies

---

20. In contrast, when $\sigma < 1$, an increase in N_Z/N_L narrows the income gap since the term in square brackets in (26) is now negative. However, when $\sigma < 1$, a lower N_Z/N_L increases the demand for Z relative to the demand for labor—i.e., it corresponds to Z-biased technical change. Moreover, in this case, the North, which is more abundant in Z, will invest in technologies with lower N_Z/N_L than is appropriate for the South. In other words, exactly as in the case with $\sigma > 1$, the North will choose "too skill-biased" technologies, since with $\sigma < 1$, lower N_Z/N_L corresponds to greater skill bias. This extends the results in Acemoglu and Zilibotti (2001) to a slightly more general model and also, more importantly, to the case where the two factors are gross complements, i.e., $\sigma < 1$. See Acemoglu (2001) for a more detailed discussion.

$$\frac{N_Z}{N_L} = \left(\frac{\eta_Z}{\eta_L}\right)^2 \left(\frac{1-\gamma}{\gamma}\right)^{\varepsilon} \left(\frac{Z}{L}\right)^2. \tag{28}$$

Substituting this into (27) we obtain

$$\frac{Y'}{Y} = \kappa \left[\frac{\gamma^{\varepsilon/2}(L')^{1/2} + \gamma_0(Z/L)(Z')^{1/2}}{\gamma^{\varepsilon/2}(L)^{1/2} + \gamma_0(Z/L)(Z)^{1/2}}\right]^2,$$

where γ_0 is a suitably defined constant. So the income gap between the North and the South will depend on the human capital gap between them, very much as in Nelson and Phelps (1966).

It is also instructive at this point to compare this approach based on endogenous-technology choice to Nelson and Phelps's original contribution. Despite the similarities, there are also a number of important differences between this approach based on the idea of directed technical change and appropriate technology, and the Nelson-Phelps approach. The first difference is more apparent than real. It may appear that in Nelson and Phelps (1966), human capital differences translate into technology differences, whereas in the simple version of the model of Acemoglu and Zilibotti (2001) that I outlined here, all countries have access to the same technology frontier, so there should be no differences in TFP/technology. This conclusion is not correct, however, because TFP differences are calculated as a residual from assuming a specific relationship among human capital, physical capital, and output. In particular, it is typically assumed that $Y = K^{0.33} (AH)^{0.67}$, and A, the TFP term, is calculated as the residual. In the presence of technology-skill mismatch as in the Acemoglu-Zilibotti model, the effect of human capital on output will be counted as part of TFP. Therefore, in both the model discussed here and in Nelson and Phelps (1966), human capital differences contribute to differences in output per worker or income per capita because of their interaction with technology adoption and the efficiency of technology use.

The second difference between the approaches is more interesting. Inspection of equation (30) from the Nelson-Phelps model given in the appendix shows that human capital should matter more when the growth rate of the world technology, g, is greater. In contrast, (27) [or less transparently, (25)] shows that human capital should matter more when new technologies are more skill-biased. This is an interesting area to investigate. A recent paper by Easterly (2001) finds that low human capital countries lagged behind the richer countries over the past 25 years. Interestingly, this period has been one of slow world growth, so according to the Nelson-Phelps view, these low human capital countries should have benefited relative to the technology leaders. On the other hand, the past 25 years have also been characterized by very rapid skill-biased technical change, which suggests that, according to the model in Acemoglu and Zilibotti (2001), low human capital countries should have lagged further behind. But, of course, many other factors could account for this pattern, and more work is required to get a better understanding of these issues.

6. CONCLUSION

This chapter revisited the induced innovations literature of the 1960s to which Phelps was a major contributor (Drandakis and Phelps, 1966). This literature provided the first systematic study of the determinants of technical change and also investigated the relationship between factor prices and technical change. I presented a modern reformulation of this literature based on the tools developed by the endogenous growth literature. This reformulation confirms many of the insights of the induced innovations literature, but reveals a new force—the market size effect: There will be more technical change directed at more abundant factors.

This modern reformulation sheds light on two recent debates: Why is technical change often skill-biased, and why has it become more skill biased during recent decades? Further, what is the role of human capital differences in accounting for income differences across countries? Interestingly, an application of this modern reformulation to these important debates also reiterates some of the insights of another important paper by Phelps (Nelson and Phelps, 1966). Despite the similarities, there are also different implications of the Nelson-Phelps approach and those of an approach based on the direct technical change model. To investigate these differences empirically appears a fruitful area for future research.

APPENDIX: THE NELSON-PHELPS MODEL

I briefly outline a version of the second model of Nelson and Phelps (1966).[21] Imagine that there is a world technology frontier, $T(t)$, advancing at an exogenous rate g, that is,

$$T(t) = T(0) \exp(gt).$$

Countries can benefit from this world technology by incorporating it into their production processes. But this is a human capital–intensive task. For example, a country needs highly skilled engineers to adapt world technologies to their conditions, to fill key positions in the implementation of these technologies, and to train workers in the use of these new techniques. So Nelson and Phelps (1966) postulated that the technology of country j, $A_j(t)$, would evolve according to the differential equation

$$\frac{\dot{A}_j(t)}{A_j(t)} = \frac{\phi(h_j)[T(t) - A_j(t)]}{A_j(t)}, \tag{29}$$

where h_j is the human capital in country j, which is assumed to be timing-variant [see their equation (8′)]. This equation states that the farther a country is from the world technology frontier, the faster its rate of progress. Most plausibly, this would be because there is more technology out there to be absorbed. But also $\phi'(h_j) > 0$

---

21. See also Welch (1970) and Shultz (1975).

so that the greater the human capital of a country, the faster this convergence. Here h_j can be years of schooling, or the fraction of highly skilled individuals, such as university graduates or engineers, or some other feature of the human capital distribution.

The first implication of (29) is that

$$\frac{\partial^2 \dot{A}_j(t)/A_j(t)}{\partial T(t)\partial \phi(h_j)} > 0,$$

so that human capital becomes more valuable when technology is more advanced. This is the reason that the Nelson-Phelps approach has provided the foundation for a number of recent papers linking the demand for skills to the speed and extent of technical change (e.g., Greenwood and Yorukoglu, 1997; Aghion et al., 2000; Galor and Maov, 2000).

Second, note that although equation (29) is in terms of technological progress, it does have a unique stable stationary distribution as long as $\phi(h_j) > 0$ for all countries. In the stationary state, all $A_j(t)$'s will grow at the same rate g, and this stationary cross-country distribution is given by

$$A_j(t) = \frac{\phi(h_j)}{g + \phi(h_j)} T(t). \tag{30}$$

Suppose now that output in each country is proportional to $A_j(t)$. Equation (30) then implies that countries with low human capital will be poor, because they will absorb less of the frontier technology. This effect is in addition to the direct productive contribution of human capital to output and suggests that human capital differences across countries can be more important in causing income differences than calculations based on private returns to schooling might suggest.

REFERENCES

Acemoglu, D. (1998), "Why Do New Technologies Complement Skills? Directed Technical Change and Wage Inequality," *Quarterly Journal of Economics* 113:1055–90.

——— (1999), "Labor- and Capital-Augmenting Technical Change," NBER Working Paper No. 7544.

——— (2001), "Directed Technical Change," NBER Working Paper 8287, forthcoming in *Review of Economic Studies* 69.

Acemoglu, D. and J. D. Angrist (2000), "How Large Are Human Capital Externalities? Evidence from Compulsory Schooling Laws," *NBER Macroeconomics Annual 2000*, pp. 9–71.

Acemoglu, D., S. Johnson, and J. A. Robinson (2001), "The Colonial Origins of Comparative Development: An Empirical Investigation," *American Economic Review* 91:1369–1401.

Acemoglu, D. and F. Zilibotti (2001), "Productivity Differences," *Quarterly Journal of Economics* 116:563–606.

Aghion, P. and P. Howitt (1992), "A Model of Growth Through Creative Destruction," *Econometrica* 60:323–51.

——— (1998), *Endogenous Growth Theory*, Cambridge: MIT Press.

Aghion, P., P. Howitt, and G. Violante (2000), "Technology, Knowledge, and Inequality," mimeo, Harvard University.

Autor, D., A. Krueger, and L. Katz (1998), "Computing Inequality: Have Computers Changed the Labor Market?," *Quarterly Journal of Economics* 113:1169–1214.

Azariadis, C. and A. Drazen (1990), "Threshold Externalities in Economic Development," *Quarterly Journal of Economics* 105:501–26.

Barro, R. J. and Jong-Wha Lee (1993), "International Comparisons of Educational Attainment," *Journal of Monetary Economics* 32:363–94.

Becker, G., K. M. Murphy, and R. Tamura (1990), "Human Capital, Fertility and Economic Growth," *Journal of Political Economy* 98:S12–37.

Benhabib, J. and M. M. Spiegel (1994), "The Role of Human Capital in Economic Development: Evidence from Aggregate Cross-Country Data," *Journal of Monetary Economics* 34:143–73.

Card, D. E. (1999), "The Causal Effect of Education on Earnings," in O. Ashenfelter and D. Card, eds., *The Handbook of Labor Economics*, Vol. 3, Amsterdam: Elsevier.

Drandakis, E. and E. S. Phelps (1966), "A Model of Induced Invention, Growth and Distribution," *Economic Journal* 76:823–40.

Easterly, W. (2001), "The Lost Decades," *Journal of Economic Growth* 6:135–57.

Foster, A. and M. Rosenzweig (1996), "Technical Change in Human Capital Return and Investments: Evidence from the Green Revolution," *American Economic Review* 86:931–53.

Galor, O. and O. Maov (2000), "Ability Biased Technological Transition, Wage Inequality and Economic Growth," *Quarterly Journal of Economics* 115:469–99.

Greenwood, J. and M. Yorukoglu (1997), *"1974"—Carnegie-Rochester Conference Series on Public Policy* 46:49–95.

Grossman, G. and E. Helpman (1991), *Innovation and Growth in the Global Economy*, Cambridge: MIT Press.

Hall, R. and C. I. Jones (1999), "Why Do Some Countries Produce So Much More Output per Worker Than Others?," *Quarterly Journal of Economics* 114:83–116.

Hendricks, L. (2002), "How Important Is Human Capital for Development? Evidence from Immigrant Earnings," *American Economic Review* 92:198–220.

Hicks, J. (1932), *The Theory of Wages*, London: Macmillan.

Jones, C. I. (1995), "R & D-Based Models of Economic Growth," *Journal of Political Economy* 103:759–84.

Katz, L. and D. Autor (2000), "Changes in the Wage Structure and Earnings Inequality," in O. Ashenfelter and D. Card, eds., *Handbook of Labor Economics*, Vol. 3, Amsterdam: Elsevier.

Kennedy, C. (1964), "Induced Bias in Innovation and the Theory of Distribution," *Economic Journal* 74:541–47.

Kiley, M. (1999), "The Supply of Skilled Labor and Skill-Biased Technological Progress," *Economc Journal* 109:708–24.

Klenow, P. J. and A. Rodriguez-Clare (1997), "The Neoclassical Revival in Growth Economics: Has It Gone Too Far?," *NBER Macroeconomics Annual*, pp. 73–103.

Lucas, R. (1988), "On the Mechanics of Economic Development," *Journal of Monetary Economics* 22:3–42.

Mankiw, N. G., D. Romer, and D. N. Weil (1992), "A Contribution to the Empirics of Economic Growth," *Quarterly Journal of Economics* 107:407–37.

Nelson, R. and E. S. Phelps (1966), "Investment in Humans, Technological Diffusion and Economic Growth," *American Economic Association Papers and Proceedings* 56:69–75.

Nordhaus, W. (1973), "Some Skeptical Thoughts on the Theory of Induced Innovation," *Quarterly Journal of Economics* 87:208–19.

Rauch, J. E. (1993), "Productivity Gains from Geographic Concentration of Human Capital: Evidence from the Cities," *Journal of Urban Economics* 34:380–400.

Romer, P. M. (1986), "Increasing Returns and Long-Run Growth," *Journal of Political Economy* 94:1002–37.

———— (1990), "Endogenous Technological Change," *Journal of Political Economy* 98:S71–102.

Salter W. E. G. (1966), *Productivity and Technical Change*, 2nd edn., Cambridge: Cambridge University Press.

Samuelson, P. (1965), "A Theory of Induced Innovations Along Kennedy-Weisacker Lines," *Review of Economics and Statistics* 47:444–64.

Schultz, T. (1975), "The Value of the Ability to Deal with Disequilibria," *Journal of Economic Literature* 13:827–46.

Segerstrom, P. S., T. Anant, and E. Dinopoulos (1990), "A Schumpeterian Model of the Product Life Cycle," *American Economic Review* 80:1077–92.

Stokey, N. (1991), "Human Capital, Product Quality and Growth," *Quarterly Journal of Economics* 106:587–616.

———— (1995), "R&D and Economic Growth," *Review of Economic Studies* 62:469–90.

Summers, L. and A. Heston (1991), "The Penn World Table (Mark 5): An Expanded Set of International Comparisons, 1950–1988," *Quarterly Journal of Economics* 106:327–68.

Trajtenberg, M., R. Henderson, and A. B. Jaffe (1992), "Ivory Tower vs. Corporate Lab: An Empirical Study of Basic Research and Appropriatability," NBER Working Paper No. 4146.

Welch, F. (1970), "Education in Production," *Journal of Political Economy* 78:312–27.

Young, A. (1998), "Growth without Scale Effect," *Journal of Political Economy* 106:41–63.

— 24 —

Comments on Acemoglu

NANCY L. STOKEY

Both the chapter by Acemoglu and the Drandakis-Phelps (1966) paper to which it is related are very thought-provoking pieces of work. They share a common motivation—the fact that U.S. data displays two startling regularities:

1. The factor shares of capital and labor have been fairly constant.
2. The real interest rate has been fairly constant.

The factor share and interest rate series display modest fluctuations at business cycle frequencies but show no secular trend, despite the fact that income has grown quite substantially.

Except in the unit-elastic (Cobb-Douglas) case, for an aggregate production function that displays constant returns to scale (CRS), (1) holds if and only if the economy is growing along a balanced growth path (BGP), where effective capital and effective labor grow at a common rate. Then, if we view all technical change as factor augmenting, (2) holds if and only if all of it is labor augmenting. But why should all technical change take that form? Does someone—firms or scientists— "direct" R&D in a way that makes it take this form? The goal in each paper is to construct a model in which such a choice is made and the resulting BGP displays features (1) and (2).

Since the Drandakis and Phelps paper has held up quite well over time, it is interesting to include it in the discussion. In the rest of this chapter I will briefly summarize the main features of each model, discuss some of their limitations, and point to two alternative (unoriginal) explanations for the evidence.

1. THE MODELS

Drandakis and Phelps (1966) postulate an innovation possibility frontier (IPF) of the type introduced in Kennedy (1964). Given a rate of capital-augmenting technical change $\hat{B}$, point $\hat{A} = \Phi(\hat{B})$ on the IPF frontier represents the maximum feasible rate of labor-augmenting technical change. Drandakis and Phelps suppose that someone (who?) chooses a point on the IPF to maximize the rate of cost

---

I am grateful to Pat Kehoe, Tim Kehoe, Ed Prescott, and Warren Weber for stimulating conversations.

reduction, or equivalently, to maximize the rate of output growth. Formally the problem is

$$\max_{\hat{B}} \left[a\hat{B} + (1-a)\, \Phi(\hat{B}) \right],$$

where a is capital's share in income. Note that the solution $\hat{B}^*(a)$ is increasing in a: A larger factor share tilts technical change more heavily in the direction of capital augmentation.

Along a BGP, factor shares are constant ($\dot{a} = 0$), the interest rate is constant ($\dot{r} = 0$), and all technical change is labor augmenting ($\hat{B} = 0$). Hence, capital's share along the BGP, call it a^*, satisfies $\hat{B}^*(a^*) = 0$, and the growth rate of per capita consumption is $g^* = \Phi(0)$. With capital's share determined, it is easy to calculate the effective input ratio k^*. Let $\overline{B}$ denote the (constant) level of the capital augmentation variable along the BGP. The split of effective capital $\overline{B}K(t)$ into its two components and the real interest rate $r = \overline{B} f'(k^*)$ depend on savings behavior. A constant savings rate s pins down $K(t)/Y(t)$, and then $\overline{B}$ and r can be calculated. An intertemporal utility function pins down $\overline{B}$ through an equation of the form $\rho + \sigma g^* = r^* = \overline{B} f'(k^*)$, where ρ is a rate of time preference and $1/\sigma$ is an elasticity of intertemporal substitution, and then $K(t)$ can be determined. Drandakis and Phelps show that if $\varepsilon < 1$, then the BGP is globally stable, and that case is the one that is empirically relevant.

The setup is an interesting one, but it leaves an important issue unresolved: Who "chooses" the point on the frontier? Alternatively, how can this model be connected with R&D by individual firms? Although the model postulates that the motive for the choice is cost reduction, in the end all of the benefits accrue to the factors of production, capital and labor. That is, in the end there are no profits, so the model provides no framework for thinking about profit-oriented R&D. Acemoglu's model incorporates profit-motivated R&D, so it takes care of that objection, but as we see next, it raises other problems.

In Acemoglu's model there are three primary inputs: $\overline{L}$ is labor, $\overline{S}$ is the supply of scientists, and the third factor Z may be interpreted, for now, as land or capital. All three are owned by households and supplied inelastically, and the first two are assumed to be in fixed supply.

There is one final good and two layers of intermediate goods. The final good Y is produced by competitive firms using a constant elasticity of substitution (CES) technology with two intermediate goods Y_L and Y_Z as inputs. Each of these intermediate goods Y_F, where $F = L, Z$, is produced by competitive firms using a Cobb-Douglas technology with an aggregate of N_F differentiated inputs, $x_F(j, t)$, $j \in [0, N_F(t)]$, and the primary factor F as inputs. The differentiated inputs are produced by monopolists using CRS technologies, and the primary factors are supplied inelastically. New differentiated products are invented by scientists using the CRS technology:

$$\frac{\dot{N}_F}{N_F} = \eta_F \left(\frac{N_{-F}}{N_F} \right)^{(1-\delta)/2} S_F, \quad F = L, Z, \tag{1}$$

$$\overline{S} = S_L + S_Z, \qquad\qquad \text{all } t,$$

where $\tilde{F}$ denotes the other factor. Prices of the differentiated inputs are set by their producers, and all other prices are determined competitively.

Since the total supply of scientists is fixed, their allocation between the two sectors depends only on the relative profitability of differentiated products in the two sectors. But profit maximization leads to the standard markup formula on all differentiated inputs, so along the BGP the relative profitability is simply $\pi_Z/\pi_L = x_Z/x_L$, where the π_F's are profit flows and the x_F's are output flows for differentiated inputs in the two sectors. The output ratio x_Z/x_L grows at the same rate as $Z/\overline{L}$, however, so balanced growth requires that $Z(t) = \overline{Z}$, and that factor must be in fixed supply. It is then straightforward to show that along a BGP, $N_Z/N_L = \Omega_N$, where Ω_N is a constant that involves η_Z/η_L and $\overline{Z}/\overline{L}$.

Consequently, this model incorporates profit-oriented R&D, but it does so at the expense of disallowing capital accumulation: The factor Z must be in fixed supply along a BGP. Hence, the return to Z cannot be interpreted as a marginal product of capital, a real interest rate. This is just as well: The returns (per unit) to L and Z grow at a common, constant rate along the BGP, a feature that would be inconsistent with stylized fact (2) if Z were interpreted as capital.

2. CRITIQUE

The Acemoglu chapter herein and the paper by Drandakis and Phelps (1966) have an excellent motivation: The stylized facts (1) and (2) are quite compelling. But though both offer thoughtful, well-executed theoretical models, in the end neither is entirely satisfying. There are two issues. The first has to do with the nature of the models, while the second involves the empirical observations that motivated them. Although the motivation for both is empirical, each model has at its center variables that are unobservable or unmeasurable. Abstract theory is useful for many purposes, but concrete, empirical motivations like (1) and (2) cry out for a theoretical model stated in terms that have empirical counterparts.

The heart of the Drandakis and Phelps model is the IPF. But note that an economy that is on the BGP generates data representing only one point on the IPF. Thus, to the extent that the time series for the United States suggests an economy on a BGP, those data are virtually useless for estimating the location or shape of the IPF. Stated a little differently, estimating the IPF requires a data set that displays substantial variation in factor shares, whereas this whole enterprise started with stylized fact (1), the constancy of factor shares.[1]

The heart of the Acemoglu model is the technology in (1) for inventing new differentiated products, which in turn are used in producing the intermediate goods

---

1. It might seem that the same argument would apply to the production possibility factor (PPF), which in fact many people have estimated. But BGPs abstract from short-run fluctuations, and there is evidently enough short-run variation in factor prices to make the PPF exercise possible. However, short-run fluctuations will not help much in estimating the IPF. In a world with stochastic shocks, choices from that frontier would presumably be guided by the (smooth) behavior of the average.

Y_L and Y_Z. But is there anything in the National Income and Product Accounts that corresponds to Y_L and Y_Z? Is there any evidence on N_L and N_Z or their rates of change, or on η_Z/η_L, or on the allocation of scientific effort S_L and S_Z? In short, is there any evidence that could refute this theory?

If an empirical motivation demands an empirically refutable theory, then it is useful to begin by asking what is measured or at least, in principle, measurable. If directed technical change is directed by a profit motive, then perhaps we should listen to Deep Throat's advice and "follow the money." That is, we should ask who pays for R&D and who uses the results. On the input side, data are available on both private and public (National Science Foundation, National Institutes of Health, Department of Defense) expenditures on R&D, and on the output side data are available on patents, licenses, and total factor productivity (TFP) growth by sector.

Casual observation suggests that many innovations are sector specific and even product specific, and the data on expenditures—which show that R&D expenditures are very unequal across sectors—confirm this view. Some sectors, such as pharmaceuticals, aerospace, and electronics, have very high ratios of R&D expenditures to total revenues, whereas others, such as food processing and clothing, have ratios that are quite low. Similarly, TFP growth shows substantial variation across industries at any point in time. In addition, TFP growth rates within an industry can display substantial variation from one decade to the next.

A second issue also arises in judging the empirical success of these two models. The data are, in some sense, too good for the models. Both theories focus on technical change within a single economy, but the empirical regularities—especially for interest rates—seem to be much broader.

The data in Homer and Sylla (1991), which cover many centuries and many countries, suggest that average real interest rates are astonishingly similar over time and across countries. An unsystematic perusal of that book suggests that rates on high-quality long-term bonds have fallen mostly in the 2–8 percent range (and for much of the time in the 3–6 percent range), for the U.S. and various European countries going back as far as the 1500s: in Medieval and Renaissance Europe (Chart 2); in England during the eighteenth century (Chart 4); in England, France, the Netherlands, and the United States during the nineteenth century (Charts 6, 14, 18, and 31), and in the United States during the first half of the twentieth century (Chart 53). These rates are nominal, but under the gold standard inflation was a minor issue. Thus, the fluctuations in real rates over many centuries and many countries have been similar in range and magnitude to those seen in (real) U.S. rates for the post–World War II war period. Wars and other major economic events evidently affected those rates, but no long-run trend is discernible. In this sense the evidence on interest rates seems "too good" for the explanations offered here.

Cross-country data on factor shares are a little more difficult to evaluate, especially if a broad set of countries is considered. In less-developed countries a much higher fraction of the labor force is self-employed, and many of those work in agriculture. Since it is difficult to distinguish the shares of farm income that should be attributed to land, labor, and capital, factor share figures necessarily involve some sort of extrapolation from the sector of the economy where wages and salaries are reported. Gollin (2002) concludes that average factor shares are quite similar across countries over a wide range of per capita income levels. The factor share of labor is more variable across countries at lower per capita income levels, but shows no trend as income increases. Other studies for highly agrarian economies conclude that factor shares are roughly equal for land, labor, and capital, whereas data for modern industrialized economies attribute a declining (and now negligible) share to land.

3. ALTERNATIVE EXPLANATIONS

In this section I discuss two other models briefly—one quite specific and one rather general—that are also consistent with stylized facts (1) and (2).

Krusell et al. (2000) study a model that disaggregates capital and labor just a little, using two types of capital and two types of labor. They postulate the nested CES form

$$y = k_s^\alpha \left\{ \mu u^\sigma + (1 - \mu) \left[\lambda k_e^\rho + (1 - \lambda) s^\rho \right]^{\sigma/\rho} \right\}^{(1-\alpha)/\sigma}$$

for the aggregate production function, where k_s and k_e denote stocks of structures and equipment, and s and u denote inputs of skilled and unskilled labor. Note that this form does not permit construction of either a capital or a labor aggregate. Instead, the form of this production function is driven by four key facts. First, estimates of the aggregate production function indicate that capital (meaning equipment) is complementary to skilled labor but highly substitutable for unskilled labor. Second, the relative price of equipment has fallen dramatically in the post–World War II period, leading to a substantial increase in the stock of equipment per capita. Specifically, Krusell et al. calculate that over the period 1963–1992 the stock of equipment grew at 6.2–7.5 percent per year, whereas the capital stock as a whole grew at only 2.6–3.2 percent per year. (Question: Is this change capital augmenting or labor augmenting?) Third, over the same period the ratio of skilled to unskilled labor more than doubled. Finally, the skill premium over the period grew quite sharply, despite the enormous increase in the ratio of skilled to unskilled labor.

The baseline model simulation, which takes the factor inputs as given, displays features (1) and (2). Indeed, the factor shares in the simulation are much smoother than in the data, and the simulated real interest rate is also quite constant. The rate of return on structures is about 4–5 percent over the whole period, whereas the return on equipment has a slightly higher mean and a much higher variance but displays no discernible trend.

Although the Krusell et al. (2000) model was not explicitly motivated by the stylized facts (1) and (2), it is consistent with them—despite the fact that the simulations do *not* mimic a BGP. As noted previously, the four factors grow at quite different rates. Moreover, the model does not permit construction of either a capital or a labor aggregate, and the shares of the individual factors are far from constant. Unskilled labor and structures had declining shares, and skilled labor a rapidly growing one. Thus, the model is an example where (1) and (2) hold despite the fact that the economy's growth path is far from balanced.

A second model that is consistent with (1) and (2) is the obvious one: If the aggregate technology is Cobb-Douglas, then all technical change that is factor augmenting can be viewed as labor augmenting, and (1) and (2) hold. But why should the aggregate production function—which after all is simply an artificial construct invented by economists—appear to be Cobb-Douglas? In a series of numerical simulations, Fisher et al. (1977) show that it may be no more than an aggregation phenomenon. Specifically, they look at artificial economies with several CES technologies, with various elasticities. They allocate capital and labor in a competitive way across technologies and calculate total output. Then they estimate an aggregate production function, with aggregate capital and aggregate labor as inputs. They find that the aggregate production functions tend to look Cobb-Douglas even when the individual technologies underlying them have nonunitary elasticities of substitution. Thus, a possible explanation for (1) and (2) is simply as an aggregation phenomenon.

What do we want from an aggregate model of technical change? The Krusell et al. (2000) model provides a parsimonious explanation for several different features of post–World War II U.S. data, and the aggregation results in Fisher et al. (1977) provide a tantalizing possibility for explaining why (1) and (2) might be observed in many different economies. However, one puzzle remains, the one posed by the data in Homer and Sylla: Why have interest rates fluctuated within the same band in so many different economies over a period of five centuries? The band is not particularly narrow—interest rates of 2–8 percent translate into prices of 12.5 to 50 for consoles that pay one unit per period, but it has been remarkably stable over a very long period. A regularity like that is rare and remains tantalizing.

REFERENCES

Drandakis, E. M. and E. S. Phelps (1966), "A Model of Induced Invention, Growth and Distribution," *Economic Journal* 76:823–40.

Fisher, F. M., R. M. Solow, and J. M. Kearl (1977), "Aggregate Production Functions: Some CES Experiments," *Review of Economic Studies* 44:305–20.

Gollin, D. (2002), "Getting Income Shares Right," *Journal of Political Economy* 110:458–74.

Homer, S. and R. Sylla (1991), *A History of Interest Rates,* 3rd ed., New Brunswick: Rutgers University Press.

Kennedy, C. M. (1964), "Induced Bias in Innovation and the Theory of Distribution," *Economic Journal* 74:541–47.

Krusell, P., L. Ohanian, V. Rios-Rull, and G. Violante (2000), "Capital-Skill Complementarity and Inequality," *Econometrica* 68:1029–53.

— 25 —

Population and Ideas:
A Theory of Endogenous Growth

CHARLES I. JONES

1. INTRODUCTION

Can exponential growth be sustained forever? How do we understand the exponential increase in per capita income observed over the last 150 years?

The growth literature provides a large number of candidate theories to address these questions, and such theories are nearly always constructed so as to generate a steady state, also known as a balanced growth path. That is, the growth rate of per capita income settles down eventually to a constant. In part, this reflects modeling convenience. However, it is also a desirable feature of any model that is going to fit some of the facts of growth. For example, as noted by Barro and Sala-i-Martin (1995, p. 34):

> [O]ne reason to stick with the simpler framework that possesses a steady state is that the long-term experiences of the United States and some other developed countries indicate that per capita growth rates can be positive and trendless over long periods of time. . . . This empirical phenomenon suggests that a useful theory would predict that per capita growth rates approach constants in the long run; that is, the model would possess a steady state.

Clearly there are many examples of countries that display growth rates that are rising or falling for decades at a time. However, there are also examples of countries, such as the United States over the last 125 years, that exhibit positive growth for long periods with no noticeable trend. It seems reasonable, then, that a successful theory of growth should at least admit the possibility of steady-state growth.

Models with this property, however, are very special and require strong assumptions. One of these assumptions is that technical change, at least in the long

I thank Daron Acemoglu, Robert Barro, Robert Lucas, Antonio Rangel, Paul Romer, T. N. Srinivasan, John Williams, Alwyn Young, and seminar participants at the Chicago GSB, Cornell, the European Science Foundation Conference on Growth, Harvard, the Minneapolis Fed, MIT, the NBER Summer Institute, Princeton, UCSD, and Stanford for insightful comments. I am grateful to the Hoover Institution and the National Science Foundation (SBR-9818911) for financial support.

run, should not be capital augmenting. Another is the presence of a differential equation that is exactly linear in a sense we will define shortly.

Now that growth theorists understand the kind of assumptions that have to be made to generate sustained exponential growth, it is possible to construct a large number of models with different "engines" of growth, ranging from physical capital accumulation to human capital accumulation to the discovery of new ideas to population growth to various combinations of these factors. Indeed, the problem now confronting growth economists is how to choose among the abundance of competing explanations. Empirical work provides some guidance, but a number of difficulties such as the accurate measurement of ideas or human capital or even growth itself lead this research to be less than conclusive.

This chapter proposes a complementary approach to judging growth models by "raising the hurdle" to which our models aspire. Specifically, the suggestion is that a successful theory of economic growth should provide an intuitive and compelling justification for the crucial assumptions that are a requirement of such a theory. That "crucial" assumptions should be justified is a time-honored strategy for making progress in the growth literature. This kind of reasoning is discussed explicitly in the introduction in Solow (1956) and is partly responsible for the discovery of the neoclassical growth model.[1] Another example relates to the requirement that technical change should not be capital augmenting in the long run. At first, this seems like a very ad hoc assumption. However, research several decades ago by Kennedy (1964) and Drandakis and Phelps (1966) and more recently by Acemoglu (2001) explains how this can be the natural outcome in a model in which researchers choose the direction of technical progress.

Just as these previous authors made progress by questioning the justification for ad hoc but crucial assumptions, I propose that additional progress toward understanding long-run growth can be made by seeking a justification for the kind of linearity that is needed in models that generate sustained growth over long periods of time. Existing growth models fall short of this ideal, providing essentially no justification for why a key differential equation should be linear. This was surely appropriate when we were searching for the first several candidate explanations of long-run growth, but perhaps it is now time to ask more of our models.

The final result of any model that exhibits long-run growth is an equation of the form $\dot{y}/y = g$, where y is per capita income and $g > 0$ is a constant. Not surprisingly, then, the key to obtaining such a result is for the model to include a differential equation that is "linear" in a particular sense, as in

$$\dot{X} = \underline{\quad} X. \tag{1}$$

---

1. "All theory depends on assumptions that are not quite true. That is what makes it theory. The art of successful theorizing is to make the inevitable simplifying assumptions in such a way that the final results are not very sensitive. A 'crucial' assumption is one on which the conclusions do depend sensitively, and it is important that crucial assumptions be reasonably realistic. When the results of a theory seem to flow specifically from a special crucial assumption, if the assumption is dubious, the results are suspect. I wish to argue that something like this is true of the Harrod-Domar model of economic growth" (Solow, 1956, p. 65).

Growth models differ according to the way in which they label the X variable and the story they tell in order to fill in the blank.[2]

Much of the work in both new and old growth theory can be read as the search for the appropriate characterization of equation (1). For example, the original models in Solow (1956) and Swan (1956) without exogenous technical change focused our attention on the differential equation for capital accumulation. However, with diminishing returns to capital, that equation was less than linear, and there was no long-run growth in per capita income. When Solow and Swan added exogenous technical change in the form of an equation that was assumed to be linear, $\dot{A} = gA$, long-run growth emerged.

The so-called "AK" growth models departed from Solow and Swan by eliminating the diminishing returns to capital accumulation. Linearity in the accumulation of physical capital or human capital (or some combination of these two) became the engine of growth.[3] Idea-based growth models by Romer (1990), Grossman and Helpman (1991), Aghion and Howitt (1992), and others returned the linearity to the differential equation for technological progress and filled the blank in equation (1) with resources devoted to research by profit-maximizing entrepreneurs.

Note that *exact* linearity of the key differential equation is critical to generating sustained exponential growth in the long run. If the exponent on X in equation (1) is slightly larger than one, then growth rates will explode over time, with the level of X (and hence income) becoming infinite in a finite amount of time. On the other hand, if the exponent on X is slightly less than one, then growth rates will fall to zero asymptotically. In other words, the growth theorist is in the strange situation of requiring a knife-edge restriction.

One can argue that too much emphasis is placed on exact linearity in the previous paragraph. The U.S. evidence suggests that trendless growth is possible for at least 125 years, at a rate of about 1.8 percent per year. Matching this kind of evidence requires a differential equation that is close to linear. For example, if the differential equation takes the form $\dot{y}_t = a y_t^{\phi}$, acceptable values for ϕ fall approximately into the range 0.95–1.05.[4] If one wants balanced growth forever at a positive rate, exact linearity is a requirement. If one only desires to match the empirical evidence

---

2. This way of summarizing growth models is taken from Romer (1995). It is important to recognize, as documented by Mulligan and Sala-i-Martin (1993), that this linearity can be hidden in models with multiple state variables. Linearity is also an asymptotic requirement rather than something that must hold at all points in time, as pointed out by Jones and Manuelli (1990).

3. The models of Romer (1987), Lucas (1988), and Rebelo (1991) fit this category.

4. Integrating the differential equation in the text for $\phi \neq 1$ and calculating the average growth rate leads to
$$\bar{g}_T \equiv \frac{1}{T} (\log y_T - \log y_0) = \frac{1}{T} \frac{1}{1 - \phi} \log[1 + g_0(1 - \phi)T],$$
where g_0 is the growth rate $\dot{y}/y$ at time 0 (corresponding here to the year 1870). Setting $\bar{g}_T = 0.018$ and $T = 125$, one can solve this equation for the value of ϕ associated with any initial value of g_0. If $\phi < 1$, then growth rates are declining; a value of $g_0 = 0.019$ implies a value of $\phi = 0.952$ and a 1995 growth rate of $g_T = 0.0171$. What we know of U.S. history suggests that growth rates were rising prior to the 125 year period, and setting $g_0 = 0.017$ leads to a value of $\phi = 1.051$ and a 1995

for the United States, this requirement can be relaxed slightly. In either case, a crucial assumption of such a model is that it deliver a differential equation that is approximately linear.

A natural requirement of a successful theory of economic growth, then, is that it provide a compelling and intuitive justification for linearity; such an assumption is crucial to the result so we might require a good explanation for why it holds. On this basis, existing models are clearly deficient. The linearity in existing models is assumed ad hoc, with no motivation other than that we must have linearity somewhere to generate endogenous growth.

That a theory of endogenous growth assumes this kind of knife-edge linearity has long been known. Stiglitz (1990) and Cannon (1998) note that this requirement made growth theorists uncomfortable with models of endogenous growth in the 1960s. Solow (1994) appeals to this same criticism in arguing against recent models of endogenous growth. What is sometimes not sufficiently well appreciated is that any model that is going to generate sustained exponential growth requires such an assumption. A productive response to the criticism, then, is to provide justifications for our crucial assumptions.

This chapter develops a new theory of endogenous growth in which linearity is motivated from first principles. The process illustrates the potential gains from forcing ourselves to jump over a higher hurdle—the model has predictions that are different from those of other endogenous growth models. The first key ingredient of this model is endogenous fertility. At an intuitive level, the reason why endogenous fertility helps is straightforward. Consider a standard Solow-Swan model. With the labor force as a factor that cannot be accumulated endogenously, one has to look for a way—typically arbitrary—to eliminate the diminishing returns to physical capital. In contrast, with an endogenously accumulated labor force, both capital and labor are accumulable factors, and a standard constant-returns-to-scale setup can easily generate an endogenously growing economy.

However, endogenous fertility in a model with constant returns to scale in all production functions will not generate endogenous growth in *per capita* variables. This leads to the second key ingredient of the model: increasing returns to scale. Endogenous fertility leads to endogenous growth in the scale of the economy. Increasing returns to scale in the production function for aggregate output translates the endogenous growth in scale into endogenous growth in per capita output.

Research on idea-based growth models provides a justification for increasing returns that is based on first principles. At least since Shell (1966), Phelps (1968), and Nordhaus (1969), economists have recognized that the nonrivalry of knowledge implies that aggregate production is characterized by increasing returns to scale. This argument has been clarified and elevated to a very prominent place in our thinking about economic growth by Romer (1990). Ideas are nonrivalrous; they can be used at any scale of production after being produced only once. For example, consider the production of any new product, say the digital videodisc player or the latest worldwide web browser. Producing the very first unit may

---

growth rate of $g_T = 0.0191$. The growth rates in this last experiment are roughly consistent with those estimated by Ben-David and Papell (1995).

require considerable resources: The product must be invented or designed. However, once the product is invented, it never needs to be invented again, and the standard replication argument implies that subsequent production occurs with constant returns to scale. Including the production of the "idea," or the design of the product, production is characterized by increasing returns. This property, rather than the assumption that the differential equation governing technological progress is linear, is the key contribution we need from the idea-based growth literature.[5]

This chapter builds on a number of earlier insights. Several papers in the 1960s contain key results that are further developed here. Phelps (1966) and Nordhaus (1969) present models in which the nonrivalry of knowledge leads to increasing returns and derive the result that long-run growth in per capita income is driven by exogenous population growth.[6] Still, neither of these papers seems to know how seriously to take this prediction, with Nordhaus calling it a "peculiar result" (p. 23). Two years later, however, Phelps (1968, pp. 511–12) stresses the implications of population for growth:

> One can hardly imagine, I think, how poor we would be today were it not for the rapid population growth of the past to which we owe the enormous number of technological advances enjoyed today. . . . If I could re-do the history of the world, halving population size each year from the beginning of time on some random basis, I would not do it for fear of losing Mozart in the process.

More recently, Jones (1995) modified the Romer (1990) model to eliminate the apparently counterfactual prediction that the growth rate of the economy is proportional to the size of the population. In the modified model, the growth rate of the economy depends on the growth rate of the population, as in the earlier models.[7] Because the population growth rate is assumed to be exogenously given, however, the long-run growth rate of the economy is invariant to policy changes.[8]

Here, the population growth rate is endogenized, and policy changes can affect the long-run growth rate of the economy through their effects on fertility. However, as the channel through which policy affects growth is fertility, the nature of the

---

5. Alternative methods for introducing increasing returns to scale in the model, such as a Marshallian externality associated with capital accumulation, will also lead to endogenous growth. I focus on the idea-based theory of increasing returns because it can be motivated from first principles.

6. The learning-by-doing models of Arrow (1962) and Sheshinski (1967) also obtain this result.

7. A large body of related research includes Simon (1981), Judd (1985), Grossman and Helpman (1989), Kremer (1993), Raut and Srinivasan (1994), Kortum (1997), and Segerstrom (1998).

8. Subsequent papers by Dinopoulos and Thompson (1998), Peretto (1998), Young (1998), and Howitt (1999) have found clever ways to eliminate the effects of scale on growth in idea-based models without eliminating long-run policy effects. These models maintain linearity in the equation for technical progress but assume that the number of sectors grows exactly with population, so that research effort per sector does not grow. See Jones (1999) for a discussion of these issues.

effects of policy on long-run growth is often counter to conventional wisdom. For example, subsidies to R&D and capital accumulation, even though they may be welfare improving, will reduce long-run growth in the model.

Section 2 of the chapter presents an extremely simple growth model that illustrates the role of population growth and increasing returns. The basic claim in this section is that if one takes the historical presence of population growth as given, then one can understand growth in per capita income without introducing any arbitrary linearity into the model.

The remainder of the chapter then examines the deeper issue of how we can understand growth more generally, both in per capita terms and in population, as an endogenous phenomenon. Section 3 explores in detail the claim that endogenous fertility can provide the linearity needed to understand per capita growth. Section 4 develops the decentralized dynamic general equilibrium model in the context of "basic science." That is, the model is based on the assumption that not only are the ideas underlying growth nonrivalrous, they are pure public goods. This assumption is employed almost entirely because it simplifies the analysis considerably. Still, it may also be of independent interest. For example, it is sometimes conjectured that basic science should be modeled as an exogenous process, like exogenous technical progress in a Solow model. The analysis here suggests that insight is gained by moving beyond this view. Even if the ideas of basic science fall from above like apples from trees, the fertility channel and increasing returns are crucial: The number of Isaac Newtons depends on the the size of the population that is available to sit under trees.

Section 5 explores the welfare properties of the model. Section 6 contains a general discussion of the model's predictions and discusses its interpretation. One point worth emphasizing from the beginning is that the model is best thought of as describing the OECD or even the world as a whole. Care is required when testing the model with a cross section of countries because countries share ideas.

2. THE ISAAC NEWTON GROWTH MODEL

The first claim in this chapter is that the growth in per capita income that has occurred in recent centuries can be understood without appealing to any extra linearity of the kind assumed in recent growth models. To make this claim, we construct an extremely simple toy economy and show how it exhibits per capita income growth.

There are two key ingredients that drive per capita growth in the toy model, both of which are readily justified. The first is population growth. For the moment, we simply take constant exogenous population growth as a given. Letting L_t represent the population or labor force at time t,

$$\dot{L}_t/L_t = n > 0, \qquad L_0 > 0 \text{ given.} \qquad (2)$$

The second key ingredient is increasing returns to scale. Let Y_t be the quantity of a single consumption/output good produced, and let A_t be the stock of ideas that the economy has discovered in the past. The production function in our toy model is

$$Y_t = A_t^\sigma L_{Yt}, \tag{3}$$

where L_Y is the number of people working to produce the output good and $\sigma > 0$ imposes the assumption of increasing returns to scale. Holding the stock of ideas constant, there are constant returns to scale: Doubling the quantity of rivalrous inputs (here only L_Y) will double output. Because ideas are nonrivalrous, the existing stock A can be used at any scale of production, leading to increasing returns in A and L_Y together.

Finally, we need a production function for ideas. This part of the model can be set up in a number of different ways. To keep the model simple, however, assume the following production function:

$$\dot{A}_t = \delta L_{At}, \qquad A_0 > 0 \text{ given}, \tag{4}$$

where L_A is the number of people working to produce new ideas (the number of Isaac Newtons) and $\delta > 0$ represents the number of new ideas that each researcher discovers per unit of time.

The resource constraint for this economy is

$$L_{Yt} + L_{At} = L_t. \tag{5}$$

As part of our simplifying assumptions, we assume that a constant fraction s of the labor force works as researchers so that $L_{At} = sL_t$ and $L_{Yt} = (1-s)L_t$, with $0 < s < 1$. This is the only allocative decision that needs to be made in this simple model.

From the production function in equation (3), consumption (or output) per worker is given by

$$y_t \equiv Y_t/L_t = A_t^\sigma (1-s),$$

and therefore the growth of consumption per worker, g_y, is equal to σg_A, where $g_x \equiv \dot{x}/x$ for any variable x.

From the production function for ideas in equation (4),

$$\dot{A}_t/A_t = \delta s \, (L_t/A_t). \tag{6}$$

It is then easy to show that there exists a stable balanced growth path for this model where $g_A = n$. For example, in order for $\dot{A}/A$ to be constant in equation (6), the ratio L/A must be constant. Therefore, the long-run per capita growth rate in this economy is given by

$$g_y = \sigma n. \tag{7}$$

This result nicely illustrates the central roles of population growth and increasing returns. Per capita growth is proportional to the rate of population growth, where the factor of proportionality measures the degree of increasing returns in the economy.

According to this model, sustained, long-run per capita growth results from population growth and increasing returns. The inherent nonrivalry of ideas means that the economy is characterized by increasing returns to scale. Economic growth occurs because the economy is repeatedly discovering newer and better ways to transform labor into consumption. However, the creation of new ideas by itself is not sufficient to generate sustained growth. For example, suppose an economy invents 100 new ideas every year. As a fraction of the (ever-evolving) existing stock of ideas, these 100 new ideas become smaller and smaller. Sustained growth requires that the number of new ideas itself grow exponentially over time. This in turn requires that the number of inventors of new ideas grow over time, which requires population growth.

If population growth is taken as given, this model suggests that per capita income growth is not a puzzle at all. More people means more Isaac Newtons and therefore more ideas. More ideas, because of nonrivalry, mean more per capita income. Therefore, population growth, combined with the increasing returns to scale associated with ideas, delivers sustained long-run growth.[9]

3. LINEARITY AND GROWTH

The previous section shows how two basic ingredients, population growth and increasing returns, can help us make sense of the presence of per capita income growth. In the remainder of the chapter, we consider a deeper question. How do we understand past and possibly future growth, both in per capita terms and in population itself, as an endogenous phenomenon?

Motivated by the discussion in the introduction, the answer must involve a differential equation that is linear. In this section, I argue that the law of motion for population is intimately tied to a linear differential equation in a way that the law of motion for physical capital or human capital or ideas is not.

---

9. The model clearly indicates that growth occurs because the effective resources devoted to producing new ideas increase over time. Jones (2002) applies a more general version of this model that incorporates both physical and human capital to uncover empirically the sources of twentieth-century U.S. economic growth. A key fact in the application is that resources devoted to research have increased for three reasons. In addition to basic population growth, the share of the labor force devoted to research and the educational attainment of the researchers have increased as well. I document that roughly 80 percent of postwar U.S. growth is due to increases in human capital investment rates and research intensity and only 20 percent is due to the general increase in population. However, the intensity effects cannot lead to sustained exponential growth—neither educational attainment nor the share of the labor force devoted to research can increase forever. So unless there is an ad hoc Lucas-style linearity in human capital accumulation, population growth remains the only possible source of long-run growth, leading that paper to predict that growth rates may slow considerably in the future. These results confirm that substantial progress in understanding growth can be made using the basic framework given earlier.

To understand this claim, imagine a world consisting of N_t (representative) individuals at time t. Each individual in this economy chooses to have a certain number of children, denoted by $\tilde{n}_t$. At each point in time, some constant, exogenously given fraction d of the population dies, as in the Blanchard (1985) constant-probability-of-death model. The law of motion for the aggregate population in a continuous time environment is then given by

$$\dot{N}_t = (\tilde{n}_t - d)N_t,$$

$$\equiv n_t N_t. \tag{8}$$

Therefore, by deciding on the number of children to have, individuals choose the proportional rate of increase in the population. The linearity of the law of motion for population is a biological fact of nature: People reproduce in proportion to their number.

This is not to say that such an equation automatically delivers sustained exponential population growth. Indeed, n may depend on the aggregate state of the economy. In the model, for example, it will depend on the wage rate and other endogenous variables. In fact, in a model with decreasing returns to scale (e.g., because of a constant technology level and a fixed supply of land), a subsistence requirement for consumption, and endogenous fertility, one easily arrives at a Malthusian result in which the size of the population is asymptotically constant—people endogenously choose $\tilde{n} = d$, delivering zero population growth.

Instead, the point of this exercise is simply that thinking about fertility delivers an equation that is linear in a way that thinking about physical or human capital accumulation or the production function for knowledge does not. To see this more clearly, consider a very rough comparison of this equation to the key linear differential equation in other growth theories:

1. AK model: $\dot{K} = sK^{\phi}$
2. Lucas model: $\dot{h} = uh^{\phi}$
3. Romer model: $\dot{A} = H_A A^{\phi}$
4. Fertility model: $\dot{N} = (\tilde{n} - d)N^{\phi}$

Each of the models maintains the assumption that $\phi = 1$ (which may be viewed as an analytically useful approximation for the crucial assumption of $\phi \approx 1$).

What does it mean for these equations to be linear? Hold constant the control or choice variable of individual agents and consider whether doubling the state variable will double, more than double, or less than double the change in the state variable. For example, in the AK model, hold constant the saving rate chosen by individuals. What happens to net investment when the stock of capital in the economy is doubled? In a neoclassical model with the usual diminishing returns, net investment is less than doubled, so the neoclassical model is less than linear. The AK model, however, eliminates these diminishing returns through an ad hoc assumption. In the Lucas-style model, hold constant the fraction of time u that individuals spend accumulating skills and double the stock of human capital. If a seventh grader and a high school graduate both go to school for 8 hours a day, does the high school graduate learn twice as much?

In the Romer-style model, let A denote the stock of ideas or designs and H_A be the total level of resources the economy devotes to research. Holding H_A constant, suppose we double the existing stock of ideas. What happens to the output of new ideas? A benchmark case of constant returns would be $\phi = 0$: The number of new ideas created by 100 units of research effort is independent of the total stock of ideas discovered in the past. One might suppose that $\phi > 0$—the productivity of research is higher because of the discovery of calculus or the semiconductor. Or one might suppose that $\phi < 0$—the most obvious ideas are discovered first, and it becomes more and more difficult to discover new ideas because of "fishing out." What one sees from this example is that the case of $\phi \approx 1$ is clearly ad hoc. There is no intrinsic justification for linearity in the production function for new ideas.

In contrast, consider finally the fertility model. Hold constant the choice variable of individuals—the number of children per person, $\tilde{n}$. What happens to the total number of offspring if we double the population? Of course the total number of offspring doubles. Linearity in the fertility equation results from the standard replication argument.[10]

One can endogenize the fertility rate $\tilde{n}$ by following the endogenous fertility literature associated with Dasgupta (1969), Pitchford (1972), Razin and Ben Zion (1975), and Becker and Barro (1988), among others. Individuals care not only about their own consumption, but also about the number of their descendants and the consumption of their descendants. This literature, especially Barro and Becker (1989), shows that the population can grow endogenously at a constant exponential rate in a neoclassical-style growth model.

This result depends in part on the production technology for children. Suppose

$$\tilde{n} = bl^\psi, \tag{9}$$

where $0 \leq l \leq 1$ is the time an individual with a fixed labor endowment of one unit spends producing offspring, and $0 < \psi < 1$. The parameter $b > d$ (for "births") represents the maximum number of children that an individual can have in a given period (i.e., if $l = 1$). With these properties, as we will see below, it is easy to get the result of positive, steady-state population growth. For example, all we need is that b be sufficiently large.

Now consider the possibility that instead of being a parameter, b depends directly on the state variables of the economy. For example, new ideas in health care might allow children to be produced with less labor effort; technological progress might increase b, although one might suspect that fertility remains bounded from above. What is critical, however, is that asymptotically b does not decrease with

---

10. One might wonder about a dependence of d on N, which could destroy the linearity. It seems most natural to think of the mortality rate d as depending on per capita consumption and on the technological sophistication of the economy. Increases in consumption or medical technology, for example, may reduce the mortality rate, perhaps leading it to asymptote to some constant level (perhaps even to zero). Incorporating these features into the model would not destroy the linearity of the fertility equation.

N. For example, to get sustained population growth, we must rule out a case like $b = N^{-\theta}$ with $\theta > 0$. Clearly, this would eliminate the linearity of the model.

Is it reasonable to believe that θ is not too far from zero? I think so. To see why, note first that people are a primary input into nearly all production functions. People are needed to produce output, people are needed to produce ideas, and people are needed to produce new people. At least so far, the AK assumption that machines by themselves can produce new machines does not seem tenable. With an exogenously given population, one needs an exact but ad hoc degree of increasing returns to scale to get constant returns to "reproducible" inputs. Thus, for example, the simple Romer equation given above requires a returns to scale of approximately two, which is difficult to justify. However, once population is itself an endogenously reproducible input, then a standard constant-returns-to-scale production function already exhibits constant returns to reproducible inputs; the two coincide so that the standard replication argument provides the key justification for linearity.

This is the situation that applies here. The standard constant-returns-to-scale benchmark in the production of offspring corresponds to $\theta = 0$. It is possible, of course, for θ to be substantially larger or smaller than zero, but *this* would require a departure from constant returns through some kind of arbitrary and difficult-to-justify external effect: As the population gets larger, why should the maximum number of children that an individual can produce decline?

4. THE DECENTRALIZED MODEL

The remainder of this chapter should be read as an extended example. We embed an endogenous fertility setup into an idea-based growth model and examine the kind of results that can arise. I have chosen a particular theory and made particular assumptions to get to the basic results easily. I will indicate in the appropriate places how the results generalize.

4.1. Preferences

One of the key insights of Barro (1974) was to think about utility-maximizing individuals who care not only about their own consumption but also about their children's consumption. This reasoning was extended by Razin and Ben-Zion (1975) and Becker and Barro (1988) to model endogenous fertility: Parents also care about the number of children that they have, and there may be costs to increasing the number of offspring.

Following Becker and Barro (1988), we assume that the time s utility of the head of a dynastic family is given by

$$U_{0,s} = \int_s^\infty e^{-\rho(t-s)} u(c_t, \tilde{N}_{0,t}) \, dt, \tag{10}$$

where c_t is the consumption of a representative member of the dynastic family at time t, and $\rho > 0$ is the rate of time preference. $\tilde{N}_{0,t} \equiv N_t/N_0$ represents the size of the dynastic family living at time t. Individuals live through their descendants, so that the death of an individual is not a remarkable event in that person's life. When an individual dies, her assets are divided evenly among the other members of the dynastic family.

With respect to the kernel of the utility function, it turns out to be convenient to assume

$$u(c_t, \tilde{N}_t) = \log c_t + \epsilon \log \tilde{N}_t, \tag{11}$$

where $\epsilon > 0$. Both the marginal utility of consumption and the marginal utility of progeny are positive but diminishing. The elasticity of substitution between consumption and progeny is one, as in Barro and Becker (1989). Within the class of utility functions with a constant elasticity of substitution between consumption and progeny, this unit elasticity guarantees that the dynastic approach is time consistent—choices made by the dynastic head of generation zero will be implemented by subsequent generations. This assumption also turns out to be required for the existence of a balanced growth path, as we will see shortly.[11]

Finally, characterizing the equilibrium of the model is much easier under the stronger assumption that $\epsilon = 1$, so that per capita consumption and offspring receive equal weight in the utility function. In the presentation of the model, we will make this assumption and indicate at the appropriate time what happens when $\epsilon \neq 1$.

4.2. Technology

The consumption-capital good in the economy, final output Y, is produced according to

$$Y_t = A_t^\sigma K_t^\alpha L_{Yt}^{1-\alpha}, \tag{12}$$

where A is the stock of ideas in the economy, K is capital, L_Y is labor, and the parameters satisfy $\sigma > 0$ and $0 < \alpha < 1$. While this kind of production function is commonly used in economics, it incorporates a fundamental insight into the process of economic growth. Specifically, the production function exhibits increasing returns to scale because of the nonrivalry of ideas. The strength of increasing returns is measured by σ.

The technology for producing offspring has already been discussed. It turns out to be convenient to invert this production function in the analysis that follows. Individuals are endowed with one unit of labor, and generating a net fertility rate of $n \equiv \tilde{n} - d$ requires $l = \beta(n)$ units of time, where

---

11. This restriction is closely related to the restriction in dynamic general equilibrium business cycle models that consumption must enter in log form if consumption and leisure are additively separable (leisure per person does not need to enter in log form because it is not growing over time). Alternative approaches to fertility can relax this assumption.

$$\beta(n) \equiv \left(\frac{n+d}{b}\right)^{1/\psi}. \tag{13}$$

The time that individuals have left over to supply to the labor market is therefore $1 - \beta(n)$. Note that $\beta(0) > 0$ (some time is required to maintain a constant level of population to compensate for the deaths at rate d), and $\beta(n)$ is a convex function. In the optimization problem, we have individuals choose n rather than $\tilde{n}$, but of course the two choices are equivalent. With N identical agents in the economy, the total change in population in an economy with net fertility n is given by

$$\dot{N}_t = n_t N_t. \tag{14}$$

We start the economy at time 0 with $N_0 > 0$ given.

Capital accumulates in this economy in the form of assets owned by members of the dynastic family. Letting v denote the per capita stock of assets ($K = Nv$ is imposed later, and $K_0 > 0$ is assumed),

$$\dot{v}_t = (r_t - n_t)v_t + w_t[1 - \beta(n_t)] - c_t - f_t, \tag{15}$$

where r is the market return on assets, w is the wage rate per unit of labor, and f represents per capita lump-sum taxes collected by the government ($f \equiv F/N$).

The final component of the technology of the economy is the production of ideas. New ideas are produced by researchers according to

$$\dot{A}_t = \bar{\delta}_t L_{At}, \tag{16}$$

where L_A denotes labor engaged in research, and $\dot{A}$ represents the measure of new ideas created at a point in time. The resource constraint on labor is

$$L_{At} + L_{Yt} = [1 - \beta(n_t)] N_t \equiv L_t. \tag{17}$$

While individual researchers, who are small relative to the total number of researchers, take $\bar{\delta}$ as given, it may, in fact, depend on features of the aggregate economy. The true relationship between new ideas and research is assumed to be given by

$$\dot{A}_t = \delta L_{At}^\lambda A_t^\phi, \tag{18}$$

where $\delta > 0$, $0 < \lambda \leq 1$, and $\phi < 1$ are parameters. This formulation allows for both positive and negative externalities in research. At a point in time, congestion or duplication in research may reduce the social value of a marginal unit of research, associated with $\lambda < 1$. In addition, the productivity of research today may depend either positively (knowledge spillovers) or negatively (fishing out) on the stock of ideas discovered in the past. Equation (18) therefore allows for increasing, constant, or decreasing returns to scale in the production of new ideas.

4.3. Market Structure

Romer (1990) and others have emphasized that ideas are nonrivalrous but partially excludable. The assumption that ideas are at least partially excludable allows inventors to capture some of the social value that they create. This feature, together with the increasing returns to scale implied by nonrivalry, leads Romer, Grossman and Helpman, and Aghion and Howitt to favor models with profit-maximizing entrepreneurs and imperfect competition—what we might call "Silicon Valley" models.

Here, we will make an alternative assumption that will have the flavor of growth through basic science. In particular, we assume that ideas are nonrivalrous and nonexcludable; that is, they are pure public goods.[12] This means that inventors cannot use the market mechanism to capture any of the social value they create. In the absence of some nonmarket intervention, no one would become a researcher because of the fundamental ineffectiveness of property rights over basic science, and there would be no growth.

This alternative assumption serves two purposes. The primary purpose is that it greatly simplifies the analysis of the decentralized model. We assume that all markets are perfectly competitive and then introduce a government to collect lump-sum taxes and use the revenues to fund research publicly. Of course, this case may also be of independent interest. Previous Silicon Valley–style models have analyzed the case in which research is undertaken by private entrepreneurs who are compensated through imperfectly competitive markets. This chapter explores the alternative extreme in which growth is associated with basic science undertaken by publicly funded scientists.

The government collects lump-sum taxes F from individuals and uses this revenue to hire research scientists at the market wage w. We assume that the government collects as much revenue as needed so that a constant fraction of the labor force, $0 < \bar{s} < 1$, is hired as researchers: that is, $L_A = \bar{s}L$.

4.4. Equilibrium

A competitive equilibrium in this model is a sequence of quantities $\{c_t, Y_t, K_t, A_t, v_t, L_{Yt}, L_{At}, N_t, n_t\}$, prices $\{w_t, r_t\}$, and lump-sum taxes $\{F_t\}$ such that:

1. The head of the dynastic family chooses $\{c_t, n_t\}$ to maximize dynastic utility in equation (10) subject to the laws of motion for asset accumulation (15) and population (14), taking $\{r_t, w_t, F_t\}$ and v_0 and N_0 as given.
2. Firms producing output rent capital K_t and labor L_{Yt} to maximize profits, taking the rental prices r_t and w_t and the stock of ideas A_t as given.
3. Markets clear at the prices $\{w_t, r_t\}$ and the taxes $\{F_t\}$. In particular, the stock of assets held by consumers V_t is equal to the total capital stock K_t, and the number of researchers is a constant fraction $\bar{s}$ of the labor force.

---

12. See Shell (1966) for an early application of this approach.

We now characterize the competitive equilibrium in steady state, that is, when all variables are growing at constant (exponential) rates.

The first-order conditions from the utility maximization problem for individuals imply that the steady-state fertility rate chosen by the dynastic family satisfies[13]:

$$\frac{(r - g_Y)[v_t + w\beta'(n)]}{\tilde{N}_t} = \frac{u_{\tilde{N}t}}{u_{ct}}. \tag{19}$$

This equation is the dynamic equivalent of the condition that the marginal rate of transformation (the left-hand side) equals the marginal rate of substitution (the right-hand side) between people and consumption. The marginal rate of transformation is based on the cost to the individual of increasing fertility, which involves two terms. First, there is a capital-narrowing effect: adding to the population dilutes the stock of assets per person. Second, there is the direct cost of wages that are foregone in order to increase the population growth rate. The total cost is scaled by the size of the population so that it is measured in terms of bodies rather than as a rate of growth, and it is multiplied by the effective discount rate $r - g_Y$ to put it on a flow basis. This marginal rate of transformation is equal to the static marginal rate of substitution $u_{\tilde{N}}/u_c$ along the optimal balanced growth path.

This relationship makes it clear why a unit elasticity of substitution between people and consumption is required. The marginal rate of transformation on the left-hand side of equation (19) will end up being proportional to $y/\tilde{N}$, where y is per capita output Y/N. Therefore, the marginal rate of substitution must be proportional to $c/\tilde{N}$ for a balanced growth path to exist; otherwise, the cost and the benefit of fertility will grow at different rates and the economy will be pushed to a corner. The equation also makes clear why the curvature $\beta''(n) > 0$ is required: with $\beta(n) = 1 - \beta n$, for example, equation (19) does not depend directly on n, and households will move to a corner solution.

Other first-order conditions characterizing the equilibrium are more familiar. For example, consumption growth satisfies the following Euler equation:

$$\dot{c}_t/c_t = r_t - n_t - \rho. \tag{20}$$

Also, the first-order conditions from the firm's profit-maximization problem, assuming no depreciation, are

$$r_t = \alpha Y_t/K_t$$

and

$$w_t = \frac{(1-\alpha)Y_t}{L_{Yt}} = (1-\alpha)y_t \cdot \frac{1}{1 - \beta(n_t)} \cdot \frac{1}{1 - \bar{s}}. \tag{21}$$

---

13. Robert Barro, in work in progress, shows that with an intertemporal elasticity of substitution equal to one, if we replace $r - g_Y$ with ρ, this condition holds at all points in time, not just along a balanced growth path.

With these first-order conditions in mind, we are ready to characterize the steady-state growth rate of the economy. Along the balanced growth path, the key growth rates of the model are all given by the growth rate of the stock of ideas:

$$g_y = g_k = g_c = \frac{\sigma}{1 - \alpha} g_A, \tag{22}$$

where g_z denotes growth rate of some variable z along the balanced growth path, y is per capita income Y/N, and k is capital per person K/N.[14]

The growth rate of ideas, g_A, is found by dividing both sides of equation (18) by A:

$$\frac{\dot{A}_t}{A_t} = \delta \frac{L_{At}^\lambda}{A_t^{1-\phi}}.$$

Along a balanced growth path, the numerator and the denominator of the right-hand side of this expression must grow at the same rate, and this requirement pins down the growth rate of A as

$$g_A = \frac{\lambda}{1 - \phi} g_{L_A}.$$

Finally, along a balanced growth path, L_A must grow at the rate of growth of the population. Therefore,

$$g_A = \frac{\lambda n}{1 - \phi}. \tag{23}$$

Combining this result with equation (22), we see that

$$g_y = \gamma n, \tag{24}$$

where $\gamma \equiv [\sigma/(1 - \alpha)][\lambda/(1 - \phi)]$.

As in Jones (1995), the per capita growth rate of the economy is proportional to the population growth rate. This is a direct consequence of increasing returns to scale: With $\sigma = 0$, there is no per capita growth in the long run. Note that balanced growth in the presence of population growth in this model requires $\alpha < 1$ and $\phi < 1$. That is, the capital accumulation equation and the law of motion for ideas must both be less than linear in their own state variables; otherwise, growth explodes and the level of consumption and income is infinite in a finite amount of time.

---

14. This relationship is derived as follows. First, the constancy-of-consumption growth requires a constant interest rate and therefore a constant capital-output ratio, yielding the first equality. Second, the asset accumulation equation in (15) is simply a standard capital accumulation equation. For the capital stock to grow at a constant rate, the capital-consumption ratio must be constant, yielding the second equality. Finally, log differentiating the production function in (12) yields the last equality.

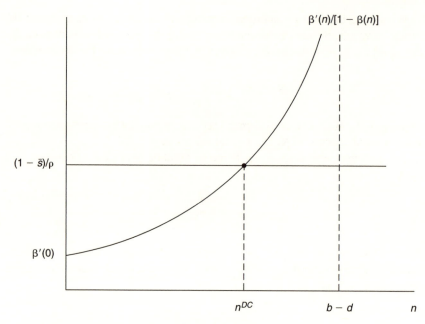

Figure 1. Solving for n^{DC}.

4.5. Fertility in the Decentralized Economy

The rate of population growth is determined by consumer optimization, as in equation (19). Using the fact that $\epsilon = 1$ and $r - g_Y = \rho$ along a balanced growth path, and substituting for the wage from equation (21), equation (19) can be written as

$$k_t + (1 - \alpha)y_t \cdot \frac{\beta'(n)}{1 - \beta(n)} \cdot \frac{1}{1 - \bar{s}} = \frac{1}{\rho}c_t. \qquad (25)$$

Some algebra then shows that along a balanced growth path, the rate of fertility satisfies[15]

$$\frac{\beta'(n^{DC})}{1 - \beta(n^{DC})} = \frac{1 - \bar{s}}{\rho}. \qquad (26)$$

The solution to this equation exists and is unique under the assumption that $\beta'(0) < (1 - \bar{s})/\rho$, as shown in Figure 1. Recall that the relationship in equation (24) that $g_y = \gamma n$ then determines the growth rate of the economy along the balanced growth path.

The steady-state growth rate of the economy is directly proportional to the net fertility rate. This rate is smaller the higher is the rate of time preference ρ or the

---

15. Specifically, divide both sides of the equation by k and use the fact that $y/k = r/\alpha$ and $c/k = y/k - g_Y = (1 - \alpha)/\alpha * r + \rho$ along a balanced growth path.

higher is the cost of fertility $\beta(\cdot)$. Interestingly, the growth rate of the economy is *decreasing* rather than increasing in the fraction of the labor force devoted to research. This is very different from the results in previous idea-based growth models and reflects the fact that growth is driven by a different mechanism. Here, changes in research intensity affect long-run growth only through their effect on fertility. A larger research sector takes labor away from the alternative use of producing offspring, which reduces population growth and therefore reduces steady-state per capita growth. It is important to note that this long-run effect is quite different from the short-run effect. In the short run, an increase in the fraction of the labor force devoted to research will lead to more new ideas and a faster rate of growth. Only in the long run is the fertility effect apparent.

5. WELFARE AND A PLANNER PROBLEM

With more than one generation of agents, it is not obvious how to define social welfare: It depends on how one weights the utility of different generations. We focus on a narrower question: Does the allocation of resources achieved in the market economy maximize the utility of each dynastic family given the initial conditions that constrain their choices?

To maximize the welfare of a representative generation (the generation alive at time zero here), the social planner solves

$$\max_{\{c_t, s_t, n_t\}} U_0 = \int_0^\infty e^{-\rho t} u(c_t, \tilde{N}_{0,t}) \, dt, \tag{27}$$

subject to

$$\dot{k}_t = A_t^\sigma k_t^\alpha (1 - s_t)^{1-\alpha} [1 - \beta(n_t)]^{1-\alpha} - c_t - n_t k_t, \tag{28}$$

$$\dot{A}_t = \delta s_t^\lambda [1 - \beta(n_t)]^\lambda N_t^\lambda A_t^\phi, \tag{29}$$

and

$$\dot{N}_t = n_t N_t. \tag{30}$$

The first-order conditions from this maximization problem can be combined to yield several equations of interest. First, optimal consumption satisfies a standard Euler equation

$$\frac{\dot{c}_t}{c_t} = \alpha \frac{y_t}{k_t} - n_t - \rho. \tag{31}$$

Second, the first-order conditions together with the equations governing the law of motion for capital and ideas can be solved to yield optimal research intensity in the steady state:

$$s^{SP} = \frac{1}{1 + \psi^{SP}}, \tag{32}$$

where

$$\psi^{SP} = \frac{1-\alpha}{\lambda\sigma}\left[\frac{\rho(1-\phi)}{\lambda n} + 1 - \phi\right].$$

To solve for the steady-state rate of population growth, we follow the steps used for the decentralized model. The first-order conditions from the planner's problem can be combined to yield a condition analogous to equation (19) in steady state:

$$\left[k_t + (1-\alpha)y_t \cdot \frac{\beta'(n^{SP})}{1 - \beta(n^{SP})} \cdot \frac{1}{1 - s^{SP}}\right]\frac{\rho}{\tilde{N}_t} = \frac{u_{\tilde{N}t}}{u_{ct}} + \mu_{2t}\lambda\frac{\dot{A}_t}{\tilde{N}_t}, \tag{33}$$

where μ_2 is the shadow value of an idea [the co-state variable corresponding to equation (29)].

The distortion that affects fertility choice can be seen by comparing this equation to the corresponding condition in the decentralized model, either equation (19) or (25). Individual agents ignore the extra benefit associated with increasing returns to scale provided by additional population. This distortion is reflected by the presence of the second term on the right-hand side of equation (33), which corresponds to the utility value of the extra ideas created by an additional person.

Some additional algebra reveals that, along the balanced growth path, the optimal fertility rate satisfies[16]

$$\frac{\beta'(n^{SP})}{1 - \beta(n^{SP})} = \frac{1}{\rho}. \tag{34}$$

Finally, the optimal steady-state growth rate of per capita income is given by $g_y^{SP} = \gamma n^{SP}$.

A comparison of equations (26) and (34) indicates that steady-state fertility and growth are inefficiently too slow in the decentralized economy, as shown in Figure 2. This results from the fact that, as noted above, individuals ignore the economy-wide benefit of fertility that is associated with increasing returns to scale: A larger population generates more ideas that benefit all agents in the economy. This is the "Mozart effect" mentioned by Phelps (1968).

In more general models that I have explored, this result can be overturned. For example, when the kernel of the utility function is generalized to place a higher weight on offspring, that is, when $\epsilon > 1$, it is possible for the decentralized economy to have a fertility rate and therefore a growth rate that is inefficiently too high. This occurs if $\bar{s}$ is sufficiently smaller than s^{SP}.[17] Second, fertility and

---

16. Once again, divide both sides of the equation by k and use the fact that $y/k = r/\alpha$ and $c/k = y/k - g_Y = (1-\alpha)/\alpha * r + \rho$ along a balanced growth path.

17. To see part of the intuition, recall that from the standpoint of the decentralized economy, a lower research intensity increases fertility.

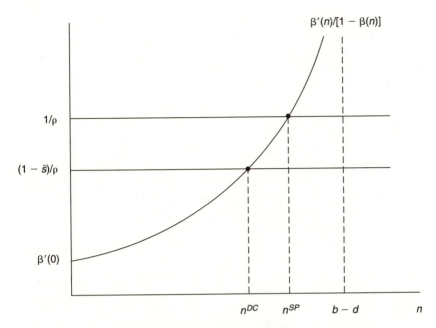

Figure 2. Comparing n^{DC} and n^{SP}.

growth can be inefficiently high in a model in which the Romer (1990) market structure is used instead of the perfectly competitive/basic science market structure. With the imperfectly competitive market structure of Romer, capital is underpaid relative to its marginal product so that some resources are available to compensate entrepreneurs. However, recall that part of the opportunity cost of fertility is the additional capital that must be provided to offspring. Imperfect competition reduces this cost and can lead to inefficiently high fertility and growth.

6. DISCUSSION

This extended example contains a number of predictions about long-run growth, some of which are found in earlier papers and some of which are new. First, the "scale effects" prediction that has been a key problem in many endogenous growth models turns out to be a key feature in this model. Increasing returns to scale implies that the scale of the economy will matter. Instead of affecting (counterfactually) the long-run growth rate, however, scale affects the long-run *level* of per capita income. Large populations generate more ideas than small populations, and because ideas are nonrivalrous, the larger number of ideas translates into higher per capita income. Endogenous growth in the scale of the economy through fertility leads to endogenous growth in per capita income.

Changes in government policies can affect the long-run growth rate by affecting the rate of fertility. For example, suppose that for each child, parents have to pay a fraction of their wages in taxes. Such a tax will reduce fertility and therefore reduce per capita growth.

Other policies can also affect population growth and per capita growth in the model, but the effects are often counterintuitive on the surface. Specifically, the imposition of many taxes in the model will increase rather than decrease long-run growth (though once again, the short-run effects and the welfare effects can go in the opposite direction). For example, a tax on labor income creates a wedge between working and child-rearing, the untaxed activity, and will increase fertility and per capita growth. A tax on capital reduces the opportunity cost of fertility by reducing the capital stock and wages and therefore will also increase growth. Finally, as we have already seen, an increase in an existing government subsidy to research will reduce long-run growth in the model. Note that increasing the research subsidy may easily be welfare improving here, but not, as is often argued, because it increases the long-run growth rate.[18] In general, these results emphasize the important point that long-run growth and welfare are different and may even respond to policy changes in opposite directions.

What policies should the government follow in this model to obtain the socially optimal allocation of resources? At least in steady state, the policy turns out to be very simple and conventional, contrary to the counterintuitive results just mentioned. Suppose the government taxes labor income at rate τ_L and uses the revenue to fund research, with no lump-sum rebates or taxes. In this case, it is easy to show that steady-state fertility achieves its socially optimal level. Moreover, the share of labor employed in research, $\bar{s}$, is equal to the tax rate τ_L. Therefore, by choosing a labor income tax rate of $\tau_L = s^{SP}$, the fraction of labor working in research as well as the steady-state fertility and growth rate match the social optimum.

A final issue worth considering is the plausibility of the way endogenous fertility is modeled. The assumption of a unit elasticity of substitution between consumption and offspring in the dynastic utility function is crucial for delivering sustained exponential growth in population, and therefore in per capita income. However, it is far from clear that future population growth will actually be sustained. For example, fertility rates throughout the world appear to be falling and demographic projections by the U.S. Bureau of the Census and the World Bank suggest that world population may stabilize at some point far into the future—maybe the twenty-third century (Doyle, 1997).

Jones (2001) examines a model with an elasticity of substitution greater than one in a study of growth over the very long run. In this case, the model generates a demographic transition similar to that observed in the advanced countries of the world and, at least for some parameterizations, suggests that population levels may stabilize. An important prediction of such a model is that exponential growth in per capita incomes would not be sustained. This does not mean that growth would necessarily cease, however. For example, a constant number of researchers could potentially generate a constant number of new ideas, leading to arithmetical rather than exponential growth.

---

18. In all of the examples in this paragraph, it is assumed that the tax revenue collected is rebated lump sum to the agents. The behavioral changes result from the substitution effects; without the lump-sum rebates, the income effect will neutralize the substitution effect.

In this sense, the framework does not necessarily suggest that sustained exponential growth must continue forever. As indicated earlier, linearity in the population equation does not guarantee growth; this depends on fertility behavior. Sustained growth seems to be a good description of the advanced economies for the last century or so. But if the model is correct, the future of per capita growth will hinge on the ability of the world economy to continue to devote more and more quality-adjusted resources to the production of new ideas.

7. CONCLUSION

Recent research has led to a large number of potential explanations for the engine of economic growth. Distinguishing among these explanations is important, both from a scientific standpoint and from a policy perspective. Some explanations suggest that increases in public investment in physical capital would be appropriate and others point to subsidies to private investment. Some suggest that imperfect competition and incentives for innovation are key and others stress the formation of human capital. Some suggest that growth rates may be much higher in the future, and others say that they will be much lower.

In order to generate sustained exponential growth like that observed in the United States for the last 125 years, models of growth require a differential equation that is linear, or at least very nearly so. Following the suggestion of Solow (1956), this chapter proposes that a successful theory of economic growth should provide an intuitive and compelling justification for this crucial assumption.

After proposing this standard to which our future models should aspire, the chapter attempts to make some progress. We begin by pointing out that, taking population growth as a given, it is possible to understand the exponential growth in per capita income without appealing to any additional linearity. Instead, the increasing returns to scale associated with the nonrivalry of ideas combined with the historical presence of population growth implies per capita growth.

The remainder of the chapter explores a model in which both population growth and per capita growth emerge endogenously. The crucial linearity appears in the law of motion for population, and the chapter argues this is a more natural location for linearity than other locations considered in existing growth models. Each family chooses a number of children to have, $\tilde{n}$. With N such agents in the economy, the net increase in population is given by $\dot{N} = nN$, where $n = \tilde{n} - d$. In other words, in deciding how many children to have, individuals choose the *proportional* rate of increase in the population. The linearity of the law of motion for population results from the biological fact of nature that people reproduce in proportion to their number. By itself, however, this linearity is not sufficient to generate per capita growth.

The second key ingredient of the model is increasing returns to scale. In line with the reasoning of Romer (1990) and others, increasing returns also seems to be a fact of nature. Ideas are a central feature of the world we live in. Ideas are nonrivalrous. Nonrivalry implies increasing returns to scale. This line of reasoning, rather than placing the key linearity in the equation of motion for technological progress, is the fundamental insight of the idea-based growth models, according to the view in this chapter. Endogenous fertility and increasing returns, both motivated from first principles, are the key ingredients in an explanation of sustained and endogenous per capita growth.

REFERENCES

Acemoglu, D. (2001), "Labor- and Capital-Augmenting Technical Change," mimeo, MIT.

Aghion, P. and P. Howitt (1992), "A Model of Growth through Creative Destruction," *Econometrica* 60(2):323–51.

Arrow, K. J. (1962), "The Economic Implications of Learning by Doing," *Review of Economic Studies* 29:153–73.

Barro, R. J. (1974), "Are Government Bonds Net Wealth?," *Journal of Political Economy* 82:1095–117.

Barro, R. J. and G. S. Becker (1989), "Fertility Choice in a Model of Economic Growth," *Econometrica* 57(2):481–501.

Barro, R. J. and X. Sala-i-Martin (1995), *Economic Growth*, New York: McGraw-Hill.

Becker, G. S. and R. J. Barro (1988), "A Reformulation of the Economic Theory of Fertility," *Quarterly Journal of Economics* 108(1):1–25.

Ben-David, D. and D. H. Papell (1995), "The Great Wars, the Great Crash, and Steady-State Growth: Some New Evidence about an Old Stylized Fact," *Journal of Monetary Economics* 36:453–75.

Blanchard, O. J. (1985), "Debts, Deficits, and Finite Horizons," *Journal of Political Economy* 93(2):223–47.

Cannon, E. (1998), "Economies of Scale and Constant Returns to Capital: A Neglected Early Contribution to the Theory of Economic Growth," mimeo, University of Bristol.

Dasgupta, P. S. (1969), "On the Concept of Optimum Population," *Review of Economic Studies* 36:295–318.

Dinopoulos, E. and P. Thompson (1998), "Schumpeterian Growth without Scale Effects," *Journal of Economic Growth* 3(4):313–35.

Doyle, R. (1997), "By the Numbers, Global Fertility and Population," *Scientific American* 276:26.

Drandakis, E. M. and E. S. Phelps (1966), "A Model of Induced Invention, Growth, and Distribution," *Economic Journal* 76(304):823–40.

Grossman, G. M. and E. Helpman (1989), "Product Development and International Trade," *Journal of Political Economy* 97(6):1261–83.

———— (1991), *Innovation and Growth in the Global Economy*, Cambridge: MIT Press.

Howitt, P. (1999), "Steady Endogenous Growth with Population and R&D Inputs Growing," *Journal of Political Economy* 107(4):715–30.

Jones, C. I. (1995), "R&D-Based Models of Economic Growth," *Journal of Political Economy* 103(4):759–84.

———— (1999), "Growth: With or Without Scale Effects?," *American Economic Association Papers and Proceedings* 89:139–44.

———— (2001), "Was an Industrial Revolution Inevitable? Economic Growth over the Very Long Run," *Advances in Macroeconomics* 1(2): Article 1. http://www.bepress.com/bejm/advances/vol1/iss2/art1.

———— (2002), "Sources of U.S. Economic Growth in a World of Ideas," *American Economic Review* 92(1):220–39.

Jones, L. E. and R. Manuelli (1990), "A Convex Model of Economic Growth: Theory and Policy Implications," *Journal of Political Economy* 98:1008–38.

Judd, K. L. (1985), "On the Performance of Patents," *Econometrica* 53(3):567–85.

Kennedy, C. M. (1964), "Induced Bias in Innovation and the Theory of Distribution," *Economic Journal* 74(295):541–47.

Kortum, S. S. (1997), "Research, Patenting, and Technological Change," *Econometrica* 65(6):1389–419.

Kremer, M. (1993), "Population Growth and Technological Change: One Million B.C. to 1990," *Quarterly Journal of Economics* 108(4):681–716.

Lucas, R. E. (1988), "On the Mechanics of Economic Development," *Journal of Monetary Economics* 22(1):3–42.

Mulligan, C. B. and X. Sala-i-Martin (1993), "Transitional Dynamics in Two-Sector Models of Endogenous Growth," *Quarterly Journal of Economics* 108(3):739–74.

Nordhaus, W. D. (1969), "An Economic Theory of Technological Change," *American Economic Association Papers and Proceedings* 59:18–28.

Peretto, P. (1998), "Technological Change and Population Growth," *Journal of Economic Growth* 3(4):283–311.

Phelps, E. S. (1966), "Models of Technical Progress and the Golden Rule of Research," *Review of Economic Studies* 33:133–45.

———— (1968), "Population Increase," *Canadian Journal of Economics* 1(3):497–518.

Pitchford, J. (1972), "Population and Optimal Growth," *Econometrica* 40(1):109–36.

Raut, L. K. and T. N. Srinivasan (1994), "Dynamics of Endogenous Growth," *Economic Theory* 4:777–90.

Razin, A. and U. Ben-Zion (1975), "An Intergenerational Model of Population Growth," *American Economic Review* 65(5):923–33.

Rebelo, S. (1991), "Long-Run Policy Analysis and Long-Run Growth," *Journal of Political Economy* 99:500–21.

Romer, P. M. (1987), "Crazy Explanations for the Productivity Slowdown," in S. Fischer, ed., *NBER Macroeconomics Annual*, Cambridge: MIT Press.

———— (1990), "Endogenous Technological Change," *Journal of Political Economy* 98(5): S71–102.

———— (1995), "Comment on a Paper by T. N. Srinivasan," in *Growth Theories in Light of the East Asian Experience*, Chicago: University of Chicago Press.

Segerstrom, P. (1998), "Endogenous Growth Without Scale Effects," *American Economic Review* 88(5):1290–310.

Shell, K. (1966), "Toward a Theory of Inventive Activity and Capital Accumulation," *American Economic Association Papers and Proceedings* 56:62–68.

Sheshinski, E. (1967), "Optimal Accumulation with Learning by Doing," in K. Shell, ed., *Essays on the Theory of Economic Growth*, Cambridge: MIT Press.

Simon, J. L. (1981), *The Ultimate Resource*, Princeton: Princeton University Press.

Solow, R. M. (1956), "A Contribution to the Theory of Economic Growth," *Quarterly Journal of Economics* 70:65–94.

———— (1994), "Perspectives on Growth Theory," *Journal of Economic Perspectives* 8(1): 45–54.

Stiglitz, J. E. (1990), "Comments: Some Retrospective Views on Growth Theory," in P. Diamond, ed., *Growth/Productivity/Unemployment: Essays to Celebrate Robert Solow's Birthday*, Cambridge: MIT Press, pp. 50–69.

Swan, T. W. (1956), "Economic Growth and Capital Accumulation," *The Economic Record* 32:334–61.

Young, A. (1998), "Growth without Scale Effects," *Journal of Political Economy* 106(1):41–63.

—— 26 ——

Another View of Investment: 40 Years Later

JESS BENHABIB AND BART HOBIJN

1. INTRODUCTION

Does it matter if the growth of productivity is driven by disembodied technological change that raises the productivity of all factors of production, including all capital in place, or by continuous improvements in the quality of new capital goods? This is the central question of the embodiment issue that has been widely debated among macroeconomists. The answer to the question must distinguish between the long and the short run.

Long-run considerations focus on the dependence of steady-state values on the composition of the sources of economic growth. This research agenda was set by Phelps (1962), who showed, among other things, that the elasticity of the steady-state level of output with respect to the savings rate does not depend on the composition of embodied and disembodied technological progress. [For the debate that followed see also Matthews (1964), Phelps and Yaari (1964), Levhari and Sheshinski (1967), Hall (1968), and Fisher et al. (1969).] Following Phelps (1962), Denison (1964) developed the empirical case for the unimportance of the embodiment question, and the spate of literature on the long-run consequences of embodied technical progress subsided.[1]

Short-run considerations focus on the business cycle implications of embodied versus disembodied technological change. Recent works on this subject by De Jong et al. (2000), Gilchrist and Williams (2000), and Greenwood et al. (2000) study the transitional dynamics of various vintage capital models. Our main focus is also on the short-run implications of embodied technological change. In particular, we are interested in whether investment-driven economic expansions stimulated by significant innovations and quality improvements in capital goods tend to produce subsequent economic slowdowns.

This question is of particular relevance for current economic developments. As Tevlin and Whelan (2000) have documented, the economic expansion of the

---

1. In more recent work, Boucekinne et al. (1999) suggest that the composition of the sources of growth may affect long-run properties of an economy if technological change is endogenous.

The views expressed in this chapter do not necessarily reflect those of the Federal Reserve Bank of New York or those of the Federal Reserve System in general.

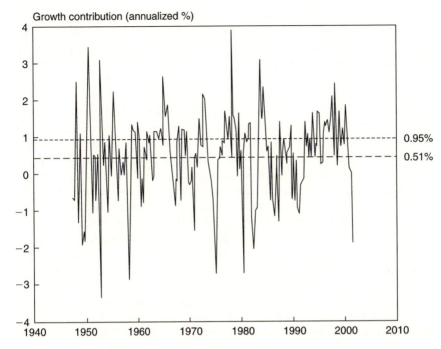

Figure 1. Contribution of investment to GDP growth.

1990s was mainly driven by an economy-wide investment boom, particularly in computers and software. To illustrate this point we plot the contribution of fixed private nonresidential investment to overall GDP growth. Apart from the significant drag that investment has on GDP growth in the first and second quarters of 2001, the most remarkable observation about the recent past is the unprecedented contribution of investment to the 1990s expansion. In particular, the average growth contribution of investment to GDP in the postwar period is about 0.51 percent, while that in the period 1992–2000 is 0.95 percent. Furthermore, this is not due to a particular outlier in the 1990s, but rather to an unprecedented sustained increase in the importance of investment in GDP growth.

On the downside, recent newspaper accounts have now claimed that the 2001 U.S. economic slowdown may be different than previous slowdowns and recessions. It is claimed that the culprit for the unexpected severity of the investment bust is the sustained investment boom of the 1990s.[2] According to this view, the current

---

2. For example, *The Economist* of June 30, 2001, suggests (in "Another Shot from Dr. Feelgood: Will the Fed's Latest Cut in the Interest Rate Get the Economy Moving Again?," pp. 26–27): "In contrast to the post-war norm the expansion was not "murdered" by the Federal Reserve. The contraction started with an invstment bust, as firms that had radically overinvested during the boom years of the late 1990s suddenly cut back. This collapse of capital spending lies behind the recession in American industry." See also Robert Reich, "How Long Can Consumers Keep Spending," *New York Times*, September 2, 2001, Week in Review Section, p. 9.

bust is indeed the result of an excessive investment boom fueled by overoptimistic expectations generated by the information technology "revolution." Another older view, advocated as early as the beginning of the last century, suggests that major aggregative technological innovations, such as the steam engine, electricity, or more recently information technology, give rise to a burst of new investment, inevitably followed by low investment activity once the initial phase of plant and equipment replacement and modernization is completed. Indeed, further down the line as these new plants and equipment have to be scrapped, damped investment echoes may be observed (see Robertson, 1915), giving rise to oscillatory transition dynamics of output and employment. A key point is that the investment boom and subsequent slowdown in economic activity need not arise entirely from mistakes of optimism (dotcom bankruptcies notwithstanding), but may represent the normal course of planned modernizations and replacement investments. No doubt techno-logical innovations that are pervasive enough to stimulate substantial investments across a wide range of industries are rare events and probably hard to observe systematically in high-frequency data. Therefore there may be some validity to the suggestion that the current slowdown differs from the recent others that have been caused and driven by declines in consumption expenditures.

The purpose of this chapter is to study economic propagation mechanisms of vintage models for economies that experience various embodied or disembodied technological innovations major enough to give rise to bursts of aggregate invest-ment activity. While technological innovations may indeed provide the rationale for sudden bursts of investment, a critical element of our analysis relies on the struc-ture of depreciation and economic obsolescence that departs from the standard radioactive exponential form. Whether scrapping old equipment is endogenous or not, to the extent that scrapping must occur owing to physical and economic obsolescence, investment booms will be followed by slowdowns in economic activity and subsequent echo effects. The induced transition dynamics in output, consumption, and employment may then be quite complex. The initial phases of technological innovations may also see accelerated replacement and adoption waves, especially if there is some persistence in the rate of innovation. We will see that if technological change is of the embodied kind, investment booms will give rise to subsequent busts, generating a hump-shaped response in output levels.

We introduce a vintage capital model that specifically allows for the scrappage of capital goods and thus for echo effects. We show that in our economy Phelps's (1962) long-run result on the independence of the elasticity of output with respect to the savings rate does not hold if labor supply is endogenous. We then show that the short-run dynamics of the economy is very different when driven by embodied technology shocks rather than by the disembodied productivity shocks that are conventionally considered in the business cycle literature. In particular, we will see that echo effects are much more profound in investment-driven expansions caused by embodied technological change than in those driven by standard Hicks neutral productivity shocks.

Our plan of action is as follows. In order to illustrate the basic mechanism for short-term propagation mechanisms, in Section 2 we give an illustrative example of a simple vintage capital model that generates echo effects. We then proceed with the introduction of our more general model in Section 3. Section 4 is devoted to the steady-state properties of our model economy, where we duplicate Phelps's (1962) result in the context of our framework but show how it fails to hold when labor supply is endogenous. In Section 5 we address the question of how embodied and disembodied technological change affects the transitional dynamics of the economy. We provide an analysis of impulse responses to technological shocks under various parameterizations to illustrate the propagation mechanisms and the main intuition behind our results. In particular we illustrate how in our model disembodied shocks generate hump-shaped impulse responses in output whereas disembodied shocks do not. Finally, in Section 6, we conclude, and a technical appendix follows.

2. A SIMPLE ILLUSTRATIVE VINTAGE MODEL

We start by presenting a simplified vintage capital model for expository purposes. In the simplified model, our economy consists of a single representative agent, supplying a fixed quantity of labor L. Output is produced by allocating labor to each vintage of capital. Each vintage of capital, and the labor allocated to it, then produces output according to a constant-returns-to-scale production function. The agent maximizes the discounted utility of future consumption:

$$\max_{k} \sum_{t=0}^{\infty} \beta^t U \left[\sum_{\tau=0}^{T} f \left(k_{t-\tau}, A_{t-\tau} l_{t-\tau}^t \right) - k_{t+1} \right],$$

where $\beta < 1$ is the discount factor, $A_{t-\tau}$ is embodied technological progress that makes newer vintages more productive, $k_{t-\tau}$ is capital of vintage $t - \tau$ used at time t, $l_{t-\tau}^t$ is labor at t allocated to $k_{t-\tau}$, and f is the constant-returns-to-scale neoclassical production function for each vintage. We take the scrappage time for vintages as exogenous: vintages last $T + 1$ periods.[3] The labor market constraint requires that labor supply exceed labor demand, such that $L \geq \sum_{\tau=0}^{T} l_{t-\tau}^t$.

The Euler equation for this problem, assuming interiority, is given by

$$U'(c_t) = \sum_{s=0}^{T} \beta^{s+1} U'(c_{t+1+s}) f_k \left(k_{t+1}, A_{t+1} l_{t+1}^{t+1+s} \right).$$

This equation simply states that the marginal utility of forgone consumption today equals the discounted value of the future marginal products, measured in utility,

---

3. This again is for simplicity. If f was a CES production function with an elasticity of substitution less than unity, then older depreciated vintages that are less efficient would not be allocated any labor. By contrast if f has an elasticity of substitution greater than unity or is Cobb-Douglas, all existing vintages would be allocated some labor, because the production function f satisfies Inada conditions in this case. Since our analysis and results only require a finite truncation, whether fixed and exogenous or variable and endogenous, we adopt the simpler exogenous specification (see also Benhabib and Rustichini, 1991). For the case where T may be endogenous see Benhabib and Rustichini (1993). Note also that for notational simplicity we suppress any ongoing depreciation that may occur before scrappage.

of a unit investment in today's vintage capital. Note that at a steady state, or if utility is linear so that U' cancels on both sides of the Euler equation above, we have the discounted sum of marginal products of a unit investment today equal to unity. Thus if there is an increase in the marginal product of the latest vintage, there will be a burst of investment in the newest vintage (nonnegativity constraints on consumption allowing) to "reequate" this composite discounted marginal product to the discount rate. Subsequent investment will drop, but when the initial vintage with a spike is finally scrapped, another smaller burst of investment will take place to maintain the equality of the discounted composite marginal product to the discount rate, resulting in damped echoes. These investment dynamics, depending on the nature of the technology shock, will have implications for the dynamics of employment, consumption, and output. In particular, output may exhibit a hump-shaped impulse response to technological innovations with a peak beyond T, the lifetime of equipment, and employment may also follow the oscillatory pattern induced by investment expenditures.

The model with linear utility, however, is likely to generate echo effects that are too pronounced. Nonlinear utility dampens echoes by introducing consumption smoothing, while at the same time preserving the impact effects of a technological innovation on investment.[4] Therefore, we generalize the model to include non-linear utility and we specify various types of shocks to more thoroughly explore the propagation mechanisms induced by technological innovations that simultaneously affect a large number of industries.

3. THE VINTAGE CAPITAL MODEL WITH TECHNOLOGY SHOCKS

We are interested in the short-run dynamic consequences of shocks to embodied and disembodied technological change in an economy in which capital goods are scrapped and give rise to echo effects. We construct a stochastic general equilibrium model with vintage capital in which: (1) there are stochastic shocks to embodied as well as disembodied technological change, (2) there is exogenous scrappage of capital goods, and (3) we allow (as an extra) for capital goods of different vintages to be complementary.

We introduce the model in three steps. The final model with which we study transitional dynamics is a reduced form of an underlying standard vintage capital model. Therefore we first introduce the underlying vintage capital model and then

---

4. A closed-form solution for a slightly different but related vintage model with nonlinear utility exists if the product of the intertemporal elasticity of substitution σ^{-1} in the utility function $(1-\sigma)^{-1}c^{(1-\sigma)}$ and the elasticity of substitution in a CES production function is set to unity (see Benhabib and Rustichini, 1994). This generalizes the closed-form solutions, with or without vintages, for the standard log utility–Cobb-Douglas production function combination. The solution reduces, as it does in the case with linear utility, to a constant-savings rate yielding a linear difference equation in vintages with all roots complex or negative, except that in this case of nonlinear utility, it also has a dominant Frobenius root that is positive and less than unity and controls the asymptotic dynamics (see Sato, 1970). Thus the curvature of utility calibrates propagation dynamics.

derive the reduced form on which our results are based. Finally, we summarize the reduced form.

3.1. Microfoundations

In our model economy a representative household maximizes the expected present discounted value of the stream of utilities. Let C_t denote consumption at time t and L_t be the fraction of time the household spends working. Given the stochastic processes that drive exogenous technological change, the household maximizes

$$E_t \left\{ \frac{1}{1-\sigma} \sum_{s=0}^{\infty} \beta^s \left[C_t^{\phi} (1 - L_t)^{1-\phi} \right]^{1-\sigma} \right\},$$

subject to the resource constraint

$$C_t = Y_t - k_{t+1},$$

the production function

$$Y_t = \left\{ \sum_{\tau=0}^{T} \left\{ \left[(1-\delta)^{\tau} k_{t-\tau} \right]^{\alpha} \left(X_t A_{t-\tau} l_{t-\tau}^t \right)^{1-\alpha} \right\}^{\theta} \right\}^{1/\theta},$$

where $\theta < 1$ and $0 < \alpha < 1$, and the labor market equilibrium condition

$$L_t = \sum_{\tau=0}^{T} l_{t-\tau}^t, \quad \text{and} \quad 0 \le L_t \le 1.$$

In this model, technological change is driven by two different sources. The first is standard disembodied technological progress, represented by X_t, which applies identically to the productivity of all capital vintages in place. The second is embodied technological change, represented by A_t, which only applies to its respective vintage.

This setup is similar to the simple model of the previous section, but differs from it in three important respects. First of all, it has an elastic labor supply. Second, it contains physical depreciation of capital, given by the exogenous rate δ. Finally and most importantly, the production function has a two-level representation. The first level is a CES aggregate of vintage-specific outputs. When $\theta = 1$, we obtain the standard case in which output is the sum of vintage-specific output levels and outputs produced using the various vintages are perfect substitutes. When $\theta < 1$, outputs produced using various vintages are complementary. For example, we could think about this as computers being complementary to other equipment already in place. The second level of the vintage production is Cobb-Douglas, which simplifies the representation and analysis of the model. The next two subsections are devoted to an exposition of these features.

3.2. Units of Measurement of Capital Goods

In the above representation we have assumed that the price of capital goods is equal to the price of consumption goods. Essentially k_t is measured in terms of consumption goods. The Cobb-Douglas specification allows us further simplification. Note that when we define $Q_t = A_t^{(1-\alpha)/\alpha}$ we have

$$k_t' = Q_t k_t.$$

We can write the resource constraint as

$$C_t = Y_t - \frac{1}{Q_{t+1}} k_{t+1}',$$

while the production function has the representation

$$Y_t = \left\{ \sum_{\tau=0}^{T} \left\{ \left[(1-\delta)^\tau Q_{t-\tau} k_{t-\tau} \right]^\alpha (X_t l_{t-\tau}^t)^{1-\alpha} \right\}^\theta \right\}^{1/\theta}$$

$$= \left\{ \sum_{\tau=0}^{T} \left\{ \left[(1-\delta)^\tau k_{t-\tau}' \right]^\alpha (X_t l_{t-\tau}^t)^{1-\alpha} \right\}^\theta \right\}^{1/\theta}.$$

Essentially, Q_t is the number of quality units of the capital good embodied in each unit of the consumption good invested at time t. Therefore, k_t' is the amount of investment measured in constant quality units of the capital good. Here Q_t is the relative price of the consumption good in terms of constant quality units of the capital good. It is the relative investment price.

Since the representation with Q_t is easier to handle than the one with A_t, in the rest of this chapter we use the representation in which investment is measured in constant quality units. For notational convenience, we drop the prime and from here on let k_t denote investment in constant quality units. This representation coincides with that chosen by Greenwood et al. (1997), who call Q_t "investment-specific technological change."

3.3. Labor Allocation and the Reduced-Form Production Function

Given this new definition of investment, the production function is

$$Y_t = \left\{ \sum_{\tau=0}^{T} \left\{ \left[(1-\delta)^\tau k_{t-\tau} \right]^\alpha (X_t l_{t-\tau}^t)^{1-\alpha} \right\}^\theta \right\}^{1/\theta}. \tag{1}$$

The optimal labor allocation problem in this economy is to choose $(l_{t-\tau}^t)_{\tau=0}^T$ in order to maximize (1) subject to the restriction that $L_t = \sum_{\tau=0}^T l_{t-\tau}^t$. This implies equating the marginal products of labor across the different vintages. This problem has a specific closed-form solution, which, after a bit of algebra, can be shown to be

$$l_{t-\tau}^t = \left\{ \frac{\left[(1-\delta)^\tau k_{t-\tau}\right]^\alpha \left(X_t l_{t-\tau}^t\right)^{1-\alpha}}{Y_t} \right\}^\theta L_t.$$

Substituting this optimal labor assignment in the production function (1), we see that the reduced-form production function satisfies

$$Y_t = \left\{ \left\{ \sum_{\tau=0}^{T} \left[(1-\delta)^\tau k_{t-\tau}\right]^{\alpha\theta/[1-(1-\alpha)\theta]} \right\}^{[1-(1-\alpha)\theta]/\alpha\theta} \right\}^\alpha (X_t L_t)^{1-\alpha}.$$

If we define $\gamma = \alpha\theta/[1 - (1-\alpha)\theta] < 1$, we can define a Jelly capital stock, similar to that conventionally derived in the vintage capital literature (see Solow, 1960):

$$J_t = \left\{ \sum_{\tau=0}^{T} \left[(1-\delta)^\tau k_{t-\tau}\right]^\gamma \right\}^{1/\gamma}.$$

Then the reduced-form production function is

$$Y_t = J_t^\alpha (X_t L_t)^{1-\alpha}.$$

Note that $\theta = 0$ implies that $\gamma = 0$. Hence, our setup generalizes the results on the existence of a capital aggregate in Fisher (1965) to the case in which total output is a CES aggregate of vintage-specific Cobb-Douglas production functions.

3.4. Reduced-Form Representation

Unlike the vintage models studied in the 1960s, the savings rate in our model is endogenous. In order to address the long-run implications derived by Phelps (1962), we introduce an investment tax credit τ_I, financed with a nondistortionary lump-sum tax denoted by τ_t. If we use the transformations of the model derived above and add the investment tax credit, in the reduced-form representation of our model, a representative household maximizes the expected present discounted value of its stream of utility levels, that is,

$$E_t \left\{ \frac{1}{1-\sigma} \sum_{s=0}^{\infty} \beta^s \left[C_t^\phi (1-L_t)^{1-\phi} \right]^{1-\sigma} \right\},$$

subject to the revised resource constraint

$$C_t = Y_t - \frac{1-\tau_I}{Q_{t+1}} k_{t+1} - \tau_t,$$

the reduced-form production function

$$Y_t = J_t^\alpha \, (X_t L_t)^{1-\alpha} = F \, (J_t, X_t L_t) \, ,$$

the Jelly capital identity

$$J_t = \left\{ \sum_{\tau=0}^{T} \left[(1 - \delta)^\tau \, k_{t-\tau} \right]^\gamma \right\}^{1/\gamma} ,$$

and the stochastic processes that drive technological change. The government is assumed to run a balanced budget such that at each point in time $\tau_t = \tau_I k_{t+1} / Q_{t+1}$.

For the stochastic processes for X_t and Q_t we choose log-trend stationary processes of the form

$$\ln Q_t = \ln (1 + q) \, t + \ln Q_t^{(t)}, \tag{2}$$

where

$$\ln Q_t^{(t)} = \rho_Q \ln Q_{t-1}^{(t)} + \varepsilon_{Q,t},$$

and, similarly,

$$\ln X_t = \ln (1 + g) \, t + \ln X_t^{(t)}, \tag{3}$$

where

$$\ln X_t^{(t)} = \rho_X \ln X_{t-1}^{(t)} + \varepsilon_{X,t}$$

and $\varepsilon_{X,t} \sim N \, (0, \sigma_X)$ and $\varepsilon_{Q,t} \sim N(0, \sigma_Q)$. We choose these processes as trend stationary purely for expository purposes because the resulting impulse responses are more easily interpretable. We have, however, generated unreported results in which $\ln X_t^{(t)}$ and $\ln Q_t^{(t)}$ followed ARIMA(1,1,0) processes in deviation of a deterministic trend, as is suggested to be the appropriate specification by Lippi and Reichlin (1994). The results using this specification were, in deviation of the trend, qualitatively very similar to the ones that we present later and are therefore omitted.

3.5. Optimality Conditions

The optimality conditions of this model are fairly straightforward variations of the standard real business cycle (RBC) model, as discussed for example in King et al. (1988). The optimal labor supply is determined by the intratemporal optimality condition. This condition implies that at any point in time the representative agent equates the marginal disutility of work to the marginal utility of consumption that can be obtained by working. In our model this implies that

$$\frac{C_t}{1 - L_t} = \frac{\phi}{1 - \phi} X_t F_L \, (J_t, X_t L_t) \, .$$

The intertemporal optimality condition implies that the representative agent chooses the investment level in order to equate the marginal utility of current consumption to the expected present discounted value of the returns to the current investment. The corresponding Euler equation for investment is

$$(1 - \tau_I) \left[C_t^{\phi - 1/(1-\sigma)} (1 - L_t)^{1-\phi} \right]^{1-\sigma} =$$

$$Q_{t+1} E_t \left\{ \sum_{s=1}^{T+1} \beta^s \left[C_{t+s}^{\phi-1/(1-\sigma)} (1 - L_{t+s})^{1-\phi} \right]^{1-\sigma} F_J (J_{t+s}, X_{t+s} L_{t+s}) \frac{\partial J_{t+s}}{\partial k_{t+1}} \right\},$$

where we assume that Q_{t+1} is known at time t. The major difference between this Euler equation and those obtained using capital aggregates based on the perpetual inventory method is that this one is not stated in terms of a co-state variable, but rather in terms of a finite sum of returns to capital. It implies that, instead of the level of the Jelly capital aggregate J_t, the relevant state variable in this model is a sequence of past investment levels $\{k_{t-\tau}\}_{\tau=0}^T$.

4. STEADY-STATE AND LONG-RUN IMPLICATIONS

To study the perfect foresight steady-state and transitional dynamics of this model, we have to transform the variables such that they are constant in the perfect foresight steady state and are stationary around it. The common trend that drives consumption and output in this model is

$$P_t = G^t,$$

where $G = (1 + g)(1 + q)^{\alpha/(1-\alpha)}$. The transformed variables in this model are

$$\tilde{Y}_t = Y_t/P_t, \quad \tilde{C}_t = C_t/P_t, \quad \tilde{k}_t = \frac{k_t}{(1+q)^{t-1} P_{t-1}}, \quad \text{and } \tilde{J}_t = \frac{J_t}{(1+q)^t P_t},$$

where, contrary to standard growth models, investment grows at a faster rate than output and consumption because of the steady decline in its relative price, represented by $(1 + q)^t$ in the correction of investment and the capital stock.

In terms of these transformed variables, we can rewrite

$$\tilde{C}_t = \tilde{Y}_t - \frac{1}{1+q} \frac{1}{Q_{t+1}^{(t)}} \tilde{k}_{t+1}, \tag{4}$$

$$\tilde{Y}_t = F\left(\tilde{J}_t, X_t^{(t)} L_t \right), \tag{5}$$

$$\tilde{J}_t = \left\{ \sum_{\tau=0}^T \left\{ (1 - \delta)^\tau \left[\left(\frac{1}{1+q} \right)^{\frac{1}{1-\alpha}} \left(\frac{1}{1+g} \right) \right]^{\tau+1} \tilde{k}_{t-\tau} \right\}^\gamma \right\}^{1/\gamma}. \tag{6}$$

The intratemporal optimality condition reduces to

$$\frac{\tilde{C}_t}{1-L_t} = \frac{\phi}{1-\phi} X_t^{(t)} F_L\left(\tilde{J}_t, X_t^{(t)} L_t; Z_t\right),$$
(7)

and for the intertemporal optimality condition we obtain

$$1 = \frac{Q_{t+1}^{(t)}}{1-\tau_I}(1+q) E_t \left\{ \sum_{s=1}^{T+1} \beta^s \left[\left(\frac{\tilde{C}_{t+s}}{\tilde{C}_t}\right)^{\phi-1/(1-\sigma)} \left(\frac{1-L_{t+s}}{1-L_t}\right)^{1-\phi} \right]^{1-\sigma} \times \right.$$

$$\left. (G)^{\phi(1-\sigma)s} F_J\left(\tilde{J}_{t+s}, X_{t+s}^{(t)} L_{t+s}; Z_{t+s}\right) \frac{\partial \tilde{J}_{t+s}}{\partial \tilde{k}_{t+1}} \right\},$$
(8)

where

$$\frac{\partial \tilde{J}_{t+s}}{\partial \tilde{k}_{t+1}} = \left\{ (1-\delta)^{s-1} \left[\left(\frac{1}{1+q}\right)^{1/(1-\alpha)} \left(\frac{1}{1+g}\right) \right]^s \right\}^{\gamma} \left(\frac{\tilde{J}_{t+s}}{\tilde{k}_{t+1}}\right)^{1-\gamma}.$$

The perfect foresight steady state of this model is a stationary point of the dynamic system implied by the transformed optimality conditions under the assumption that the variances of the shocks are zero, that is, $\sigma_Q^2 = \sigma_X^2 = 0$. It is a quintuple,

$$\left(Y^*, C^*, k^*, J^*, L^*\right),$$

that satisfies

$$C^* = Y^* - \frac{1}{1+q} k^*,$$
(9)

$$Y^* = F\left(J^*, L^*\right),$$
(10)

$$C^* = \frac{\phi}{1-\phi} F_L\left(J^*, L^*\right)(1-L^*),$$
(11)

$$J^* = \left\{ \sum_{\tau=0}^{T} \left\{ (1-\delta)^{\tau} \left[\left(\frac{1}{1+g}\right) \left(\frac{1}{1+q}\right)^{1/(1-\alpha)} \right]^{\tau+1} \right\}^{\gamma} \right\}^{\frac{1}{\gamma}} k^*,$$
(12)

$$1 = \frac{1+q}{1-\tau_I} \left\{ \sum_{\tau=0}^{T} \left\{ (1-\delta)^{\tau} \left[\left(\frac{1}{1+g}\right) \left(\frac{1}{1+q}\right)^{1/(1-\alpha)} \right]^{\tau+1} \right\}^{\gamma} \right\}^{\frac{1-\gamma}{\gamma}} \times \quad (13)$$

$$\sum_{s=1}^{T+1} \left[\beta (1+g)^{\phi(1-\sigma)-\gamma} (1+q)^{\alpha/(1-\alpha)\phi(1-\sigma)-\gamma/(1-\alpha)} \right]^s \times$$

$$(1-\delta)^{\gamma(s-1)} F_J\left(J^*, L^*; 1\right).$$

It is fairly straightforward to show that this steady state exists and is unique because the above equations can be solved sequentially. The details of this calculation are left for Section A.1 of the appendix.

4.1. The Old "New View of Investment" Revisited

A central issue in the literature on vintage capital, initially addressed by Phelps (1962), is whether the effect of changes in the savings rate on the steady-state level of output depends on the composition of embodied and disembodied technological progress. The growth rate of output on the perfect foresight steady-state balanced growth path is

$$G = (1 + g)(1 + q)^{\alpha/(1-\alpha)}, \tag{14}$$

where g represents disembodied technological change and q embodied technological change. The precise question is whether the elasticity of the steady-state level of output with respect to the savings rate depends on the composition of G, that is, whether it is independent of variations of g and q that keep G constant. In a very similar model that assumes an inelastic labor supply and an exogenous savings rate, Phelps (1962) shows that this elasticity is independent of the composition of growth.

The issue of studying an effect of an exogenous change in the savings rate is not directly appropriate for our model, so we address it in two steps. In the first step we consider the effect of a change in the investment tax credit on the savings rate. In the second step we follow Phelps (1962) and address the effect of a change in the savings rate on the level of steady-state output. The mathematical details of these two steps are given in Section A.2.

As shown in Section A.2, the steady-state savings rate in this model equals $s^* = \tilde{s}^*/(1 - \tau_I)$, where

$$\tilde{s}^* = \alpha \frac{\sum_{\tau=0}^{T} \left\{ (1-\delta)^\tau \left[1/(G(1+q))^{\tau+1} \right] \right\}^\gamma \left(\beta G^{\phi(1-\sigma)} \right)^{\tau+1}}{\sum_{\tau=0}^{T} \left[(1-\delta)^\tau \left[1/(G(1+q))^{\tau+1} \right] \right]^\gamma}$$

and $\beta G^{\phi(1-\sigma)} < 1$ is a necessary condition for the boundedness of the representative household's objective function. The elasticity of the steady-state savings rate with respect to the investment tax credit equals $\tau_I/(1 - \tau_I)$ and does not depend on the composition of G in q and g. In fact, it does not even depend on the growth rate G. What does depend on the composition of G, however, is the level of the savings rate. The bigger the share of productivity growth that occurs through embodied technological change, the higher the savings rate, simply because in that case investment becomes more important as a source of growth relative to the case where it simply adds to the existing capital stock.

The level of steady-state output as a function of the savings rate is given by

$$Y^* = \left(s^* \right)^{\alpha/(1-\alpha)} \left\{ \left\{ \sum_{\tau=0}^{T} \left[(1-\delta)^\tau \left(\frac{1}{G(1+q)} \right)^{\tau+1} \right]^\gamma \right\}^{\frac{1}{\gamma}} \right\}^{\alpha/(1-\alpha)} \times$$

$$\frac{\phi(1-\alpha)}{\phi(1-\alpha)+(1-\phi)(1-s^*)}.$$

This differs in an important way from Phelps (1962). Because we consider an endogenous labor supply, the elasticity of this expression with respect to the savings rate equals

$$\frac{\alpha}{1-\alpha}+\frac{(1-\phi)s^*}{\phi(1-\alpha)+(1-\phi)(1-s^*)}$$

and depends on the endogenous steady-state savings rate s^*. Since the steady-state level of the savings rate depends on the composition of the sources of growth, the elasticity also depends on the composition of growth, through the effect of this composition on the steady-state labor supply. Note that this result hinges on two things. The first is that we have made the labor supply elastic, that is, if $\phi = 1$ and $L_t = 1$ for all t, then this elasticity does not depend on the steady-state savings rate, and we recover exactly Phelps's result that the elasticity is given by the ratio of factor shares. The second is that we do not take the steady-state savings rate as exogenously given, but allow it to be determined by the composition of the sources of growth.

Hence, where Phelps's (1962) result suggests that the elasticity of the steady-state level of output with respect to an investment tax credit will not depend on the composition of the sources of growth, our result suggests that it does. In particular, the more important embodied technological change, the higher the savings rate and the higher the elasticity of output with respect to the savings rate. Consequently, an investment tax credit is more effective when the relative importance of embodied technological change is high.

We have now shown that the composition of growth matters in the long run, and we will proceed by considering whether it also matters in the short run.

5. TRANSITIONAL DYNAMICS
AND SHORT-RUN IMPLICATIONS

What are the short-run effects of embodied technological change? How do they differ from more commonly studied disembodied productivity shocks? In order to address this question, we will approximate the transitional dynamics of our model economy around its perfect foresight steady state. The details of our approximation method are described in Section A.3.

We study the transitional dynamics induced by the various shocks through the impulse response functions that the shocks generate for the log-linear approximation to the solution of our model. For this purpose we must specify a benchmark calibration of the parameters of our model. Table 1 summarizes this benchmark calibration.[5] In particular, we choose our Jelly aggregate in the standard additive representation ($\gamma = 1$) with no complementarities, and taxes are set to zero.

---

5. To check the robustness of our qualitative results concerning the differences in the shapes of impulse response functions induced by embodied versus disembodied shocks, we varied parameters over a wide range. In particular we varied σ and ϕ to see if these qualitative results are sensitive to

Table 1. Parameter Calibration

Parameter	Value	Varied in . . .
σ	2.00	
β	0.95	
ϕ	0.50	
α	0.33	
δ	0.05	
γ	1.00	Figure 5
ρ_Q	0.90	
ρ_X	0.90	
g	0.021	Figure 6
q	0	Figure 6
T	50	Figure 4

The recent literature (Greenwood et al., 1997; Greenwood and Jovanovic, 1998) has stressed the improvements in the quality of capital goods embodied in vintages, as reflected in the data by the falling relative price of capital goods, as critical for the proper accounting of productivity growth. The relative price of fixed private nonresidential investment relative to the PCE deflator is plotted in Figure 2. This is basically $1/Q_t$ as measured by the Bureau of Economic Analysis. The steep decline since the mid-1980s is due to the rapid quality improvements in computers and their increased importance for the capital stock. The BEA's price indexes are subject to a lot of criticism, however, because many studies, most notably Gordon (1990), have shown that the index is probably improperly quality adjusted. Greenwood et al. (1997) use Gordon's (1990) results to argue that even before 1985 the properly quality-adjusted relative price of equipment was already declining at an annual rate of about 3.5 percent.

However the relative investment price is measured, all studies suggest that shocks to Q_t are a potentially important source of economic fluctuations, and during the last decade even more than before. We therefore focus first on embodied technological progress that improves the quality of capital goods. Newer equipment is more productive than older equipment, in the sense that a forgone unit of consumption on average yields more new capital units than in the past, so the relative price of capital, Q_t, tends to decline over time. The stochastic process for Q_t is described by equation (2).

The solid line in Figure 3 depicts the impulse response to an initial shock in Q_t ($\varepsilon_{Q,0} = 0.01$). It exhibits a sharp spike in investment, a real investment boom. Consumption, after dropping on impulse, climbs smoothly and, after a temporary increase, settles back down at the steady-state level. The initial drop in consumption is caused by the increased labor supply induced by the embodied shock. Since consumption and leisure are complements, a decrease in leisure lowers the marginal utility of consumption and consumption drops on impulse. Employment tracks the investment dynamics. There is a sharp increase in labor supply in order to produce a lot of output that can be converted into new and cheap

---

the labor supply elasticity. We found that our results and conclusions are robust to wide variations in parameters.

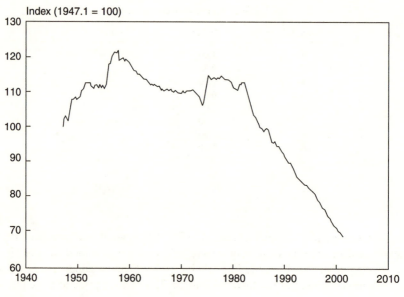

Figure 2. Relative price of investment.

capital goods. The most interesting dynamic is exhibited by output, which rises
with the initial increase in investment and continues to climb because the new
vintages of capital come online while older less-efficient vintages are scrapped.
As the investment vintage profile evens out, a hump-shaped response in output
emerges, where on the downside of the hump output and employment contracts
as if in a recession. The persistence of the transient component of the innovation,
ρ_Q, affects not only the size of the impact effect of the shock on investment and
output, but also the shape of the hump in the response of output. The effects are
small for $\rho_Q = 0$, because in that case the investment response is not sufficient to
increase the capital stock and output after the initial period. The effects become
large as ρ_Q approaches unity. Thus a more persistent rate of innovation, typical
in the early phases of the introduction of a new technology, is likely to generate
a larger hump-shaped response of output. Note that that response, caused by the
echo effects, is in stark contrast to the monotonically declining impulse responses
of output to embodied shocks reported in Greenwood et al. (2000) and DeJong
et al. (2000).

While we have modeled the economic lifetime of vintages, T, as exogenous,
an acceleration in the rate of technological innovation is also likely to reduce T
and increase the rate of adoption of new innovations, as is documented by Tevlin
and Whelan (2000). Figure 4 depicts the impulse responses to a shock to Q_t
for various lifetimes of capital. The earlier the equipment is scrapped, the more
profound the echo effects. Lengthening the economic life of equipment, that is,
making T larger, increases the initial burst of investment, because the increase in
the lifetime of capital implies an increase in the return to investment, but it dampens
as well as delays the replacement echoes. The reason for the milder echoes, which

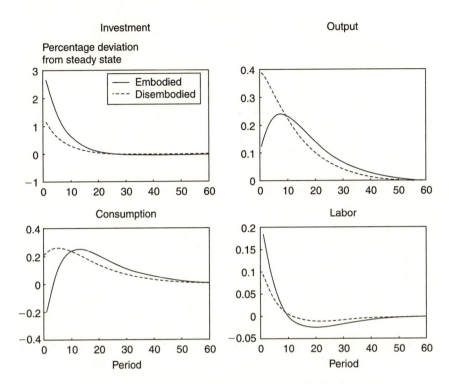

Figure 3. Impulse responses for embodied and disembodied shocks.

would disappear in the limit, is the depreciation of vintages while in use. The longer lifetime decreases the quantity scrapped and reduces investment needed for replacement. The shorter the T, the more profound the investment booms and busts caused by echo effects.

More persistence in the responses of investment, consumption, output, and labor can be introduced by adding complementarities between capital vintages. Figure 5 depicts the impulse responses for three different values of γ. The smaller the γ, the more complementary current investment levels are with future investment, hence the more incentive there is to drag out the investment response. This leads to increased persistence in all impulse responses and allows for more consumption smoothing.

So far we have focused on the impulse responses of our model to an embodied shock. However, we want to compare the relative importance of the sources of growth for economic fluctuations. There are two ways to look at this issue. The first is to ask how the different sources of shocks affect the transitional dynamics of the economy. The second is to inquire whether the transitional dynamics of the economy depend on the composition of the deterministic parts of embodied and disembodied technological change.

In order to answer the question of whether the dynamic response of the economy to an embodied shock is very different than it is to a disembodied shock, we refer

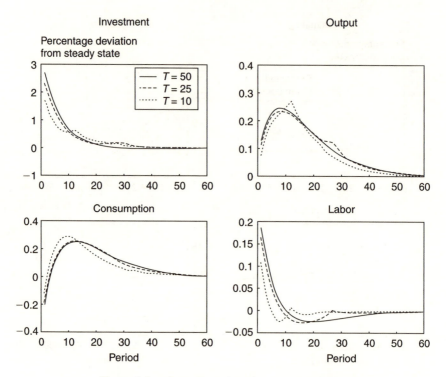

Figure 4. Impulse responses for various scrappage times.

again to Figure 3. The dashed line in this figure depicts the response of the economy to an impulse in $X_t(\varepsilon_{X,0} = 0.01)$, the disembodied shock. In this case echo effects in investment are still present, but are hardly noticeable. They are much milder than the impulse resulting from a Q-shock. Responses of output, consumption, and employment are close to monotonic in this case. The reason that the hump-shaped response of output is absent is that investment reacts much less to such a shock, leading to a much smaller increase in the Jelly capital stock. The increase in the Jelly capital stock is in fact so much less that it fails to generate any subsequent increases in output after the initial shock. The bottom line is that embodied shocks are much more likely to lead to echo effects and a hump-shaped output response than disembodied shocks.

The second way to pose the question, in a manner similar to Phelps (1962), is to inquire how the dynamic response of the economy changes if we change the composition of growth, but leave the growth rate G constant. Output in this model is measured in terms of consumption goods and the average annual postwar growth rate of PCE-deflated real GDP per capita is 2.1 percent.[6] Figure 6 depicts

---

6. There is a recent discussion in the literature on how to measure properly the growth rate of real GDP in a world with embodied technological change. See Ho and Stiroh (2001) and Licandro et al. (2001) for suggestions on how to measure real GDP growth in a way that is consistent with the National Income and Product Accounts.

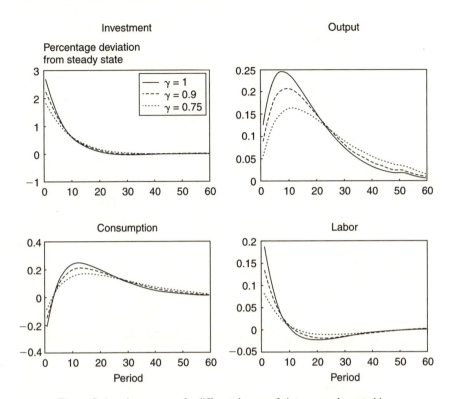

Figure 5. Impulse responses for different degrees of vintage complementarities.

the impulse responses of the model for three different scenarios. Each scenario implies that $G = 1.021$, but the first is the one in which all growth is disembodied, the second is the case considered by Greenwood et al. (1997) in which $q = 0.035$, and the last is the case in which all growth is embodied. As the figure clearly illustrates, the impulse responses are relatively insensitive to the composition of the sources of growth.

6. CONCLUSION

We opened this chapter with the question, "Does it matter if the growth of productivity is driven by disembodied technological change that raises the productivity of all factors of production, including all capital in place, or by continuous improvements in the quality of new capital goods?" Our conclusion is a resounding "Yes!," for both the long and the short run.

By endogenizing the savings rate and the labor supply, we showed that, contrary to Phelps (1962), the long-run effects of policies affecting the savings rate depend on the relative importance of embodied and disembodied technological change.

More importantly, we showed that if one considers the interaction of vintage effects with scrappage of capital goods, shocks to embodied technological change can generate echo effects that take the form of investment booms and busts and

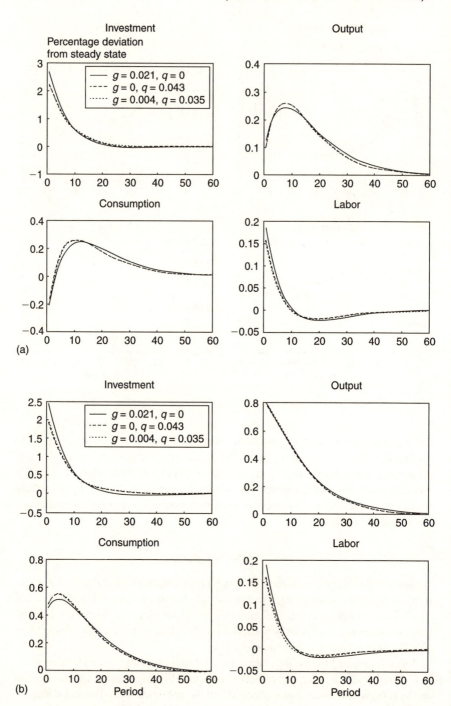

Figure 6. Effect of sources of growth on impulse responses: (a) response to embodied shock, (b) response to disembodied shock.

hump-shaped impulse responses in output, but that with disembodied shocks these effects are much more subdued. This is an important observation if one realizes that the 1990s expansion was mainly investment driven. Hence, if the source of the 1990s expansion was indeed embodied technological change rather than the disembodied technological change associated with other postwar expansions, then our results provide a possible interpretation for the different character of the transitional dynamics of the current slowdown.

The emphasis in this chapter is on the interaction between scrappage and embodied technological change in economic fluctuations. However, just like Phelps (1962) took the savings rate as exogenous, we took the scrappage time as exogenous. A worthwhile extension of this work would be to endogenize the scrappage time, as in Campbell (1998), and get a better insight for the response of T to the composition of the sources of growth.

APPENDIX: MATHEMATICAL DETAILS

This appendix contains some of the mathematical details needed to obtain the results presented in the chapter. It contains three subsections: in the first we solve for the steady-state equations (9) through (13); in the second we present the detailed derivation of the long-run effects of the composition of the sources of growth; finally, in the third subsection, we briefly describe our log-linearization procedure.

A.1. Derivation of Steady State

The system of equations (9) through (13) can be solved sequentially. We can solve for the steady-state Jelly capital-to-labor ratio by defining $f_J(x) = F_J(x, 1; 1)$ and using (13) to find

$$\frac{J^*}{L^*} = f_J^{-1} \times$$

$$\left\{ \frac{(1-\tau_I)\left\{\sum_{\tau=0}^{T}\left\{(1-\delta)^\tau\left\{[1/(1+g)][1/(1+q)]^{1/(1-\alpha)}\right\}^{\tau+1}\right\}^\gamma\right\}^{(\gamma-1)/\gamma}}{(1+q)\sum_{s=1}^{T+1}\left[\beta(1+g)^{\phi(1-\sigma)-\gamma}(1+q)^{[\alpha/(1-\alpha)]\phi(1-\sigma)-\gamma/(1-\alpha)}\right]^s(1-\delta)^{\gamma(s-1)}} \right\}.$$

Once we have the Jelly capital-labor ratio, we can easily solve for the investment ratio k^*/L^*. That is,

$$\frac{k^*}{L^*} = \left\{\sum_{\tau=0}^{T}\left\{(1-\delta)^\tau\left[\left(\frac{1}{1+g}\right)\left(\frac{1}{1+q}\right)^{1/(1-\alpha)}\right]^{\tau+1}\right\}^\gamma\right\}^{-1/\gamma}\frac{J^*}{L^*},$$

and output per hour equals

$$\frac{Y^*}{L^*} = F\left(\frac{J^*}{L^*}, 1\right),$$

while consumption per hour equals

$$\frac{C^*}{L^*} = \frac{Y^*}{L^*} - \frac{1}{1+q}\frac{k^*}{L^*}.$$

The intratemporal optimality condition can now be solved to obtain the steady-state labor supply such that

$$1/L^* = 1 + \frac{1-\phi}{\phi}\frac{C^*/L^*}{F_L\,(J^*/L^*, 1; 1)},$$

and

$$L^* = \frac{\phi F_L\,(J^*/L^*, 1; 1)}{\phi F_L\,(J^*/L^*, 1; 1) + (1-\phi)\,C^*/L^*}.$$

This is derived under the assumption that the steady state exists for appropriate restrictions on parameters. The assumption is warranted because the first-level Cobb-Douglas production function satisfies Inada conditions, in the sense that

$$\infty = \lim_{x\downarrow 0} f_J\,(x) >$$

$$\frac{(1-\tau_I)\left\{\sum_{\tau=0}^{T}\left\{(1-\delta)^\tau\left\{[1/(1+g)][1/(1+q)]^{1/(1-\alpha)}\right\}^{\tau+1}\right\}^\gamma\right\}^{(\gamma-1)/\gamma}}{(1+q)\sum_{s=1}^{T+1}\left[\beta\,(1+g)^{\phi(1-\sigma)-\gamma}\,(1+q)^{[\alpha/(1-\alpha)]\phi(1-\sigma)-\gamma/(1-\alpha)}\right]^s\,(1-\delta)^{\gamma(s-1)}}.$$

Hence, the steady state exists and is unique.

A.2. Effect of Investment Tax Credit on Steady-State Values

We decompose the effect of an investment tax credit on the steady-state values in two parts. In the first part, we consider the effect of the investment tax credit on the savings rate and show how this effect depends on the composition of the sources of growth. In the second, we derive how the savings rate affects the steady-state level of output. Throughout, we substitute G following (14) for all relevant instances. The steady-state savings rate in this economy, which we denote by s^*, is given by

$$s^* = 1 - \frac{C^*}{Y^*} = \frac{1}{1+q}\frac{k^*}{Y^*}.$$

For the investment-to-output ratio k^*/Y^* we can derive

$$\frac{k^*}{Y^*} = \frac{J^*/L^*}{\left\{\sum_{\tau=0}^{T}\left\{(1-\delta)^\tau\left\{[1/(1+g)][1/(1+q)]^{1/(1-\alpha)}\right\}^{\tau+1}\right\}^\gamma\right\}^{1/\gamma}F\,(J^*/L^*, 1; 1)}$$

$$= \frac{\alpha}{\left\{\sum_{\tau=0}^{T}\left\{(1-\delta)^\tau\left\{[1/(1+g)][1/(1+q)]^{1/(1-\alpha)}\right\}^{\tau+1}\right\}^\gamma\right\}^{1/\gamma}f_J\,(J^*/L^*)},$$

where we have used the fact that the production function is Cobb-Douglas. In the steady state

$$f_J\left(J^*/L^*\right) =$$

$$\frac{(1-\tau_I)\left\{\sum_{\tau=0}^{T}\left\{(1-\delta)^\tau\left\{[1/(1+g)][1/(1+q)]^{1/(1-\alpha)}\right\}^{\tau+1}\right\}^\gamma\right\}^{(\gamma-1)/\gamma}}{(1+q)\sum_{s=1}^{T+1}\left[\beta\,(1+g)^{\phi(1-\sigma)-\gamma}\,(1+q)^{[\alpha/(1-\alpha)]\phi(1-\sigma)-\gamma/(1-\alpha)}\right]^s\,(1-\delta)^{\gamma(s-1)}},$$

such that the savings rate equals

$$s^* = \frac{\alpha}{(1-\tau_I)}\,\frac{\sum_{s=1}^{T+1}\left[\beta(1+g)^{\phi(1-\sigma)-\gamma}(1+q)^{[\alpha/(1-\alpha)]\phi(1-\sigma)-\gamma/(1-\alpha)}\right]^s\,(1-\delta)^{\gamma(s-1)}}{\sum_{\tau=0}^{T}\left\{(1-\delta)^\tau\left\{[1/(1+g)][1/(1+q)]^{1/(1-\alpha)}\right\}^{\tau+1}\right\}^\gamma}$$

$$= \frac{1}{(1-\tau_I)}\,\alpha\,\frac{\sum_{s=1}^{T+1}\left\{(1-\delta)^{s-1}[1/G(1+q)]^s\right\}^\gamma\left(\beta G^{\phi(1-\sigma)}\right)^s}{\sum_{\tau=0}^{T}\left\{(1-\delta)^\tau[1/G(1+q)]^{\tau+1}\right\}^\gamma}$$

$$= \frac{1}{(1-\tau_I)}\,\tilde{s}^*,$$

where $\beta G^{\phi(1-\sigma)} < 1$ is a necessary condition for boundedness of the solution to the representative agents problem.

Now note that a change in g and q such that G is constant will affect $\tilde{s}^*$. This is because in case of embodied technological change the capital, measured in efficiency units, depreciates faster (owing to economic depreciation) than in the case of disembodied technological change. In fact, an increase in the importance of embodied technological change, that is, in q, will decrease the returns to capital, decrease $1/[G(1+q)]$, and this will increase $\tilde{s}^*$. The intuition behind this result is that if productivity growth can only be obtained through investing in new vintages then there is an increased incentive to invest and the savings rate will rise. Consequently, an increase in the investment tax credit τ_I will raise the steady-state savings rate more than in the case of disembodied technological change. However, the elasticity of the savings rate with respect to the investment tax credit equals $\tau_I/(1-\tau_I)$ and is independent of the composition of growth into embodied and disembodied technological change.

Now that we have considered the effect of a change in the investment tax credit on the savings rate, we will rederive Phelps's (1962) result in the context of our model by considering the effect of the savings rate on steady-state output. For the steady-state labor supply we obtain

$$L^* = \frac{\phi\,(1-\alpha)}{\phi\,(1-\alpha) + (1-\phi)\,(1-s^*)}.$$

The steady-state level of the Jelly capital-to-labor ratio has to satisfy

$$\frac{J^*}{L^*} = \left\{ \left\{ \left[\sum_{\tau=0}^{T} \left[(1-\delta)^\tau \left(\frac{1}{G(1+q)} \right)^{\tau+1} \right]^\gamma \right]^{1/\gamma} s^* \right\} \right\}^{1/(1-\alpha)}$$

such that

$$Y^* = (s^*)^{\alpha/(1-\alpha)} \left\{ \left\{ \left[\sum_{\tau=0}^{T} \left\{ (1-\delta)^\tau \left[\frac{1}{G(1+q)} \right]^{\tau+1} \right\}^\gamma \right]^{1/\gamma} \right\} \right\}^{\alpha/(1-\alpha)} \times$$

$$\frac{\phi(1-\alpha)}{\phi(1-\alpha) + (1-\phi)(1-s^*)},$$

where we have again used the fact that the production function is Cobb-Douglas. In this case the elasticity of the steady-state level of output with respect to the savings rate equals

$$\frac{\alpha}{1-\alpha} + \frac{(1-\phi)s^*}{\phi(1-\alpha) + (1-\phi)(1-s^*)}.$$

A.3. Log-Linearization Details

The problem with log-linearizing the model is that it contains a high-dimensional state space, because the relevant state variables are the shocks $X_t^{(t)}$ and $Q_{t+1}^{(t)}$, as well as the sequence of past T investment levels $(k_{t-\tau})_{\tau=0}^T$. In order to deal with this efficiently, we use a two-step procedure. In the first step we log-linearize the transformed resource constraint (4), the production function (5), the Jelly capital identity (6), and the intratemporal optimality condition (7). These four equations then allow us to solve for $\hat{C}_t$, $\hat{Y}_t$, $\hat{J}_t$, and $\hat{L}_t$ as a function of $(\hat{k}_{t-\tau})_{\tau=-1}^T$, $\hat{X}_t^{(t)}$, and $\hat{Q}_{t+1}^{(t)}$. Here the caret denotes percentage deviations from the steady state. We then log-linearize the Euler equation (8), and substitute for $\hat{C}_t$, $\hat{Y}_t$, $\hat{J}_t$, $\hat{L}_t$, and their leads. This yields a $(2T+2)$-order linear difference equation in $\hat{k}_t$ from which we eliminate the $T+1$ unstable roots to obtain the resulting linearized investment policy function that gives $\hat{k}_{t+1}$ as a function of $(\hat{k}_{t-\tau})_{\tau=-1}^T$, $\hat{X}_t^{(t)}$, and $\hat{Q}_{t+1}^{(t)}$.

REFERENCES

Benhabib, J. and A. Rustichini (1991), "Vintage Capital, Investment and Growth," *Journal of Economic Theory* 55:323–39.

———— (1993), "A Vintage Model of Growth and Investment: Theory and Evidence," in R. Becker, M. Boldrin, R. Jones, and W. Thomson, eds., *General Equilibrium, Growth and Trade II*, San Diego: Academic Press, pp. 248–300.

———— (1994), "A Note on a New Class of Solutions to Dynamic Programming Problems Arising in Economic Growth," *Journal of Economic Dynamics and Control* 18:808–13.

Boucekkine, R., F. del Rio, and O. Licandro (1999), "The Importance of the Embodiment Question Revisited," FEDEA Working Paper No. 99-13.

Campbell, J. R. (1998), "Entry, Exit, Embodied Technology, and Business Cycles," *Review of Economic Dynamics* 1(2):371–408.

DeJong, D., B. Ingram, and C. Whiteman (2000), "Keynesian Impulses versus Solow Residuals: Identifying Sources of Business Cycle Fluctuations," *Journal of Applied Econometrics* 15:311–29.

Denison, E. (1964), "The Unimportance of the Embodied Question," *American Economic Review* 54:90–93.

Fisher, F. (1965), "Embodied Technological Change and the Existence of an Aggregate Capital Stock," *Review of Economic Studies* 32:263–88.

Fisher, F. M., D. Levhari, and E. Sheshinski (1969), "On the Sensitivity of the Level of Output to Savings: Embodiment and Disembodiment: A Clarificatory Note," *Quarterly Journal of Economics* 83(2):347–48.

Gilchrist, S. and J. Williams (2000), "Putty-Clay and Investment: A Business Cycle Analysis," *Journal of Political Economy* 108:928–60.

Gordon, R. (1990), *The Measurement of Durable Goods Prices*, Chicago: University of Chicago Press.

Greenwood, J. and B. Jovanovic (1998), "Accounting for Growth," in Charles Hulten, ed., *Studies in Income and Wealth: New Directions in Productivity Analysis*, Chicago: University of Chicago Press.

Greenwood, J., Z. Hercowitz, and P. Krusell (1997), "Long-Run Implications of Investment-Specific Technological Change," *American Economic Review* 87:342–62.

———— (2000), "The Role of Investment Specific Technological Change in the Business Cycle," *European Economic Review* 44:91–115.

Hall, R. (1968), "Technical Change and Capital from the Point of View of the Dual," *Review of Economic Studies* 35:35–46.

Ho, M. and K. Stiroh (2001), "The Embodiment Controversy: You Can't Have Two Prices in a One-Sector Model," mimeo, Federal Reserve Bank of New York.

King, R., C. Plosser, and S. Rebelo (1988), "Production, Growth and Business Cycles I: The Basic Neoclassical Model," *Journal of Monetary Economics* 21:195–232.

Levhari, D. and E. Sheshinski (1967), "On the Sensitivity of the Level of Output to Savings," *Quarterly Journal of Economics* 81:524–28.

Licandro, O., J. Duran, and J. Ruiz-Castillo (2001), "The Measurement of Growth under Embodied Technical Change," mimeo. FEDEA.

Lippi, M. and L. Reichlin (1994), "Diffusion of Technical Change and the Identification of the Trend Component in Real GNP," *Review of Economic Studies* 61:19–30.

Matthews, R. C. O. (1964), " 'The New View of Investment': Comment," *Quarterly Journal of Economics* 78(1):164–72.

Phelps, E. S. (1962), "The New View of Investment: A Neoclassical Analysis," *Quarterly Journal of Economics* 76(4):548–67.

Phelps, E. S. and M. E. Yaari (1964), "The New View of Investment: Reply," *Quarterly Journal of Economics* 78(1):172–76.

Robertson, D. H. (1915), *A Study of Industrial Fluctuation: An Enquiry into the Character and Causes of the So-Called Cyclical Movements of Trade*, London: Aldwych. Reprinted by the London School of Economics and Political Science, 1948.

Sato, R. (1970), "A Further Note on a Difference Equation Recurring in Growth Theory," *Journal of Economic Theory* 2:95–102.

Solow, R. M. (1960), "Investment and Technical Progress," in K. Arrow, S. Karlin, and P. Suppes, eds., *Mathematical Methods in the Social Sciences*, Stanford, Calif.: Stanford University Press.

Tevlin, S. and K. Whelan (2000), "Explaining the Investment Boom of the 1990's," *Finance and Economics Discussion Series 2000*, Vol. 11, Federal Reserve Board.

— 27 —

General Comments on Part IV

ROBERT M. SOLOW

There was a lot of indiscriminate praise of Ned Phelps during the October 2001 festschrift in his honor. But no one seems to have noticed a genuine intellectual problem specific to the occasion and to others like it. Presumably praise is subject to diminishing marginal utility, like most things. I have observed that praise can be produced at constant—or perhaps mildly increasing—cost. So praise ought to be spread out roughly evenly over its object's lifetime, or at least over a broad span of years. Instead we choose to heap it on at age 65 and thus perpetrate an intertemporal inefficiency. Since this habit is not imposed by government but seems to emerge spontaneously, in a decentralized way, there is a nagging paradox, perhaps calling for corrective taxation. But I feel confident that someone here will soon find a set of assumptions under which what is is optimal.

I learned about Ned in real time, before many of you were born. That was when I picked up the September 1961 *AER* with his first paper, "The Golden Rule of Accumulation." (I asked my father if he knew where Solovia was; he was not sure, but thought maybe near Minsk.) That paper was a winner—neat, meaningful, and leading somewhere interesting, to the special kind of intertemporal inefficiency associated with oversaving. By the way, it did this without tedious algebra. I mention this last fact only because one of my insights from the conference was the realization that I am not now and have never been a Keynesian. I deduced this from Bob Lucas's remark that Keynesians do not like tedious algebra. I love tedious algebra. Some of my happiest moments have come when I was just sitting there doing tedious algebra. It beats thinking for sure; thinking is really irksome.

Anyway, when I learned that the golden rule paper had been written by a brand-new Yale Ph.D., I consoled myself with the thought that he was probably just an overachiever. Then I noticed that E. S. Phelps had overachieved again, after only a year or two, and I could watch him doing it during a fun year at MIT. Now, here we are 40 years later, and Ned is still overachieving. We need a new category: that of habitual overachiever.

I take it that a "general commentator" is something different from a designated nitpicker. I do not want to try to comment individually on these four excellent chapters in a few pages. So I will focus instead on three fairly broad issues that stuck in my mind after I read the chapters themselves.

The first of these is the issue addressed directly by Chad Jones. Every model that wants to be able to describe steady-state exponential growth has to make a significant linearity assumption somewhere. After all, the linear differential equation $dy/dx = y$ with $y(0) = 1$ is as good a definition of the exponential function as any. This is important, because linearity is both very special and hard to verify. The more complicated the model, the harder it may be to spot the crucial linearity, rather like the cartoon "Where's Waldo?," which asks you to find Waldo's not very distinctive face in a sea of other cartoon faces.

Jones suggests that there is indeed one entirely natural place to postulate the necessary linearity and that is in population growth. The fact of birth and death rates, even if they are endogenously determined, will automatically make the increase in population proportional to the population itself. (The fact that birth and death rates are age specific merely calls for some tedious algebra.)

I am doubtful about this, for two reasons. The first is that birth rates can and probably do depend on population size, and that is a nonlinearity. Fertility is surely a social phenomenon in rich societies. My wife and I are independent thinkers, as these things go. So why did we find ourselves, in the Eisenhower mid-1950s, living in a suburban house and having three children in 3 years? Furthermore, there are the various environmental and social factors that lead to logistic curves. Those are precisely nonlinearities. I continued to think that each key linearity needs to be justified, and it is not easy to do so.

But then how important is it to have a model that gives exponential steady states? Jones points to the fact that real growth rates in the United States have been essentially trendless for a century or more. But trendlessness and constancy are not the same thing. I wonder if models in which real growth rates are proportional to population growth rates may not run into a different empirical difficulty. Most studies seem to show convergence among the rich OECD countries. Must we believe that they converge demographically as well?

The other imperative for exponential steady states is that technological progress must be purely labor augmenting. This issue is discussed in a fascinating way by Daron Acemoglu. He shows how models of endogenously directed technological change can imply precisely this bias. The key linearity in his model is tucked into his equation (15), where both right-hand sides are homogenous of degree one in N_L and N_Z. The symmetry in (15) gives still more. If one multiplies the two left-hand sides and the two right-hand sides, it emerges that (15) implies that

$$\left(N_L^{-1}dN_L/dt\right)\left(N_Z^{-1}dN_Z/dt\right) = \eta_L\eta_Z S^2/4.$$

(Actually the last term is $S_L S_Z$, but it is obviously best to divide S evenly between them.) This is an innovation possibilities frontier such as the one in Acemoglu's Figure 1, but it has the opposite curvature.

Apart from the theory of directed technological change, it is worth wondering if observed technological progress actually is purely labor augmenting. This is not easy to test, but the one paper I know that tackles the problem head-on, by Lau and Boskin (2000), uses panel data for several large countries and concludes that it is not. I suspect that the heavy steady-state orientation of much current growth theory is excessively dependent on the Cobb-Douglas function, the one case in which the direction of factor augmentation does not matter.

I am left with the feeling that we overdo steady states and are much too free with nonrobust and nonintuitive linearity assumptions.

This leads me to a second general point, on which I can be very brief. Endogenizing technological progress is a fine idea, provided that it can actually be done in a sensible way. What little relevant experience I have suggsts two comments.

First, the growth literature proceeds as if all improvements in total factor productivity originate in research and development activities. That is what gets modeled. But it is certain that an appreciable fraction of "technological progress" has nothing to do with R&D. It originates on the shop (or office) floor and is "invented" by workers and managers who see that there are improvements to be made in the location of activities, the flow of work, the way part A is fastened to part B, and so on. I suppose this is "learning by doing," but it may be only loosely related to cumulative output, say, as empirical learning curves have it. This is the sort of thing that Japanese gurus called "continuous improvement." Other buzzwords, such as "lean production," also have little or nothing to do with R&D, but a lot to do with total factor productivity.

Second, despite what I have just said, R&D is certainly an important source of innovation. I have long wondered why growth theory makes so little use of whatever is known about what actually happens in industrial R&D activities. Does it correspond in any way to standard models of endogenous technological change, such as those in the two directly relevant chapters in this section? It would not surprise me if the answer were hardly at all. I once had the opportunity to observe a major industrial research laboratory—not intensively, but at intervals over a long period of time. I heard much discussion of the way research problems were chosen, for instance. It was never obvious what the people involved thought they were maximizing. They understood perfectly well that the ultimate goal was the long-run value of the firm, but how this got translated into decisions about the allocation of research funds across potential projects was anything but transparent. If there is systematic knowledge about this, it should be turned to use by growth theorists.

My last general point is quite different. I am surely not alone in noticing that we talk a lot about "skill," but in practice we deal empirically with schooling. Everyone understands that this identification is problematic. I want to draw attention to the lack of clarity in what we mean by "skill." We take it for granted that there is a one-dimensional hierarchy, so one can talk about more or less skill, higher or lower skill. One problem is that skills obsolesce, even very "high" skills.

Just to take one example, think about agriculture and leave aside sentimental thoughts such as that dealing with domestic animals may be as hard a skill to learn as dealing with municipal bonds. A friend of mine comes from an Iowa farm family; she once heard her grandfather say: "Farming is 10 percent agriculture and 90 percent fixing things." But he would be classified as unskilled or semiskilled today. Obviously the reality of multidimensional skills is not going to be captured in any tractable model of skill-biased technological progress or of earnings differentials by skill. That sort of thing is always true. The question that matters is whether we are using the right simplifications. In the case of the map into schooling, the answer is very likely "no." The Aghion and Howitt chapter about "adaptability" is obviously a step in the right direction; but what is the measurable counterpart? Is there no body of knowledge about this?

One last comment, relating to a casual remark by Dale Mortensen. Given our starting-point, it is probably natural to try to understand widening wage inequality in terms of the needs imposed by technology and the "skills" supplied by the labor force. What gets ignored is any serious discussion of the mechanism or process of distribution. Collective bargaining is gone in the United States. Has it really been replaced by atomistic competition? Is that the best way to understand the determination of wage differentials between and within firms? Or are we missing some institutional subtleties?

REFERENCE

Lau, L. and M. Boskin (2000), "Generalized Solow-Neutral Technical Progress and Postwar Economic Growth," NBER Working Paper No. 8023.

28

Reflections on Parts III and IV

EDMUND S. PHELPS

The birth of micro-macro and the developments in its wake, from the mid-1960s to the early 1980s, produced radical changes in the way we do monetary macroeconomics. Now it is increasingly evident that in nonmonetary equilibrium modeling, models that defiantly abstract both from money and misexpectations, changes have been occurring steadily since the early 1980s that may prove to be no less important for the conduct of macroeconomics. In focusing on the medium- and the long-term tendency rather than fluctuations around it, this kind of modeling can focus on the bedrock-level influences determining an economy's *capacity* to offer participants an economic life of enterprise and challenge and thus to achieve high participation and productivity. A whole new field is forming that is taking us well beyond the models of neoclassical spirit that dominated economic thinking over most of the past century.

Job and career are recognized in much of this new work to be the source of the most basic satisfactions and personal development that a good economic system can offer—not merely a source of income (however highly or little valued). People, most people at any rate, need the unending new problems that an entrepreneurial economy can throw out, both for their mental stimulation and as a way to discover their talents and develop their capabilities. Many also want jobs in order to experience the personal growth that comes from working with others (while others may want jobs as an escape or respite from personal interactions). Some want involvement in their society, and to be an employee in the economy's mainstream is to be a part of society's biggest project. People also value self-support: the dignity of feeling they are earning their own way and the autonomy brought by a substantial income of their own to meet their special needs. For these reasons, the *job satisfactions* as well as the *wage rates* employers can offer and *job availability*—hence the enterprise of the business sector in launching new products, new methods, or new markets and its sophistication in selecting and mastering innovations—are among life's *primary goods*, to use John Rawls's term.

These basic satisfactions from jobs and careers and, as a result, the economy's total employment rate (participation rates or unemployment rates or both) are seen in much of the new work to be a function of the economy's *dynamism* and the resulting growth rate; and both are codetermined by economic institutions: The scope and degree of enterprise in the business sector underlie much of the job satisfaction obtained by employees—the intellectual growth, the realization of talents, the stimulation—in both the industries creating the innovations and those pioneering their selection and use. The attendant investing in new products, new methods, and new markets pulls up wage rates and the availability of jobs. (Faster productivity growth may raise the wages firms can pay, too, although faster growth may not be sustainable.) Thus dynamism raises the rewards from business life in general and from employment in particular, and the increased attractiveness of jobs pulls up employment. The converse is also true: People's intellectual growth from their business experience is a part of society's economic development. Increased participation and employment is apt to result in more firms, more entrepreneurs, with benefits for productivity growth. (This echoes the idea of mine years ago that is discussed by Chad Jones: The more people there are seeing and mulling over problems, the more solutions there will be.)

My reflections here on this emerging field will go best if I organize them around the stages of my own work in this area, while bringing in the contributions of a great many others along the way.

I

My own first immersion in nonmonetary employment theory, begun in late 1985, was provoked by the deep slump that had become so visible at that time in Continental Europe. The pioneering *nonmonetary* reworking of my quitting model (with revamping) by Steve Salop in 1979 and of the customer market model by Calvo and myself in 1983 suggested that the project might be feasible. My first step was work with Jean-Paul Fitoussi. (Elements of the turnover-training and customer market models as well as a conventional two-sector model were used to argue that an overseas shock to world real interest rates would drive down the unit value placed on the business asset in the home country, "Europa," and thus depress home employment.) But these elements were embedded in static, monetary models. Soon after, I started building intertemporal nonmonetary models to verify that the results with Fitoussi were robust and to test them. This work, much in collaboration with Hian Teck Hoon and Gylfi Zoega, culminated in *Structural Slumps*[1] in 1994 and extensions.

I think that what we found and what we missed were both important. In time-series analyses of national data in OECD economies from 1955 to 1989 we regressed the annual change of the national unemployment rates on the causal forces in the theoretical models, including lagged unemployment in view of the turnover-training model. These independent variables were the models' *private market forces*, such as accumulated private wealth (or the income therefrom), the stock of business assets, and the overseas real interest rate, as well as some familiar *policy* variables, such as the direct tax rate and social wealth, also figuring in the models. We could thus see whether and how well the models' independent variables explained the data. As a by-product, we had an explanation (such as it

---

1. *Structural Slumps: The Modern Equilibrium Theory of Unemployment, Interest and Assets*, Cambridge: Harvard University Press (1994).

was) of why some countries experienced a lesser slump than others. Of the several conclusions four stand out in my mind:

1. Results in 1997 and 1998 supported the models' implication that the growth rate of productivity, both expected and actual, has important effects. So the great productivity slowdown (dating from 1974), which was severe on the Continent, where catch-up growth had been spectacular in the 1950s and the 1960s, drove unemployment up far more there, especially in Italy, Belgium, and France, than it did in the United States, the United Kingdom, Australia, and Canada, where the slowdown was mild. There are two channels: The ensuing expectation of slower trend growth of productivity operates just like a rise in expected real interest rates, as first shown in Christopher Pissarides's 1990 book[2] (and touched on here and there in *Structural Slumps*). Second, with productivity and hence wages growing more slowly, workers' asset holdings started to rise as a ratio to the wage; and, theoretically, the income or services from all these riches weakened workers' incentives not to quit or shirk at the drop of a hat. The benefits offered by social entitlements likewise rose as a ratio to the slowed-down wage, with the same effects.

2. The world real interest rate was unfailingly a significant variable and the elevation of real interest rates dating from 1981 was a sizable contractionary influence—and not just on the Continent, of course. Through this elevation, Continental saving was pulled out to finance increased investment in east Asia and to offset decreased saving in the United States. The chilling effect on Continental firms' rate of investment in new plant, new customers, and new employees reduced employment and real wages.

3. We found evidence that, given entitlement outlays and government purchases, a hike in the tax rate on wage income, in lowering the after-tax wage employers could pay as a ratio to workers' income from wealth, would move an economy down its medium-run wage curve, which takes income from wealth as fixed, thus driving up unemployment. But the models warn that the consequent fall of saving, in steadily lowering workers' income from wealth, could neutralize the wage effect, driving unemployment back to the rest point where it began.

4. Late in the day we discovered that the appearance of a milder slump in the United States and a faster recovery from its slump was the result of demographics: a steep upward trend in the proportion of U.S. workers with some college and the proportion with a college degree, groups relatively immune to joblessness. In the United States, the mean unemployment rate among high school dropouts in the 1980s was nearly double its rate in the 1970s and did not get out of "double digits" until the mid-1990s, as if it were a country on the Continent.

I was delighted that Steven Nickell in his chapter, experimenting with a similar approach and his own preferred explanatory variables, arrived at several results in

---

2. *Equilibrium Unemployment Theory*, Oxford: Blackwell (1990).

common with mine. Thanks also to the results of Olivier Blanchard and others, the view taken by *Structural Slumps* seems to have won a surprisingly broad consensus.

On reflection, however, I see that these results do not go as far as we would wish. *Structural Slumps*, intending to explain the Continent's slump, produced an alternative macroeconomics of unemployment, real interest, and real asset prices but it did not really get to the bottom of that slump. It is one thing—and very nice— to explain a greater *rise* in one economy's unemployment rate than in another's and quite another thing to explain a greater *level*. It is certain that, if you have explained why a country's unemployment (I am thinking of France) rose by 8 percentage points between the mid-1960s and, say, the mid-1990s you have gone a long way toward explaining why it was *high* in the 1990s; after all, the rate could not have been negative in the 1960s. But if we think of the *mid-1990s* as normal, the regressions Gylfi and I carried out can be said to explain why unemployment in the 1960s was *abnormally low* and to leave it a mystery why unemployment is as high as it is—in France, in Italy, in Germany, and the rest—in the 1990s. The panel methodology lets one estimate a free constant term for each country without having to introduce any determinants of the constant term and their differences across countries. We can plow along with this research without the foggiest idea of what they are.

II

In the mid-1990s I came increasingly to believe—a belief that was reinforced by research on the Italian economy I started in 1997—that widely recognized differences among the advanced economies in the framework of economic institutions created by their histories and policies had consequences for these economies' dynamism and their enlistment of the population in business life. The economies whose institutions were, by some measure, closer to the model or models of capitalism, I suspected, would have greater dynamism: They might be more innovative and their innovative investment projects, being more closely geared to prospective profitability, would be better directed. Such differences, I thought, might have major consequences for long-run economic health. But how to develop and test that entrepreneurial thesis?

Some ideas in that direction arose in the course of work I began with Gylfi a few years ago on investment booms. The background to this research was the record-breaking investment boom in the United States over the second half of the 1990s, which was not explained by existing models (at least not models that gear the expected growth rate of productivity to observation of the recent productivity growth rate). My modeling of the boom was based on the theory, which I attributed to Spiethoff and Cassel, that asset values and thus investment activity jump *off* their accustomed saddlepaths and *onto* (explosive) boom trajectories when there is the sudden expectation of new uses for capital (at normal rates of return)—in some new method, new product, or new region—*at some future date*. We cannot observe the arrival and duration of such a galvanizing vision but its presence will have effects on the value placed (by firms) on the business asset—the customer, the employee, commercial space—and these effects may be "signaled" by the value of the *stock market* per unit of the business asset. In statistical analyses reported in 2000 and 2001 this variable worked well.[3] It had a significant coefficient when entered on top of the usual explanatory variables in our unemployment-change regression equation.

These results were thought provoking. It appears that market economies are capable of being excited by expected future shocks to productivity (in the simplest formulation) that are signaled by share prices and dulled by long periods without such shocks. There may be intense exhilaration, with investment elevated by 2 or 3 percent of GDP as in the recent boom, and there may be spells of lesser stimulation. This may be how the more entrepreneurial economies in the world tend to grow, just as described by the German School—by Spiethoff, the Austrian Schumpeter, and Cassel.

I found myself proposing (in the 2001 piece) that such investment booms are healthy. Even if there is overbuilding, as realizations fall short of expectations, the "overhang" and "bust" after the boom may not outweigh or offset the benefit. A productively creative economy experiences the occasional investment boom followed by a spell of tidying up, learning by doing and research just as a productively creative person has the occasional rush of energy and focus, then returns to a relaxed and ruminative state. Investment booms may be good in general and a sign of an enterprising economy.

These thoughts led to a question: If some economies are more capable of responding to the prospects driving a boom than others, was there evidence showing that the countries having the strongest booms in the late 1990s had the more entrepreneurial economies? And, since we cannot observe and measure the degree of enterprise, what statistics in a country might proxy for the dynamism, or enterprise, of which an economy under existing arrangements was capable?

Table 1 (a revision of the table in a *Financial Times* piece on August 9, 2000) uses three measures of the strength of the investment boom. The growth since 1996 of fixed investment is one. To capture the impetus to invest in new employees and new customers the growth of labor's share and the percentage appreciation of the real exchange rate are thrown in. (Much of the force of the boom in the United Kingdom spilled into labor's share and its exchange rate.) Ranked by summing these growth rates, the countries fall into two groups: one with convincing signs of an investment boom, whatever total output and employment may be doing, and the other with few or no signs of such a boom (though expansion may have been strong for other reasons, such as employment subsidies in France and Holland and labor reforms in Spain). The unambiguous boomers were the United Kingdom, the United States, and the Netherlands, but it is reasonable to add Canada, Australia, and Sweden. Germany, Italy, Belgium, and France clearly belong in the other group, and probably Spain and Austria as well. A natural experiment seems to have been performed.

Now to the "entrepreneurial thesis" that the dynamism of economies requires economic institutions providing the necessary access and incentives. In this thinking, the economies that participated vigorously in the investment boom must have

---

3. *Brookings Papers on Economic Activity* 2000:237–311 (2000); *Economic Policy* 32:85–126 (2001).

Table 1. The 1990s Investment Boom: Measures and Some Sources

	Mean annual growth rate (%)			Stock market capitalization in % of GDP	Red tape index	Union + employer coordination	University degree in % of LF
	Fixed investment	Real exchange rate	Labor's share				
A strong general investment boom in evidence							
United Kingdom	10.8	8.5	2.0	80	0.5	2	21
United States	10.6	4.3	0.6	50	1.3	2	33
Canada	11.6	-2.2	1.3	45	—	2	37
Netherlands (1997)	7.6	0.9	0.3	40	1.4	4	22
Sweden (1997)	9.1	-2.4	2.1	50	1.8	6	28
Australia (1995)	8.5	-0.2	-0.4	50	—	—	24
Few signs of investment boom driving the expansion (if any)							
Austria	8.7	-1.4	0.1	13	—	6	8
Spain	8.8	-1.3	-0.7	25	1.8	3	16
France	6.2	-1.9	-0.3	25	2.7	4	19
Belgium	6.0	-1.9	-1.1	42	2.6	4	25
Italy	4.0	0.3	-0.7	18	2.7	4	8
Germany	3.6	-2.2	-0.1	22	2.1	5	23
Euro zone	5.7	-1.5	-0.5	—	—	—	—

Source: OECD, *Economic Outlook* June 2000, Appendix and chap. VII.

Notes: Mean growth rate is the mean of the annual growth rates up to 1999 from 1996 or the start date given in parentheses. Investment is real gross private nonresidential fixed capital formation. Compensation per employee is real total labor cost per person employed in the business sector. Labor's share is compensation per employee to output per employee in the business sector; only the growth rates from 1996 are available. The exchange rate is an index of trade-weighted nominal rates deflated by consumer price indexes. Market capitalization figures from Morgan Stanley Capital International are for 1988. The OECD red tape index is from *The Economist*, July 1999. Proportion of labor force with university degree is from the OECD.

been the "dynamic" or "enterprising" ones, and so their entrepreneurs (in start-up or existing firms) must have been operating with the right institutions: capital markets providing access to venture capital and stock exchanges offering liquidity and transparency, product markets open to start-ups and to new entrants generally, and labor markets offering opportunities to hire and boss and fire employees without large and uncertain penalties and restrictions—to mention just some of the basics. The table records for each country some statistics that are presumably signs of the presence or absence of such institutions. They are to be interpreted here as proxies that reflect the strength and nimbleness of the economy's capacity for dynamism and therefore its response to the new opportunities of the 1990s.

The table shows that the ranking of the countries by the strength of the boom correlates well with these institutional indicators of dynamism. The correlation with the red tape indicator is strong. Less strong is the correlation with the indicator of concerted action—the sum of the indexes of employer coordination and union coordination. While these slender results might be said by some to be unsurprising, they give encouragement to dig deeper.

For me, the success of the higher-education indicator is quite intriguing and, if it holds up in other uses, an important discovery. I would add that the predictive power of the education variable *is* somewhat surprising. How many of us would have been willing to bet (at even odds) that the three economies with the highest proportions of the labor force having a university degree would *all* be among the six boomers and that the four with the lowest proportions would *all* be among the six nonboomers?

The inspiration to try this indicator came from the 1966 Nelson and Phelps paper.[4] As Philippe Aghion and Peter Howitt noted in their chapter, that simple model of the diffusion of innovations emphasizing the facilitating role of advanced education is a sort of "general purpose" concept applicable to the problem-solving processes arising in an entrepreneurial economy: Managers have to use their education to solve the many problems that new ideas pose. Nelson and Phelps make explicit that adoption of new intermediate products or new consumer durables will proceed slowly, and with it the investment made by the innovators in productive capacity, where firms or households that are potential adopters do not have the sophistication to choose early among the innovations offered. (At best the "new economy" would take time, no matter how fast innovations might come on line.) The corollary I would add here is that *without* such problem-solving capacity in others, innovations will be few and far between. Entrepreneurs will innovate fewer intermediate products and new consumer goods if their diffusion is slowed or permanently limited by the dearth of sophistication among the managers, employees, or households on whom adoption and use would depend. Furthermore, entrepreneurs, who may themselves not be of sterling educational attainment, cannot design and launch commercial innovations without well-educated managers to address legal, technical, financial, and even cultural problems that come up.

It has been exciting to see the widening receptivity to the Nelson-Phelps view of education (a wave of earlier work was led by Glenn Cain) not solely because

---

4. *American Economic Association Papers and Proceedings* 56:69–75 (1966).

of my partnership interest in that paper but because of the sea change it tokens in economists' perception of the economy: from a mere market mechanism, in which productivity would benefit from the use of foreign languages and math, to an enterprise system in which growth and the very fabric of economic life depend upon well-directed innovations and their prompt selection and exploitation. (Let me refer readers to recent results from Michelle Connally showing that the states and regions in America's South that pulled themselves out of backwardness in the middle of the last century—like the nations that achieved the most modernization in east Asia—were those with a relatively high antecedent level of education. (I understand that Jess Benhabib is preparing a new round of results on Nelson-Phelps, which could not be ready for this volume.)

The revelation here, for me at any rate, is the predictive power of the stock market indicator—and 7 years before the boom. Speculating on the reasons for it, I suggested (in the *Financial Times* piece) that start-up entrepreneurs in the booming economies could launch "new economy" ventures since those economies had more developed stock markets. "That was crucial to venture capitalists, who could later sell shares in start-ups they financed. Also, a liquid market for shares was crucial to the rise of stock options to focus managers on earnings growth." It should be added that the listing of a firm's shares in a stock exchange is like a seal of approval, which boosts the price of the shares, since to gain a listing the firm has to meet requirements for financial accounting—transparency, frequency, prompt disclosure—that the exchange finds advantageous to impose.

III

Let me recap. I got to the point of stating what I called the entrepreneurial thesis—the thesis that a country's having economic institutions that provide desirable access and incentives to entrepreneurs, investors, managers, and employees is, at some level, the key to the dynamism of its economy and thus to the attractions and satisfactions of economic life there. As a first check on that thesis I looked to see whether a partial and very crude implementation of it helps to explain why, in the second half of the 1990s, some economies went into an investment boom while others did not respond. The thesis, it seems to me, did well. Perhaps it was necessary for the thesis to pass that test. However, that test is *remote* from being *sufficient* to convince skeptics.

The basic limitation of the above exercise is that it is awfully "second-order." It suggests that, in a period of new opportunities apparently regarded as extraordinary, the economies indicated to be relatively entrepreneurial in some of their institutional features responded relatively strongly to those opportunities. That does not imply, however, that these relatively entrepreneurial economies have a higher *trend path* in terms of employment or productivity. It could be that these same economies suffer bigger setbacks during an unusual drought of new opportunities. It could be too that the relatively *non*entrepreneurial economies to some degree *offset* with their cunning in importing or copying the advances elsewhere what they lack in entrepreneurship.

What we have to do, then, is to examine how and to what degree differences in the "endowment" of economic institutions among the advanced economies explain the *levels* of things. For a start we might look at levels in a relatively normal year, namely, 1995, just before the upheaval of the investment boom in several of our twelve economies—as if the economies were in a steady state that year.

For this purpose we have to shift gears a little. If we want to make use of the stock market variable, capitalization as a ratio to GDP, and thus relate the level of that variable to the *level* of productivity or of employment, we had better recognize that it is much more than an indicator of the development (both its sophistication and its penetration in the business sector) of the stock exchange as an institution. It is very close to a key macroeconomic variable in the intertemporal models of *Structural Slumps*, namely, the value (per unit) of the business asset as a ratio to the opportunity cost of producing it—the ratio known as Tobin's Q ratio (in my notation). In the turnover-training model, for example, the key variable is the shadow price attaching to one job-ready employee, q, divided by the technological parameter giving the employees' productivity when producing (instead of training) *times* the number required to prepare a new employee for his job; and this ratio is close to the capitalization-to-GDP ratio. Moreover, there is a technical, or structural, relationship between that macrovariable and the steady-state level of the business asset—hence also steady-state employment and productivity.

Consequently, I have briefly explored a simple organizing idea: Visualize the steady state as determined by the intersection of two steady-state curves in a plane with the stock of the business asset on the horizontal axis and the Q-like variable on the vertical axis, which for our present purposes we may think of as just the value (per unit) placed on the business asset by firms. One of these curves gives the steady-state *supply* of the business asset as an increasing function of the unit value placed on it by the firms. The other curve gives the steady-state asset's unit *value*, that is, what it is worth to the firms, as a function of the size of the asset stock—in view of the burdens and hazards for the firms' profitability created by the adverse institutions in the existing institutional endowment and the prospective benefits of the propitious ones; this curve may be downward sloping (as in the turnover-training and customer models) but if upward sloping it is not as steep as the steady-state supply curve. Now think of the imposition of an adverse institution (or a more adverse one) as operating like a tax in that it shifts down the unit value of the asset *as seen by the firms and their owners*. (Equivalently, it inserts a *wedge* between the two curves at the *left* of their intersection.) The result is a movement *down the upward-sloping supply curve*. Hence the unit value of the asset stock to the firms is decreased and the steady-state stock of the business asset is correspondingly reduced—whether it is job-ready employees, plant, or net foreign customers. In this formulation, then, we think of the influence of most or all economic institutions on the stock of business assets as occurring in significant part, if not entirely, *through* their creation of a bad wedge (or good wedge) that drives the value of the business asset down (or up).

I have had time to try out this organizing idea with four charts. The first part of this idea is that various institutions impact on the asset value curve. For this purpose one could reach for the familiar indicators of the welfare state, such as the Layard-Nickell "replacement ratio" or my "social wealth" variable. One could as well use supply side indicators, essentially measures of departures from the "free market," such as the tax rates on labor and the scale of government purchases. But I am attempting here to draw attention to the possible roles played in productivity and employment determination by institutions in a wholly different realm—the institutions that make up the economy's *operating system*, or its "market organization" in bygone terminology. So I investigate the effects of some of these central economic institutions on asset valuation.

The first pair of charts (Figures 1 and 2), drawing upon the same cross section of twelve economies used in Table 1, examines how two such operating institutions appear to affect the value of the business asset and thus the market-capitalization variable. In Figure 1 the stock market variable appears to decrease with the degree of "coordination" among employers and among labor unions. Of course, several economists have supposed that coordination damages investment, employment, and innovation, and thus the supply of output and of wealth. But here, perhaps, we glimpse the channel through which this effect may occur. In Figure 2 we see the effect of another institution, an index of job protection, which, though valued for its presumably favorable effect on job tenure, is also seen to have a depressing effect on business asset valuation and thus, according to the theory, on the assets

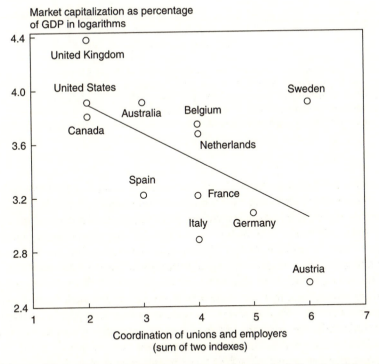

Figure 1. Coordination and market capitalization. Market capitalization is the value of shares in the corporate sector in 1988. The coordination variable is calculated as the sum of Nickell's indexes of union and employer coordination for the years 1989–1994. Employment protection is the number of months of salary that goes in mandatory redundancy payments. (Sources: Morgan Stanley International and Layard and Nickell in *Handbook of Labor Economics*, Amsterdam: North-Holland [1999].)

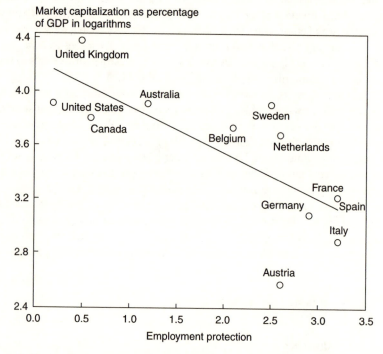

Figure 2. Employment protection and market capitalization. Market capitalization is the value of shares in the corporate sector in 1988. The coordination variable is calculated as the sum of Nickell's indexes of union and employer coordination for the years 1989–1994. Employment protection is the number of months of salary that goes in mandatory redundancy payments. (Sources: Morgan Stanley International and Layard and Nickell in *Handbook of Labor Economics*, Amsterdam: North-Holland [1999].)

accumulated—from plant to employees. (This last variable can be understood to be a product of populist desire for community and stability rather than welfarist objectives, since the latter can be and are met through the entitlement programs of the state.) Of course, my thought is that we can learn something by carrying this investigation further to include, for example, the extent of private ownership, corporate governance arrangements, and measures of financial development.

The second pair of charts (Figures 3 and 4) applies to the data the second part of the organizing idea, that the whole gamut of investments made by the firms in the business sector—the cumulative investment in fixed capital, the patents and results obtained from research, and development expenditure; in customers; and in readying workers to be functioning employees—are increasing in the value that firms place on a unit of each of these assets. If there is such a mechanism, it will presumably be displayed in the observed cross section between labor productivity and the stock market variable, since the former is a proxy for the assortment of assets per unit of labor and the latter is a proxy for some weighted average of business asset values (suitably normalized). In Figure 3 we see that

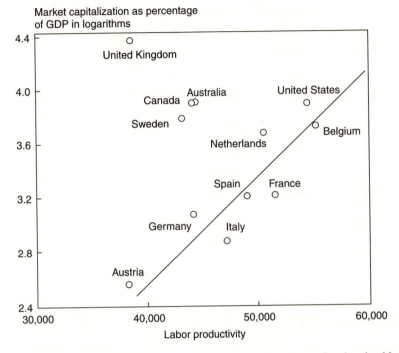

Market capitalization as percentage of GDP in logarithms

Figure 3. Market capitalization and labor productivity: business output per employed worker. Market capitalization variable measures the value of shares in the corporate sector in 1988. Labor productivity is calculated as business output per employed worker in U.S. dollars. The employment rate is the ratio of total employment to working-age population. (Sources: Morgan Stanley International and OECD.)

productivity in the business sector was indeed correlated with the considerably lagged stock market variable in our cross-sectional sample. (The "market cap" in the Netherlands and the United Kingdom is inflated by holdings of overseas business assets that do nothing to raise domestic productivity, however beneficial they might be.) In Figure 4 we find that employment as a ratio to working-age population was also noticeably correlated with the stock market variable.

I am not completely unaware of the limitations and pitfalls of this sort of analysis. An institution may be a proxy for a raft of institutions, some of which are the real source of the measured effect; a multivariate analysis is required, but there are not many countries to study. An institution may be in place only because the alternatives to it are worse, so that some more fundamental and overarching deficiency is the problem. An institution may function differently in one institutional setup than in another, so there may well be interactions that are hard to capture, and so forth. But I feel that we would make a mistake not to go down this road simply because there is not very much light there. The returns from the perhaps small number of things learned may be very high.

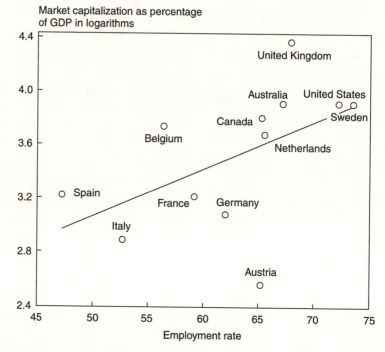

Figure 4. Market capitalization and employment: employment as a share of the working-age population. Market capitalization variable measures the value of shares in the corporate sector in 1988. Labor productivity is calculated as business output per employed worker in U.S. dollars. The employment rate is the ratio of total employment to working-age population. (Sources: Morgan Stanley International and OECD.)

The history of macroeconomics shows that, bit by bit, it has taken on board more and more of the real world: Two such additions—one the size of the public sector and consequent tax rates and the other the incentive effects of the welfare state—have been prominent. But it has given a wide berth to economic institutions. Encouraged by the above results, though, I can foresee a field of study that embeds economic institutions into the macroeconomics of employment and productivity. Some factors that were previously regarded as arcane—for example, private ownership, financial accountability, minority shareowner rights—will find a place in the new models. Where should we look for the most promising candidates? The institutional literature has grown large by now. The focus of the early institutional theorists, well represented by Douglass North, was on the poor enforcement of normal property rights: lax policing, weak courts, and poor patent protection, and, more recently, political instability and social unrest, which raise fears of expropriation. But I would not expect differences in these respects to explain many of the disparities in productivity or in employment among the advanced economies in the OECD.

For ideas on the advanced economies and their differences I think of the work of theorists over the past two decades explicitly concerned with European puzzles: say, Mancur Olson's *Rise and Decline*,[5] Roman Frydman and Andrzej Rapaczynski's *Privatization in Eastern Europe*,[6] and Edward Prescott and Stephen Parente's *Barriers to Riches*.[7] Now, in chapters in this volume, James Heckman takes an institutional perspective on the stagnation of Germany; Christopher Pissarides models the link between start-up costs and the economy's employment; and Philippe Aghion and Peter Howitt inject the Nelson-Phelps view of education into productivity growth. They identify institutions that create stakeholders to share power with stockholders, that protect managements from competition and from takeovers, and that block entrepreneurs and oppose change.

The thread running through this new school is the recognition that productivity, the stimulations and satisfactions of business life, and therefore the enlistment of working-age people into the business economy all depend on the dynamism of the economy's operating system. Among economies that are entrepreneurial by some standard, an economy will be less creative and stimulating if some of its institutions offer reduced incentive to perform for those playing entrepreneurial, managerial, and financial roles or offer less access to these roles for some who might perform them better.

Fresh winds are clearly blowing. I will be pleased if in these reflections I have succeeded in characterizing the nature of this new research perspective, in identifying a channel—asset values—through which the institutions it studies work their effects on the "real" economy, and in conveying some of the importance of this thinking.

---

5. *The Rise and Decline of Nations*, New Haven: Yale University Press (1982).

6. *Privatization in Eastern Europe*, London: Central European University Press (1994).

7. *Barriers to Riches*, Cambridge: MIT Press (2000).

INDEX

Page numbers for entries occurring in figures are followed by an *f;* those for entries occurring in notes are followed by an *n;* and those for entries occurring in tables are followed by a *t.*